Volume 1

Handbook of Work and Organizational Psychology

Volume 1

Handbook of Work and Organizational Psychology

Edited by

P. J. D. Drenth
Free University, Amsterdam

H. Thierry
Amsterdam University

P. J. Willems
Tilburg University

C. J. de Wolff
Catholic University, Nijmegen

JOHN WILEY & SONS

Chichester · New York · Brisbane · Toronto · Singapore

Library of Congress Cataloging in Publication Data:
Main entry under title:

Handbook of work and organizational psychology.

  Includes indexes.
  1. Psychology, Industrial.   I. Drenth, Pieter, J. D.
(Pieter Johan Diederik)
HF5548.8.H2655   1984   158.7   83–23316
ISBN 0 471 90344 2 (U.S. : set)
ISBN 0 471 90400 7 (U.S. : v. 1)
ISBN 0 471 90401 5 (U.S. : v. 2)

British Library Cataloguing in Publication Data:

Handbook of work and organizational psychology.
  1. Psychology, Industrial
  I. Drenth, P. J. D.
  158   HF5548.8

  ISBN 0 471 90344 2
  ISBN 0 471 90400 7   v. 1
  ISBN 0 471 90401 5   v. 2

Typeset by Thomson Press (India) Ltd., New Delhi
Printed by Page Brothers (Norwich) Ltd.

List of Contributors

Prof. Dr. Wil Albeda
Dr. Jen A. Algera
Prof. Dr. Jacques T. Allegro
Dr. Erik J. H. T. H. Andriessen
Dr. Albert van Assen
Prof. Dr. Paul M. Bagchus
Prof. Dr. J. Gerrit Boerlijst
Drs. Giel v. d. Bosch
Drs. Jan Willem Broekhuysen
Drs. George R. P. Bruining
Dr. Marc Buelens
Prof. Dr. Pol L. Coetsier
Prof. Dr. Jules J. J. van Dijck
Prof. Dr. Frans J. P. van Dooren
Prof. dr. Pieter J. D. Drenth
Prof. Dr. Maarten R. van Gils
Drs. B. Groenendijk
Prof. Dr. Aart Hazewinkel
Dr. Friso J. den Hertog
Drs. Herbert van Hoogdalem
Drs. Jaap H. Huijgen
Dr. Ir. John R. de Jong
Drs. Ben Jansen
Dr. Paul L. Koopman
Dr. Agnes M. Koopman-Iwema

Drs. Theo J. Meijman
Drs. Oscar M. Meijn
Prof. Dr. John A. Michon
Prof. dr. James F. O'Hanlon
Drs. E. Mazlies Ott
Prof. Dr. John B. Rijsman
Prof. dr. Robert A. Roe
Drs. Ph. Hans M. Sopar
Prof. dr. Henk Thierry
Prof. dr. Peter Veen
Dr. Eveat v. d. Vliert
Prof. Dr. Jos J. A. Vollebergh
Dr. Arie Vrolijk
Prof. Dr. Peter B. Warr
Drs. André F. M. Wierdsma
Prof. dr. Paul J. Willems
Prof. dr. A. Roper T. Williams
Dr. Jagnes A. M. Winnubst
Prof. dr. Charles. J. de Wolff
Dr. Harry L. G. Zanders

On January 15, 1984 our friend and colleague Paul Willems died. One of his last activities before he became ill was checking proofs for this handbook, which he did as always with utmost care and attention. We have worked together for a very long time, and we have admired and enjoyed his scholarship, his sound judgment, his helpfulness and his friendship. It is therefore that we dedicate this handbook to his memory.

PIETER J. D. DRENTH
HENK THIERRY
CHARLES J. DE WOLFF

Contents

Preface

Customarily, books begin with a preface, although in most cases it would be more appropriate to call it a postscript, a review of what happened between the original plans of the authors or editors and the actual result of their endeavor. This preface being no exception to the rule, it is written at a time when the editors are winding up their work. However that may be, it does give us the opportunity to thank all persons involved in the production of this Handbook.

The idea to produce a handbook does not usually arise overnight. When we first discussed the project—some 15 years ago—we soon came up with a number of reasons for abandoning it. The major one was, why should we even try to compete with a number of excellent textbooks produced in the United States? It seemed like we would be carrying coal to Newcastle. So, instead, three of the present editors decided to lower their sights and to aim for a more modest goal. They invited a number of colleagues to write a chapter for a volume on Work Psychology (*Bedrijfspsychologie*, 1970) and, a few years later, for one on Work- and Organizational Psychology (*Arbeids- en organisatiepsychologie*, 1973), both published in The Netherlands by Kluwer/ Van Loghum Slaterus. Although these volumes covered a reasonably large number of topics in the field, they did not claim to present a systematic coverage of the whole field of work- and organizational psychology.

The positive response to these books and the experience gained by the editors in producing them led to renewed discussions about the original plan of editing a handbook. But more important than these positive experiences was our growing conviction that the European developments in our discipline in the preceding decades warranted an attempt at consolidating the results in a systematic survey of the domain.

Starting in 1976, various proposals on matters of content and structure were discussed and rejected until, in 1978, a proposal, reflected in the structure of the present Handbook, was agreed upon. The domain of work- and organizational psychology was divided into five sections, each containing a number of chapters of a rather general nature and a number of chapters discussing applications. Then we began inviting colleagues, most of them working in The Netherlands, with a sprinkling of experts from other countries, to write one, or more, chapter(s).

The task assigned to the authors was primarily to review the research and developments in the area of their expertise, and, secondly, to pay some attention to possible future developments in that area. If possible or necessary, they should also mention differences in views between Anglo-Saxon and European scientists. This recommendation was not intended to dissociate ourselves from differing views, but to contribute to a more complete picture of the problems at hand. To the present editors it would be gratifying if at least some of the ideas and views 'from the other side of the Atlantic' would indeed serve this purpose and help to clarify the problems we are all faced with.

Now that our work is (almost) done, the editors wish to express their sincere gratitude to all the women and men who contributed to the realization of this Handbook. First of all, we should thank the authors for their patience. Although they communicated with only one of the editors, they had, in fact, to deal with a quartet of commenting and criticizing reviewers. Each editor reviewed each text; these reviews were then discussed by all editors, which resulted in a combined evaluation of the proposed chapter. This procedure inevitably, and repeatedly, led to requests for revision. Although we have been demanding taskmasters, we do hope that we did not lose too many friends in the process and that the authors will share our conviction that the results are worth the toil.

With only a few exceptions, the editors and authors did not excel in writing in English. Anna de Haas and her colleagues did their best to save the reader the trouble of having to decipher the double Dutch some of us wrote down. We are very grateful for the good-humoured way in which she kept decoding our awkward sentences.

Finally, we wish to express our deep appreciation of all that the translators, typists, printers and publishers have contributed to the production and publication of this Handbook.

May 1983

P. J. D. DRENTH
Hk. THIERRY
P. J. WILLEMS
CH. J. DE WOLFF

Part 1

Definitions, historical background, and methodological basis

1.1. What is work- and organizational psychology?

The first chapter of this Handbook of Work and Organizational Psychology is intended as an introduction. First, we want to discuss the nature of W/O psychology as a science and its areas of application. Next a brief account of the developments in W/O psychology will be given. Finally, we will consider the relation to other disciplines and future developments.

W/O PSYCHOLOGY AS A SCIENCE

W/O psychology is the science which is concerned with the behavior of working people and with the behavior of people who function in organizations. There are two aspects in this definition: work and functioning in organizations. This might suggest that the former is associated with work psychology and the latter with organizational psychology. Then this would, in fact, relate to two separate disciplines, each with its own research domain. However, there is much to be said for just one discipline instead of two. The terms work psychology and organizational psychology are indeed used separately, but the subjects to which they relate can overlap extensively. In general, the term psychology is used when the emphasis lays on the characteristics of individuals as determinants of behavior (aptitude, motivation, attitudes), while in organizational psychology the characteristics of organizations get the primary attention. In the course of time it has become quite clear that all kinds of interactions between these two categories of determinants occur and that a strict separation is impossible.

The research domain of W/O psychology has emerged from a prolonged development process. It emphasizes a large number of issues which have one aspect in common: they all relate to the world of work and to the world of organizations.

3

W/O psychology is a psychological discipline indeed, but an attempt to classify it within the system of subdisciplines, which are usually recognized, becomes problematic. Duijker (1958) presents a systematic and widely used classification of fields of psychology, distinguishing the attention on elementary functions, social behavior, developments, personality and, finally, research methods. It seems that W/O psychology does not fit very well into this classification. It comprises elements from each category formulated by Duijker. In ergonomic studies the emphasis is on elementary functions, in selection studies there are many elements of personality theory, career studies are extensively, based on development theory, and leadership studies widely use results of social behavior theory. Moreover, W/O psychology cannot be distinguished from other fields because of its own methods. From the detailed treatment in chapter 1.2 of this Handbook, it is obvious that W/O psychology utilizes methods which are also used in other areas of psychology. The difference lies in the object of study. Psychology addresses itself to the study of behavior and W/O psychology to a specific category of behavior: the behavior of working people which, in most cases, occurs in organizations.

In addition, one should keep in mind that we deal with a very large scientific field and that only part of it has yet been delineated. The enormous extent of the field is a consequence of the large differences in kinds of work, types of organizations, working conditions and development phases of working people. The differences in kinds of work are reflected in the large number of occupations and professions that exist. The *Dictionary of Occupational Titles* (1965) lists tens of thousands descriptions of occupations and professions which are divided into 22 work areas and 114 trait groups. The differences in organizations result from differences in form (private or nationalized enterprises, foundations, governmental agencies, local authorities, etc.) as well as to differences in product (industry, hospitals, churches, sports associations etc.). The variations in conditions under which work is done is immense (in war time, during economic depression, in space vehicles, in the south pole base camp, at the conveyor belt, under time pressure, in open offices, etc.). As far as the development phases of workers are concerned, one finds subjects like vocational counseling, unemployed youth, career development, mid-career crisis, retirement preparation etc. Many of these subjects have been studied at one time or another. Although some sub-areas have been extensively explored, little is known about others.

Such an extensive research area cannot be viewed comprehensively by one person, let alone that he be active in all of the sub-areas. W/O psychology is composed of many specialities (England, 1976). Dunnette (1976) attempted to classify the field by using a matrix which incorporated the 37 chapters of his handbook and 84 headings which he compiled in an analysis of the content of a large number of books. Looking at this matrix, it seems that the entire field cannot be easily divided into a limited number of sub-areas. The classification categories are too complex. In practice there are a few areas, however, where some specialization occurs, such as ergonomics, training, selection, organization development, although no institutionalized forms of specialization have been established as yet.

W/O PSYCHOLOGY AND ITS FIELDS OF APPLICATION

W/O psychology is not only a science. Scientific knowledge lends itself to application. W/O psychologists render services to clients and principals. They are involved in the selection of applicants, the development of training programs, the design of displays, the introduction of employee participation programs, the construction of job evaluation systems, organizational changes and so on.

W/O psychologists carry out research projects commissioned by others, for example on the question 'how attractive is it to work with a certain company' or 'what are the causes of turnover in a given organization'. In a great many cases the W/O psychologist is not asked to carry out research projects, but just to give advice: which applicant should be preferred; how should a re-organization be set up; how can a remuneration system be renovated and so forth. In such cases psychologist often do not restrict themselves to giving advice, but they also assist in implementing programs, often in cooperation with others (specialists, managers). Consequently, W/O psychology does not only refer to a scientific discipline but also to an established profession.

THE DEVELOPMENT OF W/O PSYCHOLOGY

W/O psychology is still a relatively young field. It is true however that a number of pioneers can be pointed out who were already active at the beginning of the 20th century (Dill Scot, Münsterberg, Lahy, Moede and others; see also Baumgarten-Tramer, 1971). But without detracting from their interesting work, it can be asserted that in Europe the growth of W/O psychology occurred to a large extent during the years after World War II. This is reflected in the fact that at Dutch universities the chair of W/O psychology was not established until the sixties. The same holds for most other European countries.

The development in Europe (with the exception of England and Germany—more on this point later) clearly started later than in the United States. In the latter, development started in the first half of this century (Ferguson, 1963). A few highlights from this period are:
—the extensive selection program during World War I in which the Army alpha and Army beta test were developed;
—the Hawthorne studies which were started in 1927 and on which Roethlisberger and Dickson published their book *Management and Worker*;
—the 'Army Aviation Psychology Program' which was mostly concerned

with the selection of pilots and to which psychologists such as Flanagan, Guilford and Thorndike contributed (1947);
—The social-psychological studies reported by Stouffer (1947) in 'The American Soldier'.

The field, which was called Industrial Psychology, was already rather developed in the thirties and forties. In this development, attention was not only paid to the content, but methodological issues were stressed as well. In 1932, the handbook *Industrial Psychology* by Viteles appeared; since then, a few dozen have followed and some have gone through a considerable number of printings. A handbook which may be considered as a mile-stone in the genre was edited by Dunnette in 1976.

The earlier development in the United States is also reflected in the number of psychologists. In 1940 the APA had 3000 members (McKinney, 1976). During World War II an estimated 2000 were involved in activities of the American armed forces. The rapid development in the United States of psychology in general and of W/O psychology in particular was also stimulated by European psychologists who fled from the Nazi regime to America during the thirties (probably the most well-known of whom was Lewin). The enormous lead built up during the thirties and forties resulted in a strong influence of American developments on work started in Europe after World War II. American psychologists came to Europe as guest professors and advisers, and European psychologists went to America for study and orientation. American literature was and still is read on a very large scale in Europe, and publications by European authors generally refer to the American literature on a large scale. A glance at *Psychological Abstracts*, a journal that also systematically abstracts non-American journals, still shows the dominance of American publications.

The situation in Europe did not develop along the same lines in all countries. In England, W/O psychology started to develop early. In 1920 Myers published a book in which such subjects as motion studies, fatigue studies, selection, restriction of output, remuneration systems and industrial unrest were treated (Myers, 1920). During this period a number of large research projects were carried out, commissioned by the Industrial Health Research Board among others. In England as in America a long tradition of measuring individual differences (Galton, Burt, Spearman) existed, whereby quite some attention was paid to selection problems. During World War II large scale selection programs were carried out (Vernon, 1947), including group observation procedures for the selection of officers. After World War II development was less intense: a well-known institute as the 'National Institute of Industrial Psychology' could not be maintained and had to be disbanded. Although much and qualitatively good work is performed, the acceptance by industry remains rather limited. Psychologists who work in industry do not advertise themselves as such but very often operate under other professional titles.

The development in Germany is characterized by discontinuity. It started very rapidly in the beginning of this century. Acceptance by industry was much greater than in England. Some companies set up their own laboratories. Psychological work was done not only be psychologists but also by engineers trained in 'psychotechnical' methods. Psychologists also played an important role in military organizations. But they came into conflict with the Nazi regime. In 1942 Hitler and Göring disbanded all of the psychological units and sent the psychologists to the front. Around 1950 the reconstruction W/O psychology began in Germany. Since, the number of W/O psychologists has sharply increased. Interest at the universities still is rather restricted however. Activities must be mainly sought in the 'Technische Hochshulen' (for further details on England and Germany see McCollum, 1960; de Wolff and Shimmin, 1976).

The situation in other European countries is very diverse. In some countries W/O psychology is still in short pants (for example, southern and south-east Europe, while in other countries (northern Europe, especially Sweden) development has been prosperous. In eastern Europe (especially Poland) development has been greatly stimulated by the government (for an overview of the development in a number of east-European countries, see Zarnek-Gliszczynska, 1980).

THE SITUATION IN THE NETHERLANDS

Compared with other European countries developments have been relatively favorable in The Netherlands. The universities have devoted much attention to W/O psychology, while acceptance by commerce and industry has always been great. It is precisely this combination which positively distinguishes W/O psychology in The Netherlands from many other European countries. Large enterprises showed an early interest in what was then called 'psychotechnics'. Philips, AKU, Hoogovens, the State Mines, Dutch Rail and the PTT all started their own psychological service very early. Some activities even date back to the thirties. The national government also started its own service, and the armed forces employed their own psychologists (often for selection). In addition, there were various institutes which rendered service in the field of selection and vocational counselors. Initially these institutes and services also employed non-psychologists. These activities were greatly expanded during the sixties and seventies.

Although during recent years, due to the stagnating economy, employment of psychologists in general has become quite problematic, unemployment of W/O psychologists still is virtually non-existent. At present the Work- and Organizational section of the Dutch Psychological Society numbers over 650 members.

We have already remarked that the domain of W/O psychology is very broad. The diversity of activities also increases with the growth in the number of W/O psychologists. Formerly, practitioners restricted themselves to a limited number of activities. Until the sixties, W/O psychologists in The Netherlands engaged mostly in selection work, so much so that W/O psychology and selection were more or less synonymous for the public. However, since then an extensive differentiation process has occurred regarding both scientific research and other professional activities, and the relative importance of selection has sharply decreased (Krijnen, 1975).

An impression of the nature of these new activities can be obtained from earlier readers, published by Drenth *et al.* (1970, 1973). Contributions to these publications are classified under headings such as: 'training and development' 'selection and placement', 'people and organizations' (including subjects like employee participation, job redesign, industrial democracy, changes in organizations), 'work satisfaction and motivation', 'evaluation of job and performance' and 'consumer psychology'. There is growth in both width and depth. Due to more extensive scientific research more elaborate and more adequate models and theories have evolved (Drenth, 1978).

RELATION TO OTHER DISCIPLINES

Due to the rapid expansion of the domain of W/O psychology the relation to other, related disciplines has become problematic. On the one hand, psychologists have become more interested in theories, concepts and methods from other fields, especially sociology and industrial engineering. In university curricula, W/O psychology students are required to read publications from other disciplines. On the other hand, there is an increasing interest in W/O psychology from other disciplines. W/O sociologists read W/O psychological literature, and some publications of W/O sociologists could be counted as psychology if the definition formulated by us is strictly used. It is not surprising that some of the authors in this Handbook of Work and Organizational Psychology are sociologists.

The research of Krijnen (1975) demonstrates that psychologists are more and more of the opinion that their function could be accepted by non-psychologists as well. Here, graduates from other social sciences come first to mind. Many recently graduated psychologists land in newly created functions, but the same is occurring with graduates from other disciplines. Thus, there is an increasing overlap of professional activities. In theory, the activities of sociologists can be distinguished from those of psychologists, if the definition is used correctly: the psychologist should occupy himself with the behavior of individuals, and the sociologist with the behavior of societal groups and systems and with developments in society. But in fact, this distinction does not hold in practice. The appearance of social psychology with its interest in the interaction of small groups has already created a sort of intermediate area.

In addition, practicing psychologists, sociologists, industrial engineers etc. are often confronted with questions which do not stem from theory but are based on concrete problems of clients and principals. 'Why is absenteeism increasing?' 'Why is this company having trouble in recruiting unskilled labor?' 'How can communication between management and the personnel staff be improved?' These problems are not restricted to the territory of one specific discipline.

In searching for explanations and possibilities of intervention, practitioners are not inhibited by any so-called boundaries of disciplinary domains. This is particularly true in the area of organizational problems.

During the last few years there has been much talk about a multidisciplinary approach, in which representatives of different disciplines co-operate. Although multidisciplinary co-operation is much applauded, very little of such activity has occurred. There is little multidisciplinary collaboration on projects in practice and publications by multidisciplinary teams are still rare.

FUTURE DEVELOPMENTS

Above, W/O psychology was described as a broad and rapidly developing area of science and application, without any sharply defined boundaries. This raises the question in which direction further developments will go or 'should' go. On the one hand, out of scientific curiosity one could be interested in how development processes take place. In this sense, the development of W/O psychology also lends itself to study. On the other hand, one can focus on the question what should W/O psychologists do in the time to come.

In every profession there are diverse opinions on the manner in which it should practiced. Mok calls this 'definitions' (Mok, 1973). One deals with questions like which services should be rendered and for which clients one should work (Thompson, 1967). The existing definitions are not always reconcilable. Usually there is one opinion or set of opinions that dominates.

In W/O psychology the contrasts between definitions were initially conceived as scientific questions, for example 'clinical' versus 'statistical'. At the end of the sixties more social questions became topical: what is the position of the W/O psychologist in society, what is his contribution to the solution of social problems, how is the relation to management and to personnel staff?

The discussion took place at the universities as well as in practice. It was carried on not only by psychologists but also by students. A much heard idea was that psychologists function in a specific social context which determines to a high degree the nature and outcomes of their work. Too often the psychologists neglected to raise the question whether they should challenge in this context or not. By changing structures other answers could become possible. It was often assumed that some organizational psychological programs (democratization, organizational change, job enrichment) could be the means for achieving such structural changes. Now, ten years later, those high-pitched expectations have for the most part disappeared. Attempts at evaluation point out that all of this has not led to spectacular changes (Schaake, 1978; van Strien, 1978).

But the discussion has made clear that psychologists do not operate in an isolated field: their work is stimulated by social forces, and it has important social implications. There are sufficient reasons to further discuss these developments more systematically. Various authors plead for a 'professional forum' (van Strien, 1978; de Wolff and Shimmin, 1976; de Wolff et al., 1980), on the analogy of the 'scientific forum' (de Groot, 1961). This forum first of all should address itself to social and professional problems. On the basis of Mok's theories it can expected that competing opinions do indeed exist. The discussion should, therefore, be carried on more systematically.

There are optimistic as well as pessimistic visions of the further developments in W/O psychology. Dunnette (1976) opens his handbook with a chapter in which he asserts 'Industrial and organizational psychology ... offers great promise, in the years ahead, for further developing and extending our knowledge of those behavioral processes which are critical to an understanding of interacting between persons and the institutions and organizations of society'. The rapid developments offer grand perspectives which raise expectations for the future.

There are also pessimistic voices. Heller (1978) points out the risk of too one-sided approaches and Wilpert (1979) refers to the insufficient infrastructure and the need for better quality norms.

This alternation of optimism and pessimism holds for the entire field of applied psychology (see de Wolff, 1977) and seems to be an expression of a reorientation process of psychologists who operate in a 'turbulent environment'. In turn they become impressed by new developments and possibilities and by the many problems which appear. Apparently, the frame of reference from which the future perspectives of W/O psychology are judged can vary greatly. If they are viewed from the perspective of science development, the rapid growth and new possibilities are especially striking. From this point of view Dunnette's optimism is quite understandable. Our insights increase and are deepened. This is also evident in this Handbook. In all respects it appears that also further progress will be made on this point in the coming years.

On the other hand, W/O psychologists work for clients and principals. They help others solve problems and contribute to the realization of 'values': i.e. they help others to achieve something that is of value to them. They construct 'better' remuneration systems, select 'suitable' candidates, set up more 'efficient' training methods, and design 'attractive' positions.

Considered from this perspective, it is not only noteworthy what psychologists think of development but also what their clients and principals think about it. Do they consider psychologists capable of helping them? Are clients and principals of the opinion that psychologists prove the usefulness of their services?

W/O psychology is no longer an activity of a small group of pioneers. Now that there are many W/O psychologists, there is a vast amount of knowledge available (although more often stored in libraries than ready for use in practice), and the salient question is: what is going to happen to it in the coming years?

This Handbook is not primarily meant to go into these questions, however important they may be. First of all, it intends to give a survey of the developments in the field of scientific W/O psychology. With which subjects do W/O psychologists occupy themselves, what is known about these subjects, where can more information about these subjects be found?

This Handbook does not pretend to present an exhaustive treatment. The field is too large for this. Although the book is systematic, it is also in a certain sense eclectic. Its purpose is primarily to orientate. It handles a number of theories, methods, approaches and lines of research which are of interest to W/O psychologists, whether they be engaged in science or practice.

The question, how can this knowledge be best used in the coming decade, remains topical. The attempt to answer this question will be an important challenge for future W/O psychology and W/O psychologists.

REFERENCES

Army Air Force Aviation Psychology Research Program Reports (1947). Washington, D. C.: Government Printing Office.

Baumgarten-Tramer, F. (1971), Chronologie der Entwicklung der Arbeitswissenschaft und der angewandten Psychologie. *Arbeitswissenschaft*, **8/9**, 165–182.

Dael, J. van (1938), *De geschiedenis der psychotechniek van het bedrijfsleven* [The history of industrial psychotechnics]. Nijmegen: Dekker & Van de Vegt.

Dictionary of occupational titles (1965), Washington, D. C.: Department of Labor.

Drenth, P. J. D. (1978), Arbeids-en organisatiepsychologie [Work- and organizational psychology]. In: Duijker, H. C. J. (Ed.), *Psychologie vandaag* [Psychology today]. Deventer: Van Loghum Slaterus.

Drenth, P. J. D., Willems, P. J., Wolff, Ch. J. de (Eds.) (1970), *Bedrijfspsychologie* [Industrial psychology]. Deventer: Kluwer/Van Loghum Slaterus.

Drenth. P. J. D., Willems, P. J., Wolff, Ch. J. de (Eds.) (1973), *Arbeids- en organisatiepsychologie* [Work- and organizational psychology]. Deventer: Kluwer/Van Loghum Slaterus.

Duijker, H. C. J., Palland, B. G., Vuyk, R. J. (1958), *Leerboek der psychologie* [Textbook of psychology]. Groningen: Wolters.

Dunnette, M. D. (Ed.) (1976), *Handbook of industrial and organizational psychology.* Chicago: Rand McNally.

England, G. W. (1976), Conceptual foundation of industrial and organizational psychology. In: Dunnette, M. D. (Ed.), *Handbook of industrial and organizational psychology.* Chicago: Rand McNally.

Ferguson, L. W. (1961), The development of industrial psychology. In: Gilmer, B. H. (Ed.), *Industrial psychology.* New York: McGraw-Hill, 18–37.

Groot, A. D. de (1961), *Methodologie: Grondslagen voor onderzoek en denken in de ge-dragswetenschappen* (English tr. 1969: *Methodology: Foundations of inference and research in the behavioural sciences*). The Hague: Mouton.

Heller, F. (1978), *Controversies in organizational psychology*. Paper presented at the 19th International Congress of Applied Psychology, Munich.

Krijnen, G. (1976a), *Ontwikkeling functievervulling van ontwikkelingspsychologen* [Development job fulfillment by psychologists]. Part I. Nijmegen: Institute of Applied Psychology.

Krijnen, G. (1976b), *Ontwikkeling functievervulling van psychologen* [Development job fulfillment by psychologists]. Part II. Nijmegen: Institute of Applied Psychology.

McCollom, I. N. (1960), Psychologists in industry in the United Kingdom and Western Germany. *American Psychologist*, **15**, 58–64.

McCormick, E. J. (1975), *Industrial psychology*. 6th ed. New York: Prentice Hall.

McKinney, F. (1976), Fifty years of psychology. *American Psychologist*, **31**, 834–842.

Meyers, C. S. (1920), *Mind and work*. London: University of London Press.

Mok, A. L. (1973), *Beroepen in actie: Bijdrage tot een beroepensociologie* [Professions in action: A contribution towards a sociology of professions]. Meppel: Boom.

Roethlisberger, F. J., Dickson, W. J. (1939), *Management and the worker*. Cambridge (Mass.): Harvard University Press.

Schaake, B. (1977), Ontwikkelingen in het werkveld en het werk van de organisatiepsy-choloog (Developments in the working domain and work of organizational psychologists]. *De Psycholoog* [The Psychologist], **12**, no. 5, 252–261.

Stouffer, S. A. (1949), *The American soldier*. New York: Princeton University Press.

Strien, P. J. van (1978), *Om de kwaliteit van het bestaan* [On the quality of life]. Meppel: Boom.

Thompson, J. D. (1967), *Organizations in action*. New York: McGraw Hill.

Vernon, P. E., Parry, J. B. (1949), *Personnel selection in the British forces*. London: University of London Press.

Viteles, M. (1932), *Industrial psychology*. New York: Norton.

Wilpert, B. (1978), *On the status of organizational psychology*. Paper presented at the 19th International Congress of Applied Psychology, Munich.

Wolff, Ch. J. de (1977), *Uit de ivoren toren* [From the ivory tower]. Deventer: Van Loghum Slaterus.

Wolff, Ch. J. de, Shimmin, S. (1976), The psychology of work in Europe: A review of a profession. *Personnel Psychology*, **29**, 175–195.

Wolff, Ch. J. de, Shimmin, S., Montmoulin, M. de (1980), *Work psychology: Contradictions and controversies*. London: Academic Press. (in press.)

1.2. Research in work- and organizational psychology: principles and methods

Pieter J. D. Drenth

1. INTRODUCTION[1]

This chapter discusses the methodology of research in work- and organizational psychology. Of course neither a comprehensive survey of the methods and instruments nor an exhaustive discussion of their pros and cons is possible in such a limited space. Nor is it intended as a guide for research design. For a survey of such more technical matters as selecting the proper design and set-up for a study, choosing samples, testing instruments, and the statistical support of interpretations, the reader is referred to the appropriate literature (e.g. Guilford, 1954; Hays, 1963; Runkel and McGrath, 1972). Rather, this chapter attempts to discuss the foundations of and assumptions inherent in the process of research in this subdiscipline of psychology. Thorough acquaintance with these principles is an important condition not only to carry out research in work- and organizational psychology, but also to be able to understand and form a critical opinion of the research of others as it is presented in the literature.

First, some basic characteristics of research in work- and organizational psychology will be discussed, and the various forms it may take will be classified. Next, the relationship between scientific research and its applications will be descanted. Then the process of interpreting research findings and various types of design will be dealt with. A summary of the different methods of data collection will conclude this discourse.

Prof. dr. P. J. D. Drenth, Subfaculteit Psychologie der Vrÿe Universiteit De Boelelaan, 1081 HV
AMSTERDAM

[1] I wish to thank the staff members of the Department of Industrial and Organizational Psychology of the Free University, Amsterdam, for their critical comments on an earlier version of this chapter.

2. WHY SCIENTIFIC RESEARCH IN WORK- AND ORGANIZATIONAL PSYCHOLOGY?

First of all one might ask why so much attention should be devoted to scientific research and its methods. Have we not, through experience, by now gained sufficient insight and practical knowledge for research to become less necessary? And is it not true also that fewer and fewer work- and organizational psychologists are directly involved in research?

A first response to this question would be that much current knowledge in the field of work- and organizational psychology is based on past research, and that, for further development of this knowledge, continued research is necessary. Thus far, many questions have received incomplete answers and many others have not been studied at all. Add to this that, because of social, technological, and organizational developments, new problems arise almost daily, which also demand solutions. In other words: the theory of work- and organizational psychology is all but complete, and new developments make past theoretical acquisitions outdated or obsolete. The scientific theory of work- and organizational psychology is ever being challenged to try and keep up with events, developments, and continuous changes, and the researcher's modesty is called upon to realize again and again how incompletely this can actually be done.

Furthermore, knowledge of scientific research methods is of great importance to the practitioner also. He, too, will be confronted with many problems which oblige him to fall back on earlier research or which demand new research. To be able to understand and evaluate this critically, knowledge of the principles of research is necessary. This is no less true if he wants to enlist the assistance of an institute or consultant to have a study carried out. Knowledge of the methodology of research will be indispensable in evaluating proposals, in understanding interpretations, and in deducing the correct implementations.

3. CHARACTERISTICS OF A SCIENTIFIC WAY OF THINKING

The foregoing remarks imply that a scientific way of thinking has something unique distinguishing it from 'common sense' psychology or lay opinions. Without wishing to pass off these two as useless, it must be said that there are a number of elements in scientific thinking which give scientific methods of acquiring knowledge at least a greater chance to lead to correct understanding. Such knowledge relates not only to existing phenomena and their relationships, but also to future developments, providing the opportunity to make predictions and to take preventive or corrective measures. In this sense there is nothing as practical as a good theory.

What, then, are the elements characterizing the process of scientific acquisition of knowledge?

In the first place, the *unbiased* way in which questions are posed and answers sought. The scientific set-up of a study requires, in any case, systematic, unbiased planning, giving data which can support a certain theory or hypothesis as well as data which give occasion to reject it equal chances. In other words, one is looking not only for data confirming the theory, but just as much—or, according to the critical rationalist Popper, rather—for data which could weaken the theory.

A second characteristic is that *research data* are collected in order to either confirm or disaffirm a theory. The word 'data' does not refer exclusively to 'hard' facts. It will become clear in the course of this chapter that the nature of the data may vary from subjective opinions or expectations (results of questionnaires, interviews) to very objective facts (number of meetings, number of members elected to a works council). The exactness of the data will, of course, vary as well, but must be weighed against their relevance and the generalizability of their interpretations. In any case, scientific research bases its conclusions as much as possible on data which are as relevant as possible. In this way, psychology, and this includes work- and organizational psychology, is an empirical science.

The next element is the fact that data are *collected systematically*. Standardization and objectivity are important criteria here. Standardization means to have as much control as possible over the circumstances which may influence the phenomenon perceived. In studying the influence of music on work, the working conditions with and those without music will have to be as similar as possible, in order to be able to ascribe differences to the factor 'music'. Complete standardization will be hard to achieve. With less standardized observations, it is necessary that, anyhow, the circumstances that do vary be described or measured, thus making it possible to generate alternative explanations for the differences perceived in the phenomenon under study.

Objectivity refers to the extent to which the data can be recorded or coded in the same manner by another observer or judge. In a scientific study, an evaluation or classification of data may not be fundamentally affected by the subjectivity of the observer. This is not to say that subjectivity on the part of the observer can be, or even should be, entirely eliminated. In a certain sense, every observation or evaluation, as a psychological process, is subjective in nature. But through standardization and systematization of the procedure, such a subjective process can lead to results which other expert observers or evaluators would arrive at as well. In psychology, a certain degree of objectivity—in the sense of intersubjectivity—can very definitely be achieved.

Fourthly, *analysis* and *interpretation* also take place in as *unbiased* a way as possible. First and foremost this means that the 'data' be allowed to speak for themselves as completely and as exclusively as possible; they are not used selectively nor are they coloured by expectations, wishes, or hopes. Values certainly play a role in scientific research, but not as guidelines for interpreting data. It is true that research is embedded in a system of societal values and ideological premises. These values may act as a stimulus to research; they are also the normative conditions in the application and use of research. But in a strict sense, scientific research itself is 'value-neutral', i.e. ideology, values, and interests may not have a part in determining the explanation and interpretation of research findings.

But at the same time this requirement means that statements, expectations, and hypotheses must be formulated in such a way that they can be tested on the basis of facts, not only by the researcher himself, but also by other researchers. This yields three important criteria for scientific research: explicitness, testability, and replicability.

The fact that values, preferences, or interests may not play a role in scientific interpretation processes also implies that power has no place in a scientific discussion. Only reasonable and rational arguments may exert any influence. Power relationships are foreign to processes of scientific influence, and only non-power or convincing relationships (Mulder, 1977, p. 68) are acceptable. De Groot (1971) for one even advocated that, in fact, only the principle of unanimity should count, leaving no room for the majority model used for problems which cannot be solved through logical and empirical arguments, but where the different standpoints derive from preferences or interests.

This is not to say that power considerations play no role at all in the daily practice of scientific activities. In discussing 'schools' and methods, accepting manuscripts for scientific journals, allocating money, and defending interpretations of (often applied) scientific research, non-scientific elements, power factors included, undeniably carry weight.

A last characteristic of scientific research is the combination of seemingly opposite aspects. This first involves *openness* for new developments, the benefit of the doubt which new initiatives deserve, and room for creative ideas. This is true both for content (new theories, new explanations) and method and approach (Kuhn, 1962; Phillips, 1973). Rigidity is fatal to both these aspects of scientific research. On the other hand, it should be realized that science is both *communicative* and *cumulative*. That is, new ideas, new approaches, and new paradigms must be tested in open communication with other scientists (the 'forum' of De Groot, 1971) or even any other reasonable person (the 'universal audience' of Hofstee, 1975) and must be evaluated in the light of existing knowledge and insights. In other words, we cannot take for granted that a renewal is an improvement and least of all can we accept it 'for its own sake', as Feyerabend (1975) seems to advocate. Scientific activity is an activity in the field of the two forces: creativity and testing, or, as Van Strien (1978) describes it, the forces openness and continuity.

Above we discussed the ideal criteria for scientific research. By no means all the work of scientists satisfies these norms, nor does the fact that persons or institutes are called 'scientific' in any way guarantee that their work is scientific in the sense described above. Using the criteria mentioned one must continuously take a critical view of whatever pretends to be scientific research. This is only possible when the requirement of openness, of publicity, or, as Hofstee (1975) puts it, of 'making oneself vulnerable' is met. Indeed, this is why this requirement may be considered as central to scientific research.

4. TYPES OF RESEARCH

The criteria mentioned above are features essential to scientific research, but this is not to say that all research is uniform in design and process. Research practice shows great variation. Below we will discuss the various types of research as they are found in work- and organizational psychology. This discussion proceeds from earlier distinctions made by e.g. De Groot (1961) and Vercruijsse (1960).

4.1. Descriptive research

This type of research is not concerned with testing general theories or hypotheses, but rather with systematically depicting a particular phenomenon, process, collection of elements, or system. It may mean studying various facets or possible determinants, but it is always a matter of analysing a specific phenomenon, group, or population at a certain time and place.

Various more specific types of research fall into this category. First of all the *case study*, which systematically describes a single case. An example would be Allegro's (1973) description of a process of change which he introduced in an organization with the aim to improve the functioning of the social system through a more adequate synchronization of the technical and social systems. The value of such case studies is two-fold: they serve as illustrations and they provide material to generate hypotheses, although the latter is often not the primary objective of case studies.

A second type of research in this category is the measuring and summarizing in descriptive terms (numerical or verbal) of various aspects of a *total population*, such as the characterization of a school's population, the employees of a firm, or the members of a club.

In the third place, the analysis of the universe can also be approximated by studying a *sample* from it. Typification of the total population then takes place through statistical inferences from the sample data. One of the first Dutch large-scale studies in work- and organizational psychology, on first-line supervisors in industry (COP, 1959), may be mentioned as an example.

4.2. Instrumental research

A second form of research is aimed at constructing and validating instruments, that may be applied in other research or used for diagnostic counseling or decision purposes. Of course, this would include the development not only of psychological tests, but also of other instruments, such as appraisal systems, interview schedules, (self-)rating scales, satisfaction questionnaires, etc. The scientific nature of this type of research lies in the analysis and evaluation of the psychological meaning of whatever the test or scale operationalizes. Merely constructing an instrument according to the rules of test construction, even if done judicially and properly, is still not scientific research. Only the evaluation of the psychological meaning of the instrument, preferably in terms of a psychological theory, can elevate that activity beyond the level of technology.

Some examples of instrumental research in work- and organizational psychology would be the development of a series of selection tests (as for instance discussed in Guion, 1965), scales for measuring work satisfaction (such as the Job Description Index, Smith *et al.*, 1967), rating scales for identifying management potential (Tigchelaar, 1974), or the many scales for organization characteristics (Price, 1972). For procedures of construction and evaluation of this type of instrument, the reader is referred to the relevant literature (see e.g. Edwards, 1957; Nunnally, 1967; Kerlinger, 1973).

4.3. Theory-oriented research

This includes all the research in work- and organizational psychology where empirical data are collected and interpreted with no specific interest in particular samples (or the population from which samples were taken) or particular instruments. The data serves to explore or test certain theoretical relationships.

In this connection the term 'theory' need not have very pretentious connotations. It only signifies that, in a theoretical explanation, a connection is made with certain concepts and conceptual systems. In doing this, the theory is used in an attempt to somehow link concrete observations together. Runkel and McGrath put it more simply: 'Theory is a guide to tell you where to look for what you want to observe' (1972, p. 23).

The extent to which a theory can be considered valid on the basis of research results may vary a great deal in theory-oriented research. It can, in fact, be viewed as a *continuum* with one pole representing the generation of possible theoretical explanations and the other the testing of these explanations. How close a position on this continuum is to one pole or the other depends on how explicitly one has been able to formulate a theory or (more accurately) a number of hypotheses. Between the two poles is a large grey area which can be typified neither as explicit hypothesis-creation nor as explicit hypothesis-testing. It is this continuum we want to discuss in more detail.

At one end there is hypothesis-generating research, also called *explorative* research. Its purpose is to generate hypothetical explanations for facts or observations. Possible relationships, possible interactions, possible causal relationships are looked for by exploring the indications in the empirical material either objectively (e.g. through factor or cluster analysis) or sub-jectively (e.g. through an inventory of expert opinions). Explorative research is never really finished: it requires follow-ups in which the hypotheses are tested. Explorative research is often the first phase of a more extensive research project.

Two types of conditions call for explorative research: firstly, when it is impossible for the researcher to formulate clear-cut hypotheses or expectations based on his own or others' experience or on existing theories. Secondly, when the research domain is so complex and many of the variables which play a role are so difficult to be kept under control, that the emerging interrelationship patterns can never yield more than hypothetical explanations, which should be tested under more narrowly defined conditions or in a better controlled setting.

It is doubtful if there are absolute examples of this pole. Theories will often, for the most part implicitly, have played a role in the choice of the relationships to be explored. And the selection of the variables to be included will usually not have taken place without theoretical justification, albeit a vague one.

A large field study is often preceded by a so-called pilot study, also referred to as the 'explorative' phase. But if a pilot study only tests the general appli-cability of the concepts used or the usefulness of questionnaires etc. (this often being the sole intention of a pilot phase), then the name 'explorative study' is not very appropriate: here, no hypotheses or expectations are generated.

At the other extreme there is *theory-testing*, the aim of which is to test for expected and predicted relationships. Such expectations and predictions may be based on theoretical assumptions and deductions, or on practical experience and observation, or on previous empirical (explorative) research. It is important that the hypothesis is tested unambiguously in the study. But often the nature of such testing does not go beyond 'lending support' to the theory, because of the never perfect reliability of the observations and measurements, the pro-babilistic nature of the test itself (e.g. the chosen level of significance), and the logical distance between the basic theory and its operationalization in the concrete hypotheses being tested. A theory can never really be accepted or rejected on the basis of a single test study. There are, of course, many examples of such research in The Netherlands. Thierry's (1968) disaffirming test of Herzberg's two-factor theory, with its distinction between satisfiers (sole determinants of satisfaction) and dissatisfiers (sole determinants of dissatis-faction), or Mulder and Wilke's (1970) experimental support of the theory of increasing power distance through participation may serve as illustrations.

Between these two extremes there is a large research field that can be classified neither as typically explorative nor as typically testing: it combines charac-teristics from both types. Many larger field studies can serve as examples: the study of the occurrence of different styles of leadership under varying circum-stances (Mulder *et al.*, 1970), the study of the influence of the nature of an issue on the relationship between participation in and effectiveness of decisions (Drenth *et al.*, 1979), or the study of the influence of formal participative systems on actual involvement in decision making in organizations (IDE, 1981). It cannot be said that in this type of research the choice of the variables or relationships studied took place without any theoretical considerations or defensible expectations. Thus, such studies are not exclusively hypothesis-generative, but neither are they pure test studies. For this qualification they too often lack explicitly formulated hypotheses, and too often an outcome is, unsurprisingly, contrary to the expectation which can be made plausible by pointing to uncontrolled influences or situation-specific 'contingencies'.

Recognition of this 'mixed form' of research, which blends elements of both exploration and testing, should, however, never lead to assumptions being presented as theories or hypotheses as proven explanations. Nor does it mean that, from carelessness or laziness, one may neglect to formulate hypotheses and expectations before collecting the data or at least before the first analysis of the data. All it does mean is that many of the careful analyses of often highly complex empirical material, as are often found in the field of work- and organizational psychology, cannot be characterized either as inferior theory testing studies or as overgrown explorative research.

4.4. Formal approaches

Finally, we should mention a form of research in work- and organizational psychology whose nature is not empirical in that no new data are collected to answer a question or to solve a problem. Here we might think of the development of a *formal theoretical* system, often in abstract symbolical or mathematical form, in which the variables often have a stochastic character so as to reflect as much as possible the probabilitistic nature of the phenomena.

A highly concrete form of this formal approach is found in the research on and development of *models* for certain behavioural systems. Such models are ontological, not heuristic. In *heuristic* models the various categories of variables to be included in the study are grouped according to their relationships. There are two reasons for this: to test the completeness of the representation and to use this as a guideline in formulating possible hypotheses on connections and cause-effect relationships. *Ontological* models simulate reality as closely as possible, and by testing such models insight into reality will be tested at the same time. Nowadays, ontological models are often simulated with the aid of computers. The advantage of such a computer model is that it allows us to study all kinds of extreme events which seldom occur in reality, or the consequences of certain influences which cannot be tested in practice because of the great risks or high costs involved. Decision making processes or the market behaviour of consumers are often studied in this way (see e.g. Engel *et al.*, 1968).

5. RESEARCH AND APPLICATION

In this section we will discuss the relationship between scientific research and its practical application. It is often said that the more field-oriented disciplines in psychology (clinical psychology, educational psychology, and work- and organizational psychology) can in fact only be characterized as applied sciences. At the same time, too, it is interesting to learn how such applied research is related to policy and action, especially in the perspective of what is generally called 'action research'. For this discussion, it seems useful to make a number of distinctions as to the viewpoints from which scientific research is undertaken, and then to see what position work- and organizational psychology takes in each case.

Firstly, we can distinguish between *applied research* and *pure scientific* research. The criterion here is what motivated the research and the origin of the research problem. If it is a practical question, a difficulty or dilemma experienced in practice, if, in short, it is 'field induced', then we have to do with applied research. But if the issue is stated by a researcher prompted by scientific curiosity, or through questions raised in previous research because of incomplete or incorrect theories, etc., then we may speak of pure scientific research.

Apart from this, scientific research can be differentiated according to its *goal and orientation*. It may be concerned with decisions or goals which in themselves are not inherent in scientific research: policy measures (policy supporting research), decisions (decision-oriented research), and applicable results. On the other hand we have free scientific research. This is done for the sake of acquiring insight and not primarily to see whether it has any practical application or yields practical results. Such research, which is intended solely to increase knowledge, is conclusion oriented. (The distinction 'decision versus conclusion oriented research' was first made by Cronbach and Suppes, 1969.)

These two dimensions do not run entirely parallel, but the two combinations pure scientific/conclusion-oriented research and applied scientific/decision-oriented research are frequently encountered. An example of the former is McClelland's study of the relationship between achievement motivation and economic development in various countries (McClelland, 1961). In work- and organizational psychology, the numerous, often short, studies which must serve to support a certain practical decision, are examples of the second type. One could think of a study of the psychological and physiological reactions of employees to various shift schedules, in order to introduce, on this basis, the best or (rather) least harmful shift schedule (see this Handbook, ch. 3.6).

But field-induced research need not always be directed at applications and practical decisions. Take, for instance, the extensive research programme of the Aston group, directed at identifying the nature and interrelationships of a large number of organization characteristics (Pugh et al., 1968). Nor will it be impossible to convert research that is primarily motivated by scientific curiosity into practical measures or policy decisions. In this connection, we may think of the theoretical research on the influence of personal factors (Franck and Hackman, 1975) or social factors (Schmitt, 1976) on appraisal processes. This research can be used directly in training or selecting raters or interviewers.

A concept like fundamental or 'basic' research, defined as research aimed at the study and clarification of basic principles in a certain target area, does not fit too well in our discussion. Generally, of course, it will fall under pure scientific research, but not necessarily so. Some 'basic' research is rather applied research (e.g. social learning theory). On the other hand, applied research may also have, or acquire, a 'fundamental' nature (space research!).

'Social relevance' does not seem to be a useful principle of classification either, and it certainly does not run parallel with either of the two mentioned. In the first place, it will, for example, not be easy to establish the social irrelevance of pure scientific research which is not *directly* applicable. Furthermore, 'relevance' is a value judgement, which fluctuates with the opinions about social values as held by various societal groups. It would thus not appear to provide useful guidelines for classifying scientific research.

We are now faced with the question whether testing job applicants, studying organizations, or the psychological analysis of a given man-machine system can also be called scientific research; and where they would fit in the scheme discussed. The criterion for scientific psychological research is whether it aims at and leads to an increase of knowledge about behaviour. Studies of individual cases or persons may sometimes be directed at such an increase in general knowledge (case study), but in most cases this is not true. It is generally a matter of gaining insight into a particular situation or a single individual (in order to improve it or to help him). It is a matter of *applying* science, not of science as such. In applying science, if done correctly, one still adheres to the norms and rules of science (accuracy and precision as a norm, verification of what is surmised, avoidance of gratuitous statements), but the objective is no longer a generalizable insight in human behaviour.

It is, again, different with decisions, actions, and policies, even if scientific data and conclusions are *used*. In this case, the scientific data is not used to increase knowledge and insight, but with a view to ... greater economic use, better chance of recovery, smoother change processes, or a higher degree of mental well-being. Psychotherapists, organizational developers, and personnel selection psychologists are (in these qualities) not scientists, but, using Linschoten's (1964) typology, 'social workers', although he did not mean this to be derogatory. Here, norms, values, and social ideologies do indeed determine decisions and actions.

A term not yet mentioned but deserving closer examination in this connection is 'action research', a term introduced by Kurt Lewin in 1946. It refers to an

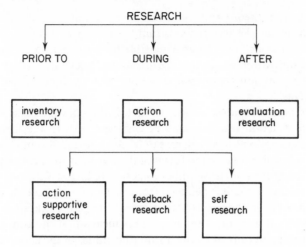

Figure 1. The relationship between research and action.

approach to social research in which the researcher actively brings about change in a social system, fully intending to change the system and to generate critical knowledge about it (see Susman and Evered, 1978). The relationship between research and action or policy[2] can take three basic forms: research *prior* to, *during*, or *subsequent* to action (see figure 1).

First, there is *inventory research*. A study of the literature, a pilot study, or an experiment will investigate as well as possible whether a certain action, a certain policy, is sensible, has a chance of success, can actually be carried out, etc. Such research has a supportive character; it is one of the determinants of the policy or line of action chosen.

Second comes *evaluation research*. Experiences, experiments, procedures are evaluated afterwards through some kind of research or another. This research can take many forms, varying from administering a simple question-naire or a few informal interviews to a well-prepared and empirically founded study (e.g. the evaluation of education by means of nation-wide achievement tests). Such an evaluation may in its turn lead to some subsequent course of action (the design of a course, the approach in an organizational development program). The feedback phase makes it cyclic in nature (Suchman, 1971). It may also have direct, i.e. preventive, effects, in the sense that people anti-cipate the outcome of an evaluation study and make their choice in accordance with it, as a teacher's style and approach may be influenced (perhaps even unconsciously) by the fact that there will be an evaluation afterwards.

In the third place, research can be more enmeshed in action or policy. Here, research does not take place before or after, but during the action.

[2] 'Action' here refers to a single act or decision, and 'policy' to a continuing series of actions.

This is the field of 'action research'. The term 'action research' is anything but simple. Wardekker (1978: 42) states that 'its presentations vary from "a form of social group work" to "the only sensible form of social scientific research", or from "co-operation with those involved" to "societal revolution". Anyone looking for a common denominator of these views will be left with only a few vague concepts'.

In an attempt to analyse in greater detail the concept of action research, three forms of action research may be distinguished. In the first place, what could be called 'action *supportive* research'. Such research is built in the various phases of an action programme, forming the basis for the next step to be taken or for correcting the course of a plan of action (Clark, 1972). It also includes a 'norm orientation', which is deduced from the goal of the action. The research is always aimed at finding out to what extent the goal or sub-goal has been or will be reached. But it still is research. This means that the conclusions of the research are not determined by the norms and values of the action or operation, but only by the empirical or logical evidence that the action goals have (not) been achieved. It is therefore incorrect to state, as De Vries (1973) does, that 'the empirical analytical researcher must share the social and human values of the policy maker to whom he lends his services'. One is even tempted to say: it is better if he does not! A voter poll carried out by a political party arouses more distrust than does a study done by an independent polling agency.

In this connection it should be stressed that Van Stren's (1975) 'regulative cycle', comprising the phases: positing a problem—diagnosis—plan—operation—evaluation, or Susman and Evered's (1978) cyclic process, with the phases: diagnosis—action planning—action taking—evaluating—specifying learning, are not essentially different from the classic approach. Admittedly, the phases 'plan' and 'operation' ('action planning' and 'action taking') are indeed deduced from the action goal and this cycle keeps recurring in the action programme in action supportive research. But such deductions also occurred in classic 'decision-oriented' research. Moreover, in many cases it is probably correct to say that action supportive research is focussed rather on individual, concrete cases, and consequently is a matter of application rather than applied research (Wardekker calls 'generalizability' one of the biggest problems in action research). But this is not necessarily true. This type of research can definitely be used to generate general laws and to discover general knowledge, which implies that it may be called scientific research.

In the second form of action research, *feedback research*, persons are studied more closely by confronting them with the actual research results and involving them in the interpretation process. At the individual level, this procedure is used, for example, when results of ability or personality tests are taken as a starting point for a joint interpretation process and further counseling (see e.g. Goldman, 1961). At the group level, researchers at the University of Michigan elaborated this principle in the Survey Feedback Method (Mann, 1957;

Seashore and Bowers, 1964; Klein *et al.*, 1971) and Heller did this in his method of Group Feedback Analysis (Heller, 1969, 1970, 1976).

In the Group Feedback Analysis (GFA) method, a questionnaire is usually administered to measure an attitude or opinion (e.g. job satisfaction or rating of leadership style) in a certain group (work groups, decision making bodies). The mean scores are fed back to the group and form the starting point for discussion. At the end of a discussion session, questionnaires are filled out and analysed for the second time. Thus three sets of scores become available: the first a series of 'objective' scores, the second a series of scores after feedback, and the third a series of difference scores between the two measurements. Heller lists three goals of GFA: first, validation of results; second, qualitative enrichment of the data; and third, stimulating change. It is especially the third goal, acting as a change agent, that makes this method a typical action research instrument in the strictest sense: research that motivates change and in which the persons involved in this change process participate. The discussions about the scale scores and the confrontation with the scores of others often are a source of inspiration for making efforts towards changing and improving the situation.

The third form of action research, described by Albinski (1978) as 'self-research', shows even more strongly the elements usually considered essential to action research: immediate usefulness to those involved, participation by the individuals and parties involved, and a focus on social change. In this third form of action research, the person or group involved participates not only in the interpretation of the data, but also in the setting up and carrying out of the study. This method originated in community work, where it is called 'community self-survey'. Self-research is the beginning of a change process. The group itself sets up and carries out the study, promoting responsibility and democratization by means of the characteristics mentioned by Albinski: awareness, self-diagnosis, and motivation. The role of the researcher has shifted to that of consultant, counselor, assistant. Obviously, the borderline between research and action has become quite blurred, or, rather it is often overstepped, as the importance conferred upon the self-activity and involvement of individuals or groups comes to override that of the accuracy of data and conclusions. It could even be said that often the balance between action and research is so much in favour of action that it is, in fact, impossible to speak of 'research' any longer. The chance that self-research will result in generalizable knowledge is even smaller than is the case with the two previous types of action research, although, in principle, it exists.

6. THE SCIENTIFIC INTERPRETATION PROCESS

In Section 2 it was said that one of the most important characteristics of research in work- and organizational psychology is the fact that its conclusions are based on empirical data. The process of selecting the variables to be studied, the choice of the operationalizations of the variables, and the interpretation of the findings is a complicated task. Some of the difficulties which may be encountered in this process will be discussed in this section.

6.1. The nature of the variables

The objects of study in work- and organizational psychology often are of a very complex nature. Generally, a great variety of aspects can be considered for study. There are four possible ways to deal with the many variables:
—Control; that is, keep the variables constant. The constant character of their influence on the behaviour to be studied eliminates the possibility of finding in this factor an explanation for any differences.
—Manipulation; that is, classify the phenomena on these variables, like for instance organized/unorganized workers, male/female employees, textile/metal industries.
—Measurement; in this case the variables are taken as they present themselves and their variation is recorded as accurately as possible.
—Ignore them. This is not actually a real treatment of the data, but not everything can always be taken into account, and if it can be reasonably assumed that the variable will not have much influence, it may be ignored. It should be noted that this may sometimes lead to unpleasant surprises. One may even not be aware of variables being ignored erroneously.

On the basis of these possibilities, Runkel and McGrath (1972) arrive at six modes of treating psychological variables which are considered relevant to the behaviour to be studied. A variable is relevant if it varies with the behaviour under study (direct relevance) or if it varies with another variable which does this (indirect relevance):
1. The K mode. The variable is kept constant and always has the same effect (control variable).
2. The X mode. The variable is manipulated so that all variables in the n classes have the values 1, 2, 3, ... n respectively (independent or 'treatment' variable).
3. The M mode. The variable is allowed to vary, but cases are assigned to samples which have to be compared in such a way that their means and variances are the same (matching variable).
4. The Y mode. The variable is measured as it occurs (dependent variables).
5. The R mode. Variables are not measured, controlled, or manipulated, but through random distribution of cases over the independent conditions, it is expected that any effect they may have will thus be equally distributed over the conditions.
6. The Z mode. In this mode, the influence of the variables is ignored. This is naturally the most risky, although in the R mode one is never sure either as to whether the randomization was entirely successful. Undesired sample

effects also fall under this last mode. These are of two types: the sample may underrepresent certain phenomena (or even not represent them at all) or it may overrepresent them. Such effects are difficult to pinpoint if the representativeness of the sample is not checked.

Above, a distinction was made between directly and indirectly relevant variables. The criterion here is whether the variables themselves co-vary with the behaviour or phenomenon under study, or whether, at most, the co-vary with the directly relevant variables, but not with the behaviour in question.

The nature of the relationship between directly relevant variables and the phenomena to be studied can vary greatly. The increasing capacity of computers and the development of more advanced data processing techniques over the past decades make it much easier to analyse complex interaction patterns. As far as co-variance is concerned, for instance, there are various forms of factor analysis to choose from (Harman, 1977). Factor analysis started out as an explorative technique, but, as Roskam (1978, p. 195) notes, it has since become a full-grown testing method, thanks mainly to Jöreskog's elaborations. In factor analysis in a stricter sense, the common variance is divided into fractions, determined by underlying dimensions, with only the common variance being analysed. In a variant of this technique, component analysis, the total variance, including unique variance, is analysed. With respect to the analysis of covariance among the variables as a whole, various forms of cluster analysis are available; for example, hierarchical forms, such as the one first presented by McQuitty (1960) and worked out in detail in The Netherlands by Elshout *et al.* (1967), or iterative forms, such as the one developed by Boon van Ostade (1969).

Over the past decades, there has been considerable progress in the field of regression analysis also. Weiss (1976) presents a systematic survey of the different forms of multivariate prediction, based on three classification principles: univariate or multivariate criteria, continuous or discrete criteria, and linear or non-linear relationships.—There is plenty of choice!

6.2. Causality

It remains an important problem in co-variance research that, although it is possible to study the relationships between relevant variables, it is often very difficult to say anything about the one aspect that is of great interest to both scientists and practitioners, that of possible *causal* relationships. It is all very well to know that there is a positive relationship between satisfaction with the firm and effective work consultation, or a negative one between productivity and standardization of work. It is, however, much more interesting to know if satisfaction is *caused* by work consultation or if, rather, effective work consultation is possible only when the employees involved have a positive attitude to the firm. As for the second example, it is much more interesting to know whether standardization *leads* to lower productivity or whether standardization

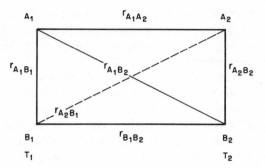

Figure 2. A model of cross-lagged panel
correlations.

is a measure taken as a *result* of a decline in productivity. In other words:
causality is often more important than correlation.

The usual correlational studies generally leave us in the lurch here. Only in
exceptional cases and with the aid of techniques which are anything but simple
can such research lead to conclusions about cause and effect. As mentioned
earlier, Jöreskog's elaboration of factor analysis has also made hypothesis
testing and causal analyses possible. Other methods are cross lagged panel
correlations and path analysis. But *cross lagged panel correlations* require
longitudinal data and ordinary transversal data cannot be used. At least two
measuring points are needed (T_1 and T_2). (See figure 2.)

If the correlations between A (e.g. intelligence) and B (e.g. school
performance) are about just as high at T_1 ($r_{A_1B_1}$) and T_2 ($r_{A_1B_2}$), but $r_{A_1B_2}$
is greater than $r_{A_2B_1}$, then it could, under certain conditions, justifiably be
concluded that the direction of the causal relationship runs from A to B. This
is an oversimplification: there are several forms and many complicating
factors. For a discussion of them, the interested reader is referred to the
literature (e.g. Cook and Campbell, 1976, pp. 228–293).

Path analysis has its origins in econometrics but has been adapted for the
social sciences by, for example, Blalock (1961) and Kerlinger and Pedhazur
(1973). Rather than an explorative technique, path analysis is a technique for
testing causal relationships that are presumed to exist on theoretical grounds.
Path coefficients between the variables in the model are calculated. Using
these, the correlation coefficients can be fractionized into direct, indirect, and
spurious relationships. To test causal chains, use is made of the direct and
indirect relationships.

Figure 3 shows an example of this. X_1 represents physical condition, X_2
motivation, X_3 work performance. According to the theoretical model, X_1
will have a direct effect on X_3, but also an indirect one via X_2. The path coefficients tell us to what extent this model is correct. The relationship between
X_2 and X_3 is partly direct, partly spurious (caused by the correlation of X_1

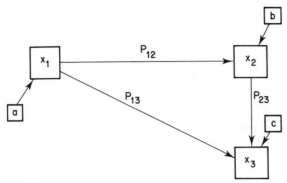

Figure 3. A path-analysis model.

with both X_2 and X_3). This is based on the assumption that exogenuous factors (a, b, and c) do not interfere in the model. This is not an easy assumption to make in work- and organizational psychology research, just as there are several other conditions which are too often difficult to fulfill (see Billings and Wroten, 1978).

6.3. The 'third factor'

In the complex field of work- and organizational psychology research, it often happens that a third variable, Z, influences the interrelationship of two variables, X and Y. Figure 4 shows four cases which frequently occur. In the following section, it will be explained what the nature of the influence of variable Z is and how it can be indentified in research.

    a. *Intervening* variable. First, the relationship between X and Y can be caused or strengthened by a third variable Z, if it is an intervening variable. X influences Z and Z influences Y, and some or all of the relationship between X and Y comes about through the effect of Z. An example: in World War II many men volunteered for the RAF out of patriotism. Of course, many more accidents occur in fighter flying than elsewhere. It cannot be claimed that there is an intrinsic relationship between patriotism and accidents, despite the fact that such a 'correlation' will be found. Such an intervening influence can be identified by calculating the partial correlation between X and Y, keeping Z constant.

    b. Element in a *circular chain*. This model is illustrated in figure 4b. X influences Z, Z influences Y, and Y in its turn influences X. (Of course the chain can also run the other way round.) To give an example: giving more formal power to a consultative body (X) may result in more competent people being attracted to it (Y) and better decisions being made (Z). This again may lead to more power being given to the consultative body, etc. Often, it is difficult to trace the 'starting point' of the circle, the correlations yielding merely a complex pattern. Here theoretical insight will have to guide the interpretation.

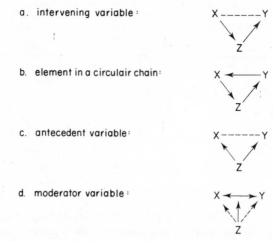

Figure 4. Various possibilities of a third factor Z
influencing the relationship between X and Y.

c. *Antecedent* variable. This model (figure 4c) is much used in social sciences and is often the source of mistaken interpretations of the relationships found. In the English literature they are called 'confounding' variables. An example from research in developing countries: socio-economic class (Z) correlates negatively with the number of children per family (X) and positively with the number of books per family (Y). It would be incorrect to think, on the basis of the resulting negative correlation between the number of books and the number of children, that there is an essential and interpretable relationship between these two variables, let alone that one determines the other (the more books one reads, the fewer children one has!).

d. *Moderator* variable. This fourth form of influence (figure 4d) is in fact the indirect form of relevance mentioned earlier (see section 6.1). The basic principle of a moderator variable is that, although it need not correlate with two others, it can nevertheless influence their relationship. The nature of the task need not correlate with a participative style of leadership nor with a subordinate's satisfaction with this leadership style, but it can nevertheless influence the relationship between them (e.g. for task related decisions this may be stronger than for personnel related decisions, Drenth *et al.*, 1979). In regression analysis, this means that a significant contribution is made by the interaction term XZ. This is, therefore, one of the methods for identifying moderator variables (Saunders, 1956). A simpler method, primarily applied to nominal or categorial variables, is that of 'subgrouping', by which the total population is subdivided on the basis of possible moderators (male-female, trade union member or not). Next, it is investigated whether the subgroups thus defined show different correlations between X and Y.

A moderator variable is not necessarily uncorrelated with X or Y. Apart from its influence as moderator variable, it may make its own independent contribution to the prediction of Y. In that case, the linear additive model is combined with the multiplicative model according to the formula $Y = aX + bZ + cXZ$, a and b being the beta weights for X and Z respectively, and c the beta weight for the interaction term XZ.

6.4. Types of errors

Lastly, we will present a brief survey of the errors in interpretations and conclusions which can play tricks on a researcher. Four categories are discussed.

1. Errors of incorrect or insufficient *operationalization* of the concepts. This can take two forms: first, the measures are not sufficiently objective and reliable or, second, the concepts are inadequately measured by the instruments chosen. The latter is a problem of construct validity. The instrument may not co-vary enough with the behaviour or phenomenon it is intended to measure (insufficient confirmative construct validity), or it may (also) co-vary with a behaviour or phenomenon which it is not intended to measure (insufficient discriminative validity; see Campbell and Fiske, 1959). For a discussion of the methods of estimating these qualities and the techniques to improve them, see the appropriate literature (Nunnally, 1967; Drenth, 1975; Campbell, 1976).

2. Errors in the statistical analysis of the data. The major errors here can be classified into two well-known types:

a. Type-one error: the null hypothesis is wrongly rejected, i.e. the existence of a relationship, cause, or phenomenon is wrongly thought proven.

b. Type-two error: the null hypothesis is wrongly accepted, i.e. the relationship, cause, or phenomenon is wrongly thought not to exist.

There are a number of statistical 'flaws' to be spotted as the causes of errors of the first type, such as too high a significance level, one-tailed rather than two-tailed testing, or the use of too insensitive tests. Conversely, errors of the second type may be caused by too low a significance level, two-tailed rather than one-tailed testing, or the use of an oversensitive test.

In work- and organizational psychology, type-one errors are often made in explorative research, when a great variety of relationships is studied. At some point certain 'significant' differences occur by chance. According to the probability distribution, five out of 100 relationships are significant at 5%!

A frequent type-two error is the consequence of the often small samples one must work with, particularly in organizational psychology. At the organizational level, large numbers are rarely available (accessibility, costs). For more on statistical errors we refer the reader to the methodological handbooks (Hays, 1963; Edwards, 1965; Runkel and McGrath, 1972).

3. Errors resulting from insufficient *internal validity*. The basic question

of internal validity is whether the results can really be ascribed to the factors held responsible (e.g. in an experiment, the independent variables). For example: a new method of bonus calculation is introduced in one department, and comparative research shows that the employees enjoy their work more than before and that absenteeism has decreased. The question of internal validity is whether this result may be ascribed to the experimental variable method of bonus calculation. Cook and Campbell (1976) give a systematic classification of the various threats to internal validity:

—History: something else has happened that is responsible for the result (e.g. a pay rise).
—Maturation: the result is a consequence of the normal process of adaptation and growth.
—Research: it is the research itself that has brought about change (being the centre of attention, the well-known 'Hawthorne' effect).
—Instrumentation: differences in research results may be due to the fact that the second measurement is not exactly the same as the first. With repeated measurements, there is often the difficulty of memory and recognition effects.
—Regression: the measurements are not very reliable, which causes regression to the mean.
—Selection: the group taking part in the study is not representative.
—Mortality: a non-random part of the research group drops out in the course of the study.
—Interaction between selection of participants and one of the above factors.

In a good experimental design (see the following section), it is always necessary to choose a control group with which to compare the results of the experimental group. This is a considerable improvement over measuring changes in one single group, but it should be realized that it creates a number of additional threats to internal validity:

—Diffusion, i.e. the experimental condition becomes known to the control group and the question arises whether the control group is then still truly non-experimental.
—Rivalry between the experimental and control groups, with positive or negative effects.
—Demoralization of the control group, to whom the experimental condition is not administered, a condition which is often favourable in many respects (otherwise it would not be studied). This problem is particularly important in, for instance, pharmacological research, where the control group has to do without a 'good' medicine. This example makes clear that demoralization often goes hand in hand with the ethical issue of whether it is right to withhold something desirable from any group of people under study.
—Local history, i.e. chance events which occur in one group but not in the other and could affect the comparison. Not all influences can be controlled or manipulated; many can at best be measured and will often just be ignored.

4. Errors due to an inadmissible *generalization* of the results (Cook and Campbell (1976) call this 'external validity'). In committing such an error, one wrongly generalizes to situations outside the research situation. Generally, there are three basic facets of research programmes which must be generalized: the research condition (the question of: what music, what system of bonus calculation, which supervisor?), the method of observation (satisfaction measured by questionnaires or interviews?, what index of absenteeism?), and the persons or objects studied (are they representative of the population to which one will generalize?). Obviously, it is primarily conclusions from case studies which allow little generalization.

Particularly in laboratory experiments, this question narrows down to that of significance and applicability of the findings in real life situations. Following Bronfenbrenner (1977:516), this source of errors is referred to as lack of 'ecological validity'.

7. DIFFERENCES IN RESEARCH DESIGN

In this section, the various designs of studies in work- and organizational psychology are discussed. We confine ourselves here to empirical research. Purely theoretical, historical, or formal logical studies are not included in this summary (see figure 5).

A first distinction is that between the study of behaviour evoked by an *experimental condition* (where the research setting is primary) and the study of behaviour evoked by *stimuli* (questions, tasks, tests), where the research setting

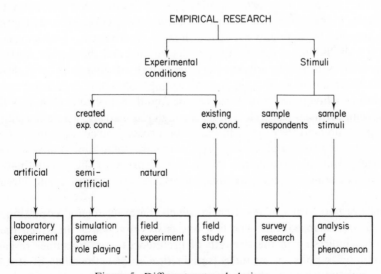

Figure 5. Different research designs.

is not primary. As to the experimental condition, we can distinguish between conditions created specially for the study and existing given conditions which are treated as experimental conditions. In the latter case we have to do with a *field study*. An example: the question whether a four-month typing course yields poorer results than a six-month course may be studied by comparing the results of two such existing courses which differ only in their duration.

There are three forms of experimental designs with the conditions created specifically for the study: an artificial condition, a semi-artificial condition, and a natural condition. In the first case we have to do with a *laboratory experiment*. The experimental condition is entirely artificial, because the experiment takes place in a laboratory, for the very reason of being able to control the many variables which play a role in natural settings. The third case is a *field experiment*: the experimental condition is created specifically for the study, but the natural character of the situation to be observed is left intact as much as possible. A new wage system (for example, a group system) is introduced in one department of an organization, while in another department, which resembles the first one as much as possible, the wage system remains the same (for example, a piece-wage system). The differences in the reactions to the two wage systems are recorded and form the basis for an evaluation of the new system.

In between these two forms there are the semi-artificial research models, such as simulation research, games, and role-playing. None of these is entirely artificial, because their natural settings are imitated to varying degrees. But they are not entirely natural either, because the imitation is only partial. In a semi-artificial design, there are three levels of manipulation of the conditions. First, external conditions can, in principle, be manipulated throughout the experiment. In that case we have to do with *simulation*, a procedure that actually is used more in training and education than in experimental research (Gagné, 1962). If only the initial situation is pre-determined and the further control of the parameters is left to the subjects, we speak of *games*, in organization contexts referred to as business games. An example of a study of decision making by means of a budget-control game can be found in Hofstede (1967). A third kind of semi-artificial research is done through *role-playing*, where the subjects are asked to pretend they are fulfilling certain roles. The conditions of 'identification with the role' and 'acting as if' are at the same time, the weak point of such experiments (Freedman, 1969). For a survey of the possibilities and limitations of semi-artificial experimental research, see Fromkin and Streufert (1976).

There are two forms of research in which the experimental condition, the setting, is *not* so important. The first one is *survey research*, in which the researcher is interested in the strength of preferences (e.g. consumer research, voter preference polls) or attitudes (satisfaction studies, the study of attitudes towards policy measures). Often the analysis of such data is of a simple univariate or bivariate type (frequency distributions, differences between groups), but this is not necessarily so. Complicated multivariate analysis designs are also possible, such as higher level analyses of variance, taxonomic analyses, etc. In survey studies the selection of the respondents is primary.

A researcher may also be interested in the nature of a *phenomenon*. Is work satisfaction a unidimensional or a multidimensional concept; what design of displays or control panels leads to the least observation or response errors; how does technical insight relate to intelligence or to education and experience; does safe behaviour depend more on the 'safety' of machines or equipment than on personality factors or environmental conditions, such as the supervisor's behaviour...? Such questions require the analysis of a carefully selected sample of stimuli. These must then be presented to a sample of respondents (which often again limits generalizability) in the hope of finding a response pattern from which conclusions regarding the psychological concept or the issue studied can be deduced.

There has been much discussion on how meaningful and useful laboratory experiments are compared to field experiments and field studies. As a rule, the semi-artificial experiments occupy an intermediate position with regard to the arguments for or against either type. In defence of the laboratory experiment it may be noted that there are two main problems in field experiments and field studies: first, the impossibility to keep undesired influences under control (no K mode) and, second, the practical impossibility to have comparable groups, departments, firms, etc. in both the experimental and the control conditions. This is of course necessary, because, if we wish to draw any conclusions about the effects of an experimental variable (e.g. job enrichment) from a comparison of the reactions in an experimental department (job enrichment introduced) and those in a control department (no job enrichment, but simply the initial short-cycle tasks), we should make sure that the differences, if any, are not brought about, increased or, conversely, reduced by causes other than those intended. And this always is a very weak point of any given field situation. The threats to internal validity are considerable, because of, on the one hand, the impossibility to eliminate undesired effects, and, on the other, the impossibility to find comparable experimental groups (the M mode) or to randomize the persons studied over the two conditions (the R mode).

The major disadvantage of laboratory experiments is, however, their artificiality. Their settings barely resemble real-life situations, which reduces the realistic value and significance of the results (the external or ecological validity), especially if they mean to study rather more complex behaviours which can hardly be understood outside their social and organizational contexts. In other words, in laboratory experiments our confidence in the accuracy of our insight into causal relationships may rise at the expense of the value this knowledge has for real-life situations. Depending on the nature of the phenomenon in question and the necessity to generalize the interpretations to situations outside the laboratory, each case will have to be considered separately as to whether confidence in the conclusions and generalizability of the results are properly balanced.

The possibility to have the subjects distributed at random over the study and control conditions only seldom occurs in field experiments and almost never in field studies. Thus, we cannot speak of a 'true experiment' if such randomization (as well as control of undesired effects) would be essential. Cook and Campbell (1976) list a number of conditions under which field experiments and field studies can still be called 'experiments, including the possibility to establish causal relationships. They use the term 'quasi experiment'. We would now like to review some of the most frequent types of quasi experiments discussed by them.

Let us start by saying that without a control group, there is no question of proper experimental research at all. This immediately eliminates two types of study often encountered in work- and organizational psychology, to wit: (a) the *One-Group Posttest-Only Design* (b) *The One-Group Pretest-Posttest Design*. If the experimental treatment is indicated by X and the observation by O, then the following models are not acceptable: $X O_1$ and $O_1 X O_2$. The first model must be rejected since we have no idea whether the observed behaviour has changed at all and, if it has, whether that is a result of X. But even the frequently used second form (pre-measurement—treatment—post-measurement) has the drawback that we do not know whether the observed changes actually are the result of the X treatment or of a normal process of maturation or change which would have occurred without X also. Wolff-Albers (1968) gives a good example. Various significant changes observed in students at a Dutch business school over one year could not be ascribed to changes in the educational programme, since the differences ran nearly parallel to similar differences among students at a number of other Dutch institutes for higher education.

The most important models Cook and Campbell mention are:
a. *The Untreated Control Group Design with Pretest and Posttest:*

$$\frac{O_1 X O_2}{O_1 O_2}$$

The only difference with laboratory experiments is that here the groups are not matched, nor are they randomly composed. Of course, the closer this ideal can be approximated, the better the experiment. In practical terms, for such an experiment, departments, study groups, etc. should be chosen which are as alike as possible, in order to keep internal validity as high as possibble. The degree to which this can be realized is an important codeterminant of the validity of the conclusions.

b. *The Reversed-Treatment Non-Equivalent Control Group Design with Pretest and Posttest:*

$$\frac{O_1 \ X + O_2}{O_1 \ X - O_2}$$

The difference with the previous design is that here the control group is also subjected to an experimental treatment, which treatment is, however, the opposite of that of the experimental group. To give a few examples: higher versus lower remuneration, a more participative versus a more authoritarian leadership style, faster versus slower working pace, etc.

c. *The Removed Treatments Design with Pretest and Posttest:*

$$O_1 \, X \, O_2 : O_3 \, \tilde{X} \, O_4$$

Any difference between O_1 and O_2 may with reasonable confidence be ascribed to X if removal of the condition shortly after has the reverse effect. O_3 need not be the same as O_2, since a change may be caused by some natural course of events (wear and tear, habituation). Experimental evidence is provided only by a noticeable 'break' between O_3 and O_4.

d. *Repeated Treatment Design.*

$$O_1 \, X \, O_2 \quad O_3 \, X \, O_4$$

An example of this design is the repeated presentation of a given stimulus (verbal stimulus or medicine). Conclusions can be drawn from this design only if O_1 differs from O_2 and O_3 from O_4 in the same direction.

These models are not all foolproof and suffer from various faults regarding internal validity (for a detailed discussion see Cook and Campbell, 1976, pp. 246–284). But under certain conditions and with certain outcomes it is certainly possible to find useful explanations, including causality, based on such quasi experiments.

8. METHODS OF DATA COLLECTION

A brief summary of the methods of data collection used in work- and organizational psychology will conclude this chapter. Space is too limited to discuss in detail the advantages and disadvantages of the various alternatives. This section is primarily intended as a first orientation.

Generally speaking, the methods of data collection can be classified according to two points of view. First, the *channel* through which information is collected. This may be the subject, who is the one directly providing the data. It may also be the researcher who provides data by means of ratings or by recording observations and impressions. An other possibility is that the initial information consists of the evaluation or opinion of a third party (an expert or

Structure Channel	Structured	Unstructured
Subject	questionnaires scales structured interviews objective tests	open interviews projection tests
Researcher	systematic observation rating	impressions participative observation
Experts/third parties	appraisals interview schedules	brainstorming Delphi-method
Recording equipment	indirect indications experimental apparatus	video, film, tape
Archives	recorded data	personal documents official documents

Figure 6. Methods of data collection.

someone involved). Then there is also the possibility to obtain information via objective registration or with the aid of experimental apparatus. Finally, information may, in principle, be already available, stored in existing documentation and files.

The second point of view concerns the extent to which the material is *structured*. Some methods first set down clearly what information is desired and how this will be categorized. These are called structured methods. When such selection and categorizing is done after data collection, we speak of unstructured methods.

Using these two points of view, the various methods of data collection can be classified into a matrix as shown in figure 6. Each of these methods will now be discussed in short, following the rows of figure 6.

8.1. Subject

First, there are methods where the *subject* is the source of information.

(i) The following techniques belong to the category *structured* methods.

Questionnaires
These are filled out by the respondents (individually or collectively, under the supervision of a researcher or independently, as in a mail questionnaires).

This is a common method, discussed extensively in the literature. For a survey of the various forms and a discussion of the technical problems involved in constructing questionnaires, see e.g. Bouchard (1976) and Oppenheim (1966).

Scales

Existing scales or, more commonly, specifically developed scales are used to measure certain attitude objects or social phenomena, such as work satisfaction (COP, 1970), hierarchy of needs (Huizinga, 1979), or participative leadership (Koopman and Werkman, 1973).

Structured interviews

In such interviews either the questions or the answer alternatives (or both) can be structured. This method strongly resembles that of questionnaires, but here the list is filled out by the researcher. This form allows some leeway, without turning into an 'open interview'. For example, the order of the questions or their wording can be adapted to the subject or the research situation (Richardson et al., 1965). Research and experience with interviews as the method of data collection (Kahn and Cannell, 1957) or as the basis for personnel guidance (Randell, 1978) is extensively covered in the literature.

Objective tests

For the measurement of a wide variety of capacities or personality factors, tests are available or can be constructed. Here we refer to tests where the evaluation of test performance or test behaviour is reasonably objective (this is the case with multiple choice tests, but it can also be achieved by means of the essay type or open ended questions). For a survey of tests in The Netherlands see Drenth (1975), NIP (1974), and De Zeeuw (1971).

(ii) Next come the *unstructured* methods where the subject acts as the channel of information.

Open interviews

There is a gradual transition between the structured and the open interview and it is not always easy to say exactly where the borderline is. But at the extremes it is quite clear. The open interview leaves the selection of topics, the order of their presentation, and the way the answers are recorded to the researcher, who follows a certain procedure dependent on the situation. Whyte (1960) extensively discussed the advantages of this form of interviewing. The researcher often makes use of a tape recorder, working out the tape later on. One of the major objections to unstructured interviews is the selectivity in the choice of topic (Mayfield, 1964) and the resulting lack of consistency, systematic coverage of the relevant domain of information and, thus, lack of comparability.

Projection tests

Another type of unstructured material is that provided by projection tests, where the subjects have to make up a story with reference to a pictured situation, or where the response to a question or remark has to be given in a 'balloon' (as in comic strips). This material is to be interpreted by the researcher. In psychodiagnostics these methods have been in use for a long time (Anderson and Anderson, 1951), although they have been subject to quite some criticism. They have also been used in attitude research (Campbell, 1950), motivation research (Drenth, 1960), and—particularly—in consumer psychological research (Smith, 1954). In work- and organizational psychology, as in psychodiagnostics, the usefulness of such techniques is primarily in the first phase of the study, in which the generation of ideas and hypotheses is emphasized.

There are obvious *advantages* to research methods with the subject as their source of information. In the first place, the subject is often the only one who can provide certain information (opinions, attitudes). It is important that he speak from his own experience or observation. Moreover, especially with the structured methods, it is possible to achieve a very satisfactory degree of reliability and objective analysis. In this respect, tests and scales, and even questionnaires, can utilize the tradition of psychometric theory and reach a high degree of methodological refinement. The force of the unstructured methods lies in the wealth of ideas and suggestions they yield. In research where this has a high priority and where the accuracy of ideas is not crucial just yet (explorative research, first phase of theory testing) these methods prove very useful.

But there are also considerable *drawbacks* to such methods. The first objection is the possibly low *relevance* of the data produced by the subject. Researchers generally are interested in behaviour itself rather than in subjective appraisals or rationalizations of behaviour. It is well known from the literature that the relationship between attitude and behaviour is often a weak one (Guilford, 1959, ch. 9). This is certainly not less true in work- and organizational psychology (see e.g. Brayfield and Crocket, 1955).

Another major difficulty with self-reports and reputational methods is their *reactivity*. By this we mean the ease with which and the likelihood that information is distorted, under the partly unconscious, partly conscious influence of the subject. In test theory, this phenomenon is known as 'social desirability' (Edwards, 1959). The results of surveys and opinion polls, especially when they concern controversial subjects or topics which may have considerable consequences for the subjects (questions about satisfaction with wages, about how an impending dismissal is experienced), may be useless if this problem is not sufficiently appreciated. The researcher hears what the subject thinks he wants to hear, the subjects chooses answers that safeguard him and his work situation, or he writes down just anything. The fact that too little attention has been paid to this phenomenon is probably a reason for the fairly negative attitudes towards such research methods (Garfinkel, 1967; Douglas, 1976; Salancik and Pfeffer, 1977), but this is not always justified (see e.g. Albinski, 1978, pp. 82–96).

With the unstructured methods, such as the open interview and the projection test, the objections just discussed appear less important. Because of their more indirect approach, the researcher's intentions may not be quite so clear and the subject is somewhat more disarmed. But, on the other hand, there is again the objection of lower reliability and validity of the information.

8.2. Researcher

The second category is that in which the *researcher* is the primary information channel. Here again there are structured methods, where the dimensions and alternatives are laid down in advance, and unstructured methods, where this is left much more to the researcher.

(i) As far as the more *structured* methods are concerned, the procedure of *systematic observation and rating* may be mentioned.

Behaviours, processes, or phenomena are recorded, using observation schedules or rating scales. The behaviour may take place in a natural or in an artificial (e.g. simulated) setting. The persons being observed or rated may or may not be aware of the fact that they are being observed (one-way mirror). The evaluation process may concern matters of content (e.g. contents of discussions; Bass, 1954) or formal process or interaction characteristics (Bales, 1950; Andriessen *et al.*, 1980). Sometimes, as in the open interview, the registration phase and the actual rating phase are separated by using a tape and/or video recorder for the registration and working out the material at a later stage.

(ii) Two methods can be classed under the *unstructured* methods.

Impressions
The researcher observes, interviews, or analyses projective material of the subject not so much with a view to a systematic analysis of the formal aspects or contents of the subject's behaviour, but primarily for his own impressions. What he, as a researcher, experiences and perceives forms the starting point for descriptions or predictions. This method is closely related to the phenomenological or clinical method in diagnostics. Research findings concerning the validity of this impressionistic approach (Wiggins, 1972) make us view the usefulness of this source of information with reservations.

Participative observation

Participative observation always consists of a combination of participating in a process and observing and evaluating that same process. The extent of participation may vary from that of a fairly aloof participant to that of a fully involved group member. According to some authors (Douglas, 1976) it is best (especially with controversial or taboo topics) to start out as a full participant and, once one has gained trust, to slip gradually into the role of observer. Douglas studied controversial issues such as nude beaches and beauty parlours in this way.

Obviously the method of 'researcher as respondent' is some sort of solution to the drawback of reactivity discussed above. Of course, this danger is still there. Having the observation and rating of behaviour done by outsiders, even experts, does not completely rule out the chance of the information being distorted by the subject. Moreover, a fresh problem crops up, namely that of distortion by the researcher. Hopefully he is well trained in unbiased observation, so he should have less difficulty with this than the subjects, but from another point of view he is certainly not without prejudices or interests (attachment to certain theories, bias as a consequence of ideology or societal value judgements). In addition, the reliability of these methods, particularly of the unstructured ones, is a point of some concern. In the more structured methods, reliability can be raised to an acceptable level by using properly designed schedules and scales.

But, on the other hand, there is the great advantage of relevance, especially with the observation methods. If, for instance, the employees being studied claim to have a certain frequency of interaction with others, but the observation data reveal that this interaction is actually more, or less, frequent, we could say that the subjective experience is a social reality and as such an interesting piece of information, but the 'objective' observation data are probably much more relevant for research purposes and practical measures. The advantages and disadvantages of objective versus participative observation have been much discussed, mostly with regard to the relationship between objectivity and replicability on the one hand, and relevance, 'realistic' character, and avoidance of reactivity on the other. For a critical evaluation of the issue see Bouchard (1976, pp. 384–392). One criterion that is particularly important in this method is that of costs in terms of personnel and time. Participation sometimes takes years, before it is fully accepted. This is no small investment, and it must be seriously balanced against the quality of the information.

Lastly, the problem of the selectivity of such information should be mentioned. Selectivity is one of the difficulties of interviews, particularly open interviews, but this objection is even more pertinent to observations. It is utterly impossible to record and use everyting one sees; there will have to be some selection. The moot question is whether such selection does not lead to biased and/or incomplete information.

8.3. Experts/third parties

Thirdly, one can fall back on the judgement of third parties, for example experts or key figures.

(i) Some of the more *structured* methods are:

Appraisals

Experts (personnel managers, supervisors, trainers) may be asked to evaluate the performance or behaviour of individuals or groups of individuals. Sometimes such evaluations are already available in the form of performance appraisals or potential assessments, sometimes they must be made specifically for the study. For the various forms of appraising and their positive and negative aspects, see this Handbook, ch. 2.4.

Interview schedules

Another possibility is to interview experts (key figures who play a crucial role in the processes to be studied) about the story behind and their perception of an event. This method includes the 'snowball technique' which starts out with an informant who has played a relevant role in an often conflictive process (for example, a negotiated decision). On the basis of the first interview, a second expert (often an opponent) is selected and asked questions. This may lead to choosing a third, fourth, etc. informant. Another example is the tracer method, in which one tries to gain insight into the historical development of a complicated process by first identifying the phases and then questioning those who had much influence (per phase) on the course of events. The phases and persons are selected on the basis of as much objective material as possible (minutes of meetings, notes, agendas, etc.). For an explication of these methods, see Koopman (1980).

(ii) Then there are the more *unstructured* methods. In this connection it is, of course, possible to use the usual open interviews to sound out the opinions of third parties. But there are two other methods which deserve to be mentioned and which are used in answering open questions, such as possible future developments or creative solutions to given problems.

The first is the 'brainstorming' method introduced by Osborn in 1941. It makes use of the following three principles:
a. free flow of ideas without attention being paid to their quality;
b. following up each other's ideas;
c. a ban on criticism.
The material thus obtained is sifted out later as to its quality.

The second technique, the Delphi method, does not make use of the cumulative effects of face-to-face interaction. On grounds of individual expert opinions averages are computed, but, at the same time, dispersions and deviations are brought to light. This is fed back to the participants for comment. The process may be repeated several times. Often these 'subjective iterative techniques' are applied in futurological research (see van Doorn and van Vught, 1978, pp. 104–117).

There are, ipso facto, advantages to using experts' judgements, because such a method relies on expertise. Obviously the quality of the information is entirely determined by the expert's knowledge and by the way in which information is recorded and used. It is known from the literature that, in offical personnel ratings, the quality of the second aspect is not very high (de Wolff, 1963).

8.4. Recording/equipment

Data collection by means of this category of instruments does not involve subjective evaluations or perceptions by people, be they respondent, researcher, or expert. Here, it is a matter of data which can be objectively recorded or registered.

(ii) The following methods can be ranked among the *structured* methods.

Objective indirect indicators
This category includes all measures which can be registered objectively and which give an indirect indication of the phenomenon to be studied. The indirect nature of the measures makes it more difficult for subjects to consciously influence the data. These methods often belong to what Webb *et al.* (1966) call 'unobtrusive measures'. They include physical traces such as the thumb-markedness of a book as an index of how much it has been read, the degree of wear of the vinyl tiles in front of certain paintings in an exhibition as an index of the paintings' popularity, the number of cigarette butts in an ashtray as an index of the amount of stress in a meeting, etc.

But they also include much simpler registrations, such as the place where someone sits down at a conference table as a measure of his dominance, the distance from certain others as a measure of congeniality and affinity (see e.g. Cook, 1970), etc. This type of measure can prove highly useful in 'real life experiments' (Bovenkerk and Brunt, 1976), as appears from a number of studies of discrimination against Surinamese in the Netherlands. This was measured by, for instance, the relative frequency with which in a streetcar the seat next to a female Surinamese researcher remained empty (Daams, 1978), or the number of times a Surinamese researcher driving an expensive car was stopped by the police for routine checks as compared to a white colleague driving a similar car along the same route (Bovenkerk and Luming, 1979).

Experimental apparatus
Such instruments are used particularly in experimental research (for instance, in engineering psychology). There is a multitude of instruments, taken directly

from experimental psychology or developed specifically for ergonomic and human factors applications (Chapanis, 1959; van Wely and Willems, 1973).

Here again, unobtrusive measures can be used to register many types of behaviour and conduct. Equipment to measure and record body movement and reactions (see Webb *et al.*, 1966, p. 152), photography and film, sometimes even infra-red film, to record reactions of groups, photo-electric cells to determine the number of times people pass a certain point—these are all means of analysing behaviour without the individuals studied being aware of it. A nice example of a complex instrument for registering the movements of individuals in a room is Bechtel's hodometer (described in Craik, 1970, p. 29). It consists of many electric switches (installed at regular intervals in the floor, under the carpet) which register each time someone passes.

It is inherent in objective measurements using often very advanced equipment that in many cases we obtain reliable data. Of course this says nothing about the validity, or, more importantly, the relevance of such data. It is primarily the indirect indicators and registrations that suffer from irrelevance or invalidity, although this is offset by the advantage of little distortion of the data. Sometimes, the logical distance between the indicator chosen and the phenomenon to be studied as so great that any conclusions with respect to the latter cannot be but extremely tentative.

With the unobtrusive measures, many feel that, in addition, it may well be asked whether they are ethically permissible. Often a method will have to be rejected solely on ethical grounds, if, that is, at least the advantage of non-reactivity should be retained!

(ii) As to the *unstructered* registration of behaviour, conduct, or interaction, equipment exists for the integral recording of conversations, movements, events, or social interaction. Such information can later be worked out, coded, and interpreted. Examples are tape recorders, film, and video equipment, which are often used to this end. In principle, this method is analogous to that of interviews or observations in vivo, but it differs from them in that tapes, films, or video tapes may be replayed as often as necessary in order to be able to clarify any obscurities or to run a recoding to assess its reliability.

8.5. Archives

A last source of information, often forgotten but easily available, is what was recorded in the past. Examples are data available from personnel files or from the files of administrative or medical departments (indicators of absenteeism, turnover) or personal or official reports, memos, agendas, minutes. The latter usually are unstructured and need to be carefully analysed and interpreted. It must not be fogotten that such information is hardly ever compiled with a view to research. Besides, there is the problem of 'selective retention' and 'selective disposal' (Webb *et al.*, 1966). Attention should be paid also to the development of scoring forms and scoring rules. It should be possible, perhaps after some training, to have them filled out reliably. For an example of such an analysis applied to work consultation and works council minutes, see Koopman *et al.* (1981). This type of documented information enriches the range of methods of data collection, as shown in the extensive discussion of this source of information by Webb *et al.* (1966).

Clearly, there is a wide range of methods of data collection for researchers in work- and organizational psychology to choose from. Each of these methods has both its problems and its advantages as the above discussion has made clear. If all of them are judged by the criteria of reliability and accuracy, validity and relevance, avoidance of reactivity, efficiency and costs, not a single method wins hands down. Moreover, in each concrete case the criteria must be weighed in light of the situation and topic to be studied. On grounds of the above critical summary, the conclusion seems justified that (a) a combination of various methods of research and (b) a combination of various instruments for each method make for a better study. The choice should therefore always be in favour of a multi-method, multi-operationalization approach, up to the point where the costs (time, money, patience of subjects) become prohibitive.

REFERENCES

Albinski, M. (1978), *Onderzoek en aktie* [Research and action]. Assen: Van Gorcum.
Allegro, J. T. (1973), *Socio-technische organisatie ontwikkeling* [Socio-technical organization development]. Leiden: Stenfert Kroese.
Anderson, H. H., Anderson, G. I. (Eds.) (1951), *An introduction to projective techniques*. New York: Prentice-Hall.
Andriessen, J. H. T. H., Cornelis, P., Flier, H. van der (1980), Participatie, invloed, satisfactie en groepseffectiviteit. Een onderzoek bij deelnemers aan een bedrijfsspel [Participation, influence, satisfaction, and group effectiveness. A study of participants in an industrial game]. *Gedrag*, **8**, 88–108.
Bales, R. F. (1950), *Interaction process analysis*. Reading: Addison-Wesley.
Bass, B. M. (1954), The leaderless group discussion. *Psychological Bulletin*, **51**, 465–492.
Billings, R. S., Wroten, S. P. (1978), Use of path analysis in industrial/organizational psychology: Criticism and suggestions. *Journal of Applied Psychology*, **63**, 677–688.
Blalock, Jr., H. M. (1961), *Causal inference in non-experimental research*. Chapel Hill: The University of North Carolina Press.
Boon van Ostade, A. H. (1969), *De iteratieve clusteranalyse* [Iterative cluster analysis]. Nijmegen: Catholic University.
Bouchard, T. J. (1976), Field research methods: Interviewing, questionnaires, participant observation, systematic observation, unobtrusive measures. In: Dunnette, M. D. (Ed.), *Handbook of industrial and organizational psychology*. Chicago: Rand McNally.
Bovenkerk, F. (Ed.) (1978), *Omdat zij anders zijn* [Because they are different]. Meppel: Boom.

Bovenkerk, F., Brunt, L. (1976), *Binnenste buiten en onderste boven; De anthropologie van de industriële samenleving* [Inside out and upside down: anthropology of industrial society]. Assen: Van Gorcum.

Bovenkerk, F., Luming, L. (1979), Surinamers en grote auto's; een levensecht experiment om rassendiscriminatie op te sporen [Surinamese and big cars; a true-to-life experiment to detect racial discrimination]. *Intermediair*, 15, 59–63.

Brayfield, A. D., Crocket, W. H. (1955), Employee attitudes and employee performance. *Psychological Bulletin*, 52, 396–424.

Bronfenbrenner, U. (1977), Towards an experimental ecology of human development. *American Psychologist*, 32, 513–531.

Campbell, D. T. (1950), The direct assessment of social attitudes. *Psychological Bulletin*, 47, 15–38.

Campbell, D. T., Fiske, D. W. (1959), Convergent and discriminant validity by the multi trait-multi method matrix. *Psychological Bulletin*, 56, 81–105.

Campbell, J. P. (1976), Psychometric theory. In: Dunnette, M. D. (Ed.), *Handbook of industrial and organizational psychology*. Chicago: Rand McNally.

Chapanis, A. (1959), *Research techniques in human engineering*. Baltimore: Johns Hopkins Press.

Clark, P. A. (1972), *Action research and organizational change*. London: Harper and Row.

Cook, M. (1970), Experiments on orientation and proximities. *Human Relations*, 23, 61–76.

Cook, Th. D., Campbell, D. T. (1976), The design and conduct of quasi-experiments and true experiments in field settings. In: Dunnette, M. D. (Ed.), *Handbook of industrial and organizational psychology*. Chicago: Rand McNally.

COP (1959), *Bazen in de industrie* [Supervisors in industry]. Den Haag: COP.

Craik, H. K. (1970), Environmental psychology. In: Newcomb, T. M. (Ed.), *New directions in psychology*. New York: Holt, Rinehart and Winston.

Cronbach, L. J., Suppes, P. (1969), *Research for tomorrow schools: Disciplined inquiry for education*. New York.

Daams, M. C. (1978), Naast wie zal ik nu eens gaan zitten? [Will I sit down beside you?]. In: Bovenkerk, F. (Ed.) (1978).

Doorn, J. van, Vught, F. van (1978), *Forecasting*. Assen: Van Gorcum.

Douglas, J. D. (1976), *Investigative social research*. Beverly Hills: Sage.

Drenth, P. J. D., (1960), *Een onderzoek naar de motivatie bij her kiezen van een beroep* [A study of motivation in choosing an occupation] (diss.). Amsterdam: Van Soest.

Drenth, P. J. D. (1975), *Inleiding in de testtheorie* [Introduction to test theory]. Deventer: Van Loghum Slaterus.

Drenth, P. J. D., Koopman, P. L., Heller, F. A., Brown, F., Rus, V., Odar, M. (1979), Participative decision making: A comparative study. *Industrial Relations*, 18, 295–309.

Drenth, P. J. D., Koopman, P. L., Hermanides, G. Heller, F. A., Brown, F., Rus, V., Odar, M. (1978), Participative decision making in industrial organisations: A three country comparative study. München, XIXth Intern. Congress of Applied Psychology.

Drenth, P. J. D., Willems, P. J., Wolff, Ch. J. de (1970), *Bedrijfspsychologie: Onderzoek en evaluatie* [Industrial psychology: Research and evaluation]. Deventer: Kluwer.

Edwards, A. L. (1957), *Techniques of attitude scale construction*. New York: Appleton Century Crofts.

Edwards, A. L. (1959), Social desirability and personality test construction. In: Berg, I. A., Bass, B. M. (Eds.), *Cognitive approaches to personality measurement*. New York: McGraw Hill.

Edwards, A. L. (1965), *Experimental design in psychological research*. New York: Holt, Rinehart and Winston.

Elshout, J. J., Elshout, M., Wijngaart, J. van de (1967), *Marimaxcor: Hiërarchische clusteranalyse uitgaande van een intercorrelatiematrix* [Marimaxcor: Hierarchical cluster analysis based on an intercorrelation matrix]. Amsterdam: ICO, University of Amsterdam.

Engel, J. F., Kollat, D. J., Blackwell, R. D. (1968), *Consumer behavior*. New York: Holt, Rinehart and Winston.

Feyerabend, P. K. (1975), Against method. London: NLB.

Frank, L. L., Hackman, J. R. (1975), Effects of interviewer interviewee similarity on interviewer objectivity in college admission interviews. *Journal of Applied Psychology*, **60**, 366–368.

Freedman, J. L. (1969), Role playing: Psychology by consensus. *Journal of Personality and Social Psychology*, **13**, 107–114.

Fromkin, H. L., Streufert, S. (1976), Laboratory experimentation. In: Dunnette, M. D. (Ed.), *Handbook of industrial and organizational psychology*. Chicago: Rand McNally.

Gagné, R. M. (1962), Simulators. In: R. Glaser (Ed.), *Training, research and education*. New York: Wiley, 223–246.

Garfinkel, H. (1967), *Studies in ethno-methodology*. Englewood Cliffs: Prentice-Hall.

Gedrag [Behaviour]. Nijmegen: Stichting Gawein.

Goldman, L. (1961), *Using tests in counseling*. New York: Harper.

Groot, A. D. de (1961), *Methodologie: Grondslagen van denken en onderzoeken in de gedragswetenschappen* (Eng. tr. 1969: Methodology: Foundations of inference and research in the behavioural sciences). The Hague: Mouton.

Groot, A. D. de (1971), *Een minimale methodologie* (A minimal methodology]. The Hague: Mouton.

Groot, A. D. de (1972), Standpunt over onderwijs, democratie en wetenschap [A viewpoint on education, democracy and science]. The Hague: Mouton.

Guilford, J. P. (1954), *Psychometric measures*. 2nd ed. New York: McGraw Hill.

Guilford, J. P. (1959), *Personality*. New York: McGraw Hill.

Guion, R. M. (1965), *Personnel testing*. New York: McGraw Hill.

Harman, H. H. (1977), *Modern factor analysis*. 3rd ed. Chicago: Univ. of Chicago Press.

Hays, W. L. (1963), *Statistics for psychologists*. New York: Holt, Rinehart and Winston.

Heller, F. A. (1969), Group Feedback Analysis: A method of field research. *Psychological Bulletin*, **72**, 108–117.

Heller, F. A. (1970), Group Feedback Analysis as a change agent. *Human Relations*, **23**, 319–333.

Heller, F. A. (1976), Group Feedback Analysis as a method of action research. In: Clark, A. W. (Ed.), *Experience in action research*. New York: Plenum Press.

Hofstede, G. H. (1967), *The game of budget control*. Assen: Van Gorcum.

Hofstee, W. K. B. (1975), De betrekkelijkheid van sociaal wetenschappelijke uitspraken [The relativity of statements in the social sciences]. *Nederlands Tijdschrift voor de Psychologie*, **30**, 373–600.

Huizinga, G. (1979), *Maslow's need hierarchy in the work situation*. Groningen: Wolters-Noordhoff.

IDE International Research Group (1981), *Industrial democracy in Europe*. Oxford: Oxford University Press.

Kahn, R. L., Cannell, C. F. (1957), *The dynamics of interviewing*. New York: Wiley.

Kerlinger, F. N. (1973), *Foundations of behavioral research*. New York: Holt, Rinehart and Winston.

Kerlinger, F. N., Pedhazur, E. J. (1973), *Multiple regression in behavioral research*. New York: Holt, Rinehart and Winston.

Klein, S. M., Kraut, A. J., Wolfson, A. (1971), Employee reactions to Attitude Survey Feedback. *Administrative Science Quarterly*, **16**, 497–514.

Koopman, P. L. (1980), *Besluitvorming in organisaties* [Decision making in organizations]. Assen: Van Gorcum.

Koopman, P. L., Werkman, B. (1973), Het verhoudingsmodel bij de meting van satisfactie [The ratio-model in measuring satisfaction]. In: Drenth, P. J. D., Willems, P. J., Wolff, Ch. J. de (Eds.), *Arbeids- en organisatiepsychologie* [Work- and organizational psychology]. Deventer: Kluwer.

Koopman, P. L., Drenth, P. J. D., Bus, F. B., Kruyswijk, A. J., Wierdsma, A. F. (1981), Context, process and effects of participative decision making on the shop floor. *Human Relations*, **34**, 657–676.

Kuhn, Th. (1962), *The structure of scientific revolutions*. Chicago: University of Chicago Press.

Linschoten, J. (1964), *Idolen van de psycholoog* [The psychologist's idols]. Utrecht: Bijleveld.

McClelland, D. C. (1961), *The achieving society*. Princeton: Van Nostrand.

McQuitty, L. L. (1960), Hierarchical syndrome analysis. *Educational and Psychological Measurement*, **20**, 293–309.

Mann, F. C. (1957), Studying and creating change: A means to understanding social organization. In: Arensberg, C. M. (Ed.), *Research in industrial human relations: A critical appraisal*. New York: Harper, 146–167.

Mayfield, E. C. (1964), The selection interview—a review of research. *Personnel Psychology*, **17**, 239–260.

Mulder, M. (1977), *Omgaan met macht* [Managing power]. Amsterdam: Elsevier.

Mulder, M., Wilke, H. (1970), Participation and power equalization. *Organisational Behaviour and Human Performance*, **5**, 430–448.

Mulder, M., Ritsema van Eck, J. R., Jong, R. D. de (1970), Het systeem van functioneren onder verschillende omstandigheden in een grote organisatie [A system of functioning in different circumstances in a large organization]. In: Drenth, P. J. D. *et al.* (Eds.) (1970).

Nederlands Tijdschrift voor de Psychologie [Dutch Journal of Psychology]. Deventer: Van Loghum Slaterus.

NIP (1974), *Documentatie van tests en testresearch* [Documentation on tests and test research]. Amsterdam: NIP.

Nunnally, J. C. (1967), *Psychometric theory*. New York: McGraw Hill.

Oppenheim, A. W. (1966), *Questionnaire design and attitude measurement*. London: Heinemann.

Osborn, A. F. (1941), *Applied imagination: Principles and procedures of creative thinking*. New York: Harper and Row.

Phillips, D. L. (1973), *Abandoning method*. London: Jossey-Bass.

Price, J. L. (1972), *Handbook of organizational measurement*. Lexington (Mass.): Heath.

Pugh, D. S., Rickson, D. J., Hinings, C. R., Turner, C. (1968), Dimensions of organisation structure. *Administrative Science Quarterly*, **13**, 65–105.

Randell, G. (1978), Interviewing at work. In: Warr, P. B. (Ed.), *Psychology at work*. 2nd ed. London: Penguin.

Richardson, S. A., Dohrenwend, B. S., Klein, D. (1965), *Interviewing*. New York: Basic Books.

Roskam, E. E. Ch. I. (1978), Methodenleer [Methodology]. In: Duyker, H. C. J. (Ed.), *Psychologie van vandaag* [Psychology today]. Deventer: Van Loghum Slaterus, 188–237.

Runkel, Ph. J., McGrath, J. E. (1972), *Research on human behavior*. New York: Holt, Rinehart and Winston.

Salancik, G. R., Pfeffer, J. P. (1977), An Examination of need-satisfaction models of job attitudes. *Administrative Science Quarterly*, **22**, 427–456.

Saunders, D. R. (1956), Moderator variables in prediction. *Educational and Psychological Measurement*, **16**, 209–222.

Schmitt, N. (1976), Social and situational determinants of interview decisions: Implications for the employment interview. *Personnel Psychology*, **29**, 79–101.

Seashore, S. Bowers, D. G. (1964), *Changing the structure and the functioning of an organization*. Ann Arbor: Survey Research Center.

Smith, G. H. (1954), *Motivation research in advertising and marketing*. New York: McGraw Hill.

Smith, P. C., Kendall, L. M., Hulin, C. C. (1967), *Measurement of satisfaction in work and retirement*. Chicago: Rand McNally.

Strien, P. J. van (1975), Naar een methodologie van het praktijk denken in de sociale wetenschappen [Towards a methodology of practical thinking in the social sciences]. *Nederlands Tijdschrift voor de Psychologie*, **30**, 601–619.

Strien, P. J. van (1978), *Om de kwaliteit van het bestaan* [On the quality of life]. Meppel: Boom.

Suchman, E. A. (1971), *Evaluative research*. New York: Russell Sage Foundation.

Susman, G. I., Evered, R. D. (1978), An assessment of the scientific merits of action research. *Administrative Science Quarterly*, **23**, 582–603.

Thierry, Hk. (1968), *Loont de prestatiebeloning?* Assen: Van Gorcum.

Tigchelaar, L. S. (1974), *Potentieel beoordeling en loopbaansuccess* [Potential assessment and career success]. Eindhoven: Geena.

Vercruijsse, E. V. W. (1960), *Het ontwerpen van een sociologisch onderzoek* [Designing sociological research]. Assen: Van Gorcum.

Vries, J. de (1973), *Dienstbaar onderzoek* [Serviceable research]. Meppel: Boom.

Wardekker, W. (1978), Actieonderzoek in de onderwijsmethode [Action research in educational methods]. *Kennis en Methode* [Knowledge and Method], **1**, 44–55.

Webb, E. J., Campbell, D. T., Schwartz, R. C., Sechrest, L. (1966), *Unobtrusive measures*. Chicago: Rand McNally.

Weiss, D. J. (1976), Multivariate procedures. In: Dunnette, M. D. (Ed.), *Handbook of industrial and organizational psychology*. Chicago: Rand McNally.

Wely, P. A. van, Willems, P. J. (1973), *Ergonomie: Mens en werk* [Ergonomics: Man and work]. Deventer: Kluwer.

Whyte, W. F. (1960), Interviewing in field research. In: Adams, R. N., Preiss, J. J. (Eds.), *Human organizations research*. Homewood: Dorsey.

Wiggins, J. S. (1972), *Personality and prediction*. Reading (Mass.): Addison-Wesley.

Wolff, Ch. J. de (1963), *Personeelsbeoordeling* [Personnel appraisal]. Amsterdam: Swets & Zeitlinger.

Wolff-Albers, A. D. (1968), *Een poging tot evaluatie van een tertiaire opleiding, of het nut van controle groepen* [An attempt at evaluating tertiary education, or the use of control groups]. Groningen: Wolters-Noordhoff.

Zeeuw, J. de (1971), *Algemene psychodiagnostiek* [General psychodiagnostics] I. Amsterdam: Swets & Zeitlinger.

Zelditch, M. (1969), Some methodological problems of field studies. In: McGall, G. J., Simmons, R. G. (Eds.), *Issues in participant observations*. Reading (Mass.): Addison-Wesley.

1.3. The role of the work- and organizational psychologist

Charles J. de Wolff

1. INTRODUCTION

Work and organizational psychologists have been engaged in many subjects in their scientific work, but they have done relatively little on their own function. That is strange, because this subject is certainly worthwhile studying. W/O psychologists do a lot in our society: they work in and for organizations and render services to clients. In their work they have much influence on others; they give advice which could have far-reaching consequences for individuals and organizations. They also have opinions about how society functions and in their work they attempt to assert their views and certain norms and values. What they pursue has consequences for the functioning of other people. In their turn W/O psychologists experience the influence of what principals and clients do and what they think about the profession of psychologist.

Although the functioning of psychologists has hardly been the subject of scientific studies, it cannot be said that psychologists are unaware of the problems in this area. There are discussions and articles on the subject, but they must be sought in annual addresses of presidents of professional associations and in journals of societies (such as 'De Psycholoog' and 'The American Psychologist'). These kinds of arguments and articles do contain analyses of the problems but mostly they also give opinions and beliefs about how the problems should be approached and on what should be pursued.

This chapter is an analysis of how W/O psychologists function. What do W/O psychologists attempt to achieve, by what is their functioning determined, which problems do they experience in their work? What are the determinants

Prof. dr. Ch. J. de Wolff, Katholieke Universiteit, Vakgroep Arbeids- en Organisatiepsychologie, Montessorilaan 3, 6500 HE NIJMEGEN of their behavior? The analysis will be mostly based on a number of social science theories which were developed to study other subjects, such as theories on professionalization, role theory and systems theory. For a general description of these theories, the reader is referred to Katz and Kahn (1978), Secord and Backman (1974) and Mok (1973). Role theory is especially useful for the conceptualization of our problem area.

Psychologists who work in organizations are in constant interaction with others. In their work these others are dependent upon the psychologist, and the psychologist in turn is dependent upon these others in performing his professional activities ('interdependency'). At work, people have expectations regarding others and they also let this be known either openly or covertly ('role sending'). People develop certain beliefs and attitudes regarding persons upon whom they are dependent; people who are dependent upon the psychologist do the same. People attribute certain intentions and characteristics to each other and behave in a certain way in relation to each other. There are continuous attempts to influence each other. Such processes occur in a 'role set': role theory distinguishes a 'focal person'—in this chapter the psychologist—and the individuals in the organization with whom the focal person interacts (the 'role senders'). Important role senders for the W/O psychologist are other W/O psychologists, principals, clients, representatives of other disciplines and government. In these mutual relationships many problems can occur. As an example: a principal needs a quick solution and therefore does not agree to a time consuming study suggested by the psychologist, or a consultant proposes a certain organizational structure and wants it implemented quickly and therefore he sees little merit in a proposal from a psychologist to choose a participative approach.

In this chapter W/O psychologists are first viewed as members of a professional group and afterwards as members of an organization (for example, as an employee of a company). The fullfilling of more than one role is a source of strain. Psychologists have a domain; they provide services to clients. Which services these are and who are the clients will be discussed, in addition to the relationship with representatives of other disciplines and the government.

2. THE PROFESSION OF W/O PSYCHOLOGIST

2.1. W/O psychologists present themselves as psychologist

W/O psychologists present themselves as such. In their relations with role senders (principals, clients, representatives of other disciplines) they clearly signify that they are not acting on the basis of private insights but on the collective insights of a larger whole. Role senders realize this. They often report that something was said by a psychologist. Speakers are often introduced as psychologist. There are even statements as 'the psychologist said that . . .'. Apparently, something that is done by a person in the capacity of psychologist has surplus value. With regard to W/O psychologists there are two capacities involved: they present themselves as 'W/O psychologist' and also as 'psychologist'. W/O psychologists are members of a larger group, to which social psychologists, clinical psychologists etc. also belong. The surplus value seems to be for the most part tied to the broader concept 'psychologist'. Not all psychologists present themselves as such. In a country like The Netherlands, the title is used quite often; but in other countries (for example England) where the profession enjoys less prestige in organizations, different titles are used (de Wolff *et al.*, 1981): for example 'management development specialist' or 'training specialist'. Different titles are also preferred in The Netherlands, for example 'director', 'professor', 'organization consultant'. Titles are used because of the prestige and reputed strengthening of a position derived from them.

2.2. Members of a profession have a special attitude

W/O psychologists practice a profession. W/O psychology is not only the name of a scientific discipline, but it is also the name of a profession. This is somewhat confusing, because in contrast to some other professions there are no distinguishing concepts available for discipline and profession (for example, medicine and physician). The profession of W/O psychologist is relatively new, only being developed in the 20th century (and in most countries especially in the second half).

The emergence of professions and the interaction between profession and professionals have been studied predominantly by sociologists. Mok (1973) gives a survey of the literature in this area. The theories developed by sociologists provide propositions for the analysis of the behavior of W/O psychologists. According to Gross (1958) the professions have the following characteristics: (1) the product is not standardized; (2) the professional shows a high degree of personal involvement; (3) the professional possesses thorough knowledge of a specialized technique; (4) there is a clear sense of duty; (5) there is a feeling of group identity; and (6) professionals make an important contribution to society. Kast and Rosenberg (1970) mention a number of characteristics whereby professions distinguish themselves:

—Professions have a 'systematic body of knowledge' available to them. The members acquire skill by means of a lengthy process of training. This involves an intellectual basis as well as practical experience.

—Professionals have acquired a high degree of authority based on superior knowledge, which is also recognized by the clients. This authority is highly specialized and is related only to the professional competence sphere.

—There is broad social sanction and approval of the exercise of this authority.

—There is a code of ethics regulating relations of professionals with clients and with colleagues.

—There is a professional culture which is sustained by organizations.

Hall (1969) mentions a number of attitudes found among professionals:
—the use of the professional group as a point of reference;
—the belief in service to the public;
—the belief in self-regulation;
—a feeling of vocation and dedication to the work;
—the need for autonomy, i.e. the conviction that the practitioner should be free from external pressure.

From the paraphrases above it would appear that professionals are characterized by a special attitude and a special social position. The attitude is constituted by involvement, vocation, dedication, sense of duty, identification with a professional group and the belief in service to the public. The social position is expressed through the possession of a high degree of authority and the important contribution to society. (But in view of the social changes of the seventies, it may be questioned if these statements—all dating from the fifties and sixties—still hold for the possession of authority and the social position.) It seems justified to assert that psychologists strongly identify with their work and profession and that they are convinced of the significance of their work for society.

2.3. The professionalization process

The attitudes and beliefs of professionals are closely connected to the manner in which a profession emerges and the way in which the professional community functions. Mok distinguishes three processes which lead to the development of a profession: differentiation, legitimation and institutionalization. The process of differentiation occurs first. The increasing complexity of organizations occasions the need for experts who are able to solve certain problems. This leads to the emergence of professions. Interaction between experts contributes to a certain feeling of community, not only in the activities performed but also in the approach and solutions developed. However, differentiation is not enough to establish a profession.

The next step is institutionalization. This process occurs when experts start to develop a specific structure around the activities and solutions, for example setting up a professional association, formalizing the training, supervision of the way members practice the profession, acquiring official recognition etc. Professionals establish the objectives they want to reach in and through the structure and seek support from the environment. Two points are important here: (1) the attempt to remain self-regulating, for example with the aid of a professional code. This involves the strong conviction that representatives of the profession should judge whether the profession is being correctly practiced. (2) The recruitment of members is important for the growth and future of the profession as well as for maintaining views, beliefs and values. Recruitment always involves a process of socialization (there will be more about this point below).

Legitimation refers to the pursuit of recognition and acceptance by others (principals, clients, government and society as a whole). Professionals have their own definition of reality; this involves perception and explanatory processes. A profession obtains credibility only when this definition is accepted by others. This is first of all connected to the knowledge attributed to the professionals and the ability to solve problems. An example: personnel psychologists assumed that success at work is determined to a large extent by aptitudes (see for example Thorndike, 1949). This is one definition of reality. Principals were successfully convinced of its validity, which led to psychologically testing applicants on a large scale (credibility). Principals were also convinced that psychologists have special knowledge and skills at their disposal in judging applicants.

Professions differ to the extent that these processes have advanced; in some cases the extent is great, for example the medical profession. This is called an established profession; in other cases the professions are still at the beginning. Whether these processes will progress depends not only upon the effort of the professionals but also upon environmental factors. Acceptance by others must be obtained and this will be closely connected to the degree wherein the professionals' definition of reality is acceptable to others. The example from personnel selection mentioned above fits very well in a period of world war, when mobilization must be quickly effected and an army must be built up. The same idea is less appropriate in a period of emancipation with emphasis on participation and 'power equalization'. Sometimes the professionalization process does not succeed: in the sociological literature the example of the social worker is described (van Doorn, 1966). Institutionalism and legitimation of W/O psychology in the Netherlands are in an advanced stage (for information on a number of other European countries, see de Wolff et al., 1981).

2.4. The attractiveness of a profession

Belonging to a profession is attractive. We have already established that one identifies with a profession: one is a psychologist. The professional group is an important point of reference. The term 'professional community' is also used. Mok cites Goode (1957) regarding a number of characteristics of the professional community:

1. the members are allied by a common identity;
2. once a member always a member, the status is terminal;
3. mutual values;
4. the role definitions concerning members and non-members are shared by all members, that is to say there are institutionalized role expectations;
5. there is a professional language which is only partially understood by outsiders;
6. the profession has power over its members;

7. there are clear borders and they are socially determined;

8. the community ensures continuity by influencing recruitment, selection and training of new members.

Mok states that 'the community is the basis for the identity of the professional functions and serves as the main point of reference'. This also applies to W/O psychologists. They identify themselves to a high degree with their profession and are convinced that they provide important services to society by practicing their profession. The identification is built up during their training and during the period in which they are introduced to practice by experienced colleagues. One sees how instructors and colleagues approach problems and hears their opinions. Instructors and colleagues function as role models and their values and norms are adopted. Training and introduction to practice constitute not only a period of knowledge transfer but also a socialization process. The beginner's self-image is changed; he becomes interested in the professional problems, is proud of his new knowledge and skills, acquires a professional ideology and internalizes the norms and values which in turn provide professional motivation (Mok, 1973). Being a member of a professional group enhances one's own position: one experiences more recognition and acceptance in practicing the profession. On an individual basis one would never succeed in gaining such a position so quickly. Clients are prepared to consult the professional on the basis of the trust which they have in the profession. One obtains credit. Remuneration also occurs on the basis of conditions which are stipulated by the profession and is almost always more favorable than what one could obtain as an individual.

For these advantages there is a corresponding price. The norms and values of the professional group have to be underwritten and the member must subject himself to 'colleague surveillance'. This concerns not only written rules such as those for psychologists laid down in a code of conduct (NIP, 1976) but also unwritten rules. Whoever does not obey the rules can be formally corrected: for instance, the Dutch Psychologists Association has a Board of Surveillance and a Board of Appeals which deal with submitted complaints. Sanctions are warnings and in the most serious cases expulsion from membership. Breaking unwritten rules can lead to reactions from colleagues. These will entail openly or covertly making the offender aware that he is not behaving according to the norms and values of the profession. The remarks could be that something is dubious or qualitatively not up to measure or scientifically 'unfounded' etc. Those who do not behave themselves according to the norms and values of the profession are not considered for attractive positions.

The professional group warrants this by asserting that in this way guarantees can be given that ensure responsible practice. By exercising surveillance the interests of clients will not be prejudiced. This is all the more necessary because the client is to a high degree dependent upon the professional. The professional is assumed to possess superior knowledge and to be capable of solving problems.

The relationship between client and professional is not symmetrical. The collective of colleagues formally organized in a professional association must provide the guarantees against the misuse of this dependence.

There is, therefore, an exchange relationship between practitioners and the professional group, which implies the existence of tension. Everyone will not experience this as such. The socialization process leads to strong identification with the profession and internalization of the values and norms. For most this will only become visible when there are conflicts with norms and values of other groups to which one refers.

2.5. The profession as a social system

W/O psychologists have been discussed above without making any further distinctions. However, W/O psychologists fullfill very different functions (Krijnen, 1975, 1976): some work at universities, others in companies and still others in organization consultant firms. Their task content is very diverse. The one is engaged in selection, the other in organizational change. To speak of *the* W/O psychologist leads to simplifications. What was discussed in the preceding sections holds in general for all W/O psychologists. But it should be taken into account that the differences between subgroups and even between individuals within a subgroup can be great. A psychologist who teaches at a university is exposed to other problems than a psychologist who does selection work in a company. The costs and profits of belonging to a professional group can be different for both categories. A profession can be seen as a social system with a number of subsystems such as professional training, professional association, institutes rendering services, research institutes, journals of the profession etc. In all of these subsystems there are W/O psychologists with their own interests, opinions, beliefs and concerns.

There are also psychologists engaged in managing the system and subsystems: directors of agencies, chairmen of professional associations and divisions, professors, editors of journals etc. Considering the variety of functions and interests, it is understandable that tension occurs within a profession. On the one hand there is a community, but on the other there are opinions, interests and goals which are in competition with each other. There are centrifugal as well as centripetal forces involved. Mok (1973) recognizes this play of forces and points out that there is a dominant segment in every profession. There are internal conflicts and there is competition within the profession. But a coalition of some segments succeeds in imposing their viewpoint on the whole profession. Most of the time this happens because the viewpoint of this dominant segment is also supported by outsiders: clients, principals, government etc. This not to say that other viewpoints become muted as a result, but one sees no chance of displacing the dominant coalition and one must accept the situation. The defenders of opinions of the dominant coalition are to be found everywhere in executive positions. Professions also have an 'establishment'; psychologists who are called to these positions can and will defend the viewpoint of the dominant coalition. However, dominant coalitions are not permanent; evolutions as well as revolutions can occur. The opinions which could be defended in the course of time are very different: an example, in the fifties 'clinical' selection methods were still widely accepted but in the sixties 'statistical' methods became predominant. This involves not only a scientific discussion but also the emergence of a new dominant segment. This is apparent in the appointment of professors, invitations to address congresses, in the composition of editorial boards, appointment of directors etc.

2.6. Conflicts between the segments

Mok observes that all professions are characterized by internal conflicts, competition between factions and dissension about values and norms. There are 'segments', groups of professionals who have an organized identity and professional situation in common, who jointly attempt to influence the professional group's development by promoting or blocking important changes.

Each segment has its own ideology in the form its definition of professional activities and common values. An important basis for segment formation within a profession is knowledge. On the basis of this a split can occur: a 'knowledge elite' emphasizing competence and formal education for the profession and a 'behavior elite' emphasizing integrity and training in practice. Mok cites a few studies on the medical profession, where this conflict between 'scientific' and 'clinical' forces is continuous. Such a conflict also exists in psychology: an illustration of this is the polemic between Duijker (1977, 1978), Van Strien (1977, 1978), Roe (1978) and Wijngaarden (1978). It was not a coincidence that precisely these people were involved in the controversy. Duijker can be considered as the architect of the training in psychology in The Netherlands; for years he was secretary of the Dutch Journal of Psychology and filled many executive positions (among others, president of the Dutch Institute of Psychology). He was, therefore, a prominent member of the dominant segment in psychology. As a professor of work and organizational psychology Van Strien has extensively published on professional issues. The title of one of his books 'On the quality of life: contours of an emancipatory psychology' clearly shows that he has outspoken ideas about social developments and the role which W/O psychologists must play therein. The other authors also fill prominent positions in the world of psychology (professor, past president of the professional association, president of the W/O division).

The contrast between the scientific approach and that of practical application is expressed in the polemic. Duijker (1977) begins by pointing out that a complete change of front has taken place in psychology. He asserts that 'psychology is what psychologists make of it' and that 'psychology is dependent upon the professional identity which psychologists assume'. He observes that more and more psychologists have become helpers and calls what they do 'salutary' activities. He does not consider this development to be proper: 'psychology is in danger of losing its scientific character. Psychologists should search for the determinants of human behavior and describe their impact and their mutual interaction. A psychologist who would like to base his professional identity on such 'salutary' activities cannot be distinguished from the countless others, who are either trained in another scientific discipline or those who are quasi-scientifically indoctrinated or those without any training at all, claiming to promote human well-being .... Descriptive psychology forms ... not just the foundation on which activities correctly considered as 'psychological' rest, but also the legitimation of the professional identity of all psychologists'.

In a reaction to this Roe (1978, p. 12) suggests that '—at least in the present state of psychology—there is no objection to the values of a psychologist playing a role in rendering services. This can be even useful, in the sense that it becomes possible for the psychologist to make statements or give advice on matters about which science offers no support'. Duijker reacted to this very angrily: 'Useful for whom? For the psychologist's bank account? If a psychologist is unable to contribute more to the solution of a client's problem than grandpa, aunt or neighbor, can he then be allowed to pretend expertise and be paid accordingly?'. These psychologists should 'be immediately kicked out of the association and brought before the judge for deceit' (Duijker, 1978). Duijker writes further: 'If there is a need for help (not necessarily from psychologists), then it should be considered how helpers can be found and utilized. It seems evident to me that for them a five-year university education will not be necessary'.

Duijker's view has not remained uncontested. Van Strien is directly opposed to the statements of Duijker: 'the maturity and analytical sharpness which normally characterize the writings of Duijker have apparently made way for a rhetoric of indignation and alarm ...'. At the end of his article he points out 'that in the coming years one can expect increasing dispute between the subdivisions of psychology departments about lectureships, staff positions and their part of the budget'. He is afraid that Duijker's approach could lead to impairment of the scientifically and organizationally well substantiated training and professional activities. He ends with the call 'psychologists watch your business!'

We have cited Duijker as well as Van Strien in some detail because their articles illustrate very well the dispute between segments reported by Mok. Here, different views of the profession collide. The views are based on evaluations of developments and on beliefs and values. Duijker emphasizes that psychology as a science has not developed so far that good answers can be formulated for many practical problems. Duijker is, by the way, not opposed to applying knowledge. In a later article he stresses that psychologists should limit themselves to their expertise: 'cobbler, stick to your last'. He mentions ergonomics as one of the fields where this is actually done. Van Strien envisages a psychology which is more socially innovative. Psychologists must be researchers as well as consultants. Both authors attempt in their articles to obtain support from others. They rouse professional colleagues to underwrite their views.

2.7. Conclusion

The professional group is an important role sender for the W/O psychologist. This group is not homogeneous, within it there are competing opinions. Those who defend these opinions attempt to convert others to their views. Even within the professional group the W/O psychologist is confronted with role conflicts.

3. THE W/O PSYCHOLOGIST AND HIS CLIENT

3.1. Two central questions

Thompson (1967) points out that every organization is confronted with two central questions: 'which products and/or services does one want to supply?' and 'for which clients does one want to work?'. These are also important questions for professions. Thompson makes it clear that the answers which one gives have great consequences for the organization's chances of survival. 'Inadequate' answers could lead to the decline and death of the organization. If one chooses a product that is not purchased by clients, for example because it is too expensive or because someone else supplies a better product, acute problems emerge. They could be so serious that the organization is ruined by them. The same holds if one chooses a client who is not prepared or able to buy the products. Thereby, one should not only look at the present but also at the future. The choices made should ensure continuity. The organization ought to be able to remain functioning even in situations where there are changes in the task environment of the system.

Psychologists provide services. Within the profession there are many—sometimes very pronounced—opinions about which services are to be provided and also which services are not to be provided (see for example the Duijker–Van Strien discussion previously referred to). There are also opinions about the point for which clients should one work. There are some W/O psychologists who think that they have been 'leased' by management, others think that they should be loyal first of all to the weakest groups in society, still others emphasize that they are working for a client-system and some even prefer to work in a workers union.

The professional code (NIP, 1976) contains many passages on the relationship with the client. Besides, opinions apparently change in the course of time. This is explicitly stated in the preamble of the Dutch professional code (article 1.2): ' ... views are subject to developments'. The choices psychologists make influence the chances for survival and the possibilities of development of the profession. They also influence the behavior of psychologists.

In this section we will discuss questions about the choice of clients. In the following section, about the domain of the psychologist, the services offered will be discussed. The two questions are, understandably, very closely connected. If one has developed a certain product for one client, one is inclined to look for other clients who are prepared to buy the product. Once one has built up a good relationship with a given client, one may subsequently attempt to adapt the package of services better to the wishes of the client.

3.2. The client is the consumer of the professional system's output

It is not so easy to establish who are the W/O psychologists' clients. A psychologist who teaches at a university will probably view his students as clients. A psychologist working for a vocational consultant firm will consider the individuals who ask his advice as clients. Organization consultants speak of client-systems, denoting that they are dealing with a complex network of relations and responsibilities. In this sense *the* client does not exist. If the profession is viewed as a social system, it is possible to restrict the scope of the question. Katz and Kahn (1978) state that providing services is the most important function of a system. Training of professionals is consequently the task of a subsystem ('maintenance subsystem') but research can also be viewed as a subsystem (a discussion about this is possible, see below). The clients are then the individuals and organizations who consume the services of psychologists (who constitute the 'production subsystem'). In view of this, the discussion is restricted to the question of who are the customers for the system's output.

3.3. Knowledge production or helping clients?

Two orientations can be distinguished within W/O psychology. The first orientation is focussed on knowledge production: W/O psychologists should concentrate especially on research and publication of research results. The second orientation is focussed on service or assistance. Clients have problems and turn to W/O psychologists for help. W/O psychologists attempt to help clients in solving those problems (at least to the extent that they fall within the profession's domain).

These two orientations are limits of a continuum, forms and combinations other than polar can be imagined. These orientations do not only occur within

W/O psychology but also within all kinds of other professions (Mok, 1973). Which orientation one will support seems on the one hand to be connected to one's position, but on the other hand it also seems to be connected to the times.

Psychologists on the staffs of universities are more inclined to support the knowledge-production orientation, whereas in contrast practicing psychologists focus more on helping clients. In addition, there are differences in relation to the times. Before the second world war, there was a distinct service orientation. An example: in lectures held for employers, Roels, a professor in Utrecht, pleaded for the use of psychologists as leaders of teams of managers, engineers and others in solving moral and social problems (ter Meulen, 1981). After 1960 the knowledge-production orientation became dominant. In that period, the number of psychologists employed by universities increased rapidly. (In The Netherlands: from 94 in 1963 to 595 in 1972; see Krijnen, 1975) The percentage of W/O psychologists employed by universities rose from 19% in 1960 to 32% in 1972. In that period there was a distinct need to develop further the methods of research and to expand the amount of knowledge. The tendency to use that knowledge in solving problems of clients is much less than in the preceding period.

It is conceivable that in the coming years the service orientation will regain more and more of the ground lost, as a result of the decreasing availability of university positions and the necessity for recently graduated psychologists to start looking for jobs in the market sector. Developments in the labor market could stimulate a reorientation.

3.4. Who is the client?

With regard to the knowledge-production orientation, it is not so clear who the clients are. In principle, they are the ones who read the publications and use the knowledge to solve problems. But who are the readers? George Miller (1969) gave an interesting example of this orientation in his presidential address to the American Psychological Association. Miller thinks that psychologists should give away their knowledge ('To give psychology away'). He observes that people use numerous inadequate theories and concepts in their approach to reality. By advancing better knowledge and insights it must be possible to achieve spectacular improvements. He mentions a few examples from the past: one is how Freud's insights into sexuality led to an entirely different view of society, once they became common property of the public. The social problems of our time could be tackled better if the people who are involved with them had better theories and concepts at their disposal.

Within W/O psychology this has been practiced on a large scale. Lots of knowledge were 'given away'. Many books and journals were written especially for managers, personnel administrators and others in the business world.

In addition, W/O psychologists provided lectures and courses which, as a result, have made the theories of McGregor, Likert, Herzberg and many others common property of organizations. W/O psychology has become part of the training programs of economists, engineers and industrial engineers.

It is also concievable that the knowledge is used by practicing psychologists. In practice this happens on a large scale. With regard to the increase of knowledge-production orientation, there is ambiguity concerning the question 'who is the client'. On the one hand it seems that especially nonpsychologists should use the knowledge, on the other that precisely psychologists ought to do this. Combinations are also conceivable. George Miller is one of few who explicitly states which strategy ought to be followed, based on this orientation.

In the service orientation at least, the client is visible. W/O psychologists render their services to numerous individuals and organizations. Here, however, problems arise as to who should be designated as client and which clients one is allowed to work for.

At the end of the sixties the question 'who is the client' became an especially burning question for W/O psychologists. Before that time the problem did indeed exist but it was discussed only to a limited extent. It was recognized very early that there can be a conflict of interests between principal and applicant. The first code of conduct (1960) approved by the Dutch Institute of Practicing Psychologists contained a number of clauses that were intended to clarify the positions of principal, applicant and psychologist. Thus it was stipulated that the psychologist must inform the applicant of the test results if the applicant request it. Towards the end of the sixties there was a wide discussion on the acceptability of these selection procedures. Not only psychologists but also nonpsychologists participated in this discussion. The question where the loyalties of the psychologist lay was posed. Must he primarily feel responsible for the interest of the organization and the principal or should he identify himself especially with the employees, with whom he is professionally involved, and the applicants. It was also observed that in the application situation the applicant is at a disadvantage. The organization has created a favorable position for itself by means of elaborate procedures and staff support. It is very difficult for the applicant to adequately counter this situation. University and academy students insisted on an arrangement whereby loyalty to the 'weaker party' (the employees) is manifested. W/O psychologists were surprised by these criticisms. They took the service to principals for granted and they were hardly inclined or prepared to discern a conflict of interests between the principal and individual employees. In the beginning of the seventies, more radical standpoints were voiced by the Theme-group North Netherlands, a group of psychologists working at the university of Groningen, 'who wanted to make science subservient to the struggle of the working population in the north (of The Netherlands) in improving their position' (van Strien, 1978). Although only few psychologists have taken such an extreme position, it has attracted many students. Many of the ideas of that time and utopian expectations about the future can be found in Van Strien's book 'On the quality of life' (1978).

The discussion on the relationship with the client led to the approval of an amended code of conduct by the Dutch Institute of Psychologists in 1975. This code has the merit of being more clear about the relationship of psychologists with principals and applicants.

3.5. The client system also socializes the W/O psychologist

Most psychologists who render services are in the employment of their client organization or of a consulting firm. The organization in or for which one works has a socializing effect like that of the profession. Psychologists are also confronted with norms and values in the client organization. Clients are important role senders; they have expectations from the W/O psychologist. The statement of Secord and Backman (1974) that 'Socialization is thought of as an interactional process whereby a person's behavior is modified to conform with expectations held by members of the groups to which he belongs .... Socialization processes are especially active each time a person occupies a new position, as when he joins a fraternity or sorority, gets promoted in a business organization ... ' clearly holds for the client organization. W/O psychologists are more or less compelled to identify themselves with the client organization. Sometimes this goes so far that when they speak of the organization in which they work, the term 'we' is used.

In organizations, management formulates the objectives and establishes the norms. Because of this managers constitute an important reference group for W/O psychologists, and it is understandable that they tend to adopt the ideas of the managers. Organizations regulate the behavior of their members, just as professions do. Organizations are oriented towards the realization of values. They provide goods and services to customers, an income and other benefits to employees, interest to investors and so on. All this is possible only through the cooperation of all of those involved with the organization. It is the task of the 'managerial subsystem' to realize this cooperation. This is done by rewarding behavior that is positive for the organization. The esteem for the psychologist will primarily depend upon the extent to which he contributes to the realization of the organization's objectives. As there are conflicts between segments in the profession, they also occur in organizations. There are also within the 'managerial subsystem' differences of opinion about objectives, and there are coalitions which are formed in order to assert certain ideas. Complete unity in the client organization is just as absent as in a profession. Opinions differ as to how the organization can best adapt to the changing task environment; individual and group interests can also play a role here. The psychologist who renders services is also involved because of his work, and he can get pulled into the conflicts.

3.6. Serving two masters

The W/O psychologist who renders services is continuously involved in multiple loyalties: on the one hand to the profession, on the other to the client organization. Both pose demands, have expectations and judge his behavior. They demand that he behaves according to the norms and values they use. Scientists first look at the correctness of the psychologist's propositions and methods. First of all, they want him to associate himself with objectivity and scientific responsibility.

Those who consume his services expect to receive his help. Organizations are oriented towards the realization of values and they expect the psychologist to contribute to this. Often it happens that something must be urgently taken care of, and the psychologist is expected to keep in mind the urgency of cases. The differences in expectation are difficult to reconcile with each other. Work done for the one group of role senders may be appreciated but may be considered as less relevant by the other group. Attempts to do good work in one area can lead to alienation in another area. A few examples may clarify this.

Client organizations as a rule are not or only to a limited extent interested in scientific publications. The W/O psychologist who does scientific research in the client organization scores sooner with professional colleagues than with clients. It becomes even more difficult if he, for the sake of a good research design, thinks he needs more than what is at hand. This can obviously lead to negative reactions on the part of the client.

Another example: on the basis of his knowledge the W/O psychologist is often a good person for management to talk to when complex social problems have to be solved. But this knowledge is often fragmentary and he can only partly depend upon theories and research findings. If he attempts to formulate explanations and models in such conversations, they will probably be so speculative that he runs the risk of becoming alienated from his academic colleagues.

3.7. The legitimation of rendering services

A psychologist who offers services claims, be it often implicit, that he can do something better than others. He thinks that the client can realize certain objectives better by taking advantage of his services. In one way or another he must be able to reasonably support this and make it clear to the client. A statement by Thorndike (1949, p. 312) clarifies this:

'A basic fact that every personnel psychologist needs to appreciate, whether he is working in industry, in civil service, or in the armed forces is that the broad administrative decisions which determine the conditions under which he is to work and even the question of whether he is to continue to work will be made not by him but by his administrative superiors. Some person or persons in the top levels of management will have the power to decide that there is to be a personnel selection program and that psychological tests are to be used. . . . This dependence on others for the continuing support of his activities raises a new set of practical problems which the psychologist must face. They are problems of salesmanship. A personnel program necessarily includes a selling program, to guarantee continuing acceptance of and support for the program. It is of critical importance to sell the program to those members of top management who have powers of life or death over the program'.

Selling does not occur exclusively with scientific arguements. The seller is not exclusively concerned with the client but also with other role senders. With the sales pitch he often attempts to convince the client as well as other role senders. The vocabulary plays an important role in this connection. A few examples: in the first half of this century psychologists attempted to emphasize especially the scientific character of their work: W/O psychologists who did selection work did this in 'a laboratory' and called the applicants 'subjects'. In the fifties and sixties many psychologists tried to make the utility of their services clear by pointing out that they contributed to the 'increase of productivity'. In the seventies, industrial democracy came to the fore. A fine example is to be found in the blurbs on the cover flaps of a book by Van Strien (1978): he wants an 'emancipatory psychology' which should contribute primarily to the 'quality of life'. He wants 'democratization of work' and 'greater responsibility on the part of the employee', etc. Science should be a 'liberating emancipating force'. Van Strien is loyal to the 'less powerful in the organization'. The vocabulary clearly indicates what values and norms W/O psychologists underwrite and where their loyalties lay. The choice of words contributes to the sale of programs and services to clients and to the acquisition of support from important role senders. Naturally, the arguments they use in presenting their services are also of great importance. The examples above are meant to show that less rational processes also occur in attempting to influence role senders.

4. THE DOMAIN OF W/O PSYCHOLOGY

4.1. How are decisions about the domain made?

In section 3 of this chapter it was pointed out that in every social system there are two important questions that must be answered: 'Who is the client?' and 'Which services are to be provided?'. In this section we will go further into the second question: every profession must choose a domain and defend it (Thompson, 1967). First, the process of choosing will be gone into; how do practitioners choose? Within a profession a 'managerial subsystem' that would be engaged in such activities is wanting. There is no director to make decisions about such matters, and the members of a profession do not meet periodically to discuss this kind of decision. However, the members of the profession do have some idea about what belongs to the domain, and W/O psychologists take this into account when accepting commissions. All of them would consider personnel selection activities as belonging to the domain. They would, however, hesitate to include or might even reject head hunting activities; labor relations would be included by some and rejected by others. This indicates that psychologists do have notions about the domain but its borders are not fixed. There is consensus on the nucleus of the domain, but its border areas are still a source of hesitation.

It seems that many decisions on the domain are made at the individual level. It is in interaction with clients that practitioners accept commissions and offer services. Thereby the needs of the client, but also the opinions of practitioners about their own knowledge play a role. In this interaction, the domain is not sharply demarcated. In discussing problems of clients, solutions are liable to come up which do not belong to the domain of the practitioner. Sometimes the W/O psychologist will refer the client to others; he can also take an active part by helping to find a solution. An example: in 'The American Soldier' (Stouffer, 1949), a member of a field team was helpful in setting up an improved method of predicting the man-power replacement needs due to personnel turnover in an army unit. The practitioner has knowledge and methods at his disposal and, in interaction with the client, he discovers that they are useful for objectives apparently outside of his domain. In such situations the psychologist might be very aware that he is engaged in activities outside of his domain. But there is a rather large area in which it is difficult to say whether he is acting in the function of W/O psychologist or not.

In addition, new knowledge is continuously becoming available which lends itself to successful application and in turn to domain expansion and innovation. The initiatives of pioneers are often followed, leading to domain development.

There are a number of activities in which professional colleagues are engaged, especially the dominant segment, that guide the development of the domain: invitations to give addresses, acceptance of material for publication in journals etc. In this way recognition becomes visible, and what is important for the domain choice becomes apparent for others outside of the profession. Hereby notions about what should or should not be regarded part of the domain are re-enforced and adapted to new developments in the task environment of the profession. During discussions at meetings these items are worked out further, and the practitioners have the opportunity to establish what is controversial, what is to be accepted and what is to be rejected. In this way regulation of members' behavior occurs.

4.2. The domain is dynamic

Perhaps the most striking feature of W/O psychology's domain is its broadness. The most diverse subjects are handled; a look at the contents of this handbook supports this. In the opening chapter of his handbook Dunnette (1976) observes that 'Industrial and Organizational Psychology's scope is so broad and so diverse that I have been frustrated in efforts to develop a conceptually satisfying or dimensionally clean structure'. This applies to W/O psychology as a science, but it also applies to the professional activities.

This was not always the case. Still in the fifties and sixties the domain was restricted to personnel selection in many countries. For many clients W/O psychology and personnel selection were synonymous. In the second half of the sixties all kinds of new activities were initiated, especially in organizational psychology. For The Netherlands, a documentation of this can be found in Krijnen (1975). This is indubitably connected to the increase in the number of W/O psychologists which became apparent precisely during that period in most European countries. This led to a differentiation process which is still continuing today. It is difficult if not impossible to delineate the borders of the domain, the only certainty being its extensiveness.

A broad domain is difficult to defend, since practitioners are not always able to master all of its various subdivisions. This could lead to a reduction in quality, but to some extent this might be prevented by specialization. However, it is also possible that outsiders can take over parts of the domain or that split-off segments will form a separate profession. Consequently, broadness is not just simply an advantage, it confronts the professional group with new problems.

4.3. The domain is not exlusive

The domain of the W/O psychologist is not exclusive. This applies to scientific as well as professional activities. Graduates in W/O psychology as well as graduates in other disciplines are applying for the same positions. In advertisements it is often indicated that for a given posstion applications will be considered from graduates in various disciplines. Many W/O psychologists (just as other psychologists) think that their positions could be filled by other specialists, especially from other social science disciplines. There is a long line of professionals who can compete with the W/O psychologist: sociologists, personnel administrators, organization consultants, social workers, company physicians (this list does not pretend to be complete).

There have, indeed, been attempts to distill what is unique in the domain and to demarcate this from other sciences. Duijker (1977) asserts that the main preoccupation of psychologists should be the search for determinants of human behavior: 'Psychology wants to make human situations understandable and discussable'. For W/O psychologists this will mean occupying themselves primarily with determinants relevant to work and organizations. Such a description still does not lead to completely acceptable demarcation lines. Sociologists describe their domain as 'the scientific study of the social behavior or the social action of human beings' (Gould and Kolb, 1964). This kind of formulation rules out any clear demarcation based on the description given by Duijker. In addition, some sociologists give an even broader interpretation: 'a general social science which systemizes all scientific knowledge produced by the special social sciences'. They see psychology as a 'competitor' for this sort of general role but call psychology 'a poor claimant'. Such quotes illustrate the competition element and the difficulty in establishing reasonable boundaries.

One trend to be observed in W/O psychology and in the other social sciences is the interest in system theory and organizational behavior, with 'organizational effectiveness' as an important point of attention (Katz and Kahn, 1978). Connected to this is the interest in improving the fit between individual and organization whereby both individual and organizational behavior are investigated (see for example this Handbook, ch. 2.4). Both psychologists and other social scientists have this orientation.

The attempt to demarcate domains is most obvious at the universities. In rendering services there is a strong tendency to work in the border areas because of the needs of the client (see section 4.1). There are but few professional activities over which exclusiveness can be claimed by W/O psychologists; personnel selection is one of them. Claims by others to this activity (for example graphologists) are considered as unjustified. But when it comes to other activities, such as organization development, it is more difficult to reject the claims. The large extent of overlap is confusing to the client. He does not know whom to turn to and who can help him best. Here also, the broadness of the domain avenges itself. Customers are not prepared to choose arbitrarily between professionals and to become involved in discussions between them.

4.4. The choice of the domain is not neutral

Thompson (1967) clearly states that the choice of the client as well as that of the service package has important consequences for the survival of the profession. Needs of clients can change, sometimes competitors offer a better product, the government can demand that the services satisfy certain requirements. The task environment changes, necessitating adaptation of the services.

Thompson describes the strategies which social systems have at their disposal for surviving. It seems that W/O psychologists have absorbed the changes primarily by developing new services and adapting the existing service package. Thus, in the seventies organization development and job design emerged in answer to the efforts of society to give workers more influence on the activities in the organization. Selection procedures were adapted as a result of, among other things, different societal attitudes and governmental regulations. These changes and adaptations have a more or less *ad hoc* character. Various authors (de Wolff *et al.*, 1981 among others) have pleaded for a more systematic way of working. Here, the 'marketing' approach comes to mind, whereby the needs of (potential) clients are mapped and how the services can be fitted best to these needs is studied. One attempts to survey the entire domain and to estimate what development possibilities are there. Research, development work and training activities could be aimed at that part of the domain where one expects the greatest yields. Such studies could be carried out best by the professional associations. In 1959 and 1964, Division 14 (Industrial/Organizational Psychology) of the American Psychological Association published guidelines for training practitioners. These were based on estimates of developments in the domain. Later planning commissions also carried out studies.

4.5. One domain or various domains?

Psychology is pre-eminently an international activity. Psychologists read the professional literature from abroad and attend international congresses. They converse with colleagues from other countries. An inspection of the lists of references in this handbook clearly shows the international character of psychology.

Psychology as a science is not restricted by national borders. Theories developed in one country are also used in other countries. But is this also true for the professional domain? In the preceding sections it was emphasized that the domain emerges through interaction between W/O psychologists and their task emvironment. But some factors are indeed restricted by national boundaries. Government policy in the one country need not be the same as that in another country. The activities in a professional association in a given country can differ from those in another country. Although psychologists from different countries utilize in principle the same knowledge, it is quite obvious that there are differences in the choice of clients and domain.

It seems that striking differences do exist between countries (see de Wolff *et al.*, 1981; de Wolff and Shimmin, 1976). In France much attention is paid to ergonomics but relatively little to organizational psychology. Sociologists are more active in the latter. In The Netherlands the profession is highly developed; many psychologists work as such in companies and consultant firms. During the seventies the Polish government stimulated the employment of psychologists in industry. In Spain many psychologists find work in employment offices. Although the profession has the same name, there are per country differences in domain choice and development.

5. THE RELATIONSHIP WITH GOVERNMENT

In previous parts of this chapter, the development of the profession and services to the client were discussed; in doing so the relation to the government has come up several times already. In this section we will go further into the matter. The government exercises directly and indirectly influence on the profession. It does this directly by providing employment, functioning as principal for research, and financing university training and research. It does this indirectly by carrying out a social-economic policy which has great influence on the activities in organizations and therewith the behavior of clients.

W/O psychologists are, just as many other groups, dependent upon the government to a high degree. And, as Thompson (1967) emphasizes, dependencies should be 'managed'. In the history of W/O psychology there are numerous examples of government interventions which have had great influence on the functioning of psychologists. The Dutch government changed the minimum duration of university training for psychologists from six to four years in 1982. The financing of an important part of the research at universities depends upon the size of the project and external evaluation. In many countries there are retrenchment programs whereby allocations are cut back and sections of departments are dropped. Vacancies at universities are not allowed to be filled, disciplines and sub-disciplines are reorganized. Such actions have not only immediate consequences for the profession but also for the competition positions between professions. The interventions can affect some professions more than others, whereby the position in the labor market may be influenced.

The socio-economic policy of the government has great influence on the profession. Initially, this policy was kept in low profile (see the recommendation of the Social Economic Council on Social Policy, SER, 1981). The government intervened in organizations only to a limited degree, and when it did the actions were restricted to regulations on which there was wide societal consensus (for example the safety laws). This policy was changed during the sixties and seventies. The government attempted to change the relations within organizations by actively intervening through legislation: greater powers for the works and employees' councils, regulations meant to create equal opportunities for all groups in the labor market and legislation in the area of health and well-being. This position of the government forces organizations to adapt their social policies and to develop them further. On the one hand, this policy creates new needs through which new possibilities for domain development emerge (e.g. work consultation); on the other hand, the services provided by the psychologist must be adapted (e.g. methods of personnel selection).

It is doubtful whether W/O psychologists have sufficiently appreciated how great the influence of the government is and whether they have begun to influence the actions of the government. It often seems that some sort of aversion to promoting their own interests exists. The necessity of critically following and influencing the actions of government is recognized by the American Psychological Association (Kiesler and Zaro, 1981; Pallak, 1982;

DeLeon *et al.*, 1982). They have set up an organization (the Association for the Advancement of Psychology) with the task 'to promote human welfare through the advancement of the science and profession of psychology by the promotion of the interest of all psychology; by the representation of psychology before public and governmental bodies, by seeking out and contributing to the passage of important social and psychological issues in current legislation and to advocate to the legislative, judicial and executive branches of government the ethical and scientific views of the American Psychological Community' (DeLeon *et al.*, 1982).

The APA clearly discerns that this is a political activity but considers promotion of their interests essential to the practice of the profession and the realization of personal ideals. Another example of 'managing' the dependency upon government is to be found in The Netherlands. In 1971, the issue of the manner in which applicants were psychologically tested was discussed in parliament. This led the minister of social affairs to set up a commission to draw up guidelines for selection procedures. In 1980, this commission presented to the minister its final report. The Dutch Institute of Psychologists anticipated this development by extensive discussions on professional ethics. In 1975, a new code of conduct was approved which went into effect January 1, 1976. This code contains detailed guide-lines on selection procedures. By taking the initiative themselves, the tendency of the government to regulate through legislation has decreased somewhat. This last example involves one-time activity, and in contrast to the APA example there is no systematic program to critically follow and influence the actions of the government.

6. THE RELATION TO OTHER PROFESSIONS

In discussing the domain it was noted that there is overlap in the domain claims of W/O psychologists and other professions. In this section we will go further into the consequences of this for mutual relations. Two different views are possible of where there is overlap: the professionals can view each other as competitors who are operating in the same market and who are in competition for scarce employment. Another opinion is that disciplines can supplement each other and that better results are achieved through cooperation. The last opinion occurs more often than the first one. In recent years there has been much discussion about multidisciplinary cooperation. However, it happens but little that projects are set up with the idea of recruiting people from different disciplines. It is conceivable that the preference for cooperation stems from an aversion to conflicts and from the pursuit of harmony. Scott (1967) asserts that this tendency occurs often in organizations. Mok (1973) remarks that in the professions 'gentleman-like behaviour' is a norm, and 'gentlemen don't argue'. Professionals, therefore, will not readily conduct a hard competitive campaign.

This is not to say, however, that cooperation between professions is probable, let alone that mergers of professions will come about. At the individual level it seems that cooperation does often occur. Sociologists work in psychological sections, and psychologists work in pedagogical departments; but identity problems seem to be a hindrance for more formal forms of cooperation. Earlier in this chapter it was stated that the profession socializes, and that new members take over the norms and values of the profession. Levine and Campbell (1972) present a theory of group conflict in which they fall back on Sumner (1906). They distinguish the existence of an 'ingroup' ('we') and 'outgroups' ('others'). Within the 'ingroup' peace is preserved by keeping distance from the 'outgroup'. They emphasize their own identity, see themselves as strong and superior and consider their own values to be valid for every one. In contrast, the 'outgroup' is seen as inferior. They attempt to increase the distance from this group. This behavior is especially manifested when a group feels threatened. This theory could explain why one profession dissociates itself from another.

Members of professions are not the only ones who make decisions on cooperation. Government interventions can have great influence on mutual relations. The government may force cooperation in educational programs. New university curriculums may be set up in which W/O psychologists and members of other professions have to cooperate (e.g. business schools, management academies) and whereby the graduates claim parts of the W/O psychologist's domain. It is conceivable that, through interventions, a professional group can become so weak that it is no longer capable of successfully defending its domain; the profession dwindles away or disappears.

7. OTHER ROLES AND RELATIONS

W/O psychologists not only practice a profession, they also are citizens, parents, members of political parties, neighbors, church members etc. They fulfill a multiplicity of roles and maintain numerous relations. There are those who participate in the peace movement, who are active for Amnesty International or who are on the board of directors of the Association for Sexual Reform. They embrace ideas, take positions and have views on how society should be. It is difficult to keep all of this separated from the professional role. Convictions cannot be only reserved for one specific role. Soon, one wants to assert certain ideas through the profession. In the seventies, diverse examples of this were to be seen. Those who are convinced attempt in turn to convince others.

The period 1968–1978 was, in The Netherlands, characterized by attempts to change societal relationships, involving the equalization of knowledge, power and income and improvement of the position of the weakest. These attempts greatly influenced relations within companies (the fight for employees' participation). Management was often accused of only being interested in 'economic' values and of having an unsatisfactory conception of 'social' values. W/O psychologists were called 'the lackeys of management'. They should have promoted the interests of the employees more and not let themselves be used by management. Discussions on the role of management and on relationships within organizations took place primarily via the mass media. Television and radio paid a lot of attention to these subjects. That meant that W/O psychologists were confronted with opinions more often in their living rooms than in their professional relations.

There were also attempts to mobilize the professional group for more specific problems. In the beginning of the seventies a motion was submitted to the general meeting of the Dutch Institute of Psychologists in which the noise of air traffic around Schiphol airport was declared unhealthy for the people living in the area. During a meeting of the International Union of Scientific Psychology, it was attempted to get a motion approved in which the behavior of Russian psychiatrists who 'treated' dissidents was condemned.

It is understandable that psychologists attempt to bring their diverse roles into some kind of agreement. Their activities do have consequences for their relations to role senders in their work. Business men and managers are very hesitant to make statements about subjects that do not directly involve the domain of the organization. As a rule they wish to keep the production of goods and services strictly separated from political activities, which are considered to be the business of parliament. Attempts in The Netherlands to hold up the university and its democratic structure as an example for other organizations (van Strien, 1978) have not been met with sympathy everywhere. Especially the tendency to be at odds with management has caused mistrust. The NIP's code of conduct (1976) has the merit that a number of rules for the relations to clients are given, so that it is clearer what they should expect from each other. The above examples clearly show that W/O psychologists (and others) are also confronted with expectations which do not stem from their work but from general social developments. These could contribute to tensions with role senders.

8. CONSEQUENCES FOR THE PSYCHOLOGIST

In the previous sections it was made clear that W/O psychologists are involved with many role senders, who have their particular expectations concerning their behavior. The many demands are often not to be reconciled with each other. Some expectations are urgent; if they are not satisfied sanctions follow. Some are veiled: it is not so clear what the contents are exactly and what the consequences will be if they are not satisfied. This involves role conflict as well as role ambiguity (Kahn *et al.*, 1964).

Differences in opinion between W/O psychologists and their role senders cannot be just simply qualified as negative. Conflicts can be a challenge for the parties concerned, which may lead to solutions of problems. In this way innovation of and adaptation to a changing task environment come about. When conflicts reach a level where solutions to problems are impossible, the functioning of the psychologist will become problematic. Kahn *et al.*, (1964) describe the effects of role ambiguity and role conflict. Both cause strains. If this lasts too long, dissatisfaction and injury to self-esteem follow. Role conflict might lead to 'withdrawal' and decreased trust in the relations to role senders. Role ambiguity leads to feelings of futility, i.e. a lack of confidence that one can improve something through one's own actions. 'Withdrawal', an increase in the psychological distance from the person with whom one is in conflict, is a well-known coping mechanism.

Little is known about how W/O psychologists handle role ambiguity and role conflict. One can only speculate about this on the basis of findings in studies on other professions. It is to be expected that if the strain becomes too much, W/O psychologists will attempt to avoid those situations which cause strain. This might explain why in that period, when many had negative attitudes towards industry, graduates sought positions at the university or with government agencies as civil servants. Others tried for positions with the unions. It is conceivable that in those times W/O psychologists employed by industrial organizations left them for functions in other organizations where there was less role conflict (the university for example). The change of name from industrial to work and organizational psychology was perhaps not only inspired by the need to express that the services rendered are not restricted to industrial organizations but cover other organizations also. It could have also been a form of 'coping', whereby it was attempted to discard the industrial image.

It would be interesting to have more specific insights into the 'coping' behavior of W/O psychologists. Research in this area seems urgently desirable. Coping does not only occur at the individual level, groups also react to conflict. The theory of Levine and Campbell cited earlier makes this clear. Feelings of being threatened can lead to stronger identification with the 'ingroup' and to more distance from other groups. In reorganizations in social science departments of universities, psychologists emphasize research and would like to have the allocation of funds coupled to this. They dissociate themselves from other disciplines that do not emphasize research as much. Many forms of 'coping' do not contribute to the solution of conflict but are limited to the reduction of tension. By increasing the distance from the party with whom they have conflicts, they avoid being continuously confronted with threats. The capacity to solve problems actually decreases, which is ultimately disadvantageous for all parties concerned.

9. THE FUTURE OF THE PROFESSION

If we look at the possible developments in the coming years within the profession of W/O psychologist, both negative and positive aspects can be observed.

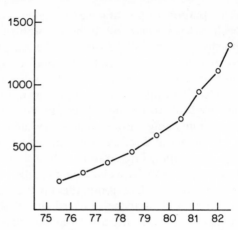

Figure 1. Unemployed psychologists in The Netherlands (source: Ministry of Social Affairs and Employment).

It is positive that the profession has become very developed during the last decades. In all developed countries there are university training programs in W/O psychology. A large amount of knowledge is available, and numerous institutions are carrying out research. The methodology is much advanced. There are large numbers of W/O psychologists who practice the profession and in coming years to come many will graduate in W/O psychology. All of this contributes to the growth of the profession and the expansion of its domain. But there are also negative aspects. The profession is vulnerable on a number of points. Unemployment among psychologists is rising rapidly. (see figure 1). The situation is more favorable for W/O psychologists than for other categories of psychologists, because the demand is greater and supply is not as large as that of clinical psychologists for example. Initially (up to 1982), graduate W/O psychologists formed approximately 1% of all registered unemployed psychologists in The Netherlands. In the meantime this has gone up to 2%. Now, it is becoming noticeable that other psychologists (for example clinical psychologists) are applying for positions previously filled exclusively by W/O psychologists. In the coming years, this will mean more problems also for the W/O psychologist in seeking appropriate work. In addition, the prospects in the labor market for academics in general are deteriorating rapidly, because of large-scale cut-backs by the government. The number of available positions with the government and at universities is decreasing (Ritzen, 1982). Therefore, it will become more and more difficult for recent graduates to find a position. This will result in W/O graduates accepting positions that do not belong to the profession.

The consequences of this seem to be that (a) the borders of the domain will become less clear and (b) the contacts between (a considerable part of) graduates and the professional group will become less intensive, resulting in less identification with the profession. The situation can become even more critical because graduates in other disciplines have the same sort of problems and will try for the same positions as W/O psychologists. The profession is, therefore, being confronted with important changes in the task environment. This constitutes a challenge for any social system, and if the system is to survive it is essential that appropriate answers be found.

De Wolff *et al.*, (1981) have compiled a number of scenarios for possible developments within the profession, in which the possibilities for 'coping' are described. Aspects which deserve special attention in seeking answers are: (a) the possibility of influencing the decision-making process regarding the domain. Here, the government must be considered first of all and also health insurance funds, employers, trade unions etc. The domain is not only determined by scientific knowledge and methods but also to a high degree by political processes. The latter requires promotion of interests and systematic activities in order to make the opinions of the professional group known to others. (b) Support seems to be a very important variable in many studies; it facilitates or makes functioning possible even in difficult circumstances (House, 1981). In a period when many recent graduates find it difficult to obtain positions or land in positions where there is less contact with professional colleagues, it seems worthwhile to find out whether the profession can give more support to recent graduates during this critical period. (c) There are various areas where the domain of W/O psychology can be further developed. The service package offered to clients can be enlarged, for example work and health (Kahn, 1981) and the influence of modern technology on work. In addition to research activities this also requires development activities, such as the construction of instruments (e.g. questionnaires) and methods. Universities should be able to play an important role here.

REFERENCES

Amir, A., Ben-Ari, R., (1981), Psychology and society in Israel. *International Journal of Psychology*, **16**, 239–247.

APA, Division of Industrial Psychology (Committee on Professional Education Policy) (1959), Professional education in industrial psychology: A statement of policy. *American Psychologist*, **14**, 233–234.

APA, Division of Industrial Psychology (1965), Guidelines for doctoral education in psychology. *American Psychologist*, **20**, 822–831.

Commissie Hessel (1977), *Een sollicitant is ook een mens* [An applicant is also a human being]. The Hague: Staatsuitgeverij.

DeLeon, P., O'Keefe, A., Vandenbos, G., Kraut, A. (1982), How to influence public policy. A blueprint for activism. *American Psychologist*, **17**, 476–483.

Doorn, J. A. A. van (1966), *Organisatie en maatschappij. Sociologische opstellen* [Organization and society. Sociological essays]. Leiden: Stenfert Kroese.

Dunnette, M. D. (Ed.), (1976), *Handbook of industrial and organizational psychology*. Chicago: Rand McNally.

Duijker, H. C. J. (1977), De psychologie en haar toekomst [psychology and its future]; Wat gebeurt er met de psychologie? [What will happen to psychology?]; De verantwoordelijkheid van de psycholoog [The psychologist's responsibility]. *De Psycholoog*, **12**, 353–358, 415–422, 556–562.

Duijker, H. C. J. (1978a), Competentie en verantwoordelijkheid van de psycholoog [The psychologist's competence and responsibility]. *Nederlands Tijdschrift voor de Psychologie*, **33**, 493–511.

Duijker, H. C. J. (1978b), Dramatisering vs nuchterheid. Bij wijze van dagsluiting [Dramatization vs sobriety. By way of calling it a day]. *De Psycholoog*, **13**, 3–9, 256–266, 561–565.

Goode, W. J. (1957), Community within a community: The professions. *American Sociological Review*, **22**, 194–200.

Gross, E. (1958), *Work and society*. New York: Crowell.

Hall, R. H. (1969), *Occupations and the social structure*. Englewood Cliffs (N.J.): Prentice-Hall.

House, James S. (1981), *Work stress and social support*. Reading (Mass.): Addison-Wesley.

Kahn, R. L. (1981), *Work and health*. New York: Wiley.

Kahn, R. L., Wolfe, D. M., Quinn, R. P., Snoek, J. D., Rosenthal, R. A. (1964), *Organizational stress: Studies in role conflict and ambiguity*. New York: Wiley.

Kast, F. E., Rosenzweig, J. E. (1970), *Organization and management: A systems approach*. New York: McGraw-Hill.

Katz, D., Kahn, R. L. (1978), *The social psychology of organizations*. 2nd ed. New York: Wiley.

Kiesler, A., Zaro, S. (1981), The development of psychology as a profession in the United States. *The International Review of Applied Psychology*, **30**, 341–353.

Krijnen, G. (1975), *Ontwikkeling functievervulling van psychologen* [Development job fullfillment by psychologists]. Part I. Nijmegen: Institute of Applied Sociology.

Krijnen, G. (1976), *Ontwikkeling functievervulling van psychologen* [Development job fullfillment by psychologists]. Part II. Nijmegen: Institute of Applied Sociology.

Levine, R. A., Campbell, D. T. (1972), *Ethnocentrism: Theories of conflict, ethnic attitudes and group behavior*. New York: Wiley.

Meulen, R. ter, Hoorn, W. van (1981), Psychotechniek en menselijke verhoudingen [Psychotechnics and human relations]. *Grafiet*, **1**, 106–155.

Miller, G. A. (1969), Psychology as a means of promoting human welfare. *American Psychologist*, **24**, 1063–1075.

Mok, L. A. (1973), *Beroepen in actie: Bijdrage tot een beroepensociologie* [Professions in action: A contribution towards a sociology of professions]. Meppel: Boom.

NIP (Nederlands Instituut van Psychologen [Dutch Institute of Psychologists]) (1976), *Beroepsethiek voor psychologen* [Professional ethics for psychologists]. Amsterdam: NIP.

Nederlands Tijdschrift voor de Psychologie [Dutch Journal of Psychology]. Deventer: Van Loghum Slaterus.

Pallak, M. S. (1982a), Psychology in the public form. *American Psychologist*, **37**, 475.

Pallak, M. S. (1982b), Report of the Executive Officer: 1981. *American Psychologist*, **37**, 621–624.

Psycholoog, De [The Psychologist]. Amsterdam: NIP.

Ritzen, J. M. M. (1982), *Hoger opgeleiden in de knel* [Professionals in a jam]. Nijmegen: Catholic University, Inst. of Economics.

Roe, R. A. (1978), Psychologen en de psychologie [Psychologists and psychology];

Psychologen in het midden [Psychologists caught in the middle]. *De Psycholoog*, **13**, 10–19, 355–364, 370.

Scott, W. G. (1967), *Organizational theory. A behavioral analysis for management*. Homewood (Ill.): Irwin.

Secord, P. F., Backman, C. W. (1964), *Social psychology*. New York: McGraw-Hall.

SER (1981), *Advies inzake sociaal beleid in de onderneming* [Recommendation on social policy in the firm]. Publication 8104. The Hague: SER (Social Economic Council).

Stouffer, S. A., *et al.* (1949), *The American soldier*. Boston: Princeton University Press.

Strien, P. J. van (Ed.) (1976), *Personeelsselectie in discussie* [Personnel selection under discussion]. Meppel: Boom.

Strien, P. J. van (1977), Regulering van de beroepspraktijk [Regulating the professional practice]. *De Psycholoog*, **12**, 486–495.

Strien, P. J. van (1978a), Vermaatschappelijking van de psychologie. [The socialization of psychology]; Psychologen in de voorhoede [Psychologists in the forefront]. *De Psycholoog*, **13**, 211–219, 365.

Strien, P. J. van (1978b), *Om de kwaliteit van het bestaan. Contouren van een emanciperende psychologie* [On the quality of life. Contours of an emancipatory psychology]. Meppel: Boom.

Sumner, W. G. (1906), *Folkways*. New York: Ginn.

SWOV (Stichting Wetenschappelijk Onderzoek Vakcentrales [Unions' Foundation for Scientific Research]) (1973), *De afhankelijke sollicitant* [The dependent applicant]. Utrecht: SWOV.

Thompson, J. D. (1967), *Organizations in action*. New York: McGraw-Hill.

Thorndike, L. (1949), *Personnel selection*. New York: John Wiley & Sons.

Wijngaarden, H. R. (1978), Wat is een psycholoog? [What is a psychologist?]. *De Psycholoog*, **13**, 103–108.

Wolff, C. J. de (1977), *Uit de ivoren toren* [From the ivory tower]. Deventer: Van Loghum Slaterus.

Wolff, C. J. de, Shimmin, S. (1976), The psychology of work in Europe: A review of a profession. *Personnel Psychology*, **29**, 175–195.

Wolff, C. J. de, Shimmin, S., Montmollin, M. de (1981), *Conflicts and contradictions*. London: Academic Press.

Zamek-Gliszczynska, X. (Ed.) (1980), *Work psychology in Europe*. Polish Academy of Science, Committee of Organization and Management Science. Warsaw: Polish Scientific Publishers.

Handbook of Work and Organizational Psychology
Edited by P. J. D. Drenth, H. Thierry, P. J. Willems and C. J. de Wolff
© 1984, John Wiley & Sons, Ltd.

1.4. Psychologist and policy

J. J. A. Vollebergh

INTRODUCTION

To many people the image of the psychologist, just like that of the medical practitioner, is determined by his concern and care for clients, within a private confidential relationship. In the field of work- and organizational psychology a gradual breakthrough to an organization-oriented approach has taken place, and yet here, too, the approach is mainly determined by an interest in individual behaviour. Veen's recent introduction to organizational psychology (1982) testifies to this. Motivation, problems of power, impacts of specialization on the individual, participation and leadership are among the main subjects. A study of participation such as conducted by Koopman–Iwema (1980) focuses on power and motivation, thus differing fundamentally from a sociological study of control (and a share in the control) in hospitals, such as Meurs's study (1982), in which structures and parties dominate. Therefore, it is not so very surprising that the psychologist should still have the image of being specialized in matters and problems of individual human behaviour.

Some outsiders link this image to the slightly negative view that psychologists show a lack of interest in organizations or are even at times hostile to organizations. The interest in processes of, for example, change, decision-making and management also seems to be dictated by care for the people involved rather than by interest in, for example, the productivity of organizations. Many managers are of the opinion that such care costs rather a lot of time and money without yielding clear and convincing results.

Prof. Dr. J. A. Vollebergh, GITP, Berg en Dalseweg 127, 6522 BE NIJMEGEN

This problem of image seems to be inherent in the angle of approach of the psychologist, i.e. human behaviour in its involvement in the human and non-human environment. It would probably not be right for the psychologist to be deterred from this original purpose and to strive to become a manager of people. The orientation to individual behaviour and interaction between individuals as such and in or with groups is of paramount importance in our increasingly organized society, and the psychologist is the pre-eminent scientist when it comes to rendering those services, just because of his care for the individual. However, this means that the importance of more thorough contact with policy-making in organizations increases, as otherwise the psychologist will more and more be confronted with systems built up by other people that are very hard to change.

Incidentally, the psychologist also comes into contact with policy by way of his own work environment. Many psychologists have never practised their work as an (independent) profession, but always as professionals in an organization. A great many of these organizations have expanded to such sizes that policy-making grew to be a separate task. The organization may be one of psychologists, e.g. a psychological consulting agency, or one of related professionals, e.g. a (psychiatric) hospital, a school or organizational consulting agency, but sometimes also a department or company. In all these cases the psychologist will come into contact with policy and policy-making. In most cases he is only partially prepared for this. He may have some experience in research, but policy-making is not the same as research, even through there are similarities between policy-making and experimenting. In both cases the essence is insight into the connections between phenomena, which enables us to foresee what we may expect in certain situations or as a result of certain actions.

In both cases we are dealing with hypotheses that need to be tested and results that need to be evaluated. Both preparing a policy decision and designing an experiment require thorough analysis and a lucid design. The formulation of a policy decision is not a safe and trustworthy starting-point, but rather an assumption concerning the result of the policy, just as the hypothesis is for the experiment. Policy-making and experiment both have to provide clues for the future, after evaluation, even if it were only the negative certainty that this is not the way to do it. In other words, the model for policy-making and that for experimental research resemble each other more than policy-makers like to admit. Especially when a policy may have harsh results, in which one would like to have more certainty. However, so many uncontrolled and uncontrollable influences play a part that each situation is unique, and that is why policy-making will continue to be experimenting. In this respect the scientific experiment has the added advantage that the variables can be manipulated under controlled circumstances, though even then it is still often a problem in how far the conclusions can be generalized.

To give a closer description of the connection between psychologist and policy, we look first of all to the specific characteristics of policy-making, and, subsequently, to the position the psychologist may take in this field. Finally, some marginal notes may be added on the relationship between the psychological profession and policy-making.

1. THE CYCLE OF POLICY

The greatest problem in policy-making is that, without much certainty about the effects in the near future and certainly in the long run, we bring about changes that are often irreversible. By putting the contraceptive pill on the market we have thoroughly changed our society and there is no way back. Policy is hardly ever non-committal. In this respect it differs from research, though the latter, too, may at times have immediate social consequences. To go back to the example: as soon as the invention of the pill became common knowledge, its introduction could hardly have been stopped. The Catholic church can testify to that. However, with the help of research we usually try to gain insight by evaluating our finding as impartially as possible, whereas by means of policy we try to realize values.

So, apart from similarities between research and policy there are also clear differences between the two, and these will show especially when the object of policy and research are values, as in the case of social policy and social research. Drenth (this Handbook, ch. 1.2) may ask whether for judging research results a universal forum (Hofstee in Drenth, art. cit.) is needed or desired, but there is no doubt about this as far as policy-making is concerned. In a democratic society such as ours, the forum in policy-making is in fact always universal in the sense that a great many people express themselves on the subject and exercise their influence, through formal authorities, but also by means of actions by those directly involved, varying from lobbying and lawsuits to demos and actions in the street. It is not quite clear in what way such actions, and the fear of them, actually influence policy-making. However, an important question is always whether the universal forum shows sufficient consensus to base a policy on, which turns policy-making into a political subject.

The political context of policy-making, the balance of power and changes in it, are the reasons why policy-making is no smooth process developing according to a fixed pattern (this Handbook: Koopman et al., ch. 4.6; Veen, ch. 4.2; Vollebergh, 1982). Therefore the phases outlined in this chapter do not pretend to be a description of the actual course of the process. They underline aspects of policy-making that should be dealt with in a normative model. The sequence of the phases is right logically, but in practice neither the individual nor organizations will proceed so strictly according to rules. People jump to conclusions, evaluate beforehand by way of presumptions, and only afterwards do they realize what image they let themselves be guided by. In organizations there is the added circumstance that the individual participants in such processes have different wishes, starting-points, and pace. Therefore a normative model is useful. It may contribute to an orderly and clear course of such complicated processes, especially so if we strive to make policy more transparent.

In this model the emphasis is on policy in a wider sense, i.e. viewed as a complex of values that we try to realize within a framework of limitations set by the environment and ourselves (Vollebergh, 1982). It seems to involve views on and expectations of the future, as well as planning and execution of actions that are oriented to concrete aims. Policy-making thus conceived has a broader basis than decision-making. Policy provides the context within which decision-making takes place about concrete aims and the ways to achieve these. This appears in more detail from the normative description of the phases.

1.1 The starting-position is described

The starting-position depends on those standards and values that either superior authorities or the policy-makers themselves on higher order considerations, premise prior to determining policy aims. They act as limitations to the freedom of policy and therefore are sometimes called limits or 'constraints'. The reasons for explicitly incorporating these in the policy-making process is that they tend to be often less evident in policy discussions, so that the understanding of the process may be obscured.

1.2 Selection of a perspective

Goals are basically images of a situation to be attained. Such images of the future roughly take two forms: perspectives and prospective analysis. These two can be shown to be clearly and importantly different.

A perspective is an image of the future, a situation to be attained, based on intuition, being a rough reflection of our hopes and fears regarding the future. Because of their emotional load, such perspectives may have a strongly motivating effect and give a major impulse to policy-making. The fact that many people consider them too speculative to allow for them in policy-making may, consequently, lead to impoverishment and single emphasis on the economic aspects of policy. On the other hand, perspectives will be taken seriously only if they are elaborated and translated into concrete measures and, consequently, are imbued with realism.

1.3 A prospective analysis

This type of analysis, based on extrapolation of existing trends, offers a more analytical way of policy-making. People who think perspectives are too speculative believe in analysis. They use models and their policy is usually not based on an explicit image of the future, but on a notion of 'natural' development without a clear end, allowing for timely adjustments if important values tend to be overruled. They are less concerned with images and often do not elaborate the analysis into images, so that their policy is not understood and in the view of many people seems to consist of separate, unconnected measures. A prospective analysis, too, should be transformed into an appreciable image, in so far as possible.

1.4 Selection of operational objectives

In a democratic society, policy-making is influenced by a number of divergent groups, each with its own perspective and its own idea of the future situation. Consequently, policy-making will take place in a field of tension between divergent images of the future and their defendants.

In order to get some idea of the real value of these images, a critical analysis is required of the possible outcome of a policy based on them. To that purpose we try to translate the images and expectations into concrete, operational objectives which may function, so to speak, as hypothesis in what could be called a natural experiment. So we are dealing with a provisional line of action, offering us an opportunity to use those objectives, formulated as concretely as possible, as parameters for an evaluation of the underlying images.

Many analyses of decision processes can be almost completely placed in this phase of policy-making. It applies, for example, in case of the Mintzberg model, about which Mintzberg himself says that his analysis mainly refers to singular strategy decisions and that the process of strategy formulation is not considered in his study—and in the literature in general (Mintzberg *et al.*, 1976, p. 273). In the policy-making model discussed here a start has been made with this broadening, to which the previous phases provide the context, which is not a 'neutral' environment, but a field of tension between images and 'image-bearers'. The formulation of an objective, perhaps better defined as the narrowing down or the concretization of a 'goal' to an 'objective' (van Doorn and van Vught, 1978, p. 63 ff.), is a separate process. If, however, too little attention is paid to the more general aspects of policy mentioned before, complaints about absence of policy may be brought to the fore even after careful decision-making.

1.5 Evaluation and adjustment

Eventually it may be more closely determined what, based on our experience with the objectives, we think about our images of the future and parameters. Thus the policy cycle keeps developing. Our images are adjusted and new objectives can be selected.

So the first characteristic feature of this cycle is that in principle the images of the future are made explicit, analysed and criticized. They are not permanently fixed; their very evolution and the willingness to adjust them become corner-stones of our line of thinking. The second important point is the introduction, at all vital stages in the cycle, of the values and value judgements of all the persons involved. This leads to political processes and to the introduction of negotiations and of problems of power. In that sense, it means an extension of the classic paradigm of policy, which is essentially based on a clear selection of goals, that are subsequently realized in a purposeful and effective way (van der Schroeff, 1968, p. 30 ff.).

2. PSYCHOLOGIST AND POLICY CYCLE

This brief description of the policy cycle was necessary in order to be more precise about the contribution to it by psychology and the psychologist. It is obvious that variables of behaviour play an important role throughout the cycle. Thus, it would be interesting to know what psychological back-grounds there are to images of the future. Why does a director choose for a particular image and is his choice dependent on his views on organization and co-operation? What psychological factors influence the choice between intuitively anticipating the future and predicting it on the basis of analysis? The relationships between certain aspects of images of the future can be very important. Thus, a society in which there is no competition or unsafety may evoke problems of motivation or induce people to be dependent or passive. Cultivating a works council might lead to a climate of consultation that reduces alertness. Even analysing such connections and finding differentiated solutions sometimes calls for a change in view. Problems of organization may be tackled by making better agreements or setting effective rules, but also by improving the problem-solving ability of the organization.

In addition, there are numerous practical questions with a psychological background. Examples are selection of goals, use of power, power-play over-ruling policy content, selection of evaluation criteria, belief in these criteria, accessibility to inspiration and innovation, and the willingness to start a new and different policy cycle.

So we are concerned here with questions regarding the motives and behaviour of persons involved in policy-making, as well as with questions regarding the processes as such, for in these processes also expectations about the behaviour of groups and of certain categories of people play a part. Shifts in coalitions, determinants of the process, the various dimensions and levels of intervention, all these factors evoke questions that are also relevant for the psychologist. A good review of these factors can be found in the works of Bennis *et al.* (1969), French and Bell (1973) and Hackman (in: Dunnette, 1976, p. 1455 ff.).

With regard to policy three different roles seem to be identifiable for the psychologist: the role of scientific researcher, of consultant, and of director.

2.1 The role of scientific researcher

The essence of this role does not differ from that in any other field of research. The point is to clarify connections and interactions between various aspects of policy. A condition is that this clarification should be free from prejudice and be executed in a systematic and testable way. However, in studies concerning policy, scientists are seldom really unprejudiced or uncommitted. Especially among the numerous 'exposing' studies which have been published in recent years, there are rather a few that clearly show the scientist's personal choice, in some cases to an extent that it may impair the conclusive force of the study, though sometimes unjustly so.

The problem is understandable. Policy is important to us and, especially in social issues on which relatively much money is spent, social scientists too are often vitally involved and, by exposing, have in fact provided for progress in many fields. Examples are the emancipation of the workers and nowadays of women, the role of the churches, and the meaning of sexuality.

Research in these fields may be either focused on the structures within which the policy is established and on the course of the processes, or on the behaviour of the participants. The latter aspect is still rather underdeveloped. Many studies make clear what happens and what, for instance, the course of decision-making is, but there is less interest in the motives of the participants. Thus, one can often read that structures in the health care system are rigid mainly because directors want to keep their power and doctors their incomes. The weak point of these studies is that the interest of the social scientists and especially of the psychologists was, in general, more directed to structures, in association with the social policy and problems of organization. When the work- and organizational psychologists, who originally were occupied mainly with problems of selection gradually widened their scope of interest (Vollebergh, 1972, 1974), they may have been too fast and too intensive followers of the fashionable trend of 'structures and processes' and their influences on individuals and especially on those who have little power. The interest in the individual motives of behaviour of the policy-makers did not increase to the same extent, and yet, knowledge of such motives is vitally important if the insight into the course of processes and the degree to which they can be influenced is to be increased. Directors and doctors in the health care system, employers, employees and trade-union leaders, members of the Works Council, civil servants and politicians usually react as wisely or unwisely as other people. Their motives are complex, their views of the situation limited, and their powers of resistance to the impact of structures and processes seldom adequate.

However, supposing the behaviour of policy-makers is viewed in an unprejudiced way, what can be said about their policy? That question might be specifically intended for psychologist-researchers to answer. It goes without saying that attention to the whole context is still essential and so is multidisciplinary co-operation, but the psychologist's own contribution forms an almost indispensable part of it. A very good illustration of this point is Mintzberg's study of the manager (1973).

A special aspect of the role of researcher becomes evident in research in direct connection with and on behalf of policy-makers. Such studies are usually carried out by order of policy-making bodies, with the purpose to analyze the situations so that a better insight into the actual relationships and views may lead to improvement of the quality of the policy. It really is a smooth transition to the role of consultant, so that part of the problems described in that section is applicable.

A complicating factor is the political colouring of a great number of studies, and, of course, especially if the study is policy-supporting. This leads particularly to an active interference of various interested parties with problem definition and elaboration of the study and the interpretation of the results. If such parties (government departments, municipalities, trade unions, and employers' organizations) have a major social influence, the interference is sometimes difficult to handle. Even the acquisition of new assignments may be at stake, so that the researcher's attitude may appear to be a confusing mixture of ethics and pragmatism, even to those for whom a nod is as good as a wink.

In Part 4 of Bennis's handbook (Bennis *et al.*, 1969, p. 529 ff.) this problem is clearly illustrated. The same happens in individual organizations with respect to the possible tensions between top management, executive staff, works councils, or groups of trade-union members in the company. A closer psychological analysis of the behaviour of the participants in such a study would constitute a meaningful contribution in itself. Case studies can be good instruments in this respect (cp. Zwart, 1972).

2.2 The role of consultant

If practising psychologists are at all concerned with policy, it is mainly in this role. Professional consultants are expected to gather, classify and interpret data in an unprejudiced way and for all those involved, so as to enable the latter persons to react sensibly to the situation they are in. What matters is the client's behaviour and actions. The consultant should refrain from exerting influence. He plays no active part in determining the policy, for what matters is the policy to be decided on by the client, including the entire client-system and all its interactions.

The consultant is concerned with the organization involved and its structure, with the processes within the framework of policy-making, and with the individual persons involved. It is his task to clarify the impact of each of these aspects. He carefully identifies forces inherent in the structure, he clarifies the processes, and assists in experiencing and recognizing how structures and processes in fact force people to assume certain roles and allow them no choice, even if they would like to decide differently. He also shows how one's personal behaviour elicits other people's behaviour, or even provokes it, and, alternatively, what effect individual behaviour has on structures and processes. In other words, as a 'prudent assistant without interests of his own' he helps other people to become aware of their own situation and function optimally in it.

Of course, not all of these objectives will be achieved, as a consultant has limits of his own. He has his own personal opinions, must make an income, is sensitive to criticism and appreciation, may make mistakes, and dislikes some clients. Moreover, he has his own opinion of the situation, which is sometimes very pronounced. Therefore, consultants say that, before signing a contract, they need to be explicit about their own attitude. Only if the client-system (but then, *who* forms part of it?) does not object to that attitude can an assignment be accepted. But the immediate implication is that from then onwards the role of consultant is no longer neutral regarding the policy, since influencing policy-making is (seems?) legitimate.

Thus, the different roles may become confused (see also Bruining and Allegro, this Handbook, ch. 4.9). On the one hand there may be a virtually soundless transition to the role of director, but on the other hand, a consultant may take the stand of an impartial researcher with a semblance of objectivity that in a consulting role is sometimes the very source of power. The heart of this matter is (still) adequately represented by Kelman and Benne (in Bennis *et al.*, 1969).

In the attempt to make the role(s) of consultant explicit, the differentiation in types of roles is pertinent. The role of 'expert' is closest to that of researcher, the one of 'lawyer' is the most explicitly partial; the 'referee' mediates and, if necessary, makes a choice between parties. The 'coach' comes closest to the role of consultant described here; the 'catalyst' plans his actions in such a way that all those involved reach a joint analysis. And one may think of a number of other roles, all containing elements that at one time or another dominate in the role of consultant, but are also at times incompatible with each other. Besides, consultants have, for a number of reasons, more or less affinity to particular roles.

The very study of these roles, of their interaction within one single person or within a team the members of which have different roles, is within the competence of the psychologist. This problem-field is sometimes still too much confined by ethical questions, i.e. how should the consultant behave? But practical questions such as: can anyone adopt a stand that other people think he should, are the expectations realistic, is such an attitude credible and, if so, under what conditions, are certainly equally important. Their analysis, without the immediate pressure or threat exerted by words such as unethical, inadmissible and improper, is in the line of the psychologist.

On the other hand, the psychologist's view of the structures of the organization and the context within which it operates is often limited. As it is, he may have less affinity to these, which puts him in a slightly disadvantageous position compared to consultants who are, on account of their job, more familiar with organizational dimensions, as is the case with industrial economists, accountants, management consultants and engineers. Directors of organizations, too, are often more fully alive to the organizational aspects of policy-making, and to economic conditions and outcomes of that policy. They often make easier contact with consultants talking about work efficiency and procedures than with consultants whose attention is directed to the relational approach, which they think of as rather 'soft'. Moreover, professionals from other disciplines, especially the management consultants have meanwhile oriented themselves fairly well in the field of behavioural sciences. As long as all people, and this applies certainly to directors, think they understand human behaviour to a certain extent and as long as their traditional consultants know how to work with that common-sense insight into human nature, the psychologist will find it slightly difficult to hold his own against them.

That is the reason why the psychologist in the role of consultant should be aware of two points. He must orient himself concerning organizational and structural aspects of this problem-field, to be able to contribute substantially in a discussion. But it is even more important that he build up a good-co-operation with professionals from other disciplines. In that way he can concentrate best on the dimensions of the problem that he is familiar with, without the danger of gaps for the other dimensions. The opposite holds true for the representatives of other disciplines. Consultancy work is no longer solitary or monodisciplinary.

2.3. The role of director

A director is not the same as a manager. Managers are leaders at various levels, but they do not always make policy. At times they only carry it out, without any more additions other than practical adjustments. Directors, however, are people who are responsible or at least co-responsible for longer-term policy determination. In industry, for example, the Board of Directors is responsible for determining the policy. An outside director assumes co-responsibility by approving the policy, without being involved in the management. Incidentally, an analysis of such (co-)reponsibility is worthwhile, as the transitions may be very subtle (Bloembergen, 1974, p. 119 ff.; van

Wersch, 1979, p. 96 ff.). Here we should also mention the responsibility of a Works Council: although it is only entitled to give advice in matters of policy, yet the influence of its advice is real, and at least some sort of feeling for policy-making is required.

However, in the present contribution the role of director is limited to that of a professional director, whether or not as manager in charge of day-to-day management, who is formally authorized to decide on or approve policy on his own or jointly with his colleagues. His role is not limited to 'aspects of policy' with tasks divided between persons or groups of persons, for the final determination of the general policy comprises the total set of work goals for the short(er) term within their framework of long-term positions and objectives, including their evaluation and adjustment. General policy is indivisible, although directors and managers may approach it from different angles (see also Bagchus and van Dooren, this Handbook, ch. 4.7).

There will hardly be any difference of opinion on the fact that psychologists playing this role are still very few in number. This is hardly surprising as the reason for becoming a psychologist will have been, in most cases, an interest in the human individual and in his living conditions and work environment. It has gradually dawned upon us that the influence of the environment in which people live and work is essential to a positive development of the individual. As a result, the attention of the psychologist in his roles of researcher and consultant is no longer exclusively directed to the individual; but in the function of director in the field of social policy and especially general policy, psychologists are still fairly unusual, though their number is gradually increasing.

Psychologists have, however, found the way to the role of director in their own profession. They can be found as heads of psychological services, members of the board of a psychological agency, or deans at universities. But in all these cases the professional character is predominant, and understandably so, for from the very start the psychologists were intent on professionalism, clearly inspired by the medical profession. Autonomy with respect to, for example, economic policy was and still is highly valued, as in the medical profession. The relationship with administrators in organizations tends to be slightly antagonistic. For the medical profession this is gradually being adjusted through the development of large medical institutes which make the doctors realize how important management is for their work. But it is still difficult to find qualified medical managers for these institutes. For the time being, psychologists feel less urged to become involved in management, because there are few large psychological organizations, and, consequently, in his professional environment the psychologist is less motivated to become a director or manager.

Yet, the psychologist could certainly play a valuable role as director, that is if he would be able and willing to take the plunge. His affinity to several essential aspects of policy-making, acquired through education and added to by experience, can be very useful in boards of management. It holds true for problems of social policy, such as participation, motivation, structuring of work, or organization. It equally holds true for management problems relating to team-formation and co-operation. It finally holds true for problems of policy-making itself, such as managing social processes, the presentation of policy, and the establishment and handling of communication and consultation structures. Almost any traditionally composed board of management will acknowledge that policy-making in more or less democratic organizations evokes such problems, and that a managerial contribution based on socioscientific knowledge would certainly serve a purpose.

Such a contribution cannot simply be provided by specialists from the personnel or Organization departments. If a psychologist, however, aspires to a task of this kind, it is a prerequisite that he changes his career in time, for he will have to be able to perform a director's task that equals the other tasks in size and weight. Boards of companies and institutions do not have directors who are solely occupied with social studies or process guidance. Ultimately, each director is responsible for the entire policy.

There are two main roads to a task as director: by choosing a career in the Personnel and Organization field, or by timely taking up the work of organizational consultant, preferably in a service or institute with a broad and interdisciplinary set-up, where experience can be gained in co-ordinating tasks. The choice should not be made by halves. It requires changing over to other work with a different attitude. Someone who wants to be a psychologist, i.e. a professional with a confidential relationship with the individual, and at the same time perform a co-ordinating task or fill a consultancy job oriented to the organization as a whole, will not only become entangled in conflicts of roles, but also never gain optimum experience in either of the roles. Both his role and experience will remain incomplete.

There is a third road for psychologists which can be found in the field of health care in its widest sense, including general and psychiatric hospitals, homes for the mentally deficient, nursing homes and service homes. In such institutes psychologists work professionally, but their professional activities from part of or are closely linked with the central processes in these institutes. Just like medical men, they may find their way to general policy positions via their professional work.

However, in all these situations the psychologist should realize that there are fundamental differences between the attitude of a director and that of a researcher or consultant. The core problem is that directors cannot take a stand that is unprejudiced, objective, devoid of value judgements or whatever one would like to call it, because basically they want to realize values. Moreover, they operate in a strongly politicized field, comprising a large number of more or less powerful co-operating or opposing participants. Effecting sufficient consensus of opinion in order to continue is essential to them, because they mean to achieve something, and when they strive to do so in an almost fanatical and, consequently, one-sided conviction, their chances are often better than when they take an objective view of their work. What is called 'unprejudiced' in a researcher should present itself as courage and honesty in a director. He must look reality in the eye, even if he does not like it and would like to change it. And he needs other people, his whole organization, for realizing something, so he will have to be trustworthy, which requires sound judgement. Consequently, one is bound to find in such a personality a certain tension between conflicting qualities, e.g. equilibrium and calm versus drive or long-term thinking versus short-term alertness. This phenomenon is called 'complementarity' by Van Lennep (1967). Even though a good composition of the teams and proper mutual attuning of the personalities of the team-members may partly compensate for what are traditionally called 'entrepreneurial' qualities, a certain affinity to managerial tasks is still desired. Anyone who has such affinity and, to some extent, the creative attitude of a 'policy-maker' should timely attune his life to it. Otherwise a future career as researcher or consultant offers better perspectives.

3. THE ROLE OF THE PROFESSION

One is tempted to enlarge on the role of a profession, but that would be far outside the present scope. On the other hand it is certainly worthwhile to state that psychologists, just like doctors, can ascribe a role to their professional associations in this respect. Such a role would be dual.

3.1.

In society as a whole the psychologists together with their colleagues from the other social sciences are capable of rendering a critical contribution to the numerous social issues of these times. We may think of a number of concrete matters.
—Participation in a scientific forum, preferably not restricted to psychology, which supports the role of researcher. It may involve both the planning of research and its critical assessment and evaluation. Questions concerning the applicability and practical significance of scientific research are only too often left out of consideration. A judgement on these would be valuable from a social point of view, even if the researcher himself cannot or will not always (be able to) provide it. Seeing to the formation of such a judgement might even be considered part of the researcher's responsibility. In policy-related research this task is often fulfilled by special committees, but their position is often far from clear. Sometimes they assume a fair share of responsibility for the research as such, and, inherently, for a society-oriented presentation of the results. At other times they dissociate themselve from the contents of the research and add little to

its presentation. It would certainly be worthwhile for a 'scientific forum' to give its judgement on this issue and simultaneously review the possible role of such special committees.

—The improvement of scientific communication with the other social sciences: at a fundamental level, e.g. with respect to methodology, as well as in special fields such as health care education, participation, etc. An especially valuable contribution would be the improvement of communication between largely overlapping disciplines such as organizational psychology and organizational sociology.

—Active co-operation in policy-making in social and political fields, not only by means of individual publications—their number is rather large—but also by way of integrated publications, either from one's own circle or from multi-disciplinary committees. Under the auspices of the Dutch professional medical association (Koninklijke Nederlandse Maatschappij tot Bevordering der Geneeskunst) and its affiliated organizations, committees have been active on subjects such as abortion and euthanasia. For industrial and organizational psychology there are also important subjects, e.g. further elaboration of the notion of well-being ('welzijn') as expressed in the Act on Labour Conditions (ARBO-wet). A subject such as stress is already receiving more attention (Winnubst, this Handbook, ch. 3.4), but also issues such as (youth) unemployment and related problems of a psychological nature centring on the meaning of work for man, and the attitude to work and leisure time should receive more attention (see also this Handbook, Warr, ch. 2.13, and Thierry and Jansen, ch. 3.6).

In all this, the intention is not to establish co-operation in scientific or professional fields, but to collect whatever the profession can offer to society in this respect. It may take the form of well-described insights, or be limited to doubts or gaps in the knowledge. But each clear stand taken and each pinpointing of the problem can be of importance to such as make policy. And, alternatively, each comment by policy-making bodies, including rejection and criticism, may contribute to professional thinking.

3.2.

Within the profession—universities and the Dutch professional psychological association NIP (Nederlands Instituut van Psychologen)—there is a similar problem: the subdisciplines develop independently and all the above remarks about psychology and society with respect to the function of a forum, communication and joint publications, equally applies within the psychological profession. It is partially understandable because psychologists are active in greatly differing social environments, with few mutual contacts. However, it is also a sign of short-sightedness. The study of stress is also dependent on contributions by clinical psychology and personality psychology (cp. Winnubst, this Handbook, ch. 3.4). Psychotherapy will certainly profit by a more structural approach to influencing behaviour, as is offered in social and organizational psychology. Career problems cannot be studied without contributions from child and adolescent psychology and psychogerontology (Janmaat *et al.*, 1976; Boerlijst, this Handbook, ch. 2.9). However, the university structures with their still dominant disciplinary subdivisions are not conducive to such a study. Incidentally, the NIP is clearly actively engaged in promoting communication in these fields, which is evidenced by, for example, the congresses for psychologists.

Of even more importance, however, seems the communication between the different types of role-players within the world of psychologists. Researchers tend to have quite a few mutual contacts. Their contacts with consultants are fewer, and those with directors very scarce. This can again be partially explained by the actual difference in work-address, but it also seems to result from prejudices, in all probability partly based on reality. 'Consultants are persons who are manipulated by their clients, they are not professionally independent'. 'Researchers live in an ivory tower'. 'Policy-makers have been corrupted by power'. 'The new elite-groups live in a reserve, in which they decide on their own privileges'.

Psychologists might within their profession pursue a policy, in which the problems and needs of directors and consultants can be used as an introduction to research. Alternatively, the outcomes of research by consultants and directors can be translated to aid practical action. The gap between research and action is so large that it can only be bridged by a well-organized profession or professional organization. Particularly social problems such as the decreasing employment possibilities call for such studies. Sometimes, based on the viewpoints of economists and organizational experts, an approach is agreed upon that is already so fixed that the psychologist's role is restricted to providing guidance in, for example, 'the social effects of automation'. This does not only set bounds to his own role, but also to his horizon, so that the problems of work creation will be hidden from his view (van Assen and den Hertog, this Handbook, ch. 4.8; Vollebergh, 1981). He should familiarize himself with the way of thought of his 'colleagues' in other roles. This also applies to, for example, the problems concerning the costs of health care. The appeal to expensive facilities can be extended almost indefinitely. A reduction in provisions for economic reasons and by economic means such as price increases and own contributions, without supplementary measures in information and health-education, meets with some grave objections, also from a psychological point of view. But this remark should be elaborated more concretely in co-operation with psychologists who, as policy experts or consultants, work in such fields.

The conclusion of this contribution will have to be: psychologists are involved in policy, but they still make too little policy, either in or outside their profession. They seem too scared of soiling their hands, they are too unfamiliar with the matter, and sometimes still too impractical. Some may still be too intent on finding their inspiration with the medical profession which can still provide for at least part of its activities—though that, too, is ever decreasing—within a domain of its own, whereas psychology in all its forms is knitted to people, organizations, and society as a whole. Both as to content and form, psychologists can supply an important contribution. They can choose from three respectable roles and they can assist each other in these roles in such a way that the contribution of their profession to society will gain by it.

REFERENCES

Annalen van het Thijmgenootschap [Annals of the Thijm-society]. Baarn: Ambo.
Bedrijfspsychologie [Industrial Psychology]. Leiden: Stenfert Kroese.
Benne, K. D. (1969), Some ethical problems in group and organizational consultation. In: Bennis *et al.* (1969), 595–604.
Bennis, W. G., Benne, K. D., Chin, R. (Eds.) (1969), *The planning of change.* New York: Holt, Rhinehart & Winston.
Bloembergen, E. (1974), *De raad van commissarissen* [The board of directors]. Utrecht/ Alphen a/d Rijn: Het Spectrum/Samsom.
Doorn, J. van, Vught, F. van (1978), *Planning.* Assen: Van Gorcum.
Dunnette, M. D. (1976), *Handbook of industrial and organizational psychology.* London: Rand McNally.
Feltman, E. (1976), Een oog over OO. Een organisatiepsychologische bijdrage over en aan organisatie-ontwikkeling [Running an eye over OD. An organizational-psychological contribution on and to organization development]. Deventer: Kluwer.
French, W. L., Bell, Jr., C. H. (1973), *Organization development.* Englewood Cliffs (N.J.): Prentice-Hall.
Kelman, H. C. (1969), Manipulation of human behavior: An ethical dilemma for the social scientist. In: Bennis *et al.* (1969), 582–595.
Koopman-Iwema, A. M. (1980), *Macht, motivatie en medezeggenschap* [Power, motivation and co-determination]. Nijmegen: Stichting Studentenpers.
Janmaat, J. F. J., Remmerswaal, P. W. M., Hullenaar, R. H. J. van 't (1976), *Verslag van een vooronderzoek naar de problematiek van oudere werknemers* [Report of a preliminary study on the problems of older employees]. Nijmegen: GITP.
Lennep, D. J. van, Muller, H. (1967), Worden managers geboren of gemaakt? [Managers, are they born or made?]. *Tijdschrift voor Vennootschappen, Verenigingen en Stichtingen,* **10,** 10/11, 248 ff.
Meurs, P. (1982), *Zeggenschap in het ziekenhuis* [Co-determination in hospitals]. Leiden: Vuga.
Mintzberg, H. (1973), *The nature of managerial work.* New York: Harper and Row.
Mintzberg, H., Raisinghani, D., Théorêt, A. (1976), The structure of 'unstructured' decision processes. *Administrative Science Quarterly,* **21,** 2, 246–274.
Schroef, H. J. van der (1968), *Leiding en organisatie van het bedrijf* [Managing and organizing firms]. Amsterdam: Kosmos.
Tijdschrift voor Vennootschappen, Verenigingen en Stichtingen [Journal for Ltd. Companies, Associations and Foundations]. Deventer: Kluwer.

Veen, P. (1982), *Mensen in organisaties, een inleiding in de organisatiepsychologie* [People in organizations, an introduction to organizational psychology]. Deventer: Van Loghum Slaterus.

Vollebergh, J. J. A. (1972), De bedrijfspsychologie tussen mensen en systemen [Industrial psychology between people and systems]. *Bedrijfspsychologie*, no. 59, 5–24.

Vollebergh, J. J. A. (1974), Van psycho-techniek naar sociale wetenschappen [From psychological techniques to social science]. In: *GITP—in ontwikkeling* [The development of the Joint Institute for Applied Psychology]. Nijmegen: Gebr. Janssen.

Vollebergh, J. J. A. (1981), Waarheen met onze arbeid? [What happens to our jobs?]. *Annalen van het Thijmgenootschap*, **69**, 2, 40–70.

Vollebergh, J. J. A. (1982), Beleidsvorming: Onderhandelen over wensdromen [Policymaking: Negotiating about wishful thinking]. In: Huppes, T., Berting, J. (Eds.), *Transformatie door informatie* [Transformation through information]. Leiden: Stenfert Kroese, 247–269.

Wersch, P. J. M. van (1979), Demokratisering van het bestuur van non-profit instellingen [Democratization of boards of non-profit organizations]. Alphen a/d Rijn: Samsom.

Zwart, C. J. (1972), *Gericht veranderen van organisaties* [Planned change of organizations]. Rotterdam: Lemniscaat.

Part 2

The interaction between person and work

Handbook of Work and Organizational Psychology
Edited by P. J. D. Drenth, H. Thierry, P. J. Willems and C. J. de Wolff
© 1984, John Wiley & Sons, Ltd.

Introduction

Charles J. de Wolff

The chapters of this handbook are grouped into sections, each section consisting of an A-part, which centres on elements and process variables, and a B-part, whose focus is on applications. Section 2 concerns the interaction between person and work, section 3 covers the interaction between person and group and section 4 the interaction between person/group and organization. The last section, section 5, deals with interaction between organizations and their environments.

The editors made this categorization to somehow organize and structure the great variety of subjects, but they are well aware that any such attempt will always be rather arbitrary. Also, these categories had been established before the authors were invited to write their chapters. So, it turned out that for some of them it was impossible to strictly observe the boundaries set by our plan. For example, writing on personnel selection—which belongs in section 2—one cannot avoid writing about government intervention—which belongs in sections 4 and 5.

Thus, the categorization somewhat resembles a cluster analysis. Chapters are included in that part with which they are most closely related, while they may have links with other parts as well. Even so, the whole picture is a rather kaleidoscopic one. It reflects the thought processes by which W/O psychologists have taken up new subjects or continued older ones. Some subjects do have a rather long history. For 70 years now, personnel selection has been holding our attention. It is the subject of numerous studies. But other subjects, such as employment, have—with the exception of a few pioneering studies—only recently begun to attract our attention: such subjects cannot yet boast many research results.

We do not claim that all five parts together present a complete survey of all topics in W/O psychology, but we have aimed to include at least the most important ones, that is: those on which extensive research has been done.

In a way, section 2 may be said to represent the oldest domain of W/O organizational psychology: it mainly comprises subjects with a longstanding research tradition. The other sections cover a newer part of the domain. They mainly concentrate on issues that have come to our attention only in the past two decades. This does not mean that the traditional domain are to be left aside. On the contrary! Views and theories have greatly changed. In this respect too, the field of W/O psychology is very much alive.

Section 2 contains a number of chapters that could rightly be expected to appear under its heading. These concern selection, training, ergonomics, and motivation. Such topics are encountered in almost all handbooks. In addition, this section has chapters on individual characteristics and task characteristics. In W/O psychology, the process of adjustment between person and work constitutes a central theme. For this reason, the editors felt that these two subjects should be discussed in part A on elements and process variables.

In both the theory and practice of W/O psychology, personnel appraisal takes up a central place. The research frequently makes use of appraisals. Doing this, one is faced with methodological problems. Appraising is very important to personnel management, because it can, among other things, help to improve the fit between the interests of organizations to those of individual employees.

In the past years, 'workload' has received much attention from those working in the field of psychonomics. It has major implications for practical work. In these days of the government paying more attention, through legislation, to the quality of work and to mental and physical health, it is necessary to gain more insight into the nature of the workload and the processes resulting from it.

In the past decade, it has become more and more clear that employees are not ageless. During those years of his life man spends working, various processes take place which both theory and practice should take account of. Obviously, a chapter on career development cannot reasonably be omitted.

W/O psychologists not only are concerned with the study of behaviour and working man, they also try to influence that behaviour by means of interventions. In that case, a command of interview techniques is indispensable— these are discussed in chapter 2.9.

Part B includes a chapter on job evaluation. Dutch W/O psychologists have done quite some work in this area and it seemed useful to include such a chapter.

Section 2 as a whole makes clear that W/O psychology is all but standing still and even growing. There is considerable knowledge available, ready to be applied to practical problems. And the field continues to grow—much research is being done and many publications are appearing. This may make for great expectations for the future.

2.1 Individual characteristics

Robert A. Roe

INTRODUCTION

In studying the interaction between individuals and organizations a distinct
need is felt to describe individuals in a standardized and meaningful way.
This chapter is devoted to the possibilities to do so. I will try to give a survey
of individual characteristics relevant to the world of work and organization
and make clear what roles they can play. This task is harder than it looks.
One might have expected that, in the course of its 100 years existence, empirical
psychology would have created a systematic taxonomy, from which we only
had to make our choice. But such an expectation is completely unwarranted.
To be sure, there has been extensive research directed at individual characteristics—especially 'basic' ones—but the results are far from satisfactory. It has,
on the contrary, given rise to fundamental questions having to do with the
concept of personal characteristics itself.

Because of this, I will first have to discuss the theoretical status of the
'individual characteristic' concept. This exploration leads to a distinction of
some classes of individual characteristics, among which 'personality traits'
appear to take a special position. In the survey, which is given next, individual
characteristics are treated as theoretical concepts. The operationalization of
these concepts is discussed only briefly, because much is known about it
from other sources. Finally, some remarks are made on the meaning of
individual characteristics within psychological theory on work and organization and on their possible use in practical interventions.

Prof. dr. R. A. Roe, Technische Hogeschool Delft, Onderafdeling der Wijsbegeerte en Maatschappij-
Wetenschappen, Kanaalweg 2b. DELFT.

INDIVIDUAL CHARACTERISTICS FROM A THEORETICAL POINT OF VIEW

In this section three subjects are discussed. First the question is posed how individual characteristics may be defined. Next an attempt is made to create some order in the realm of individual characteristics by introducing a number of distinctions. And finally personality traits are considered in some detail, taking into account some points of critique that have been put forward.

What are individual characteristics?

Although the term 'individual characteristic' seems to be self-explanatory, we do well to reflect on its meaning for a moment. To start with, it should be noted that this term refers to some *postulated* attribute characterizing one or more individuals. In other words: individual characteristics are not given as such, but have their basis in assumptions and/or suppositions. This may be a matter of a simple operational definition, as is the case with characteristics like body length and sex. But they may also be constructs that are part of a more or less comprehensive theoretical framework, like the need to achieve or ego-strength. In this latter case, suppositions are made concerning the validity of the theory involved and the operationalization of constructs. Another usual supposition, derived from the parsimony-principle, is that constructs are basic in character, i.e. cannot be reduced to other, more fundamental constructs.

Apart from these assumptions and suppositions relating to the 'existence' of the attribute, a typical supposition is that of a more or less durable *boundedness* to the individual. By saying that a person carries a characteristic, one expresses that the attribute is maintained for a certain time and is insensitive to the circumstances to which the person is exposed. From here on, I will speak of 'constancy'. A clear example is the person's sex, a characteristic retained during the whole lifetime, exceptional circumstances excluded. For the majority of individual characteristics, the time interval and the array of conditions under which no changes are observed are limited however.

Within the perspective of psychological theory and intervention (thus leaving direct clerical uses out of account), it makes sense to conceive of individual characteristics as *theoretical constructs* serving to explain and predict behavior. Their position within the nomological networks relevant to the behavior involved is thereby partly fixed: from the hypothesized constancies it may be derived that with some constructs relations will exist, while with others no relations will be found. Of course, it would not be justified to consider any individual attribute as a personal characteristic. It is essential that the suppositions, especially those about constancy, have been shown to be valid in empirical research. What is needed is in other words *construct validation.* One should establish whether the construct may be operationalized unambiguously and whether relations with other constructs are adequately reflected in associations between operational measures. The general purpose is to verify whether convergent and discriminant relationships that are supposed to exist between constructs are found at the empirical level. This research may be executed according to the multitrait-multimethod design, which calls for the operationalization of each construct by a number of methods (Campbell and Fiske, 1959; Schmitt *et al.*, 1977).

For the sake of completeness it should be said that another type of research may also be required, i.e. *inductive research* aimed at construct and hypothesis development. As far as constructs are concerned, one may speak of 'analysis of meaning' (Drenth, 1975). Logically speaking this type of investigation precedes construct validation and should not be confounded with it. Its goal is to help weave the nomological net which is tried in construct validation. By means of explorations (e.g. with factor analysis) one tries to identify theoretical constructs (the knots) and hypotheses (threads). Furthermore, means for operationalizing constructs are sought.

Types of individual characteristics

Individual characteristics may be classified in a number of ways. In this section two dimensions are introduced: the level of abstractness and the degree of constancy. With the help of these dimensions three classes of individual characteristics are distinguished.

ABSTRACTNESS

The foregoing already showed that individual characteristics may differ in their distance to the empirical world, in other words in their level of abstractness. Although in fact a continuous scale underlies these differences, it is customary to use the following dichotomy (e.g. de Groot, 1961):

(1) Individual characteristics as empirical concepts. These characteristics are purely descriptive. They are directly connected to empirical phenomena by means of an operational definition. Examples are: body length and sex, but also reaction time and I.Q.

(2) Individual characteristics as theoretical concepts (constructs). These characteristics can not be observed directly, but only by means of a hypothesized relationship to one or more empirical concepts. They are abstract, but at the same time general, because they cover a wider range of empirical phenomena than empirical concepts. Further, they may play a role in theoretical explanations, as components of hypotheses or theories. Examples are: the need to achieve, authoritarianism, neuroticism.

CONSTANCY

By definition, individual characteristics are bound to the individual. They possess a certain constancy over time and under situational changes. The degree of constancy varies however. Perfect time constancy (*stability*) is rather exceptional. Apart from a number of genetically given physical characteristics like sex and blood type, changes are usual. If one confines oneself to certain phases in the individual's life span (in case of work- and organizational psychology: adulthood), some characteristics show little and others great variability. For constancy under changing circumstances (*transsituational constancy*) the same applies. There are a number of characteristics being maintained within a wide class of situations, while others easily disappear or arise.

THREE CLASSES

A global classification, which also takes the theoretical content into account, is the following:

(1) *Dispositional characteristics*. These characteristics, which may also be denoted as 'personality traits', possess a relatively high degree of constancy, attributable to heredity and early experiences. Once present, there is a large probability that they will be present at later times and in other situations also. Examples are: several intellectual abilities and so-called style characteristics.

(2) *Habitual characteristics*. These characteristics are acquired in interaction with the situation, in a process of learning, training or habituation. Once formed, they possess a relatively high degree of stability. The degree of transsituational constancy varies, dependent on the specific characteristic. Examples are: several types of knowledge, aptitudes, skills, attitudes, expectations and habits.

(3) *Motivational characteristics*. These characteristics refer to shorter or longer enduring physical and/or mental conditions giving rise to a certain level of activity and a specific directedness of behavior. Most of these characteristics are unstable and change easily under influence of situational changes. Examples are: needs like hunger and thirst, but also aspiration level, degree of cognitive dissonance, etc.

A sharp delineation of these classes of individual characteristics is not possible. On the contrary, there is an unmistakable overlap (see figure 1). Some motivational characteristics are so typical and show so little change, that they might be classed as dispositional as well. Others may be shaped during a learning process and hence fall within the class of habitual characteristics at the same time. Of these last mentioned characteristics a number is sufficiently stable to be considered as dispositional.

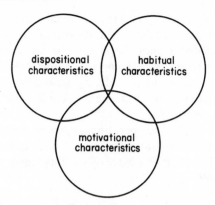

Figure 1. Relationships between different types of personal characteristics.

In the remainder of this chapter personality traits will be put in the foreground. The other types of characteristics will be mentioned, but not extensively discussed. They will be dealt with in other chapters. Motivational characteristics are treated in chapter 2.2; habitual characteristics in chapter 2.3.

The personality trait concept

DEFINITION

The description of personality traits as individual characteristics with a relatively high degree of constancy does not specify how to recognize an individual characteristic as a trait. The answer to this question may be derived from the foregoing. Firstly, a definition of the characteristic is needed, specifying a certain (high) degree of constancy. Secondly, it should be specified which instruments may be used to operationalize the construct; in other words, 'observational hypotheses' should be formulated. And thirdly, there should be results from empirical research with these instruments, showing the definition to be adequate and the supposed constancy to be present.

It is decisive that convergent relations be shown, i.e. that repeated measurements with comparable or different operationalizations of the postulated trait appear to be related. More specifically, signs of *stability* and *generality* are required, the first meaning a correspondence between measurements at different times now, and the second the congruence between measurements in different situations.

Another condition, often mentioned, is that there should be *differentiation* in measurements, which means that it should be possible to distinguish people according to the degree in which the trait is shown. This presupposes traits to be 'universal', i.e. discernible in every individual. Although this presupposition does not always make sense at the individual level—certain traits like color blindness or left-handedness happen to be found in a limited number of people—it does not pose any problems at the operational level. Universality may be present by assumption, considering individual characteristics to be variables on which some, or even many people, get an extreme score, corresponding to the zero point.

With the help of the mentioned operational concepts a more precise definition is now possible. A personality trait is an individual characteristic which shows, as hypothesized, a relatively high degree of stability, generality and differentiation (cf. Guilford, 1959).

Personality traits and behavior

The psychological meaning of personality traits lies in the fact that they can help to *explain* and *predict* human behavior. At least when tested hypotheses are available relating traits to specific forms of behavior. It has been put forward that here circular reasoning is involved (cf. Feij, 1978), because traits are inferred from behavior first and behavior is subsequently from traits. However, this gives a wrong picture of what is happening in explanation (or prediction), as may be shown with an example. Suppose a worker performs a certain task poorly. His behavior may then be considered to be explained[1] if it is known that a low intelligence level is generally associated with poor performance on the task, and the worker has a low intelligence level. The intellectual capacity is inferred from the behavior, i.e. in a test situation, but this is different from the behavior which is explained.

The course of things in explanation, shown in this example, differs only slightly from that in prediction. The difference is that in the case of prediction the hypothetical intelligence-performance relation and the intelligence levels of the worker are given, while the performance is unknown and has to be derived. This picture of explanation and prediction is only very crude. A more complete exposition is presented elsewhere (Roe, 1983).

In order to understand properly the role of personality traits, it should be recognized that human behavior is caused by a large number of determinants, operating simultaneously (Duijker, 1972). While some of these *multiple determinants* may correspond to personality traits, others will reside in more changeable individual characteristics and in aspects of the situation in which an individual finds himself. The diagram of figure 2, although very rough, may elucidate this. It gives a rough classification of behavior determinants:

---

[1] As Fey (1978) remarks correctly, one cannot speak of a 'causal' explanation in any strict sense here. However, it should be noted that there are other types of explanation, causal explanations being relatively rare within psychology (Ruimschotel, 1979; Stegmüller, 1969).

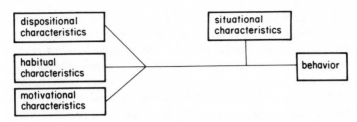

Figure 2. Personal characteristics and situational characteristics
as behavior determinants.

on the one hand dispositional, habitual, and motivational characteristics,
on the other hand situational characteristics.

In interpreting this diagram three points are of interest. First, it should
be noted that the different determinants may have *interactive* as well as additive
effects on behavior. This is indicated by the points at which the lines meet.
In the second place, there is a *multiplicity* of determinants within the four
classes also. For instance, several dispositional characteristics will be active
at the same time: character traits like intelligence, shrewdness, emotional
stability, as well as physical traits like length, muscular strength and reaction
speed. Mutatis mutandis the same applies to habitual and motivational
characteristics. In the same way there may be a variety of situational determinants: material determinants such as a work environment with machines,
tools and materials, a certain temperature, humidity, etc., and immaterial
ones like tasks, competencies, the reward structure, the presence of other
people having their own attitudes, expectations, etc. Finally, the diagram is
general, it may take a *variety of concrete forms*, depending on the specific
type of behavior one is interested in and the time episodes chosen.

The influences that personality traits exert within this whole are limited.
It would, in any case, be unrealistic to assume that one could perfectly predict
behavior from a series of traits (cf. Roe, 1983). At the same time, it should
be said, that for many practical purposes personality traits may be of more
importance than one would think. This is mainly because of their stability,
which opens up the possibility to predict behavior across longer time intervals,
a possibility absent from most of the other determinants, situational ones
included.

The general model presented above embodies a view known as *interactionism*.
This approach has been contrasted to both *personologism* (or the classical
trait model), which assigns a predominant role to personality traits, and
situationism, which assumes situational determinants to be of major importance
(cf. Ekkehammer, 1974; Endler and Magnusson, 1976; Magnusson, 1981).
However, the term interactionism carries many meanings (Krauskopf, 1978;

Buss, 1977) all of which certainly do not apply here. One meaning is that behavior is thought to take place in an interactional (also transactional) process, in which person and situation influence each other in a dynamic way. Another meaning is that within an analysis-of-variance model interaction-terms account for the larger part of the variance. In my opinion, the dynamic view has not yet attained the scientific status required in order to be under-written; further elaboration and empirical support are required first. I would not dare to draw any conclusion about the importance of traits, situational characteristics and interactions, in the sense of percentage of variance explained. Apart from the fact that adequate statistical data are lacking (Golding, 1975), it would not make much sense to draw such conclusions, because every kind of behavior and every set of explanatory variables would yield different results.

Criticism of personality traits

The trait concept and its application meet two kinds of criticism. The first one concerns the importance of traits, the second one their 'existence'.[2]

Doubts about the stability and transsituational constancy of traits, easily supported by impressions from everyday life and examples from empirical investigations, constitute the basis of the first kind of criticism. Its essence may be summarized in two statements:
—Supposed traits lack the required constancy.
—The role of traits in explaining or predicting behavior tends to be a minor one.
Both statements should be seen in contrast to the classical trait model, which, according to its critics, assumes that traits play a predominant (if not completely determining) role. Authors like Hunt (1965), Hettema (1967) and Mischel (1968) have stressed the first aspect. They present examples of correlations between repeated or parallel measurements of supposed traits, pointing to far from perfect relationships. A much cited example is a study of Hartshorne and May (1928), reporting an average correlation of .23 between nine measures of dishonest behavior in children. The generalizability of other traits would be just as limited as was the case for 'honesty' here.

Critics showing interest in other behavior determinants as well have mainly pointed to the second aspect. For a few types of behavior they have tried to establish the role of one or more situational factors and, in some cases, the importance of person-situation interactions, usually taking the percentage of explained variance as the standard of judgment. Well known are studies

---

[2]Other points of criticism have been put forward also (see the review by Hogan et al., 1977). It has been argued, for instance, that the trait concept does not help to gain an understanding of behavior processes (Hettema, 1967). However, traits and process variables do not lie in the same theoretical plane. It is possible to use both in a way to supplement each other (cf. Feij, 1978). In the same vein it may be argued that traits may exist along with variables from learning theory.

by Endler *et al.*, (1962) and Endler and Hunt (1966, 1969), using a special type of questionnaire in which subjects were asked to indicate how anxious they would feel in certain situations. In the first study an analysis of variance led to the (by the way, wrong) conclusion that the situations described in the questionnaire items explained a major part of the variance of the anxiety-scores, while individual differences explained just a small part. In the other studies it was concluded that the interaction effects were stronger than the main effects.

Putting the available data next to each other, it appears that only a small number of behaviors and supposed traits were covered and that the choice of situational factors was very arbitrary indeed. Taking into account the shortcomings of the methods used for operationalization and data analysis (Jackson and Paunonen, 1980; Lanterman, 1978; Golding, 1975; Bowers, 1973), the conclusion seems justified that the criticism was phrased in a much too general way. Neither the absence of constancy nor a minor explanatory or predictive power have been demonstrated regularly and convincingly.

In as far as it conveys a warning against overestimation and unrestricted use of the trait concept, this criticism should be taken seriously. Postulated traits must be submitted to systematic construct validation. At the same time it should be kept in mind, that several types of traits have been shown to possess a considerable degree of constancy (e.g. Thomae, 1960; Bloom, 1964; Mischel, 1968; van der Werff, 1979; Brim, 1980).

The composition of the model to be used for explaining or predicting behavior will vary according to the type of behavior, the reliability and validity of available measuring instruments, the costs of using these instruments, etc. In one case, a combination of a situational variable and a number of traits will be required, while in another only traits will suffice (cf. Hofstee, 1978). A decision-theoretical discussion of this problem of choosing a model is presented by Roe (1983).

The second kind of criticism seems more fundamental. It stems partly from the findings of research on attribution processes, showing that observers tend to explain other people's behavior in terms of traits which may in fact be irrelevant or even non-existent (Jones and Nisbett, 1972; Nisbett *et al.*, 1973). This might also apply to the psychologist as an observer, his traits being mere phantasies. Further, there is the observation, made in a number of studies, that analyses of the semantic similarity of terms used to describe individual differences tend to yield a stable structure which may or may not be comparable to the structure found in an analysis of factual differences between individuals (d'Andrade, 1965, 1974; Schneider, 1973; Shweder, 1975). It has been argued, referring to this observation, that a rater may force a conceptual structure upon his description of other people, and thus introduce 'dimensions of personality' (cf. traits) having nothing to do with empirical facts. A person responding to a personality questionnaire may structure his answers in the same way. The consequence would be that traits found by means of judgement data or responses to questionnaire items are artificial in character.

The core of the criticism seems to lie in the risk that raters or psychologists confuse their descriptive notions with real personality traits. Or, to quote d'Andrade (1965, p. 215), that 'propositions about theory are confused with propositions about the world'. Although the critics have tended to reject the trait concept as such, it will be clear that only the *induction* of traits is at stake here: the establishing of theoretical constructs on the basis of observations (cf. Block *et al.*, 1979). The risk concerns the possibility that the constructs may be 'wrong', i.e. do not take their presupposed position within the nomological network and lack the operational characteristics of stability, generality and differentiation. Apart from questions concerning the relationships between the rater's conceptual structure, his behavior ratings (Lamiell *et al.*, 1980) and empirical patterns of behavior (a.o. Mischel, 1979), it should be noted that the risk may be eliminated in the process of construct validation taking place after the trait construct has been defined. When researchers reveal convergent relations with other variables, including external criteria, using divergent operationalizations within different populations, it appears of itself whether a certain trait does or does not exist. Castles in the air have little chance to survive here.

The criticism is not without importance however. It underlines the importance of construct validation of traits, which often is not sufficiently recognized. Further, it implies a warning to the psychologist to keep away from the layman's path and to confine himself to traits whose meaning and validity have been properly assessed. This requires rather strict preconditions concerning the use of ratings (see p. 121).

To recapitulate, it may be concluded that so far the criticism on personality traits has cut little ice. The main problem appears to be the lack of adequate trait descriptions and systematic construct validation efforts in the past. It seems to me that the chaotic situation resulting from these shortcomings, which has left many supposed traits with an obscure status, has needlessly given room to doubt and criticism.

A REVIEW OF INDIVIDUAL CHARACTERISTICS

Below, a review is given of individual characteristics that seem relevant to the psychology of work and organization. As was said, a certain emphasis is laid on personality traits, although some other characteristics are mentioned also. Furthermore, the description is confined to concepts at the theoretical level.

Considering the incomplete and badly ordered knowledge gathered so far, to present a review is a precarious affair, because it creates the illusion of order. Because of this, it should, with the exception of some parts (see 1 and 4), not be considered a taxonomy, but rather a somewhat optimistic provisional sketch. The list of individual characteristics is more or less arbitrary. For example, characteristics found in various studies (using different operationalizations) predominate, which implies that less often identified characteristics could be added. Further, relatively broad characteristics are preferred over fine distinctions. My general aim has been to present a picture of the more fundamental characteristics identified in empirical research, with some emphasis on their diversity. The nomenclature is rather arbitrary also, especially in the section of character traits, where many divergent names have been proposed.

The classification of personal characteristics is pragmatic; it does not rely on any consistent logic. First, mental traits are mentioned, divided as usual into modalities (Cattell, 1968): intellectual abilities, character traits and interests/values. Next, physical traits are presented, distinguishing motor and sensory traits. Finally a number of other individual characteristics are described: habitual characteristics belonging to the realm of knowledge and skills, and biographical characteristics.

1. Intellectual abilities

The intellectual domain may be characterized in a number of ways. The most detailed and comprehensive classification system is offered by the well-known 'structure-of-intellect' model (S.I.-model), which presupposes 120 independent ability dimensions (Guilford and Hoepfner, 1971). Most of these dimensions, each of which indicates a specific type of mental activity, have been identified empirically (e.g. Elshout, 1976); others still are the subject of investigation. The dimensions of the S.I.-model are generally thought to be too specific for practical use, although there are examples of successful applications in personnel selection.

Many less detailed systems are known (cf. Dunnette, 1976), most of them relating to specific test batteries constructed on the basis of factor analysis. Thurstone (1938) distinguishes five Primary Mental Abilities; the General Aptitude Test Battery (U.S. Department of Labor, 1967) counts ten factors. De Wolff and Buiten (1968) have found ten factors also in an analysis of four test batteries. Greater numbers are found as well. The well-known 'kit' devised by French et al., (1963) covers 24 dimensions. Theologus et al., (1970) distinguish 19 intellectual (besides 18 physical) dimensions. And Hakstian and Cattell (1975) describe 20 correlated dimensions.

Although these classification schemes differ from each other, they have much in common. Quite a number of dimensions can be found in several studies. The differences mainly have to do with the level of abstraction: what is a single dimension in one scheme, is split into several dimensions in another. The most frequently found dimensions are the following.

Reasoning (R): the ability to solve all kinds of reasoning problems; on the one hand discovering a rule or a principle and applying it in solving a problem, on the other hand deducing conclusions from certain premises, following rules of logic; distinctions are made according to the type of material involved: verbal, numerical, abstract (figurative), mechanical reasoning.

Verbal comprehension (V): being able to understand the meaning of words and their relationships, as well as verbal expressions.

Numerical ability (N): proficience in handling numbers and performing simple arithmetic operations (addition, subtraction, multiplication, division).

Spatial ability (S): being able to visualize spatial figures and objects and to orient oneself with respect to them.

Perceptual speed (P): being able to discover symbols quickly and to manipulate (a.o. compare) them; may be distinguished according to the type of symbol involved: in the case of alphanumerical symbols the term 'clerical perception' is used, in the case of figures the term 'form perception'.

Word fluency (W): the ability to find and/or make quickly and easily words that have certain characteristics.

Visualization (Vz): being able to catch on figures, retain them and manipulate them mentally.

Memory (M): being able to remember series of words, symbols, numbers, etc.; remembering 'what goes with what'; may be distinguished according to the time interval: immediate, short term, and long term.

Creativity (C): the ability to produce divergent solutions to given problems.

One may also use the compound notion of *general ability* (G), which embraces a number of the dimensions mentioned above. The precise meaning of this notion varies. The General Aptitude Test Battery defines general intelligence as a weighted composite of scores on the verbal, numerical and reasoning factors. At any rate, general ability should not be seen as a common denominator of all aspects of intelligence; many of Guilford's dimensions are not covered by it (cf. Guion, 1965).

2. Character traits

For a number of reasons, it is not easy to give an overview of character traits. To begin with, there are large differences in terminology, each group of researchers using its own vocabulary. Secondly, most of the research has been devoted to separate tests, giving little attention to possible interconnections. Conceptual differences play a role also. Some traits refer to specific types of behavior, while others are quite abstract (see the distinction between 'surface traits' and 'source traits'; Cattell, 1950). Also, there are differences in the psychological processes referred to: needs, habits, cognitive styles, etc.

Below, I will indicate in descriptive terms to what aspects of personality the many trait dimensions found in the literature relate. There is one important limitation: only aspects discernible in 'normal' adult individuals are mentioned; the countless concepts used to indicate pathological traits are disregarded.

The list contains temperament traits as well as other character traits. Although one might prefer to make some distinction here, this has not been attempted, because of the difficulties involved in giving adequate, i.e. unambiguous delineations (Feij, 1978). It is left to the reader to introduce his own distinctions, if he likes. However, I have made a pragmatic division, which should make it easier to effect an overview. There are four categories: (I) traits relating to the general functioning of the individual; (II) traits referring to the relation which the person maintains to himself; (III) traits referring to social relations, and (IV) the relationships with in a wider social context.

The following list is a crude inventory, based on dimensions found in well-known personality questionnaires and rating scales and on results of comparative and factor-analytic studies (a.o. Cattell, 1973; Adcock *et al.*, 1974; Browne and Howarth, 1977; Powell and Royce, 1981; see also Pawlik, 1968; Feij, 1978). As a whole, this list has not been corroborated by empirical research. The traits mentioned may interrelate and hence be reduced to more fundamental trait dimensions. Some of them may be split into lower-level dimensions.

The names are chosen in such a way, that only one pole of each trait dimension is reflected. So the name 'emotional stability' instead of 'neuroticism' is used, 'dominance' instead of 'submissiveness', etc. The other, mostly the weak or unfavorable, pole might be emphasized also, of course. This leaves the trait dimensions unaffected however.

I. *General functioning*

Energy level: the amount of energy produced, the level of activity, vitality, mental speed (opposite: inertness).
Determination: having a clear picture of one's purposes (opposite: incertitude).
Rhatymia: the tendency to proceed energetically in carrying out actions (opposite: restraint).
Sensation-seeking: the need for variety, dislike of monotony.
Emotionality: tendency to react emotionally, sensitivity to emotional stimuli.
Psychological differentiation: the degree of differentiation in cognitive functioning, self-perception, social relationships, etc.; analytical vs. global style, field-independence.
Intellectual functioning: speed and quality of thinking, originality, imagination.

II. *Relations to oneself*

Conscientiousness, responsibility: the way in which conscience is functioning, i.e. the observance, strict or less strict, of moral norms; possibly self-defensiveness.
Persistence: the tendency to continue activities under difficult circumstances.
Emotional stability, maturity: control of oneself, control of emotional impulses (opposite: neuroticism, impulsiveness, agressiveness, enthusiasm).
Reflectiveness: the inclination to think about and render account of one's behavior.
Flexibility: the openness to self-correction (opposite: rigidity).
Self-esteem: the judgement about oneself, self-confidence; also self-sufficiency, self-compassion (opposite: self-denial).

III. *Social relations*

Sociability, extroversion: the need to be with others, the dislike of being alone.

Dependence: the tendency to behave in accordance to what others think or like (opposite: independence, autonomy).

Dominance: wanting to dominate other people, to exercise authority, also showing this want in an aggressive manner.

Ascendance: the ability to dominate, to demonstrate authority.

Empathy: the ability to understand others, to have insight into their behavior and feeling.

Trust: having trust in others, believing their good intentions (opposite: suspicion).

Friendliness: behaving friendly to other people, treating them charitably.

Cooperativeness: the ability to cooperate with others without causing conflicts.

Machiavellianism: the inclination to influence others in such a way that own preconceived goals may be reached.

IV. *Social context*

Adaptation, conformity: the congruence between one's own behavior and social norms, a.o. with respect to sex roles (femininty-masculinity).

Authoritarianism: the tendency to lay stress on rules of conduct (especially those defining decency) and demanding strict observance by oneself and others.

Achievement motivation: the orientation to achieve, the tendency to excel.

Internal-external control: the attribution to oneself or the environment of the capacity to exert a decisive influence on one's own life.

3. Interests and values

Interests and values, together representing the dynamic side of personality, are conceptually closely related. Values used to be characterized as 'what is important to the individual'; general goals that he is pursuing or outcomes he is trying to obtain. Interests reflect 'what the individual likes'; they are more specific and connected more directly to patterns of activity. One may speak of a goal-means relationship (Super, 1973) in the sense that several interests may serve to realize one and the same value.

There are some differences in character traits, although not very sharp ones. The main point of difference lies in the 'content-like' character of interests and values, their directedness to specific activities and goals (outcomes), although the fact that they stem from the individual's own experience may be called typical also (Vroom, 1964). As far as the content is concerned, only the world of work is relevant here: the description is limited to vocational interests and work values.

Vocational interests may be defined either in terms of occupations or in terms of activities. The dimensions produced by these two approaches may be translated into each other without much difficulty. Occupational dimensions clearly relate to activity dimensions (Holland, 1976; Super and Crites, 1962). The dimensions found in the literature are bound to specific tests as was the case with character traits. But as the number of tests is much smaller and terminological differences are less profound, there is much more congruence. The dimensions found by American researchers like Guilford *et al.* (1954), Roe (1956), Holland (1965) and Kuder (1970) correspond well to those identified by European reseachers like Irle (1955) and Welten (1969). From the research, which has been summarized by Holland (1976) and Van Geffen (1977), it appears that a small number of dimensions (or categories) suffices to represent the spectrum of vocational interests.

The main activity dimensions mentioned by these last authors are: *scientific, theoretical, social, altruistic, business, artistic, technical, literary and cultural, clerical.* The review by Van Geffen (1977; p. 92) makes clear how these dimensions correspond to occupational dimensions. It should be noted that some dimensions may be split up again; see for instance Rounds and Davis (1979), and Guilford *et al.* (1954).[3]

Work values have been factor-analyzed only on a limited scale and without connections between instruments having been laid. The results reveal some points of agreement, but on the whole the picture is not very clear. Values have been examined also within the context of job satisfaction (see Locke, 1976), but here the same conclusion applies. The common dimensions that have been identified most frequently (van Geffen, 1977; Hendrix and Super, 1968; Gable and Pruzek, 1969; Rosenberg, 1957; with respect to satisfaction: Smith *et al.*, 1969; Kilpatrick *et al.*, 1964; Friedländer, 1963; Gurin *et al.*, 1960) are the following.

Security: pursuing a high income, economic security, good fringe-benefits.
Autonomy: the desire to act independently, to exert (rather than undergo) influence.
Affiliation: the desire to maintain social contacts, either active (helping, directing, persuading) or passive (being helped, directed, persuaded) ones.
Respect: the wish to gain recognition, esteem, respect and status.
Self-expression: the desire to express oneself in one's work, to accomplish given tasks.

The last four dimensions correspond to a number of 'higher needs' from the theory of Maslow (1954). 'Lower needs' are not represented, except for the security dimension. For the greater part they will lack the required stability and differentiation. Once again, the dimensions may be split up into a number of more specific dimensions, as is shown in the review of Van Geffen (1977, pp. 110–111).

4. Motor abilities

Psychomotor abilities—having to do with muscular activity—have been investigated extensively by Fleishman and his co-workers. His research has produced useful classifications. A distinction is made between: (1) performances with the limbs, especially in manipulating certain objects; and (2) performances

---

[3] Less general than vocational interests are interests for specific types of jobs as these exist within given organizations. An example of research devoted to such interests, offering leads to classification, may be found in Boerlijst (1974).

involving the whole body. The first category is designated as 'psychomotor abilities' to indicate the fact that performance takes place under voluntary and perceptual control. The second category involves aspects of 'physical fitness'.

In *manipulating objects* the following items play a role (Fleishman, 1962; Theologus *et al.*, 1970):

Choice reaction time: the ability to select and initiate a response when the response is selected from two or more alternatives relative to two or more stimuli.

Reaction time: the speed with which a single motor response can be initiated relative to a single stimulus.

Speed of limb movement: the speed with which discrete movements of the arm or leg can be made.

Wrist-finger speed: the speed with which discrete movements of the fingers, hands, and wrists can be made.

Finger dexterity: the ability to make skillful, coordinated movements of the fingers where manipulation of objects may or may not be involved.

Manual dexterity: the ability to make skillful, coordinated movements of the hand, or of a hand together with its arm.

Rate control: the ability to make timed, anticipatory motor adjustments relative to changes in the speed and/or direction of a continuously moving object.

Control precision: the ability to make controlled muscular movements necessary to adjust or position a machine or equipment control mechanism.

Multi-limb coordination: the ability to coordinate the movements of a number of limbs simultaneously.

Arm-hand steadiness: the ability to make precise arm-hand positioning movements that do not require strength.

The dimensions underlying *performance involving the whole body* (based on Fleishman, 1964, 1972) are:

Static strength: the maximum force that can be exerted during a short time.

Dynamic strength: the force that can be exerted continuously or repeatedly, especially in moving one's own body.

Explosive strength: the ability to mobilize energy effectively for bursts of muscular effort (e.g. sprints).

Trunk strength: the force that can be exerted with trunk muscles.

Extent of flexibility: the ability to flex or stretch trunk and back muscles.

Dynamic flexibility: the ability to make repeated, rapid, flexing trunk movements.

Gross body coordination: the ability to make coordinated movements with several parts of the body (including movements while the body is in motion).

Gross body equilibrium: the ability to maintain balance while moving.

Stamina: the capacity to sustain maximum effort requiring cardiovascular exertion.

5. Sensory abilities and attention

Sensory functioning plays a role in intellectual and psychomotor abilities, but they may also be considered separately. Because there has hardly been

any research on basic dimensions in this area, it is impossible to give a satisfactory review. One could summarize aspects of sensory functioning from
physiological literature, but this would yield a less adequate picture. Because
of this, only some fundamental aspects of vision and hearing are presented
(cf. McCormick and Tiffin, 1975; Pawlik, 1968). In relation to *vision* the
following aspects may be mentioned.

Visual acuity: the ability to discern symbols at variable distances (myopia–presbyopia).
Phorias: the position of the eye in a condition of physiological rest (vertical and hori-
zontal).
Color discrimination: the ability to recognize colors of different brightness, saturation
and shade.
Depth perception: the ability to estimate distances using both eyes.

And in relation to *hearing*:

Auditory sensitivity: the sensitivity to tones of different pitch and loudness.
Pitch discrimination: the ability to discriminate tones of different pitch.
Loudness discrimination: the ability to discriminate tones of different loudness.
Duration discrimination: the ability to discriminate tones of different duration.

In connection with sensory perception also some specific aspects of central
nervous system functioning are relevant. These aspects, all having to do with
attention, are the following.

Closed attention: being able to keep perception directed at a specific object or event.
Open attention: being able to keep perception directed at various objects or events simul-
taneously.
Mental capacity: being able to perform several mental tasks simultaneously.

6. Knowledge and skills

Knowledge refers to the ability to reproduce or recognize specific facts or
relationships, while skills are abilities to perform specific tasks in a prescribed
manner. These characteristics bear some relationship to intellectual (as well
as motor and sensory) abilities, because these abilities are prerequisites for
their acquisition. However, there is an important difference also: knowledge
and skills are specific achievements. They constitute, so to say, the result of
what the individual has accomplished using his mental capacities.

Because of the large number of subjects that people may have knowledge
about and the variety of activities in which they may be skillful, a review can
hardly be given. One could of course resort to research on intellectual abilities
and set up a classification system along the lines of ability dimensions, but
in doing so the distinctive character of knowledge and skills, its content-
directedness, would get lost. Another option would be to make use of didacti-

cally oriented taxonomies (e.g. Bloom, 1965; de Block, 1975). However, this would preserve even less of the contents and bring along the risk of loosing oneself in the vast domain of less stable individual characteristics.

To me, the best solution seems to lie in the design of an ad hoc classification system, taking its theoretical and practical aims into account. By way of example, I want to point to a crude system that may be used within the context of personnel selection (Roe, 1983). Here, knowledge and skills are divided into 'parcels' such as tend to be acquired within educational programs or during one's working career. Two main categories are distinguished: (1) knowledge and skills resulting from *general education* (2) knowledge and skills acquired in *vocational training, specific courses* and *actual job performance*. Within these categories a series of 'parcels' are distinguished, following the educational structure. Within the first category, parcels are distinguished according to *level* and *composition*, the latter in terms of academic subjects. The second category is divided into *sectors* first (agriculture, printing technology, health care) and *levels* of programs next. Knowledge and skills resulting from the fulfillment of certain jobs or specific life experiences take a separate position. Aspects to be mentioned are: *oral and written expression, mastery of foreign languages, social skills, driving skills, clerical skills*, etc.

7. Biographical characteristics

A last category comprises a series of heterogeneous characteristics relating to the individual's life career. A number of these characteristics, like educational background, have been mentioned before. A review by Owens (1976) shows that most biographical characteristics may be considered as intellectual or character traits.

Characteristics not mentioned before that may be relevant to work behavior are (cf. Super, 1960; Lawshe and Balma, 1966): Sex, age, socio-economic status, geographical-cultural background, ethnic origin, childhood experiences, family situation, social contacts, leisure activities, cultural experience, experiences under exceptional circumstances (like war, military service, travels, etc.), political, religious and philosophical convictions.

OPERATIONALIZATION

The characteristics that have been listed above may be operationalized in several ways. The main methods are tests, ratings and direct inquiry.

TESTS

First of all, a large number of ready-to-use tests is available, distributed by publishers and test designers. There are several reviews of tests, Buros' Mental Measurements Yearbooks (e.g. 1978) probably being best known.

Apart from existing tests, tests may be also developed by oneself. This option may be chosen for instance when no instruments avail to measure given characteristics. Treatises on test construction may be found in Thorndike (1971), Anastasi (1976) and Nunnully (1978).

Generally speaking, tests compare positively to other instruments, because of their specific orientation to selected constructs and their high degree of standardization. Their construction guarantees a certain level of construct validity and reliability, although of course every instrument has its own merits and shortcomings. Finally, it should be noted that costs of test administration (and development) are also of influence on the utilization of tests.

RATINGS

Rating procedures have to be developed by the prospective user almost without exception. One should not primarily think of the design of rating scales here. Rather, a set of rules is needed concerning the rating process as a whole. Because ratings are always based on perceived behavior (or perceived outcomes), it is important that aspects like the observation of behavior, the procedure of conducting interviews, etc. be covered (cf. Roe and Daniëls, 1984).

Rating is a versatile method of measurement, applicable at least in principle to a wide array of individual characteristics. But at the same time this method is afflicted with serious problems, giving it a bad record on the whole (de Wolff, 1970; see also this Handbook, Ch. 2.4). Useful results may only be expected if stringent conditions are observed, making the rating process as objective as possible. And besides, considerable research efforts are required to guarantee sufficient construct validity (see p. 112).

DIRECT INQUIRY

Characteristics having a more tangible nature may be established by means of direct inquiry. Examples are: age, sex, educational qualifications, etc. One should be mindful, however, of possible distortions that can make reports of biographical data less reliable (e.g. Cascio, 1978, p. 201).

THEORETICAL ROLE

TWO PARADIGMS

The role of individual characteristics in theories on organizational behavior is very much dependent on the research paradigm opted for and the type of behavior one is interested in. In the psychology of work and organization, just like in other fields of psychology, two paradigms prevail which have led to separate developments, in spite of the fact that they may be reconciled quite well (Vale and Vale, 1969). These are (a) the paradigm of differential psychology, which aims to explain differences in behavior from individual characteristics, and (b) the paradigm of general psychology, which looks for explanations of behavior mainly in terms of processes holding for every individual (cf. Cronbach, 1957). The first paradigm assigns a central role to individual characteristics, especially traits and other stable characteristics; they constitute the basis for explaining behavior. The second one places individual characteristics in the background; at best, changeable characteristics in the sphere of learning and motivation play a role.

The differential paradigm, with its interest in variability and correlation, is clearly represented in former industrial psychology and present-day *personnel psychology*. Both strongly emphasize the importance of abilities, skills, character traits, etc. for the individual's behavior. With the help of these characteristics it is attempted to predict what behavior will be shown in given situations. There is a vast literature with data on these types of relationship (e.g. Ghiselli, 1966, 1973; Lent et al., 1971; Pearlman et al., 1980). Of course this is not the only approach being followed. In connection with performance appraisal, career development, training etc., also the paradigm of general psychology is followed.

For *organizational psychology* the reverse pertains: there the paradigm of general psychology prevails, with its experimental, comparative approach. The emphasis is on motivation, perception, attitudes, etc., seen as dynamic characteristics related to situational characteristics. In older theories on organizations individual characteristics are even completely neglected and personality is considered as a constant. 'Man' is supposed to be lazy, inclined to self-actualization, etc. (Lichtman and Hunt, 1971).

Looking back at figure 2, it appears that different parts of the behavior model are stressed: while personnel psychology takes dispositional and habitual characteristics as its main independent variables, organizational psychology confines itself almost exclusively to motivational and situational variables.

INTEGRATION

In the foregoing, the theoretical role of personal characteristics is indicated only sketchily. Within the psychology of work and organization a process of integration has been going on for a number of years now, which is slowly eroding the differences between the two paradigms. Personnel psychology demonstrates an increasing interest in motivation and situational characteristics (e.g. Dunnette, 1963; Terborg, 1977; Schneider, 1978), while organizational psychology shows an increasing interest in individual differences, mainly relating to motivation (e.g. Oldham, 1976; Mitchell, 1979; Cummings, 1982). There have been pleas for a fully integrated approach which would do justice to all components of the model (a.o. Campbell et al., 1970; James, 1973; James and Jones, 1976; Terborg, 1981), but no such approaches have been developed so far.

Present-day interaction models break up into a few categories. Within *organizational psychology* one finds models that explain (or predict) satisfaction and/or performance from motivational or organizational characteristics. In the first place there are models relating task characteristics to performance, satisfaction, turnover, etc., while taking into account personal characteristics like the need for personal growth or the need to achieve (e.g. Hackman and Oldham, 1976; Oldham *et al.*, 1976; Steers and Spencer, 1977; Stone *et al.*, 1977; Mowday *et al.*, 1979; Morris and Snyder, 1979).

Further, there are models that use in an analogous way personal characteristics as moderator variables in the relationship between aspects of goal setting and satisfaction and/or performance. These are characteristics like the need for achievement, independence, self respect, internal-external control (a.o. Latham and Yuhl, 1976; Steers, 1976; Dossett *et al.*, 1979) or general educational level (Latham and Yuhl, 1975; Ivancevich and McMahon, 1977). Lastly, 'expectancy models' may be mentioned. They infer motivation from cognitive variables, i.e. expectancies and outcomes, leaving room for a moderator effect of values in the sense that these may determine what outcomes are relevant in the eyes of the individual (van Geffen, 1977).

Within *personnel psychology* models have been developed in which individual characteristics, mostly abilities, are connected with performance criteria, and situational characteristics play the role of moderators. Examples are organizational climate (e.g. Frederiksen *et al.*, 1973; Bray *et al.*, 1974), level and differentiation of payment (e.g. Weinstein and Holzbach, 1973; Dunnette, 1973). Somewhat older is the leadership model devised by Fiedler (1967), which hypothesizes a relationship between the individual characteristic 'leadership style' and group performance, that is influenced by three situational conditions: group atmosphere, task structure, and position power, together defining the variable 'situational favorableness'. An interesting interaction model is described by Bagozzi (1978), who relates selling performance and satisfaction of salesmen to self-esteem, other-directedness and verbal intelligence as individual characteristics and sales potential within the area and workload.

These examples make clear that there are still considerable differences, the specific field of research determining whether personal characteristics are used, and if so, which of them are chosen. But at the same time it should be noted that there is, on the side of personnel psychology, a distinct trend to de-emphasize individual characteristics, whereas, on the side of organizational psychology, the tendency is to emphasize them.

In making connections one may profit from studies that are explicitly directed at the discovery of interrelationships. Some studies show, for instance, that expectancies, while serving as independent variables in expectancy models, are related to individual characteristics like self-esteem and internal-external control (see Mitchell, 1979). A study by Stone (1979) shows that the perception of task characteristics—variety, autonomy, feedback, etc.—is related to psychological differentiation (field-dependency).

ROLE IN APPLICATIONS

The role that individual characteristics may play in practical interventions may be clarified best with the help of a diagram given by Pawlik (1976) for categorizing intervention strategies. This diagram (see figure 3) makes a distinction between strategies based on choice and those based on modification. Both may relate to either people or conditions (situations). Thus there are four possibilities: selection of persons or conditions and modification of persons or conditions.

Although individual characteristics may play a role within all four strategies, it is evident that their importance is greatest in the selection of people, in other words in personnel selection. The rationale behind making choices is the presence of individual differences with a certain degree of stability. These differences may involve the whole range of individual characteristics, so: abilities, character traits, interests, values, etc. In the selection of conditions, individual characteristics may play a role when congruences of conditions and persons are sought after. This holds in the case of placement and classification in a traditional sense, i.e. when different jobs are assigned, but also when working conditions (like shift work) are chosen, or, within the context of job redesign, jobs are looked for, that differ in a specific respect only.

For modification of persons something comparable holds. Depending on its specific goal, intellectual, motor and perceptual abilities, or motivational characteristics, may play a role in training and development. Modification of conditions, a strategy underlying measures as diverse as task redesign, changes in the work environment, changes in payment and appraisal systems, democratization, organization development, has on the whole little to do with individual characteristics. The rare exceptions may be found within the field of ergonomics.

The general picture resembles that on the theoretical side. Within *personnel psychology* selection, placement, and training are common interventions. For *organizational psychology*, modification of conditions is typical, and, to a lesser degree, selection of conditions and modification of people. Thus, the theoretical importance assigned to stable characteristics and other behavior

	Persons	Conditions
Selection	Selection of persons	Selection of conditions
Modification	Modification of persons	Modification of conditions

Figure 3. Intervention strategies according to Pawlik (1976).

determinants is reflected in the intervention methods. Given this relationship, it may be expected that the practical role of individual characteristics will change in the future. The process of theoretical reconciliation justifies the expectation that individual characteristics will increasingly be dealt with in changing organizations, while, conversely, organizational characteristics will be incorporated into personnel selection. At present, there are already clear signs that such a development is taking place. Values and needs are taken into account in job design projects, task characteristics are included in selection procedures, and training programs are differentiated on the basis of abilities and interests.

REFERENCES

Adcock, N. V., Adcock, C. J., Walkey, F. H. (1974), Basic dimensions of personality. *Int. Rev. Appl. Psychol.*, **23** 131–137.

Anastasi, A. (1976), *Psychological testing*. 4th ed. New York: MacMillan.

Andrade, R. G. d' (1965), Trait psychology and componential analysis. *Am. Anthropol.*, **67**, 215–228.

Andrade, R. G. d' (1974), Memory and the assessment of behavior. In: Blalock, H. (Ed.), *Measurement in the social sciences*. Chicago: Aldine-Atherton, 159–186.

Bagozzi, R. P. (1978), Sales performance and satisfaction as a function of individual differences, interpersonal, and situational factors. *J. Market. Res.*, **15**, 517–531.

Bennett, G. K., Seashore, H. G., Wesman, A. G. (1972), *The Differential Aptitude Tests*. Rev. ed. New York: Psychological Corporation [1947].

Block, A. D. de (1975), *Taxonomie van leerdoelen* [Taxonomy of learning goals]. Antwerpen: Standaard Uitgeverij.

Block, J., Weiss, D. S., Thorne, A. (1979), How relevant is a semantic similarity interpretation of personality ratings? *J. Pers. and Soc. Psychol.*, **36**, 1055–1074.

Bloom, B. S. (1956), *Taxonomy of educational objectives. Handbook I: Cognitive domain*. New York: McKay. 1956.

Bloom, B. S. (1964), *Stability and change in human characteristics*. New York: Wiley.

Boerlijst, J. G. (1974), *Werk met perspectief* [Work with a perspective]. Amsterdam: Academische Pers.

Bowers, K. S. (1973), Situation in psychology: An analysis and a critique. *Psychol. Rev.*, **80**, 307–336.

Bray, D. W., Campbell, R. J., Grant, D. L. (1974), *Formative years in business: A long-term AT&T study of managerial lives*. New York: Wiley.

Brim, O. G. (Ed.) (1980), *Constancy and change in human development*. Cambridge (Mass.): Harvard Univ. Press.

Browne, J. A., Howard, E. (1977), A comprehensive factor analysis of personality questionnaire items: A test of twenty putative factor hypotheses. *Multiv. Behav. Res.*, **12**, 399–428.

Buros, O. K. (Ed.) (1978), *The Eighth Mental Measurements Yearbook*. Vols. 1 and 2. Highland Park (N. J.): Gryphon Press.

Buss, A. R. (1979), The trait-situation controversy and the concept of interaction. *Pers. Soc. Psychol. Bull.*, **3**, 196–201.

Campbell, D. T., Fiske, D. W. (1959), Convergent and discriminant validation by the multitrait-multimethod matrix. *Psychol. Bull.*, **56**, 81–105.

Campbell, J. P., Dunnette, M. D., Lawler, E. E., Weick, K. E. (1970), *Managerial behavior, performance and effectiveness*. New York: McGraw Hill.

Cascio, W. F. (1978), *Applied psychology in personnel management*. Reston (Vir.): Reston.

Cattell, R. B. (1950), *Personality*. New York: McGraw Hill.

Cattell, R. B. (1968), Traits. In: Sills, D. L. (Ed.), *International Encyclopedia of the Social Sciences*, vol. 16. London: MacMillan, 123–128.

Cattell, R. B. (1973), *Personality and mood by questionnaire*. San Francisco: Jossey-Bass.

Cronbach, L. J. (1959), The two disciplines of scientific psychology. *Am. Psychol.*, **12**, 671–684.

Cummings, L. L. (1982), Organizational behavior. *Ann. Rev. Psychol.*, **33**, 541–579.

Dossett, D. L., Latham, G. P., Mitchell, T. R. (1979), Effects of assigned versus participatively set goals, knowledge of results, and individual differences on employee behavior when goal difficulty is held constant. *J. Appl. Psychol.*, **64**, 291–298.

Drenth, P. J. D. (1975), *Inleiding in de testtheorie* [Introduction to test theory]. Deventer: Van Loghum Slaterus.

Duijker, H. C. J. (1972), *De meervoudige gedetermineerdheid van menselijk gedrag* [The multiple determinacy of human behaviour]. Mededelingen van de Koninklijke Nederlandse Akademie van Wetenschappen [Communications of the Royal Dutch Academy of Science], New Series, vol. 35, no. 3.

Dunnette, M. D. (1963), A modified model for test validation and selection research. *J. Appl. Psychol.*, **47**, 317–332.

Dunnette, M. D. (1973), *Performance equals ability and what?* Technical Report No. 4009. University of Minnesota, Department of Psychology.

Dunnette, M. D. (1976), Aptitudes, abilities, and skills. In: Dunnette, M. D. (Ed.), *Handbook of industrial and organizational psychology*. Chicago: Rand McNally, 473–520.

Ekkehammer, B. (1974), Interactionism in personality from a historical perspective. *Psychol. Bull.*, 1974, **81**, 1026–1048.

Elshout, J. J. (1976), *Karakteristieke moeilijkheden in het denken* [Characteristic problems in thinking]. Amsterdam, doctoral dissertation, University of Amsterdam, 1976.

Endler, N. S., Hunt, J. McV. (1966), Sources of behavioral variance as measured by the S-R Inventory of Anxiousness. *Psychol. Bull.*, 1966, **65**, 336–346.

Endler, N. S., Hunt, J. McV. (1969), Generalizability of contributions from sources of variance in the S-R Inventories of Anxiety. *J. Person.*, 1969, **37**, 1–24.

Endler, N. S., Hunt, J. McV., Rosenstein, A. J. (1962), *An S-R Inventory of Anxiousness*. Psychol. Monogr., 76 (17 Whole no. 536).

Endler, N. S., Magnussen, D. (1976), Toward an interactional psychology of personality. *Psychol. Bull.*, 1976, **83**, 956–974.

Feij, J. A. (1978), *Temperament: Onderzoek naar de betekenis van extraversie, emotionaliteit, impulsiviteit en spanningsbehoefte* [Temperament: A study of the meaning of extroversion, emotionality, impulsiveness and need of tension]. Amsterdam: Academische Pers.

Fielder, F. E. (1967), *A theory of leadership effectiveness*. New York: McGraw Hill.

Fleishman, E. A. (1962), The description and prediction of perceptual-motor skill learning. In: Glaser, R. (Ed.), *Training research and education*. Pittsburgh: University of Pittsburgh Press.

Fleishman, E. A. (1964), *The structure and measurement of physical fitness*. Englewood Cliffs (N.J.): Prentice-Hall.

Fleishman, E. A. (1972), On the relation between abilities, learning and human performance. *Am. Psychol.*, **27**, 1017–1031.

Frederiksen, N., Jensen, O., Beaton, A. E. (1973), *Prediction of organizational behavior*. New York: Pergamon.

French, J. W., Ekstrom, R. B., Price, L. A. (1963), *Kit of reference tests for cognitive factors*. Princeton: E.T.S.

Friedländer, F. (1963), Underlying sources of job satisfaction. *J. Appl. Psychol.*, **47**, 246–250.

Gable, R. K., Pruzek, R. M. (1969), *Super's Work Values Inventory: Two multivariate studies of interitem relationship*. Albany: State Univ. New York.

Geffen, L. M. H. J. van (1977), *De keuze van werk* [Occupational choice]. Culemborg: Schoolpers.

Ghiselli, E. E. (1966), *The validity of occupational aptitude tests*. New York: Wiley.

Ghiselli, E. E. (1973), The validity of aptitude tests in personnel selection. *Personnel Psychol.*, **26**, 461–478.

Golding, S. L. (1975), Three flies in the ointment: Methodological problems in the analysis of the percentage of variance due to persons and situations. *Psychol. Bull.*, **82**, 278–288.

Groot, A. D. de (1961), Methodologie (Eng. tr. 1969: Methodology). The Hague: Mouton.

Guilford, J. P. (1959), *Personality*. New York: McGraw-Hill,

Guilford, J. P., Hoepfner, R. (1971), *The analysis of intelligence*. New York: McGraw-Hill.

Guilford, J. P., Christensen, P. R., Bond, N. A., Sutton, M. A. (1954), *A factor analysis study of human interests*. Psychol. Monogr., 68 (4. Whole no. 575).

Guion, R. M. (1965), *Personnel testing*. New York: McGraw-Hill.

Gurin, G., Veroff, J., Feld, S. (1960), *Americans view their mental health*. New York: Basic Books. 1960.

Hackman, J. R., Oldham, G. R. (1976), Motivation through the design of work: test of a theory. *Organiz. Behav. and Hum. Perf.*, **16**, 250–279.

Hakstian, A. R., Cattell, R. B. (1975), *The Comprehensive Ability Battery*. Champaign (Ill.): Institute for Personality and Ability Testing.

Hartshorne, H., May, M. A. (1928), *Studies in the nature of character Vol. I: Studies in deceit*. New York: MacMillan.

Hendrix, V. L., Super, D. E. (1968), Factor dimensions and reliability of the Work Values Inventory. *Vocat. Guid. Q.*, **17**, 269–274.

Hettema, P. J. (1967), Trekken, processen en persoonlijkheidstests [Traits, Processes and personality tests]. *Ned. Tijdschr. Psychol.* [Dutch Journal of Psychology], **22**, 618–641.

Hofstee, W. K. B. (1978), Persoonlijkheidsleer [Personality theory]. In: Duijker, H. C. J. (Ed.), *Psychologie vandaag* [Psychology today]. Deventer: Van Loghum Slaterus/NIP, 70–84.

Hogan, R., DeSoto, C. B., Solano, C. (1977), Traits, tests, and personality research. *Am. Psychol.*, **32**, 255–264.

Holland, J. L. (1965), *Manual for the Vocational Preference Inventory*. Palo Alto (Cal.): Consulting Psychologists.

Holland, J. L. (1976), Vocational preferences. In: Dunnette, M. D. (Ed.), *Handbook of industrial and organizational psychology*. Chicago: Rand McNally, 521–570.

Hunt, J. McV. (1965), Traditional personality theory in the light of recent evidence. *Am. Sci.*, **53**, 80–96.

Irle, M. (1955), *Der Berufs Interesse-Test*. Göttingen (dissertation).

Ivancevich, J. M., McMahon, J. I. (1977), Education as a moderator of goal setting effectiveness. *J. Vocat. Behav.*, **11**, 83–94.

Jackson, D. N., Paunonen, S. V. (1980), Personality structure and assessment. *Ann. Rev. Psychol.*, **31**, 503–551.

James, L. R. (1973), Criterion models and construct validity for criteria. *Psychol. Bull.*, **80**, 75–83.

James, L. R., Jones, A. P. (1976), Organizational structure: A review of structural dimensions and their conceptual relationships with individual attitudes and behavior. *Org. Behav. and Hum. Perf.*, **16**, 74–113.

Jones, E. E., Nisbett, R. E. (1972), The actor and the observer: Divergent perceptions of the causes of behavior. In: Jones, E. E. *et al.* (Eds.), *Attribution, perceiving the causes of behavior.* Morristown (N.J.): General Learning Press, 79–94.

Kilpatrick, F., Cummings, M., Jennings, M. (1964), *The image of the federal service.* Washington, D. C.: Brookings Institution.

Krauskopf, C. J. (1978), Comment on Endler and Magnusson's attempt to redefine personality. *Psychol. Bull.*, **85**, 280–283.

Kuder, G. F. (1970), *Manual for the Occupational Interest Survey, Form D. D.* Chicago: Science Research Associates.

Lamiell, J. T., Foss, M. A., Cavenee, P. (1980), On the relationship between conceptual schemes and behavior reports: A closer look. *J. Person*, **48**, 54–73.

Lantermann, E. D. (1978), Situation × Person: interindividuelle Differenzen des Verhaltens als Folge und Ursache ideosynkratische Konstruktion von Situationen. In: Graumann, C. F. (Ed.), *Oekologische Perspektiven in der Psychologie.* Stuttgart: Huber, 143–160.

Latham, G. P., Yukl, G. A. (1975), Assigned versus participative goal setting with educated and uneducated wood workers. *J. Appl. Psychol.*, **60**, 299–302.

Latham, G. P., Yukl, G. A. (1976), Effects of assigned and participative goal setting on performance and job satisfaction. *J. Appl. Psychol.*, **61**, 166–171.

Lawshe, C. H., Balma, M. J. (1966), *Principles of personnel testing.* New York: McGraw-Hill.

Lent, R. H. Aurbach, H. A., Levin, L. S. (1971), Predictors, criteria, and significant results. *Personnel Psychol.*, **24**, 519–533.

Lichtman, C. M., Hunt, R. G. (1971), Personality and organization theory: A review of some conceptual literature. *Psychol. Bull.*, **76**, 271–294.

Locke, E. A. (1976), The nature and causes of job satisfaction. In: Dunnette, M. D. (Ed.), *Handbook of industrial and organizational psychology.* Chicago: Rand McNally, 1297–1349.

McCormic, E. J., Tiffin, J. E. (1975), *Industrial psychology.* London: Allen & Unwin.

Magnusson, D. (1981), *Toward a psychology of situations: an interactional perspective.* Hillsdale (N.J.): Earlbaum.

Maslow, A. H. (1954), *Motivation and personality.* New York: Harper.

Mischel, W. (1968), *Personality and assessment.* New York: Wiley.

Mischel, W. (1979), On the interface of cognition and personality: Beyond the person-situation debate. *Am. Psychol.*, **34**, 740–754.

Mitchell, T. R. (1979), Organizational behavior. *Ann. Rev. Psychol.*, **30**, 243–281.

Morris, J. M., Snyder, R. A. (1979), A second look at need for achievement and need for autonomy as moderators of role perception-outcome relationships. *J. Appl. Psychol.*, **64**, 173–178.

Mowday, R. T., Stone, E. F., Porter, L. W. (1979), The interactions of personality and job scope in predicting turnover. *J. Vocat. Behav.*, **15**, 78–79.

Nisbett, R. E., Caputo, C., Legant, P., Maracek, J. (1973), Behavior as seen by the actor and as seen by the observer. *J. Pers. and Soc. Psychol.*, **27**, 154–164.

Nunnally, J. (1978), *Psychometric theory.* New York: McGraw Hill.

Oldham, G. R. (1976), Job characteristics and internal motivation: The moderating effects of interpersonal and individual variables. *Hum. Relat.*, **29**, 559–569.

Oldham, G. R., Hackman, J. R., Pierce, J. L. (1976), Conditions under which employees respond positively to enriched work. *J. Appl. Psychol.*, **61**, 395–403.

Owens, W. A. (1976), Background data. In: Dunnette, M. D. (Ed.), *Handbook of industrial and organizational psychology*. Chicago: Rand McNally, 609–644.

Pawlik, K. (1968), *Dimensionen des Verhaltens*. Stuttgart: Huber.

Pawlik, K. (1976), Modell- und Praxisdimensionen psychologischer Diagnostik. In: Pawlik, K. (Ed.), *Diagnose der Diagnostik*. Stuttgart: Klett, 13–43.

Pearlman, K., Schmidt, F. L., Hunter, J. E. (1980), Validity generalization results for tests used to predict job proficiency and training success in clerical occupations. *J. Appl. Psychol.*, **65**(4), 373–406.

Powell, A., Royce, J. R. (1981), An overview of a multi-factor theory of personality and individual differences. *J. Person and Soc. Psychol.*, **41**, 818–829.

Roe, A. (1956), *The psychology of occupations*. New York: Wiley. 1956.

Roe, R. A. (1983), Grondslagen der personeelsselectie [Foundations of personnel selection]. Assen: Van Gorcum.

Roe, R. A., Daniëls, M. J. M. (1984), *Beginselen van personeelsbeoordeling* [Principles of personnel appraisal].

Rosenberg, M. (1957), *Occupations and values*. Glencoe, (Ill.): Free Press.

Rounds, J. B., Davis, R. V. (1979), Factor analysis of Strong Vocational Interest Blank items. *J. Appl. Psychol.*, **64**, 132–143.

Ruimschotel, D. (1979), *Causal explanation in psychology*. Amsterdam: University of Amsterdam, Psychological Laboratory.

Schmitt, N., Coyle, B. W., Saari, B. B. (1977), A review and critique of analysis of multi-trait-multimethod matrices. *Multivar. Behav. Res.*, **12**, 447–478.

Schneider, B. (1978), Person-situation selection: A review of some ability-situation interaction research. *Personnel Psychol.*, **31**, 281–297.

Schneider, D. J. (1973), Implicit personality theory. *Psychol. Bull.*, **79**, 294–309.

Shweder, R. A. (1975), How relevant is an individual difference theory of personality? *J. Person.*, **43**, 455–484.

Smith, P. C., Kendall, L. M., Hulin, C. L. (1969), *The measurement of satisfaction in work and retirement*. Chicago: Rand McNally.

Steers, R. M. (1976), Factors affecting job attitudes in a goal setting environment. *Acad. Manag. J.*, **19**, 6–16.

Steers, R. M., Spencer, D. G. (1977), The role of achievement motivation in job design. *J. Appl. Psychol.*, **62**, 472–479.

Stegmüller, W. (1969), *Probleme and Resultate der Wissenschaftstheorie und analytischen Philosophie, Band I: Wissenschaftliche Erklärung und Begründung*. Berlin: Springer.

Stone, E. F. (1979), Field independence and perceptions of task characteristics: A laboratory investigation. *J. Appl. Psychol.*, **64**, 305–310.

Stone, E. F., Mowday, R. T., Porter, L. W. (1977), Higher order needs strength as moderators of the job scope-job satisfaction relationship. *J. Appl. Psychol.*, **62**, 466–471.

Super, D. E. (1960), L'inventaire biographique à choix-multiple comme méthode pour la description de la personnalité et pour le pronostic du succès. *Bull. Ass. Int. Psychol. Appl.*, **9**(1), 12–39.

Super, D. E. (1973), The Work Values Inventory. In: Zytowski, D. G. (Ed.), *Contemporary approaches to interest measurement*. Minneapolis: University of Minnesota Press.

Super, D. E., Crites, J. O. (1962), *Appraising vocational fitness*. New York: Harper.

Terborg, J. R. (1977), Validation and extension of an individual differences model of work performance. *Organiz. Behav. and Hum. Perf.*, **18**, 188–216.

Terborg, J. R. (1981), Interactional psychology and research on human behavior in organizations. *Acad. Managem. Rev.*, **6**, 569–576.

Theologus, C. G., Romashko, T., Fleishman, E. A. (1970), *Development of a taxonomy of human performance: A feasibility study of ability dimensions for classifying human tasks.* Washington D. C.: American Institudes for Research.

Thomae, H. (1960), Das Problem der Konstanz und Variabilität de Eigenschaften. In: Lersch, Ph. *et al.* (Ed.), *Handbuch der Psychologie, Band IV: Persönlichkeitsforschung und Persönlichkeitstheorie.* Göttingen: Hogrefe, 281–353.

Thorndike, R. L. (Ed.) (1971), *Educational measurement.* Washington D. C.: Am. Council of Education.

Thurstone, L. L. (1938), *Primary mental abilities.* Psychometric Monogr., no. 4.

U. S. Department of Labor (1967), *General Aptitude Test Battery.* Washington D. C.

Vale, J. R., Vale, C. A. (1969), Individual differences and general laws in psychology. *Am. Psychol.,* **24,** 1093–1108.

Vroom, V. H. (1964), *Work and motivation.* New York: Wiley.

Weinstein, A. G., Holzbach, R. L. (1973), Impact of individual differences, reward distribution, and task structure on productivity in a simulated work environment. *J. Appl. Psychol.,* 58, 296, 301.

Welten, V. J. (1969), *Konstruktie en scoringssysteem van de I.S.I.-Interessetest, vorm I en II* [Construction and scoring system of the ISI-Interest-test, forms I and II]. Gronigen: Wolters-Noordhoff.

Werff, J. J. van der (1979), De stabiliteit van persoonskenmerken [The stability of individual characteristics]. In: Koops, W. (Ed.), *Overzicht van de ontwikkelingspsychologie* [Survey of developmental Psychology]. Groningen: Wolters-Noordhoff, 253–281.

Wolff, Ch. J. de (1970), Beoordelingen als criteria [Appraisals as criteria]. In: Drenth, P. J. D., Willems, P. J., Wolff, Ch. J. de (Eds.), *Bedrijfspsychologie* [Industrial psychology]. Deventer: Kluwer, 677–694.

Wolff, Ch. J. de, Buiten, B. (1963), Een factoranalyse van vier testbatterijen [A factor analysis of four test batteries]. *Ned. Tijdschr. Psychol.* [Dutch Journal of Psychology], **18,** 220–239.

Handbook of Work and Organizational Psychology
Edited by P. J. D. Drenth, Hk. Thierry, P. J. Willems and C. J. de Wolff
© 1984, John Wiley & Sons, Ltd.

2.2. Motivation and satisfaction

Henk Thierry and Agnes M. Koopman-Iwema

1. INTRODUCTION

What is it that motivates us? What incites us and keeps us going? Why is it that what appeals to the one, is avoided as much as possible by another, for example, the opportunity to work independently and to make decisions? And how can we account for the fact that certain people perform better when they have arrears to clear off, whereas others would feel hampered under such circumstances? What is the reason why some, when confronted with a relatively difficult task, are inclined to give up soon, while others become intrigued and continue to work on that task for a prolonged period? Which of the latter two categories is more satisfied? More generally, what causes job satisfaction in the first place? Has it primarily to do with the characteristics of the job, or rather with typical qualities of the person himself? And what effects does satisfaction have: does it influence performance, absenteeism and turnover?

Such questions are merely a brief illustration of the kind that turns up when dealing with the themes of motivation and satisfaction. Because themes as the 'why' (need) and the 'what for' (goal) of human (and animal) actions may be regarded as among the main determinants of behaviour, it is small wonder that in psychology the topic of *motivation* has always received a great deal of attention. This does not imply that the interest in motivation is exclusively psychological in nature: in other behavioural and social sciences, as well as in theology and philosophy, the question as to motives and concomitant processes

Prof. dr. Hk. Thierry, Universiteit van Amsterdam. Vakgroep Arbeidspsychologie, Weesperplein 8, 1018 XA AMSTERDAM.
Dr. A. M. Koopman-Iwema, Universiteit van Amsterdam. Vakgroep Arbeidspsychologie, Weesperplein 8, 1018 XA AMSTERDAM.

on which behaviour is based, is discussed regularly. In this chapter we will have to leave out of consideration the viewpoints from which motivation is regarded in other disciplines, as far as they are non-psychological.

The interest in motivation, in psychology, is reflected for instance by the considerable number of yearly publications on this subject. Yet we cannot maintain that there exists a widely acknowledged, comprehensive theory on motivation; on the contrary. In fact there is a large number of 'partial theories', which differ from one another in various respects. Some theories are concerned with rather specific characteristics of behaviour, or with specific situations, whereas others are more general (or at least pretend to be so). There is also a great variety of processes which are supposed to 'energise' behaviour. It must be understood, however, that the impression of a great variety of theories is made stronger by a general tendency to stress the special, different quality of a new theory, while the connection with, and the resemblance to other theories is frequently understated. It is not surprising that a comparable characteristic holds for empirical research on motivation: the great majority of the studies restrict themselves to a few aspects of behaviour, and research programs aiming at a coherence or even integration of theories are rarely taken up. Then there is an extra difficulty, as in other fields of psychology: there is far too little agreement about, and coherence among the definitions and the operationalizations of core concepts, appropriate research designs, suitable statistical methods etc.

Naturally we cannot but discuss a limited number of motivational theories in the scope of this chapter. In section 2 we shall deal with several theories of a rather general nature, and especially with a number of approaches important in the field of work and organization. We shall restrict ourselves to the major lines (and suggest to the reader additional literature for each theory). This section will end with some observations on issues cutting through motivational theories.

The theme of *satisfaction*, too, has caused psychologists to speak up. Locke (1976) in his survey estimates that by the middle of the seventies approx. 3400 publications existed on the subject, and that an average of 111 is added each year. Since this estimation is based almost exclusively on English contributions, we may assume that the real figures will be higher. Nevertheless, the interest in satisfaction is less widespread among psychologists than that in motivation: a great many publications are concerned with a specific field of psychology, as particularly that of work and organization. Another remarkable difference is that relatively few theories on satisfaction are up to par. Some 'theories' consist of no more than a verbalization of the manner in which satisfaction was measured. On the other hand, a relatively large number of measuring instruments has been developed and validated, whose applicability in all kinds of situations is often quite reasonable.

We have also had to limit the discussion of this topic to a considerable extent. Section 3 starts with a brief account of several theories that are of importance for propositions in the field of work and organizational psychology. We will then go into various kinds of methods and instruments for measuring satisfaction. These will be accompanied by several more technical aspects with which one is often faced in the practice of satisfaction research. We conclude this paragraph by exposing the familiar issue whether there is any relationship between satisfaction and performance, and if so, how one is to interpret this relation in terms of cause and effect.

With a view to optimal clarity, we have so far pretended as if there were no connection between the concepts of *motivation and satisfaction*, as if they just happen to appear in this chapter together. Authors are by no means of one mind about the mutual relation between the two themes. In many cases the (potential) relationship is not mentioned at all, in other cases both concepts are declared to be of virtually equal meaning; not infrequently explicit conceptual distinctions are made. In spite of this it will become clear, in sections 2 and 3, that when discussing the one concept, we shall often have to refer to the other. Consequently, in the fourth and last section we wish to deal briefly with the relationship between the two concepts, and its benefit to future research.

2. MOTIVATION

2.1. Introduction

In every theory dealing with the explanation as well as changing of the motivation to perform a task, three central questions need to be answered, according to Cummings and Schwab (1973):
1. What is it that attracts someone's attention? How is he activated?
2. In what way is motivation channelled to performance?
3. How can motivation be sustained, e.g. after a need has been satisfied or a goal achieved?

Lawler (1973) also mentions three questions, which have a great deal of overlap with the previous ones, but he adds that a sound motivational theory should also deal with the question as to what general classes of outcomes are (un)attractive to individual human beings.

In section 2.4 we shall return to these questions, which are a basis for assessing the value of different theories. Another question which requires an answer is what is in fact understood by such concepts as motive and motivation. As opinions vary widely, they have often led to confusion. There are, on the one hand, the so-called *'need'-theories*, whose point of departure is that, whenever deprivation occurs in a particular area (e.g. of food), the individual will be motivated to satisfy that 'need'. He is, as it were, 'pushed' to behave in a way which will restore the balance. On the other hand, there are the so-called *'goal'-theories*: because the individual considers certain goals or results to be attractive or valuable, he becomes motivated to achieve them. He is, as it were, 'pulled' by those goals, challenged to make an effort.

Our definitions of motive and motivation are conceptually related to the latter type of theory. It implies that we attach great significance to the role of cognitive processes in human behaviour (which does not exclude recognition of the importance of physiological processes). By the concept of *motive* we understand: the systematic preference for or aversion to a particular category of outcomes (see also Vroom, 1964). There is, for example, the motive of being recognized by others: it refers to the interpretation of such behaviour in an individual, which systematically aims at achieving (or avoiding) outcomes in the nature of 'recognition by others'. In later sections, several other categories of outcomes will be mentioned.

Motivation is concerned with an important aspect of behavioural dynamics. It refers to what is attractive (or unattractive) to a person, and at the same time, to the way in which he intends to achieve that (or avoid; see also Lawler, 1973). We define motivation as: the process concerning both those goals on which someone is oriented, either approaching or withdrawing, and the specific actions aimed at achieving that goal. We recognize similar aspects in the definitions phrased by various other authors: according to Vroom (1964) it is concerned with 'the process that controls, both in direction and in strength, the choice made by a person among alternative courses of action'. The central part of Duijker and Dudink's (1976) definition says: 'the total number of inducements active at a particular moment'. Like Campbell *et al.* (1970), Campbell and Pritchard (1976) emphasize those factors which account for the direction, strength and persistence of individual behaviour. They are right to point out that, in order to appreciate the motivational components of behaviour, the effects of aptitude, skill, and constraints operating in the environment really ought to be kept at a constant level. These things imply that such aspects as 'level of deprivation', 'general level of activity of an organism', 'effort made' etc. may form part of a definition of motivation, but are, in our opinion, not its essence.

With a view to all this, it is not surprising that also in practice—for example among managers and other employees—the concept of motivation is interpreted in all kinds of ways. Here, too, the absence of agreed terms would lead to confusion. At times motivation is considered to be a *feeling* ('I feel highly committed to my work'), a form of observable *behaviour* ('people refuse to make an effort nowadays'), *the pursuit of a goal* ('I want to make a career') etc.

Lawler (1980) holds that the confusion among practitioners about the concept of motivation is also brought about by the large number of theories, which, as we stated in the previous section, emphasize moreover the unique element in each approach. He underlines, however, major similarities—which often remain unmentioned—between various motivational theories. These similarities are:

1. Motivation is determined by a combination of forces in the individual (e.g. his experience) as well as in the environment (e.g. in the structure of the organization).
2. People repeatedly make decisions about their behaviour.
3. People have goals and rewards that they try to achieve and punishments that they try to avoid.
4. Behaviour is determined by the connection between the outcomes that people value and their behaviour.
5. The rewards that people receive can be both internal (e.g. the feeling of doing meaningful work) and external to the person (like gaining status; we shall return to this distinction presently).
6. People sometimes misperceive the situation; hence much attention has to be paid to making clear behaviour-outcome connections.

Lawler holds that it is especially the fourth item which determines the effectiveness of motivation. An additional similarity, in a sense, is that the majority of theories are highly unclear as to how outcomes may be linked with performance: they are of only little use in practical circumstances.

Lawler's views are indeed quite interesting. The reader is asked to bear them in mind while we discuss the theories below. We shall return to Lawler's ideas in section 2.4.

Henceforth we mean to distinguish between *content* and *process theories* (see also Campbell *et al.*, 1970). Content theories focus on *what* it is about the individual and/or about his environment that attracts his attention, what incites and sustains behaviour. They specify what needs man has, what categories of outcomes he pursues, etc. Process theories, however, are related to the question *how* behaviour is energised, how it is channelled, how it is continued or changed. They emphasize the dynamic quality of motivation, its course and the way in which the main variables are related to one another. For those readers who wish to have further general information on motivation, or on theories not included in this chapter, we recommend: Vroom (1964); Campbell *et al.* (1970); Lawler (1973); Campbell and Pritchard (1976); Staw (1977); Naylor *et al.* (1980); Koopman-Iwema (1980); Nuttin (1981); Orlebeke (1981); Petri (1981); Smits (1982).

2.2 Content theories

2.2.1. NEED FOR ACHIEVEMENT

This theory was designed by McClelland (1951, 1961, 1971) and Atkinson (1964, 1974); we shall focus on Atkinson's work chiefly in this chapter. Both start from the principle that human behaviour is determined by two needs: one for success and one for avoiding failure. Thus the individual's tendency to engage in a task and to complete it successfully may be regarded as the result of a conflict between approach and avoidance. In a formula:

$$T_A = (M_s \times P_s \times I_s) - (M_f \times P_f \times I_f).$$

In this equation the three terms with the symbols (of success) refer to the tendency to approach, whereas the other three terms (with the symbol f, of failure) refer to the tendency to avoid. The motivation to engage in a task and to complete it successfully (T_A) firstly depends on the motive for success (M_s); M_s is taken as a relatively stable personality dimension and is usually referred to as need for achievement (henceforth: n-Ach). What is important, besides M_s, are the subjective probability of succeeding in the task (P_s) and the incentive value of success to the individual (I_s); these three are multiplied. According to Atkinson, I_s and P_s are interdependent as follows: $I_s = 1 - P_s$. Secondly, T_A is determined by the motive to avoid failure (M_f); as with M_s, M_f—often referred to as: fear of failure—is regarded as a personality dimension. M_s and M_f are considered to be mutually independent. Other factors are the subjective probability of failure (P_f) and the incentive value of failure (I_f), as held by the individual; the three terms M_f, P_f and I_f are also multiplied. I_f and P_f are mutually dependent as follows: $I_f = - (1 - P_f)$; whereas $P_s + P_f = 1$.

Since both I_s and P_s, and I_f and P_f are related, it appears that the value of success or failure depends on the expected degree of difficulty of the task. Therefore, the value of success will be higher in a difficult task than in a simple task. Similarly, failure will strike harder in tasks with a low probability of failure than in complicated tasks with a higher probability of failure. In short, an individual's eventual behaviour is considered to be the result of his motivation to succeed in a task and his fear of failing to accomplish it.

We may conclude from the explanation of the formula that for those whose M_s is greater than M_f, the motivation to engage in a particular task and to complete it successfully is strongest when faced with tasks of intermediate difficulty. The fear of failure will then be strongest, too. We already found that $I_s = 1 - P_s$. If, for the moment, we do not consider all other terms, T_A turns out to be highest (viz. .25) when P_s as well as I_s equal .50; every other value of P_s will lead to a lower product. A similar argument holds for P_f.

Since $P_s + P_f = 1$, we can simplify the formula:

$$T_A = (M_s - M_f)[P_s \times (1 - P_s)]$$

In later work Atkinson (1964) pointed out that *external* factors which are not achievement related (M extrinsic), may equally influence activities engaged in by an individual. Let us suppose that M_s is smaller than M_f: if a person expects to earn quite a lot of money for his achievement, he is likely to undertake the task after all, etc. Moreover, a fourth component has been added (Atkinson and Cartwright, 1964): the *inertial tendency* (M inert). It refers to an aroused, but unsatisfied need to achieve a particular goal, which remains active nevertheless.

This theory has proved to be a fertile basis for a great deal of empirical, and particularly experimental, research. Results reveal that the theory is useful in a number of areas, such as in occupational choice, in education, in risk-taking etc. Besides, it carries the possibility of extension in a differential-psychological direction, as the behaviour of differently motivated people (high n-Ach, or high fear of failure) can be adequately explained.

This is not to say that the theory has no shortcomings. For example, objections have been made to the equalization of I_s and P_f (both are determined by $1 - P_s$), which makes it impossible to distinguish between value (of success) and probability (of failure). Another objection is that the meaning of the extrinsic factor is quite unclear: it really refers to 'all circumstances conceivable', whereas the other terms are concerned with particular 'states' of the individual. What has also been criticized, is the neglect of processes that cause particular types of behaviour to occur (for further detail, see Weiner, 1972; Duijker and Dudink, 1976; Campbell and Pritchard, 1976; Koopman–Iwema, 1980; Carver and Scheier, 1981; Petri, 1981).

2.2.2. MASLOW

The premise of this theory—which has got widespread reputation, in particular in industry, through McGregor's publications (see e.g. 1960)—is a hierarchy of human needs. In it, Maslow (1954) distinguishes five categories. Although each category is denoted by a simple label, it should be kept in mind that each type of need involves a rather large number of behavioural phenomena; we shall mention several examples for each one of the five needs:
1. Physiological needs: among other things, hunger, thirst, fresh air, sex.
2. Needs for safety: for example, a regular and orderly life, security.
3. Needs to belong: social needs, such as affection, friendship, personal contacts, love.
4. Needs for recognition and esteem. A distinction between:
    a. the needs for self-respect, confidence, achievement, competence;
    b. the needs to be respected, for reputation, status, power.
5. Needs for self-actualization, i.e. personal growth and development, for 'realizing what's inside of you'.

The individual, according to Maslow, will seek to satisfy these needs, in the order mentioned. He will not try to satisfy a need from a 'higher' category, until the needs of the 'lower' category (or categories) have been satisfied. Hence the motivation for a certain type of behaviour is determined by the lowest need operating at a particular moment. As soon as this need has been met, it will lose its motivating force and be replaced by a 'higher' need as motivator. The need for self-actualization, however, will hardly ever reach a final stage of satisfaction, Maslow says. The more this need is satisfied, the stronger it is going to be. Maslow states that in a sound development, people will go through all categories of needs, to finally get down to realizing the need for personal growth and development. In his view, the development of any individual can be defined according to the level of needs he is trying to satisfy.

The fact that this theory has gained tremendous popularity is probably due to its clarity (at least, at first sight) and to its structure, which is intuitively appealing. Nevertheless, objections have come from various quarters, especially to its content and ethical aspects; indeed, there is very little empirical support for this theory (see, however, ten Horn, 1983). Firstly, each category is of a rather complex composition and, also because of this, the operationalization of (partial) needs causes problems: it will therefore also be difficult to categorize behavioural elements in an unambiguous way. A second criticism concerns the assumed hierarchical structure, in that the 'next' need will not motivate behaviour until the 'previous' one has been satisfied: quite regularly, however, it appears that behavior is aimed at satisfying various categories of needs simultaneously. And it may occur that certain behaviour is aimed at 'higher' needs, while the 'lower' ones have not been satisfied yet, or have even been neglected. Thirdly, the very categories of needs have been questioned. For instance, Alderfer's research (1969, 1972, 1977) points out that a tripartite division of categories is more correct than the five elements of Maslow's division. Alderfer distinguishes existence needs, needs for relatedness, and needs for personal growth; he sees no hierarchical relationship between the three. Maslow's proposition that it would be possible to ascertain whether someone's development is 'sound', was qualified by Duijker (1975, 1976) as scientifically untenable and ethically intolerable. After all, Maslow states that men can be characterized according to the level of needs they have satisfied: by this he implies that there is a hierarchy among people. It is along the same lines that we observe that this theory really has no room for the role of all kinds of individual characteristics, such as personality variables, biographical data, capacities, etc. (for further detail on the previous matter: Alderfer, 1969, 1972, 1977; Huizinga, 1970; Lawler, 1973; Duijker, 1976; Koopman-Iwema, 1980; ten Horn, 1983).

2.2.3. INTERNAL-EXTERNAL CONTROL

Rotter (1966, 1967) designed a social learning theory which focuses on the concept of 'locus of control of reinforcement'. In his view, human behaviour is a function of past experiences and situational characteristics. This leads to the following premise: 'The potential for a specific behavior directed toward a reinforcement to occur in a particular situation is a function of the expectancy of the occurrence of that reinforcement following the behavior in that situation and the value of the reinforcement in that situation' (Rotter, 1967, p. 117).

This means, in short, that behaviour in a particular situation depends on the one hand on the expectancy that this behaviour in that situation will lead to a particular outcome (reinforcement), and on the other hand on the value of that outcome. (As we found in section 2.2.1, and as we will see in later sections, this view of motivation plays an important part in various theories, although a variety of terms are used for the same concepts.)

According to Rotter, it is on the grounds of experiences and learning processes in specific situations, that people develop over-all, so-called generalized expectancies and norms concerning the connections between behaviour and its outcomes. An example of such an expectancy is the dimension of 'internal-external control' of outcomes (the so-called I-E dimension). Rotter considers it to be a personality variable, in order to measure which he has designed a by now widely known scale. This dimension applies to the degree to which people feel themselves to be the cause of their behaviour and think that they are capable of influencing their conditions and environment, or feel themselves to be at the mercy of external forces, which are beyond their influence. Internally oriented individuals deem that they themselves can influence their situation and the outcomes of their behaviour. Externally oriented individuals, however, believe that the situations and events facing them are the workings of external forces, which are beyond their power (e.g. fate, fortune, the powers of others). Faced with a similar situation, the former category will behave differently from the latter.

A fair quantity of research has been based on the I-E scale, for example in The Netherlands, where Andriessen's (1972) adaptation was used. One of the outcomes was that a stronger internal orientation may be accompanied by a stronger tendency to take initiatives, to model one's environment, and a lesser tendency to remain passive and to conform (see Minton, 1972).

This theory, too, has met with criticism, three points of which we shall deal with. Firstly, rather a great deal of research was concentrated exclusively on I-E as a personality variable, without any attention for the interaction with situational variables. The latter point would involve, for example, that not only the I-E expectancies are to be measured, but at least also the value of reinforcements. Secondly, it is doubted whether specific modes of behaviour can be predicted on the basis of a general personality variable. On these grounds the construction of more specific locus of control scales is called for.

The third critical comment touches the core of the theory: those supporting attribution theory declare the I-E dimension to be of merely secondary importance. Thus Weiner (1974) holds that people can ascribe the cause of the outcome (success or failure) of their performance to one or more of the following four sources: (1) their capacities, (2) their efforts, (3) the difficulty of the task, and (4) luck. On the basis of these, Weiner says, their expectancies concerning future outcomes can equally be predicted. In fact, these sources can be categorized along two dimensions: 1 and 2 are I-oriented, 3 and 4 are E-oriented; 1 and 3 refer to relatively stable characteristics, whereas 2 and 4 are more variable. Research—carried out with respect to performance behaviour mainly—has shown more than once that the stability dimension has a stronger influence on changes in the expectancies concerning future outcomes, than the I-E dimension. This implies that previous experiences (in particular: performance) will not affect the expectancies concerning the outcomes of future behaviour, unless the causes of these previous experiences are attributed to stable characteristics. As Rotter did not distinguish the stability dimension, some assume that his scale must measure both I-E and stability aspects in a confounding manner (for further detail, see: Weiner *et al.*, 1976; Andrisani and Nestel, 1976; Carver and Scheier, 1981; Klandermans and Visser, 1983a, b; Andriessen and van Cadsand, 1983).

2.2.4. THE COGNITIVE EVALUATION THEORY

Some aspects of Rotter's theory were developed earlier by, for example, Heider (1958) and De Charms (1968). Deci's cognitive evaluation theory (1975) is based primarily on the views of these two authors. He states that individuals aim at deciding about their own behaviour and that they like to regard themselves as the cause of that behaviour (the so-called locus of causality): that is decisive for motivation. Deci developed his theory on the basis of the outcomes of a series of laboratory experiments, in which the subjects had to solve puzzles. The theory implies that if behaviour which is in itself (intrinsically) motivating is linked to certain outcomes by others (extrinsic rewards), the locus of causality will shift from the individual to his environment. The individual will be less inclined to regard himself as the cause of his behaviour and, as a consequence of a 'cognitive process of revaluation', will be less interested in the task, or less intrinsically motivated.

If this theory is tenable it may entail quite some implications for the practice of work and organization, since 'being employed' involves that every employee regularly gets extrinsic outcomes due to others. But Deci also assumes that one category of extrinsic outcomes in particular leads to an unfavourable causality-shift: the provision of *contingent monetary* rewards—i.e. rewards directly related to performance—causes a decline of intrinsic motivation. However, fixed, non-contingent monetary rewards will not affect intrinsic motivation as there is no relationship with the efforts made. Non-monetary (e.g. verbal) contingent rewards, by contrast, will raise motivation, in his view. But this is true for men only: they will tend to derive an increased self-esteem from such rewards, whereas among women the locus of causality will tend to shift towards those giving praise.

These findings have encouraged a rather large number of empirical studies into the validity of Deci's theory. They reveal that the connection between intrinsic motivation and (whatever) extrinsic rewards is much more compli-cated than Deci had assumed. It appears from various studies that intrinsic and extrinsic motivation may indeed be mutually reinforcing, which, consequently, increases intrinsic motivation. Other sources disprove the relationship between the two, and there are research results from which we may conclude a decrease in intrinsic motivation. Serious criticism has also been expressed against Deci's method of interpreting various data from his own experiments (for further detail, Hamner and Foster, 1975; Calder and Staw, 1975; Staw, 1976; Pritchard *et al.*, 1977; Koopman-Iwema, 1982).

In this context Carver and Scheier's criticism (1981) should be mentioned separately. They point out that the concept of reinforcement has two compo-nents—an informative and a rewarding ('reinforcing') component— and that the former is often neglected by psychologists. If we pay attention to the information transmitted, we find that an extrinsic reward provides some knowledge as to the outcomes so far. Then, if the individual believes his goal has not yet been reached, he will continue to apply himself to it. If, however, the information makes evident that the goal has been achieved, the individual will no longer exert himself. He may then regard the reward as the motive for his efforts and conclude from that, that the task was not really interesting. Yet, the extrinsic reward may just as well increase his intrinsic motivation, especially if it informs him that others find him competent, doing a good job, etc. Thus the individual may be incited to continue his activities. What attracts us in this criticism is not only its more coherent interpretation of Deci's findings, but also that it provides good grounds for explaining the seemingly contradictory results of later research, as mentioned above.

2.2.5. The two-factor theory

This theory, which Herzberg originally developed with Mausner and Snyder-man (1959), has gained widespread renown in science as well as in industry. Like Deci, he distinguishes between intrinsic and extrinsic motivation; it will nevertheless become evident that both authors do not attach the same meanings to these concepts.

With a view to objections expressed later, we shall first deal briefly with Herzberg's research method. In it, the concepts of Factor-Attitude-Effect are distinguished. The respondent is first requested to ask himself what situa-tional *factors* gave rise to certain attitudes regarding his work at any time in his career. He is then asked to state what *attitudes* had arisen and what *effects* they had caused, for instance in his job, as regards his health or social relation-ships.

In the first place, positive attitudes turned out to be caused almost entirely, according to the respondents, by the following five factors: being able to achieve; getting recognition; being creative in the work itself; having responsibility for new work and for others; being promoted. All these factors causing satisfaction are, according to Herzberg, work-related: they are intrinsic. They create a sense of self-actualization, of being able to grow.

In the second place, negative attitudes appeared to arise primarily as a result of such factors as company policy and management; technical aspects of supervision; inter-personal relationships; recognition; the work itself; promotion; salary; physical working conditions. These dissatisfaction-causing factors, Herzberg says, do not concern the work-content, but its context: they are extrinsic. Extrinsic factors especially may cause feelings of being treated unfairly. According to Herzberg, such factors as the work itself, recognition and promotion, which we also found in connection with satisfaction, now have another meaning: they are often accompanied by dissatisfaction with the company's policy and management.

In the third place, the main effects mentioned were: performance; turnover; health; private life. Here there are no qualitative differences between satisfaction and dissatisfaction.

Herzberg wishes to stress, by means of the term 'two factor', that the effects of a (situational) factor upon work attitudes are viewed too much as being located on a single continuum. For it is generally assumed that whenever a factor is operating more forcefully, it will lead to more satisfaction, whereas a weaker operation will cause more dissatisfaction. However, satisfaction and dissatisfaction are not opposite to each other but are essentially different. Moreover, two categories of causal factors need to be distinguished. One category concerns work content and task performance: these are the variables originating satisfaction (and called *motivators*). If these variables are not in operation (e.g. when there is a lack of recognition), this will not lead to dissatisfaction, but to an indifferent state of mind. The other category of variables refers to the context and the organization of work: these may cause dissatisfaction. These variables are referred to as *hygiene-factors*: dissatisfaction will arise unless they are met. If there is nothing lacking about these variables (e.g. the work is well organized), it will not lead to satisfaction, but again to an indifferent state of mind.

In the 1959 study this theory is qualified as a hypothetical explanation, partly because the empirical data are not quite conclusive. But this reticence does not characterize Herzberg's later work: in 1966 he generalizes the two-factor-hypothesis into an over-all theory of human nautre.

As was noted above, this theory has made quite an impression. The emphasis on job-content aspects, with a view to motivation, was acclaimed in industry. Besides, in the course of the sixties there was an increasing interest in the opportunities for enlarging and enriching jobs (see also this Handbook, ch. 4.8). Herzberg's call for job enrichment (see e.g. 1968, 1976) was a logical consequence of his theory. More satisfaction may be gained from tasks to which more 'vertical' task elements have been added involving, and enhancing, the opportunities for having responsibility and for decision-making and growth. But Herzberg's work also meant a challenge with respect to designing new theories, particularly as it broke away from the classical view that satisfaction and dissatisfaction are located on a single continuum and have no essentially different causal factors. As could be expected, it gave rise to a large quantity of empirical research on the validity of this theory.

The research data have caused what is commonly called the 'Herzberg controversy'. Many authors have pointed to weaknesses in the theory's structure and coherence, asking, for example, if not the malfunctioning of an intrinsic factor is by definition 'unsatisfactory' and thus refers to dissatisfaction? An analogous argument holds for the 'satisfactory' operation of an extrinsic factor: is that not identical to satisfaction? Are 'causal' factors as feelings (e.g. of recognition) and work aspects (e.g. being promoted) not confused in a conceptionally incorrect way, etc.? Others revealed the discrepancy between Herzberg's own data and his interpretation. But the outcomes of hypothesis testing research contain the most far-reaching criticism: Herzberg's theory can usually be sustained as long as his own research method is followed; as soon as some other (generally less vulnerable) method is applied, the theory hardly ever appears to be supported. This implies that Herzberg's findings are method-bound, and that his 'theory' is probably founded on some artefact in this method: when an individual is satisfied, he will attribute the causes to himself; when he is dissatisfied, he will be inclined to attribute the causes to his environment. Nevertheless, we wish to emphasize that Herzberg was among the first to point out the importance of the distinction between intrinsic and extrinsic variables (for further detail, see Thierry 1968, 1969; Thierry & Drenth, 1970; Campbell *et al.*, 1970; Locke, 1976).

Before concluding this survey of content theories on motivation, we wish to underline once more the fact that we have by no means been able to provide a complete picture. We have had to leave out of consideration, for example, many theories postulating one particular motive or need, such as those concerning power (see Mulder, 1972; Koopman-Iwema, 1980), affiliation (Schachter, 1959), competence (White, 1959). But we deem it to be a representative survey, providing sufficient clues for interpreting other theories, as, for example, regarding self esteem (Korman, 1971; Lefkowitz, 1967; Tharenou and Harker, 1982) and self-enhancement (Dipboye, 1977).

2.3. Process Theories

2.3.1. HULL'S DRIVE THEORY

This theory may be regarded as a quite consistent attempt at accounting for (human and animal) behaviour in terms of physically defined variables (see e.g. Orlebeke, 1981) without using cognitive or any other 'mental' constructs and processes. In Hull's opinion (1943, 1951), behaviour is a function of the number of times this behaviour has successfully satisfied a need (the 'habit'), as well as of the strength of the drive caused by that need (see also Koopman-Iwema, 1980). Consequently, there are two components: a *learning* and a *drive* (or motivational) component.

The learning component in Hull's theory is based on Thorndike's law of effect: i.e. learning is a result of reinforcement. Of all the different responses (reactions) to a similar situation the response causing satisfaction (being 'effective') will be more closely associated with that situation. When that situation (stimulus) arises again, the probability for that response to occur will have risen. Thus, when the organism has a particular need which can be satisfied by particular behaviour, the probability of recurrence of that behaviour is heightened in the case of a return of that need. So the probability of that behaviour occurring is defined by the frequency of this stimulus-response connection (the habit), as well as by the extent of ensuing satisfaction.

Apart from primary reinforcement, Hull distinguishes the principle of secondary reinforcement: a stimulus which is no primary reinforcer in itself, can acquire the properties of a reinforcer when it regularly and simultaneously accompanies a reinforcing stimulus. Thus it is evident that the habit specifies the *direction* of behaviour under a particular stimulus. However, an adequate explanation of behaviour also requires indicating its *strength*.

It is the latter issue with which the drive component is concerned, according to Hull. An organism will be motivated to manifest certain behaviour when there are needs to be satisfied. It is inclined to aim at a situation of balance, of satisfaction. If the balance is upset—that is, a state of deprivation, a need occurs—drives will arise which, as it were, supply the organism with the energy to manifest certain behaviour. The organism will become 'attentive' to the possibilities in the environment for supplying what is needed. The more the need is satisfied, the more the strength of the drive will be reduced.

These drives may be either of a biological nature, or 'acquired'. The biological (or primary) drives involve those which follow from a need for food, fluids, rest, activity, the care of offspring, etc. The acquired (or secondary) drives develop due to their simultaneous occurrence with primary drives (e.g. drives based on the need for social contacts or status, which develop along with the satisfaction of the primary need for activity).

According to Hull it is the drives and the habits which, in an interactive manner, are decisive for the ultimate behaviour. The drive is the 'propelling' power, or motivation, for satisfying the need; the habit is decisive for the way (stimulus-response connection) in which the need will be satisfied.

Changes in the strength of reinforcements can only gradually influence behaviour, since the component of 'habit' changes only gradually. As this provides no explanation for abrupt changes in behaviour, Hull later inserted a separate motivational variable, viz. the incentive K. The (perhaps altered) value of a particular object or goal may immediately affect motivation. Spence (1958) has elaborated this addition, assuming that the so-called anticipatory goal response lies at the root of the incentive: while the drive 'pushes' the organism to certain behaviour, the value of a set goal 'pulls' the organism to behaviour.

It stands to reason that this theory has encouraged in particular a miscellany of laboratory experiments, mainly on animals. They lend some empirical support to Hull's theory. Yet, the critical comments prevail in the literature. These apply to the alleged immediate relationship between the proportion of a need's deprivation and the organism's activity level aimed at satisfying it; to the joint occurrence of drive and incentive in a single theory; and to its restricted predictive value for learning to cope with simple or difficult tasks. The mechanistic character of Hull's approach has met with a great deal of criticism, because of its limited applicability in explaining or predicting human behaviour, and particularly the 'conscious' ignoring of cognitive and other mental variables. Nevertheless, we would say that the addition of the concept of incentive, particularly, seems to show the way to the latter type of variables. But this theory plays virtually no role in the field of problems concerning work and organization (for further detail, see Cofer and Appley, 1968; Weiner, 1972; Cofer, 1972; Lawler, 1973; Campbell and Pritchard, 1976; Koopman-Iwema, 1980; Orlebeke, 1981; Petri, 1981).

2.3.2. THE SOCIAL COMPARISON THEORY

In this theory, which has gained a wide reputation, Festinger (1950, 1954) takes as a starting-point the human drive to evaluate oneself. According to him, this is true both for someone's opinions and for his capacities. If there are no objective standards available for this evaluation, the individual will want to compare his opinions and capacities to those of others (often called 'comparison others'). If the result of the comparison is positive, he will find it agreeable. A negative result will be experienced as disagreeable. If the opinions or capacities of the comparison-other are somewhat different from this individual's, he will tend to adjust his opinions or capacities. For a comparison process one tends to select such 'others' as do not deviate too much from oneself. In other words, one will select others having similar opinions and capacities. As the difference is greater, the individual will be less inclined to compare himself with the comparison-other.

Evidently there is a tendency towards *consistency* concerning the selection of the comparison-others as well as the behaviour of the comparing individual when detecting a difference in opinion or capacity. Still, in the case of opinions, the comparing process is not quite analogous to that in the case of capacities. When comparing our opinion on a particular issue with (an)other(s), we prefer to select others holding a similar opinion, while adjusting our opinion to that of others as much as possible. This latter process will occur all the more as the opinion is considered to be more important. Moreover, this *uniformity tendency* will grow as we are more attracted to the other. Capacities, on the other hand, can be considered as much valued in our culture, Festinger says: people will seek to extend their capacities. In this respect, therefore, they compare themselves with others who are slightly more capable, seeking to distinguish themselves from those others: they want to surpass them just a little. This is based on the so-called *discrimination tendency*. Both tendencies are active at the same time.

This theory has proved to be a fertile source of much empirical research. As a rule, the theory is supported and its applicability in various situations demonstrated. Besides, it caused new theories to be designed (see e.g. section 2.3.3), e.g. as regards the elements and processes which play a more particular role in social comparisons (for further detail, see Wilke and Kuiper, 1977; Koopman-Iwema, 1980; Rijsman and Wilke, 1980).

2.3.3. THE EQUITY THEORY

In this theory, which came from Adams (1963, 1965), we recognize the central theme discussed in the previous section: the general human tendency to evaluate oneself by means of comparison with one or more others. In Adam's terms, men aim at a *balance* between their inputs and their outcomes compared with the relationship between the two as they perceive it, in comparison-others. The inputs (investments) may be: education, experience, intelligence, effort. The outcomes may be: performance; payment; recognition; status. Whether or not a particular attribute turns into an input or outcome variable depends primarily on the question if the comparing individual recognizes that attribute at all. It then depends on his judgment whether the attribute is relevant to the comparison. What is decisive for the selection of the comparison other(s) is also its relevance to the comparing individual in the process of comparing. Thus he may select colleagues, friends, people sharing his occupation or others, but it can also happen that he chooses the firm's policy as a referent, or his own person in earlier days or (as expected to be) in the future, etc. (see e.g. Goodman, 1972).

According to Adams, the degree of equity is defined by the relationship between one's own inputs and outcomes in relation to that of the comparison-other. There is equity when this relation is viewed as *equal* ('consonance'). When there is an unequal relation, an experience of inequity, there is 'dissonance': the resulting dissatisfaction will motivate the individual to such behaviour as will restore the balance (under certain circumstances—see below—he will be motivated to increase the dissonance).

The various forms of (in)equity are illustrated in Figure 1. We take it as given that an individual compares the relationship between his effort and his payment to someone else's. If the resulting relationship is found to be inequit-

	Individual	Other	Result
a. Effort Payment	high high	high high	consonance
b. Effort Payment	high low	high high	dissonance (being 'underpaid')
c. Effort Payment	low high	low low	dissonance (being 'overpaid')
d. Effort Payment	high low	high low	consonance
e. Effort Payment	high high	low low	consonance
f. Effort Payment	high low	low high	dissonance (maximal)

Figure 1. Examples of consonance and dissonance in Adam's theory.

able by the individual, what behaviour he is going to manifest will depend partly on the type of dissonance. Another factor is the characteristics of the attributes in question: some attributes are additive (e.g. more training), while several others are interchangeable. For example, it can be concluded from Figure 1 that in case of b the individual is likely to try to get more pay. In this or any other case he could also attempt to adjust his input, or to make the other one adjust his input and/or outcome.

If this does not produce the desired effect, he may do any of the following things:

—The individual makes cognitive changes. He re-interprets his own, and/or the other's inputs and/or outcomes (and, for example, explains away the differences).

—He will be absent, applies for a transfer, or gives notice.

—He selects another comparison-other.

The latter two possibilities are examples of the individual no longer aiming at consonance, but perhaps even increasing the dissonance with a view to changing the comparison situation as a whole.

This theory has formed the basis of many laboratory experiments. They reveal, for example, that the theory receives more support when the individual and the comparison-other are in a direct exchange relationship, than when they are indirectly related, by way of a third party, for instance their employer. It also appears that the motivation for pursuing consonance is stronger in the case of under-rewarding, than when over-rewarding is perceived. Objections have been made to the lack of explicitness as to what factors are decisive for the selection of the comparison other(s) as well as under what conditions exactly the increase of dissonance will occur. It is considered a major handicap that the application of the theory in real life situations has met with little success. More than once, it is true, the theory was able to supply a useful explanation after all, but there is still much to be desired about its predictive value in non-laboratory situations (for more details, see Pritchard, 1969; von Grumbkov and Wilke, 1974; Campbell and Pritchard, 1976; Koopman-Iwema, 1980; von Grumbkov, 1980).

2.3.4. THE EXPECTANCY THEORY

This theory on motivation has won itself a dominant place in the last 15 years, among others in work and organizational psychology. It has not only originated a vast quantity of empirical research, but it has also encouraged the application in various other fields, such as leadership and remuneration (see this Handbook, ch. 3.2 and 4.11). We shall therefore pay some more attention to it, dealing especially with the way in which Vroom (1964) originally designed this theory. We shall then pass quickly over the main additions and revisions made by others in later years.

Conceptionally speaking Vroom's approach is akin to Lewin's views (1935, 1938, 1951), while the ideas of Edwards (1954) are recognizable at several points. Vroom distinguishes three models: the motivation, the valence (or job satisfaction) and the performance models.

According to the *first model*, motivation for particular behaviour depends on:
—the expectation that this behaviour will lead to particular outcomes, and
—the valence or attractiveness of these outcomes in the eyes of the individual.
An example: the motivation to make a considerable effort depends on the extent to which it is expected to result in performance of a fair quality, as well as on how attractive good performance is to the individual.

Vroom uses the term value, as distinct from valence, of an outcome: it refers to the actual degree of satisfaction derived from achieving it; the valence of the outcome is the 'expected' degree of satisfaction.

The *valence model* is concerned with the way in which the valence of outcomes is brought about. An individual's preference, neutral attitude or dislike as regards particular outcomes, Vroom says, is a function of the instrumentality of these outcomes to achieve other outcomes, and the valence of these other outcomes. Again an example: to an individual, the valence of a fair performance is decided by such a performance's instrumentality to earn money, to gain status and to enhance possibilities of promotion, as well as by the valence, in his eyes, of money, status and possibilities of promotion. The instrumentality of an outcome, therefore, is concerned with the extent to which the individual expects that outcome to lead to other outcomes. It is a so-called outcome-outcome relation and differs from the concept of expectancy (as found in the motivation model) which involes the relation between behaviour and its outcomes.

The *performance model* is based on the idea that someone's performance is not only determined by his motivation, but also by his capacity.

The valence model has frequently served the study of job satisfaction; it has changed little throughout the years. A great many alterations, however, have been made in the motivation model which, of the three, is the one most applied in research. The main changes in both models deal with:

1. *Distinguishing between intrinsic and extrinsic outcomes.* Vroom deals mainly with extrinsic outcomes. Although he does not dismiss the fact that, to the individual, certain actions may 'in themselves' be of some value, he sees externally mediated rewards as being most decisive for motivation. The valence, to the individual, of extrinsic outcomes is partly defined by external factors, by other people playing a mediating role in achieving the outcome. Also, the value of an outcome is partly dependent upon other people.

2. *Distinguishing between first and second level outcomes.* First-level outcomes refer to working behaviour itself and the resulting performance. These outcomes gain valence provided that they cause obtaining a second level of outcomes (e.g. money, status). This distinction between first-level and second-level outcomes merges Vroom's valence and motivation models. First-level outcomes (e.g. a particular level of performance) are explained in the motivation model as a function of the expectation that certain efforts will lead to this level of performance as well as to the valence of that performance level. The valence of the performance level is explained in the valence model as the extent to which this performance level is instrumental to achieve second-level outcomes (money, status) as well as the valence of those outcomes.

3. *Distinghishing between various sorts of expectancy.* Expectancy-1 (also named Effort → Performance) is identical to Vroom's expectancy concept, whereas Expectancy-2 (also called Performance → Outcome) corresponds to the concept of instrumentality. With Vroom, expectancy is a probability estimate, whose values range from 0.00 to 1.00; instrumentality relates to a correlation (between outcomes), hence varying from − 1.00 to + 1.00. In some versions of this model the difference between probability and correlation is maintained, while various others deal with correlational relations exclusively.

4. *Adding to the model a number of variables derived from the work situation, together with various feedback loops.* It is likely that the model has grown considerably more complicated by this addition, despite the assumption that this operation would mean a more contingent approach which would promote the predictive value of the model. Figure 2 provides an example of this; it is partly derived from Lawler's work (1971, 1973).

The main line in this model is the relationship between (1) someone's motives and expectancies, (3) his efforts, (8) his performance, (10) the achieved outcomes

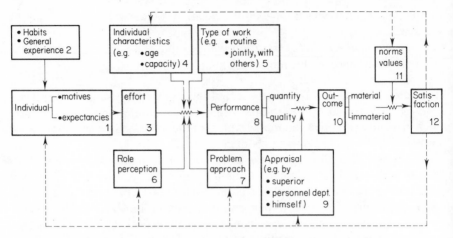

Figure 2. Work motivation model derived from expectancy theory.

and (12) the degree of satisfaction. This relationship is modified by several variables (the solid lines), whereas the degree to which the behaviour has brought about satisfactory outcomes feeds back to various components of the motivation cycle (the dotted lines). A brief explanation:

—The individual's motives and expectancies as regards the outcomes of his efforts and performance (1) are modified by his habits, his experience in similar situations, observations of others, etc. (2). The resulting action is referred to as effort (3).

—The extent to which his effort leads to performance (8) is affected by individual characteristics (4), such as his capacity, the type of work (5), his perception of what he is expected to do (6), and his manner of dealing with a problem (7), e.g. as a whole or item by item.

—The extent to which his performance affords him outcomes (10) is due to the appraisal of his performance (9).

—The relation between achieved outcomes and his satisfaction with them (12) is, in its turn, modified by the norms and values (11) concerning how effort and performance on the one hand and outcomes on the other should relate.

—The less satisfactory the result, the more the person will try to change his own and, if possible, others' behaviour (9).

As a matter of fact, there are hardly any examples of research analysing the meaning of all types of variables, mentioned in Figure 2, simultaneously: after all, such a model makes high demands which often cannot be entirely met, e.g. for practical reasons. This may in part be the reason why the suggested sophistication and extensions of the expectancy theory have not resulted in a better explanation and prediction of behaviour after all. The average correlation between predictions, based on the expectancy model, and criterion behaviour (often performance) still turns out to be between .25 and .30. Besides, the application of this theory involves several 'technical' problems, which can rarely be solved satisfactorily within a single research design. Some of the main points are:

—The outcomes which are included in any research are not in advance relevant to all respondents. To how many levels (first, second etc.) should they relate? Is it necessary to include equal numbers of positively and negatively valent outcomes, etc. ?

—If instrumentality (and not infrequently expectancy) is regarded as a correlation between two variables, it should, in principle, be capable of adopting any value between -1.00 and $+1.00$. But this implies, in fact, that a great many interval positions ought to be distinguished per variable, not merely one or two (e.g. 'high' and 'low' performance), as is often the case.

—Although the concept of effort may be theoretically meaningful, it is often hard to identify and, hence, to operationalize, in a respondent's behaviour cycle.

—The terms in the model—such as performance, expectancy, outcome—are not to be multiplied haphazardly.

Although there is much more empirical support for the valence model (satisfaction) than for the other two models, the interest in the expectancy theory as a whole remains considerable, especially because the chief components of motivation are claimed to be prominent in its central themes. Nevertheless, these central themes have gradually become subject to more criticism:

1. Expectancy and valence are not necessarily mutually independent. When assessing the former, the respondent is bound to take the valence into account (or the other way round).

2. The influence of 'other parties' (colleague, superior, quality controller, etc.) is taken into account far too little. The respondent has considerably less grip on his own behaviour than is assumed in the theory.

3. Along the same line as the previous point: expectancies do not only play a role 'at the start' to the cycle (see Figure 2) but throughout its entire course, e.g. as regards the relationship between appraisal and outcome. Therefore, it is necessary to distinguish and measure more aspects of expectancy.

4. Expectancies occur under special conditions only, that is in case of deviations from the usual pattern. Carver and Scheier (1981) mention as such a condition uncertainty about the course of action to be taken; Galbraith (1972) refers to it as a 'discrete' situation of decision. (For further detail, see Galbraith and Cummings, 1967; Porter and Lawler, 1968; Graen, 1969; Campbell *et al.*, 1970; Mitchell and Biglan, 1971; Mitchell and Albright, 1972; Lawler, 1973; Andriessen, 1974; Mitchell, 1974; Koopman-Iwema and Thierry, 1975; Sheridan and Slocum, 1975; Campbell and Pritchard, 1976; Staw, 1976; Koopman-Iwema, 1980.)

2.4. Motivation theories in perspective

In section 2.1 we mentioned four central questions to which a sound motivation theory needs to provide an adequate answer. If we take those as our starting-point, the various theories appear to differ in many respects. In particular, most theories give little or no satisfactory attention to the question as to how behaviour remains motivated after the need or goal has been satisfied. The process theories, almost by definition, leave out of consideration the question what classes of needs or motives there are. It is with due reservations that we state that such theories as 'need for achievement', those based on social comparison processes, and, to some extent, expectancy theory, are more 'up to the mark'. Which does by no means remove the often serious critical comments.

In the same section we mentioned the six points of similarity existing, according to Lawler, among motivation theories. Admittedly, there is a considerable degree of consensus on the issue that people aim at rewards and attempt to avoid punishment, as well as on the idea that behaviour is decided by the relationship between that behaviour and attractive outcomes. But there is really general consent only about the point that motivation is determined by the mutual influence of individual and environmental characteristics. It is, by the way, remarkable that all of the six points are dealt with in expectancy theory only. In addition, those supporting the latter theory are as a rule (with the exception of Herzberg) most explicit about the nature and the meaning of environmental characteristics. This, in its turn, is a consequence of the view that in the environment—i.e. the work situation—'other parties' may strongly affect motivation: as we saw in section 2.3.4, the linking of outcomes to behaviour (expectancy) or to previous outcomes (instrumentality) is of essential importance. The characteristics mentioned in this context are usually those concerned with leadership, the work group, the work content, remuneration and the possibilities of promotion.

We feel that there is still another point of similarity: in all theories the concept of *consistency* (or conformity, balance) plays a prominent part. The motivation for a certain type of behaviour is then usually concerned with reducing some sort of deviation (again, theories may differ as to its determinants and results).

Possibly the well-known recommendation to expand a theory by means of (more) contingency variables does not lead the way to a 'full-fledged' and generalizable motivation theory as much as the (re-)analysis of existing approaches in terms of such over-all concepts. An intriguing attempt to this effect was made by Carver and Scheier (1981); we shall conclude this section with a summary of it.

A typical aspect of human behaviour is self-regulation. Exactly what is perceived and how reality is constructed is defined by the 'attentional focus': the things in ourselves and in our environment on which we focus our attention. This focus is also decisive for what is stored in our memory and what is reproduced from it.

This process of storing and reproducing information can best be described as a cybernetic cycle: the behaviour is continuously tuned to one standard by means of negative feedback.

Besides this type of process, a model of motivation processes is required for the sake of accounting for the self-regulation of behaviour. What characterizes motivation is, on the one hand, a standard indicating the goal to which behaviour is oriented. On the other hand, there is the aim to reduce the gap between the standard and the present situation (or: negative feedback). The more an individual's attention is focused on himself, the stronger will be this tendency to reduce. It is Carver and Scheier's assumption that standards, like all other information, are stored in the memory in code. They are part of the same cognitive schemes used in storing and reproducing information. The schemes are ordered according to hierarchy: the lowest level of information deals with the intensity of the stimulus. The next level refers to the transformation of intensity into stimulus qualities; after that comes the classing of configurations (such as objects) etc. One of the highest levels is that of conceptual and moral principles. Each level in the hierarchy has its own type of standard defined by the next-higher information level.

It is evident that Carver and Scheier apply the same concepts for defining both motivation and self-regulation. Their study proceeds with an attempt to re-define several motivation theories in terms of these concepts (which we cannot enlarge upon in this context).

In our view such an approach could prove to be of use not only for the sake of theorizing on motivation in general, but also for the sake of motivation on the job. One might suggest the probably pluriform meanings (in terms of the relevant information levels) of such outcomes as recognition, security and remuneration. It might be possible to make more coherent distinctions between types of motives by means of an analysis of the level of information which is at stake at any particular moment.

3. SATISFACTION

3.1. Introduction

We came across this concept a number of times in section 2. In fact, it plays a role in all motivation theories whenever, generally speaking, it is a question to what extent a particular need has been met or a goal achieved. However, in several of the theories discussed here, satisfaction has yet another, more specific and pronounced meaning: in Maslow's terms it decides whether a higher level of need, in the hierarchy, is going to evoke behaviour. Herzberg's two factors—motivators and hygiene variables—have even frequently been labelled by the exclusive effects they are assumed to cause: satisfiers and dissatisfiers. It has led several authors (Locke, 1976, among them) to categorize

Maslow's and Herzberg's approaches under the heading of satisfaction theory.

This often happens to Adam's theory too, because it pays special attention to behaviour caused by dissatisfaction (dissonance). In the context of the expectancy theory, we dealt with Vroom's satisfaction (valence) model. It is evident that, as was stated in the introduction, the concept of satisfaction cannot possibly be excluded from any exposé on motivation. Similarly, in this section, section 2 will be often referred to (the relationship between motivation and satisfaction will be dealt with in the fourth and last section).

In its most direct sense we define job satisfaction as the degree of well-being experienced in the work or work situation. This means that for the sake of brevity we use the general term 'satisfaction' to indicate *the degree of* satisfaction or dissatisfaction; only when it is felt to be empirically or conceptually necessary, will the term dissatisfaction be applied. This type of definition is favoured by a great many authors (see e.g. Locke, 1976); in section 3.2 it will be demonstrated that several theories particularly deal with the causal factors of the 'degree of well-being'. Furthermore, we distinguish four perspectives on satisfaction (some of which can be derived from Figure 2, section 2.3.4):

1. Firstly, satisfaction may be regarded as the 'result' of a behavioural cycle, reflecting the individual's way of aiming at attractive outcomes. It represents that which he *has achieved and gained*.

2. Secondly, satisfaction may cause *changes* to occur—see the feedback lines in Figure 2—in the behavioural cycle, partly in the short run (e.g. role perceptions), partly in the long run (e.g. greater capacity deemed to be required by the individual).

3. Along the same line: satisfaction may refer to the individual's cognitions of *valent outcomes*, i.e. to what he intends to achieve or avoid in future.

4. Finally, satisfaction may have certain *effects* (other than those mentioned in 2), such as concerned with absenteeism, health, turnover, complaints.

Thus we consider satisfaction to be a dynamic concept referring to past, present and future aspects, and applicable both as a 'dependent' and as an 'independent' variable. Besides, satisfaction may be regarded as valuable in itself (see Drenth *et al.*, 1970, Introduction section V).

We will proceed with, firstly, a discussion of various satisfaction theories, some of which directly reflect how satisfaction is measured, while others (those mentioned last) are also referred to as 'causal' theories. An interesting question in this context is whether each theory is quite concerned with the four perspectives mentioned by us. Secondly, we shall discuss several types of measuring instruments, followed by the issue whether satisfaction had better be viewed as a global concept or as one composed of specific facets. The section will be concluded by a discussion of the relationship between satisfaction and performance. (For those readers who wish to go further into satisfaction, or any theories not mentioned here, we refer to Herzberg *et al.*, 1957; Vroom, 1964; Lofquist and Dawis, 1969; Campbell, *et al.*, 1970; Lawler,

1973; Cherrington, 1973; Seashore and Taber, 1975; Locke, 1976; Taylor, 1977; O'Brien and Dowling, 1980; Ben-Porat, 1981; Francès and Lebras, 1982).

3.2. Satisfaction theories

3.2.1. NEED FULFILLMENT

According to this theory, satisfaction is determined by the extent to which the individual's work and working situation afford him outcomes which he holds as valuable (Vroom, 1964; Lawler, 1973). The essential points here are, in terms of the expectancy theory (section 2.3.4), value and valence: satisfaction is not only related to the already achieved outcomes, but also to those which are expected to be achieved or to be possibly avoided. The type of question by which satisfaction is measured, is the so-called 'is now' type. The respondent is asked to assess descriptions which are as factual as possible, for instance: How often does your superior consult with you? Thus, in this much used approach, it is assumed that the degree of satisfaction is reflected in the assessment of factual descriptions: in his description the individual at the same time indicates what he considers valuable and attractive, or unimportant.

Various authors (see e.g. Lawler, 1973) have suggested, however, that this type of question does not sufficiently enable the individual to be quite clear about what he wishes or thinks is attractive (see section 3.2.2). It is unfortunate that some authors (among them Korman, 1971) refer to the subsequent discrepancy model—which has in fact met the objection mentioned—with the term 'need fulfillment'. Locke (1976) makes another point: in his opinion the majority of researchers fail to adequately specify the concept of 'need'; with a somewhat uncommon use of terms he understands 'needs' as the objective requirements for survival (of a physical as well as psychological nature), with 'values' representing human wants and preferences.

3.2.2. DISCREPANCY

The following argument is the starting-point of much satisfaction research: satisfaction depends on the extent to which the outcomes, which an individual thinks he gets from his work, correspond with those pursued in his work. One of the elaborations on this notion is found in the discrepancy model, which has become known in particular through the writings of Morse (1953), Porter (1961), Porter and Lawler (1969) and Locke (1969). In it, satisfaction is seen as a 'degree of difference'. The larger the distance between the pursued and the perceived outcomes of the work, the lesser the satisfaction.

The ways in which the concept of discrepancy has been operationalized in research, are highly varied nevertheless. An initial question is to what *components* the discrepancy is related. One component is almost invariably concerned with the factual outcomes as perceived by the individual (as reflected in the 'is now' type of question; see section 3.2.1). But the other component is concerned, now with what he wants, now with what he finds attractive, then again with what he prefers, what he considers important, what he thinks should be, what he expects, or what he has himself adapted to. Another question is *which* of these components should be linked: the perceived outcome is balanced against, for example, what the individual wants, but in quite a few cases also against its importance, etc. A third question is concerned with *how* the components are related: quite often the discrepancy between 'want' and outcome is defined (which is where the model derives its name), but it also occurs that the product is calculated, or that the discrepancy is corrected by means of a weighing factor, etc. It appears from many studies, however, that such variants frequently produce mutually different outcomes (see e.g. Wanous and Lawler, 1972; Wall and Payne, 1973; Sheridan and Slocum, 1975; Ferratt, 1981). We shall return to some of these problems in section 3.3.

Another discrepancy theory is the *Personality-Environment fit* (P-E) model (see e.g. French *et al.*, 1974; Kahn, 1981). It relates satisfaction to the individual's degree of 'adjustment'. His adjustment depends on the extent to which the characteristics of himself as a person and those of his environment (e.g. his work) are attuned to each other. Either can be divided into objective and subjective characteristics: objective in the sense that others (for instance impartial observers) identify the characteristics, the subjective characteristics referring to what is perceived by the individual himself. If the (objective as well as subjective) so-called 'goodness of fit' is not up to the mark, there will not be a high degree of satisfaction; the individual may even experience strains which can negatively affect his health. These effects may occur whenever the work is more demanding than he can handle (overload) as well as when he has better qualifications than is required by the job (understimulation).

This model is applied especially in connection with research on stress on the job (see also this Handbook, ch. 3.4). These studies reveal that we are still in the dark as to the exact relationship between the lack of adjustment on the one hand and strain and satisfaction on the other.

In section 2.4 we noted that the motivation theories discussed in that section resembled each other as to the view that motivation is decided by the mutual influence of individual and environmental characteristics. A comparable statement can be made as regards the satisfaction theories discussed here (in spite of their differences, e.g. in the nature of the assumed relationship between both types of characteristics). This mutual influence is apparent in, for example, the P-E fit model, described above; it is emphatically embedded in the title of the next theory to be discussed.

3.2.3. EVENT-AGENT

Prompted by their criticism of Herzberg's classification of intrinsic and extrinsic factors (section 2.2.5) Schneider and Locke (1971) suggested that a categorization be made of all events that may give rise to more or less satisfaction, along two dimensions:
—'Event', relating to the things that happen.
—'Agent', relating to the cause of the event.
Thus, satisfaction is regarded as the result of the interaction between the two dimensions. Locke rightly points out (1976) that this clears the way for making use of concepts from attribution theory.

Either dimension can be sub-divided in several ways. It is possible to distinguish, in research, as many kinds of Events as there are types of outcomes in expectancy theory (section 2.3.4). The Agents may be the individual himself or others, who may in turn be specified. A good example of this theory is found in Ben-Porat's study (1981): he demonstrated, with the aid of smallest space analysis, that satisfaction is best represented by a radex-structure (i.e. a particular type of circular structure between variables).

3.2.4. THE SOCIAL REFERENCE GROUP

Both need fulfillment and discrepancy theories are based on the notion that an individual balances his outcomes against what he pursues. The social reference group theory, however, maintains that this balancing is done with regard to the viewpoints and characteristics of one's group or (socio-economic) category.

Especially the latter aspect has received attention in the specification of the theory. It has caused the themes that already played a part in the study of *social indicators*—particularly with regard to the quality of working life—to become more and more involved in satisfaction research. The following have been distinguished: size of the place of residence; number of employees; number of trade union members; level and differentiation of income; level and distribution of spending power; quality of housing, etc. The idea is that the individual tends to evaluate the characteristics of his work(ing situation) in terms of his frame of reference. An example: two people are in the same income bracket. In the organization employing him, the one person's income is classed as top level, whereas the other person's income in his organization rates as medium level. These two people are bound to show different degrees of satisfaction.

Naturally, the researcher ought to have some notion (or rather: partial theory) of the relationship between satisfaction and the topics on which he collects data. Setting norms on the basis of preceding research is also required. With the help of these it can be ascertained what degree of satisfaction is

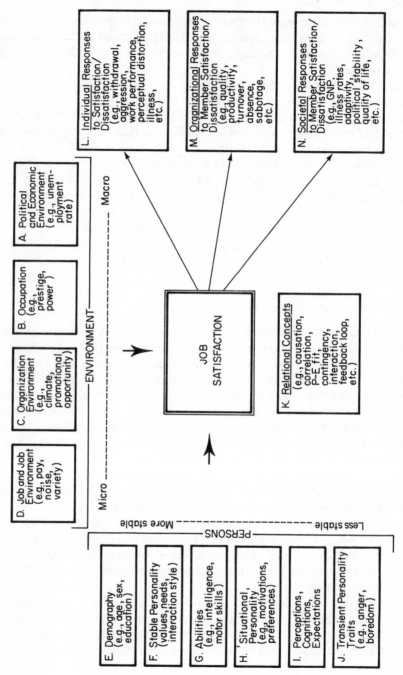

Figure 3. Satisfaction model according to Seashore and Taber (1975).

indicated by the answers to a questionnaire, usually of a decriptive type (sections 3.2.1 and 3.3).

In the above examples, the frame of reference was primarily of a socio-economic nature, but it may also refer to someone's personal past and future: a combination of both—referred to as adaptation level—was attempted in the construction of the well-known Job Descriptive Index (see also section 3.3; for general reading see Katzell *et al.*, 1961; Kendall, 1963; Hulin, 1966; Blood and Hulin, 1967; Orpen, 1974; Francès and Lebras, 1982).

Although, strictly speaking, it does not really belong in this section we would like to call attention here to Seashore and Taber's model (1975), as it is an interesting combination of several social indicators and some more well-known variables from satisfaction research (see Figure 3).

According to this model—in which some connecting lines (especially the feedback relations) are omitted for the sake of clarity—satisfaction is due to both individual and environmental characteristics. As to the *way* in which this happens, various theories may be taken as a basis (e.g. the P-E fit theory; see section 3.2.2). The persons are ordered according to degree of stability, with the environmental characteristics ranging from micro to macro; the authors emphatically state that the characteristics mentioned are not exhaustive, but have been selected for the sake of illustration. The effects of satisfaction may take place on three levels: that of the individual, of the organization and of society. This type of model has been applied in satisfaction research on a modest scale only (for the meaning of other 'objective' and 'subjective' work and organization characteristics, see Ronan, 1970; Korman, 1971; Lawler, 1973; Seybolt, 1976; Locke, 1976; Penn *et al.*, 1980; James and Jones, 1980; Caldwell and O'Reilly, 1982; for the effects of satisfaction we refer to Vroom, 1964; Ronan, 1970; Bass and Barrett, 1972; Lawler, 1973; Porter and Steers, 1973; Jeswald, 1974; Locke, 1976; Taylor, 1977).

3.2.5. THE FACET-SATISFACTION MODEL

This model, designed by Lawler (1973), combines equity theory (section 2.3.3) and discrepancy theory (section 3.2.2). Reading figure 4 from right to left, we see first of all that satisfaction is determined by the discrepancy between what should be received, according to the individual, and what he perceives he is actually getting. His idea of what he should receive, secondly, depends on the inputs (qualifications) which he claims to have, on the job requirements as well as on the perceived relation between inputs and outcomes of referent others. The perception of actually received outcomes is determined on the one hand by his own actual outcomes and on the other by the outcomes of others. Furthermore, we see that several aspects make an inpact upon the perception of inputs and job characteristics.

One very rarely reads of studies investigating the applicability of this model;

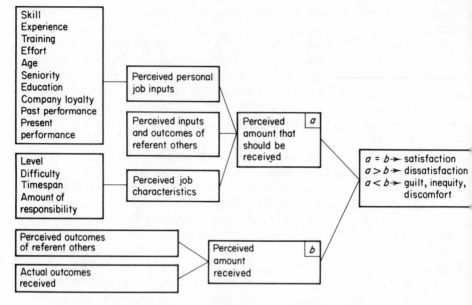

Figure 4. Facet-satisfaction model (Lawler, 1973).

quite a few partial studies have been made, however. A study of pay satisfaction (Metsch, 1980) showed that the variables mentioned in the top-lefthand column were of no predictive value to personal inputs, but that the perceived inputs and outcomes of others were evidently related to the degree of satisfaction.

Our survey of theories may not be exhaustive, we consider it to be representative: the large majority of satisfaction studies makes use of the concepts or assumptions mentioned above.

3.3. Measuring satisfaction

Satisfaction can be measured in several ways. We distinguish (see e.g. Bass and Barrett, 1972; Locke, 1976):

—*Questionnaires*: respondents describe aspects of their work(ing situation) and/or evaluate them and/or list their preferences and/or state their action tendencies, etc. As a rule, this is done by means of standard forms—designed as a scale—on which the most applicable answer to each item can be indicated. Apart from these, semi-structured and open-end forms are used (the latter e.g. by way of a projective technique).

—*Interviews*: with the aid of standard questions, or depending on the course an interview takes, the interviewer seeks to gain insight into, for instance, the

background, nature and effects of (dis)satisfaction. Content-wise, this method
is not necessarily different from the questionnaire.

—*Observation of behaviour*: on the basis of the individual's options and
actions, etc. 'other parties' infer his degree of satisfaction.

—*Objective data*: this somewhat unfortunate term refers to indices not derived
from the respondents' answers. They may refer to absenteeism, turnover,
income distribution in a work organization (see further section 3.2.4).

—*Critical incidents*: this refers to the selection of certain notable and representative events which confront, or have confronted the respondents.
Then follows an analysis of aspects of their behaviour, as e.g. their attitudes
towards these incidents. The incidents are usually selected by the researcher (the
external criterion), in order to define the incident and the resulting behaviour
in a mutually independent fashion. Naturally there can be no question of
independence if the respondent himself selects the incidents (internal criterion),
for example in Herzberg's study (section 2.2.5).

The selection of measuring methods depends on a number of considerations, of
which we shall list a few. There is no flawless method (see also this Handbook,
ch. 1.2.): each has its particular weak spots, which makes it advisable to apply,
if possible, more than one method in each study. A second consideration is
how knowledgeable the researcher is, at the start, about his subject, about the
peculiarities of the population or the sample, etc. As he is less familiar with
these, a more open method—such as the interview—is to be recommended,
possibly by way of a pilot study. A third consideration often is related to the
previous point: to what extent does he make use of instruments whose reliability
and validity have been demonstrated in earlier studies? Of similar importance,
in this connection, are considerations of the availability of time and financial
means. In the fourth place, there is the question whether the nature of the
subject under investigation may possibly render the use of certain types of
method undesirable or impossible: sometimes, a study may become useless
when filling out a questionnaire prematurely informs the participants of its
intention, etc.

　　In practice, however, it is questionnaires that have been used most to measure
satisfaction. In our opinion, this is often for good reasons. In this section
we shall restrict ourselves to this method, dealing with three types of scale in
particular (see Koopman and Werkman, 1973):
—simple evaluation;
—description;
—weighted evaluation.

Simple evaluation: the respondent is given statements or questions, to be
evaluated by choosing one of the alternative answers. An example of a statement
is: 'My superior gets on well with his men'. On the basis of this type of scale,

quite a large number of instruments have been developed, for example in The Netherlands: 'What do you think of your job' (NIPG, 1958), 'Attitudinal Scale for Industrial Work' (ASIA, 1969), and the 'Industrial Survey of Staff and Managerial Personnel' (van der Graaf and Huizinga, 1969). Instruments developed later were, in The Netherlands, often founded on these 'models'. An example from the USA is the 'Survey of Organizations' (Taylor and Bowers, 1972). This method is based on the need fulfillment theory of satisfaction (see section 3.2.1).

Description: the respondent is asked to assess the adequacy of descriptions of his work(ing situation) in the form of statements or adjectives. Prior to that, the weight of these statements as regards satisfaction has been determined. One of the best-known examples is the 'Job Descriptive Index' (Smith *et al.*, 1969), which is generally considered to be one of the best-validated questionnaires. It distinguishes five facets, viz. work, supervision, co-workers, pay, promotion. It has such items as: 'my work is useful'; 'my wages are bad'.

The way in which this scale has been designed is a good example of the social reference group theory (section 3.2.4). Satisfaction is here regarded as a function of the difference between what the individual expects and what he experiences in relation to his *perceived actual or potential alternatives* in any given situation. For this purpose the respondents initially had to answer each item three times, on the subject of (1) the present job; (2) the job they would most like to have; (3) the job they would least prefer, but would still accept. The results showed, however, that the scores with respect to the present work yielded the most valid data (the so-called triadic scoring was useful only in connection with higher-level respondents); that is why the definitive scale is concerned with that only. A series of norms could then be developed, differentiating according to sex, income, education, tenure and community prosperity (the latter consisting of five indices).

Weighted evaluation: the respondent's opinion about some aspect of his work(ing situation) is related to his wants with respect to it, or with what he finds attractive or important, etc. As we saw in the case of the discrepancy model (section 3.2.2), this can be done by computing the difference between either scores, or the products, or by weighing the discrepancy score, etc.

Although the *discrepancy model* is used quite frequently, it has occasionally been objected to; moreover, it has to meet several requirements which often are not met in practice. We illustrate this with the following:

Item: frequency of information on one's own work performance

Desire: often   5 4 3 2 1   rare

Perceived reality: often   5 4 3 2 1   rare

These are two five-point scales: the degree of satisfaction can range from + 4 to − 4; in our example it is + 2. What is curious, first of all, is that the values satisfaction may adopt in theory, may differ per item: if the perceived outcome is 3, satisfaction varies from + 2 to − 2. If the outcome is 2, there is a range from + 3 to − 3, etc. Another remarkable fact is that the size of the difference is important, not the component scores. In other words: the 5 − 3 difference is identical to e.g. 3 − 1; maximal satisfaction (when the discrepancy score is 0) in the case of 5–5 equals that of 1–1. This has provoked quite a few objections. Thirdly, a dissatisfaction score of e.g. + 2 (when an individual wants more than he has) is equalled to a score of − 2 (when he has more than he wants). This assumption raises doubts, owing to the results of research on the validity of the equity theory (section 2.3.3).

To apply the discrepancy model is to presume that the two scores are mutually independent, but regularly the opposite is the case. The desire score often tends to increase as the perceived outcome is greater. This may be due to a tendency always to score higher on the desire. Also, a matter of content may be at stake: the individual grows accustomed to a particular level of outcomes—as, for instance, exercising influence—and gradually comes to desire more of it. Or it may indicate that a third factor is influencing both scores (e.g. a change of jobs). Besides, satisfaction is often related to a criterion variable, e.g. work performance. The condition is then that either score be independent of that criterion score, a condition which is often not fulfilled (for more detail, see Pelz and Andrews, 1966; Hoekman, 1971; Wall and Payne, 1973; Koopman-Iwema, 1980).

In the product or *interaction model* the two scores are multiplied. In the previous example satisfaction would amount to $4 \times 2 = 8$. It is an attempt to remove the objection against the discrepancy model (the absence of interaction between desire and outcome). However, it may raise other problems. Let us suppose the desire score is 1. The greater the perceived outcome (e.g. 3, 4 or 5), the greater the satisfaction (viz. 3, 4 or 5). This makes it hard to find out why someone having a satisfaction score of 1 is less satisfied than someone scoring between 2 and 5. Another point is that the product scores need to be standardized: after all, several values between 1 and 25 cannot occur. In addition, the amount of error is greatly enhanced when the product is correlated to a criterion score, which is often the intention in research studies (for further detail, see Koopman-Iwema, 1980).

We conclude that, in practice, it is often preferable to apply the method of description (or simple evaluation).

The second half of this section has largely dealt with verbal methods of measuring satisfaction. Yet, we recommend to consider the use of *non-verbal* methods. As a rule they are not concerned with separate items, but with facets that are differentiated in a study (such as work, physical working conditions, etc.)

or with overall satisfaction. A well-known method is Kunin's 'Faces Scale' (1955): these faces—11 in the original version—range from expressions of the greatest bliss to the deepest misery. The respondent selects the face which best reflects his attitude or feelings. Research has proved this scale to be of high validity (see e.g. Smith *et al.*, 1969; Dunham and Herman, 1975).

The respondent can also be asked to indicate his degree of satisfaction on a straight line of which merely the extremes are defined, or with the aid of a diagram, etc, etc.

3.4. Weighing facets?

So far in this section, satisfaction has mainly involved the degree of satisfaction about *facets* of the job (as work content, leadership, etc.): each facet can be sub-divided again (e.g. into elements on a scale). An essential question is, however, how one is to gain insight into an individual's overall satisfaction about his work(ing situation). We distinguish two approaches:

The first one involves the researcher presenting the respondent with this problem: the latter has to qualify his job with the aid of a single *global* question (or a very limited number of questions). A formulation frequently used runs something like: 'All in all, how satisfied are you with your job?' It is likely that Hoppock (1935) was the first to use this type of question. Many have followed his example since then, at times using different formulations, such as: 'If you were to choose all over, would you do this work again?' In various countries the outcomes of such studies reveal in the first place that the percentage of respondents reporting to be satisfied is always high, and furthermore that this percentage has gradually increased, with the exception of the period during World War II. In the last few years 80–85% have indicated to be satisfied.

Several researchers have been faced with a dilemma owing to such results, particularly as they often appear to diverge considerably from specific (satisfaction) data on the various facets separately. Besides, such a high degree of satisfaction quite unexpectedly appears to be accompanied by a high degree of absenteeism, considerable turnover, large numbers of complaints, etc. Whether or not partly due to De Swaan's 'Bare slice of bread' ('Boterham met Tevredenheid') (1972), some researchers have concluded not only that this kind of data is not of much use, but also that such a concept as (global) satisfaction is of little help.

In our view, it is not the concept of satisfaction, but the answers to such global questions which are usually hard to interpret. For one thing, the gradual rise, during the last 30–35 years, of the percentage of satisfied workers creates the impression that such a thing as economic prosperity is tapped on here (too). For another: it may well be a threatening question. For if the individual is indeed not satisfied (e.g. with his career) but reconciled to the idea, a negative response might unsettle this 'adjustment' and urge him to undertake changes which he would rather omit, or which would arouse fear of receiving notice.

In the third place, a positive answer may imply that he has 'something to do', that he is 'at any rate employed', that 'things are not that bad', etc. A fourth possibility is that the individual is satisfied with what his present job has to offer, but that he would rather work somewhere else, or that, in contrast, he is dissatisfied with his living conditions outside the job. These things imply that the answer to this type of question leaves open far too many possibilities of interpretation, and that the choice of the global method—for the objective mentioned that is—is not suitable without restrictions (see e.g. Kahn, 1972; Porter *et al.*, 1975).

The second approach involves regarding general job satisfaction as a *composite* concept, connecting the satisfaction scores on different facets. The question as to the best procedure for this raises the problem of weighing: are all facets really equally important?

If we go by intuition or content, it seems only natural to have the respondent weigh the facet satisfaction scores. It is generally felt that if one places a facet such as 'responsibility in the job' beside e.g. a facet like 'physical working conditions', the former will usually weigh more heavily as regards the degree of general satisfaction. Consequently, respondents have regularly been asked also to supply a weighing factor for each of the different facets in a study by means of ranking or rating (which may also be done for each separate item, as we saw in the preceding section). This factor is multiplied by, divided by or added to the facet satisfaction score by the researcher.

On the grounds of the results of a great deal of empirical research, however, this can by no means be regarded as a legitimate approach. They reveal, in short, that weighing either means no improvement, or leads to metrically misleading data. On the other hand, unweighed summation of facet satisfaction scores produces more reliable and valid data (for further detail, see Ewen, 1967; Mikes and Hulin, 1968; Smith *et al.*, 1969; Mobley and Locke, 1970; Blood, 1971; Quinn and Mangione, 1972; Wanous and Lawler, 1972; Sheridan and Slocum, 1975; Ferratt, 1981).

How could these results be accounted for? Discussing the method of 'weighted evaluation' (section 3.3) we mentioned various conditions with respect to weighing, which often cannot be met in research. And it was Hoekman (1971) who demonstrated that the mere summation of facets (or items) is enough to produce effective score differences (weights), and that extra weighing—especially when, as usual, quite a number of facets are included in the research—enhances the amount of covariance in particular. In this connection, we remind the reader of what was revealed by studies applying the expectancy theory (section 2.3.4): the addition of a valence score to an instrumentality score frequently causes a lower correlation with the criterion than the mere use of instrumentality scores.

We conclude this section by another observation on the global and the composite method. In our view, global measurement of general (job) satisfaction—by means of one or a few questions—can be justified only when it can be proved by *prior* research that the question or index is sufficiently reliable and valid, and that it is, for example, part of a predictive model. If such is the case, the selection of the method mainly depends on the *object* of the research. If it is mainly concerned with the effects of satisfaction—e.g. with respect to absenteeism, turnover, health—the global method will suffice in many cases. If, however, specific information on satisfaction is needed, as in the event of 'broad spectrum' diagnosis (e.g. what are the organization's main problems?), of shaping a proposed policy (e.g. what specific forms of shorter working weeks are preferable?), of the evaluation of certain interventions, then one should include various facets in the research. General job satisfaction is then determined by simply adding up the scores, but one might also compose—e.g. with the aid of factor analysis—a short list of scale items predicting the general score (see e.g. the abridged version of the ASIA, 1969).

3.5. Satisfaction and performance

So far, we have dealt only briefly with the effects of satisfaction. It has been demonstrated by a great amount of empirical research that there is often some relation to such aspects as absenteeism and turnover. But we hasten to add that statements in terms of cause and effect are often impossible to make, as they are not allowed by the research design chosen. Moreover, there is considerable variation in the size of the correlations found, while these may also be modified by a mixture of individual, job, organizational, and environmental characteristics.

Nonetheless, we wish to pay attention to a question which is much more puzzling, relatively speaking: is there a relationship between satisfaction and performance? Especially when the human relations movement had much influence on the ideas about behaviour in organizations (see this Handbook, ch. 4.2), this question was answered positively. But this assumption is hardly supported by the results of much empirical research: at times the relations are found to be negative, then again positive, or no relation can be detected at all. Based on the survey of a large number of studies, Vroom (1964) ascertains an average correlation of .13. Later studies did not essentially change this picture, though they have repeatedly emphasized the role of moderator variables (for further detail, see Brayfield and Crockett, 1955; Herzberg *et al.*, 1957; Ronan, 1970; Schwab and Cummings, 1970; Korman, 1971; Bass and Barrett, 1972; Lawler, 1973; Wanous, 1974; Baird, 1976; Lopez, 1982).

Various authors have explained that there is not much sense in relating general job satisfaction to performance, because it is important to learn with respect to what facet an individual is more or less satisfied. Thus, satisfaction with work-related facets is assumed to be more closely related to performance than e.g. satisfaction with physical working conditions. Others have suggested that there may be a third variable influencing both satisfaction and performance, but in opposite directions. Triandis (quoted by Schwab and Cummings, 1970) stated that e.g. the pressure put on production decreases satisfaction but increases performance, in the short run, that is. Suggestions have also been made concerning the influence of many kinds of individual, organizational and job characteristics, the relationship between them, and concerning the frequently unjustified assumption that there be a linear relationship between satisfaction and performance.

Those supporting expectancy theory (section 2.3.4) change the order round: performance causes a certain degree of satisfaction. After all, the performance is the means by which outcomes can be acquired, satisfaction reflecting the degree to which outcomes have been achieved. This relationship can again be moderated by several variables, such as appraisal in figure 2 (section 2.3.4). Theoretically speaking this view may be more satisfying, but it does not make the empirical data look better.

In our opinion a twofold division is to be recommended on theoretical and empirical grounds: it will represent some of the perspectives distinguished in section 3.1 (see also March and Simon, 1958; Lawler, 1973; Sheridan and Slocum, 1975).

1. *Performance causes satisfaction.* This idea corresponds to the expectancy theory. As the performance resembles what was pursued, satisfaction increases (*positive* correlation). It encourages the individual to repeat that particular behaviour cycle as much as he can. The relationship may be moderated by several variables connected with the person, the working group, the job, the organization, etc. Hence, satisfaction refers to what was achieved.

2. *Dissatisfaction causes performance.* This approach also resembles the nature of the expectancy theory. It is characteristic of someone's motivated behaviour that he seeks to realize needs or motives not yet satisfied; we have ascertained before that satisfaction is determined by the individual's valent motives (i.e. by what he hopes to achieve in future). As a consequence, he will always be dissatisfied to a certain extent. If he expects that he will be able to realize his motives by means of successful performance, we speak of a *negative* correlation between satisfaction and performance. This relationship can of course be moderated by several variables. In this case the degree of satisfaction refers to what has not been achieved yet.

All this means that future research on the relationship between satisfaction and performance will need to distinguish better between the various components of satisfaction, which is also decisive for the type of causal relationship that is assumed. It also dismisses as unjustified the summary of all studies of this relationship into a single average correlation coefficient.

4. MOTIVATION AND SATISFACTION

In our introduction to section 3 we observed that the concept of satisfaction plays a general part in all the motivation theories discussed by us, having a more specific meaning in some theories. In the discussion on the subject of satisfaction this close mutual connection became even more prominent: time and again we were made to refer to a motivation theory. Several theories are even closely akin; to mention one example: in the social reference group theory (satisfaction) one detects significant concepts and ideas from the social comparison theory and the equity theory (motivation).

There are more points of similarity: all satisfaction theories attach great importance to the influence of individual and environmental characteristics (i.e. work and working conditions). Such appeared to be the case also with the motivation theories. The concept of consistency (however formulated and defined) plays an essential part in several satisfaction theories; a similar conclusion was drawn as regards motivation theories.

It is our conviction, therefore, that closer theoretical and empirical relations will greatly benefit either theme. Satisfaction research will be improved especially by a far more sound theoretical basis, relatively speaking, of motivation approaches. What may prove to be of use to motivation research is primarily the enormous set of empirical instruments developed for measuring satisfaction. Such an integrated approach really involves incorporating satisfaction, as an essential component, into a wider motivation cycle. Naturally, these components can hardly ever all be part of a single study at the same time. The essence is, however, that it is possible to make a more justifiable selection of antecedent, moderating and effect variables for research.

REFERENCES

Adams, J. S. (1963), Toward an understanding of equity. *J. of Abnormal and Social Psychology*, **67**, 422–436.

Adams, J. S. (1965), Inequity in social exchange. In: Berkowitz, L. (Ed.), *Advances in Experimental social psychology*. Vol. 2. New York: Academic Press.

Alderfer, C. P. (1969), An empirical test of a new theory of human needs. *Organizational Behavior and Human Performance*, **4**, 142–175.

Alderfer, C. P. (1972), *Existence, relatedness and growth: Human needs in organizational settings*. New York: The Free Press.

Alderfer, C. P. (1977), A critique of Salancik and Pfeffer's examination of need-satisfaction theories. *Administrative Science Quarterly*, **22**, 658–669.

Andriessen, J. H. T. H. (1972), Interne of externe beheersing [Internal or external control]. *Ned. Tijdschrift voor de Psychologie*, **27**, 173–198.

Andriessen, J. H. T. H. (1974), *Veiligheid—een kwestie van motivatie* [Safety—a matter of motivation]. Amsterdam: Free University (dissertation).

Andriessen, J. H. T. H., Cadzand, J. P. van (1983), Een analyse van de Nederlandse I-E schaal [An analysis of the Dutch I-E scale]. *Ned. Tijdschrift voor de Psychologie*, **38**, 7–24.

Andrisani, P. J., Nestel, G. (1976), Internal-external control as contribution to and outcome of work experience. *J. of Applied Psychology*, **61**, 156–165.

ASIA: Attitudeschaal voor industriële arbeid [Attitudinal scale for industrial work] (1969). The Hague: Commissie Opvoering Productiviteit/SER.

Atkinson, J. W. (1964), *An introduction to motivation*. Princeton: Van Nostrand.

Atkinson, J. W. (1974), The mainsprings of achievement-oriented activity. In: Atkinson, J. W., Raynor, J. O. (Eds.), *Motivation and achievement*. New York: Wiley.

Atkinson, J. W., Cartwright, D. (1964), Some neglected variables in contemporary conceptions of decision and performance. *Psychological Reports*, **14**, 575–590.

Baird, L. S. (1976), Relationship of performance to satisfaction in stimulating and nonstimulating jobs. *J. of Applied Psychology*, **61**, 721–727.

Bass, B. M., Barrett, G. V. (1972), *Man, work, and organizations*. New York: Allyn & Bacon.

Ben-Porat, A. (1981), Event and agent: Toward a structural theory of job satisfaction. *Personnel Psychology*, **34**, 523–534.

Blood, M. R. (1971), The validity of importance. *J. of Applied Psychology*, **55**, 487–488.

Blood, M. R., Hulin, C. L. (1967), Alienation, environmental characteristics and workers' responses. *J. of Applied Psychology*, **51**, 284–290.

Brayfield, A. H., Crockett, W. H. (1955), Employee attitudes and employee performance. *Psychological Bulletin*, **52**, 396–424.

Calder, B. J., Staw, B. M. (1975), Self-perception of intrinsic and extrinsic motivation. *J. of Personality and Social Psychology*, **31**, 599–605.

Caldwell, D. F., O'Reilly, C. A. (1982), Task perceptions and job satisfaction: A question of causality. *J. of Applied Psychology*, **67**, 361–370.

Campbell, J. P., Dunnette, M. D., Lawler, E. E., Weick, K. E. (1970), *Managerial behavior, performance, and effectiveness*. New York: McGraw-Hill.

Campbell, J. P., Pritchard, R. D. (1976), Motivation theory in industrial and organizational psychology. In: Dunnette, M. D. (Ed.), *Handbook of industrial and organizational psychology*. Chicago: Rand MacNally.

Carver, C. S., Scheier, M. F. (1981), *Attention and self-regulation: A control-theory approach to human behavior*. New York: Springer.

Cherrington, D. J. (1973), Satisfaction in competitive conditions. *Organizational Behavior and Human Performance*, **10**, 47–71.

Cofer, C. N. (1972), *Motivation and emotion*. Glenview: Scott, Foreman.

Cofer, C. N., Appley, M. H. (1968²), *Motivation: Theory and research*. New York: Wiley.

Cummings, L. L., Schwab, D. P. (1973), *Performance in organizations: determinants and appraisal*. Glenview: Scott, Foreman.

De Charms, R. (1968), *Personal causation: The internal affective determinants of behavior*. New York, Academic Press.

Deci, E. L. (1975), *Intrinsic motivation*. New York: Plenum Press.

Dipboye, R. C. (1977), A critical review of Korman's self-consistency theory of work motivation and occupational choice. *Organizational Behavior and Human Performance*, **18**, 108–126.

Drenth, P. J. D., Willems, P. J., de Wolff, Ch. J. (Eds.) (1970), *Bedrijfspsychologie: Onderzoek en evaluatie*. [Industrial psychology: Research and evaluation]. Deventer: Kluwer.

Dunham, R. B., Herman, J. B. (1975), Development of a female faces scale for measuring job satisfaction. *J. of Applied Psychology*, **60**, 629–631.

Duyker, H. C. J. (1975), *Norm en descriptie in de psychologie* [Norm and description in psychology]. Amsterdam: North-Holland Publ. Co.

Duyker, H. C. J. (1976), De ideologie der zelfontplooiing [The ideology of self-actualization]. *Pedagogische Studiën* [Pedagogical Studies], **10**, 358–373.

Duyker, H. C. J., Dudink, A. C. (1976), *Leerboek der psychologie* [Psychology text-book]. Groningen: Wolters-Noordhoff.

Edwards, W. (1954), The theory of decision making. *Psychological Bulletin*, **51**, 380–417.

Ewen, R. B. (1967), Weighting components of job satisfaction. *J. of Applied Psychology*, **51**, 68–73.

Ferratt, T. W. (1981), Overall job satisfaction: Is it a linear function of facet satisfaction? *Human Relations*, **34**, 463–473.

Festinger, L. (1950), Informal social communication. *Psychological Review*, **57**, 184–200.

Festinger, L. (1954), A theory of social comparison. *Human Relations*, **7**, 117–140.

Francès, R., Lebras, C. (1982), The prediction of job satisfaction *International Review of Applied Psychology*, **31**, 391–410.

French, J. R. P., Rodgers, W. L., Cobb, S. (1974), Adjustment as person-environment fit. In: Coelho, G., Hamburg, D., Adams J. C. (Eds.), *Coping and adaptation*. New York: Basic Books.

Galbraith, J. R., Cummings, L. L. (1967), An empirical investigation of the motivational determinants of task performance: interactive effects between instrumentality-valence, motivation and ability. *Organizational Behavior and Human Performance*, **2**, 237–257.

Goodman, P. S. (1972), *An examination of referents used in the evaluation of pay*. GSIA. Carnegie-Mellon University. Working paper 83-72-3.

Graaf, M. H. K. van der, Huizinga, G. (1969), *Bedrijfsenquête staf- en kaderpersoneel* [Industrial survey staff and managerial personnel]. The Hague: Commissie Opvoering Productiviteit, 1969.

Graen, G. (1969), Instrumentality theory of work motivation. *J. of Applied Psychology* (Monograph), **53**, 1–25.

Grumbkow, J. von (1980), *Sociale vergelijking van salarissen* [Social comparison of salaries]. Groningen: University of Groningen (dissertation).

Grumbkow, J. von, Wilke, H. A. M. (1974), Sociale uitwisseling en billijkheid: Toetsing en evaluatie van de billijkheidstheorie. [Social exchange and equity: Test and evaluation of the equity theory]. *Ned. Tÿdschrift voor de Psychologie*, **29**, 281–316.

Hamner, W. C., Foster, L. W. (1975), Are intrinsic and extrinsic rewards additive: A test of Deci's cognitive evaluation theory of task motivation. *Organizational Behavior and Human Performance*, **14**, 398–415.

Heider, F. (1958), *The psychology of interpersonal relations*. New York: Wiley.

Herzberg, F. (1966), *Work and the nature of man*. Cleveland: World Publishing Co.

Herzberg, F. (1968), One more time: How do you motivate employees? *Harvard Business Review*, **46**, (1), 53–62.

Herzberg, F. (1976), *The managerial choice: To be efficient and to be human*. New York: Dow Jones-Irvin.

Herzberg, F., Mausner, B., Peterson, R. O., Capwell, D. F. (1957), *Job attitudes: Review of research and opinion*. Pittsburgh: Psychological service of Pittsburg.

Herzberg, F., Mausner, B., Snyderman, B. B. (1959), *The motivation to work*, New York: Wiley.

Hoekman, K. (1970), Satisfactie-meting: Over-weging en modellen [Measuring satisfaction: Over-weighing and models]. In: P. J. D. Drenth *et al.* (1970).

Hoppock, R. (1935), *Job satisfaction*. New York: Harper & Brothers.

Horn, L. A. ten (1983), *Behoeften, werksituatie en arbeidsbeleving* [Needs, working situation and job attitudes]. Delft: Technological University (dissertation).

Huizinga, G. (1970), *Maslow's need hierachy in the work situation*. Groningen: Wolters-Noordhoff.

Hulin, C. L. (1966), Effects of community characteristics on measures of job satisfaction. *J. of Applied Psychology*, **50**, 185–192.

Hull, C. L. (1943), *Principles of behavior*. New York: Appleton-Century-Crofts.

Hull, C. L. (1951), *Essentials of behavior*. New Haven: Yale University Press.

James, L. R., Jones, A. P. (1980), Perceived characteristics and job satisfaction: An examination of reciprocal causation. *Personnel Psychology*, 33, 97–135.

Jeswald, T. A. (1974), The case of absenteeism and turnover in a large organization. In: Clay Hamner, W., Schmidt, F. L. (Eds.), *Contemporary problems in personnel*. Chicago: St. Clair Press.

Kahn, R. L. (1972), The meaning of work. In: Campbell, A., Converse, P. E. (Eds.), *The human meaning of social change*. Washington: Russell Sage Foundation.

Kahn, R. L. (1981), *Work and health*. New York: Wiley.

Katzell, R. A., Barrett, R. S., Parker, T. C. (1961), Job satisfaction, job performance, and situational characteristics. *J. of Applied Psychology*, 45, 65–72.

Klandermans, P. G., Visser, A. Ph. (1983a), Interne-externe beheersing en de theorie van het sociaal leren [Internal-external control and social-learning theory]. *Ned. Tijdschrift voor de Psychologie*, 38, 1–6.

Klandermans, P. G., Visser, A. Ph. (1983b), Interne-externe beheersing. Nabeschouwing [Internal-external control. Epilogue]. *Ned. Tijdschrift voor de Psychologie*, 38, 65–69.

Kendall, L. M. (1963), *Canonical analysis of job satisfaction and behavior, personal background, and situational data*. Cornell University (doctoral dissertation).

Koopman, P. L., Werkman, B. (1973), Het verhoudingsmodel bij de meting van satisfactie [The ratio model in measuring satisfaction]. In: Drenth, P. J. D., Willems, P. J., Wolff, Ch. J. de (Eds.), *Psychologie van arbeid en organisatie* [The psychology of work and organization]. Deventer: Kluwer.

Koopman-Iwema, A. M. (1980), *Macht. motivatie. medezeggenschap* [Power, motivation, co-determination]. Assen: Van Gorcum.

Koopman-Iwema, A. M. (1982), De puzzel van het prestatieloon—arbeidsgedrag en motivatie [The puzzle of incentive payment—work behaviour and motivation]. *Psychologie* [Psychology], June, 15–21.

Koopman-Iwema, A. M., Thierry, Hk. (1977), Participatie, motivatie en machtafstand [Participation, motivation and power distance]. *Mens en Onderneming* [Man and Enterprise], 5, 263–284.

Korman, A. K. (1971), *Industrial and organizational psychology*. Englewood Cliffs: Prentice-Hall.

Kunin, Th. (1955), The construction of a new type of attitude measure. *Personnel Psychology*, 8, 65–78.

Lawler, E. E. (1971), *Pay and organizational effectiveness*. New York: McGraw-Hill.

Lawler, E. E. (1973), *Motivation in work organizations*. Monterey: Brooks/Cole.

Lawler, E. E. (1980), Motivation: Closing the gap between theory and practice. In: Duncan, K. D., Gruneberg, M. M., Wallis, D. (Eds.), *Changes in working life*. London: Wiley.

Lefkowitz, J. (1967), Self-esteem of industrial workers. *J. of Applied Psychology*, 51, 521–528.

Lewin, K. (1935), *A dynamic theory of personality*. New York: McGraw-Hill.

Lewin, K. (1938), *The conceptual representation and the measurement of psychological forces*. Durham: Duke University Press.

Lewin, K. (1951), *Field theory in social science*. New York: Harper & Row.

Locke, E. A. (1969), What is job satisfaction? *Organizational Behavior and Human Performance*, 4, 309–336.

Locke, E. A. (1976), The nature and causes of job satisfaction. In: Dunnette, M. D. (Ed.), *Handbook of industrial and organizational psychology*. Chicago: Rand McNally.

Lofquist, L. H., Dawis, R. V. (1969), *Adjustment to work*. New York: Appleton-Century-Crofts.

Lopez, E. M. (1982), A test of the self-consistency theory of the job performance-job satisfaction relationship. *Academy of Management Journal*, **25**, 335–348.

McClelland, D. C. (1951), *Personality*. New York: Holt, Rinehart & Winston.

McClelland, D. C. (1961), *The achieving society*. Princeton: Van Nostrand.

McClelland, D. C. (1971), *Assessing human motivation*. New York: General Learning Press.

McGregor, D. C. (1960), The human side of enterprise. New York: McGraw-Hill.

March, J. G., Simon, H. B. (1958), *Organizations*. New York: Wiley.

Maslow, A. H. (1954), *Motivation and personality*. New York: Harper & Row.

Metsch, J. C. (1980), *Loonsatisfaktie en variable beloning* [Pay satisfaction and variable payment]. Amsterdam: University of Amsterdam, Dept. of Work- and Organizational Psychology.

Mikes, P. S., Hulin, C. L. (1968), Use of importance as a weighting component of job satisfaction. *J. of Applied Psychology*, **52**, 394–398.

Minton, H. L. (1972), Power and personality. In: Tedeschi, J. T. (Ed.), *The social influence processes*. Chicago: Aldine Atherton.

Mitchell, T. R. (1974), Expectancy models of job satisfaction, occupational preferences and effort: A theoretical, methodological and empirical appraisal. *Psychological Bulletin*, **81**, 1053–1077.

Mitchell, T. R., Albright, D. W. (1972), Expectancy theory predictions of the satisfaction, effort, performance and retention of naval aviation officers. *Organizational Behavior and Human Performance*, **8**, 1–20.

Mitchell, T. R., Biglan, A. (1971), Instrumentality theories: Current uses in psychology. *Psychological Bulletin*, **76**, 432–454.

Mobley, W. H., Locke, E. A. (1970), The relationship of value importance to satisfaction. *Organizational Behavior and Human Performance*, **5**, 463–483.

Morse, N. C. (1953), *Satisfaction in the white-collar job*. Ann Arbor: University of Michigan.

Mulder, M. (1972), *Het spel om macht* [The play for power]. Meppel: Boom.

Naylor, J. C., Pritchard, R. D., Ilgen, D. R. (1980), A sequential view of behavior and motivation. In: Duncan, K. D., Gruneberg, M. M., Wallis, D. (Eds.), *Changes in working life*. London: Wiley.

Nederlands Tijdschrift voor de Psychologie [Dutch Journal of Psychology]. Deventer: Van Loghum Slaterus.

NIPG (1958), *Hoe denkt u over uw werk?* [What do you think of your job?] Leiden: Dutch Institute of Preventive Medicine.

Nuttin, J. (1981), *De menselijke motivatie* [Human motivation]. Deventer: Van Loghum Slaterus.

O'Brien, G. E., Dowling, P. (1980), The effects of congruency between perceived and desired job attributes upon job satisfaction. *J. of Occupational Psychology*, **53**, 121–130.

Orlebeke, J. F. (1981), Motivatie [Motivation]. In: Orlebeke, J. F., Drenth, P. J. D., Janssen, R. H. C., Sanders, C. (Eds.), *Compendium van de psychologie* [Compendium of psychology]. Vol. 4. Muiderberg: Coutinho, 1981.

Orpen, C. (1974), Discrimination, work attitudes and job satisfaction: A comparative study of whites and coloureds in South Africa. *International Review of Applied Psychology*, **23**, 33–45.

Pelz, D. C., Andrews, F. M. (1966), *Scientists in organizations*. New York: Wiley.

Penn, R., Sheposh, J. P., Riedel, J. A., Young, L. E. (1980), Job and organization characteristics and how they pertain to job satisfaction and work motivation. In: Duncan, K. D., Gruneberg, M. M., Wallis, D. (Eds.), *Changes in working life*. New York: Wiley.

Petri, H. L. (1981), *Motivation: Theory and research*. Belmont: Wadsworth.

Porter, L. W. (1961), A study of perceived need satisfaction in bottom and middle management jobs. *J. of Applied Psychology*, **45**, 1–10.

Porter, L. W., Lawler, E. E. (1968), *Managerial attitudes and performance*. Homewood: Irwin.

Porter, L. W., Steers, R. M. (1973), Organizational work and personal factors in employee turnover and absenteeism. *Psychological Bulletin*, **80**, 151–176.

Porter, L. W., Lawler, E. E., Hackman, R. (1975), *Behavior in organizations*. New York: McGraw-Hill.

Pritchard, R. D. (1969), Equity theory: A review and critique. *Organizational Behavior and Human Performance*, **4**, 176–211.

Pritchard, R. D., Campbell, K. M., Campbell, D. J. (1977), Effects of extrinsic financial rewards. *J. of Applied Psychology*, **62**, 9–15.

Quinn, R. P., Mangione, T. W. (1973), Evaluating weighted models for measuring job satisfaction: A Cinderella story. *Organizational Behavior and Human Performance*, **10**, 1–23.

Rijsman, J. B., Wilke, H. A. M. (1980), *Sociale vergelijkingsprocessen* [Social comparison processes]. Deventer: Van Loghum Slaterus.

Ronan, W. W. (1970), Individual and situational variables relating to job satisfaction. *J. of Applied Psychology*, **54** (monograph).

Rotter, J. B. (1966), Generalized expectancies for internal versus external control of reinforcement. *Psychological Monographs*, **80**, 1–28.

Rotter, J. B. (1967), Beliefs, attitudes and behavior: A social learning analysis. In: Jessor, R., Feshbach, S. (Eds.), *Cognition, personality and clinical psychology*. San Francisco: Jossey Bass.

Schachter, S. (1959), *The psychology of affiliation*. Stanford: Stanford University Press.

Schneider, J., Locke, E. A. (1971), A critique of Herzberg's incident classification system and a suggested revision. *Organizational Behavior and Human Performance*, **6**, 441–457.

Schwab, D. P., Cummings, L. L. (1970), Theories of performance and satisfaction: A review. *Industrial Relations*, **9**, 408–430.

Seashore, S. E., Taber, T. D. (1975), Job satisfaction indicators and their correlates. *American Behavioral Scientist*, **18**, 333–369.

Seybolt, J. W. (1976), Work satisfaction as a function of the person-environment interaction. *Organizational Behavior and Human Performance*, **17**, 66–75.

Sheridan, J. E., Slocum, J. W. (1975a), The direction of the causal relationship between job satisfaction and job performance. *Organizational Behavior and Human Performance*, **14**, 159–172.

Sheridan, J. E., Slocum, J. W. (1975b), Motivational determinants of job performance. *J. of Applied Psychology*, **60**, 119–121.

Smith, P. C., Kendall, L. M., Hulin, C. L. (1969), *The measurement of satisfaction in work and retirement*. Chicago: Rand McNally.

Smits, B. W. G. M. (1982), *Motivatie en meetmethode: Een cognitieve benadering* [Motivation and measuring method: A cognitive approach]. Lisse: Swets & Zeitlinger.

Spence, K. W. (1958), Behavior theory and selective learning. In: Jones, M. R. (Ed.), *Nebraska Symposium on Motivation*. Vol. 6. Lincoln: University of Nebraska Press.

Staw, B. M. (1976), *Intrinsic and extrinsic motivation*. Morristown: Northwestern University General Learning Press.

Staw, B. M. (1977), Motivation in organizations: Toward synthesis and redirection. In: Staw, B. M., Salancik, G. R. (Eds.), *New directions in organizational behavior*. Chicago: St. Clair Press.

Swaan, A. de (1972), *Een boterham met tevredenheid* [A bare slice of bread]. Amsterdam: Van Gennep

Taylor, J. C. (1977), Job satisfaction and quality of working life: A reassessment. *J. of Occupational Psychology*, **50**, 243–252.

Taylor, J. C., Bowers, D. G. (1972), *Survey of organizations*. Ann Arbor: Institute for Social Research.

Tharenou, Ph., Harker, Ph. (1982), Organizational correlates of employee self-esteem. *J. of Applied Psychology*, **67**, 797–805.

Thierry, Hk. (1968), *Loont de prestatiebeloning?* [Does incentive payment pay off?]. Assen: Van Gorcum.

Thierry, Hk. (1969), *Arbeidsinstelling en prestatiebeloning* [Job attitude and incentive payment]. Utrecht: Het Spectrum.

Thierry, Hk., Drenth, P. J. D. (1970), De toetsing van Herzbergs "two factor" theorie [Testing Herzberg's 'two factor' theory]. In: Drenth *et al.* (1970).

Vroom, V. H. (1964), *Work and motivation*. New York: Wiley.

Wall, T. D., Payne, R. (1973), Are deficiency scores deficient? *J. of Applied Psychology*, **58**, 322–326.

Wanous, J. P. (1974), A causal-correlational analysis of the job satisfaction and performance relationship. *J. of Applied Psychology*, **59**, 139–144.

Wanous, J. P., Lawler, E. E. (1972), The measurement and meaning of job satisfaction. *J. of Applied Psychology*, **56**, 955–105.

Weiner, B. (1972), *Theories of motivation from mechanism to cognition*. Chicago: Markham.

Weiner, B. (1974), An attributional interpretation of expectancy-value theory. In: Weiner, B. (Ed.), *Cognitive views of human motivation*. New York: Academic Press.

White, R. W. (1959), Motivation reconsidered: The concept of competence. *Psychological Review*, **66**, 297–333.

Wilke, H. A. M., Kuijper, H. (1977), Sociale vergelijkingsprocessen [Social comparison processes]. *Ned. Tijdschrift voor de Psychologie*, **32**, 385–392.

Handbook of Work and Organizational Psychology
Edited by P. J. D. Drenth, Hk. Thierry, P. J. Willems and C. J. de Wolff
© 1984, John Wiley & Sons, Ltd.

2.3. Task characteristics

Jen A. Algera

1. INTRODUCTION

At the beginning of this century, the chief aim of production organization design was to split up the work as much as possible into simple tasks. The principles of 'scientific management' (Taylor, 1911) were intended to increase productivity, obtain better control of production, and lower production costs.

As soon as these principles were applied to production systems, it was discovered that the resulting tasks gave the task performer hardly any satisfaction. Ford, for instance, had many personnel problems (turnover) in his automobile works, despite the high unemployment rates and his high wages. But people regarded these problems as the price to be paid for achieving mass production of goods which would raise the general level of prosperity, so that the worker as consumer would profit by it. Fry (1976) observed that, due to an improper use of Taylor's ideas, scientific management very quickly got a bad name in some circles. Time and motion studies were used to increase work pace and to simplify tasks, rather than to establish the best working method and a reasonable working rate. This improper use was so glaringly obvious that in 1915 the American Congress passed a bill outlawing the use of time-keeping devices to clock work performance in governmental offices. Nonetheless, Taylor's ideas had an enormous influence on designers of industrial production installations, engineers and work analysts. Willems (1970) notes that the interest on the part of social scientists for work design is fairly recent. At first, work psychology was strongly oriented to the selection and placement of personnel on the basis of individual differences: the job to be done

Dr. Jen A. Algera, Vrije Universiteit Amsterdam. Vakgroep Arbeids- en Organisatiepsychologie De Boelelaan 1081, 1081 HV Amsterdam. Tel.: 020–5485514.

was accepted without question. Later more socio-psychological issues also came into play, such as the role of leadership and relationships within groups. It was not until the fifties and sixties that social scientists began to show an interest in the design of production systems and the work situation as determinants of the reactions, chiefly negative ones, of task performers.

Over the past years, this mode of thinking has given rise to developments referred to by terms such as job enrichment, work design, quality of work life, etc. What these trends have in common is their reaction to the problems that occur in organizations designed according to the scientific management approach. Problems such as low productivity, high absenteeism, low work satisfaction, and high turnover are ascribed in part to Taylor's method of work organization and the control systems associated with it.

Several theories may serve as a starting point for studying the relationships between aspects of the work situation and the behavior and attitude of task performers. In this chapter we will confine ourselves to theories on the effects of task characteristics; other determinants of behavior and attitude in work situations, such as characteristics of groups and styles of leadership, are discussed elsewhere in this handbook.

For a definition of terms we can start out with Hackman (1969), who suggests: 'A task may be assigned to a person (or group) by an external agent or may be self-generated. It consists of a stimulus complex and a set of instructions which specify what is to be done vis-à-vis the stimuli. The instructions indicate what operations are to be performed by the subject(s) with respect to the stimuli and/or what goal is to be achieved.'

Hackman also points out that a distinction can be made between the objective elements of a task and the way they are perceived by the task performer ('redefined task input'), which may differ from person to person.

Various approaches can be taken to describing or measuring tasks or jobs. Hackman (1969) names four:

1. *Task qua task*: this approach concerns the 'objective' characteristics of tasks (for example, the physical nature of a task). According to Hackman, not only the physical nature of the stimuli, but also *any* aspect of the actual task materials presented to a subject or group (for instance, a dimension such as 'goal clarity') falls under this heading.

2. *Task as behavior requirement*: 'what responses *should* the subjects emit, given the stimulus situation, to achieve some criterion of success?' A parallel approach is used in systems analysis in determining the function of a particular system component.

3. *Task as behavior description*: 'responses which the performer *actually does* emit, given the stimulus conditions'. Unlike point 2, what counts here is not what behavior should occur in order to reach a certain goal, but what behavior actually does occur.

4. *Task as ability requirement*: what abilities of the performer are called upon?

As an example of a model that takes this approach, Hackman cites the Structure of Intellect-model of Guilford (1967), with its 120 components of intelligence, corresponding to 120 elementary tasks, that can be distinguished on the basis of three dimensions (operation, content, product).

For the goal of studying how tasks affect the behavior of performers, Hackman discards points 3 and 4. These approaches actually measure dependent rather than independent variables. In his view, approaches 1 and 2 (task qua task and task as behavior requirement) open up good perspectives, because they relate more to task than to performer. The task qua task approach would seem to be the most profitable; the chief argument against this approach is that it can prove difficult to work with because of the very many descriptive dimensions possible.

Some dependent variables, which have been used in studies as indicators of reactions by task performers to various task characteristics, are: satisfaction with the work in general, satisfaction with opportunities for personal development, intrinsic work motivation, job involvement, psychosomatic complaints, absenteeism due to illness, turnover, and performance.

Below we will discuss a number of studies in which task characteristics are viewed as determinants of the behavior and attitude of task performers. We will also consider the chief questions they raise. A short summary of research results follows. Finally, we will go into the relationship between task characteristics and other variables such as technology and organization structure.

2. STUDIES ON TASK CHARACTERISTICS

2.1. Turner and Lawrence

A classic study on the reactions of task performers to different task characteristics is the study by Turner and Lawrence (1965). Before formulating a descriptive framework for jobs, Turner and Lawrence posited serveral criteria which it should satisfy:

—it should provide the means to describe jobs in all branches of industry;
—it should yield quantitative data;
—it should describe jobs in terms of behavior: what concrete human behavior is required for task performance?; this should include not only motor activities but also social and cognitive components of behavior;
—it must be convenient to use and yet satisfy the requirement of inter-judge reliability.

Turner and Lawrence felt that existing task description frameworks (for example, from a technical, organizational, or job-evaluation point of view) did not put enough emphasis on the description of human behavior required for task performance.

ELEMENTS OF BEHAVIOR

		activities	interactions	mental states
ELEMENTS OF TASK	prescribed	variety (object and motor)	required interactions	knowledge and skill
	discretionary	autonomy	optional interaction (on or off the job)	responsibility

Figure 1. Requisite task attributes: descriptive scheme. Source: Arthur N. Turner and Paul R. Lawrence, *Industrial Jobs and the Worker: An Investigation of Response to Task Attributes*. Boston: Division of Research, Harvard University, Graduate School of Business Administration, 1965, p. 20, Exhibit 1.3. Reprinted by permission.

In their descriptive scheme, Turner and Lawrence utilize a two-sided grid, the columns representing categories of behavior ('activities', 'interactions', and 'mental states') and the rows categories of task elements ('prescribed' and 'discretionary') (see figure 1).

The term 'prescribed' refers to task elements that are predetermined. The term 'discretionary' refers to behavior, within the limits of the prescribed task, where the individual must make independent choices or decisions. Both terms refer to behavior that is required for task performance. For example, 'autonomy' means the amount of discretion inherent in the task design which the task performer is expected to exercise in carrying out the task assigned to him. The six 'requisite task attributes' corresponding to the cells of figure 1 are:

1. *variety* (for example, in tools, equipment, machinary used, in prescribed work pace);
2. *autonomy* (for example, amount of latitude in determining the method of work);
3. *required interactions* (contact necessary for proper task performance);
4. *optional interaction* (possibilities or limitations (e.g. due to noise) of contact both on and off the job);
5. *knowledge and skill* (learning time necessary);
6. *responsibility* (for example, ambiguity of remedial action).

In addition, Turner and Lawrence distinguish a number of other attributes, closely associated with the job but not required for task performance, which they term 'associated task attributes'. Primary among these is the 'task identity index', defined as the extent to which a task is a 'unique and visible work assignment'. The other associated task attributes are: pay, working conditions, cycle time, level of mechanization, and capital investment.

Most of the attributes are measured by determining the mean score on several scales which are considered indicators for a certain attribute. For example, motor variety is determined by the mean score on the following three scales:

1. variety in prescribed work pace;
2. variety in physical location of work;
3. variety in prescribed physical operations of work.

Turner and Lawrence developed a total of 18 scales to measure the six requisite task attributes. Each scale had five or nine points, each point being described in words. The majority of the scales had five points with values of 1, 3, 5, 7, and 9, respectively. The scores on each scale were determined through observation by the researchers and interviews with the direct supervisor. Because of the fairly high intercorrelations among the six attributes one total score was computed (the RTA index).

This study by Turner and Lawrence (1965) inspired later researchers in this field (Cooper, 1973; Hackman and Lawler, 1971; Hackman and Oldham, 1975; Carnall *et al.*, 1976). It is surprising how many different names different authors use for task characteristics of very similar content. Some authors also extend the domain of characteristics considered relevant.

2.2. Cooper

Cooper (1973) made a valuable contribution to our thinking on task characteristics. On the basis of a hierarchical cluster analysis, he reduced the requisite task attributes of Turner and Lawrence to two underlying concepts: 'physical variety' and 'skill variety'. He also introduced two new concepts, namely 'transformations' and 'goal structure'. The former is related to Turner and Lawrence's 'task identity', the latter is an extension of the domain.

An essential characteristic of most tasks is that the performer must transform a given situation into another one. For example, he must transform a problem into a solution. In Cooper's view, transformations represent operations relating to the stimulus material of the task, and imply motion towards a goal. Transformation acquire their motivational power from the fact that they bring about changes in the structure of the task as a whole. The greater the contribution of a transformation to the task as a whole, the greater its motivational value. To maximize their motivational value, the effects of transformations must furthermore be unambiguously perceived by the task performer. Thus, Cooper feels, transformations must be seen in terms of *a.* their contribution to the task as a whole ('transformational value') and *b.* the distinctness of their effects ('transformation feedback').

The transformational value depends on whether a task is central or peripheral to the final product (or service). According to Cooper, two aspects of the transformation, distance and direction, determine the motivational value of transformation feedback. Distance is the total amount of activity required for the transformation. In this connection Cooper cites research which he feels shows that the efforts of subjects are inversely related to the task distance. The aspect direction concerns information on progress toward (or away from) the goal. Cooper also states that the concept of 'task identity' of Turner and Lawrence (1965) is a combination of transformational value and transformation feedback, which they described as being able to distinguish a task 'as a unique and visible work assignment'.

The concept 'goal structure' that Cooper introduces consists of two components (apart from the goal content): *a*. 'goal clarity', and *b*. 'goal difficulty'. Goal clarity means the specificity with which the performance criteria are defined. Goal difficulty is closely related to the concept of level of aspiration, which also plays an important role in the achievement motivation theory. Level of aspiration refers to the future achievement level an individual strives for, given his past achievements. Atkinson (1957) assumes that the difficulty of a task can be deduced from the subjective probability of successful performance. He then postulates that the intrinsic motivational value of a difficult task (a task with a low subjective probability of success) is high. The achievement motivation theory is primarily oriented to the difficulty of the task as the primary stimulus in motivated behavior for persons with a high achievement motivation (Steers and Spencer, 1977). Hermans (1976) defines achievement motivation as a relatively stable personality disposition which, in specific situations, leads to achievement: 'The achievement motivation is present in task situations which challenge the person, or put him in a position to excel.' People with high achievement motivation are said to prefer situations with challenging work, personal responsibility, and feedback on their achievements. People with a low need for achievement, on the contrary, generally prefer situations where little can go wrong and where they can share responsibility with others.

Other authors also reckon 'goal structure' to the domain of task characteristics which influence motivation and performance of task performers. Carnall *et al.* (1976) distinguish the following three components of goal structure: *a*. 'clarity of goal', *b*. 'goal difficulty', and *c*. 'feedback of results'. Umstot *et al.* (1976) mention two task characteristics related to goal structure: 'goal specificity' and 'goal difficulty'. These authors base themselves primarily on Locke's (1968) treatise. Research has shown that specifically formulated and difficult goals have a positive effect on individual performance. The relationship with satisfaction is more ambiguous.

2.3. Hackman and Lawler

Hackman and Lawler (1971) also elaborate on the work of Turner and Lawrence. They stress the need to develop a theoretical framework from which predictions about the relationship between task characteristics and reactions of task performers under varying conditions can be derived and tested. With this in mind, Hackman and Lawler propose a conceptual framework for the interaction between task characteristics and individual differences. Based on the expectancy theory of work motivation (as developed by Vroom, 1964; Porter and Lawler, 1968; and others), Hackman and Lawler formulate five propositions specifically related to how the motivation of task performers can be improved through task design. They base the contents of individual needs on the ideas of Maslow (1954) and Alderfer (1969), the 'higher order needs' (for example, the need for personal growth and development, or for the feeling of achieving something valuable). They reach the conclusion that the conditions for 'internal work motivation' (that is, individual efforts on the basis of intrinsically valued results) are fulfilled when a job meets the following criteria: *a*. the job must put the task performer in a position to feel personally responsible for a visible work assignment: *b*. the job must lead to results that are experienced as intrinsically meaningful; and *c*. the job must provide feedback on the effectiveness of task performance. In other words, task characteristics can create the conditions which further the intrinsic motivation of individuals with a need for personal growth and development.

Hackman and Lawler base the operationalizations of these three broadly formulated criteria on the task attributes of Turner and Lawrence (1965). Hackman and Lawler distinguish four core dimensions: 'variety', 'autonomy', 'task identity', and 'feedback'. They also distinguish two interpersonal dimensions, 'dealing with others' and 'friendship opportunities'. These two variables are derived from the task attributes 'required interactions' and 'optional interaction' of Turner and Lawrence. Hackman and Lawler do not consider the last two dimensions directly relevant to work motivation on the basis of task characteristics, so they make no specific predictions about them.

Although Hackman and Lawler start out from the task attributes of Turner and Lawrence, their approach and their method of measurement are quite different. Basic to the theoretical views of Hackman and Lawler is that the reactions of task performers are determined by the perception of the task by the task performer rather than by 'objective' characteristics of the task. For this reason, in their study task performers were the chief judges in scoring 13 jobs on the six task characteristics. The jobs were also scored by two other groups of judges (first and second level supervision and the researchers) to investigate how well the perception of task performers agreed with that of other sources. But only the scores assigned by the task performers were used in computing correlations between the six task characteristics and dependent variables such as satisfaction, absenteeism, and work performance. In the original study by Turner and Lawrence, the relationship between dependent variables and task attributes is primarily determined on the basis of scores assigned by outsiders (researchers). The scales used in the two studies are also quite different. While the 'requisite task attributes' are generally described quantitatively (for example: the number of persons with whom interaction is required for task performance, in exact numbers), the scale points used by Hackman and Lawler have qualitative descriptions. The number of points per scale is also different.

2.4. Hackman and Oldham

Further elaborating previous work by Turner and Lawrence (1965) and Hackman and Lawler (1971), Hackman and Oldham (1975, 1976) developed their 'job characteristics model' of work motivation. Basic to this model (see figure 2) is that positive results (high motivation, high satisfaction, low absenteeism and turnover) are achieved when three 'critical psychological states' are present in the individual ('experienced meaningfulness', 'experienced responsibility', 'knowledge of results'). The theory further states that these critical psychological states are brought about by the presence of five task characteristics, to wit 'skill variety', 'task identity', 'task singnificance' (which are primarily responsible for experienced meaningulness), 'autonomy' (related to experienced responsibility), and 'feedback' (related to knowledge of results). Since not every individual will react in the same way to a job with a high 'motivating potential', the variable 'individual growth need strength' acts as a moderator in the relationships 'job dimensions'—'psychological states' and 'psychological states'—'outcomes'.[1]

Following the model diagrammed in figure 2, a summary score was generated

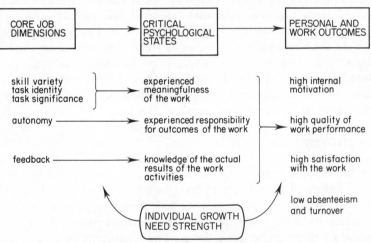

Figure 2. The job characteristics model (from Hackman and Oldham, 1975, 1976). *Copyright 1975 by the American Psychological Association. Reprinted by permission of the author.*

[1] In a later publication (Hackman and Oldham, 1980) two other moderators are mentioned, namely 'knowledge and skill' and 'context satisfactions'.

that reflects the overall motivating potential of a job: the Motivating Potential Score (MPS).

$$\text{MPS} = \frac{\begin{array}{c}\text{Skill} \\ \text{variety}\end{array} + \begin{array}{c}\text{Task} \\ \text{identity}\end{array} + \begin{array}{c}\text{Task} \\ \text{significance}\end{array}}{3} \times \text{Autonomy} \times \text{Feedback}$$

Hackman and Oldham (1975) constructed an instrument for measuring the variables in their model: the Job Diagnostic Survey (JDS). The JDS and the model are for the explicit purpose of task redesign (Hackman *et al.*, 1975). One of the discussion points concerning this model, directly related to the task characteristics it measures, is the issue of the dimensionality of 'job dimensions'. For example, Dunham (1976) wonders whether instead of the five 'core job dimensions' the model posits, it would not be better to work with one single dimension, namely 'complexity'. If capturing the five core job dimensions in a single dimension were to be justified, the problem of how to combine the five dimensions (via a multiplicative model as postulated in the MPS, or via a simple additive model as in the RTA index) would not exist.

3. DISCUSSION POINTS IN RESEARCH ON TASK CHARACTERISTICS

3.1. The dimensionality of task characteristics

Hackman and Oldham (1975) report that the five a priori task characteristics are not entirely independent, but nevertheless useful as separate characteristics. Just as in the study by Hackman and Lawler (1971), the correlation between the characteristics 'skill variety' and 'autonomy' is the highest (.51).

Dunham *et al.* (1977) studied the factor structure of the Job Diagnostic Survey in 20 different samples of respondents. The results of this study indicate that the underlying dimensionality of the JDS is inconsistent across the samples. The five-factor structure postulated by Hackman and Oldham (1975) was found in only two of the 20 samples. Usually a smaller number of dimensions (four, three, or even two) was found.

The issue of the dimensionality of task characteristics can also be posed regarding the original study by Turner and Lawrence (1965). They distinguish six different requisite task attributes, but in their analyses they employ one single weighted score (the RTA index score), in which the characteristics 'autonomy' and 'variety' receive twice as much weight as the others. The authors justify this combination by pointing out the high rank correlations among the attributes. These were higher than they had expected. They regard the RTA index score as a single independent variable that is related to the dependent and intervening variables.

Cooper (1973) did a cluster analysis on the rank correlations among the attributes in the study by Turner and Lawrence. This analysis yielded three clusters of attributes: 'physical variety', 'task uncertainty', and 'response uncertainty'. The last two also form a cluster at a lower level of similarity that Cooper calls 'skill variety'. Cooper therefore assumes a more differentiated dimensionality than Turner and Lawrence.

In the study by Hackman and Lawler (1971) the correlations between the six a priori dimensions—the four core dimensions ('variety', 'autonomy', 'task identity', and 'feedback') and the two interpersonal dimensions ('dealing with others' and 'friendship opportunities')—were generally lower than in the study by Turner and Lawrence. The authors concluded that the six a priori dimensions are useful as separate task characteristics. However, they found a rather high correlation (.67) between variety and autonomy. To Cooper (1973), the height of this correlation means that Hackman and Lawler are actually measuring 'skill variety'. Even if variety and autonomy are viewed as one characteristic, than there are still three sufficiently independent characteristics left of the four core dimensions. Later research (Sims et al., 1976), using questionnaires (the Job Characteristic Inventory) based on the study by Hackman and Lawler, also showed a multi-dimensional structure.

In a recent study by Algera (1981) the mean correlation among 24 a priori task characteristics turned out to be surprisingly low. The definitions of the task characteristics in this study were generally less abstract than those of Hackman and Oldham (1975); they more closely resembled the subscales from the original study by Turner and Lawrence. Unfortunately, these authors report only data on rank correlations among the requisite task attributes and give no information on correlations among the subscales which were regarded as indicators for an attribute. The subscale scores were averaged to obtain the score on an attribute, as is illustrated in section 2.1.

But this leaves us not much wiser on the issue of dimensionality of task characteristics. There are two main problems in comparing research results. First of all, the instruments used in the various studies are not identical. Second, there is quite a broad range of jobs in the samples. At one extreme, correlations among task characteristics are computed on the basis of perceptions by task performers of a variety of jobs from different branches of industry and at different organizational levels. At the other extreme, there are studies where the sample of task performers is much more homogeneous and is limited to one department of a factory (Wall et al., 1978).

3.2. Objective or perceived task characteristics

Another question that comes forward in the literature on task characteristics is whether the starting point for study should be the objective task characteristics or the perception of them by task performers. Schwab and Cummings (1976), for the purpose of task design, advocate the objective task characteristics approach, because changing tasks involves changing objective reality, not the perception of it. These authors reject what they term 'psychological' definitions of task characteristics, mentioning as one example the Job Diagnostic Survey of Hackman and Oldham (1975). Their objection to this approach is that the attributes are not objectively observable characteristics of the task.

Hackman and Lawler (1971) and Hackman and Oldham (1975), on the contrary, stress the use of perceived task characteristics. Their argument for this is that reactions of task performers are not primarily determined by objective reality, but by the individual's perception of objective reality. Objective task characteristics are only important in so far as they influence the perceptions and experiences of task performers. Hackman and Lawler (1971) caution that when the objective characteristics of a task are changed, this does not necessarily mean that the subjective perception of the task performer also changes. But both Hackman and Lawler (1971) and Hackman and Oldham (1975) do compare the perception of task performers with that of outsiders, such as supervisors and researchers. There is generally a good deal of convergence between the perceptions of task performers and outsiders. Hackman and Lawler (1971) conclude from this that apparently task performers are able to give unbiased descriptions of their jobs, and that these descriptions are adequately founded on reality. In fact, the authors do not contest that knowledge about the relationship between objective task characteristics and their subjective perception is very useful. They simply take a different vantage point in viewing task performers' reactions to their situations.

The standpoint of Schwab and Cummings, or the objective task characteristics approach, is not as simple as it seems. In experiments in psychophysics it is probably quite evident what physical stimulus, external to the individual, is responsible for a certain psychological reaction. But in a concrete and more complex work situation this will be more ambiguous. Hill (1969) points this out, for example, in relating 'work variety' to the psychological correlate 'perceived variety' by means of psychophysical scaling procedures. The chief difficulty is that there is no clearly defined physical correlate of perceived variety to which a scaling procedure could be applied; it is not possible to specify directly the nature of the physical stimulus that occasions the perception of variety, except perhaps to say that it has to do with the structure of the work. In a series of experiments, Hill formulated the four indices below and studied which of them would be the most appropriate as a physical correlate of perceived variety:

1. the number of different tasks in a certain period of time;
2. the total number of changes in task in a certain time period;
3. the entropy of the set of tasks, whereby time proportions are used as 'probabilites' instead of frequency ratios, expressed in bits;
4. the entropy of the total number of tasks, expressed in bits.

The two entropy indices come from information theory. This theory concerns the quantity of information contained in a given message or a separate signal in a communication system. The entropy or uncertainty of a system (expressed in bits) is the average amount of information per signal. The entropy of a system or a collection of information in non-metric scales is comparable to the standard deviation in metric scales. Just as the standard deviation, entropy can be regarded as a measure of differentiation. It is in this sense that Hill uses the entropy indices, to express the amount of differentiation in the task structure.

On the assumption that the relationship between perceived variety and its physical correlate is curvilinear, Hill reaches the conclusion that the fourth option, the entropy of the total number of tasks, would be the most suitable objective index. This conclusion was valid for most subjects, but there were individual differences.

Globerson and Crossman (1976) also attempt to establish a relationship between objective task characteristics and subjective reactions to them. They take 'monotony' as the opposite of 'variety', and their basic hypothesis is that the objective time structure of a task shows a monotonic relationship to the subjectively experienced monotony. One of the objective indices used by Globerson and Crossman is NRT = non-repetitive time,

$$t_n = \sum_{j=1}^{m} t_e(j)$$

where t_n = non-repetitive time (expressed in minutes); m = number of *different* elements within the cycle time of a task; and $t_e(j)$ = time for element j (minutes).

NRT as an indicator of variety is based on the sum total of the durations of different task elements within the cycle time. Frequently occurring task elements are counted only once. The authors find a positive relationship between NRT and the perceived characteristics 'complexity', 'variety', and 'interest'. But the question remains how objective NRT really is, because the cycle time of a task is determined arbitrarily. In brief, even with 'objective' indices such as NRT, one must be on the lookout for any subjective decisions.

These attempts make quite clear how difficult it is to establish the physical correlate of perceived variety. However, knowledge about the relationship between objective task characteristics and their perception by task performers or outsiders is indispensable to a better understanding of the effects of tasks. Aldag et al. (1981) argue for some focus on relatively more objective measurement strategies, without abandoning perceptual indices. They feel the approaches advocated by Globerson and Crossman (1976) and by Schwab and Cummings (1976) should be viewed as promising complements to a continued focus on task perceptions. A number of publications (Weiss and Shaw, 1979; White and Mitchell, 1979; O'Reilly and Caldwell, 1979) address the question of the effects of social influences on the perception of task characteristics. Also the personality trait 'field independence' has been examined as an additional determinant of task perceptions (Stone, 1979). These laboratory studies, mostly using an experimental design, are complementary to field studies which employ often correlational designs. It is clear that more research is needed on the way in which individuals redefine their tasks and on the variables which may influence this, such as the social context and individual differences.

4. RESULTS OF RESEARCH

The main hypothesis in the study by Turner and Lawrence (1965) was that workers would react favorably (high satisfaction and low absenteeism) to work that was complex, responsible, etc., and unfavorably (high absenteeism and low satisfaction) to work that was less demanding. The hypothesis was confirmed on the aspect of absenteeism, but for satisfaction, cultural background (urban or rural) acted as a moderator variable. Workers who came from a rural area ('town workers') reacted positively to complex tasks, but workers from urban areas ('city workers') were less satisfied with jobs which scored high on the RTA index.

Hulin and Blood (1968) assert that employees in small towns have incorporated the pattern of norms and values of the American middle class along with its work ethos. In the bigger cities, such a pattern of values would be less dominant. Alienation from the middle class work ethos is, in the view of these authors, an explanation for the findings of Turner and Lawrence. Hulin and Blood (1968) submit a three-dimensional model specifying the relationship between complexity of the job, work satisfaction, and alienation from the middle class work ethos.

Hackman and Lawler (1971) advocate measuring differentiation within a sample at the individual level, rather than distinguishing subgroups on the basis of sociological concepts (subgroups that differ in terms of cultural background or alienation from a value pattern). They introduce a conceptual framework on the interaction between task characteristics and individual differences where 'higher order need strength' acts as a moderator. The results of their study lend some support to this.

Most empirical data currently available have been collected on the 'job characteristics model' of Hackman and Oldham (1975, 1976). In a test of their model, Hackman and Oldham (1976) found support for it on a number of points, but their study also showed that several relationships between variables do not behave exactly as the model predicts. The job dimension 'autonomy', for example, had a direct effect on some outcome variables which was greater than or equal to the postulated indirect effect through 'experienced responsibility'. These findings raise questions on the causal relationships predicted by the model. Research on the validity of the MPS formulation (Dunham, 1976; Arnold and House, 1980) did not support the current MPS formula.

The job characteristics model was recently tested by Wall *et al.* (1978). Data was collected on a homogeneous group of fairly simple jobs, contrary to the heterogeneous group of jobs on which the results of Hackman and Oldham were based. Wall *et al.* analysed not only their own data but also that of Hackman and Oldham by means of path analysis, a statistical method which allows a priori postulated causal relationships between variables to be described and tested. This study showed that some findings of Hackman and Oldham in a heterogeneous group of jobs are also valid in a more homogeneous group of jobs, a situation more likely to occur in actual task design. Results on the causal relationships of the model, however, were less favorable. Much of the data, chiefly on 'critical psychological states', did not conform to the model. When the job characteristics model was tested against an alternative model, the alternative model accounted for a significantly greater portion of the variance than the job characteristics model. This was true for the data of Wall *et al.* and for the data of Hackman and Oldham (1976). An important difference between the two models was that the alternative model did postulate direct causal relationships between task characteristics and outcome variables.

Because direct relationships between 'core job dimensions' and outcome variables would have the same implications for task design as would be the case if the 'critical psychological states' had behaved in accordance with the model, Wall *et al.* do not reject the model entirely. They do suggest some reformulations, such as ascribing an intermediate role to 'internal work motivation' as a 'critical psychological state'.

Research in The Netherlands has also been directed at the validity of the job characteristics model. Foeken (1979) found little empirical support for the model on a number of points, but he observes that the jobs in his study were very homogeneous, which may have stood in the way of a true test of the model. Algera (1981) also investigated the validity of the model. That study evaluated the model by means of a statistical technique which makes it possible to test the causal relationships among the variables in the model simultaneously (LISREL, Jöreskog and Sörbom, 1978). The model was evaluated on the basis of data from Wall *et al.* (1978), Hackman and Oldham (1975), and his own data on 61 jobs in the Dutch steel industry. The model was not consistent with empirical data, but there was a strong relationship between task characteristics and reactions of task performers (satisfaction, psychosomatic complaints, job involvement, absenteeism). The Dutch sample showed these relationships when task characteristics were based on task performers' perceptions as well as on perceptions of others (mainly supervisors) (see also Algera, 1983). These findings provide a basis for a reformulation of the model. Steers and Mowday (1977) found the model of some use as a practical instrument in task design, but incomplete from a conceptual point of view. This was particularly true for the specification of how the critical psychological states influence motivation, and for the lack of construct validity for the broadly defined moderator variable 'growth need strength'. Katz (1978a, 1978b) studied the effect of yet another variable supposed to moderate the relationship of the model's five job dimensions with satisfaction, the length of time a task performer has been doing the job. It indeed appeared to act as a moderator, chiefly for the job dimension 'autonomy'. The correlation between autonomy and satisfaction was negative for new task performers (on the job 0–3 months); it was positive for task performers who had been on the job somewhat longer, and it was highest for task performers who had been on the job for about one year, slowly decreasing to almost zero for task performers with over 15 years' service. Although Katz (1978a, 1978b) used a transversal design, the results of his study point up an important aspect, the dimension of time, and the likelihood that reactions of task performers are not invariant in time. Of course individual differences can occur here, too.

In a critical review of the job characteristics approach Roberts and Glick (1981) conclude that the model's theoretical statements are not entirely clear and that the associated empirical work frequently fails to test the relations discussed by the researchers. Three kinds of relations are often inappropriately assumed to be isomorphic: *within-person* relations, among perceptions of tasks and of other attitudinal and behavioral characteristics of the individual; *person-situation* relations, linking independently assessed characteristics of jobs or situations with characteristics of individuals; and *situational* relations, which involve only characteristics of objective jobs or situations that are invariant across people. They catalogue the research in this area and arrive at the conclusion that task design research has not moved beyond an exploratory stage.

To sum up, let us state that the job characteristics model does offer pointers for diagnosing work situations, but from a theoretical perspective the model is still fairly obscure. This is particularly true for the critical psychological states and the role of moderator variables. As to the latter, many authors examined the importance of individual differences as moderators in the relationship between task characteristics and behavior and attitude of task performers. But in his survey, White (1978) comes to the conclusion that the generality of effects of individual differences is limited. Shepard and Houghland (1978) also stress the fact that results of research on this subject are not consistent.

Beer (1976) points out the importance of better instruments for measuring task characteristics, for the benefit of research on the relationship between task characteristics and satisfaction, motivation, and performance of workers. He feels the scales of Turner and Lawrence (1965) are the precursors of more sophisticated instruments which will be needed in the future.

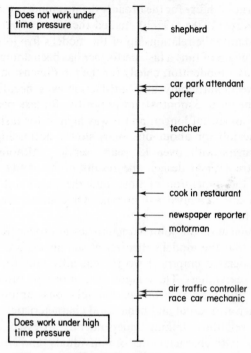

Figure 3. Example of a graphic scale, representing the task characteristic 'working under time pressure'.

Recently Algera (1981) developed an instrument for measuring task characteristics which affect a worker's behavior and attitude. This instrument consists of 24 graphic scales for which common occupations or working conditions are used as anchors (see figure 3). The scale value of each anchor is empirically determined. In the construction phase of this instrument very much effort was put into boosting the psychometric properties of the scales.

The definitions of the scales are comparable to the scales in the original Turner and Lawrence study (not to the attributes, which are more abstract), supplemented by relevant task characteristics mentioned by other authors. The results obtained in a field study using this instrument were rather encouraging. Especially important was the finding that task performers of rather simple jobs have no trouble using the graphic scales in evaluating their own jobs, which leads to psychometrically acceptable results.

5. RELATIONSHIPS BETWEEN TASK CHARACTERISTICS AND OTHER VARIABLES

5.1. Technology

Task characteristics are not isolated, but are related to other variables. Turner and Lawrence (1965) see their task characteristics as primarily determined by technology: 'By "intrinsic task attributes" we meant such characteristics of the job as the amount of variety, autonomy, responsibility, and interaction with others built into its design'. From this viewpoint, task characteristics can be regarded as dependent on the technological task design chosen. In the design phase, a system designer will generally have at his disposal several solutions which often have different implications for the resulting tasks and the task characteristics associated with them. In other words, there are task characteristics which have automatically come about through a particular choice of technology by the designer.

There is quite a difference of opinion in the literature on the concept of technology. A literature study by Andriessen and Van Baren (1976) showed that it is operationalized in very different ways. These authors feel such differences are due to the following:

a. the term is sometimes applied at the organizational level, where it refers to the entire production process, and sometimes at the level of individual task performance, where it refers to task characteristics;

b. it sometimes refers to machinery, equipment, etc. ('hardware' approach) and sometimes to such concepts as standardization, cognitive complexity, etc. ('software' approach);

c. it is used with regard to different aspects of the input-throughput-output system, namely, the materials, the processing, or the products;

d. it is described generally (based on only a few variables) or specifically (based on a farily large number of variables).

In this connection it is interesting to know at what organizational level differentiation in technological characteristics shows the strongest relationship with reactions by task performers. Rousseau (1978) carried out a study in 19 different production departments of 13 different organizations. Technological differentiation was determined at departmental level (using Thompson's (1967) classification scheme, a fairly general method) and at the level of the individual task performer (using a variant of the Job Diagnostic Survey). The study showed that technological differentiation at departmental level was related to the satisfaction of task performers, but that the relationship between task characteristics and satisfaction was considerably stronger. Despite some methodological flaws, the study suggests that prediction of the reactions of task performers is better on the basis of technological differentiation at the task level than at the departmental level. This is only logical: even if one, like

Rousseau (1978), limits oneself to tasks which are directly related to the production process, it is to be expected that there still is some variance in task structure within departments, which accounts for an extra portion of the variance in satisfaction.

5.2. Organization structure

Organization structure, like technology, may not be an easily delineated concept (Gerwin, 1979), but it is another variable which can influence task characteristics. Some authors in this field (Nemiroff and Ford, 1976; Hackman, 1977) distinguish mechanistic and organic types of organization, as proposed by Burns and Stalker (1961). The former refers to organizations with a strong hierarchical structure, where the power is centralized in the top of the hierarchy and there are clear-cut rules and procedures. The latter relates to organizations with generally much less precise rules and procedures, and where different parts of the organization may have different working methods.

It seems plausible that organization structure may imply limitations for task design. Organizations with a mechanistic character are not very compatible with tasks where an employee has a great deal of autonomy and decision power. Both Nemiroff and Ford (1976) and Hackman (1977) present models through which reactions of task performers (such as absenteeism, satisfaction, and performance) can be predicted from the congruence or incongruence of three classes of variables: organization structure, task design, and individual characteristics of task performers.

6. CONCLUSION

It is clear that the relationship between task characteristics and reactions of task performers depends on several variables. Although there is sufficient indication that task characteristics affect the behavior and attitude of task performers, there are as yet few consistent findings that specify the relationships and take different moderator variables into consideration. Despite this, organizations are routinely designed or changed, which inevitably affects task design. Assumptions about human behavior, be they implicit or explicit, play an important role. Still today, organizations (often administrative information systems) are being designed on the principles of scientific management. The assumptions of system designers about human behavior can lead to task designs which minimize the role of task performers, employees thus being given the work for which engineers or systems analysts have not yet found technical answers. We agree with Willems (1975) that even our limited psychological knowledge must be applied in the design phase, so that the evaluation of a system is founded on better, or at least different, criteria which will allow for newer and better means of achieving system goals. 'Preventive' work design

(Dekkers, 1977), which takes into account the task characteristics and their influence on the behavior and attitude of task performers resulting from a specified design, can play an important part here.

REFERENCES

Aldag, R. J., Barr, S. H., Brief, A. P. (1981), Measurement of perceived task characteristics. *Psychological Bulletin*, **90**, 415–431.

Alderfer, C. P. (1969), An empirical test of a new theory of human needs. *Organizational Behavior and Human Performance*, **4**, 142–175.

Algera, J. A. (1981), *Kenmerken van werk* [Characteristics of work] (with English summary). Lisse: Swets & Zeitlinger.

Algera, J. A. (1983), 'Objective' and perceived task characteristics as a determinant of reactions by task performers. *Journal of Occupational Psychology*, **56**, 95–107.

Andriessen, J. H. T. H., Baren, C. van (1976), *Technologie, een inventarisatie van enkele betekenissen, problemen en meet instrumenten* [Technology, an inventory of some of its meanings, problems, and measuring instruments]. DOK project, paper nr. 2. Amsterdam: Free University, Dept. of Industrial and Organizational Psychology.

Arnold, H. J., House, R. J. (1980), Methodological and substantive extensions to the job characteristics model of motivation. *Organizational Behavior and Human Performance*, **25**, 161–183.

Atkinson, J. W. (1957), Motivational determinants of risk-taking behavior. *Psychological Review*, **64**, 359–372, quoted in: Cooper, R. (1973), Task characteristics and intrinsic motivation. *Human Relations*, **26**, 3, 387–413.

Beer, M. (1976), The technology of organization development. In: Dunnette, M. D. (Ed.), *Handbook of industrial and organizational psychology*. Chicago: Rand McNally College Publishing Company.

Burns, T., Stalker, G. (1961), *The management of innovation*. London: Tavistock Publications.

Carnall, C. A., Birchall, D. W., Wild, R. (1976), The design of jobs—an outline strategy for diagnosis and change. *Management Services*, **20**, 6, 48–51.

Cooper, R. (1973), Task characteristics and intrinsic motivation. *Human Relations*, **26**, 387–413.

Dekkers, J. M. M. (1977), *Produktiesysteem en taakstructuur* [Production systems and task structure]. Nijmegen: Catholic University, Dept. of Industrial and Organizational Psychology.

Dunham, R. B. (1976), The measurement and dimensionality of job characteristics. *Journal of Applied Psychology*, **61**, 404–409.

Dunham, R. B., Aldag, R. J., Brief, A. P. (1977), Dimensionality of task design as measured by the job Diagnostic Survey. *Academy of Management Journal*, **20**, 209–223.

Foeken, H. J. (1979), *Arbeidsvoldoening van operators: Het model van Hackman en Oldham nader beschouwd* [Job satisfaction of operators: A closer look at the model of Hackman and Oldham]. Eindhoven: Technological University.

Fry, L. W. (1976), The maligned F. W. Taylor: A reply to his many critics. *Academy of Management Review*, **1**, 3, 124–129.

Gerwin, D. (1979), The comparative analysis of structure and technology: A critical appraisal. *Academy of Management Review*, **4**, 1, 41–51.

Globerson, S., Crossman, E. R. F. W. (1976), Non-repetitive time: An objective index of job variety. *Organizational Behavior and Human Performance*, **17**, 231–240.

Guilford, J. P. (1967), *The nature of human intelligence*. New York: McGraw-Hill.

Hackman, J. R. (1969), Toward understanding the role of tasks in behavioral research. *Acta Psychologica*, **31**, 97–128.

Hackman, J. R. (1977), Work design. In: Hackman, J. R., Lloyd Suttle, J. (Eds.), *Improving life at work: Behavioral science approaches to organizational change*. Santa Monica (Cal.): Goodyear, 98–162.

Hackman, J. R., Lawler III, E. E. (1971), Employee reactions to job characteristics. *Journal of Applied Psychology Monograph*, **55**, 259–286.

Hackman, J. R., Oldham, G. R. (1975), Development of the Job Diagnostic Survey. *Journal of Applied Psychology*, **60**, 159–170.

Hackman J. R., Oldham, G. R. (1976), Motivation through the design of work: Test of a theory. *Organizational Behavior and Human Performance*, **16**, 250–279.

Hackman, J. R., Oldham, G. R. (1980), *Work redesign*. New York: Addison-Wesley.

Hackman, J. R., Oldham, G. R., Janson, R., Purdy, K. (1975), A new strategy for job enrichment. *California Management Review*, **17**, 57–71.

Hermans, H. J. M. (1976), *PMT (Prestatie Motivatie Test), handleiding* [A manual to the Achievement Motivation Test]. Amsterdam: Swets & Zeitlinger.

Hill, A. B. (1969), The measurement of work variety. *The International Journal of Production Research*, **8**, 1, 25–39.

Hulin, C. L., Blood, M. R. (1968), Job enlargement, individual differences, and worker responses. *Psychological Bulletin*, **69**, 41–55.

Jöreskog, K. G., Sörbom, D. (1978). *LISREL IV, A general computer program for estimation of linear structural equation systems by maximum likelihood methods*. University of Uppsala.

Katz, R. (1978a), Job longevity as a situational factor in job satisfaction. *Administrative Science Quarterly*, **23**, 204–223.

Katz, R. (1978b), The influence of job longevity on employee reactions to task characteristics. *Human Relations*, **31**, 703–725.

Locke, E. A. (1968), Toward a theory of task motivation and incentives. *Organizational Behavior and Human Performance*, **3**, 157–189.

Maslow, A. H. (1954), *Motivation and personality*. New York: Harper and Row.

Nemiroff, P. M., Ford, D. L. (1976), Task effectiveness and human fulfillment in organizations: A review and development of a conceptual contingency model. *Academy of Management Review*, **1**, 4, 69–82.

O'Reilly III, Ch. A, Caldwell, D. F. (1979), Informational influence as a determinant of perceived task characteristics and job satisfaction. *Journal of Applied Psychology*, **64**, 157–165.

Porter, L. W., Lawler, E. E. (1968), *Managerial attitudes and performance*. Homewood, Ill.: Irwin.

Roberts, K. H., Glick, W. (1981), The job characteristics approach to task design: A critical review. *Journal of Applied Psychology*, **66**, 193–217.

Rousseau, Denise M. (1978), Measures of technology as predictors of employee attitude. *Journal of Applied Psychology*, **63**, 213–218.

Schwab, D. P., Cummings, L. L. (1976), A theoretical analysis of the impact of task scope on employee performance. *Academy of Management Review*, **1**, 2, 23–35.

Shepard, J. M., Hougland, J. G. (1978), Contingency theory: 'complex man' or 'complex organization'? *Academy of Management Review*, **3**, 3, 413–427.

Sims, H. P., Szilagyi, A. D., Keller, R. T. (1976), The measurement of job characteristics. *Academy of Management Journal*, **19**, 2, 195–212.

Steers, R. M., Mowday, R. T. (1977), The motivational properties of tasks. *Academy of Management Review*, **2**, 645–658.

Steers, R. M., Spencer, D. G. (1977), The role of achievement motivation in job design. *Journal of Applied Psychology*, **62**, 472–479.

Stone, E. F. (1979), Field independence and perceptions of task characteristics: A laboratory investigation. *Journal of Applied Psychology*, **64**, 305–310.
Taylor, F. W. (1911), *The principles of scientific management*. New York: Harper and Row.
Thompson, J. D. (1967), *Organizations in action*. New York: McGraw-Hill.
Turner, A. N., Lawrence, P. R. (1965), *Industrial jobs and the worker. An investigation of response to task attributes*. Boston: Harvard University.
Umstot, D. D., Bell, Jr., C. H., Mitchell, T. R. (1976), Effects of job enrichment and task goals on satisfaction and productivity: Implications for job design. *Journal of Applied Psychology*, **61**, 379–394.
Vroom, V. H. (1964), *Work and motivation*. New York: Wiley.
Wall, T. D., Clegg, C. W., Jackson, P. R. (1978), An evaluation of the Job Characteristics Model. *Journal of Occupational Psychology*, **51**, 183–196.
Weiss, H. M., Shaw, J. B. (1979), Social influences on judgments about tasks. *Organizational Behavior and Human Performance*, **24**, 126–140.
White, J. K. (1978), Individual differences and the job quality-worker response relationship: review, integration, and comments. *Academy of Management Review*, **3**, 267–280.
White, S. E., Mitchell, T. R. (1979), Job enrichment versus social cues: A comparison and competitive tests. *Journal of Applied Psychology*, **64**, 1–9.
Willems, P. J. (1970), Werk ontwerpen [Designing work]. In: Drenth, P. J. D., Willems, P. J., Wolff, Ch. J. de (Eds.), *Bedrijfspsychologie, onderzoek en evaluatie* [Industrial Psychology, research and evaluation]. Deventer: Van Loghum Slaterus, 273–289.
Willems, P. J. (1975), Psychologen: Systeemfitters of constructeurs? [Psychologists, fitting people to systems or systems designing?]. In: Gils, M. R. van (Ed.), *Werken en niet-werken in een veranderende samenleving* [Working and not-working in a changing society]. Amsterdam: Swets & Zeitlinger.

Handbook of Work and Organizational Psychology
Edited by P. J. D. Drenth, Hk. Thierry, P. J. Willems and C. J. de Wolff
© 1984, John Wiley & Sons, Ltd.

2.4. Personnel appraisal

Pieter J. D. Drenth

1. INTRODUCTION

In many respects, the appraisal of employees is a constant source of concern for the personnel department. This can be partly traced to the fact that, in practice, the appraisal of others is and will remain a sensitive matter, especially when the appraisal is negative and this must be communicated to the person in question. These factors may activate all kinds of psychological mechanisms (resistance, denial, aggression, discouragement) in the person appraised that can seriously upset the relationship between judge and judged. The fear of these consequences may activate, in the appraiser too, all kinds of psychological mechanisms, which in their turn may fail to do justice to the objectivity and fairness of the judgment.

These problems can be partly traced to the applied system, which does not sufficiently meet certain technical or psychometric requirements. It is hard to play billiards with a bent cue, albeit a surprising and artful shot will always be a possibility.

Perhaps they are more importantly due to the organizational and social context, in which the appraisal process and its implementation take place. Employee appraisals are part of the system of control and stimulation regarding the employees of an organization and cannot be isolated from that system. If the system of 'personnel management' is unsound or if a number of important organizational or social prerequisites for its functioning are not met, the appraisal system, however good in itself, will not work.

In this chapter, we will systematically discuss some of the above-mentioned

Prof. dr. P. J. D. Drenth, Subfaculteit Psychologie der Vrije Universiteit De Boelelaan 1981, 1081 HV AMSTERDAM

197

topics. The aims of appraisals, the question of what should be appraised, and the requirements an appraisal system should meet will be discussed, in that order. In addition, we will present a brief review of various systems in use with their pros and cons. The chapter will be concluded by a discussion of what conditions are to be met or are beneficial for an appraisal system to function well.

Before actually discussing the subject, first this: in the introduction the appraisal system was referred to a few times. One might well ask, whether the appraisal in fact requires a system and whether part of the problem would disappear if the often impersonal, bureaucratic 'cross-the-square forms' (or, as they are sometimes called: lotto forms) were not used.

Obviously, the larger and more complex an organization becomes, the harder it is for a person evaluating employees to draw on his own experience or observations in order to gain insight into the employee's actual performance and potential performance. And yet, such insight should be the basis of such measures and decisions. If, for this, one has to go by the experience and observations of others, it is difficult to see how it can be done without the information having been *recorded* in a fair, comparative manner. In fact, this is the justification for the use of appraisal systems.

This is why industrial companies and organizations of some size show a distinct preference for and an increasing use of appraisal systems. Thus, in a study in the Netherlands (COP, 1955), it was found that supervisors and subordinates both positively appreciated the use of a system. 'Some sort of system is better than no system at all'—this was the majority's reaction. According to a survey we did among middle- and upper-level employees in the early seventies, it appeared that appraisals of managers took place systematically in 88 of the 127 companies responding to an industrial questionnaire (van Ginniken, 1974, p. 89). An in-depth survey of middle managers in four large organizations (private, semi-governmental, and governmental) revealed that appraisals do not take place as often and as regularly as would appear from the first industrial survey. The data in table 1 shows that in only half of the cases appraisals took place annually.

Table 1. Frenquency of appraisals (N = 545)
(van Dam and Drenth, 1976, p. 208).

	N	%
2x per year	12	0.2
1x per year	289	53
1x per two years	109	20
irregular	135	24.8

The frequencies are approximately the same as those for managers in England and the United States. The developments for rank and file as compared to staff and line managers, however, do not run quite parallel. Rowe concluded that 74% of the 460 English companies used a system of employee appraisal (Rowe, 1970). Surveying the trends between 1950 and 1957, Whisler and Harper (1963) showed that, in the USA, the percentage of companies claiming to use an appraisal system decreased from 95.3% to 77% for rank and file and rose from 45.6% to 58% for managment. According to the conclusion of Campbell *et al.* (1970), this trend has continued for middle- and upper-level personnel in the USA. Only a few companies do not use some sort of system, although its nature and use many vary not only between but also within companies. On the basis of a recent review, Lazer and Wikstrom (1978) set the percentage for lower management at 74, for middle management at 71, and for upper management at 55.

2. THE GOALS OF EMPLOYEE APPRAISALS

In his 'Uneasy look at performance appraisal' McGregor (1957) expressed what many a practicioner had already experienced: it is difficult to combine the roles of judge and counselor. In other words, the goal 'control and management' is hardly compatible with the goal 'guidance and development'. Thus, McGregor (1957, 1960) and Maier (1963) strongly oppose this dual role of appraisals.

These two comprehensive goals do appear regularly in the literature on the goals of appraisals (Anstey *et al.*, 1976; Cummings and Schwab, 1973). At a more specific level, one could make still more refined distinctions which even more clearly delineate the 'multi-purpose' character of appraisals. Thus, Spriegel (1962) mentions guidance, promotion, training and development, discharge and remuneration in order of frequency, based on a sample of 400 companies in the USA. Lazer and Wikstrom (1978) use other terms: management development, performance measurement, performance improvement, remuneration, potential assessment, feedback, personnel planning, and improvement of communication and relations, also in order of frequency. These classifications overlap somewhat. On the other hand, not all goals mentioned in the classification of Lazer and Wikstrom are coordinate. Thus one could successfully argue that performance measurement is a phase preceding performance improvement, and that feedback is one of the means for improving both development and communication.

Moreover, it does not readily appear from surveys of companies that appraisals are used as criteria, because this is usually not an operational objective for the company. However, the purpose of providing criteria can be really seen as an important function of employee appraisals from the viewpoint of organization research. Criteria for selection (and for validating selection instruments)

Scheme 1. Goals and characteristics of employee appraisals

Goal / Characteristics	Personnel management	Guidance, development	Potential assessment	Criterion
What is appraised	Results	Work behavior	Personality characteristics and capacities	Performance behavior
Point of view	Relation goal-means	Qualitative aspects	Predictive aspects	Quantitative aspects
Time orientation	Previous period	Past and near future	(Far) future	Present
Emphasis	Positive aspects	Positive and negative aspects	Expected growth	Neutral representation
Important requirements	Comprehensiveness, objectivity	Specificity, clarity for person concerned	Predictive validity	Objectivity, relevance

or for training come to mind here. In an attempt to identify the main elements of what was said above, purposes of appraisals can be divided into four main categories:

a. Use in decisions concerning the organization and management of personnel, e.g. measures in the area of salaries and wages, (extra) allowances, normal promotions, permanent appointments, transfers, dismissals, and the like.

b. Use with a view to performance improvement, motivation, and development. These effects will occur mainly through feedback and the appraisal interview.

c. Use in the framework of trying to identify potential candidates for upper management positions. Here the often mentioned (management-)potential assessment is involved.

d. Use as a criterion, e.g. for selection and training.

In scheme 1 we have plotted these four purposes on the horizontal axis and the various aspects and characteristics of the appraisal systems on the vertical one. The scheme itself provides typologies of the various characteristics for the different goals. In this presentation the differences are somewhat sharpened, but in practice there are gradual transitions between them. However, the differences in orientation and emphasis are so distinct that one suspects it will not be easy to combine them into one coherent program.

The first type of appraisal, *personnel management* oriented, will be based primarily on actual performance and results. The basic idea of incentive wages, for example, is that a remuneration is felt to be unfair if it is not somehow coupled to the output (directly or relative to one's own input; see Lawler, 1981). This involves the relation between ends and means, or costs and benefits, and the extent to which the person appraised manages to optimize them. Here, the appraiser will turn to the period past; he is appraising what has been achieved so far, without considering all kinds of possibilities for development or aspects of expected growth.[1] The emphasis is, to be sure, upon positive aspects: what was achieved by the person concerned, what has he managed to do. Here, two points of view are of importance: firstly, whether the achievement was rated in a reliable manner (preferably in a measurable or numerical form), and, secondly, whether the information can be consolidated into one comprehensive rating. Ultimately, decisions regarding promotions, bonus allowances, and dismissals should be based on 'unidimensional' information. In practice, this will often amount to the requirement of a comprehensive, overall appraisal.

Matters are quite different with respect to the majority of these characteristics if the purpose is *guidance and development*. Employee appraisal, in this context to be called 'job appraisal', is then mainly concerned with work behavior, especially its qualitative aspects. Suggestions for improvement or readjustment will have to be linked to these qualitative aspects. In this case, one will of course first turn to the preceding period. However, particularly during the appraisal interview, the (near) future will be frequently discussed.

In fact, an attempt by superior and subordinate to jointly formulate new objectives and behavioral guidelines based on the results of the preceding period is one of the most important characteristics of the appraisal methods proposed by both McGregor and Drucker (Management by Objectives). For an effective evaluation and discussion both positive and negative aspects will have to be raised. Probably, for the many who live by the adage that one can learn from mistakes only, the emphasis will be on the less positive and improbable aspects of work behavior. Here we would like to remind the reader of the experiences of Meyer c.s. (1955, 1977) at General Electric; there-from it appears that criticism provokes many defensive reactions but few behavioral changes!

The extent to which the appraised has a clear insight into the appraisal is very important. The appraisal will be useful as a guideline for improvement, only if he is able to understand it and to relate appraisal to behavior. As a guideline for readjustment and improvement an overall appraisal will not suffice either. The appraisal must be specific and definite.

A sound *potential assessment*, on the other hand, will again be quite different. In this case, the appraisal is aimed at those aspects that anticipate future developments. Aspects of behavior and achievements making such predictions or extrapolations possible should be emphasized. Since these predictions nearly always concern future behavior in a situation and context different from the current one, there will be little room for a very literal extrapolation of current

[1]This does not in the least mean that remuneration systems are just control systems or that remuneration may not refer to future performance; see also this Handbook, ch. 4.11.

behavior. Rather, the emphasis will be on constant determinants in the behavior of the appraised, involving personality factors and capacities. Clearly, it is the (far) future one has in mind. In appraising, then, one will be looking for indicators for further growth. Expected growth and development possibilities are at issue here. The only criterion for the quality of a potential assessment is, in fact, its predictive value (predictive validity). The effectiveness of the system is measured by the extent to which it can accurately identify future successful managers, judges of law courts, professors, field officers, etc.

In using appraisals as *criteria* for evaluating selection procedures or training we are concerned particularly with the requirements of objectivity and relevance; objectivity because this is a requirement of an evaluation criterion anyway and relevance because such a norm for selection and training should in itself adequately operationalize what is essential to the organization. The emphasis should be on aspects that are crucial in view of the aims of the organization. What is to be appraised can be deduced from the objectives. In many cases, this will be performance or output. It may also imply behavioral changes (medicare, social work).

Since the assessment must be as objective as possible, it is obvious that the emphasis will be on quantitative aspects. The assessment should be as objective and neutral as possible and it should not primarily emphasize positive or negative aspects, as is the case with salary or job appraisals.

The descriptions of the four goals and the requirements derived therefrom imposed upon the system, on the one hand, and the divergent orientations of the appraisers on the other, seem to be sufficient arguments *against* integrating all of these goals into a single appraisal system and procedure. In the literature there is an increasing tendency to propose that separate systems, procedures, and times be used for these different purposes. This applies to both the separation of 'salary appraisal' and 'job appraisal' (McGregor, 1960; Maier, 1963; Meyer *et al.*, 1965; Kane and Lawler, 1979) and for the separation of 'job or salary appraisal' and 'potential assessment' (de Quay, 1973). Such separations attempt to disentangle all sorts of undesirable mixtures, e.g. 'expected growth' co-determining the current salary or 'intelligence' being a subject in a discussion about work. At the same time, these separations try to avoid various conflicts that may arise from the union of incompatible goals. Think of the conflict within the individual between the desire for fair feedback about what went wrong (work improvement) and the desire for the most positive appraisal possible (salary increase) or of the conflict within the appraiser between the desire for an objective and comprehensive evaluation (dismissal) and the desire for a comprehensible, specific and discussible appraisal for a guidance interview.

We are afraid that, in practice, these goals are often mixed up and that these matters are not sufficiently kept apart in the systems, procedures or appraisal interviews.

Not infrequently it may be observed that establishing the (variable part of) salary is directly coupled to the job appraisal and the appraisal interview.[2] And not infrequently the job appraisal contains a series of questions about performance, attitudes, and the like, followed at the end by a question about 'future development possibilities'. Through this question, an element of 'potential assessment' crops up in the regular job appraisal. In all likelihood there are various practical considerations lurking behind this 'mixing' of goals (costs, time, effort).

It is probably not that easy to keep these issues separated. In a survey of 33 large companies in the USA, Campbell *et al.* (1970) found that the majority was characterized by being primarily oriented towards one of the following three personal policies: Selection-orientation, Training-orientation, or Motivation and Development-orientation. In the first orientation, for example, both potential assessments and the use of appraisals in decisions about appointments and allocations play a predominant role. In the second orientation, the emphasis is on training and development as well as on the capability to identify (through appraisals) such needs in individuals and organizations. In the third orientation, the administrative use and the selection goal of appraisals have faded into the background altogether; the stimulation and guidance roles of the supervisor and manager have instead become the issue. The authors found only one company where these three orientations were well integrated and where the instruments (including appraisals) used for various 'roles' were adequately prepared.

It seems useful, at the end of this section, to note the difference between the *goal* and the *function* of an appraisal. If an appraisal is designed for a specific goal, it does not mean that it functions exclusively as such. An appraisal can have numerous side effects: confirmation of a certain power distribution, adaptation of employees to an existing structure, particular regulation of conflict or prevention of unrest. In this connection, Grunow (1976) speaks of the latent functions of appraisals. Insofar as these functions are unintended, Grunow's suggestion to pursue awareness of them appears worth following. To the extent that here consciously used sub-goals of appraisals are concerned, readjustment seems desirable if in the long run one does not want the credibility of appraisals to be seriously affected.

3. WHAT SHOULD BE APPRAISED?

In the scheme discussed in the above section, one aspect was mentioned that needs further elaboration: the issue of what should be appraised. In fact we

---

[2] In some remuneration systems such an integration is appropriate (e.g. forms of contract wages), but often they are separate circuits and the openness of the interview is clouded by thoughts about wage/salary consequences.

can choose from three possibilities: results, (work) behavior, and personality traits.

The advantages of *personality traits* seem obvious: one deals with more or less constant characteristics, so that the appraisals offer the possibility to make predictions. This concurs with the need to make decisions about promotions and transfers. Furthermore, personality traits are highly abstracted from incidental events and facts and, since they can be generalized, they seem to carry more weight. For the appraiser it is, so to speak, safer to discuss personality traits, illustrating them by means of a number of incidents, than to discuss the incidents themselves, in which case the appraised may argue or criticize. It is, therefore, not surprising that on appraisal forms one keeps stumbling over personality traits such as reliability, flexibility, independence, decisiveness, self-confidence, etc.

In addition, the psychological literature (see e.g. Hofstee, 1974) prompts us to be very wary of judging 'personality traits'. In the first place, we know that determining the strength of personality traits by means of observational methods, without the latter being based on a large number of concrete behavior observations, is neither very reliable nor valid. This is partly due to the fact that it often involves rather complex concepts that do not easily and unequivocally refer to concrete behavior, which in its turn causes the inter-rater agreement to be low.

Moreover, the concepts used are often situation-dependent and not unequivocally defined. The concept of reliability may serve as an example. What do we mean by an unreliable person? Someone who does not return borrowed books, someone who does not keep his appointments, someone who fills out his tax forms rather carelessly, or someone who cannot be trusted when in charge of the cash register? The relation between these various operationalizations of unreliability is very low (Mischel, 1968). Raters, when appraising 'reliability' with different elements in mind, will not easily agree in their judgements about one and the same person.

A discussion about personality traits will not be very fruitful, because of the above-mentioned semantic and conceptual obscurities. Moreover, many personality traits are difficult to change since they belong to the habitus of the individual, and feedback interviews will often lead to irritation, defensiveness, and denials, offering but few starting points for coaching and counseling.

Kavanagh (1971) attempted to salvage personality traits by pointing out that some of them certainly possess construct validity and can have their place in some nomological network around the ultimate criterion for work performance. Kane and Lawler's response (1979) seems devastating: this may be so, they say, but they are, at best, causes or limiting factors for the performance with which the organization is ultimately concerned. They are surrogates for performance criteria just as much as an intelligence test is a surrogate for the appraisal of school performance. They describe a person rather than his performance and thus can have no place in an appraisal system.

We should, however, make one exception. In the previous section it appeared that, for the goal of *potential assessment*, the emphasis is in fact on personality traits and capacities. In potential assessments two forces are active, enhancing this emphasis. Firstly, the prediction is often oriented towards behavior in a very different context and under completely different conditions. Thus, attention should be paid to those aspects that determine the behavior in different situations, and this need for generalization causes the emphasis to shift to (more trans-situationally constant) capacities and personality traits.

Secondly, it is not only generalization over situations that is involved, but also generalization over time. Often, assessments of growth and development have to be made covering a substantial period. Therefore, again, the emphasis tends to shift more towards (temporally constant) personality factors. Thus, in the well-known systems for potential assessments one encounters qualities such as analytic ability, realism, ability to anticipate, helicopter view, cooperation, self-esteem, effectiveness, expressive skills, initiative, self-control, tenacity, and the like.

Of course, the above-mentioned objections against appraising personality factors remain. It is therefore an illusion to think that one can effortlessly compile a list of such personality factors and then decide that one has a workable system for personality appraisals. The construction of a potential-assessment system requires extensive and careful empirical research. From an analysis of the ultimate job requirements it should be deduced which characteristics and traits are involved. Next, one should compile a sufficiently large number of items for these factors. These items should be selected on the basis of their intercorrelations and possible validities and carefully composed into scales. These scales, then, should be tested for their reliability and predicitive validity.

To test validity, one may use to kinds of criteria, i.e. subjective or objective criteria. Muller's (1970) study is an example of a validity study with subjective criteria. He compared his items and scales with the criterion 'expected ultimate level' of the person in the organization, operationalized as the probable attainable salary-group, estimated on the basis of an extrapolation of the individual's salary curve. The problem in Muller's research was that in all likelihood the subjective criterion rating was known to the raters, so that the risk of contamination cannot be excluded. As a result, it is not really an (external) validating study we have here, but rather an analysis of the determinants of overall subjective potential assessments.

An example of validation using an objective criterion is the study of Tigchelaar (1974); he validated his items and scales against the criterion: salary growth corrected for age and seniority. After a careful selection of the items and construction of the scales, 40 to 50% of the variance in career success could be predicted by means of potential assessments.

A warning seems appropriate here. From the above it would appear that one could conclude that the validity of items and scales is the most important criterion for potential assessments. That is correct. But it does not mean, that all valid items can be used just like that. One should realize that selecting future managers on the basis of a validation of the predictors using a criterion based on behavior and performance of *current* management leads to the continuation of current policy and approach. In any case, a critical analysis of 'valid' predictors seems appropriate. Does one wish to continue current management policy or, putting it more sharply, freeze it?

For the sake of completeness, we wish to point out that procedures for identifying future management should, of course, never be based on just one source of information, the potential assessment. In the literature, a variety of methods is mentioned, such as recording interests, biographical information, cognitive tests and personality inventories, situational tests and clinical interviews, that are or are not applied in special 'assessment centers' (for a survey see Campbell *et al.*, 1970). In this respect, both the more actuarial approaches, such as the EIMP-study of Standard Oil Co., NJ (Laurent, 1962, 1970) or the study of the Industrial Relations Center at the University of Minnesota (Mahoney *et al.*, 1969), and the more clinical approaches, e.g. the well-known management progress study at AT & T (Bray, 1964), have been fruitful.

Appraisals that do not aim at assessing potential are left with the choice between *performance/results* and work *behavior/activities*. It was noted in the previous section that in using appraisals as a criterion as well as for administrative decisions (remuneration, tenure/dismissal) objective results are considered the most just and thus more useful. In guidance and coaching, however, one should preferably pay attention to activities and behavior, because they provide the best basis for an appraisal interview.

However, it does not seem commendable to emphasize one of the two alternatives too explicitly. Firstly, we wish to refer to an idea presented by Kane and Lawler (1979): sometimes there are several roads leading to the same goal and qualitatively one could be just as good as the other. The appraisal of a job that, as they call it, can be characterized by equifinality (more than one acceptable road) must emphasize results. The appraisal of a job without equifinality should, however, emphasize work behavior.

Porter *et al.* (1975) also note the importance of both aspects. They suggest that appraisal systems have a distinct directional influence. The appraised are influenced by the fact that certain aspects of their work and performance will be either positively or negatively judged, just like tests and exams at school determine the nature of learning behavior. An appraisal that exclusively emphasizes results may well evoke behavior that clashes with other goals that are also important to the organization. It may lead to high production at the cost of morale to increased quantity at the cost of quality, to high sales at the cost of customer satisfaction, etc. Conversely, sole emphasis on work behavior may also have undesirable influences, in the sense that activities rather than achievements are stimulated. For instance, a manager's people-oriented approach may be rather unproductive, and working strictly according to rules or agreements may, in emergency situations, have harmful effects.

In a large number of cases the choice is not difficult, simply because no direct or measurable results are available (service jobs, control jobs, panel watching). This number is rapidly increasing, due to the current tendency in commerce and industry to introduce automation and computerized systems. In such cases, one is necessarily dependent on the appraisal of work behavior or activities. Here, two problems occur which are not mutually independent: first, how concrete or abstract should the appraisals of behavior be; second, how many factors should be included in the system. The first problem involves balancing the pros and cons of too extreme alternatives. In scheme 2 a number of examples of the alternatives involved here are presented.

The advantages of emphasizing more concrete behavior factors (left column in scheme 2) are that they can be perceived more objectively, are closer to observable behavior, and do not presuppose any personality theory. The

Scheme 2.   A number of (random) examples of three levels of behavior descriptions.

Incidental activities	Habitual behavior	Abstract factors
—is always on time	—keeps agreements	—attention to duty
—takes too long breaks	—quality of work preparation	—independence
—has reports ready in time	—dealings with clients	—sociability
—desk is a mess	—prepared to put in extra effort	—motivation
—cannot stand criticism	—work speed	—flexibility
—is sloppily dressed	—technical competence	—analytic ability
—has difficulty finding words in cases of disagreement	—openness to new ideas	—ability to organize
	—stimulation of subordinates	—leadership
—admits mistakes	—prepared to delegate	—creativity
—is able to chair meetings of Works Council well	—being able to make decisions when necessary	
—argues with maintenance mechanics	—knows own shortcomings	
	—way of formulating problems	
—is too buddy-buddy with the secretaries	—is knowledgeable in his/her professional field	

drawbacks are: the behavioral factors are too incidental and cannot be easily generalized, which implies a danger of a high degree of irrelevance.

These objections do not pertain to the factors in the right-hand column. Here, however, a problem arises which was mentioned earlier in connection with personality traits as a basis for performance appraisal: a high degree of semantic opacity and lack of clear-cut definitions, because the traits are too far removed from observable behavior. This results in insufficient agreement, not only between raters but also between the judgments of rater and ratee, which may have all kinds of unpleasant consequences for the appraisal interview.

Obviously, both the Scylla of too much concreteness and the Charybdis of too much abstraction should be avoided; one should try to find a solution at some intermediate level, i.e. in the area of *habitual behavior*. Then one does not, so to speak, dive too deeply into the personality structure at the risk of losing touch with reality, nor does one stay too near the surface at the risk of getting lost in irrelevant details. In the middle column of scheme 2 several examples of such habitual behavior are listed, indicating in what direction we think solutions should be sought.

In this connection the optimum *number* of aspects to be rated is the second problem deserving attention. We will present a survey of the various systems of performance rating in one of the following sections. Among these are a few where the numbers of factors is not problematic (overall appraisals, free interview). But most systems contain some specific factors or aspects which are subject to appraisal. The question then is, what is the optimum number.

The answer depends partly on the job of the person to be appraised. If a job has many relevant aspects (head of a department, academic staff member, independent agent), these should be reflected on the appraisal form.

The question of optimum number is also associated with the problem of abstraction just discussed. To the extent that one works with more abstract, 'summary' characteristics or traits (more abstract according to the right-hand column of scheme 2), fewer factors will be available and needed. In principle, however, there is an inexhaustible number of concrete incidental-behavior descriptions that could be considered in the first column of scheme 2.

There have been frequent attempts to resolve this problem by means of factor analysis. This method, however, is so much the fruit of a number of assumptions and a priori choices (does the input consist of items or scales, which items or scales, how are they rotated, what criterion is used to stop the extraction, what type of communalities are selected) that a conclusive criterion for answering the question posed is not easily found in factor analysis.

Besides, the results of various factor analyses of appraisal systems do not yield much that can be used in practice. In the relevant literature, it is repeatedly demonstrated that factor analyses of ratings yield only a very limited number of factors, the first factor generally accounting for by far the greatest part of the variance. This first factor can usually be explained as a kind of general, overall appraisal of 'performance level'; in most cases, it is followed by factors that are likely to much less explain variance, e.g. quality of performance (see Tiffin and McCormick, 1966, p. 231) or some personality traits like motivation or adaptation (see de Wolff, 1963, p. 97). In most cases, factor analysis of existing rating scales leads to a poorly differentiated basis for guidance or coaching. A slightly more differentiated picture may be occasionally obtained if the rating list is compiled very specifically and carefully and for a homogeneous group (see e.g. the four factors task performance, contact, professional knowledge, and accuracy in the rating list for job analysts in Andriessen and Drenth (1973) or the components creativity, productivity, professional knowledge, and social adaptation, as identified by Elshout et al. (1973) in appraisals of academic researchers). But even this does not simply mean that one should confine oneself to the scales found.

Factor analysis or cluster analysis can, however, be helpful in removing all kinds of unrealistic assumptions. It is an illusion to think that a rating system of twenty aspects actually represents twenty separate, discernible facets of work behavior. The analyses mentioned can certainly help to identify a smaller number of factors than there are scales and thus to reduce the number of characteristics involved in the appraisal. This kind of analysis can also help select possible items intended to measure those various aspects or items that should constitute a comprehensive rating dimension (e.g. items that load highest on the first non-rotated factor). Again, however, factor or cluster analysis does not provide definitive answers to the questions of 'how many and which'. An understanding of the behavior to be rated and other metric criteria (see below) must co-determine the choice as well.

The same holds for potential problems in weighting the various aspects for reaching an overall appraisal. Here too, factor analysis may be helpful, but in the end it is the subjective evaluation of what is important to a particular position that forms the basis for this weighting. It would be wise, however, not to lose sight of statistical considerations. Thus, weighting is not only determined by the weight factor assigned to a certain trait, but also by, first, the number of items per trait in the scale (if, that is, one adds up the (un)weighted items and not the mean scale scores), and, second, the variance of the item or scale scores.

4. CRITERIA FOR APPRAISAL SYSTEMS

In this section we will discuss criteria for evaluating appraisal systems. Two categories of criteria may be distinguished: psychometric criteria and utilization criteria (see scheme 3).

The psychometric criteria can be further differentiation in relevance, validity, generalizability, and discriminating power.

Scheme 3. Criteria for rating systems.

Psychometric criteria:	
—Relevance	—Deficiency (−) —Excessiveness (−)
—Validity	—Predictive validity —Construct validity
—Generalizability	—Across methods —Across raters —Across situations —Across items
—Discriminating power	
Utilization criteria:	
—Transparency	
—Acceptability	
—Informational value	

Relevance

By relevance is meant the degree to which the system provides an adequate representation of the domain of the behavior to be appraised. Thus we are concerned with the question as to how adequate the system is in facilitating a reflection of the behavior to be appraised.

Two questions, then, are of further importance. The first one is whether important parts of this domain are adequately considered. If this is not the case, we speak of *deficiency*. The second is whether care has been taken that the system does not include irrelevant aspects of the behavior to be appraised. If these aspects are included, we speak of *excessiveness*.

Thus, relevance is determined mainly by the extent to which both deficiency and excessiveness are avoided.

This concept is related to content validity, as known from test theory. Like content validity, relevance is ultimately based on subjective judgment and not on empirical testing, although the latter may provide some support for this judgment (see e.g. Cronbach, 1971).

Validity

The concept of validity comes straight from test theory and is used in this context in exactly the same sense. We can distinguish between predictive validity and construct validity (Drenth, 1975). The *predictive validity* of an appraisal is the degree to which the appraisal is capable of predicting future performance or behavior. Predictive validity is a relevant criterion only when there is something which has to be predicted. This occurs primarily in potential assessments, in which case it may even involve a criterion that lies in the fairly remote future. In addition, administering personnel changes on the basis of performance appraisals also involves a (implicit) prediction. For it is alleged that the person involved will satisfactorily fulfil another or higher position, due to an assumed matching of his individual qualities with the job requirements.

As with psychological tests, predictive validity should be tested by empirical correlational research. We discussed this criterion in the previous section in connection with potential assessments. De Wolff (1963) presents an extensive survey of predictive validities against external criteria (other appraisals, training results or performance criteria, as the case may be) of the appraisals currently used in organizations. From this survey it may be concluded that although there is considerable variance (depending also on the nature of the appraisal and the criterion), there is no particular reason for enthusiasm about the predictive powers of the appraisal systems currently used.

Regarding *construct validity* the question is whether an item or scale does indeed cover the underlying characteristic. As in test theory, the question of construct validity can be answered only through empirical research. Construct validity is higher as the correlation between the rating and the other indices of the same behavior or the same performance is higher; this is the so-called *convergent validity*. Construct validity is also higher as the rating has a lower correlation with the indices of behavior aspects which are assumed to have no connection with the characteristic to be rated, the so-called *discriminant validity*.

It comes as no surprise that the validity of 'overall ratings' is lower than that of more specifically defined attributes. Nearly all work which people perform is complex and multidimensional (Ronan and Prien, 1966); it is next to impossible to adequately represent the various aspects, to weight them and to integrate them in one overall appraisal in a subjective manner. Without one being aware of it, some aspects are weighted too heavily and others forgotten. In American air force ratings, Thorndike found that rating effectiveness correlated highest with sympathy for the person involved, although by itself this aspect was given the lowest score for importance by the raters (Thorndike, 1949). More specific ratings, however, often are not valid enough either. In their summary, Ronan and Schwartz (1974) report that such validity is seldom above 40 and if it is, the criterion often turns out to be contaminated: the raters were informed about the (objective) performance scores, which were being used as the criterion for validation. Objections may be raised against a number of these studies, in the sense that conceptually the criterion is too far removed from the behavior rated. In such a case, a low correlation is to be expected and is even desirable in view of the criterion of discriminant validity. This is true, for example, of Fleishman *et al.*'s (1955) study, in which performance ratings are compared with absenteeism, accidents, and personnel turnover. In a certain sense, it also holds for the many validity studies which relate ratings with results on psychological tests (e.g. Woodworth and McKinnon, 1975) or on vocational tests (e.g. Whitla and Tirrel, 1953).

However, this does not alter the fact that the validity of ratings is generally not impressive, even in those cases where the aspects to be rated and the criteria are closer to one another. Henceforth, when appraisals are required to be as correct and as just as possible and there is a choice between more objective performance criteria and subjective ones the preference for the former seems very defensible.

Generalizability

Thirdly, there is the criterion of 'generalizability' or consistency, across methods, across raters, across situations, and across items.

The first form, generalizability across *methods*, is tested by constructing two parallel forms of the instrument and intercorrelating them. Thus the specific instrument-bound variance is eliminated.

This way of assessing generalizability is seldom encountered in personnel appraisals not only because there would exist but few parallel forms of rating systems in practice. These could be constructed somehow. But the main problem is that the problems with respect to consistency of ratings are always twofold, i.e. as regards the instrument and as regards the rater. By definition, registration of the behavior rated takes place via the double channel of system and rater. The latter is probably a much more important source of variance than the instrument. If this source were removed by having the two parallel ratings carried out by one and the same person, the resulting agreement between the ratings would be too spurious.

Because of this, more attention has been given to the second form, consistency across *raters*, than to the first one. Generally, the literature is not very positive about the degree of agreement among different raters as measured by correlational research or analysis of variance. Ronan and Schwartz (1974) summarize a large number of such studies in this field and conclude that, in general, raters show little agreement in their assessments of performance and behavior. This was found to hold for a diversity of raters, tasks, and rating instruments. In truly independent ratings the correlations rarely exceed .20.

However, some critical remarks should be made here. First, this kind of research requires two raters who are equally well acquainted with the person concerned. This requirement is not very frequently met, at least not in industrial practice. In addition, there is the more important argument which casts much doubt on whether low agreement between two ratings may in fact be called error variance. In a series of studies, de Wolff (1965, 1970) demonstrated that appraisals continue to be strongly interactional in nature. In other words, the ratee actually behaves differently with different raters and different ratings do reflect some true variance. An important consequence of this finding is the difficulty of predicting from an appraisal how someone will behave and be rated in the future under another superior/rater:

A similar problem occurs with the third criterion, consistency across *situations* and, possibly, across *time*. The coefficient indicating this consistency is the stability coefficient. Under different conditions and at different times people actually behave differently. It is not surprising that these differences are also reflected in the appraisals. And these differences do not let themselves be explained away as error variance. It is for this reason that Kane and Lawler consider stability as an unsuitable measure of reliability for rating systems (Kane and Lawler, 1979).

They go even further and argue that most systems take insufficient account of the fact that people exhibit large variations in the degree of consistency of their behavior and that this fact should be a major aspect of the appraisal. They advocate what they call a completely new paradigm in appraising, which takes into account the distributional aspects of behavior or performance to be rated over a given appraisal period. The question still remains whether the advantages of this more informative 'distributional measurement' counterbalance the drawbacks of its construction (complicated) and particularly of its application (how should this information be utilized for decisions, for instance, about remuneration and placement?). There is still no empirical data available.

The fourth form of consistency, across *items*, should not be used too formally either. The utility of this criterion (also called the homogeneity criterion), indexed by the inter-item-consistency formulae or Cronbach's alpha (see Drenth, 1975, pp. 214–217), depends on the homogeneity or heterogeneity of the characteristic to be rated. In rating a complex concept or a heterogeneous field, homogeneity would lead to lower construct valdity or relevance. It is, of course, true that, given homogeneous attributes, the inter-item consistency of the scales measuring these attributes should be as high as possible. This is enhanced by having a sufficient number of items with high item-test correlations.

Discriminating power

The fourth psychometric aspect that can be used as a criterion for the quality of appraisal systems is the discriminating power of the scales: the extent to which the scales permit adequate expression of differences between people. This is enhanced by three conditions.

First, the extent to which the scales themselves offer enough possibilities for variation (sufficient scale positions) to reflect the variations in behavior. If, for example, there are ten clearly distinguishable performance levels, a scale with only three or four scale positions would be inadequate.

Second, the extent to which the various scale positions are actually used. There are scales whose extreme positions are formulated in such a way that they are hardly ever chosen. The choices accumulate in a few categories in the middle, mostly on the positive side of the scale. Although this can be also caused by other psychological mechanisms (central tendency error, see section 5.4), it can certainly be enhanced by the form of the list and the formulation of the behavioral alternatives.

Third, one may think of the context in which the appraisal takes place rather than of the technical aspects of the scale itself. A possible cause of diminishing discriminating power occurs when a reference group is being used which that is not very comparable with the persons to be appraised. As an example we take Glickman's (1955) description of appraisals in the American army, where 97% of the colonels were judged to be 'superior' or 'excellent' (the reference group was the total officers population!); this is why they changed to another appraisal system whereby the desired differentiation could be obtained (the forced-choice system, see Sisson, 1948).

Besides the psychometric criteria there are the utilization criteria mentioned earlier. As the term indicates, these criteria are coupled to specific goals of the appraisal system. It was explained in section 2 that, unlike the psychometric criteria, the utilization criteria will not have general applicability because the goals are diverse. The goal 'guidance and coaching' in particular has its specific requirements, above all in the area of its discussibility and its usefulness for beginning an interview. In general there are three utilization criteria:
—Transparency, the extent to which the relationship between behavior or performance and rating score is transparent to the rater and (especially) the ratee.
—Acceptability, to both the rater and the ratee; this criterion is, for example, a very negative point in peer ratings that are otherwise (on metric grounds) considered positive (see e.g. Love, 1981).
—Information value, particularly focusing on guidance and improvement of work behavior.

In the following evaluation of various systems currently used, these criteria as well as the psychometric criteria will be applied.

5. SYSTEMS

In this section, we will present a discussion and evaluation of the various systems currently in use or advocated. There are numerous types and the space available here does not allow a detailed discussion of all of them. For a discussion of the specific characteristics and construction we refer the reader to the relevant literature (de Wolff, 1963; Cummings and Schwab, 1973; Landy and Trumbo, 1980; McCormick and Ilgen, 1980). A systematic survey is given in scheme 4.

The main distinction is made between the *overall* systems, in which the appraisal is eventually summarized in one single score or overall appraisal, systems that are based on *objective* data, *differentiated* systems which provide a

Scheme 4. Classification of appraisal systems.

Overall appraisal systems	—Overall ratings
	—Rank-order systems
	—Forced-choice systems
	—Critical incident systems
Systems based on objective data	—Output, cost/benefit figures
	—Behavioral indices
	—Comprehensive index systems
Differentiated systems	—Graphic/numerical scales
	—Descriptive scales
	—Anchored scales
	—Checklists
Other systems	—Free interview
	—Free-written description
	—Goal-setting interviews

profile or typology of the ratee, and finally other systems which differ somewhat in character, e.g. the open interview, the free-form essay, or management by objectives. We will now pass these systems in review.

5.1. Overall systems

Here belong first of all the overall *absolute* appraisals and the *rank-order* systems. The absolute systems lead to an overall appraisal reported on an absolute scale (e.g. running from adequate to excellent). In the rank-order systems the ranking may be obtained by directly asking the rater to rank-order the ratees in the group or by having him choose first the best, then the worst, then again the best and the worst from the remaining ones, etc. (alternate ranking). With a larger group, one can also use simplifying procedures, such as comparing ranking orders (form a number of random groups, establish the order within each, and compare the tops of the columns) and paired comparisons (compare two ratees each time). If one disposes of a number of raters, one can also apply one or the other nomination techniques (pick–x).

One of the overall systems, forced choice, was developed in the US army in order to stop the positive bias in appraisals of higher officers mentioned above. Sisson (1948) was the first to describe this system. In the early fifties it received quite some attention in the literature, precisely because of the psychometric qualities it claimed (Taylor and Wherry, 1951; Travers, 1951; Baier, 1951; Berkshire and Highland, 1953; Taylor *et al.*, 1954). In The Netherlands, the National Post and Telegraph experimented with the system (Brandts and van der Poll, 1963).

This rating system consists of a number of 'blocks' of descriptive statements (their number varying from two to five), from which the rater must choose one

	PI	DI
Reads his / her professional literature	3.8	1.3
Is good at designing research	3.9	2.9
Is able to distinguish good ideas from bad ones	3.8	3.1
Is an accurate experimenter	3.7	1.2

Figure 1. Forced-choice block from an appraisal system of the 'Research and Development' department.

or two of the most appropriate statements. Variations in the composition of the blocks are discussed in the literature (see Berkshire and Highland, 1953). An example of a block with four positive statements is shown in figure 1.

The statements are followed by two columns of figures. These are two indices regarding the statements, based on preliminary research. The first index, the preference index, indicates how positive it is for the ratee if the statement is thought to apply to him or her. The index is the average evaluation of a sample of raters.[3] The second column, the discrimination index, indicates the validity of the statement. This index is based on the differences, found in experimental research, between the mean ratings of a group of high performing employees and a group of low performing employees.

In our example, the statements are more or less equivalent with respect to the preference index, but are diverse as far as the discrimination index is concerned. If, in an actual appraisal situation, two statements must be selected from the four in the block, the rater will find it difficult to express his positive (or negative) bias, because all four statements appear equally 'favorable'. The idea is that he will then choose the two statements that really apply to the behavior or performance of the ratee. The system consists of, say, 30 such blocks. The overall (comprehensive) appraisal is determined by the number of times that positively discriminating statements were chosen from the blocks.

Finally, another empirical method of the overall systems is the *critical incident* method, developed by Flanagan (Flanagan, 1954; Flanagan and Burns, 1955). In this system, the emphasis is not 'how' but 'what'. Instead of a subjective judgment about the degree to which the ratee is assumed to possess a given trait or characteristic, the system establishes the frequency of the occurrence of certain critical incidents. Which incidents are critical (good or bad) is determined in preliminary empirical research of successful and unsuccessful performances. This system was initially a job analysis method, whereby the subjective assessments of a number of job characteristics were replaced by the

---

[3]There has been quite some research on the question of how these indices should be determined and how the questions should be formulated (Bartlett, 1960; Berkshire, 1958; Waters and Wherry, 1962).

positive or negative incidents reported. The appraisal method was developed from this system of job analysis. The incidents are condensed into a (still large) number of categories. The actual appraisal consists of registering the number of critical performances during the period to be appraised. The appraisal thus results in one score, this being the sum total of positive and negative incidents.

In connection with the evaluation of these overall appraisal systems, the following may be noted: If the goal of the appraisals requires the ratees to be compared on a single dimension (using the appraisal as a unidimensional criterion for validation or making yes-no decisions) one has to depend on overall appraisals. But remember that the psychometric qualities of the various systems are not equally satisfactory. In section 3 it was noted that the reliability and validity of overall ratings are very poor. Moreover, it is often not at all clear what is hidden behind such an overall, implicit appraisal; in other words, the appraisal may well be irrelevant, without this being noticed or there being a possibility to test it.

The psychometric qualities (distribution, reliability, validity) of both empirical systems generally are somewhat more favorable than those of the overall ratings. The quality of the preliminary empirical research will of course become manifest in the quality of the concrete appraisals. The requirement of empirical research, however, often constitutes a relatively major stumbling block. Often, such research is time consuming and not always easy to carry out in respect to available test groups and to the necessity of having an objective criterion for good and poor performance. Regarding the critical incident method we may add that the actual appraisal phase is both time consuming and complicated.

The major objections to the overall systems, however, are in the area of the utilization criteria, if, that is, the goal one has in mind is that of guidance, coaching, and work improvement. For this, the overall appraisal does not provide any foothold, because of the lack of diagnostic information. As to the forced choice method it may be added that, since the 'descriptive' and the 'rating' elements of the appraisal are split up, even the rater himself does not know whether he is assessing the ratee well or badly. From the point of view of the guidance criterion, this system is then, defeated, so to speak, by its own qualities.

5.2. Systems based on objective data

To this category belong those systems that primarily emphasize quantifiable results. One may think, in the first place, of output data: number of pieces produced, number of arrests (police), number of complaints from clients (service jobs) and the like. One can also make use of various cost/benefit analyses.

Next, there are objective data that do not particularly reflect the immediate output of some person or department, but rather function as an indication of certain (desirable) behavior. Thus, in appraising a manager, one makes use of data such as the rate of turnover or absenteeism in his department, questionnaires on organizational climate (Litwin and Stringer, 1968), or the 'morale' (Giese and Ruter, 1949) of his subordinates. Merrihue and Katzell (1955) developed a specific 'employee relations yardstick', a complex framework of indicators regarding atmosphere and climate in the department.

Thirdly, measures such as salary, salary growth, and level reached in the organization, belong here. The latter two variables are often corrected for factors like age, seniority, educational level, and so on.

Such objective systems certainly have their attractive side. Because often they are directly linked up with the organizational goals, they seem to have a high degree of validity. The objectivity of the data guarantees the reliability of the indices. For the goal of 'guidance' an emphasis on output may be desirable, although, as we pointed out earlier, a too exclusive attention to results also has its drawbacks.

The greatest problem with this kind of data, however, concerns its relevance. The kind of measures involved often are both deficient and excessive. They are deficient insofar as the goals desired by the organization are not reflected in the objective results. This is true both of the frequently restricted output criteria and of the measures mentioned for morale and atmosphere. The third category (salary-(growth) or level in the organization) may be an exception, because such indices reflect a fairly complex background themselves. They form, so to speak, a summary of the appraisals of a large number of partial aspects of behavior—that often are reported or influenced by many different raters— and thus will reflect a rather broad field of behavior. This is also one of the reasons why this category is assessed positively as a criterion for potential assessments (Tigchelaar, 1974).

These objective measures suffer not only from deficiency, but also often from excessiveness, probably with the exception of, again, the third category. A (large) part of the variance of the measures cannot be traced to the behavior of the person concerned, but to other factors often beyond his sphere of influence. The number of arrests depends also on the crime rate in the neighborhood; sales depend on, among other things, economic conditions or the cost of wages; turnover is determined also by relatively more favorable wage conditions in other companies; morale often depends more on the nature of the work than on working conditions that can be influenced by the leader, etc.

5.3. Other systems

In view of our conclusion regarding the differentiated systems of employee appraisal, we will first discuss the 'remaining methods', such as the free-form essay, the open interview, and goal-setting interviews.

In a way, the method of the *free-form essay* is found in the 'free space', varying in size, at the end of many conventional appraisal forms, where the rater may formulate an overall impression or add something to the profile 'in his own words'. Such a sketch—often somewhat personal—may be a useful supplement to an otherwise objective form. If, however, the whole appraisal consists of such unstructured descriptions in a personal style, the problems of incomparability, subjectivity, and unreliability become so great that this system cannot really compete with more objective systems.

A more or less related method is the *open interview*. Here, the unstructuredness is not in the reporting but rather in the method of assembling the data and impressions, on which subsequently a typology or a person's profile is based. Obviously, this method is realistic only when the rater is not the immediate supervisor. The latter should, of course, need no interviews to be able to appraise the work of his subordinates. One could think of the independent expert who is commissioned in some systems (e.g. Dutch government). This method was also favorably evaluated in making potential assessments, whereby the assembling of, on the one hand, information concerning the possibilities and desires of the employees and, on the other, information about vacancies and placement possibilities (now and in the near future) in the organization is put into one hand, that of the career coordinator (see de Quay, 1973).

Finally, we should mention an appraisal system which, in fact, does not primarily aim at appraising but rather at motivating the person concerned. This system, developed by Drucker (1954) and being in the spirit of McGregor's view of appraising described above, is the goal-setting interview or *management by objectives* (MBO). The idea is that classic appraisals as such bring about little change and motivate little and that, therefore, the appraisal should be replaced by an interview, in which the goals for the coming period are established. This would motivate the 'ratee' much more to try to actually reach that goal. An 'appraisal interview' would then consist in jointly analyzing the question, if appropriate, as to why the goal was not attained and again establishing specified goals (and ways) for the next period. In the Netherlands there are some forms of appraising in which this element is strongly present. At Enka Glanzstof they speak of 'task interviews', at KBB/Hema of 'individualization', and at NS of 'task fulfilment interviews' (see Roe *et al.*, 1977).

It should be noted that one might argue about the question as to exactly what it is in the method of goal-setting interviews that is responsible for its possible success. According to McGregor and Drucker, it is the motivating effect of being personally involved in the goal-setting. There is, however, another, fairly realistic alternative explanation which says that it is the fact that specific goals are established. MBO requires an accurate analysis and assessment of the goals and of the chances that they will be attained as well as a specified plan of the ways by which they can be realized. It is precisely this element that tends to be lacking in classic appraisals and appraisal interviews.

Undoubtedly, the fact that this kind of interview is not really an appraisal interview plays a role as well. When problem behavior or the failure to meet a norm or deadline are brought up in a discussions, the primary concern is to find ways to prevent, to improve, and so on, not to pin someone down with an inadequate appraisal. The job requirements may be too high and the norm may have to be adjusted. According to some experts current appraisal systems are so ineffective in changing behavior, that they consider such goal-setting or problem interviews the only solution (see section 6). Of course, in this kind of goal-setting or problem interviews, the system's psychometric qualities are less important, as long as a good and constructive discussion gets under way.

However that may be, the goal-setting interview is tailor-made for the purpose of guidance and coaching. It is very difficult to base placement or transfer decisions on it. Nor may this kind of interview be expected to furnish objective measures for the validation of selection and training.

5.4. Differentiated methods

Among the differentiated methods, which provide a differentiated 'picture' or profile of the ratee, are various scale types as well as the so-called checklists. To begin with the latter: *checklists* are lists of statements of which the rater has to indicate whether they are applicable to the ratee, mostly in the form of a simple 'yes-no' dichotomy. The statements are listed in random order, although they do refer to various underlying factors.

As to this 'reference', empirical and non-empirical checklists may be distin-

Table 2.

	I	*II*	*III*	*IV*
—Is not a fast worker	62			
—Knowledge of statistics moderate			66	
—Becomes uncertain when having to carry out instructions independently	56			
—Gets along excellently with superiors		73		
—Is good at explaining technical problems			− 42	
—Careful manner of reporting				62
—Spends much time on details	64			
—Uses statistics a lot			− 60	
—Does not keep up with developments in professional field			59	
—Often does not dare oppose superiors	55			
—Does not associate easily with employees		58		
—Quality of work highly fluctuating				− 51
—Insufficient use of ergonomics				− 45
—Able to work well in a team		83		
—Makes clearly arranged graphs and tables				63
—Occasionally approaches employer unwisely		72		

guished. The latter kind consists of statements that are classified on logical grounds. With the empirical checklists, the classification is achieved on grounds of empirical research. An example is the afore-mentioned appraisal system for job analysts constructed by Andriessen and Drenth (1973). On the basis of the factor analysis of a large number of statements about the work of job analysts, four factors were established, i.e. task performance, contacts, know-how with respect to statistics, literature, and technology, and accuracy. The list was compiled with statements which covered as 'factor purely' as possible one of the four factors and ordered randomly. The scores on these four dimensions for any one individual are indicated by the number of statements considered applicable. It is in principle also possible to weight the statements, for example on the basis of their factor loadings. Usually this does not yield much additional value, while its actual implementation is much more difficult.

As an illustration, a number of these statements and their factor loadings are presented in table 2.

In the practice of appraising, *graphic and numerical* scales are by far the most frequently used. A number of behavior aspects, whether or not classified according to main categories—which in its turn may or may not rely on preliminary empirical research—are listed and the rater has to indicate on a graphic or numerical scale to what extent he thinks these characteristics are applicable (for an example see figure 2).

In *descriptive* scales, the positions on the scales are not indicated by a number or place on a continuum, but by means of a behavior description or an indication of intensity (for an example see figure 3).

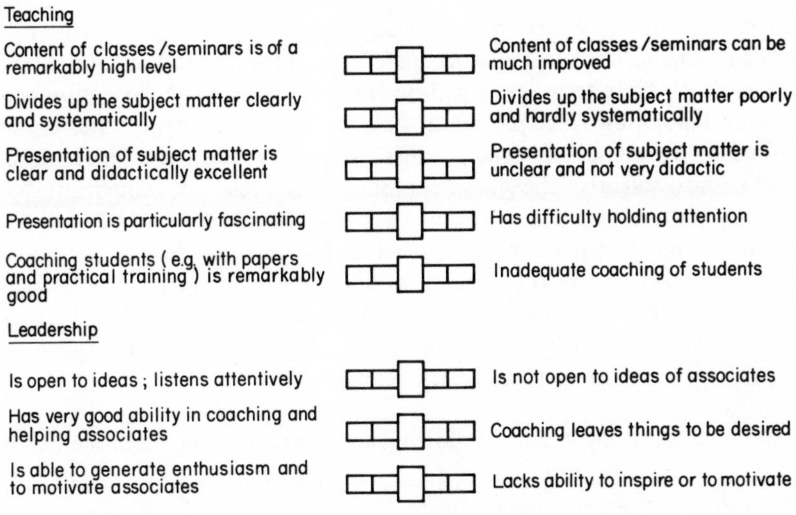

Figure 2. Parts of the appraisal form 'academic personnel' Free University.

I	THEORETICAL PROFESSIONAL KNOWLEDGE	Possesses more knowledge than is required	Sufficient theo-retical knowledge to fulfil job satisfactorily	Occasionally lacking in theo-retical knowledge	Insufficient theoret-ical knowledge
II	CAPACITY	Has the job at his fingertips	Fulfils job satisfactorily	Has trouble with certain parts of the job	Has an overall insufficient command of the job
III	INTEREST	Is totally devoted to the job	Does the job with sufficient interest	Does the job with moderate interest	Does not care
IV	INDEPENDENCE	One can leave the work to him	Brief instructions will do	Fairly often in need of support	Requires guidance all the time
V	MANNER OF WORKING				
	1. Speed	Works fast	Works at speed required	Does not always attain required speed	Seldom attains required speed
	2. Regularity	Keeps working solidly	Usually attains reasonable regularity	Does not always work regularly	Unable to work regularly
	3. Accuracy	No need of control	Sample controls suffice	Requires regular control	Makes many mistakes, thus requiring constant control

Figure 3. Example of (part of) a descriptive rating scale.

Here   the same distinction obtains as for checklists, i.e. empirically and non-empirically based descriptions. The non-empirically chosen alternatives are in fact nothing but subjectively indicated scale positions, comparable to a school report card using, instead of grades, words like: excellent, good, adequate, etc. If there is a communicative gain, this often is only apparent. The scale positions themselves are, in most cases, less clear than they are in graphic or numerical scales.

One can, however, establish empirically the scale value of the statements beforehand. One of the most elaborate methods is the method of equal appearing intervals of Thurstone (see e.g. Edwards, 1957, ch. 4). A large number of statements belonging to a particular category (e.g. quality of the work) is submitted to a number of 'expert raters' who are requested to indicate how positive or how negative the statements rate on the relevant dimension. Next, an average score (usually the median) and the distribution across raters are calculated. Then statements with variance as low as possible (to raise consistency of the items across raters) and with intervals as equal as possible are selected. In the final appraisal these statements are listed in random order and the rater must indicate which of them apply;[4] the score will be the mean scale value of the statements considered applicable.

Anchored scales are constructed following a similarly careful, empirically based

----

[4] In this respect, this system is basically a 'checklist', which is why it is sometimes called 'weighted checklist' in the English literature on the subject.

procedure for selecting behavioral alternatives, the anchors. In principle, this method, originally developed by Smith and Kendall (1963), starts from the idea of critical incidents. The anchors are derived from a description of a large number of critical behavior descriptions generated by a group of raters, 'critical' meaning that they are crucial to good or poor performance. Next the pool of items is cleared up qua formulation by a second group of experts and supplied with scale values (e.g. through group discussions or the so-called retranslation method; for a full description of the latter see Campbell et al., 1970, pp. 119–124). This results in a scale, whose anchors not only are carefully formulated, but also yield an exact level indication of the behavioral aspect to be rated. Campbell et al. (1970, pp. 122, 123) give some examples for the dimensions 'handling customers' complaints' and 'meeting deadlines'.

In some of these scales, an assessment must be made of the behavior to be expected from the ratee. This type is called the 'Behaviorally Anchored Rating Scale' (BARS). One of its variants, in which the frequency of occurrence of the relevant behaviors in the appraisal period is observed and scored, is the so-called 'Behavioral Observation Scale' (BOS).

Bernardin and Smith (1981) warn against the increasingly sloppy designs and implementations of the anchored systems and do not consider the criticism levelled at them (e.g. Atkin and Conlon, 1978) always applicable to the original idea and implementation.

According to Burke and Goodale (1975), the obvious objection to these systems, that they are rather specific and allow little generalization, is not necessarily always valid. They present a BAS-system which can indeed be applied to different jobs. Considering the great effort required for constructing these anchored scales, their advantage over the good 'classic' scales is quite limited—as a review of the literature shows (Schwab et al., 1975); however, the theory and the idea behind the system are certainly appealing.

But let us not forget one thing: the comparison was made with 'good' conventional rating scales. It is no exaggeration to say that these are rare. Because of the subjective and a priori character of these types of scaling, it is, in principle, possible to construct them off-hand. It takes a lot of discipline and time to construct a good, non-empirical, descriptive scale. The advantage of the empirical systems mentioned is that they are, *by definition*, carefully constructed. One is forced to concentrate on the careful wording of the aspects to be rated and the score levels. Inaccurate constructions will come to light of their own accord. This means that, on the average, empirically constructed systems will definitely be better than the generally used classic rating scales!

In attempting to evaluate the whole category of 'differentiated systems', first of all it should be said that they come out best, judged by the utilization criteria. They are transparent, manageable, acceptable to rater and ratee, and form a sound basis for an interview or action program. Because of their informational, differentiated character, moreover, they provide a starting point for measures in the areas of training, selection, or organization design. As criteria for selection or training research they are also usually more satisfactory than other systems.

As to its psychometric characteristics, this category is greatly varied. As was just pointed out, in most cases empirical systems are superior to the conventional systems as encountered in practice. As a result of the accuracy inherent in the empirical process and the testing of chosen aspects, the scale positions, and the weight values, they more adequately meet the requirements of relevance, validity, and generalizability.

The psychometric qualities of conventional rating scales (graphic, numerical, or descriptive) often are (very) deficient. The most frequently occurring deficiencies are:

(i) Irrelevance. The traits to be rated inadequately reflect the behavior or performance concerned.

(ii) Non-validity. Because the traits are too abstract or the terms used polyvalent, raters use their own 'psychological theories' as a guideline for assigning scores to particular dimensions. These private theories are often incorrect and thus invalidate the system.

In addition, the tendency to let appraisals of specific traits be influenced by a conspicuously good or specially bad trait or, more vague, by a general good or bad 'impression', is often cited as an invalidating rating error. The first type of error is called the 'halo-effect' and the second the 'horn-effect'. This often accounts for a considerable part of the variance (see Lee et al., 1981).

(iii) Tendency to reduce variance. In connection with, among other things, the previous point, raters tend to play it safe and to use only a limited width of the range of scoring possibilities, preferably slightly above the median score. This 'central tendency' reduces the variance and thus differentiating capability as well as reliability.

(iv) Bias and rating errors, coupled to rater. In this case, one might think of various social and societal prejudices, the effect of expectations, fear of confrontation with the ratee ('leniency effect'), diverse perceptions of what is 'good', the type of 'performer' the rater himself is, all kinds of individual characteristics of the rater, the question as to how well one has been rated oneself, etc.

An example of the effect of individual characteristics on an appraisal is given in the study of Schneider and Nayroff (1953), which demonstrated that an intelligent appraiser appreciates other aspects in his subordinate than does a less intelligent rater. An example of the effect of how a rater himself is appraised is provided by the research of Kirchner and Reisberg (1962); it appeared that a rater, who was himself judged as effective, appreciates initiative, planning, and know-how, whereas a rater, who was judged as less effective, will rather appreciate factors such as cooperation, loyalty to the company, and the like.

(v) Fluctuation of norms per rater. Even if performance or behavior aspects are correctly rated, the norms for 'adequate' or 'good' performance may fluctuate so strongly among raters as to render the final appraisal arbitrary. We know this phenomenon also from the education field. In his 'Fives and sixes', De Groot (1964) has brought this to light unequivocally.

(vi) Interaction with various organizational factors. Above, we saw that generalizability across situations, time, and raters as such cannot always be acquired that easily and that the variance found in the various consistency measures cannot always simply be labelled as error variance. We saw that people do not always show a stable behavioral pattern and that, under certain circumstances, with certain tasks, under supervision of certain people, their reaction will be different from that under other circumstances, tasks, and leaders. This is, in fact, the major problem in interpreting all kinds of interaction variance: interaction with the company, the department, the job, seniority, age, rank (McCormick and Ilgen, 1980), and even with year of appraisal (de Wolff, 1965).

Very frequently the question is how to distinguish true variance from error variance. That differences would always reflect errors of judgment is, in any case, not true.

This means that various technical corrections also do not solve the problem. For then it is assumed that the differences do indeed reflect errors of judgment. Thus, it has been proposed to equalize the means and distributions per department, per year, per rater, etc., by using standard scores within the defined groups. Such corrections, however, eliminate true differences between the groups!

In the literature one finds numerous suggestions for reducing the errors mentioned. Among them are the technical corrections just mentioned, various practical rules for scale construction (see e.g. Lazer and Wikstrom, 1977), the training and coaching of raters (Borman, 1979; Bernardin, 1978), calling in more than one rater or the assistance of a coordinator (Dutch government), and many others.

The advice of Campbell et al. (1970) may, however, be the most realistic. They say that it is important to ask good questions, which the rater can answer honestly: questions concerning aspects of behavior that can be adequately observed and evaluated by the rater. Most errors are made because the rater does not know what to fill in or how to put it if he wishes to be honest. A lack of understanding and the idea that the traits to be rated are irrelevant lead to distrust and lack of motivation. This is the main cause of the 'errors' of judgment mentioned above. The remedy they suggest is to use the BARS-technique. We would like to put it more broadly: Do, in any case, practice the same accuracy as that practiced in constructing the BARS-, BOS, and also the EAI-scales. Such accuracy appears to be a necessary, though not sufficient, condition for any appraisal system to be effective.

6. CONCLUSION

We would like to conclude this chapter with some remarks about the develop-ments in the theory and practice of personnel appraisals.

In the first place, the appraisal of employees is in fact nothing but a para-graph from the chapter 'rating of people', albeit that the former is colored by the specific context of work organizations, where one will actually run into the general rules of human judgment and appraisal (Hofstee, 1974) and social perception theory (Jaspars, 1964). Curiously enough, however, the contribution of psychology has tended to be mostly of an instrumental and technical nature. Thus, there is a continuous flow of studies on the improvement of instruments, the technical sophistication of scales, and how to avoid errors of judgment. Their usefulness is obviously beyond doubt. Too often, however, one fails to establish a relation with more general psychological theories about judgment formation and how ratings of persons are made. An example of what we consider desirable in this respect is a study by Feldman (1981) who looks at individual ratings from the viewpoint of attribution theory and the theory of information processing. In our opinion, there is clearly a stronger need for such a theoretical base for this practical issue.

Secondly, we wish to draw attention to developments in both policy and practice of personnel appraisal. Organizations have always considered ap-praising primarily a controlling and signalling mechanism, where the higher level makes decisions on the basis of information about the performance and behavior of employees at lower levels. The contribution of psychology, then, was looked upon mainly from the tradition of measurement: how do I attain the most reliable and the most valid judgment?

By now, another view of appraisal has come into existence, originating from the goals of performance improvement and guidance. One started to realize that personnel appraisal involves the interaction between two adult individuals and that the input of the one being appraised in this process of interaction is a condition for this instrument of policy to have a useful effect. Maier (1958) was one of the first to draw attention to this fact, through an analysis of the appraisal interview. He describes the three well-known forms of interview: Tell and Sell, Tell and Listen, and Problem Solving.

In the first method, the rater is also the leader in the appraisal interview. He wishes to communicate his appraisal as accurately as possible to the person appraised and hopes to convince him of its correctness. Confronted with the usual resistance of the appraised, he will tend to start preaching and lecturing, which in its turn will reinforce negative reactions. The underlying view that changes and innovations should be initiated and implemented from the top downwards is essentially a conservative one.

The Tell and Listen method entails a less directive attitude. Once the appraisal has been stated, the rater's attitude becomes that of an active listener. The ratee may speak out and defend himself and thus has the feeling of being respected. It is possible, too, that in this way ideas come up from below. Yet, the manager is still the rater. He determines whether something was done well or inadequately. All that has changed is the way the feedback is 'packaged', which is, indeed, much more tolerant and humane. Though it often results in a good relationship between manager and subordinate, it does not guarantee improvements.

In the third method, the Problem Solving approach, the role of the manager is essentially different. It is important to note that, in essence, the process of appraising does not agree with that of 'helping'. Here we are primarily concerned with the development of the ratee. The first thing is to stimulate the appraised to think up solutions and improvements himself, instead of presenting them to him. This requires openness and a complete absence of defensiveness on the part of the subordinate. Communication should not take place unidirectionally and attention is strongly focused on problems rather than persons. The basic idea is that real change can be achieved only if those concerned participate in it themselves.

Participation is a pivotal concept here. In the sixties, a group of researchers, supervised by Meyer, studied the effects of the classic appraisal process, which to a large extent was characterized by one-way traffic (Meyer *et al.*, 1965; French *et al.*, 1966). They were not very positive about these effects. They argue in favor not only of separating the goals 'determination of pay' and 'improvement of work' ('split roles in the performance appraisal'), but also of a considerable input of the person appraised and joint goal setting or problem solving. A later version (Meyer, 1977) again focuses on these elements of 'two-way communication' and 'problem orientation'. For suggestions about the manner of interviewing, which centers on the elements 'goal' and 'problems', we refer the reader to the literature mentioned and to this handbook, the chapters on interviewing (ch. 2.5) and management development (ch. 3.5). That such skills can be acquired by training is demonstrated in a recent study by Ivancevich and Smith (1981).

Obviously, in this last view the manager is assigned a very different role. Instead of appraiser, he becomes helper, instead of judge, coach. This last role is also cogently stipulated by McGregor, whose views we discussed earlier. The appraisal system of Management by Objectives (MBO), discussed above, is also wholly in this line.

It is remarkable that, despite its sympathetic and, considering the research, useful elements, MBO never really came off. In a sample of 216 organizations Locher and Teel (1977) found that for only 13% MBO was the main appraisal technique. In The Netherlands, MBO is encountered only sporadically. Maybe the objections raised by, for example, Flippo (1976) are responsible for this. He notes, among other things, that individual results are emphasized at the expense of other important goals of working in organizations. Furthermore, MBO cannot really be applied to jobs where the person concerned has little influence on the concrete 'output'. Finally, MBO does not lead to a comparative appraisal and thus is less appropriate for the organization's more administrative purposes.

It is, in this connection, useful to mention a proposal of Teel (1978), which combines the participation of the person appraised with the desirability of having comparative rating scores or profiles at hand. He argues for coupling the supervisor's and the self-appraisals. By itself, the self-appraisal technique is not very useful. Thornton (1980) demonstrates that qua psychometric qualities self-appraisals are inferior to appraisals by superiors. The positive aspect is its motivational effect and the stimulus for self-development. This element is picked up in Teel's proposal, where he has both rater and ratee complete an appraisal form independently before the appraisal interview, in which the final appraisal will be effected. The appraisal interview, then, begins with a discussion of the various points of view, with first the person appraised explaining his opinion and then his superior. Next, the forms are compared. When (on a five-point scale) there is a difference of only one point, the highest score is taken. If the difference is greater, a solution, usually a compromise, is reached via discussion.

Teel's experiences indicated that in two-thirds of the cases there was no difference between appraisals and that only in a very small number of cases the difference was more than one point. The persons appraised responded very positively to this procedure and they took part in the discussion more freely and more constructively than in the more classic appraisals.

The reason why we have explained this procedure a bit more extensively is that, on the one hand, it secures the advantages of the MBO approach, i.e. the ratee's participation and contribution, and, on the other, also makes available completed rating forms, on the basis of which it is possible to make comparisons and administrative decisions.

By way of summary, we wish to mention four preconditions for an appraisal system to function well.

In the first place, the *technical qualities* of the system. In this chapter we have formulated a number of requirements that appraisals should meet. We have also seen that part of the requirements' content varies according to the goal of the appraisal. A close attuning of the technical and utilization aspects to the goal of appraising and, subsequently, the qualitative optimalization of the system as such are of crucial importance here.

Secondly, we should take note of the *organizational conditions* for the design, construction, and introduction of the appraisal system. Earlier in this section we noted the importance of participation of the appraised in the appraising process. However, we are now alluding to another aspect of this involvement— in this case of both the appraiser and the appraised—namely, the involvement in the design and selection of the system as such, the way it functions in the organization, the formulation of the conditions for application and secrecy, controls to ensure adherence, etc.

In 1980, a new appraisal system was introduced at the Free University in Amsterdam—also for academic personnel—only after several years of consulting, experimenting, and evaluating, in which (representatives of) all levels had their say. We are convinced that this constituted a major condition for the acceptation and effective application of the system.

Among the organizational conditions we also wish to include the availability of an efficient appeal procedure. From a labor union point of view, Top argued for this in a critical report on 'the vulnerable ratee' (Top, 1974). This appeal facility has already been realized in government departments and at universities in The Netherlands.

Thirdly, a number of conditions in the area of *organization structure* may be mentioned here. If people must be rated on a number of job criteria and performance norms, this can obviously be done better if these criteria and norms are specified, uniform, clear, and accepted by those involved. This means that such a system works better in an organization structure in which it is clear what everybody's responsibilities are, what goals one should try to realize, and how information should be gathered about the question as to what extent the goals are reached. In other words, appraisal systems function better in organizations with clear-cut task structures, distinct goals, and unequivocal measurement procedures.

As a final precondition, we suggest a good and open *social climate*. However good the system is, if there is no trust, if fair communication is not possible, if policy and hidden motives determine the behavior, appraisals will never function well. In this connection Kane and Lawler (1979) mention the importance of the participation of the lower echelons in the setting of goals and in the formulation of norms. If the latter is done unilaterally by management, the openness required for the appraisals to function well will never materialize.

If the last two conditions regarding the organizational and social contexts are met, appraisals will be much less a 'tool of management' than they used to be. Appraising will then become a rather more continuous activity and an integral part of the leader's task. It will become more closely linked with matters like task setting and task arrangements. The transition from appraisal to work consultation will be a smooth one.

Also, from the perspective of the employee there is more integration with other personnel facilities. The appraisal of work performance is put in a broader framework, as part of career planning or coaching. In a career development plan as much information as possible is accumulated: individual wishes and needs, necessity of further training and schooling, potential qualities and possibilities for advancement, and, of course, the present manner of task fulfilment.

Viewed thus, employee appraisal acquires a central position in personnel policy, in which, on the one hand, stimulation and continuous guidance of the employee are enhanced and, on the other, development of the organization together with satisfying present and future personnel needs are promoted.

REFERENCES

Andriessen, J. H. T. H., Drenth, P. J. D. (1973), Een beoordelingslijst van arbeidsanalisten [A rating form for job analysts]. In: Drenth et al. (1973).

Anstey, E. Fletcher, C., Walker, J. (1978), Staff appraisal and development. London: Allen & Unwin.

Atkin, R. S., Conlon. D. J. (1978), Behaviorally anchored rating scales: Some theoretical issues. Academy of Management Review, 3, 119–128.

Baier, D. E. (1951), Reply to Travers. Psychological Bulletin, 48, 421–433.

Barlett, C. J. (1960), Factors affecting forced-choice response. Personnel Psychology, 13, 399–406.

Berkshire, J. R. (1958), Comparisons of five forced choice indices. Educational and Psychological Measurement, 18, 553–561.

Berkshire, J. R., Highland, R. W. (1953), Forced choice-performance rating; A methodological study. Personnel Psychology, 6, 355–378.

Bernardin, H. J. (1978), Effects of rater training on leniency and halo errors in student ratings of instructors. Journal of Applied Psychology, 63, 301–308.

Bernardin, H. J., Smith, P. C. (1976), A classification of some issues regarding the development and use of behaviorally anchored rating scales (BAS). Journal of Applied Psychology, 66, 458–463.

Borman, W. C. (1979), Training raters in performance appraisal. Journal of Applied Psychology, 69, 410–420.

Brandts, H. J., Poll, A. N. J. van der (1963), Personeelsbeoordeling volgens de methode van de gedwongen keuze [Appraising personnel according to the forced choice method]. Nederlands Tijdschrift voor de Psychologie 18, 131–145.

Bray, D. W. (1964), The management progress study. American Psychologist, 19, 419–420.

Campbell, J. P., Dunnette, M. D., Lawler, E. E., Weick, K. E. (1970), Managerial behavior, performance and effectiveness. New York: McGraw-Hill.

COP/SER (1959), Bazen in industrie [Supervisors in industry]. The Hague: COP.

Cronbach, L. J. (1971), Test-validation. In: Thorndike, R. L. (Ed.), Educational measurement. Washington D. C.: American Council on Education.

Cummings, L. L., Schwab, D. P. (1973), Performance in organizations. Glenview: Scott, Foresman and Co.

Dam, A. G. van, Drenth, P. J. D. (1976), Hoger beroep [Middle and higher management]. Amsterdam: COP/Free University.

Drenth, P. J. D. (1975), Inleiding in de testtheorie [Introduction to test theory]. Deventer: Van Loghum Slaterus.

Drenth, P. J. D., Willems, P. J., Wolff, Ch. J. de (Eds.) (1973), Arbeids- en organisatie-psychologie [Work- and organizational psychology]. Deventer: Kluwer.

Drucker, P. F. (1954), The practice of management. New York: Harper.

Edwards, A. L. (1957), Techniques of attitude scale construction. New York: Appleton-Century-Crofts.

Elshout, J. J., Boselie, F. A. J. M., Berg, J. van de, Boerlijst, G., Schaake, B. (1973), De validatie van een testbatterij voor de selectie van wetenschappelijke onderzoekers [Validation of a test battery for the selection of scientific researchers]. In: Drenth et al. (1973).

Feldman, J. M. (1981), Beyond attribution theory: Cognitive processes in performance appraisal. Journal of Applied Psychology, 66, 127–148.

Flanagan, J. C. (1954), The critical incidents technique. *Psychological Bulletin*, **4**, 337–357.
Flanagan, J. C., Brooms, R. K. (1955), The employee performance record: A new appraisal and developmental tool. *Harvard Business Review*, **33**, 95–102.
Fleishman, E. A., Harris, E. F., Burt, H. E. (1955), *Leadership and supervision in industry*. Bureau of Educational Research Monograph, **33**.
Flippo, E. B. (1976), *Principles of personnel management*. New York: McGraw-Hill.
French, J. R. P., Kay, E., Meyer, H. H. (1966), Participation and the appraisal system. *Human Relations*, **19**, 3–21.
Giese, W. J., Ruter, W. H. (1949), An objective analysis of morale. *Journal of Applied Psychology*, **33**, 421–427.
Ginneken, P. J. van (Ed.) (1974), *Verdiensten van hoger personeel* [Income of higher personnel]. Deventer: Kluwer.
Glickman, A. S. (1955), Effects of negatively skewed ratings on motivations of the rated. *Personnel Psychology*, **8**, 39–47.
Goodale, J. G., Burke, R. J. (1975), Behaviorally based rating scales need not be job-specific. *Journal of Applied Psychology*, **60**, 389–391.
Groot, A. D. de (1964), *Vijven en zessen* [Fives and sixes]. Groningen: Wolters.
Grunow, D. (1976), *Personalbeurteilung*. Stuttgart: Ferdinand Enke Verlag.
Hofstee, W. K. B. (1974), *Psychologische uitspraken over personen* [Psychological statements about persons]. Deventer: Van Loghum Slaterus.
Ivancevich, J. M., Smith, S. V. (1981), Goal setting interview skills training; Simulated and on-the-job analyses. *Journal of Applied Psychology*, **66**, 697–705.
Jaspars, J. M. F. (1964), *On social perception*. Leiden: University of Leiden (dissertation).
Kane, J. S., Lawler, E. E. (1979), Performance appraisal effectiveness. In: Staw, B. M. (Ed.), *Research in organizational behavior*. Greenwich: Jai Press.
Kavanagh, M. J., MacKinney, A. C., Wolins, L. (1971), Issues in managerial performance: Multi-trait multi-method analysis of ratings. *Psychological Bulletin*, **75**, 34–49.
Kirchner, W. K., Reisberg, D. J. (1962), Differences between better and less effective supervisors in appraisals of subordinates. *Personnel Psychology*, **15**, 295–302.
Landy, F. J., Trumbo, D. (1980), *Psychology of work-behavior*. Homewood: Dorsey.
Laurent, H. (1962), *The validation of aids for the identification of management potential* New York: SONJ.
Laurent, H. (1970), Cross-cultural cross-validation of empirically validated tests. *Journal of Applied Psychology*, **54**, 417–423.
Lawler, E. E. (1981), *Pay and organizational development*. Reading: Addison-Wesley.
Lazer, R. I., Wikstrom, B. (1978), *Appraising managerial performance: Current practices and future directions*. New York: The Conference Board.
Lee, R., Malone, M., Greco, S. (1981), Multitrait-multimethod-multirater analysis of performance ratings for law enforcement personnel. *Journal of Applied Psychology*, **66**, 625–632.
Litwin, G. H., Stringer, A. (1968), *Motivation and organizational climate*. Boston: Harvard Business School.
Locher, A. H., Teel, K. S. (1977), Performance appraisal—a survey of current practices. *Personnel Journal*, **56**, 245–254.
Love, K. G. (1981), Comparison of peer assessment methods; Reliability, validity, friendship bias, and user reaction. *Journal of Applied Psychology*, **66**, 451–457.
McCormick, E. J., Ilgen, D. (1980), *Industrial psychology*. Englewood Cliffs: Prentice-Hall.
McGregor, D. (1957), An uneasy look at performance appraisal. *Harvard Business Review*, **35**, 89–94.
McGregor, D. (1960), *The human side of enterprise*. New York: McGraw-Hill.

Mahoney, T. A., Jerdee, T. H., Nash, A. N. (1960), Predicting managerial effectiveness. *Personnel Psychology*, **13**, 147–163.

Maier, N. R. F. (1958), *The appraisal interview*. London: Wiley.

Merrihue, W. V., Katzell, R. A. (1955), ERI: Yardstick of employee relations. *Harvard Business Review*, **33**, 91–99.

Meyer, H. H. (1977), The annual performance review discussion. *Personnel Journal*, **56**, 508–511.

Meyer, H. H., Kay, E., French, J. R. P. (1965), Split roles in performance appraisal. *Harvard Business Review*, **43**, 123–129.

Mischel, W. (1968), *Personality and assessment*. New York: Wiley.

Muller, H. (1970), *The search for the qualities essential to the advancement in a large industrial group*. Utrecht: University of Utrecht (disseration).

Nederlands Tijdschrift voor de Psychologie [Dutch Journal of Psychology]. Deventer: Van Loghum Slaterus.

Porter, L. W. Lawler, E. E., Hackman, J. R. (1975), *Behavior in organizations*. New York: McGraw-Hill.

Quay, C. L. M. de (1973), Management development en beoordelingen [Management development and appraisals]. In: Drenth *et al.* (1973).

Roe, R. A., Kesteren, R. A. van, Hofstee, E. N. B., Raay, A. de, Haner, G. P., Daniëls, M. J. M. (1977), *Beoordelingen en beoordelingsgesprek* [Appraisal and appraisal interview]. Deventer: Kluwer (NVBP).

Ronan, W. W., Prien, E. P. (1966), *Toward a criterion theory: A review and analysis of research and opinion*. Greensboro: Rich. Fnd.

Ronan, W. W., Schwartz, A. P. (1974), Ratings as performance criteria. *International Review of Applied Psychology*, **23**, 71–81.

Rowe, K. H. (1970), An appraisal of appraisal. *Journal of Management Studies*, **10**, 1–25.

Schneider, D. E., Bayroff, A. G. (1953), The relationship between rater characteristics and validity of ratings. *Journal of Applied Psychology*, **37**, 278–280.

Schwab, D., Heneman, H. G., Decotiis, T. (1975), Behaviorally anchored rating scales: A review of the literature. *Personnel Psychology*, **28**, 549–562.

Sisson, E. D. (1948), Forced choice—the new army rating. *Personnel Psychology*, **1**, 365–387.

Spriegel, W. R. (1962), Company practices in appraisal of managerial performance. *Personnel*, **39**, 77–83.

Smith, P. C., Kendall, L. M. (1963), Retranslation of expectations: An approach to the construction of unambiguous anchors for rating scales. *Journal of Applied Psychology*, **47**, 149–155.

Taylor, E. K., Wherry, R. J. (1951), A study of leniency in two rating systems. *Personnel Psychology*, **4**, 39–47.

Teel, K. S. (1978), Self-appraisal revisited. *Personnel Journal*, **57**, 364–367.

Thorndike, R. L. (1949), *Personnel selection*. New York: Wiley.

Thornton, G. C. (1980), Psychometric properties of self-appraisals of job-performance. *Personnel Psychology*, **33**, 263–273.

Tiffin, I., McCormick, E. J. (1966), *Industrial psychology*. London: Allen.

Tigchelaar, L. S. (1974), *Potentieelbeoordeling en loopbaansucces* [Potential assessment and career success]. Amsterdam: Free University (dissertation).

Top, W. (1974), *De kwetsbare beoordeelde* [The vulnerable ratee]. Utrecht: Sociaal Wetenschappelijk Instituut van de Vakcentrales [The Unions' Social Science Institute].

Travers, R. M. W. (1951), A critical review of the validity and rational of the forced choice technique. *Psychological Bulletin*, **48**, 62–70.

Waters, L. K., Wherry, R. J. (1962), The preference index and responses to forced choice pairs. *Personnel Psychology*, **15**, 99–102.

Whisler, T. F., Harper, S. F. (Eds.) (1962), *Performance appraisal: Research and practice.* New York: Holt.

Whitla, D. K., Tirrel, J. E. (1953), The validity of ratings of several levels of supervisors. *Personnel Psychology*, **6**, 461–466.

Wolff, Ch. J. de (1963), *Personeelsbeoordeling* [Personnel appraisal]. Amsterdam: Swets & Zeitlinger.

Wolff, Ch. J. de (1965a), Factoranalyse van beoordelingen [Factor analysis of appraisals]. *Nederlands Tijdschrift voor de Psychologie*, **20**, 95–100.

Wolff, Ch. J. de (1965b), Een factoranalyse van beoordelingen afkomstig van verschillende beoordeelaars [A factor analysis of appraisals made by different appraisers]. *Nederlands Tijdschrift voor de Psychologie*, **20**, 283–292.

Wolff, Ch. J. de (1970), Beoordelingen als criteria [Appraisals as criteria]. In: Drenth, P. J. D., Willems, P. J., Wolff, Ch. J. de (Eds.), *Bedrijfspsychologie* [Industrial psychology]. Deventer: Kluwer.

Woodworth, D. G., McKinnon, D. W. (1957), The measurement of intellectual efficiency in an assessment of 100 A. F. captains. *AFPTRC-TN-57-128.*

2.5. Human engineering—ergonomics

Paul J. Willems*

Shortly after the turn of the century psychologists began paying attention
to problems of working life. The first decades of applied psychology were
characterized by a predominant interest in test development, selection, and
placement. In addition to these activities much effort was invested in the
development of training programs.

All these activities were based on the psychologists' notion that a job was
a fixed entity, shaped by tradition or by industrial engineers, and certainly
not to be changed by an outsider like a psychologist. A psychologist had to
select men or women who could perform a task satisfactorily and—if
necessary—to develop training programs. For several generations this idea
dominated the attitudes and activities of psychologists dealing with the relation
between man and his work. Changing a job or altering the job content was
beyond their scope.

During the second world war a completely different way of thinking about
jobs emerged: now the job, the tools, and the working environment were
considered to be changeable. This fundamentally different view comes to the
fore in two investigations by Fitts and Jones (1947a, 1947b). In the introduction
to the first of their reports they state: 'Aircraft accidents usually are classified
as due to pilot error, to material failure, to maintenance, or to supervision,
with a large proportion of all accidents attributed to the "pilot-error" category.
It has been customary to assume that prevention of accidents due to material
failure or poor maintenance is the reponsibility of engineering personnel
and that accidents due to errors of pilots or supervisory personnel are the
responsibility of those in charge of selection, training, and operations. The

Prof. dr. Paul J. Willems, Katholieke Hogeschool, Hogeschoollaan 225, 5037 GC TILBURG.

235

present study was undertaken from a different point of view; it proceeded on the assumption that a great many accidents result directly from the manner in which equipment is designed and where it is placed in the cockpit, and therefore can be eliminated by attention to human requirements in the design of equipment' (quoted from the reprint in Sinaiko, 1961).

As a matter of fact, this different way of thinking about the relationship between man and his work did not come out of the blue. One of the main reasons for this change of approach becomes visible from the problem which Fitts and Jones encountered: in modern aircraft, the pilot becomes a bottleneck in the operating of the system. The equipment becomes unmanageable due to the limitations of the operator, notwithstanding the quality of selection and training.

A second reason for this change of view is the growing body of knowledge on human abilities and limitations. both physiological and psychological, and on the effects of different environmental influences on human performance.

Thirdly, working methods and technologies change rather rapidly nowadays. This severely restricts possibilities to develop and use selection and training methods. Sometimes a working method has already disappeared before the psychologist has had a chance to develop sound selection and training programs.

These and other developments prompted psychologists to develop a different approach to the relationship between man and his work. In the United States these notions are known under a number of more or less equivalent labels, like human engineering, engineering psychology, human factors engineering. In Europe the word ergonomics was coined, composed of the Greek wordt 'ergon' (work) and 'nomos' (law, rule). Thus, the literal meaning of ergonomics could be described as: the set of laws or rules which govern (human) work.

Designing human tasks is not exclusively a psychologist's job, although in the United States psychologists have always played a leading part in these activities. In Europe the contributions of anthropometricians and physiologists are somewhat more pronounced as can be inferred from published work on the subject. The development of ergonomic activities in Europe shows an increasing awareness of the need to recruit different kinds of expertise, apart from psychologists and industrial engineers, in designing relations between man and his equipment. To mention just a few examples: De Jong's work at Schiphol (Amsterdam) airport (1973), and Wagenaar's research on handling large ships (1970, 1973, 1975) both show that teams made up of architects, industrial designers, industrial engineers, shipbuilders, mathematicians, navigation experts, and psychologists were necessary to solve problems of design and instrumentation.

Another difference between the United States and Europe is attributable to the different starting points of practitioners of the discipline. In the United States much of the work in this area has a somewhat military flavor, in Europe the bulk of the early work comes from industry. Over the years, however, these differences have tended to diminish, although the different background of the members of the family remains recognizable.

Although recognizing the multi-disciplinarian nature of human engineering, the remainder of this chapter will be restricted to the role of the psychologist in designing human tasks.

Any task performance is a goal directed activity. For the time being it may be left undecided whether the goal is attained by means of a fully automated system or through human action. To reach the goal a number of operations have to be carried out. In describing a goal directed action in general terms the following elements can be distinguished:

1. Action presupposes an information input (data, materials, instructions, etc.).

2. This information must be registered or perceived and it must be retained during a certain amount of time ('memory').

3. The information must be processed, transformed into an action-decision. Again: during these transformational activities the information and the decision have to be stored for some time.

4. The decision has to be executed. Storage is again required, at least until the action is performed.

5. Execution of the decision results in some kind of output.

In some systems there is a sixth element: information about the output is fed back to the information registering part of the system. Presence or absence of this element distinguishes closed-loop from open-loop systems. In an open-loop system intervention in the course of developments, once the execution of the decision has started, is not possible. In a closed-loop system adjustive or corrective actions can be initiated if the preceding action did not lead to the desired goal.

The foregoing is Schematically summarized in figure 1.

The terminology used is very general, applicable to automated goal directed systems as well as to man-machine systems. Limiting the discussion to this last category, the form and the terminology of figure 1 can be slightly changed

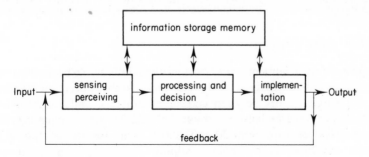

Figure 1. Schematic representation of a goal directed action.

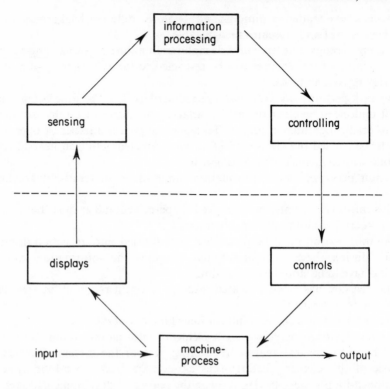

Figure 2. Schematic representation of a man-machine system.

to elucidate the role of the human operator interacting with the non-human system components (see figure 2).

In this diagram the different aspects of human functioning are grouped above the dotted line, the non-human parts of the system below. The closed-loop character of the system is symbolized by arrows, indicating that changes in the state of the process, caused by some preceding control action, are signalled back to the human operator, who subsequently decides whether to take some further action.

SENSING AND PERCEIVING

A change in the environment is not necessarily a stimulus. To become a stimulus such a change has to satisfy several conditions. To mention a few: the human senses are effective only between certain boundaries. Only electromagnetic waves with wavelengths between about 400 and 700 nanometers are visible; only vibrations between about 20 and 20.000 cycles per second can be heard as sounds; etc. Further, to become a stimulus, a change in energy in the environment has to be of a certain magnitude, or it should be possible to transform such a change by technical means (microscopes, radar, sonar, and so on) to a mode and a magnitude that can be perceived by the human senses. Basic data on capacities and limitations of the human senses can be found in numerous sources, for example in Van Cott and Kinkade (1972) and McCormick (1976). What these properties of the sense organs imply for the solution of practical problems can be gathered from sources like Woodson and Conover (1966). This literature shows that in the domain of visual presentation of information a large and diversified fund of applicable knowledge is available: form and dimensions of dials, pointers, scale-markers; methods for coding visual information; design of typographical features, and numerous other aspects of information presentation have been investigated. A specialized branch of research in this area relates to information transmission making use of signal-transforming devices, like television sets and similar types of cathode-ray tubes.

Another rather well developed area of research is auditory presentation of information. Advantages and disadvantages of different forms of auditory stimulus presentation (warning and alarm signals; radio communication; speech), as well as effects of noise, filtering, and other forms of signal transformation have been investigated extensively, as well as masking and coding of auditory information. For a detailed orientation the reader is referred to Deatherage (1972), and Kryter (1972).

Information transmission through other senses has attracted less attention. Although problems of the visually handicapped stimulate research in tactile presentation of information, unfortunately up to the present the results are not yet very encouraging in the way of developing practical aids for the handicapped.

Instead of reviewing American research on these topics, with which the reader might be familiar, some examples of work done in Europe on these subjects might be more worthwhile.

Different aspects of visibility and conspicuity of traffic lights have been investigated at the Institute for Perception (Soesterberg, The Netherlands): wavelengths of traffic light that can be used to accommodate people with different types of color-vision deficiencies; form, dimensions, and color of background shields to enhance the conspicuousness of traffic lights; forms and dimensions of directional instructions on traffic lights (like direction-indicating arrows); adjustable luminance levels for day- and night-time operation of traffic lights; patterning of traffic light-poles to enhance their visibility in different atmospheric conditions (Walraven, 1978).

A different line of research is aimed at designing effective signposts in public facilities, offices, hospitals, railway stations, and the like; especially the design of directional and informational graphic symbols ('pictograms') is investigated. The main problem in this line of research, already mentioned by Dreyfuss (1972), is the discrepancy between what designers judge to be understood by people and how people actually interpret their products, especially if the symbols are aimed at people of different cultural origins.

One line of human engineering effort in The Netherlands is addressed to alleviating the situation of the handicapped. For the visually handicapped a reading aid in the form of a print-magnifier, which makes use of a television set, was developed at the Institute for Perception Research (Eindhoven). At the same institute a relief drawing set was developed which can be used, for example, to teach geometry to the blind.

At Delft Technical University a typewriter was developed that can be operated by means of a head-mounted light beam, so that even patients para-lyzed from the neck down can operate it at a reasonable speed.

Another research effort is aimed at developing a device which presents visual information about the identity and the articulation of vowels in spoken language, to aid deaf people in improving their pronunciation of language.

To conclude this section on information presentation, an example will be given which illustrates that even a beginner's knowledge of psychology some-times will do to solve a vexing practical problem. When the Dutch government introduced a new series of coins, the public started complaining about two coins from the set—diameters 25 and 29 millimeters respectively—which were very hard to tell apart. If often happened that one paid with the larger one (value about one dollar) when the smaller one (value about 40 ¢) would have been enough. A government spokesman in parliament repudiated the com-plaints: people never had any trouble with two other, smaller coins—diameters 16 and 20 mm—and as the difference in diameter was 4 mm in both cases this 'proved' that the objections were not reasonable. Anyone remembering Weber's law will see the error in the argument. It took just a few simple psychophysical experiments (done by Vroon, 1978) to show that the diameter of the 29-mm coin had to be increased to 33 mm to reduce the number of mistakes made with the previous set of coins from 20 to 2 per cent.

INFORMATION PROCESSING

All goal directed activity implies some kind of information processing. Informa-tion entering through the senses is transformed into decisions which (some-times) lead to certain actions. Although these aspects of behavior can be distinguished conceptually, this does not imply that these different aspects can be studied separately. Perceiving, processing, and acting are so fundamentally intertwined that it is impossible to study them separately.

The way in which information is processed depends on the characteristics of the information as well as on the kind of action that has to be taken. The decision to stop at a road crossing is simpler than the decision whether or not to reorganize a large production facility. To decide whether or not to stop at an intersection is much more difficult on a rainy night than in broad daylight.

If the responses required are simple repetitive actions, like pressing a button as soon as a stimulus is perceived, processing activities and decisions are comparatively easy. But in less structured and less predictable tasks, like driving a car in heavy traffic, an adequate performance clearly requires a much more comprehensive and complicated processing activity.

As indicated earlier, processing of information requires some kind of 'memory', a temporary storage of information lasting—at least—from the intake of information to the completion of a resulting action. Effectivity of human performance depends on the properties of this storage. Memory research, although primarily motivated by theoretical problems, contains a wealth of information that is immediately applicable to human engineering problems. A few examples: memory research on primacy and recency effects (in a stream of incoming information the items that are presented at the start and at the end of the message have a better chance to be retained than items in the middle of the message) is very useful. In our daily lives we are increasingly confronted with alfanumerical codes, like zip-codes, telephone numbers, and bank account numbers, sometimes of considerable length. Experience shows that some codes are more easily forgotten, or reproduced incorrectly, than others. It has been shown by Ten Hoopen (1978) that codes of the type 1 2 A B 3 4, as used in some countries for car license plates, are harder to remember correctly than codes of the type 1 2 3 4 A B, which was chosen for the postal zip-code in The Netherlands.

Wagenaar (1979) has demonstrated that people can reproduce only a very limited number of statements from a radio weather forecast. The forecast used by the experimenter contained 32 facts, eight of which could be reproduced by the subjects. Regrouping facts in a more logical fashion and shortening the message to the most important items improved performance.

Information processing not only depends on the quality of the storage 'facility', but also on characteristics and qualities of the information presented. A few examples: if the information presented to the operator is difficult to interpret, the quality and speed of performance will suffer (Forbes, 1972; Näätänen and Summala, 1976). Driving a car at night is difficult because many depth cues that are available in daylight are lacking. There only are two cues available to judge the distance and changes in distance of a car ahead during night-time driving: changes in the visual angle of the tail lights and changes in apparent size and luminosity of these lights. The second cue is of minor importance. Janssen (1978) not only confirmed this in laboratory experiments, but also in actual night driving tests. One of the conclusions of his research is a recommendation to make the (horizontal) separation between tail lights as large as possible to improve the quality of the night driver's judgment of distance and distance-changes. This research exemplifies an important and often neglected feature of good human engineering research: checking laboratory results in field tests.

Difficulties of interpretation of information of a very different nature are found in a problem investigated by Wagenaar (1970, 1973, 1975). Operator performance in controlling a dynamic system deteriorates appreciably when a time lag is inserted between a control action and feedback of the results of this action to the operator. When driving a car or riding a bicycle, the effects of any control movement are immediately perceived. But changing the course of a big ship is a very different task: an appreciable amount of time elapses before a change in the position of the rudder results in a *visible* change of the course of the ship. This time lag has a very detrimental effects on performance, where no instrumental aids are available to counteract the effects of this lag.

Another type of difficulty in processing information is encountered in situations where the number of relevant stimuli per unit of time is small. Such situations increasingly occur in modern industry, where many processes are more or less automated. As long as relevant process-values do not exceed the boundary values for effective operation, no intervention by the operator is required. If the process is sufficiently stable, the amount of operator intervention is minimal. In such jobs performance decrements can be observed soon after the operator starts monitoring the process: when a relevant signal appears it might be overlooked, or it might take an undesirable amount of time before action is taken, or the operator becomes more 'conservative' in his actions (Mackworth, 1950). All sorts of 'tricks' have been devised—presenting information through different senses, administering stimulating drugs, presenting artificial and non-relevant stimuli—to keep performance at an acceptable level. The trouble with tricks is, however, that they rapidly lose their effectiveness.

Practical and pressing problems have stimulated research in this area. Although the volume of research in this area is rather impressive (for a survey see Mackie, 1977), the contribution of this vast effort to improve human performance is still disappointing. The reasons for this unsatisfactory state of affairs are not clear, but Meister may be right when he said that ' ... the laboratory vigil is extremely specific, and conclusions reached from it do not necessarily generalize to other types of situations' (1976, p. 114).

The speed of information processing also depends on the complexity of the information the operator has to deal with. In a simple reaction task, where the subject has to deal always with one and the same stimulus, to which one kind of reaction is always required, the extent of information processing is minimal. But if the subject has to choose the correct response when, for example, five different stimuli are presented, each stimulus requiring a different response, 40 per cent more time is needed than in the simple task.

According to Hick (1952) the relationship between reaction time and the amount of information to be processed can be expressed in the form of a linear function: $RT = a + bH$, a being the simple (no choice) reaction time, b a constant factor and H the logarithm of the number of equiprobable alternatives from which one has to choose.

Further research, however, has demonstrated that human choice behavior is not that simple. When an operator has a chance to develop some skill, his reaction time in choice situations gradually decreases, sometimes even to the simple no-choice level. Another factor that plays an important role in determining the speed of information processing is the degree of stimulus-response compatibility. This concept, introduced by Fitts and Seeger (1953), is defined by these authors as follows: 'A task involves compatible S–R relations to the extent that the ensemble of stimulus and response combinations comprising the task results in a high rate of information transfer'. Less precise, but somewhat easier to understand is the statement that some ways of responding to certain stimuli are more natural, or more obvious, than others. When turning the wheel of a vehicle clockwise, one expects the vehicle to turn to the right, not to the left.

There are several different forms of compatibility. Some of the more important kinds are: 1. spatial compatibility, e.g. grouping together on an instrument panel all displays and controls which functionally belong together; 2. movement compatibility, a similarity in the direction of movement in controls and in display indicators or in system response; 3. conceptual compatibility, a match between certain stimuli and concepts people often associate with these stimuli: sounds of high and low frequency refer to 'up' and 'down' respectively. The color green is associated with safety or 'go', red with danger or an emergency.

The importance of compatibility in human information processing is illustrated in an experiment by Fitts and Seeger (1953) where subjects were confronted with one of three different stimulus sets, A, B, and C (see figure 3), in which four or eight lights were arranged in different configurations. Responses were given by means of a stylus which could be moved along different channels.

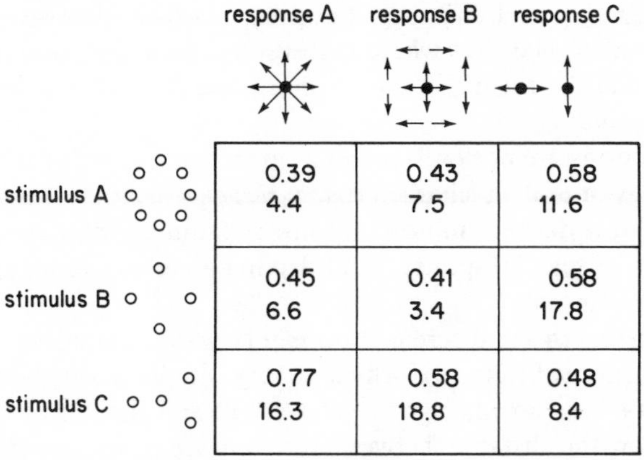

	response A	response B	response C
stimulus A	0.39 / 4.4	0.43 / 7.5	0.58 / 11.6
stimulus B	0.45 / 6.6	0.41 / 3.4	0.58 / 17.8
stimulus C	0.77 / 16.3	0.58 / 18.8	0.48 / 8.4

Figure 3. Reaction times in seconds (upper numbers), and percentage errors (lower numbers) for different stimulus-response combinations (adapted from Fitts and Seeger, 1953).

As soon as a light would come on, the subject was supposed to move the stylus to the end of the appropriate channel(s). As can be seen from figure 3, reaction times and percentage of erroneous responses were lowest when there was a correspondence between the patterns of stimuli and responses.

Human capacity for information processing is very limited, as Miller (1956) has convincingly argued. Attempts to enlarge this processing capacity have generally not been very successful. Nevertheless certain advantages can be realized by introducing redundancy in the information to be processed: although this does not enlarge capacity or speed up processing, it augments the reliability of processing (Van Cott and Kinkade, 1972).

The possibilities in combining stimuli and required control actions are almost limitless. As has been shown, human performance can be improved considerably by choosing the right combination of stimulus and control. A large volume of applied work has been done and is being done in this area. For a first orientation in this field chapters 3 and 8 in McCormick (1976) are very useful.

EXECUTING DECISIONS

Depending on the goal to be reached, and on the information available to the operator, a decision to act is reached which must then be executed. Except in situations where one decides not to act, the decision will be translated into some kind of bodily movement. Generally, this will be some hand-, arm-, or leg-movement, although other forms are possible, like making speech sounds or changing one's facial expression.

Fitts and Posner (1969) proposed a distinction between different temporal patterns of stimulus events: *discrete* events, characterized by having a clearly observable beginning and end; *serial* events, in which also separate units of activity can be identified, but where the events follow one another in a rapid sequence; *continuous* events, where a continuously varying input requires continuous responding.

These distinctions are not only useful in identifying types of *stimulus* events, they are equally useful in characterizing *response* events. Throwing a dart is an example of a discrete motor response; reading, writing, or playing the piano are types of serial responses, and driving a car is a familiar example of a continuous motor task.

Pioneering research on discrete movements was initiated by Fitts (1954). In his experiments subjects performed a very simple task: moving a stylus from a starting area to an adjacent target area. The results show that movement time depends on the distance between the two areas and on the size of the target area. A controversial point is whether the reaction time (RT), the time between the appearance of the stimulus and the start of the movement, depends on the type of task which had to be performed. A review of research by Kerr

(1978) shows that RT for a complex movement pattern is longer than for a simple movement: more time is required for the timing of the movement sequence.

Experiments by Schmidt *et al.*, (1978) show that subjects trade off speed of movement against accuracy: a larger target area allows for speedier action. Although research on these topics is not primarily prompted by practical problems, it obviously has implications for human engineering work: speed and quality of work of keyboard operators depend primarily on the dimensions and spacing of the keys.

Research on serial movements has led to ample and penetrating discussions and investigations to answer the question whether serial movements are primarily centrally controlled—an open-loop type of control—or whether movements are controlled by response produced feedback stimuli: a closed-loop kind of control (Adams, 1971, 1976; Glencross, 1977). Answers to these questions, though seemingly remote from the more mundane pursuits of applied science, are important for solving practical problems; consider e.g. the development of *effective* training programs for keyboard operators.

The driver of a car has to handle a continuously changing stream of information about his vehicle, the road, traffic signs, and other road users. This continuously changing situation requires constant activity. The perception and processing of stimuli requires a certain amount of time, and the question arises whether a driver can react continuously to this changing stream of information. One could imagine the driver to behave as an intermittent correction servomechanism: he takes a sample of the stimulus situation, acts on this information and subsequently takes a new sample (Craik, 1947).

When the driver has aquired some skill in driving, a different mode of operation could be imagined: a continuously operating transmission system with a time lag (McRuer and Jex, 1967). The effectiveness of the driver's performance will of course be different, depending on whether he acts continuously or intermittently.

Responding effectively to a continuously changing environment presupposes not only a skilled operator but also a more or less predictable task. Some kind of temporal or spatial regularity in the sequence of stimuli is necessary for the operator to be able to predict, more or less, when or where the next stimulus will come (Schmidt, 1968). In other words, the task should permit a certain degree of perceptual anticipation to allow for effective action. But *perceptual* anticipation is not the only prerequisite for effective continuous performance: some degree of *receptor* anticipation should also be possible. If the driver can see the road ahead—if some 'preview' is possible, as Sheridan and Ferrell (1974) call it—he is able to react without delay to changes in the situation, he can anticipate a road curvature, a slope, or an oncoming vehicle.

Continuous control tasks require different types of performance, depending on the nature of the control task. One can, for instance, instruct a driver to keep his vehicle always in the middle of a traffic lane. This type of task is called *pursuit* tracking. Or one could instruct the driver to keep the vehicle-speed constant in spite of any change in the slope of the road. This is a *compensatory* tracking task. In a pursuit task two different kinds of information are available to the driver: the position of the car on the road, and the effects of his control actions. In a compensatory task he is only informed about the difference between the desired and the actual output of the system.

Research shows performance in pursuit tasks usually to be superior to performance in compensatory tasks in position control (zero-order) systems (Poulton, 1974, table 9.2). In higher-order control systems this superiority does not always hold (Obermayer *et al.*, 1962).

Regardless of the order of the system, human tracking ability appears to be very limited. Experiments show that following a simple sine-track becomes too difficult at frequencies above two cycles per second (Noble *et al.*, 1955).

The degree of difficulty of a control operation sometimes depends on the relationships between the extent of a control movement and the magnitude of the effect of this movement. This subject is generally discussed under the label of control-display ratio's (C/D ratio's). Because displays are not necessarily involved it would be better to talk about control/controlled element ratio's. Changing gears while driving a car is an example of changing ratio's without any display coming into it.

The quality and/or speed of control performance depends on the C/D ratio used. If this ratio is low, a relatively small control movement results in a relatively large effect—a sensitive control: if the ratio is high, a relatively large control movement results in a relatively small effect (e.g. hoisting a load by means of a tackle). Depending on the nature of the task, a certain C/D ratio optimizes performance, in terms of time used or accuracy attained. Choice of a specific C/D ratio depends on which performance criterion, speed or accuracy, is the more important. Experiments of Jenkins and Connor (1949) show some of the relationships between the factors involved.

To conclude this paragraph, one other area of research should be mentioned, which parallels introducing multidimensionality in stimulus presentation. In executing movements the quality of performance can be increased if the visual perception of the movement can be supplemented by augmenting proprioceptive and kinesthetic feedback of the ongoing movement. Generally, it is technically possible to vary the resistance that has to be overcome in operating controls. The construction of almost frictionless controls is feasible, and on the other hand certain types of resistance can be built into controls. Spring loading, viscous damping, and inertial resistance are examples of the possibilities to change the quality of the feedback.

Research shows that proprioceptive feedback during the execution of movements is important in the timing of subsequent movements (Keele, 1968; Schmidt, 1971). Practical applications of this type of research in the design of controls are amply treated in the human engineering literature (e.g., Poulton, 1974; McCormick, 1976).

ENVIRONMENTAL INFLUENCES ON PERFORMANCE

Any goal directed performance always occurs in a certain environment that possibly influences the quality of a performance. The concept environment not only refers to the spatial aspects of a situation but includes climatic factors, vibrations, sounds, and other factors as well.

Research shows that it is not easy to pose simple and straightforward questions about environmental influences on performance. For example: certain types of noise have negative effects on certain kinds of performance, but have negligible effects on other types of work. There are even situations where noise has a relatively beneficial effect on performance, for example when operators have to work after having been deprived of sleep (Wilkinson, 1963).

Another complicating factor is that there are large individual differences in susceptibility to environmental influences. Some people hardly show any performance decrement when working in hot or noisy surroundings, while others almost feel paralyzed in such circumstances.

The nature of the task also plays an important role: performance in a monitoring task generally suffers in hot surroundings, but when a job is interesting possibly negative influences in the environment do not deteriorate performance for an appreciable amount of time.

The picture is further complicated when the duration of the task and the level of skill of the operator are taken into consideration: even in a very unpleasant environment a skilled worker shows no performance decrement during a brief working spell.

These complexities account for the lack of theory in this area, and there are no simple rules of thumb to summarize the effects of environmental factors on performance.

The alternative would be to review the voluminous research literature. Although this has been tried, e.g. Poulton (1970), at best it results in a loosely organized string of facts, leaving out interactions with many of the variables mentioned earlier. How complicated relationships between variables in this area are will be illustrated in three short examples.

Weinstein (1977) had his subjects perform a proofreading task, both in quiet and in noise (a tape recording of news items). The noise significantly impaired the detection of grammatical errors, but it did not affect the speed and the quality of detecting spelling errors.

Reviews by Grether (1971), Shoenberger (1972), and Collins (1973) show that vibrations sometimes impair performance in tracking tasks, but often have a negligible effect on reaction time tasks.

Environmental factors that impede performance in many different tasks show only minor or negligible effects when the subject considers his task interesting (Wilkinson, 1969).

Over the years many attempts have been made to accommodate the facts on environmental influences in an arousal framework. Based on the so-called Yerkes-Dodson 'law', an inverted U-type of relationship is assumed between quality of performance and the level of arousal, caused by environmental factors. These views are increasingly subject to criticism: The 'law' is a plausible but hardly explored generalization (Bartoshuk, 1971); the inverted-U relationship often depends on artifacts in experimentation (Näätänen, 1973), the unidimensionality of arousal has been challenged (Lacey, 1967), and the arousal concept itself is under attack (Cohen, 1980).

All this leads to the very unsatisfactory situation that no comprehensive theory on the effects of environmental factors on performance is in sight, and that many experimental results in this area should be regarded with suspicion, because of various methodological shortcomings. The situation has not changed for the better since Wilkinson unpromisingly stated: 'In the short term, the very complexity of the picture that arises before us may argue the case for strictly ad hoc experiments, designed to provide a specific answer for a specific question—how much will performance be debased by this particular combination of stress and task conditions' (1969, pp. 270–271).

FROM HUMAN ENGINEERING TO SYSTEM DEVELOPMENT

Earlier in this chapter the difference was noted between a psychologist who looks at the relation between man and his job from a human engineering viewpoint and his colleague who tries to optimize performance by means of selection and training. This change of view developed gradually, not only in time, but also in scope. The first step in the direction of human engineering was to abandon the idea that a human task is something given to the psychologist as a basis for selection and training, which he should not modify. If a task becomes modifiable, the psychologist could try to 'fit the job to the worker', as an early, popular definition of ergonomics has it. But he still talked about *the* job, without considering the possibility that—no matter what degree of task-modification—this job *never* could be transformed into an effective combination of man and tool to reach the goal. The budding human engineer suffered from a special form of nearsightedness: he considered the man-machine combination at best as modifiable, but not to be rejected completely. When he looked at the job of a key-punch operator, for example, he examined the operator's seating position, the key-board design, the lighting conditions, the noise situation, and the like. But it took quite some time before he started asking himself very different questions: could such a job—punching holes in paper for about forty hours a week—in any combination of man and machine whatsoever, be transformed into an acceptable job for a human being?

Putting the question this way, a different approach to work design presented itself. Why should he direct his efforts at improving today's results of a long history of combining a man and his tool to reach a certain goal? Why not start thinking about *designing* a system that realizes the goal? Asking such questions means to consider the possibility that different, even better, ways exist to reach the goal of the system than the present design.

In taking this track the role of the psychologist in human engineering changes from supplier of data for the remodelling of a task to co-designer of a man-machine system. This implies a very different approach to modelling human work.

Prior to thinking about specific tasks in a system, an exact and exhaustive definition of the system's aims should be formulated. When this is done, it usually becomes evident that the goal of the system can be reached in a number of ways. Chapanis (1965) describes different methods to collect the money a car driver has to pay for driving on a toll road. It can be done by toll collectors, who handle the money and operate the barrier. A different way to do the job is to install a machine that opens the barrier as soon as the right amount of money has been inserted. When the car passes the barrier it activates a switch that resets the machine for the next cycle.

Going back to the example of the key-punch operator: his job consists of transforming information from one kind of coding into another, usually in some kind of information processing system: for example, an accounting system. The purpose(s) of such a system can be accomplished in many different ways: by a combination of bookkeepers and adding machines; or by a combination of key-punch operators and computers; users of the system could enter information vocally, or by dialling or keying information in coded form directly into a computer, without any intervention by a specialized operator; or one might use processors equipped with optical reading devices; etc.

Before deciding on a particular system the advantages and disadvantages of different systems can be determined in the light of many and manifold criteria, often without setting up costly experiments. In this phase of choosing a system the psychologist should play an important role. He should start with a thorough analysis of human functions to be performed in a number of possible system designs. Next, he should evaluate the implications of each of the different design alterations in terms of human performance requirements to determine whether these requirements can be met by human operators. Ideally, he should not confine himself to determining the limits of human performance capacity, but rather set himself to prevent the creation of dull and impoverished jobs.

In this phase of system development decisions on task allocation have to be made which will have far-reaching consequences for the system's ultimate utility and effectiveness.

These decisions having been taken, the process of design and development then proceeds in two parallel streams, one relating to the technical components of the system (process instrumentation) and one bearing on the design and development of the human share in the system performance.

This phase is fraught with hazards, because often *parallel* is wrongly interpreted as *separate*. Obviously, this mistake results in bad designs because one overlooks that the initial task allocation is tentative, subject to revision when design problems necessitate allocation changes. When such problems are not discussed among the designers and when no action is taken to change task allocation, stagnation or poor solutions result.

A continuous dialogue between participants prevents another type of failure: design and development often require an appreciable amount of time. It often happens that in this period new technical or technological developments turn up that lead technicians to incorporate these innovations in their part of the design. When these changes are not communicated, sooner or later the psychologist discovers that he is doing useless work on yesterday's system design.

In developing the human system component, the first, essential tasks of the psychologist are to develop a thorough task analysis, to determine what human abilities and skills will be required, and what level of competence is necessary for effective system operation. Task design then needs to be supplemented by job design, combining ('packaging') the task into a job, a *human* job.

Subsequently it is up to the psychologist to find out how and where the required knowledge and skills can be obtained. Will selection be necessary? Is development and implementation of training programs necessary? Can selection or training requirements be reduced by developing job aids?

At a later stage performance measures have to be developed to determine the effectiveness of his job design and of his selection and training activities. And finally, after the human and non-human system components have been combined, he will have to participate in developing measures for evaluating the performance of the integral system.

For a thorough and detailed exposition of the different roles and tasks of the psychologist in system design and development the reader should consult Gagné (1966).

This approach to designing human work is much more radical than the activities earlier referred to as 'fitting the job to the worker'. It steers clear of prematurely accepting an existing process instrumentation or system design, and thereby avoids the pitfalls which threaten the knobs-and-dials variety of human engineering: changing human jobs only marginally, resulting only in minor improvements in system performance.

To supplement this very brief and sketchy treatment of systems psychology, the reader is referred to Meister (1971, 1976), De Greene (1970), and Beishon and Peters (1972).

HUMAN ENGINEERING RESEARCH: METHODS AND PROBLEMS

The first psychologists to enter the field of human engineering considered themselves to be applied experimental psychologists as the title of one of the first books on the subject shows (Chapanis et al., 1949). The way they tackled problems in this area was as simple as their philosophy. When they found pilots making mistakes in reading altimeters, they took the instrument out of the airplane and into their laboratories to search for the source of the errors. The results of their research sometimes were converted into an improved version of the instrument that had caused the trouble.

Over the years, however, they were confronted with performance problems that were not (easily) transferable to a laboratory setting, like car driving in dense city traffic, or handling a large ship at high sea. These developments forced psychologists to add new methods of investigation to their repertory. Chapanis (1959) provides a survey of methodological and statistical tools for different types of problems. Since his survey, several new tools have been added: research by means of simulation; psychometric methods such as rating and ranking; methods based on signal detection theory; measurement of physiological variables, like heart-rate, blood pressure, muscle tension, body fluid levels (e.g. catecholamine levels), and many others, which are reviewed by Wierwille (1979).

Along with laboratory methods the two most important tools are field research and simulation. The fundamental problem with all these types of research is the (degree of) validity of the research results for the real-life problem: are the results translatable into sound prescriptions for performing the task?

In field research controlling the experimental situation remains a chronic problem. Resorting to simulation again introduces the problem of verdicality of the results obtained in the simulated task.

Even if there are no problems about the quality of research results, errors easily creep in when these results are applied to human performance. A simple example will suffice to illustrate the problem: experimental research has shown the importance of binocular cues for correctly judging the distance of objects in the environment. Erroneously, this has led to the conclusion that good binocular vision is an essential prerequisite for successfully operating a travelling overhead crane. But there are excellent one-eyed crane operators! This type of error results if a sound task analysis is lacking. Actually, many crane operators do not use binocular cues at all in their job. In fact they use positional information: they mark certain positions on the crane jib; or they rely on certain conspicuous features of the surrounding space ('when I see the load in front of the third pillar, I am exactly on the spot where I have to dump the load').

A related pitfall which threatens the unwary user of results of laboratory research consists in applying data from a specific experiment in a seemingly very similar situation. Sleight (1948) found that presenting information by means of an open window meter (fixed pointer, moving scale) was excellent if *quantitative* information was required. A manufacturer of aircraft instruments thought he could use the same type of indicator to present *qualitative* information. To his distress he discovered that about 13% of the readings were wrong, instead of the expected 0.5%. If he had consulted the appropriate data (Grether, 1948), he would never have used an open window meter for his purpose, because Grether's work found this type of instrument rather unsuitable for conveying *qualitative* information.

A particularly vexing problem, mentioned by Chapanis (1976) in his review of methodological issues in human engineering research, is the choice of relevant dependent variables in applied research. He lists 12 different dependent variables that have been used in evaluating the legibility of type. The trouble with different dependent variables is, however, that they are often unrelated. This has major implications for the applicability of laboratory results to real-life problems, two of which are mentioned by Chapanis: 'First, although investigators may use the same words in describing their respective experiments, this does not mean that they are really talking about the same things. So when you see a number of experiments that purport to have measured the effects of something on psychomotor performance, or on complex decision making, or on vigilance, it is important to look closely at the exact dependent measures that have been used in those experiments. The data may or may not refer to the same human functions. The second implication is that we have to choose carefully and wisely when we plan applied research. If our experiments are to be meaningful, our dependent measures must have some relation to the tasks in the real-life problem that we are investigating' (1976, p. 733).

However serious these problems may be, laboratory research has the incontestable advantage that the experimental situation can be kept under control by the experimenter, which is hardly possible in field research. The same advantage holds for task simulation, although here the problem is the degree of veridicality of the simulation. But sometimes simulation is almost unavoidable: the psychologist would not have much of a chance to find a shipping company willing to put a supertanker at his disposal for some research on effects of time lag!

But how to simulate? One could substitute a supertanker by a scaled down version of such a ship. But maneuvering with a model, let us say to the scale of 1 to 25, has the disadvantage that there is a big difference between the behavior of the model and that of the real ship. From physics we know that reducing the size to 1/25 results in a reduction of the time scale to 1/5. This means that, in the model, we are dealing with speeds and accelerations that never occur in the real ship. Detecting direction or speed changes is more difficult in a slowly moving big ship than in a (faster) model: the slower the ship, the more performance suffers because of threshold problems. This means that one cannot extrapolate from the performance with the model to performance in the real task (see Wagenaar, 1970, 1973, 1975).

Finally there is the ever present problem whether the behavior of an experimental subject is comparable to his behavior in a real job situation. There may be differences in the level of motivation, in the degree of anxiety, in the amount of risk taking behavior, and in other variables that impede any attempt at extrapolating from experimental results.

These manifold difficulties have led some research workers to question the usefulness of experimental research for human engineering problems. Illustrative of this gloom is the complaint from Chapanis (1971), who considered 'much less than a fraction of one percent' of the experimental literature useful for solving practical problems. Even if some experimental research is not immediately usable, one might entertain a slightly more optimistic view in noting that laboratory experiments often are very useful because they facilitate the generation of applied experiments that *are* useful.

There is no reason to be taken aback by methodological difficulties of or by some unsuccessful attempts at applying results of experimental research to practical problems. On the contrary, discovering that human engineering research takes somewhat more than a few 'quick and dirty' experiments should be interpreted as a mark of its maturity. A growing concern about problems of validity and relevance of experimental results, an increasing emphasis on of importance of a thorough job analysis, and a growing awareness of the specific nature of applied research are signs of a more critical and more mature approach to the problems at hand.

The problems are soluble and we do not have to face them empty handed. An observation Christensen made a decade ago still holds: 'The primary problem is to get the information that is already available more generally applied, and to go out and use the tools already available' (1971, p. 182).

REFERENCES

Adams, J. A. (1971), A closed-loop theory of motor learning. *J. Motor Behavior*, **3**, 111–149.

Adams, J. A. (1976), Issues for a closed-loop theory of motor learning. In: Stellmach, G. E. (Ed.), *Motor control: Issues and trends*. New York: Academic Press.

Baddeley, A. D. (1976), *The psychology of memory*. New York: Harper and Row.

Bartoshuk, A. K. (1971), Motivation. In: Kling, J. W., Riggs, L. A. (Eds.), *Experimental psychology*. New York: Holt, Rinehart and Winston.

Beishon, J., Peters, G. (1972), *Systems behaviour*. London: Harper and Row.

Bekey, G. A. (1970), The human operator in control systems. In: De Greene, K. B. (Ed.), *Systems psychology*. New York: McGraw-Hill.

Chapanis, A. (1959), *Research techniques in human engineering*. Baltimore: The Johns Hopkins Press.

Chapanis, A. (1965), On the allocation of functions between men and machines. *Occup. Psychol.*, **39**, 1–11.

Chapanis, A. (1971), The search for relevance in applied research. In: Singleton, W. T., Fox, J. G., Whitfield, D. (Eds.), *Measurement of man at work*. London: Taylor and Francis.

Chapanis, A. (1976), Engineering psychology. In: Dunnette, M. D. (Ed.), *Handbook of Industrial and organizational psychology*. Chicago: Rand McNally.

Chapanis, A., Garner, W. A., Morgan, C. T. (1949), *Applied experimental psychology*. New York: Wiley.

Christensen, J. M. (1971), Human factors engineering considerations in systems development. In: Singleton, W. T., Fox, J. G., Whitfield, D. (Eds.), *Measurement of man at work*. London: Taylor and Francis.

Cohen, S. (1980), Aftereffects of stress on human performance and social behaviour: A review of research and theory. *Psychol. Bulletin*, **88**, 82–108.

Collins, A. M. (1973), Decrements in tracking and visual performance during vibration. *Human Factors*, **15**, 379–393.

Craik, K. J. W. (1947), Theory of the human operator in control systems. *British J. Psychol.*, **38**, 56–61, 142–148.

De Greene, K. B. (1970), *System psychology*. New York: McGraw-Hill.

Deatherage, B. H. (1972), Auditory and other sensory forms of information presentation. In: Van Cott, H. P., Kinkade, R. G. (Eds.), *Human engineering guide to equipment design*. Washington D. C.: American Institutes for Research.

Drenth, P. J. D., Willems, P. J., Wolff, Ch. J. de (Eds.) (1973), *Arbeids- en organisatiepsychologie* [Work- and organizational psychology]. Deventer: Kluwer.

Dreyfuss, H. (1972), Symbol sourcebook: An authoritative guide to international graphic symbols. New York: McGraw-Hill.

Fitts, P. M. (1954), The information capacity of the human motor system in controlling the amplitude of movement. *J. Exp. Psychol.*, **47**, 381–391.

Fitts, P. M., Jones, R. E. (1947a), *Analysis of factors contributing to 460 'pilot-error' experiences in operating aircraft controls*. Memorandum Report TSEAA-694-12, Aero Medical Laboratory, Air Material Command, Wright-Patterson Air Force Base, Dayton, Ohio, July 1, 1947.

Fitts, P. M., Jones, R. E. (1947b), Psychological aspects of instrument display. In: *Analysis of 270 'pilot-error' experiences in reading and interpreting aircraft instruments*. Memorandum Report TSEAA-694-12A, Aero Medical Laboratory, Air Material Command, Wright-Patterson Air Force Base, Dayton, Ohio, October 1, 1947.

Fitts, P. M., Posner, M. I. (1969), *Human performance*. Belmont: Brooks Cole.

Fitts, P. M., Seeger, C. M. (1953), S-R comptability: Spatial characteristics of stimulus and response codes. *J. Exp. Psychol.*, **46**, 199–210.

Forbes, T. W. (Ed.) (1972), *Human factors in highway traffic safety research*. New York: Wiley.

Gagné, R. M. (1966), *Psychological principles in system development*. New York: Holt, Rinehart and Winston.

Glencross, D. J. (1977), Control of skilled movements. *Psychol. Bulletin*, **84**, 14–29.

Grether, W. F. (1948), *Psychological factors in check-reading of single instruments*. U.S.A.F. Aeromedical Lab. MCREXD-694-17A.

Grether, W. F. (1971), Vibration and human performance. *Human Factors*, **13**, 203–216.

Hick, W. E. (1952), On the rate of gain of information. *Quart. J. Exp. Psychol.*, **4**, 11–26.

Hoopen, G. ten (1978), Om te onthouden: postcodes [To remember: zip codes]. In: Wagenaar et al. (1978).
Janssen, W. H. (1978), Achterlichten en 's-nachts rijden [Taillights and driving at night]. In: Wagenaar et al. (1978).
Jenkins, W. L., Connor, M. B. (1949), Some designs factors in making settings on a linear scale. J. Appl. Psychol., 33, 395–409.
Jong, J. R. de (1973), De toepassing van de ergonomie bij het ontwikkelen en evalueren van productiesystemen [Application of ergonomics in the development and evaluation of production systems]. In: Drenth et al. (1973).
Keele, S. W. (1968), Movement control in skilled motor performance. Psychol. Bulletin, 70, 387–403.
Kelly, C. R. (1968), Manual and automatic control. New York: John Wiley.
Kerr, B. (1978), Task factors that influence selection and preparation for voluntary movements. In: Stellmach, G. W. (Ed.), Information processing in motor control and learning. New York: Academic Press.
Klatzky, R. O. (1980), Human memory: Structures and processes. San Francisco: Freeman.
Kryter, K. D. (1972), Speech communication. In: Van Cott, H. P., Kinkade R. G. (Eds.), Human engineering guide to equipment design. Washington D. C.: U.S. Government Printing Office.
Lacey, J. I. (1967), Somatic response patterning and stress: Some revisions of activation theory. In: Appley, M. H., Trumbull, R. (Eds.), Psychological stress: Some issues in research. New York: Appleton.
McCormick, E. J. (1976), Human factors in engineering and design. New York: McGraw-Hill.
Mackie, R. R. (1977), Vigilance: Theory, operational performance and physiological correlates. New York: Plenum Press.
Mackworth, N. H. (1950), Research on the measurement of human performance. Med. Res. Council Special Report Series. H. M. Stationary Office, no. 268.
McRuer, D. T., Jex, H. R. (1967), A review of quasi-linear pilot models. IEEE Trans. Human Factors in Electronics, HFE-8, no. 3, 231–249.
Meister, D. (1971), Human factors: Theory and practice. New York: Wiley.
Meister, D. (1976), Behavioral foundations of system development. New York: Wiley.
Miller, G. A. (1956), The magical number seven, plus or minus two: Some limits on our capacity for processing information. Psychol. Review, 63, 81–97.
Näätänen, R. (1973), The inverted-U relationship between activation and performance: A critical review. In: Kornblum, S. (Ed.), Attention and performance, IV. New York: Academic Press.
Näätänen, R., Summala, H. (1976), Road-user behavior and traffic accidents. Amsterdam: North-Holland Publ. Co.
Noble, M., Fitts, P. M., Warren, C. E. (1955), The frequency response of skilled subjects in a pursuit-tracking task. J. Exp. Psychol., 49, 249–256.
Obermayer, R. W., Swartz, W. F., Muckler, F. A. (1962), Interaction of information displays with control system dynamics and course frequency in continuous tracking. Percept. Mot. Skills, 15, 199–215.
Poulton, E. C. (1970), Environment and human efficiency. Springfield: Thomas.
Poulton, E. C. (1974), Tracking skill and manual control. New York: Academic Press.
Schmidt, R. A. (1968), Anticipation and timing in human motor performance. Psychol. Bulletin, 70, 631–646.
Schmidt, R. A. (1971), Proprioception and the timing of motor responses. Psychol. Bulletin, 76, 383–393.

Schmidt, R. A., Zelaznik, H. N., Frank, J. S. (1978), Sources of inaccuracy in rapid movement. In: Stellmach, G. E. (Ed.), *Information processing in motor control and learning.* New York: Academic Press.

Sheridan, T. B., Ferrell, W. R. (1974), *Man-machine systems: Information, control and and decision models of human performance.* Cambridge (Mass.): MIT Press.

Shoenberger, R. W. (1972), Human response to whole-body vibration. *Percept. Mot. Skills*, **34**, 127–160.

Sinaiko, H. W. (1961), *Selected papers on human factors in the designs and use of control systems.* New York: Dover Publications.

Sleight, R. B. (1948), The effect of instrument dial shape on legibility. *J. Appl. Psychol.*, **32**, 170–188.

Taylor, F. V. (1957), Simplifying the controller's task through display quickening. *Occup. Psychol.*, **31**, 120–125.

Van Cott, H. P., Kinkade, R. G. (1972), *Human engineering guide to equipment design.* American Institutes for Research, Washington D. C.: U.S. Government Printing Office.

Vroon, P. A. (1978), Het verwarren van munten [Confusing coins]. In: Wagenaar *et al.* (1978).

Wagenaar, W. A. (1970), Human aspects of ship maneuvering and simulation. *International Shipbuilding Progress*, **17**, 11–14.

Wagenaar, W. A. (1973), Besturing van grote schepen als een ergonomisch probleem [Handling of large ships as an ergonomic problem]. In: Drenth *et al.* (1973).

Wagenaar, W. A. (1975), Supertankers: Simulators for the study of steering. *American Psychologist*, **30**, 440–444.

Wagenaar, W. A. (1979), Recalling messages broadcast to the general public. In: Grüneberg, M., *et al.* (Eds.), *Practical aspects of memory.* London: Academic Press, 128–136.

Wagenaar, W. A., Vroon, P. A., Janssen, W. H. (Eds.) (1978), *Proeven op de som* [The proof is in the pudding]. Deventer: Van Loghum Slaterus.

Walraven, P. L. (1978), Verkeerslichten [Traffic lights]. In: Wagenaar *et al.* (1978).

Weinstein, N. D. (1977), Noise and intellectual performance: Confirmation and extension. *J. Appl. Psychol.*, **62**, 104–107.

Wierwille, W. W. (1979), Physiological measures of aircrew mental load. *Human Factors*, **21**, 575–593.

Wilkinson, R. T. (1963), Interaction of noise with knowledge of results and sleep deprivation. *J. Exp. Psychol.*, **66**, 332–337.

Wilikinson, R. T. (1969), Some factors influencing the effects of environmental stressors upon performance. *Psychol. Bulletin*, **72**, 260–272.

Woodson, W. E., Conover, D. W. (1966), *Human engineering guide for equipment designers.* Berkeley: Univ. of California Press.

2.6. Workload
An introduction to psychological theories and measurement methods

Theo F. Meijman and James F. O'Hanlon

1. INTRODUCTION

Work psychology may be defined as the study of the organization of working activity, i.e. the study of its mental structure and regulation. Working activity is described as the systematic and motivated execution of tasks, conforming with an assignment and occurring within a specifiable working situation (Hacker, 1978; Sperandio, 1980; Willems, 1981). The systematic character of working activity derives from the anticipation of the result to be achieved during the course of this activity. This requirement is formally specified by the assignment, together with known quantitative and qualitative achievement norms. The assignment, norms, goals of work and ways of achieving the latter in particular situations are represented at the cognitive level in the worker. The motivational character of work behavior derives from the worker's acceptance of the formal assignment as his or her personal task. The readiness to do this—which, more frequently than not, has a compelling nature in real occupations (Leplat, 1980)—limits the extent to which individual performance variations are manifested.

The execution occurs by means of coordinated perceptual-motor and cognitive operations, often involving the use of specific procedures and tools This execution may be more or less efficient, and is in any case limited by the worker's performance potential of the moment. By this we mean the physical and mental functional systems which are available to the worker and which he must mobilize in order to execute task demands. The psychological study of workload now means attention to the mental structure and regulation changes that affect performance potential and/or the readiness or motivation

Prof. dr. J. F. O'Hanlon, Rijks Universiteit Groningen, Verkeerskunde, GRONINGEN.

for applying that potential. These changes are studied in functional relation to the type and intensity of demands which the worker is charged with in a real-life work situation.

Work behavior is always productive in more than one aspect. That activity changes not only situations or material things, but also the worker himself. This is to say, the execution of task demands always follows two paths. Simultaneously with achieving a particular service or product, the work behavior results in one or another development of the worker's potentials and/or their means of expression and organization. These results can be benificial. What was specified in the work assignment is indeed achieved and possibly much more. Moreover, through the fulfillment of task demands, individuals may develop their performance capabilities in a number of ways. For instance, they may acquire new problem-solving techniques. Or they may find gratification in the knowledge that their participation will result in a good product, encouraging their continued effort. In these circumstances one shouldn't too hastily speak in terms of workload as 'taxing', even though compliance with task demands always has a loading aspect. There is always the appeal to the worker's persently available performance potentials and his readiness to mobilize them. A one-sided conception of workload as a particularly negative occurrence is not necessary and may be misleading.

Meeting task demands is an essential aspect of every interaction of man with his environment, without which the development of human skill is impossible. We come across this concept particularly in the European literature of work psychology (e.g. see Sperandio, 1971; Leplat, 1972; Bachmann et al., 1973). But still, it is more customary to associate the workload question with such things as performance decrement, interference with performance potential, or a reduction of the readiness to apply existing performance capacity (Ettema, 1968, 1973).

As a consequence of the dominant perspective, research on workload has been largely ad hoc for defining a particular negative effect and seeking a specific solution. Theories based upon such demonstrations would only be useful for designing tasks to avoid negative consequences, but not to encourage human development which could be the positive consequence. This point was raised repeatedly in the 1970s (Sperandio 1971, 1972, 1978; Bainbridge 1974, 1978; Hacker 1976, 1978).

By these introductory remarks we wish to establish a special area within work psychology for research on workload. In the following section (2), we shall summarize previous definitions of the term 'workload' and discuss some general aspects of workload research. We give much attention in the next section (3) to the guiding models of human information processing as these have evolved from experimental psychology. We feel that knowledge of these theories is essential for every work- and organizational psychologist who is confronted with the practical workload problems. In section 4 we discuss the various measurement methods and their relationships to the theories. Finally (section 5) we conclude with a number of practical applications of the theories and methods.

2. CONCEPT DEFINITION

Research on the functional relationships between human performance, on the one hand, and task difficulty or other situational factors, on the other, was already present in 19th century industrial sciences from which work- and organizational psychology originated. Fredric Taylor's efforts to develop systematic task prescription may apply as the first examples of research in work psychology, particularly as it pertains to workload research. Taylor's dual purpose for optimizing work methods through systematic observation and experimentation was to achieve the highest level of individual productivity in every task situation, while at the same time minimizing the personal cost of working in terms of fatigue symptoms and the like. Although the latter aspect of his approach is frequently overlooked, it laid the foundation for modern work psychology (e.g. see Ydo, 1955; Volpert et al., 1977).

It is interesting that at about the same time the German psychiatrist, Emil Kraepelin, formulated a number of principles on mental fatigue and work hygiene that very much resembled those implicit in Taylor's work. (Hinrichs, 1981). Kraepelin utilized the then current methods of work physiology for defining the 'work curve' as a graphic barometer of performance diminishing over time under conditions determined by the task difficulty. This decrement was the inferred, direct indication of fatigue.

2.1. Processing potential

Kraepelin's work curve was the exemplary functional description of the relationship between workload and fatigue until the end of World War II (Haider, 1962). It served as a worthwhile example, in a heuristic sense, but led to dubious conclusions regarding the direct relationships between task difficulty and performance efficiency; and concerning the validity of deteriorating performance as a direct index of increasing fatigue. Vernon (1921) and Musico (1921) had already argued that performance can be sustained, or even improved, as task difficulty increases, so long as the workers were highly motivated. Their opinion was confirmed by later work indicating that performance efficiency is not directly dependent upon task difficulty or other situational factors, except perhaps in extreme situations; and, that fatigue resulting from a constant heavy workload does not invariably produce a measurable performance decrement (Murrell, 1965; Bartenwerfer, 1970; Cameron, 1973; Simonson et al., 1976; Blitz et al., 1978).

There seems to be a necessity to postulate a connecting link. Of critical importance is the ability and readiness of the worker to continuously adjust to the task demands. This ability occupies a central position in research on workload. It is not a static or abstract notion. The following example serves to illustrate the point. A man has, under normal circumstances, two hands, making it impossible to turn three knobs at the same time. His ability is limited in this respect, unless he can learn to use his mouth to turn the third knob. Ability can be expanded by the choice of a different operative strategy. Thus stipulation of any ability limit must be made contingent upon the operative strategy. In fact, Taylor's contribution was an outstanding example of the 'rules' for selecting the most efficient operative strategies. What he apparently failed to realize was that the prescribed 'one best way' to accomplish a task objective not only varies between tasks, but also for the same task performed in different environments and by different workers. The worker-task-environment interaction determines the optimal strategy and not one of these factors alone.

The effectiveness of a given strategy depends upon execution possibilities in the operational environment and within the worker himself. New strategies must be chosen to adjust for changes in the environment or worker, such as a sudden increase in objective workload or as the result of fatigue. Sperandio (1971, 1972) observed the effect of increasing numbers of aircraft on the strategies chosen by air traffic controllers. Simplifying strategies were chosen to handle the workload change. Bauju et al. (1978) further demonstrated that controller experience determined strategy change under such circumstances: the less experienced persisted in employing the more precise but time-consuming strategy. In a study employing crane operators, Wendrich (1973) showed that strategy changes can also occur when the psychophysiological state of the operator changes under the influence of fatigue. The operators changed their work methods without a change in the workload and without much change in the level of their final performance.

In practical work situations individuals are not passively influenced by loading factors. Instead, they will try with every means possible to actively deal with these in a dynamic system (Bainbridge, 1974; Hacker et al., 1978; Sperandio, 1978, 1980). This is to say that the operator, in the application of particular operative strategies, realizes his operational capacity. He does not function as a stimulus-response automation. Workload may then be described (see Ogden et al., 1979) as the discrepancy between the system input and the system processing potential to deal with this input. We use the concept 'processing potential' in a broad sense; i.e. as the total ability of the processing system in the execution of complex task demands. We shall reserve the concept of 'capacity' for those situations which are concerned with the limits of specific functions or functional systems having to do with the execution of specific task demands. This distinction makes sense for a number of reasons. Work load factors have a specific effect on particular functional systems making an analytic approach necessary. This means that the capacity of each functional system concerned, as well as the relationship between the changes in specific loading factors and system output up to capacity limits, must be separately examined. This distinction is reasonable in order to show that no linear relationship is necessary between the total processing potential and the capacity of composite functional systems. That the operator's processing potential seems unaffected does not necessarily mean that separate functional systems cannot be nearly overloaded. Problems result from long-lasting overloading of a particular function. For these reasons it is also important to know the capacity of separate mental and/or physical functions.

2.2. External load and functional load

In the preceding section we have mentioned one previous definition of 'workload'. Described as the discrepancy between system input and system potential to process this input, workload is not defined in terms of one or more dependent or independent variables, but in terms of an intervening variable. Other definitions (see Chiles *et al.*, 1979) make reference to observable effects and not to the process from which they are assumed to result. Monod *et al.* (1976, p. 11) preferred a similar definition of workload: 'the effects upon the organism of the burden borne literally as well as figuratively by men in connection with work'. Their definition is rather vague but, by referring to the effects, tends toward a more operational level than the process definition.

However, in both cases load is expressed in terms that suggest the possibility of its measurement specifically in humans, as parameters revealing the mobilization and/or disregulation of functional systems. In the literature of work physiologists they speak similarly of functional or relative load. This they distinguish from external or absolute load, described as the combination of factors inherent in the type of work—intensity and duration and the work circumstances which lead to human reactions (Bink, 1962; Bonjer, 1965). The latter are not represented as quantities measured in humans but in mainly physical quantities such as kilograms, Herz, etc. In work physiology (Ettema, 1973) and work sociology (de Ruigh, 1973) several categories of external load are distinguished. In relation to the type of work one may differentiate between metabolic load (dynamic and/or static muscle work) and mental load (information processing). In connection with situational factors one may distinguish environmental/physical factors (heat, cold, noise), chemical/physical factors (toxic substances, radiation) and psycho-social factors producing emotional reactions.

In work and organizational psychological literature we find these factors of external load for the most part under the term 'stressors' (e.g. Landy *et al.*, 1976; Winnubst, 1981). We feel that within the framework of work-load research this is an unfortunate term. From the relevant literature (among others,

Kasl, 1978; Sanders, 1980; Kleber, 1981; Sharit, 1982) it is clear that the various descriptions of the concept of 'stress' are usually associated with awareness of a threat. Stress has been psychologically defined as the reaction accompanying the perceived or assumed inability to deal with the system input (Welford, 1973; Sanders, 1980). The term 'stressor' refers to those task demands and/or work circumstances which are perceived or anticipated as threatening on the basis of the awareness of the absence of performance potential or its development. Defined thus, a stress reaction always implies load but load does not necessarily imply a stress situation.

Every workload study begins with the analysis of task demands and the circumstances under which the tasks must be performed. Several formal methods exist for the analysis of task demands and work conditions. In addition to the ergonomic checklists and related instruments, such as the checklists developed in France for working conditions and function-content of the LEST (Guélaud et al., 1975), or SAVIEM (Vandevijver, 1978), there is a number of more psychologically oriented analysis tools which can be used. Among these is The Position Analysis Questionnaire (McCormick et al., 1972), versions of which are being developed by (among others) the Dutch Rail and PTT. There is also the Job Diagnostic Survey (Hackman et al., 1975), in a Dutch version translated by Van der Graaf et al. (1978). Algera (1980), inspired by the JDS, has developed a Dutch language instrument for this study of task features. Further, there are German language instruments such as the Arbeitswissenschaftliche Erhebungsverfahren zur Tätigkeits-Analyse, the AET (Rohmert et al., 1979), and the Tätigkeits Bewertungs System, the TBS (Baars et al., 1981), neither of which exists, unfortunately, in either a Dutch or English version. Finally, we have the recently developed group diagnostic Periodic Research of Functions, the POF (Dijkstra et al., 1981), which may be employed as the initial screening instrument in the analysis of tasks demands and working conditions. An instrument such as the Question List for Organization Stress, VOS (Reiche et al., 1980) may also be used for this purpose.

2.3 Load effects, susceptibility and recovery

The term load, as previously mentioned, implies some limitation of the operator's capacity in some function or functional system. Overload occurs whenever the limit of a particular capacity is exceeded. Overload means, then, an excess of the loading factors concerned. The opposite, 'under-loading', poses a number of problems. With regard to many external loads it is hardly reasonable to refer to under-loading. What might one think, for instance, of the under-loading of toxic substances, temperature or radiation. The concept of under-loading is reserved for one specific loading situation: the absence of challenging stimuli or the continual repetition of the same type of stimuli in a task and/or task situation. The question remains why monotonous and unchallenging tasks and situations are loading, certainly over a long period, and result in the particular state of boredom which also seems to have physiological correlates (see among others, O'Hanlon, 1981). There is much to be said for the least possible use of the term under-loading and call the loading situation to which it pertains by its name, monotony.

Much research on workload may be characterized as the study of 'threshold crossing' from a still tolerable load level to a situation of 'over-loading'. In this 'testing the limits' an effort is made to define the capacity limits for respective functional systems. In such research, the criteria sought are the appearance of specific loading effects in the form of deterioration of mental and/or physical functions. These may be a quantitative and/or qualitative decrease in observable performance (for example, no longer picking up the signals in a detection task). It can also be the mobilization of a (psycho-)physiological system (for example, increased adrenaline production over a base-line). Finally, it can be changes in subjective feeling.

For the most part research is concerned with a combination of various types of criteria. In this regard, a one-dimensional work-load concept is practically abandoned and a modern interpretation emphasizes the multidimensional character in a system approach (Meister, 1976). In general, short-term criteria are considered: performance changes in a given task, pulse rate under a given workload, mood change at a given moment. In the seventies, we see a renewed orientation toward epidemiological research and, although sporadic, increasing use of longitudinal criteria. This followed from the recognition of long-term pathological consequences (e.g. myocardial heart disease, Jenkins, 1971), of sustained heavy mental or physical loading which never exceeds capacity at any given moment. Kasl (1978) gives an outstanding overview of epidemiological research with regard to workload. Broadbent (1979) discusses the possibility of using long-term criteria in fatigue research. Rohmert et al. (1979) argue that one should not only be interested in the execution of a task at a particular moment, but also, especially in the day-to-day repetition of work during the normal work period and throughout the course of the working life.

In this connection use could be made of turnover rate, absenteeism and morbidity as the first indications of possible workload problems in work situations (see Meijman et al., 1982; Vroege, 1981). The highest level of task demands that can be endured throughout the working life, without work-related damage to health, is defined by Rohmert et al. (1979) as the level of 'tolerability'. This is a particularly important concept in work-load research. Hacker (1976) likewise felt that the limits of processing capability are only interesting from the standpoint of long-term effects in the practice of work psychology. He added the observation that the 'tolerability' level may only be studied from the aspect of recovery from workload effects over short and long terms. This leads to the establishment of an important criterion: 'recovery time' or period that must elapse before a particular function or the whole processing system returns to the resting or base-line level. Though generally ignored, this concept was advanced earlier. In 1894 Kraepelin introduced recovery-time in his study of fatigue symptoms in mental tasks (Hinrichs, 1981). It was later repeatedly mentioned in general review articles with emphasis on fatigue research (e.g. Bartenwerfer, 1970; Cameron, 1973). Nevertheless, there has been still little systematic research on this important topic. Our inattention to recovery probably has to do with previous excessive attention for defining the capacity limits of various mental functions under extreme conditions (an orientation which prevailed in vigilance research of the 60s). Moreover, establishing a resting level is not always simple, certainly not in the case of mental functions.

Work physiologists, on the other hand, have long known of the necessity for relating the metabolic cost of working under a specified physical load over a specified period to the time that must elapse after work until complete metabolic restoration can occur (e.g. Ettema, 1973). The extension of the recovery time concept and implementation of its measurement in work psychology seems an important future objective.

2.4. Multiple load

Another important point is implicit in the above remarks. It concerns the multiple and cumulative action of separate loads. Separate loading factors have specific actions depending upon the function or functional system on which they act. In practice, however, a separate load is seldom, if ever, placed upon only a single function or functional system. Noise, for example, acts not only on the hearing organs but interferes as well with the ability to concentrate. During a task which demands a high level of concentration, noise can lead to an increased percentage of errors which may in turn lead to mood changes in the operator. Colquhoun (1962) showed that the influence of a combination of two loads on performance in a signal detection task was greater than the influence of both loads calculated separately. From a recent literature review, however, (Poulton, 1978) it seems that the so-called 'super-additive effect' of loads (Broadbent, 1971) may be adequately described with the aid of a linear additive model in which it can be seen that synergistic or multiplicative effects do not generally occur.

A final point concerns the accumulation of workload effects over time. Men should daily recover from the effects of loading between repetition of a task. The time necessary for recovery depends on the type of the load effects and the individual's resilience. Incomplete recovery may lead to greater effort requirements to continue performance. The need for recovery shall then be greater and the time for recovery longer. When there is inadequate recovery, time a cumulative effects can develop (van der Helm et al., 1982).

2.5. A methodological problem

There is a conceptual and methodological problem in research on workload. This concerns the description of workload as a discrepancy between the system-input and the system-potential to process the input. Workload is defined in terms of a relationship. We shall give an example. Lifting a 1.5 kilogram brick with one hand is impossible for a boy or girl of six. This demand is too great. The individual's capacity is exceeded simply because the hand cannot contain the brick. An adult would have less difficulty, unless he had already lifted 100 bricks and this were the 101st. And even then an expert bricklayer would have less difficulty with a 1.5 kilogram brick than the authors of this article. In the case of the expert bricklayer, the effects would differ at least quantitatively and perhaps also qualitatively. This difference is not only the result of more developed biceps (as well as the remaining functional systems which make this motor coordination possible). Close observation shall show that the expert bricklayer processes the demand, 'lifting a 1.5 kilogram brick with one hand' in another manner than the authors: more even tempo, smoother movement, optimal grasp, slight bending of the knees at the right moment, etc. The expert bricklayer regulates his performance better than the authors. Consequently, meeting the task demand means a different load for him.

What we wish to illustrate with this prosaic example is that the distinction between external versus functional load is of theoretical importance but not always maintainable. The problem becomes worse when we realize that psychologists wish to measure loading factors in the work situation which are not expressable in such handy amounts as kilograms, Herz, degrees Celcius and the like. Even if this were possible it is not so much a question of the quantitative level of these factors. Rather, the processing of them and in particular the mental regulating of the processing is the question of interest for psychologists (Sperandio, 1971, 1972; Hacker, 1978). In this area the problem becomes particularly clear. It is not unusual in the psychological literature to define 'mental workload' in terms of a particular manner of information processing: (the) controlled processing mode (see section 3.3; Shiffrin et al., 1977). Within this specific model of information processing, mental workload may be defined as the time in the 'controlled mode' (Mulder, 1980). A task may now be said to be proportionately more mentally loading as a function of increased time spent in this mode.

It is clear that in this instance it is difficult to speak of external load, which is not expressed in terms of measurement in humans. The load is explicitly operationalized only in human measurements; in a parameter which is significant within a particular model of information processing. It is important to note that in cases such as this external load may not be studied independently from functional load. A second important point is that these particular forms of measurement of mental load assume a particular theory. Outside this theory, the measurement procedure may have no, or in any case another meaning. For this reason we shall pay considerable attention to theoretical models, with regard to human information processing, which form the theoretical foundations for the various concepts of mental workload.

3. MENTAL LOAD

3.1. Definition

With developments in the production process, in which supervisory and control tasks are assuming an increasing prominence, mental load has become one of the most important areas in the study of workload. What is meant when someone says that he feels mentally burdened? We shall discuss this in the following section. People can speak fairly easily about mental workload. They also can give significant and reliable subjective estimates of the mental workload of a task (Moray, 1982). Yet, there is no generally accepted operational definition of the concept, either in terms of task variables or in terms of measurement of effects. Opinions in the literature are also divided over the prospect of whether this is even possible. The question is whether we can present mental workload as a one-dimensional, simple amount, thus making the search for a single measurement unreasonable from the outset. Rather, we should think in terms of qualitatively differing workload patterns. These may be associated with the various constellations of functional systems, concerned with the execution of various tasks. Sanders (1977, 1980), argues that the functional systems involved must be known for the formulation of such workload patterns. And psychology still has a long way to go in achieving this. Be that as it may, it is generally accepted that the conceptual definition of mental workload must have a bearing on the processing of information in the central nervous system relative to the capacity limits of the processing mechanisms. Thus, information is the loading factor that concerns us when we speak of mental workload (Kalsbeek, 1967).

The estimated intensity of processing information in some way should be scale-able. The highest point on such a scale would be reached at the maximum intensity of information processing for a particular individual in the execution of a particular task under specific conditions and with the use of particular operational strategies. We have already suggested that the search for such a scale is problematic. Nevertheless, upto the late 70s this was the area in which numerous researchers occupied themselves (see Moray, 1979). The vast majority came from experimental psychology and systems engineering, others from more applied disciplines such as ergonomics.

What would be obvious to anyone reading this literature for the first time is its lack of reference to data from practical work situations or realistic simulations of real work. The relevance of this literature is therefore not always clear to the practicing work or organizational psychologist. But it would be incorrect for them to entirely disregard the present theories and models of human information processing. They should be of considerable heuristic value. Modern theories are robust enough to explain many, if not all, problems associated with mental workload. Under some circumstances they yield interesting predictions that could readily be tested in field situations.

For these reasons, we shall discuss the development of theories underlying the concept of mental workload. We shall begin with the earliest models of human information processing as occurring within a single channel between sensory input and motor output. We shall continue through the development of multi-channel models that explain simultaneous processing of several input streams; and then, with theories that are less concerned with invariant stages of information processing but more with step-changes in operative strategies that qualitatively alter the process. Finally we shall comment upon the relationship between information processing and the psychophysiological status of the individual in order to explain how the interaction might affect mental workload even while the task remains constant.

3.2. Information processing models based upon the notion of a single processing channel

The simplest analogy for these models is a single communication line over which serial, equally-long messages are transmitted. The processing speed is merely a function of the time necessary to encode and transmit each message and the minimal necessary pause between messages. System capacity is a simple rate limitation. Depending upon the fundamental message length (i.e. information contained in each and every message) there exists a maximum rate which limits the total amount of information transmitted over time. The same sort of limitation was seen in human information processing by telecommunication engineers and experimental psychologists in the late 1940s and early 1950s.

3.2.1. LIMITING OF CHANNEL CAPACITY

The theory that men act like digital computers in their information processing functions was particularly emphasized in the early work of George A. Miller (1953, 1956). In his research it appeared that there was an upper limit for human capacity to react with a specific motor response, at various levels of one-dimensional sensory stimulus, for instance the brightness of a light signal or the intensity of a tone. Miller considered a limited perceptual-motor channel capacity probable. The number of reliable associations for a great number of various stimuli is around seven and never exceeds twelve. Multi-dimensional sensory stimuli make a greater number of reliable associations possible, never more than 128 however.

It would seem then that humans, as computers, know a fundamental limit to their channel capacity. This enables them to process a maximum amount of information in each message, and no more than that. As opposed to the computer, in which the maximum length of the code is the permanent length, humans can also, within a single information processing cycle, process an amount of information which is below the maximum channel capacity. This makes the analogy with the digital computer somewhat less attractive. Neverthe-less, studies by Hick (1952) and Sternberg (1969) among others showed that the reaction time is indeed related to the information-load of the input units. It matters little whether the information concerned originates from sensory stimulation or from memory.

3.2.2. THE FILTER THEORY

The implied serial stages of human information processing were originally modeled by Broadbent (1952). He recognized that the senses present far more information to the brain than can possibly be processed in a manner leading to decisions and discrete motor responses. This sensory information proceeds in parallel channels to a very short-term or buffer memory repository from which old information is constantly replaced by that more recently acquired. A small part of the information is, however, permitted to pass through to the next stage where encoding of the message occurs. This code is something that enters the simultaneous processes of perception and memory search to establish meaning, and exits through final serial stages of decision and response execution. According to Broadbent, the selective passage of information is controlled by a gating mechanism. The function of the gate is not random, but is in part determined by properties of the information in buffer storage (novel, biologically relevant or intense stimulus information has precedence) and in part by the directives of a higher process which establishes continuity of perception (information which is congruent with that previously encoded has precedence).

Perception theoreticians such as Triesman (1969) modified Broadbent's 'filter theory' by showing that an active processing of incoming information must already be occurring in the short-term buffer system. In these models of information processing the rate-limiting step was located just before the entry of information into the perceptual process. However, Deutsch and Deutsch (1963) offered a competing version of the single-channel model, wherein the sensory information is encoded and perceptually analyzed in parallel streams and where rate-limiting occurs in the stage of response selection. A different sort of continually refreshed, working memory enables the system to maintain a tendency to respond in task appropriate ways, and no other; i.e. a limited number of response routines are held in a relatively high state of activation. One of these is triggered by the arrival of a particular perceptual transmission. The 'decision' is automatically taken and recorded in memory.

3.2.3. MENTAL WORKLOAD ACCORDING TO THE SINGLE CHANNEL THEORY

Though certainly not inclusive of every version of the single-channel model, this summary indicates its basic tennants. Information processing is data-driven. The capacity of the system is first limited by the time information can exist in buffer storage before being replaced by new information. In most versions of the model, discrete codes of limited length or duration are either transmitted or synthesized in a serial manner to permit subsequent comparison with codes actively drawn from long-term memory. This memory search again proceeds in a linear manner with each recorded memory code being compared to the input code in turn. Eventually the meaning of the input is established. It is then matched to an appropriate output routine that must be initiated before the next input code can enter the process. The entire sequence represents a single decision.

Two concepts of mental load arise from this model. Both are time dependent. The simplest is the frequency of serial decisions made in response to the input load during the course of the task (Welford, 1968). However, the decision rate is inversely related to the information content of sequentially encoded input transmissions and to the number of operations, such as memory search, that occur before response selection and execution. It is illogical to suppose that mental load would be greater when the task requires more frequent decisions based upon repetitions of simple inputs, than when it requires fewer decisions based upon complex inputs that must be dealt with in longer operations. Therefore an alternative concept of mental load must be developed. A more logical proposition is that mental load is proportional to the relative time the system spends in processing any input transmission, simple or complex (e.g. Kalsbeek, 1975). The human who is continuously active in processing input data is loaded to the maximum of his capacity, and if his information processing system has any 'down time', this translates over the task period as a proportionate reduction in his mental load.

Although the strict, single-channel model of human information processing was totally rejected before the end of the 1960s, the notion of a direct relationship between decision frequency and mental load has lingered on. Indeed, Moray (1979) noted that among a group of experts at a recent conference on the topic, the *only* agreement was upon the assumed direct relationship between decision frequency and mental workload. The support for this assumption was lacking in the single-channel era and is still lacking today.

3.3. Multiple channel models

The single-channel model was ultimately rejected for the simple reason that it could not explain experimental results or real life behavior; specifically the following:

1. Increasing independence of stimulus input load and response latency with prolonged practice; reaction times tend to shorten to the same limit, irrespective of the number of alternative stimuli and contingent responses, after the task of identifying stimuli becomes 'routine'.

2. Increasing independence of stimulus input load and response latency with increasing compatibility of displays and controls; so long as stimulus sources and response switches are located in close spatial proximity it does not matter how many alternatives exist with respect to response latency.

3. Concurrent continuous performance of two or more tasks during the same period without apparent performance discontinuities; expert pilots simultaneously control air speed, roll, yawn and pitch using separate throttle, rudder and aileron controls while at the same time receiving and sending complex information via radio.

4. Gradual or sudden deterioration in performance that is in no way related to variation in input information or motor response capabilities; the occurrence of 'skill fatigue' (Bartlett, 1943), or 'blocking' (Bills, 1931; Kogi and Saito, 1973) that, respectively, disorganizes or interrupts continuous performance in tracking tasks.

5. Spontaneous and complete changes in task strategy that imply adoption of different input-output relationships in spite of constant task conditions.

To explain these findings, a remarkably large number of theorists have offered variants of a multiple-channel model of human information processing. Space here permits only a general recapitulation of elements common to different versions of the model, with occasional specific reference to unique and potentially valuable individual contributions. For complete information the interested reader should refer to the following, major theoretical expositions (Moray, 1967; Allport et al., 1972; Kahneman, 1973; Kerr, 1973; Norman and Bobrow, 1975; Legge and Barber, 1976; Rassmussen, 1976; Broadbent, 1977; Schneider and Shiffrin, 1977; Shiffrin and Schneider, 1977; McClelland, 1979; Mulder, 1979—this list is representative and not exhaustive).

3.3.1. AUTOMATIC INFORMATION PROCESSING

To begin with, a distinction must be made between types of information processing that are normally invariant with respect to input-output those which are not and the transfer function that relates the two. Automatic feedback loops involved in the maintenance of vital parameters around homeostatic set-points rarely receive the attention of psychologists, but certainly involve this sort of invariant information processing which coexists with every other sort. Automatic regulation apparently involves a relatively small proportion of the brain's total capacity and is generally not considered as a source of mental load. At least, this is true in resting man, it may not be so when a very heavy burden is placed upon several homeostatic regulatory systems as during intense physical exercise or immediate recovery from the same.

Certain learned behaviors arising from the relatively invariant S-R associations that are only acquired after long practice closely resemble innate automatic control. Thus, a particular complex sensory input, representing both a critical event (i.e. requiring a response) and the normal contextual non-critical events that reliably occur together in space and time, directly comes to a routine response without further operations being performed on the data. This process relies upon the formation of a special purpose processing channel that transmits messages with an informational content which is independent of the full range of S-R possibilities in the given situation. For example, transcription of either randomly ordered numbers or letters proceeds at approximately the same rate for an experienced typist in spite of the fact that the number of S-R possibilities is in the former case 10, and in the latter, 26. Apparently, typists viewing a number or letter have no need to exhaustively search their long-term memories for the respective character-sets before selecting the appropriate motor response. Each input representing a character directly initiates a particular motor routine which is responsible for one key-stroke response and no other.

The special-channel concept is now widely accepted in a number of models (Legge and Barber, 1976; Rassmussen, 1976; Shiffrin and Schneider, 1977; Mulder, 1979). It was mainly developed to explain the independence of stimulus information load and response latency that occurs after long practice, but it also explains how it might be possible for the brain to direct two motor operations at the same time. So long as different effectors (muscles controlling the hand and foot) are used, each can respond to the outputs of separate special-channels. The temporal coordination of special-channel operations, however, is an activity that has never been thoroughly explained.

Special-channel information processing has become known as 'automatic'. Its obvious advantages are speed and reliability. Less obvious is its lack of dependence upon information retention in short-term memory. That system capacity is apparently untapped by automatic processing and therefore remains fully available for commitment to other concurrent activities. The limit to the volume of information that can be represented in a single special-channel transmission is apparently very great. Still, a limit must exist if for no other reason than the rapid decay and/or replacement of information held in buffer storage as a prelude to encoding. Information that develops over several seconds is unlikely to be encoded in a single transmission. A further limitation might involve the number of special-channels that can be developed in training.

3.3.2. CONTROLLED INFORMATION PROCESSING

Automatic processing is now commonly distinguished from that involving the retention of information in short-term 'working' or 'active' memory where various operations are performed in a 'controlled' process. The dependence of this process upon short-term memory establishes its fundamental capacity limit. After coding enables the entry of a message into this process, it must maintain the information in short-term memory, while searching for and retrieving codes from long-term or 'passive' memory to establish the meaning of the input. Having identified the input, the similar process of response selection must transpire before a decision enables the execution of a response routine. The greater the informational content of the input, the longer the duration of the process. Although the opinions of various theorists differ with respect to possibilities of parallel processing within this system, all agree that the decision stage is unitary. Simply stated, this process cannot lead to multiple simultaneous decisions following the same series of operations. This process, and not its automatic counterpart, is considered to be the basis of consciousness.

3.3.3. MENTAL WORKLOAD DEFINED IN TERMS OF CONTROLLED INFORMATION PROCESSING

The advantage of controlled processing is greater flexibility in dealing with unfamiliar inputs that require non-stereotyped responses. Because it presumably utilizes a far greater proportion of the brain's resources in correspondence with task demands, it has been identified as the source of mental load. Mulder's (1980, p. 13) definition is the most explicit.

> 'Mental task load will be a function of the number of processing stages or processes required for adequate task performance and in particular the amount of time during which the subject is required to use control processes in working memory.'

Considering mainly the type of information processing now defined as controlled, other authors have offered alternative definitions of mental load. Moray (1967) and Norman and Bobrow (1975) developed models wherein the entire process was divided among functional parts, each occupying a share of 'space' within the system at any moment in time. By 'space', the authors refer to the number of units involved and not simply to discrete and separate brain areas. Within a capacity limit, space is allocated to each functional part in correspondence with its information load and also the program of operations that must be performed upon the data. If the load is great, or the program complex, the entire available space will be filled by a single operation. On the other hand, several operations can be performed simultaneously if their combined space does not fill the system to capacity and if these do not compete for the same indivisible resources (access to special-purpose perceptual or motor mechanisms).

These models seem particularly applicable for explaining why operators feel mentally loaded in proportion to the size of the queue of 'clients' awaiting their services (Moray, 1982). Although service to the first in line presumably occupies the greatest space in the information processing system, the presence of subsequent clients entails some allocation of space to determine if any one has a problem of such urgency as to demand immediate attention, superseding priority assigned solely on the basis of arrival. Eventually, the limited capacity models would predict a loss of capability to either service the first client or recognize some difficulty of one who follows at a critical queue length. The importance of this prediction for tasks such as air traffic control need not be emphasized.

3.3.4. KAHNEMAN'S MODEL

Kahneman (1973) likewise developed a model for controlled information processing. However, his model differed from the others in one essential point. He had accepted the concept that there is an upper limit to the *total* information processing capacity, but insisted that the available capacity is not constant. According to Kahneman, it varies, depending on the activation level of the organism. This process, known as 'arousal', is influenced by a number of factors. Specific properties of the sensory input increase arousal, and, consequently, system capacity. The important properties are intensity, novelty, complexity and incongruence (i.e. an otherwise known stimulus in an unusual context). Arousal itself also varies according to a 24-hour cycle and can be lowered by continuous exposure to heavy task demands or by sleep deprivation. Specific drugs can also lower or raise arousal. This model also accepts that a specific part of the processing system itself is able to regulate arousal in a feedback loop. Depending on the demands of the task and the influence of the factors given above, the arousal level of the individual varies, and with it the available capacity for the execution of the task.

In Kahneman's model reserve capacity can be used to attend to the (surrounding) area outside that of the principal task. With higher task demands more capacity is given to the task itself. Therefore less attention is given to the surroundings. Kahneman suggests that neither more nor less capacity may be allotted a task than the execution of the task requires. This presents problems not only in the case of too high task demands where the maximum capacity is exceeded or threatens to be. There are also problems with too low task demands in which little effort is required. Consequently, the arousal level of an individual drops to below the minimum required for reasonable task execution.

Whatever capacity arousal permits was divisible in Kahneman's model among a parallel set of information processing channels. Segregation of information into respective channels was the work of some undefined mechanism which was programmed according to the system's 'allocation policy'. The latter was determined prior to the initiation of operations upon input data as the individual adopts a particular task set or strategy for dealing with data. It can be changed during the task as the result of adopting another set to compensate for changing capacity to improve performance or as the result of the arrival of totally new input.

Mental load in Kahneman's model is the amount of capacity used relative to the amount available. Physiological indices of arousal, such as pupillary dilation, can be used to infer momentary changes in capacity in use. And, conceivably, careful application of graduated information loads would permit one to calibrate increasing capacity to some limit from an appropriate physiological index of arousal. However, without knowledge of the relationship between the physiological index and the information processing load, simple measurement of the former would be virtually meaningless. An individual might show low signs of arousal as the result of either low information processing demands, the state of fatigue or for a number of reasons and yet feel himself heavily loaded because he is using nearly all of his available capacity. Contrarily, in a very demanding task or when the individual is well rested, he may already show high arousal while using a modest proportion of his available capacity and while he is experiencing feelings of boredom. In these two situations uncalibrated measures of arousal could yield a completely misleading impression of mental load.

3.4. Multiple-strategy models

All recent models, except the last one above, have at least implied the possibility that humans possess the capability of suddenly abandoning a particular information processing strategy and adapting a radically different one. Because this seems very typical of human behavior in real life, the more practical minded theorists have recently attempted to explain why and how this occurs (Sperandio, 1971, 1972; Bainbridge, 1974, 1978; Hacker, 1976). Their theoretical orientation is firmly in the tradition of the 'cognitive revolution' in psychology which came from the classic by Miller, Galanter and Pribram: *Plans and the structure of behavior* (1960).

Fundamental to these considerations is the premise that human operators in a practical task always possess some criterion level of output performance, and adapt a particular information processing strategy to achieve this. They furthermore continually use available feedback to evaluate performance in respect to this criterion. Employment of a particular strategy is accomplished within a capacity limit and use of information processing capacity below the limit results in a proportional mental load.

Another premise is that the operator always attempts to achieve the criterion level of performance using the most economical strategy in terms of minimal mental load. Should the information load increase in volume or rate, or should the operator's capacity diminish as, for example, the result of fatigue, he will adapt a more economical strategy, accept a lower efficiency criterion, or both. The change in mental load is discontinuous and non-linear. The resulting change in performance may be in the direction of an impairment, though not necessarily.

By adopting a new strategy or criterion, the operator would accept a greater processing load, his performance would change in a manner indicating less attention to individual inputs, but more attention to a greater number of inputs. Perhaps also the speed of his operations would increase at a cost of diminished precision. Whether in an overall sense the change in strategy is for better or worse would depend upon the stringency of task demands. It is obvious that strategy alternation depends upon other factors beside information input and the state of the operator's arousal. The operator's motivation and his experience are equally critical (Bainbridge, 1974; Hacker, 1978). Low motivation could result in adopting a low performance criterion and/or a simple adherence to the least loading strategy. Low experience could force the operator to adopt an inappropriate strategy, involving a commitment of capacity that is more or less than needed for meeting a reasonable performance criterion (Bouju et al., 1978).

Naturally, the operator's choice of strategy depends also upon his working environment and the facilities it contains for expediting various choices. Where these are abundant, it should be expected that the most motivated and intelligent operators will gradually, over the course of extended practice, come to selectively employ them, with respect to varying task demands and their internal condition, in the optimal manner predicted by the theorists. The status of multiple-strategy models is clearly different than for the earlier described models. These latter are more analytic. The multiple-strategy models have a more descriptive character.

3.5. Mental load and strain

The need for or the anticipation of a prolonged information processing near capacity is seen as a source of stress, leading to a syndrome of mental and psychosomatic complaints. It is evident from the above that mental (work)load is a poorly defined concept. This applies even more to the term 'strain' (see a.o.

Kleber, 1982). Thus it is not surprising that their relationship remains exceedingly obscure. But as the ergonomist must concern him or herself with this relationship, some mention of this difficult issue should be included.

Luczak (1971, 1975) and Bainbridge (1974) felt that strain increases with the proportion of capacity used in information processing, i.e. the mental workload. The short-term effect of excessive workload is the subjective feeling of fatigue coupled with the reduction of capacity. This implies of course that performance will eventually deteriorate as the result of strain, unless the individual adopts a strategy utilizing less capacity. If Kahneman's (1973) theory is correct the deleterious long-term effects of workload arise as a side-effect of the high level of central arousal required to maintain a high capacity. The brain's arousal level determines the level of peripheral activation of autonomic (primarily sympathetic) effector mechanisms that, for example, raise cardial output, blood pressure, blood carbohydrate and lipid levels and so forth.

However, the central and peripheral side-effects of mental workload also affect the information processing system in return. The anxiety process might be excited in an especially critical task by adopting a strategy that facilitates speed at the expense of accuracy, as a higher error rate would be anticipated. According to Hamilton (1975), anxiety also constitutes informational input the processing system. If task demands prohibit a return to the original strategy, the processing of anxiety information would occupy system capacity, keeping arousal high and perpetuating strain. Moreover, the peripheral components of strain are often perceptible and demand a further allocation of capacity (Mandler, 1979). As the individual attends to these internal events, the less processing capacity is left for task information processing. A mental load that produces strain also tends, through central and peripheral positive feedback loops, to increase and perpetuate strain. Task information processing can never reach the full capacity limit under these circumstances and may often be much less.

4. THEORETICAL IMPLICATIONS AND METHODS OF MEASUREMENT

Given the present state of theory on mental load, we can only conclude that we are able to recognize what mental load is not. Mental load can certainly not be equated to the task information load offered to the operator. At any moment the operator deals with only a fraction of the task information. He does this not as a passive perceiver processing only what is offered, but as an active organizer and manipulator of the task and its information content (Sperandio, 1978; Hacker et al., 1978). His information processing system begins at an early preconscious stage to select, modify and reorganize the information for later stages in the process. He interprets the information of the moment in the light of information already in memory and in the light of anticipated possibilities. Moreover, the operator is capable of repeated assessments of the whole situation in terms of the past, present and future in relation to his own changing resources.

Whether and to what extent he will employ various resources in response to changing input information depends upon his criterion for successful performance. Resources and criterion may vary as a function of task demands and in any case differ between operators as the result of motivation, training and knowledge of the environment wherein the task is performed. Except in cases where task information loading is so great as to overwhelm any operator's capabilities, or where a lesser load can only lead to a single correct reaction, there seems no simple way to describe how the individual processes the information or to predict what response he will make.

4.1. Decision rate

Many authorities have expressed the hope that it might be possible to infer mental load from the decision rate of operators performing a task. Even supposing that it would be possible to objectively measure the occurrence of every decision the operator makes in a task, there are good reasons to reject this hope. Decisions occur most frequently when the input or the operations performed upon the input are simple. A high decision rate can therefore indicate a low mental load. However, it does not follow that the converse is true. A low decision rate can indicate a heavy mental load, interruptions in task information processing or both. This is particularly true for inexperienced operators who may arrive at the same decisions as more experienced colleagues, but only after a longer period of deliberation (Bainbridge, 1974).

Finally, 'automatic' information processing occurs without decisions that represent the selection of a response option from among alternatives. Some authors (e.g. Mulder, 1979) believe that this type of information processing does not contribute to mental load. However, 'automatic' processing must dominate the operations of a race-car driver during competition and a pilot during air combat, because there simply is no time available for 'controlled' processing. Few would describe such tasks as constituting a low mental load on the operator.

4.2. Behavioral measurement of mental load

The use of behavioral methods for assessing mental workload has never been completely successful. The usual approach has been to superimpose an artificial or 'secondary' task demand upon an operator already engaged in his normal or 'primary' task. The idea is to use secondary task performance as an indicator of the residual operator capacity (Ogden *et al.*, 1979). As the mental load imposed by primary task increases and consumes capacity, residual capacity diminishes, causing a performance deterioration in the secondary task. Two examples of secondary tasks include rythmic tapping to repeatedly produce a time interval (Michon, 1966) and reacting as quickly as possible to different auditory signals with contingent motor responses (Kalsbeek, 1967). Yet, every variation of this method makes the same assumptions about human information processing.

According to Senders (1970) these entail (a) single channel processing system whereby (b) information proceeds through a linear series of processing stages having (c) respective, strict capacity limits; and (d) that the primary task is always performed according to the same strategy, regardless of changing conditions within the environment or operators. Strictly speaking, hypotheses (a) and (b) are superfluous, but for the secondary task measures to be valid, (c) and (d) must be true. Yet, neither are popular among modern theorists.

Another problem mentioned by Kerr (1973) is that the secondary task demands should in no way facilitate or degrade performance of the primary task, and vice versa. This was almost never determined by those who have employed the method. Neisser (1977) even suggests that any secondary task approach which could somehow satisfy all of the above must still be considered invalid. The ability to perform two tasks simultaneously implies greater capacity than the sum of capacities to perform both separately. Ether that or the individual must learn a new skill which at first requires greater capacity, but after training, much less.

In spite of these objections, Kamphuis (1977) believes that the secondary task approach might be useful when employed, not too frequently, for evaluating relative changes in the operator's status while he continues to perform the same primary task. In this case, the approach is atheoretical and cannot be used for inferring mental load.

From the discussion of various theories concerning mental load, it should be clear that the quantitative and/or qualitative level of performance in the (primary) task is the least promising measure for estimating load. The highly motivated operator will use every means and strategy at his disposal in order to avoid deterioration of his performance. Depending on the task demands and his own state, he will process more or less information without observable changes. If a performance deterioration does occur, it may mean that the task demands have exceeded the operator's capacity. It may, however, also mean that within a particular strategy a momentary failure can be accepted so that an overall performance criterion can be achieved. Efficient performance does not necessarily imply anything about the load level, except that it was within the range of the operator's capability.

4.3. Physiological measurement of mental load

It is still unclear how psychophysiological activation is related to information processing for the execution of a particular task (Ursin, 1979; Hick *et al.*, 1979). Here, there are at least two problems. It is doubtful whether there exists a one dimensional relationship between activation and information processing load (as postulated in Kahneman's model, described above). Furthermore, there is a question of what physiological measure to use as an index of activation since changes in different measures are not highly correlated. Sanders (1980, p. 188) asserts that 'the activation and the organization of behavior, in physiology as well as performance, are connected in such a way that the assumption of one simple unidimensional dimension is very dubious'. This means that no single physiological measure can serve as an index of mental load. The concern of modern research is now to determine reaction patterns of physiological activity which underlie various phases in the processing of information.

Yet, the effects of excessive mental load upon peripheral physiological systems may be inferrable from certain physiological indices of long-standing strain, such as the urinary excretion rates of adrenal medullary and adrenal cortical hormones (e.g. adrenaline and cortisol, respectively). Theoretically, the elevation of these indices or the time taken for their recovery to baseline levels should provide a reasonable basis for comparison of workloads in different situations or of the succeptibility of different individuals within the same situation. However, such measures do not specifically identify the task or individual factors contributing to workload strain and are influenced by a number of factors in addition to workload. Studies that employ them should therefore involve systematic manipulation of the workload factors and control of all others.

Cardiovascular measures have been used quite often in the study of mental load. A simple parameter, mean pulse frequency, is extremely useful in work physiology but without much significance in mental load research. The variability of pulse frequency has, however, received much favorable attention since it was related to mental load in Kalsbeek's (1967) pioneering studies. The initial high expectations were somewhat tempered by subsequent research (see among others, Kalsbeek, 1973; Opmeer, 1973). A recently developed refinement of the measurement seems most promising in laboratory situations (Mulder, 1980; Mulder *et al.*, 1981). Experiences in the field are still fragmentary. For the time being, the measure must be considered tentative and still promising but certainly not as a standard index of mental load.

Other physiological variables such as obtained from blood pressure, electroencephalography (EEG), galvanic skin response (GSR), electromyography (EMG), electro-occulography (EOG), and critical flicker frequency (CFF) are used in various studies on mental load. Their theoretical status in relation to information processing and mental load is still unclear. Moreover, they do not lend themselves easily to practical application in field situations.

4.4. Subjective measurement of mental load

Subjective assessment by the operator is the final method for measuring mental load. In recent years, this method has enjoyed increasing popularity, after a period when it was viewed with skepticism (for example, Kinsman et al., 1976; Moray, 1982). Variations of the method all contain a fundamental limitation in that not all the components of mental load are accessible for introspection. 'Pre-attentional' information processing (Neisser, 1967) and the rapid execution of motor routines after the decision is taken to respond are definitely not.

Automatic information processing is equally inaccessible. To a certain degree, the experienced mental load is determined by the amount of controlled information processing over a given period. Also, it must be difficult for individuals to differentiate their feelings, separating cause and effect with regard to mental load. It is likely that their subjective impressions are based, to a large extent, on all sorts of secondary peripheral effects as a consequence of a particular mental load (Johannson et al., 1979). Although subjective measurements are certainly useful in the study of mental load, it would be unwise to treat them as the only measurement.

5. CONCLUSIONS AND PERSPECTIVES

The current situation with regard to psychological theories of mental load does not allow one to draw detailed, straight-forward conclusions. An important problem in this research is the relatively separate developments in the laboratory and the practice of work- and organizational psychology. Psychological research in the field of workload can surely profit through better interaction between basic scientists and practitioners.

We conclude this chapter on workload with four general observations relevant to real-life situations.

A. *Factors that normally contribute to mental load are not limited to task parameters.*

Information, directly acquired from elements of the tasks certainly not all that is processed by the operator at any given moment. Not only must the operator acquire task-relevant information from his own memory, he may voluntarily or involuntarily process information from his environment which is task-irrelevant. If he is attempting to cope with some problem which has transpired before the task or is anticipated after its conclusion, he can be expected to devote much of his capacity to that effort. Emotional information, arising in the states of hostility or anxiety is now recognized as an extremely important contribution to mental load (Hamilton, 1979). Finally, the greater the volume of information input from whatever source, the greater must be the commitment of capacity for the internal regulation of information processing. One should not expect a linear increase of mental load with increasing task demands. In the practice of work- and organizational psychology this means that steps taken to optimize mental load in work situations should not be limited to the task. Work surroundings, organizational factors, personality traits and interpersonal relationships must also be considered.

B. *Experienced operators can make use of other information processing strategies than inexperienced operators to reach the same task objective.*

Whether they will do this depends on two factors: their perception of their performance relative to an effectiveness criterion and the relative amount of capacity that will be used. An operator receiving immediate feedback about his performance compares his efficiency level at that moment with a personal criterion. Whenever a large difference exists between the two, as a consequence of excessive task demands or temporarily reduced capacity (i.e. fatigue) he will either lower his own criterion or switch to another processing strategy which calls for less of his processing capacity. Lowering the criterion may lead to performance deterioration. Changing strategy results in a qualitative change in performance, but does not necessarily mean that the ultimate task goal can not be achieved in a satisfactory manner. In both cases mental load can remain at the same level, unless the new strategy results in new task demands with a different information content, or when anticipation of performance lowering creates anxiety.

It should be clear that individuals in all types of work situations must have a number of strategies at their disposal in order to be able to respond to changing demands. We must realize that in the course of normal work situations task demands are never static. The demands change qualitatively and quantitatively following changes in environmental factors which may or may not be under the operator's control. Finally, at a subjective level, the difficulty of the task demands depends on the state of the operator who is himself continually changing (Hacker, 1978).

The study of strategy changes in task execution seems especially important. Experienced operators flexibly use alternative strategies, thus availing themselves of a means for actively regulating the load level while maintaining an acceptable performance level. Recent attempts to discover the principles of strategy selection and to employ the same in directional training programs showed much promise (see among others, Matern, 1979a, 1979b; Matern et al., 1978; Triebe, 1977; Bouju et al., 1978).

C. *There is no single valid measure of mental load.*

Inference of changes in mental load can best be accomplished using multiple measures. Task performance is an illogical index of mental load in almost every practical working situation. This is because the worker attempts in every way to maintain stable, or at least acceptable performance, in spite of variations in his task demands. Performance deterioration can only be expected when the worker is overwhelmed by demands or when, for reasons that may as easily imply mental load reduction as the opposite, he has chosen to accept a lower efficiency criterion.

All physiological measures of mental load are at this moment unvalidated in practical working situations. None is more than an index of physiological system activation that is imperfectly correlated with variations in information processing. Scaling of physiological changes is always difficult, and without calibration it is impossible to say what any physiological changes indicates in terms of mental load change. Finally, different physiological changes are themselves poorly correlated and patterns of change are highly idiosyncratic among different individuals.

Subjective assessments of mental load are accepted as a good single index and scaling of such measures has reached a respectable level of sophistication (Moray, 1982). However, subjective measures are not readily comparable across different task situations. More troublesome are the theoretical arguments that the worker is usually (1) unable to discriminate among causal factors that produce mental load and their relative contributions; (2) unconscious of some; (3) unaware of his internal condition as it affects his capacity; and (4) tends to make decisions on the basis of the most recent peior experience.

Just as there are multiple causes of mental workload, there are multiple effects. None of the latter may be reliably correlated with any of the former, but there may be a reliable relationship between all causes and effects combined. The practical implication is that the applied scientist should seek to identify and control as many sources of mental workload as possible while measuring simultaneously performance, physiological and subjective reactions of the worker during the task. Modern multivariate statistical procedures are available that allow testing the interaction of the independent variables upon all dependent variables, together and separately. These should be applied to group-results and also to repeated observations of the same individuals. It is entirely possible that subgroups of workers may react in respectively consistent ways, but that different subgroups will react in different or even opposite ways.

D. *The effects of excessive mental loads might best be measured during recovery periods after work.*

Certain signs of excessive mental loading appear to persist after the cessation of the work that imposed the load. An elegant demonstration of this was offered by Schmidtke (1976). Subjects were repeatedly tested to determine what level of information processing they could sustain, without increasing errors, during a four-hour mental arithmetic task. By pacing, their load was increased beyond that limit, but it was imposed for shorter periods (5, 10, 15, 20 and 30 min.). The subjects were then briefly allowed to work at their preferred pace after rest pauses of various durations. The length of pause necessary to recover completely to optimal performance level increased in an exponential manner with the duration of the period of excessive mental loading.

Physiological signs of strain in workers performing mental work in real tasks sometimes persist for a day or longer. Meijman *et al.* (1982) first selected two groups of high and low strain intracity bus drivers on the basis of respective absence due to illness histories. Though the groups performed the same task over the working day, the apparently more susceptible group required two free days before their adrenaline excretion rates returned to normal. The less susceptible group's recovery was complete within the first free day.

Results such as these (see also Rissler's, 1977) indicate that it should be possible to define the difficulty of tasks by studying recovery time of specific performance and/or physiological parameters.

It should also be possible in this way to identify individuals who for one reason or another are particularly sensitive to mental loading in 'normal' task situations. A general conclusion for normal work situations is that a loading level is tolerable when the time necessary for recovery does not exceed the time of exposure to the load (Ettema, 1973; Hacker *et al.*, 1978). Yet there remains a need for research in this area. Too little is known about the important parameters. These may be either (a) performance measurements with reference to mental functions that play a role in information processing; (b) more general behavioral measurements related to normal living activities (e.g. sleep, see Meijman, 1981); or (c) biomedical measurements pertaining to well-being and health. The measurement of recovery functions perhaps provides the best method at present for identifying unacceptable mental working situations, in spite of its limited utility for explaining reactions during the task. In any case, this method seems assured of a permanent place in workload research.

Finally, we agree with many authorities (Ettema, 1973; Hacker, 1976; Rohmert and Luczak, 1979; Teiger, 1978). Research on workload should not exclusively concern itself with the question of whether an individual can process information to meet task demands. It must also define the costs associated with meeting any task demand and these, in terms of health and well-being, over the short- and long-term.

REFERENCES

Algera, J. (1980), *Kenmerken van werk* [Characteristics of work]. Leiden (dissertation).
Allport, D. A., Antonis, B., Reynolds, P. (1971), On the division of attention: A disproof of the singel-channel hypothesis. *Quarterly Journal of Experimental Psychology*, **24** 225–235.

Baars, A., Hacker, W., Hartman, W., Iwanova, A., Richter, P., Wolff, S. (1981), Psychologische Arbeitsanalyse zur Erfassung der Persönlichkeitsförderlichheit von Arbeitsinhalten. In: Frei, F., Ulich, E. (Eds.), *Beiträge zur psychologischen Arbeitsanalyse*. Bern: Huber, 127–164.

Bachman, W., Meister, W. (1973), Zur Erfassung und Bewertung von Arbeitsbeanspruchungen und Beanspruchungsfolgen. In: Hacker, W., Timple, K. P., Vorwerg, M., (Eds.), *Arbeits-, Ingenieurs- und Sozialpsychologische Beiträge zur Sozialistischen Rationalisierung*. Berlin (DDR): VEB-DVW, 94–99.

Bainbridge, L. (1974), Problems in the assessment of mental load. *Le Travail Humain*, **37**, 279–302.

Bainbridge, L. (1978), Forgotten alternatives in skill and work-load. *Ergonomics*, **21**, 169–185.

Bartenwerfer, H. G. (1970), Psychische Beanspruchung und Ermüdung. In: Mayer, A., Hertwig, B. (Eds.), *Handbuch der Psychologie*, Bd. 9. Verl./Psych., 168–209.

Bartlett, F. C. (1943), Fatigue following highly skilled work. *Proceedings of the Royal Society of Britain*, **131**, 247–254.

Bills, A. G. (1931), Blocking: A new principle of mental fatigue. *American Journal of Psychology*, **43**, 230–245.

Bink, B. (1962), The physical work capacity in relation to working time and age. *Ergonomics*, **5**, 25–28.

Blitz, P., Moorst, A. van, (1978), Psysical Fatigue and the perception of differences in load; A signal detection approach. *Perception and Motor Skills*, **46**, 779–790.

Bonjer, F. H. (1965), *Fysiologische methoden voor het vaststellen van belasting en belastbaarheid* [Physiological methods for determining load and loading level]. Assen: Van Gorcum.

Bouju, F., Sperandio, J. C. (1978), *Effects du niveau de qualification et de la charge de travail des contrôleurs d'approche sur leur stratégies opératoires*. Rocquencourt: IRIA.

Broadbent, D. E. (1958), *Perception and communication*. Oxford: Pergamon.

Broadbent, D. E. (1971), *Decision and stress*. New York: Academic Press.

Broadbent, D. E. (1977), Levels, hierarchies, and the locus of control. *Quarterly Journal of Experimental Psychology*, **29**, 181–201.

Broadbent, D. E. (1979), Is a Fatigue test now possible? *Ergonomics*, **22**, 1277–1290.

Cameron, C. (1973), A theory of fatigue. *Ergonomics*, **16**, 633–648.

Chiles, W. D., Alluisi, E. A. (1979), On the specification of operator or cooccupational workload with performance-measurement methods. *Human Factors*, **21**, 515–528.

Colquhoun, W. P. (1962), Effects of hyoscine and meclozine on vigilance and short-term memory. *Brit. J. of Ind. Medicine*, **19**, 287–296.

Deutsch, J. A., Deutsch, D. (1963), Attention: Some theoretical considerations. *Psychological Review*, **70**, 80–90.

Dijkstra, A., Grinten, M. P. van der, Schlatmann, M. J. Th., Winter, C. R., de (1981), *Functioneren in de arbeidssituatie* [Functioning in the work situation]. Leiden. NIPG. 1981.

Ettema, J. H. (1968), Arbeidsfysiologie en mentale belasting [Work-physiology and mental load]. *Tÿdschrift voor Sociale Geneeskunde*, **46**, 486–542.

Ettema, J. H. (1973), Het model belasting en belastbaarheid [The load and loading level model]. *Tijdschrift voor Sociale Geneeskunde*, **51**, 44–54.

Graaf, M. H. K. v. d., ten Horn, L. A., Putten M. D. van (1978), *Vragenlijst Funktie-Kenmerken* [Questionnaire job characteristics]. Delft: Technological University.

Guélaud, F., Beauchesne, M., Gautrat, J., Roustang, G. (1975), *Pour une analyse des conditions du travail ouvrier dans l'entreprise*. Paris: A. Colin.

Hacker, W. (1976), Psychische Regulation von Arbeitstätigkeiten: Innere Modelle,

Strategien in Mensch-Maschine-Systemen, Belastungswirkungen. In: Hacker, W. (Ed.), *Psychische Regulation von Arbeitstätigkeiten.* Berlin (DDR): VEB-DVW.

Hacker, W. (1978), *Allgemeine Arbeits- und Ingenieurs Psychologie.* Berlin (DDR): VEB-DVW.

Hacker, W., Plath, H. E., Richter, P., Zimmer, K. (1978), Internal representation of task structure and mental load of work: Approaches and methods of assessment. *Ergonomics,* **21**, 187–194.

Hackman, J. R., Oldman, G. R. (1975), Development of the job Diagnostic Survey. *J. Appl. Psych.,* **60**, 259–286.

Haider, M. (1962), *Ermüdung, Beanspruchung und Leistung.* Wien: F. Deuticke.

Hamilton, V. (1975), Socialisation anxiety and information processing: A capacity model of anxiety-induced performance deficits. In: Sarason, J. G., Spielberger, C. D. (Eds.), *Stress and anxiety.* Vol. 2. Washington D. C.: Wiley. 1975.

Hamilton, V. (1979), Personality and stress. In: Hamilton, V., Warburton, D. M. (Eds.), *Human stress and cognition.* New York: Wiley.

Helm, K. v. d., Meijman, T. (1982), Arbeidsomstandigheden, arbeidstijden en arbeidsbelasting [Working conditions, working hours and work load]. In: Vreemen, R. (Ed.), *De kwaliteit van de arbeid in de Nederlandse industrie* [The quality of work in Dutch industry]. Nijmegen: SUN.

Hick, W. E. (1952), On the rate of gain of information. *Quarterly Journal of Experimental Psychology,* **4**, 11–26.

Hicks, T., Wierwille, W. (1979), Comparison of five mental workload assessment procedures in a moving-base simulator. *Human Factors,* **21**, 129–144.

Hinrichs, P. (1981), *Um die Seele des Arbeiters. Arbeitspsychologie, Industrie- und Betriebssoziologie in Deutschland.* Köln: Pahl Rugenstein.

Jenkins, C. D. (1971), Psychologic and social precursors of coronary disease. *Nw. Engl. J. Med.,* **284**, 244–255 and 307–317.

Johannsen, G., Moray, N., Pew, R., Rasmussen, J., Sanders, A., Wickens, C. (1979), First step towards a designer's mental workload checklist. In: Moray, N. (Ed.), *Mental workload: Theory and measurement.* New York: Plenum.

Kahneman, D. (1973), *Attention and effort.* Englewood Cliffs (N.J.): Prentice-Hall.

Kalsbeek, J. W. H. (1967), *Mentale belasting* [Mental load]. Amsterdam (dissertation).

Kalsbeek, J. W. H. (1973), Do you believe in sinus-arrytmia. *Ergonomics,* **16**, 99–104.

Kalsbeek, J. W. H. (1975), Le concept de la capacité réduite et la charge mentale. In: Laville, A., Teiger, C., Wisner, A. (Eds.), *Age et contraintes de travail; Aspects sociologiques, psychologiques.* Jouy Josas: N. E. B.

Kamphuis, A. (1977), *Mentale belasting: Theorieën en modellen* [Mental load: Theories and models]. PTT-SWOl Rapport 595/1. The Hague.

Kasl, S. V. (1978), Epidemicological contributions to the study of work stress. In: Cooper, C. L., Payne, R. (Eds.), *Stress at work.* New York: Wiley, 3–48.

Kerr, B. (1973), Processing demands during mental operations. *Memory and Cognition,* **1**, 401–412.

Kinsman, R. A., Weisner, P. C. (1976), Subjective symptomatology during work and fatigue. In: Simonson, E., Weiser, P. C. (Eds.), *Psychological aspects and psychological correlates of work and fatigue.* Springfield: Thomas, 336–405.

Kleber, R. J. (1982), *Stressbenaderingen in de psychologie* [Stress approaches in psychology]. Deventer: Van Loghum Slaterus.

Kogi, K., Saito, Y. (1973), Rhythmetic fluctuations of orientation to a continuous manual control task. *Journal of Human Ergology,* **2**, 169–184.

Landy, F. J., Trumbo, D. A. (1976), *Psychology of work behavior.* Homewood: Dorsey.

Legge, D., Barber, P. J. (1976), *Information and skill.* London: Methuen.

Leplat, J. (1972), La psychologie du travail et ergonomie. In: Reuchlin, M. (Ed.), *Traité de psychologie appliquée*. Paris: PUF, tôme 3, 63–136.

Leplat, J. (1980), La psychologie du travail, un apercu. *Bull. de Psych.*, **23**, 195–200.

Luczak, H. (1971), The use of simulators for testing individual mental working capacity. *Ergonomics*, **14**, 651–660.

Luczak, H. (1975), Untersuchungen Informaterische Belastung und Beanspruchung des Menschen. *Fortschrift-Berichte der VDI*, **10**–2, 1–172.

McClelland, J. (1979), On the time relations of mental processes: A framework for analyzing processes in cascade. *Psychological Review*, **86**, 287–320.

McCormick, E. J., Jeanneret, P. R., Mecham, R. C. (1972), A study of job characteristics and job dimensions as based on the Position Analysis Questionnaire (PAQ). *J. Appl. Psychl.*, **56**.

Mandler, G. (1979), Thought processes, consciousness and stress. In: Hamilton, V., Wartburton, D. M. (Eds.), *Human stress and cognition*. New York: Wiley.

Matern, B. (1979a), Bedeutung und Effektivität von Trainungsverfahren für Anlagenfahrer. *Textiltechnik*, **29**, 247–252.

Matern, B. (1979b), Verzögertes Wirksamwerden von Eingriffen in der Automatisierten Industrie—Konsequenzen für die Arbeitsgestaltung, *Arbeitswissenschaft*, **3**, 224–229.

Matern, B., Fechner, F., Lehmann, B., Uebel, H. (1978), Zur Qualität Psychischer Regulationsgrundlagen bei Tätigkeiten des Anlagenfahrers. *Probl. u. Ergeb. der Psych.*, **65**, 5–16.

Meijman, T. F. (1981), Analyse subjective de la récupération après les postes de nuit dans le cas de rotation lente (7 jours). *La Travail Humain*, **44**, 315–323.

Meijman, T. F., Linden, A. v. d., Mulders, H., Bussel, M. van, Steensma, L. (1982), Effecten in de ontwikkeling van voortdurende belasting en onvoldoende herstel bij buschauffeurs van het GVB Groningen [Effects in development of continuous load and insufficient recuperation in busdrivers in Groningen]. In: Vrooland, V. (Ed.), *Werk en gezondheid, over ziekteverzuin en humanisering van de arbeid* [Work and health, on absenteeism due to illness and the humanization of work]. Alphen a/d Rijn: Samsom.

Meijman, R. F., Mulders, H., Bosker, F., O'Hanlon, J., Kompier, M. (1983), Belastingseffekten en belastbaarheid: een onderzoek naar differentiële psychofysiologische reaktiviteit [Load effects and loading level: A study of differential psychophysiological reactivity]. *Tijdschrift voor Sociale Gezondheidszorg* (in press).

Meister, D. (1976), *Behavioral foundations of systems development*. New York: Wiley.

Michon, J. A. (1966), Tapping regularity as a measure of perceptual motor load. *Ergonomics*, **9**, 401–412.

Miller, G. A. (1953), What is information measurement? *American Psychologist*, **8**, 3–11.

Miller, G. A., Galanter, E., Pribram, K. H. (1960), *Plans and the structure of behavior*. New York: Holt.

Monod, H., Llle, F. (1976), L'évaluation de la charge de travail. *Arch. des Maladies Professionelles, de Médecine du Travail et de sécurité Sociale*, **37**, 1–96.

Moray, N. (1967), Where is Capacity limited? A survey and a model. *Acta Psychologica*, **27**, 84–92.

Moray, N. (1979), *Mental work load: Its theory and measurement*. New York: Plenum.

Moray, N. (1982), Subjective mental workload. *Human Factors*, **24**, 25–40.

Mulder, G. (1979), Mental load, mental effort and attention. In: Moray, N. (Ed.), *Mental workload. Its theory and measurement*. New York: Plenum.

Mulder, G. (1980), *The heart of mental effort*. Groningen (dissertation).

Mulder, G., Mulder, L. (1981), Information processing and cardiovascular control. *Psychophysiology*, **19**, 392–402.

Mulders, H., Meijman, T, O'Hanlon, J., Mulder, G. (1982), Differential psycho-physiological reactivity of busdrivers. *Ergonomics* (in press).
Murrell, K. F. H. (1965), Le concept de fatigue: une réalité ou un gêne? *Bull. du C.E.R.P.*, 14, 103–110.
Muscio, B. (1921), Is a fatigue test possible? *Brit. J. Psychol.*, 12, 31–46.
Neisser, U. (1967), *Cognitive psychology*. New York: Appleton.
Neisser, U. (1977), *Cognition and reality*. San Francisco: Freeman.
Norman, D. A., Bobrow, D. G. (1975), On data-limited and resource-limited processes. *Cognitive Psychology*, 5, 44–64.
Ogden, E. D., Levine, J. M., Eisner, E. J. (1979), Measurement of workload by secondary tasks. *Human Factors*, 21, 529–548.
O'Hanlon, J. F. (1981), Boredom: Practical consequences and a theory. *Acta Psychologica*, 49, 53–82.
Opmeer, C. H. J. M. (1973), The information content of successive RR-intervals in the ECG. Preliminary results using factor analysis. *Ergonomics*, 16, 105–122.
Posner, M. J. (1973), Psycho-biology of attention. In: Gazzania, M. S., Blakemore, C. (Eds.), *Handbook of psychobiology*. New York: Academic Press.
Poulton, E. C. (1978), Blue collar stressors. In: Cooper, C. L., Payne, R. (Eds.), *Stress at work*. New York, 51–79.
Rassmussen, J. (1976), Outlines of a hybrid model of the process plant operator. In: Sheridan, T. B., Johannsen, G. (Eds.), *Monitoring behavior and supervisory control*. New York: Plenum.
Reiche, H. M. J. K. I., Dijkhuizen N. van (1980), *Vragenlijst Organisatie Stress: testhandleiding* [Questionnaire Organizational Stress: test guidebook]. Stressgroep Nijmegen. Nijmegen: Catholic University.
Rissler, A. (1977), Stress reactions at work and after work during a period of quantitative overload. *Ergonomics*, 20, 13–16.
Rohmert, W., Landau, K. (1979), *Das Arbeitswissenschaftliche Erhebungsverfahren zur Tätigkeitsanalyse* (AET). Bern: Hüber.
Rohmert, W., Luczak, H. (1979), Stress, work and productivity. In: Hamilton, V. Wartburton, D. M. (Eds.), *Humanstress and cognition: An information processing approach*. New York: Wiley.
Ruigh, A. de (1973), *Milieu-faktoren en gezondheidsbeleving*, [Environmental factors and the experience of health]. Nijmegen (doctoral thesis).
Sanders, A. F. (1977), De meetbaarheid van mentale belasting [Measurability of mental load]. *Projket Tijdschrift van Toegepaste Wetenschappen* 5–9, 301–305.
Sanders, A. F. (1979), Some remarks on mental load, In: Moray, N. (Ed.), *Mental workload: Its theory and measuremect*. New York: Plenum, 41–77.
Sanders, A. F. (1980), Stress, activatie en verrichtingen [Stress, activation and performance]. *Nederlands Tijdschrift de Psychologie* [Dutch Journal of Psychology], 35, 185–199.
Schmidtke, H. (1976), Disturbance of processing of information. In: Simonson, E., Weisner, P. (Eds.), *Psychological aspects and physiological correlates of work and fatigue*. Springfield (Ill): Thomas.
Schneider, W., Shiffrin, R. M. (1977), Controlled and automatic human information processing: I. Detection, search and attention. *Psychological Review*, 84, 1–66.
Senders, J. W. (1970), The estimation of operator workload in complex systems. In: de Greene, K. B. (Ed.), *Systems psychology*. New York: McGraw-Hill.
Sharit, J., Salvendy, G. (1982), Occupational stress: Review and reappraisal. *Human Factors*, 24, 129–162.

Shiffrin, R. M., Schneider, W. (1977), Controlled and automatic information processing: II. Perceptual learning, automatic attending and a general theory. *Psychological Review*, **84**, 127–190.

Simonson, E., Weiser, P. C. (1976), *Psychological aspects and physiological correlates of work and fatigue*. Springfield (Ill.): Thomas.

Sperandio, J. C. (1971), Variation of operators' strategies and regulating effect on workload. *Ergonomics*, **14**, 571–577.

Sperandio, J. C. (1972), Charge de travil et régulation des processus opératoires. *Le Travail Humain*, **35**, 85–98.

Sperandio, J. C. (1978), The regulation of working methods as a function of work-load among air traffic controllers. *Ergonomics*, **21**, 195–203.

Sperandio, J. C. (1980), *La psychologie en ergonomie*. Paris: PUF.

Sternberg, S. (1969), The discovery of processing stages: Extensions of Donder's method. In: Koster, W. G. (Ed.), *Attention and performance, II*. Amsterdam: North-Holland.

Teiger, C. (1978), Regulation of activity: An analytic tool for studying work load in perceptual motor tasks. *Ergonomics*, **21**, 203–213.

Tijdschrift voor Sociale Geneeskunde [Journal of Social Medicine].

Triebe, J. K. (1977), Entwicklung Handlungsstrategien in der Arbeit. *Z. Arb. Wiss.*, **31**-4, 221–228.

Triesman, A. M. (1969), Strategies and models of selective attention. *Psychological Review*, **76**, 282–299.

Ursin, H., Ursin, R. (1979), Physiological indicators of mental workload. In: Moray, N. (Ed.), *Mental workload, its theory and measurement*. New York: Plenum.

Vijver, B. van de (1978), Construction et utilisation de grilles d'évaluation des conditions de travail. *Le Travail Humain*, **41**, 81–99.

Vroege, C. (1981), *Ziekteverzuim in Nederland, een bedrijfsgeneeskundige visie* [Absenteeism due to illness in The Netherlands, a view from industrial medicine]. Rotterdam: B.R.G.D.

Vernon, H. M. (1921), *Industrial fatigue and efficiency*. London.

Volpert, W., Vahrenkamp, R., Taylor, F. W. (1977), *Die Grundsätze Wissenschaftliche Betriebsführung*. Basel: Beltz.

Welford, A. T. (1973), Stress and performance. *Ergonomics*, **16**, 567–580.

Wendrich, P. (1973), Methodische Probleme bei der Anwendung von Algorithmen zur Strukturanalyse von Arbeitshandlungen bei Belastungsuntersuchungen. In: Hacker, W., Quaas, W., Raum, H., Schulz, H. J. (Eds.), *Psychologische Arbeitsuntersuchung*. Berlin (DDR): VEB-DvW, 92–108.

Willemsu P. J. (1981), *Inleiding in de psychologie van de menselijke verrichtingen* [Introduction to the psychology of human performance]. Deventer: Van Loghum Slaterus.

Winnubst, J. A. M. (1981), Stress in organisaties: Naar een nieuwe bendering van werk en gezondheid [Stress in organizations: Towards a new approach of work and health]. In: Drenth, P. J. D., Thierry, Hk., Willems, P. J., Wolff, Ch. J. de (Eds.), *Handboek voor arbeids- en organisatiepsychologie* [Handbook of work- and organizational psychology]. Deventer: Kluwer.

Ydo, M. G. (1956), *Taylor, over het karakter van chefs en ondergeschikten* [Taylor, on the character of supervisors and subordinates]. Alphen a/d Rijn: Samsom.

2.7. Personnel selection

Charles J. de Wolff and Giel van den Bosch

1. INTRODUCTION

The term 'personnel selection' has been in use for many decades. Since the beginning of this century, psychologists have been intensively concerned with selection.

The first time tests were applied on a large scale was in the United States during World War I. The army's alpha and beta tests were administrated to no less than 1,500,000 people. This number was greatly surpassed in World War II, when in the USA more than 14,000,000 people were tested and selected. These programmes turned out to be very effective; the pilot selection programme (Thorndike, 1949) especially has become famous. Thanks to this programme the effectiveness of training could be improved considerably.

By the mid-forties a 'selection technology' had been developed consisting of the methods and techniques described by Thorndike (1949) and tests as described in the Mental Measurements Yearbooks of Buros (published regularly since 1938). Because of its enormous success in World War II this technology received much attention and was increasingly applied both in and outside the United States. In Europe, where until then 'impressionistic' methods were used, the American technology was adapted and widely applied. In The Netherlands, the turning point came at the end of the fifties (van der Giessen, 1957). The application process, however, brought a number of problems to light. In developing the technology, a number of (partially implicit) assumptions and beliefs (among them the unidimensional criterion and the permanent

Prof. dr. Ch. J. de Wolff, Katholieke Universiteit, Vakgroep Arbeids- en Organisatiepsychologie. Montessorilaan 3, 6500 HE NIJMEGEN.
Drs. Giel v.d. Bosch, Hoogovens B. V., Psychologische Dienst, Ymuiden.

nature of individual differences) were accepted as self-evident. These were to be repudiated later, when in the sixties and seventies, one came to realize that the tests could well be a violation of individual privacy or a source of discrimination. These and other objections to the technology will be dealt with below.

Both psychologists and non-psychologists took part in the discussions about these objections and possibilities to remove them were examined. At the end of the seventies the limitations of these technologies were gradually becoming apparent, and although this was an impetus to find a better approach, no satisfactory answer to the objections raised has yet been found.

In this chapter we will discuss the following topics, in this order:
—the model which was the basis of the early selection technology (section 2);
—objections to this model as originally raised by psychologists (section 3);
—the societal ideas that were in conflict with the beliefs on which the model was based (section 4);
—some attempts at innovation (section 5);
In section 6, we shall attempt to attain some measure of integration by indicating what direction would be desirable and possible for further development.

Although we feel the term 'personnel selection' is not fully satisfactory in our context, we have retained it, rejecting the alternative 'engaging personnel'. However, the reader should keep in mind that we will not be dealing with the complete selection procedure from recruitment to introduction: our emphasis will be on the fact that a psychological test (as it is understood in personnel advertisements) cannot be regarded an isolated activity. If an applicant and an organization decide to join hands, they are both hoping for long-term cooperation. The quality of such cooperation is determined by many factors, one being the way in which the psychologist administers the psychological test.

2. THE AMERICAN SELECTION MODEL

The selection technology developed in the first half of this century had a solid empirical basis. The method prescribes a number of steps to be followed and the authors describing this technology made quite clear that the rules should be strictly adhered to: 'A personnel selection program which does not involve empirical checks of the selection procedures against criteria of job success is at best a static and untested one. At worst it might be outright charlatanism' (Thorndike, 1949). And: 'The feature that distinguishes reputable work in personnel selection from that of the mass of self-styled 'psychologists', 'personnel experts' and other quacks is that the reputable worker in the field is continuously concerned with testing, verifying and improving the adequacy of his procedures'.

The steps to be taken were:
—analysing the job;
—selecting or, if necessary, constructing predictors;

—developing criteria (measures for performance on the job);
—testing the validity of the predictors on a random sample of applicants;
—putting together the most favourable combination of predictors and determining the cutting scores;
—using this combination for personnel selection.

In principle, one could still continue trying out new predictors. Besides rules for setting up selection programmes there were also rules and techniques for test construction and statistical analysis (Lindquist, 1954). The development of selection technology was closely linked to that of psychometrical methods. Correlation computations, regression analysis and, later, factor analysis were applied extensively. The reader who would like more information on this technology is referred to Thorndike (1949), Guilford (1959), Guion (1965), Drenth (1975), and Roe (1983).

The model was based on a number of assumptions considered more or less self-evident during the first years of its development.

The most important assumption was that differences in job performance were attributed entirely or almost entirely to individual differences in ability. Attention was paid almost exclusively to establishing the nature and size of these individual differences, whose measurability became the main focus, whilst the unquantifiable variables were avoided (Argyris, 1976).

Another major factor was the belief in the existence of 'the' criterion. Thorndike based his approach on the 'ultimate criterion': 'the complete final goal of a particular type of selection or training' which is 'multiple and complex in almost every case'. He realized that such a criterion was not easy to find ('it is rarely, if ever, available for use in psychological research') but one could in any case strive to come as close to it as possible.

Thorndike emphasized that much time and attention should be spent on constructing the criterion scores as adequately as possible. The basic idea was that an individual's success in his job could be measured and that the resulting scores could be used for validation purposes. The measure of success of a selection programme was judged by its ability to predict future performance (for other assumptions contained in this model see de Wolff, 1966).

Cronbach and Gleser (1957) considered these assumptions in greater detail. They believed that selection is a form of decision making, that has a number of pros and cons. It is possible to design rational strategies in order to obtain the most favourable combination of these pros and cons and thus to achieve greatest utility. Making good predictions is, therefore, less important than making good decisions, that is, balancing, as well as possible, the pros and cons and the risks involved.

At first, attention was focussed mainly on developing series of tests and collecting validation data. In the fifties, a number of test batteries became available

(Guilford, 1959). Instructions for test construction and test administration were also published, among them the 'Technical recommendations for psychological tests and diagnostic techniques' (American Psychological Association, 1954, 1966, 1974). From 1954 to 1965 the journal 'Personnel Psychology' had a section called 'validity information exchange', publishing findings concerning the validity of predictors (the editors insisted that negative as well as positive experiences be reported).

In The Netherlands, the test research commission of the Dutch Institute of Psychologists (NIP) was founded in 1959. In 1961 it published its first review of tests and test research, and several such reviews have been published since (NIP, 1961, 1964, 1969, 1974). The most recent publication of this commission, meanwhile renamed COTAN (Commissie Test Aangelegenheden Nederland), is 'Guidelines for the development and use of psychological tests and achievement tests' (1978).

Despite strong insistence that great care be taken in applying the technology ('Thou shall validate') this has been done only on a modest scale. Although this technology has been taught at Dutch universities for at least 20 years and ample literature is available, impressionistic methods are still widely used in practice, (Evers and Zaal, 1979), whereas validation studies are relatively scarce. We will return to this subject at the end of this chapter.

3. CRACKS IN THORNDIKE'S PARADIGM

In the course of time, objections began to be raised against this selection technology. It appeared that the (partly implicit) assumptions were not (fully) watertight and had to be supplemented or substituted. It also appeared that what applied in the particular circumstances of World War II did not necessarily apply to the completely different socio-economic climate of the post-war years.

3.1. Objections to the emphasis on individual differences

Psychologists have long believed that differences in achievements at work were attributable exclusively to differences in capacities and individual characteristics. Reviewing management selection, Cowley wrote that 'The approach to the study of leadership has usually been, and perhaps must always be through the studies of traits' (Cowley, 1928). It was also believed that higher validaties could be attained if these traits could be recognized and made measurable. The technology developed implied that validity could always be improved by applying more and better predictors. Traits were considered to be constant. They were either inherited or acquired at an early age. However, errors could be made in measuring them, thus obscuring their 'real magnitude'

(Gulliksen, 1950). By eliminating these measurement errors it would be possible to determine this 'real magnitude' more accurately. This is in fact a static approach: characteristics are regarded as not subject to change.

The optimistic idea that validity would gradually 'grow' was not confirmed. Although progress was made in the area of test construction, the validity coefficients reported did not improve. It was even thought there was a 'ceiling' of approx. .50 for predicting training criteria and .35 for job performance (Rundquist, 1969).

Selection psychologists did not sufficiently take into account that job performance depends also on factors other than suitability. Social and psychological studies of that time noted the influence of the style of management on performance and the relation between work and motivation as well as its influence on individual performance. Ergonomic studies, for example, which adapt human activities to machines in 'man-machine systems' could no longer be confined to the 'study of traits' only, if, that is, individual performance was to be improved.

Moreover, in the sixties the interest in system theories increased; the organization was regarded as an 'open system' geared to the relevant environment. This train of thought is difficult to reconcile with an 'ultimate criterion' based on the 'complete final goal'. When predicting performance, one tries to take into account the whole of a person's contribution to the organization. The open-system theory shows that this contribution is not absolute. New and other requirements are made all the time and individuals must ever meet new challenges. Thorndike's model is applicable only in a closed system.

3.2. Objections to 'the' criterion

Although Thorndike (1949) called attention to 'the' criterion, this was largely neglected in practice. If validity studies are to be carried out, criterion scores should be available (usually at short notice). Those available usually consist of employers' appraisals or results of training programmes and generally these are accepted. There are many objections to appraisals; they are often very unreliable (de Wolff, 1963, 1967, 1970). It is no easy task to develop objective criteria—it entails many problems. Score differences often cannot—or can only partially—be attributed to individuals. The number of tons a crane driver hoists depends on the type of crane used and the kind of material transported rather than on the skillfulness of the crane driver himself. Often, appraisal procedures cannot be avoided, but they should at least be structured better than is usually the case (Elshout, 1973; de Wolff, 1970).

Particular attention should be paid to a better content-analysis of the criterion. The concept of a simple, unidimensional criterion must be abondoned and replaced by multiple criteria (Dunnette, 1963; Wallace, 1965; de Wolff, 1967).

Furthermore, it is questionable whether only performance criteria based on an organization's objectives should be applied. Employees, too, make demands regarding their work, and social indices such as job satisfaction can be used as a criterion as well.

3.3. Influence of the labour market

The model does not bear any relation to the labour market. It just assumes that it is possible to select, that is, that the number of applicants exceeds the number of vacancies, else there would be no cutting scores to consider. It appears that the selection ratio—i.e. the proportion of the number of vacancies to the number of applicants—determines the utility of the test procedure. If, for example, the ratio would be approximately 1.0 (the number of vacancies equals the number of applicants) utility will be negative. Administering tests requires expenses but these are practically never compensated by, say, better performance. In wartime, low ratios could be used. In the selection programme for pilots, one could sometimes afford to reject more than 70% of the subjects.

During the sixties, there was a chronic shortage of labour in The Netherlands. The so-called 'labour reserve' was mostly below 1%. In the seventies, too, there were still sectors whose demand exceeded the supply. Applying the strategies of Cronbach and Gleser, it would not be necessary to select in such a case of unfavourable ratios. However, organizations often continued using their selection procedures.

The shortage of labour, though, did draw attention to something else. While the selection model suggested that one should mainly concentrate on individual differences and selection, questions arose such as 'why do some people want to work in a particular organization, and others do not?', 'why are some people staying on and are others leaving?'. In psychology, the emphasis shifted from differential/psychological questions to questions of a more social and organizational/psychological nature.

3.4. The influence on later employment

The model regarded the selection process as a unique event. The decision to engage or to reject constituted the main focus. The various parts of the programme were considered according to their contribution to a better prediction. If interviews do nothing to improve the multiple correlation, they should be omitted. At best, a 'face validity' argument was used. It might contribute to a better acceptance of the procedure.

The selection procedure itself was almost entirely 'mechanical'. The unfavourable experiences with the validity of appraisals and interviews led to a rejection of human intervention. Such appraisals had usually resulted in a decreased validity of the decision.

Another aspect was that one only concentrated on the organization's decision-making. The model did not take the applicant's decision-making into account. It seems as if it was implicitly believed that an applicant would unconditionally accept the organization's decision. Thus the selection procedure was isolated from other activities such as recruiting, introducing, training, and career-guidance. It was only much later that it was realized that the manner of selection could influence an applicant's willingness to work in an organization and consequently his motivation. This resulted in a re-appraisal and a restructuring of the selection interview.

3.5. The applicant's position

In the model, applicants were regarded as objects. He or she was a 'subject' to be examined in a 'laboratory', a 'system' with 'properties' (Ferguson, 1952; Torgerson, 1958). The psychologist mainly busied himself with how these 'properties' could be measured: this could then contribute to a correct 'allocation' of personnel. In 1950, Bingham summarized this in the question 'Persons or guinea pigs?'. As a matter of fact, this approach stirred up reactions in those who were tested. They, however, were presumed to be content because the approach would lead to better decisions—which would be to their advantage. (In The Netherlands a number of rights were laid down in professional ethics, among them the right to a post-interview discussion and to information about the results.) It will be clear, that psychologists were operating very much from the perspective of organizations and had little idea of the position and interests of the applicants.

4. HOW SOCIETY REACTED

The development of selection technology gave rise to a method that had great potential. Its basic principles, however, proved to be too one-sided and to disregard a number of important factors (to be discussed below), so that dissatisfaction grew and gave rise to complaints about infringements on privacy and about discrimination. In the sixties and seventies this became a topic of public discussion, starting in the United States where later it concentrated on 'equal employment opportunities'. The Netherlands followed some years later: there the vulnerable position of the applicant became the main focus. Psychologists anticipated this and responded to it (van Strien, 1976).

4.1. Objections to psychological tests, violation of privacy

At the end of the fifties, an anti-test movement started in the United States. Dissatisfaction with psychological tests was conveyed by various means. In books like *The tyranny of testing* (Hoffmann, 1962), *The brain watchers* (Gross, 1962) and *The naked society* (Packard, 1964) psychological testing was bitterly attacked. It even came to the burning of test papers. In 1965, commissions from the American Senate and the House of Representatives investigated the use and abuse of psychological tests, concentrating mainly on personality questionnaries and problems concerning the 'violation of privacy' ('American Psychologist', November 1965).

It cannot be denied that some tests do enter into aspects of the private lives of individuals, though the extent to which they do that should not be overestimated.

Conrad (1967) mentions a study which, of the 5300 questions investigated found only ten to be unacceptable. However, one should take into account why psychologists are interested in such aspects: it is not the anamnesis as such, but the psychological implications that are important (van Strien, 1966). Drenth (1967) assumes that here a balancing of interests is involved. From the viewpoint that it is desirable for an organization to make the best possible use of the individuals' qualities, abilities and know-how, it will be necessary to judge the admissibility of the questions put to applicants. Drenth urges psychologists to be extremely careful, because the applicant's position is usually a dependent one. However, the interests should be in balance and for that reason a too one-sided approach of the privacy-problem is rejected. 'Privacy, but not at all costs' (Drenth, 1970).

4.2. Concern about discrimination (Equal Employment Opportunities)

Initially, the discussion focussed on privacy-aspects, but later the 'discrimination' theme came to the fore, especially in the United States. Cultural factors and legislation came to play a major role in the discussion. Ethnic minorities (e.g. the blacks and the Spanish-speaking people) stood up for their own emancipation. In 1964, Congress passed the Civil Rights Act, in which a separate paragraph was dedicated to 'Equal Employment Opportunity' (EEO). This was followed by more detailed prescriptions from the EEO-commission and the Office of Federal Contract Compliance (in 1966, 1968, and 1970), such as the Guidelines on Employment Testing Procedures. These created the possibility to exercise sanctions against employers who discriminate against minorities. Their effect on selection psychology was enormous and is well documented in the Annual Reviews. In 1969, hardly any attention was paid to this subject, but in 1972 Bray and Moses note that the three previous years had been dominated by the Test Fairness Controversy. In 1975, Ash and Kroecker mention that annually 70,000 claims were lodged with the EEO-commission, of which 15–20% concerned discrimination on account of an unfair use of tests.

According to Bray and Moses (1972), this development was embarrassing to many psychologists. Not only had they failed to pay much attention to minority-groups, but also the quality of the tests administered to the majority-group often left much to be desired. Handling the complaints, the judges needed to verify many selection procedures and psychologists had to substantiate their claims.

Juridical considerations began to play a much bigger role in selection procedures. In certain cases, lawyers rather than psychologists had to be consulted. A number of employers responded to this development by suspending psychological selection. Others chose to support large-scale and carefully planned selection-research programmes.

4.3. Vulnerability of the applicant

In the Netherlands, the discussion took another direction than in the United States. In 1971, a member of Parliament submitted a resolution stating that there are objections to psychological tests with respect to the individual interests of applicants. It was couched in terms like: 'invading the private sphere', 'insufficient discussion of conclusions with the persons tested' and 'insufficient guarantee that the results will remain in the hands of the expert and appropriate persons only'.

In 1973, the SWOV (the unions' research foundation) published a report entitled 'The dependent applicant' (Top, 1973), emphasizing the applicant's vulnerability. This is caused by, among other things, the applicant's ignorance of his market-value and of his commitment to the company, the necessity to find a job at short notice, or the impossibility for one individual to stand up against an organization that has carefully designed procedures and an expert staff. The report argues in favour of strengthening the applicant's position. Also in 1973, the Association of banking, insurance and administrative personnel published a report called 'Applicant, application, applying', which advocates a stronger position for the applicant. The report concludes by formulating a sample 'code of conduct' for the selection procedure. In November of the same year, as a result of the 1971 resolution, the Minister of Social Affairs set up the so-called Hessel-commission to advise the government on the desirability of regulations to safeguard the privacy of applicants during the selection and engagement procedures. In 1977, this commission published its final report under the title: 'An applicant is also a human being'. This report proceeds from two main principles:

a. The criterion for selection is the applicant's suitability for the job in question.
b. All parts of the entire selection procedure should be consistent with human dignity.

The latter point is elaborated in a number of rights:

—The right to a fair chance to be engaged; selection decisions must be reached on grounds of careful considerations and fairness and it must always be possible to justify them.

—The right to information; both parties in the selection procedure must be informed in such a way that they can arrive at a justified decision. Apparently, this right is but inadequately realized in many procedures. Attention is paid to, among other things, information about the procedure, the job itself and the work organization, data about the applicant which the work organization receives from third parties, and the reasons for rejection.

—The right to privacy; the commission recognizes the necessity of the applicant supplying information about himself to enable the work organization to judge his capacities and suitability. 'If the information asked has a bearing on the job, such a violation of privacy is admissible'.

—The right to confidential treatment of personal data; such data are not to be passed on to an unnecessarily large number of persons and are not to be used for other purposes than those they were obtained for.

—The right to an instrumentally efficient procedure; the selection instruments must meet the requirements of validity and reliability.

—The applicant should have the right to lodge a complaint when he feels he has been treated carelessly, unfairly, or incorrectly, or if he thinks the selection decision was not made on solid grounds. In this connection, the commission recommends to make those carrying out psychological selection-tests subject to legal disciplinary measures.

Jansen (1979), a member of this commission, has elaborated many of these points in his *Ethics and Practice of Personnel Selection*, in which 'just procedures' are strongly emphasized.

Psychologists have, in many respects, anticipated this changing attitude towards psychological testing. At the 1970 conference of the Dutch Institute of Psychologists on the theme of 'The new role perception of the psychologist regarding the social aspects of his profession', it was decided to revise the code of conduct. In 1975, after long discussions on the draft versions, a revised code was accepted, which took effect on 1 January 1976.

The Division of Work- and Organizational psychology accepted an even more elaborate code. In formulating this code, use was made of the results of an inquiry among practising psychologists (van Strien, 1973). The general code comprised the following points: the kind of information clients and research subject are entitled to, voluntary participation of the subjects, confidentiality and the right to lodge complaints. The code also states that a client may demand that the psychologist refrains from reporting to third parties (NIP, 1975). Whereas by 1983 the government had still not responded to the Hessel-report, the Dutch Association for Personnel Officers has meanwhile formulated a code of conduct, which roughly follows the recommendations of this commision.

4.4. Participation in selection procedures

In the early seventies, a development started in The Netherlands, by which the applicant's future colleagues and subordinates gained more influence on the decision-making in the selection procedures. This development ran parallel to current ideas about participation, work consultation, and industrial democratization.

There is hardly any professional literature on participation in engaging personnel. The present chapter is based partly on our own experience and partly on the topics discussed at conferences of personnel managers. There exists, moreover, a report of the Stichting Stuurgroep Sociaal-Watenschappelijk Onderzoek (1976).

Our impression is that many organizations practise some form of participation, be it mostly on an experimental or informal basis. A discussion between the applicant and his future colleagues and/or subordinates is usually part of their application procedure. Such discussions, which may in some cases be quite long, concern the content of the task and how it is to be carried out. Universities—especially when appointing professors—employ more formal procedures.

Strictly speaking, participation procedures and psychological tests do not need to be incompatible. In practice, however, it appears that they sometimes can be reconciled only with difficulty.

Participation procedures can make a decision-making process complex and lengthy; this may have the consequence that the psychological tests are rejected. And it is, furthermore, difficult to advise on what the part of the psychologist is. Formerly, it sufficed to report to the employer and, if required, to discuss this report with the applicant. In the case of participation, the psychologist's recommendation may deviate considerably from that of the colleagues and/or subordinates. If that is so, it is almost impossible to inform all parties concerned about the outcome of the tests as this would infringe on the rules set by the Hessel-commission (privacy, confidential treatment).

Very likely, participation may have some advantages. The parties concerned are more competent to judge whether they will be able to work together. The expectations on both sides can be explored in detail and may contribute to a good understanding of what will be expected from all concerned (reduction of role-ambiguity). Nevertheless, the privacy problem will continue to exist. A selection commission—as recommended by the Hessel-commission—might solve the problem in such a way that a balance obtains between the recommendations of the psychologist and those of future colleagues and/or subordinates. In any case, it seems desirable to examine more emphatically the course of participation procedures as well as their effects.

5. ATTEMPTS AT NEW APPROACHES

Above we have paid special attention to the objections against the classic selection model. The question arises as to what improvements are feasible. How can such objections be removed? Some points already became manifest in the discussion on professional ethics. In this section, we wish to deal with several attempts as described in the literature.

5.1. The model of Lofquist and Dawis

In 1969, Lofquist and Dawis published their book on work adjustment, which appeared in a series of reports known as the 'the Minnesota studies'. The model they present in this study is illustrated in figure 1.

Their point of departure is that an individual has, on the one hand, 'abilities' and, on the other, 'needs'. An organization, on the one hand, makes 'demands' and, on the other, offers 'rewards' (in the widest sense of the word: both material and immaterial). According to the model, two adjustment processes are called for, the one concerning the abilities of the individual and the demands of the organization, the other the 'needs' and 'rewards'. In the first case, successfull adjustment will lead to satisfactoriness, that is: the organization will be satisfied. In the second case, successful adjustment will lead to satisfaction, that is: the individual will be satisfied. Dissatisfaction will make both parties wish to break off the relation. The individual may start looking for another job; the organization may consider the possibility of firing or transferring the individual.

Both adjustment processes have to be successful. If only one succeeds, one of the parties will remain dissatisfied and feel inclined to discontinue the rela-

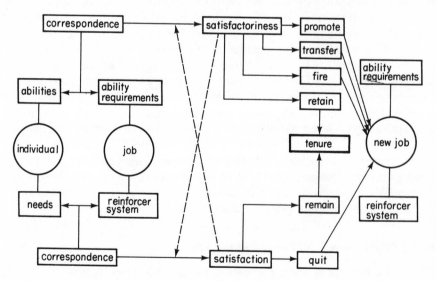

Figure 1. The Work Adjustment model of Lofquist and Dawis (from: Lofquist and Dawis, 1969; by permission of the publisher).

tion. Satisfaction on both sides leads to stabilization of the relation ('tenure'). Lofquist and Dawis mention several studies supporting this view. They also point out that one kind of satisfaction acts as a moderator on the other (which in fact follows from their theory); in other words: the correlation between 'satisfaction' and 'tenure' is higher for people with high 'satisfactoriness' scores; the same is true of the correlation between 'satisfactoriness' and 'tenure' for those with high 'satisfaction' scores.

Lofquist en Dawis further point out that the adjustment processes are dynamic, not static processes. Employees will learn from experience and/or training, so their skills will change. Organizations will reorganize, so their 'demands' and 'needs' will undergo changes. This will have its effects on the adjustment processes and may disturb them. Maintenance will always be necessary in order to maintain the balance.

When comparing this model with the classic model, two aspects in particular should be emphasized.

a. *The two adjustment processes.* In the classic model, predictions are linked to criteria, which to a great extent corresponds with the first adjustment process (the one determining the organization's satisfaction). The work adjustment model, however, also refers to another adjustment process, viz. that between demands and rewards (determining the individual's satisfaction).

b. *The dynamic character of the adjustment processes.* The adjustment is not static. It is not enough to have just one successful adjustment (upon entering the organization), it should be worked on continuously.

Curiously enough, the work adjustment model has not received much attention in the literature; it is, for instance, not discussed in the Annual Reviews, nor is it mentioned in Guion's chapter on selection in Dunnette (1976).

5.2. Motivation theories

In the first half of the sixties, several important publications appeared emphasizing 'performance' in a way entirely different from the selection model. In 1959, Herzberg's book *The motivation to work* was published. Between 1962 and 1964, Adams published several articles dealing with 'inequity' and in 1964 Vroom's *Work and Motivation* appeared. Each of these authors has his own theory about motivation; what they have in common, however, is that they relate performance not solely to individual differences (e.g. in ability), but that they also introduce other independent variables. We shall not discuss these theories here; the reader is referred to chapter 2.2. of this Handbook and Steers and Porter 1975).

Steers and Porter present a detailed description of the theories, and in their discussion they mention three important factors connected with performance: 'motivation', 'ability and skills' and 'role clarity'. Being interested in motivation, they are induced to study such variables as reward, job design, leadership, group influences, organization climate, and 'the individual's objectives', thereby introducing yet another factor: 'attachment to the organization'. On introducing this factor they state the following: 'We are concerned then with what organizations want from their employees, and what employees want in exchange from their employers'. Employees are seen as individuals who want to make sure that they will be able to satisfy their individual objectives by means of their work, 'or else there is little purpose in their coming to work'.

Later, Steers and Porter replaced the concept of 'attachment' by that of 'commitment'. They also constructed a scale with 15 items for measuring this concept. In five of their studies they correlate 'commitment' and 'turnover'; three of these are predictive studies, the other two are longitudinal in design. In all five studies, a very significant correlation is found between 'commitment' and 'turnover' (Steers et al. 1978).

Steers and Porter's findings are in conformity with those of Lofquist and Dawis. 'Tenure', the dependent variable of Lofquist and Dawis, is in fact the opposite of 'turnover'. Where the one speaks of two adjustment processes, the other speaks of an exchange-relationship which must lead to 'commitment'. In their publications, Steers and Porter do not establish a direct connection between 'commitment' and the engagement procedure. They do note, however, that there is a relation between commitment and individual characteristics and between job characteristics and work experience. As appears from the study, the relation between 'commitment' and work experiences especially yields high correlations. That a selection procedure could influence commitment is obvious. Both the expectations about the opportunity to contribute (role clarity) and those about what 'rewards' may be expected from the organizations will be based on, among other things, the matters discussed during the engagement procedure.

Two points stand out particularly clearly:
a. Performance depends not only on capacities and abilities, but also on motivation and role clarity.
b. Motivation is viewed as the resultant of a process. Thus, the expectations with which one comes to the job should be in accordance with the experiences one acquires on the job.

5.3. Results of studies on interviews

When examining the literature on interviews, it becomes evident that, originally, interest was focussed on the validity issue. As early as the twenties and thirties, it appeared that the results of validity studies were very disappointing. As a rule, the correlations between appraisals based on interviews and 'performance criteria' were low and did not show a significant deviation from zero. It turned out that interviews did not possess high predictive value. On account of these unfavourable experiences, the image of interviews became a negative one: should interviewers in any way influence selection decisions, the value of the procedure as a whole would decrease (Mayfield, 1964).

In the sixties, the interview became the object of renewed attention. LIAMA, a research organization working for American life insurance companies, prepared a research programme (for summaries see Carlson and Mayfield, 1966). Interestingly, the programme included a more systematic approach to the interview. One of the things investigated, by means of experiments, was the way in which interviewers responded to both verbal and non-verbal information and how they arrived at their judgement. The results were incorporated into the 'Agent Selection Kit', which assigns an important place to a highly structured interview to be conducted by the employer. In an explanatory comment on this selection procedure, the authors point out that their approach is based on different ideas about management. Selection is no longer seen as a unilateral decision problem of management, but as part of a personnel development programme. Together with recruitment, introduction, training, and supervision it should form an integrated entity. The parts should not be independent of each other: what is done in the framework of one part, should be coordinated with what takes place in another.

Thus, much value is attached to mutual consent concerning career decisions as well as to joint exploration so as to arrive at these decisions. The complete procedure, especially the selection interview, is structured in such a way that supervisor and applicant will systematically discuss all aspects of the job in question. The interviews are meant to investigate whether the applicant can be expected to meet the job requirements and also whether the job will give him satisfaction. Employers will have to take a course of thorough training to learn how to conduct such interviews.

The availability of extensive job analyses makes a well-structured engagement procedure possible. The supervisors have very detailed manuals at their disposal, which, among other things, list all aspects that are to be discussed in the selection-interview. Moreover, informative booklets are made available to the applicant to help him in making his decision. This method really seems to make it possible to arrive at decisions on which both parties can agree.

This method differs considerably from the traditional model, particularly on the following points:
1. its recognition that the selection procedure should be treated, not as an isolated element, but as part of a larger whole;
2. its orientation towards personnel development;
3. its aiming to pursue joint exploration by both employer and applicant as well as mutual consent;
4. this method is, like the traditional approach, based on careful job analysis. But the information obtained from this analysis is also used to structure other parts of the engagement procedures.

5.4. Personnel recruitment

In the course of the seventies, personnel selection came steadily more into the open. In 1977, Schneider published his *Staffing Organizations*. Bij 'staffing' he meant 'processes in identifying, assessing, evaluating and developing individuals at work'. His aim is to achieve a more integrated approach of personnel recruitment. For instance, he emphasizes that where job analysis is concerned, the discussion should be about the abilities an applicant should have if he is to perform a job successfully, but also about the rewards he or she may receive in doing the work. He points out that while organizations do organize individuals the reverse is also true, that is: individuals organize organizations.

Organizations should therefore ask themselves what they are able to offer. They should, for instance, know what applicants imagine them to be: what kind of image is evoked by advertisements and other publicity? Recruitment efficiency can sometimes be improved considerably if one is alive to such aspects. The way organizations approach selection problems should logically result from the personnel policy pursued.

6. ATTEMPTS AT INTEGRATION

Above we described the criticism exercised on the classic selection model, presenting at the same time a number of new approaches. But these new approaches do not stand all by themselves: the direction they are taking fits into a broader pattern that became manifest in the past two decades. The deterministic model had to give way to approaches that more specifically draw attention to an individual's development and his relation to his environment. This is happening not just in personnel selection but everywhere in work- and organizational psychology.

We will here attempt to list the elements of an integrated approach of personnel selection. The following points will be discussed successively:
a. There are two decision-making procedures.
b. In order to make a decision, one should have information available.
c. The procedure should be based upon joint exploration.
d. Participation of future colleagues and/or subordinates.
e. Fitting the man and his job is an ongoing process.
f. Organizations should set up integrated systems for improving this fit.
g. This approach will change the psychologist's role perceptions.
h. Consequently, this will bring about other forms of validation.

a. *The two decision-making processes*
In the past decade, it has become clear that in engaging personnel there are two decision-making processes playing a part. This was discussed above. In the past, psychologists have occupied themselves with decision-making from the organization's perspective. However, optimizing the decision-making process,

also from the applicant's perspective, will require more. The entire selection procedure will have to be structured in such a way that both the applicant and the organization are able to arrive at a good decision.

In the same way as psychologists have been concerned with—and have investigated—the question as to how organizations should make decisions, they should do this on behalf of the applicant. Not only the organization, but also the applicant needs help.

b. *Information to facilitate decision-making*

Adequate decision-making will be possible only when the appropriate information is available. Again and again it turns out to be very difficult to obtain such information. Organizations as well as applicants often make decisions on the basis of impressions and global information without carefully analyzing their needs or systematically collecting and evaluating the, in principle, available information. The model of Lofquist and Dawis indicates what kind of information is required. The category 'abilities' can be measured reasonably well by means of tests.

The category 'requirements' can be explicated in detail by means of job-analysis methods. Useful information on this subject is given in articles by Morsh and Madden (1961) and McCormick (1976). A useful manual on job analysis is the *Handbook for Analyzing Jobs* (1972). The *Dictonary of Occupational Titles* (1977) should be mentioned also. In test literature the category 'needs' has been treated poorly. There exist, in fact, many interest tests; however, these are thought of predictors in the first place.

In The Netherlands, Algera (1978) developed a questionnaire for measuring job preference. In the field of vocational guidance one became gradually more interested in 'vocational counseling': helping the client in making his choice (van Geffen, 1977).

Information about what a job could offer in terms of the applicant's requirements (the category 'rewards') is as a rule hardly available. Such information should concern the nature of the work itself as well as the work situation. Examples of the latter are: management style of the employer, insecurity because of reorganizations, etc. Lofquist and Dawis try to solve this problem by means of simple scales on which the judges (or the employers) indicate to what extent the jobs include such aspects as growth opportunities and associated with colleagues. One may well wonder how reliable and valid such information can be. A closer examination will be necessary.

c. *Joint exploration*

In the LIAMA-procedure, the element of joint exploration is emphasized. It involves several aspects, for example that of becoming aware of one's preferences. What is the applicant looking for in his new job and what does the organization expect from the new employee?

The applicants will wish to explore the situation too. They do not want to rely only on the information supplied by the psychologist, but they also wish to obtain information through interviews and observation in the organization. Because the parties concerned are ultimately responsible for the decisions, everything is strongly in favour of such an exploration. In most cases, the psychologist will be of more help if he assists in the *structuring* of this exploration process than if he takes over the decision-making from the parties. Both parties usually have but a faint idea of what they actually want: they are sometimes clearer about what they do not want than about what they do want. An exploration may shed more light on what their actual preferences are. Once it has become clear what one *wants* to achieve, it will be easier to find out whether, in the new situation, this aim *can* be attained and on what this might depend. It will be useful to have this exploration carried out jointly by both parties, because the results will often be determined by both parties alike and because joint exploration may lead to a more accurately formulated 'psychological contract'.

d. *Participation in selection procedures*

In section 4 we mentioned several possibly positive effects of participation in selection procedures. Participation could be especially helpful in harmonizing the expectations on both sides and in explaining clearly the tasks to be performed to the parties concerned.

However, there may also be some disadvantages attached to such participation. The procedure may be time-consuming. The privacy of the applicants may be violated. In some cases the procedure may cause a considerable loss of time and a lack of resoluteness.

e. *Adjustment of the parties is an ongoing process*

It has become increasingly clear that should both parties decide to join hands the selection procedure is only the beginning. Open systems are not static and in order to maintain the balance it is necessary that both the organization and the individual make continuous efforts. In this case, joint exploration should continue so that both parties can investigate what adjustments will be possible in future. One should bear in mind that the balance may be disturbed, not only as a result of external developments, possibly of a threatening nature, but also because of the 'growth' of the employee due to learning or training, or because of the advent of new perspectives that offer a challenge. Once a person is accepted, adjustment is effected through work discussions on the one hand, and appraisal and career-development interviews on the other.

f. *Integrated procedures and systems*

The recognition that adjustment is an ongoing process requires the organiztion to set up and construct integrated procedures and systems in order to bring about this adjustment. Recruitment, selection, training/introduction, appraisal, career planning, etc. cannot be taken as loose parts that can be controlled separately, but must be looked upon as an integrated system.

In such a system, the immediate supervisor plays an important role. In the first place, he represents the interests of the organization and is the interlocutor of the employee. The supervisor makes many decisions on behalf of the organization, in which case he will often feel the need to consult personnel specialists and psychologists. Training-specialists can advise on the available training programmes; a career-guidance department can supply information about vacancies or take care of the registration of interests; a psychologist can be consulted in case of ineffective performance, etc.

Parts of the organizational procedures may be carried out by these consultants (testing, conducting interviews with employees, etc.). Ultimately, however, there should exist just one system, representing a consistent policy and providing clarity as to who does what. In practice, these requirements are by no means fully met.

g. *The psychologist's role*

The approach indicated above will bring about changes in the position and role perceptions of the psychologists. In the classic model, the psychologist was in the first place an expert who, on the basis of his knowledge of a certain technology, advised management how to decide. In this situation he could perform his tasks outside the organization (in his 'laboratory').

The approach recommended by us will require involvement in a much wider range of activities. The selection test being integrated into the engagement-process as a whole, it should be coordinated with the various parts of the process. Besides, codes of conduct, based on the guidelines of the Hessel-commission, will strengthen the applicant's position. He will be able to introduce himself as an articulate, critical applicant who will be gathering information about the course of the entire selection-process.

The way in which one wishes to arrive at adjustment is directly linked up with the organization's personnel policy. The psychologist, as an adviser on how to design procedures and systems, is required to have a considerably more thorough understanding of the functioning of organizations. Though his work will continue to be based on knowledge and scientific insight, this extension of his task will also demand a greater awareness of social developments in society. He must be able to assess to what extent these developments will influence the policy to be pursued.

Besides, much more emphasis will be laid on the services to be rendered during decision-making. A recommendation alone will no longer suffice; the psychologist will have to assist the parties in determining their position and in making their decisions. For this, he will have to master social and interview skills.

h. *Consequences for research programmes*

Thorndike emphasized the necessity of validation. Selection decisions should be based on empirical tests. For him, the responsibility for the validation lay with the individual psychologist ('the reputable worker in the field', see section 2). This meant that practically all tasks connected with the design and implementation of selection-procedures had to be performed by either the psychologist himself or under his supervision.

In practice, there has been only a limited amount of validation research. It is true that in the past decades countless correlations between tests and criterion scores were computed, but it is decidedly untrue that the majority of the selection recommendations were based on validation studies carried out according to the method prescribed by Thorndike.

This is partly due to conditions that cannot (or can hardly) be met. Samples are too small or their composition is too heterogeneous; criteria either are not available or can be developed only after large-scale investigations (de Wolff, 1966). Often, however, an individually operating psychologist will not succeed in bringing such an extensive operation, i.e., the setting up of a satisfactory selection-programme, to a successful close. Mainly very big organizations have been able to implement a systematic approach (United States Employment Service, military forces). Some examples for management selection can be found in Campbell et al. (1973).

The approach we described in section 6 above will also require much research, some of it of the kind described by Thorndike. But other research will also be necessary, for instance on the relations between parts of the selection procedure and 'commitment', on the influence of participation in selection procedures and on the decision-making process on the part of the applicant.

It is not very realistic to put the burden of this research exclusively upon the shoulders of psychologists working individually. It should nevertheless be pointed out that they are (and remain) responsible for the quality and usefulness of the methods they use and recommend. Considering its complexity, such research will have to be carried out by large teams of researchers.

CONCLUDING REMARKS

To find new avenues and to abandon methods that are no longer adequate, will generally take far more time than we are prepared to admit. An example is the transition from the 'impressionistic' to the 'statistical' approach at the end of the fifties. Though research had shown many tests to be impracticable, they remained in use for a long time. At first, new instruments constructed according to the rules were only reluctantly accepted. The specialized literature on selection does not go into this matter, although we know from the organizational psychological literature we know there is such a thing as 'resistance to change'. We should bear in mind that changes always need quite some time before being effected, which means that situations considered undesirable continue to exist.

Forms of external pressure can sometimes promote change processes. The introduction of new codes of conduct for psychologist (NIP, 1975) and personnel officers (Nederlandse Vereniging voor Personeelsbeleid, 1971; Vereniging van Nederlandse Gemeenten, 1978) could stimulate the above-mentioned changes.

REFERENCES

Adams, J. S. (1963), Toward an understanding of inequity. *Journal of Abnormal and Social Psychology*, **67**, 422–436.

Adams, J. S., Jacobsen, P. R. (1964), Effects of wage inequities on work quality. *Journal of Abnormal and Social Psychology*, **69**, 19–25.

Adams, J. S., Rosenbaum, W. B. (1962), The relationship of worker productivity to cognitive dissonance about wage inequities. *Journal of Applied Psychology*, **46**, 161–164.

Algera, J. A. (1978), *Constructie van de 'Vragenlijst Werk preferentie'* [Construction of the 'Work preference questionnaire']. IJmuiden: Hoogovens (internal publication).

American Psychological Association (1966), *Standards for educational and psychological tests and manuals*. Washington: APA.

American Psychological Association, American Educational Research Association, National Council on Measurement Used in Education (Joint Committee) (1954), Technical recommendations for psychological tests and diagnostic techniques. *Psychological Bulletin*, **51**, 201–238.

American Psychological Association, American Educational Research Association, National Council on Measurement in Education (1974), *Standards for educational and psychological tests*. Washington: APA.

Argyris, C. (1976), Problems and new directions for industrial psychology. In: Dunnette, M. D. (Ed.), *Handbook of industrial and organizational psychology*. Chicago: Rand McNally.

Ash, P., Kroecker, L. P. (1975), Personnel selection, classification and placement. *Annual Review*, **26**.

Bingham, W. V. (1950), Persons or guinea pigs? *Personnel Psychology*, **3**, 305–400.

Bray, D. W., Moses, J. L. (1972), Personnel selection. *Annual Review*, **23**, 545–576.

Buros, O. K. (Ed.) (1938), *The 1938 mental measurements yearbook*. New York: Gryphon Press (also published in 1941, 1949, 1953, 1959, 1965, 1972).

Buros, O. K. (Ed.) (1979), *The eighth mental measurements yearbook*. New York: Gryphon Press.

Campbell, J., Dunnette, M. D., Lawler, E. E., Weick, K. E. (1970), *Managerial behavior, performance and effectiveness*. New York: McGraw-Hiil.

Commissie Hessel (1977), *Een sollicitant is ook een mens* [An applicant is also a human being]. The Hague: Staatsuitgeverij.

Conrad, H. S. (1967), Clearance of questionnaires with respect to invasion of privacy, public sensitiveness, ethical standards, etc. *American Psychologist*, **22**, 356–359.

Cowley, W. H. (1928), Three distinctions in the study of leaders. *Journal of Abnormal and Social Psychology*, **23**, 144–157.

Cronbach, L. J., Gleser, G. C. (1957), *Psychological tests and personnel decisions*. Urbana: University of Illinois Press.

Dictionary of occupational titles (1977), 4th ed. US Department of Labor. Employment and Training Administration. US Employment Service.

Drenth, P. J. D. (1967), *Protesten contra testen* [Protests against tests]. Amsterdam: Swets & Zeitlinger.

Drenth, P. J. D. (1970), Sociale en ethische aspecten van het testgebruik [Social and ethical aspects of the use of tests]. In: Drenth *et al.* (1970), 114–127.

Drenth, P. J. D. (1973), *De psychologische test* [The psychological test]. Deventer: Van Loghum Slaterus.

Drenth, P. J. D., Willems, P. J., Wolff, Ch. J. de (Eds.), *Bedrijfspsychologie: Onderzoek en evaluatie* [Industrial psychology: Research and evaluation]. Deventer: Kluwer.

Dunnette, M. D. (1963), A note on the criterion. *Journal of Applied Psychology*, **47**, 251–254.

Elshout, J. (1970), De constructie van een multivariaat criterium [The construction of a multivariate criterion]. In: Drenth *et al.* (1970).

Equal Employment Opportunity Commission (1966), *Guidelines on employment testing procedures.* Washington D. C.: Equal Employment Opportunity Commission.

Equal Employment Opportunity Commission (1970), *Guidelines on employee selection procedures.* Federal Register.

Evers, A., Zaal, J. (1979), De derde NIP-enquête onder testgebruikers [The third NIP-inquiry among test users]. *De Psycholoog* [The Psychologist], **14**, 509–528.

Ferguson, L. W. (1952), *Personality measurement.* New York: McGraw-Hill.

Geffen, L. H. M. J. van (1977), *De keuze van werk* [Occupational choice]. Culemborg: Schoolpers.

Giessen, R. W. van der (1957), *Enkele aspecten van het probleem der predictie in de psychologie* [Some aspects of the problems of predicting in psychology]. Amsterdam.

Graen, G. (1976), Role-making processes within complex organizations. In: Dunnette, M. D. (Ed.), *Handbook of industrial and organizational psychology.* Chicago: Rand McNally.

Gross, M. L. (1962), *The brains watchers.* New York.

Guilford, J. P. (1959), *Personality.* New York: McGraw-Hill.

Guion, R. M. (1965), *Personnel testing.* New York: McGraw-Hill.

Guion, R. M. (1976), Recruiting, selection, job placement. In: Dunnette, M. D. (Ed.), *Handbook of industrial and organizational psychology.* Chicago: Rand McNally.

Gullikson, H. (1950), *Theory of mental tests.* New York: Wiley.

Handbook for analyzing jobs (1972). Manpower Administration, US Department of labor. Washington D. C.: US Superintendent of Documents.

Herzberg, F., Mausner, B., Snyderman, B. (1959), *The motivation to work.* 2nd ed. New York: Wiley.

Hoffmann, B. (1962), *The tiranny of testing.* New York.

Jansen, A. (1979), *Ethiek en praktijk van personeelsselectie* [Ethics and practice of personnel selection]. Deventer: Kluwer.

LIAMA (1968), *Agent selection kit.* Hartfort.

Lindquist, E. F. (Ed.) (1951), *Educational measurement.* Washington D. C.: American Council on Education.

Lofquist, L. H., Dawis, R. V. (1969), *Adjustment to work.* New York: Appleton.

McCormick, E. J. (1976), Job and task analysis. In: Dunnette, M. D. (Ed.), *Handbook of industrial and organizational psychology.* Chicago: Rand McNally.

Mayfield, E. C. (1964), The selection interview: A re-evaluation of published research. *Personnel Psychology*, **17**, 239–260.

Mayfield, E. C., Carlson, R. E. (1966), Selection interview decisions: First results from long-term research project. *Personnel Psychology*, **19**, 41–53.

Morsh, J. E., Madden, J. M., Christal, R. L. (1961), *Job analysis in the United States Air Force.* Lackland Air Force Base, WADD, TR, 61–113.

NIP = Nederlands Instituut van Psychologen [Dutch Institute of Psychologists].

NIP (1961, 1964, 1969, 1974), *Documentatie van tests en testresearch in Nederland* [Documentation of tests and test research in The Netherlands]. Amsterdam: NIP.

NIP (1975a), *Gedragsregels voor de bedrijfs- en organisatiepsychologie* [Code of conduct for work- and organizational psychology]. Amsterdam: NIP.

NIP (1975b), Beroepscode voor psychologen [Professional code for psychologists]. *De Psycholoog*, **10**, 279–285.

NIP (1978), *Richtlijnen voor ontwikkeling en gebruik van psychologische tests en studietoetsen* [Guidelines for the development and use of psychological tests and achievement tests]. Amsterdam: NIP.

Office of Federal Contract Compliance (1968), *Validation of tests by contracters and subcontracters subject to the provisions of Executive Order*. Federal Register.

Packard, V. (1964), *The naked society*. New York.

Roe, R. A. (1983), *Grondslagen der personeelsselectie* [Foundations of personnel selection]. Assen: Van Gorcum.

Rundquist, E. A. (1969), The prediction ceiling. *Personnel Psychology*, **22**, 109–116.

Schneider, B. (1976), *Staffing organizations*. Pacific Palisades: Goodyear.

Steers, R. M., Porter, L. W. (1975), *Motivation and work behavior*. New York: Mc-Graw-Hill.

Steers, R. M., Porter, L. W., Mowday (1978). *Work commitment*. Paper presented at the IAAP Congress, Munich.

Stichting Stuurgroep Sociaal-Wetenschappelijk Onderzoek [Foundation Steering Group Social Science Research]. (1976), *Inspraak bij benoemingen* [Consultation in appointments]. The Hague.

Strien, P. J. van (1966), *Kennis en communicatie in de psychologische praktijk* [Knowledge and communication in psychological practice]. Utrecht: Bijleveld.

Strien, P. J. van (Ed.) (1976), *Personeelsselectie in discussie* [Personnel selection under discussion]. Meppel: Boom.

Strien, P. J. van, Cools, E., et al. (1973), *Speelruimte en spelregels: Verslag van een enquête over beroepspraktijk en beroepsethiek onder de bedrijfspsychologie in Nederland* [Boundaries and rules of the game: Report on an enquiry on professional practice and ethics in industrial psychology in The Netherlands]. Groningen/Utrecht.

SWOV (Stichting Wetenschappelijk Onderzoek Vakcentrales [Unions' Foundation of Scientific Research]) (1973, *De afhankelijke sollicitant* [The dependent applicant]. Utrecht: Lumax.

Thorndike, L. J. (1949), *Personnel selection: Test and measurement technique*. New York: Wiley.

Thorndike, R. L. (Ed.), *Educational measurement*. Washington D. C.: American Council on Education.

Torgerson, W. S. (1958), *Theory and methods of scaling*. New York: Wiley.

Vereniging van Werknemers in het Bank- en Verzekeringsbedrijf en Administratieve Kantoren [Association of Banking, Insurance and Administrative Personnel] (1973), *Sollicitant, sollicitatie, solliciteren* [Applicant, application, applying]. Utrecht.

Vroom, V. H. (1964), *Work and motivation*. New York: Wiley.

Wallace, S. Rains (1965), Criteria for what? *American Psychologist*, **20**, 411–417.

Wolff, Ch. J. de (1963), *Personeelsbeoordeling* [Personnel appraisal]. Amsterdam: Swets & Zeitlinger.

Wolff, Ch. J. de (1967), *Het criteriumprobleem* [The criterion-problem]. Deventer: Kluwer.

Wolff, Ch. J. de (1970), *Beoordelingen als criteria* [Appraisals as criteria]. In: Drenth et al. (1970).

Wolff, Ch. J. de (1973), *Selectie van managers* [The selection of managers]. In: Drenth, P. J. D., Willems, P. J., Wolff, Ch. J. de (Eds.), *Arbeids- en organisatiepsychologie* [Work- and organizational psychology]. Deventer: Kluwer.

2.8.   Career development and career guidance

J. Gerrit Boerlijst

A. CAREER AS A THEME IN WORK- AND ORGANIZATIONAL PSYCHOLOGY

It is only recently that work- and organizational (W & O) psychology began taking a greater interest in the systematic study of careers with a view to forming a career theory. In the 'Handbook of industrial and organizational psychology' (Dunnette, 1976) no direct reference to the concept 'career' is yet to be found.[1] Until 1976, the 'Annual review of psychology' too remained silent on the subject. The tide has turned since, as a consequence of the rapidly increasing amount of relevant professional literature.[2] It would be an error to claim that no work was done on career theory before—we shall report about such work in this chapter—, but those studies were for the most part concerned with episodes or aspects of careers that were isolated in time, e.g. the choice of career in adolescence. The career-as-a-whole began to receive greater attention only in the seventies. A plausible explanation for this can only be guessed at. Let us try to.

In selecting its subject matter and issues, W & O psychology tends to be guided by the questions and needs of the client system. Finding a methodically justifiable, instrumentally oriented solution to a problem, then, will often have

Dr. J. Gerrit Boerlijst, T. H. Twente, Vakgroep Soc. Bedrijfskunde, Postbus 217, Enschede, Tel.: 053-892688.

[1] A thorough reading of this handbook will, however, yield some reference to it (Holland, 1976; Owens, 1976; Finkle, 1976).

[2] Cf. Heller and Clark (1976): 'Personnel and human resources development'; Super and Hall (1978): 'Career development: Exploration and planning'; Krumboltz et al. (1979): 'Counseling psychology: Developing skill for career transitions'; Baltes et al. (1980): 'Life-span developmental psychology'; Holland et al. (1981): 'Counseling psychology: Career interventions, research, and theory.'

primacy over theoretical reflections, the latter being more time-consuming. At first, W & O psychology approached the career-theme in a practical manner. In the sixties, those concerned with personnel management in large industries began to feel the need for psychological aids in making justifiable decisions on the continuation of individual careers, which should fit into the broader framework of management development (usually abbreviated MD). As such decisions are usually made only once in a person's career, it seemed that the required psychological instruments (tests, questionnaires, and the like) could be constructed without going into thematic reflections on 'career' as a process of growth and development. Besides, at that time no suitable developmental-psychological framework was available. (Developmental psychology has long more or less confined itself to studying non-adults and only in the past decade has it been concerned with the subject of 'development of adults' on a larger scale.)

After 1970, personnel managements became more alive to the limitations of (momentary) *ad hoc* career decisions and shifted the emphasis to the more continuous steering and guiding of careers (and career occupants, respectively) on the basis of a 'career policy'. The psychological instruments had to be adapted to this revised objective. W & O psychology saw the necessity to form a (policy-) supporting theory, based on empirical career research, to serve, in particular, 'career guidance'. The professional literature has since been showing clear traces of this.

This chapter will proceed as follows. There are two parts. Part A presents a historical survey of the development of personnel work in relation to career guidance and career development (section A1). Next, some aspects of policies regarding careers are discussed (section A2) as well as the position W & O psychology has assumed in the course of time on the theme of 'career' (section A3). This is followed by a discussion of some developmental-psychological results that may be important to career development (section A4) and of some methodological aspects of theory formation and empirical research on careers (section A5). Finally (section A6) we will take a look at the possible future contributions of W & O psychology to 'career development' and draw attention to the problem of the lack of agreement on what the concept 'career' means.

Part B contains an exposé about the various views on the concept 'career' as encountered in the literature (sections B1–9) resulting in a brief exposition about an attempt of ours towards synthesizing the definitions—which is intended as a contribution to the integration of research and theory on careers and their development (section B10).

A1. From 'management development' to 'career guidance'

In the early sixties, at the time of the economic boom, larger organizations and industries began to feel more and more the need for policy instruments geared to promoting the internal mobility of middle management and higher personnel and to securing the continuity and quality of (top) management.

The rapid developments in products, services, and markets brought about a great demand for all kinds of specialized tasks to be carried out by relatively highly qualified, specifically skilled, but not necessarily managerial personnel. Various specialized sectors in industries and services filled up with middle and higher management. As long as these sectors kept offering jobs—and until recently that was still the case—the managerial personnel concerned lacked the incentive or motive to broaden their outlook or to move beyond their own jobs. Our own research (Boerlijst, 1974) has shown that around 1970 the mainly specialized middle and higher management of a large production organization, when asked to state their expectations of the future, was still strongly fixed on 'further growth in their *present* position'.

Generally, this category enjoyed good incomes, social security, status, and the like. Despite their ties with the organization, they did not have to worry about its managerial aspects, such as outlining the organization's development, maintaining continuity, or safeguarding the unity of administration and management. They could or had to leave such things to the proportionally much smaller group of (top) managers, whose tasks and responsibilities increased in size and especially in complexity during that period.

The two groups, of old traditionally linked together—not only in business, but often also more personally, e.g. in the sphere of mutual interest promotion—gradually grew apart. Not only were they divided by a widening gap as regards knowledge and interest, but also the social distance between the top and the lower hierarchical levels increased.

In many industries and organizations one came to realize that the strength of (top) management could be consolidated only if the gap between management and the top were bridged. The solution was sought in categorial personnel management, offering promising 'potential growers' an opportunity to prepare themselves so as later to be able to function as professionally trained managers. In order to give this policy substance, numerous industries and organizations developed diverse[3] procedures which are usually designated as 'management development' (MD).

In the first half of the sixties, a MD policy was generally assumed to proceed from, above all, the protection of organizational interests, i.e. to provide a guarantee that management positions shall be occupied by capable employees, who are up to date and from the organization's own ranks. In behalf of 'potential growers'—a group selected from middle or higher management—conditions were created through MD to realize a specially devised 'individual career plan',

---

[3]The diversity of MD programs in The Netherlands is demonstrated by the publications of Van der Wolk (1971) and Kuip (1979). Although each and every organization tends to express its own policy views in its MD program, they still have characteristics and principles in common (cf. van Hoesel, 1969; van der Giessen, 1970; de Quay, 1973; also Schein, 1972; Taylor and Lippitt, 1975; Yuill and Steinhof, 1975; Beach, 1980).

ensuing from a stock-taking of future vacancies expected to occur in the (top) management.

W & O psychologists have been involved in MD right from the start. Their first contributions were concerned with solving problems with respect to the selection of suitable and interested 'potential growers' and, furthermore, with rigging up, helping to implement, and, through empirical research, evaluating MD programs. The tradition of work-psychology put them ahead of other disciplines both as to proficiency in methods of selection and appraisal and as to research on interests and motives, learning processes and training methods, and intervention techniques. They also had a theoretical and methodical lead in the field of leadership in organizations and, last but not least, in designing and implementing empirical validation- and evaluation research.

In The Netherlands, scientific contributions concerning the means of selection were, at that time, confined to rating-questionnaires on the growth expectations of the organization's individual employees (Mulder, 1970; Tigchelaar, 1974). Compared to other countries there has been, to date, little interest in the so-called 'assessment centers'. Such centers are specialized in spotting young managerial talents in an organization. They make use of a wide range of predictors: interviews, tests, biographical questionnaires. Special emphasis is put on behavior observations in simulated management situations, e.g. reactions in group discussions. Both the scores on tests etc. thus gathered and the (subjective) assessments of observed behavior are converted into predictions by a team of specifically trained raters, who are well aware of the job requirements and circumstances in the management of the organization concerned. Exposés on this subject may be found in Finkle, 1976; Kraut, 1976; Moses and Byham, 1977.

Van Hoesel (n.d.) blames the minimal interest of Dutch industries in such centers on the fact that in The Netherlands, more so than elsewhere, they do not really expect much from premature attempts to spot managerial abilities, i.e. already when they are just getting acquainted with that young employee. Supposedly there is, on the one hand, a desire to avoid forming an army of 'crown princes' who, on grounds of such assessments, might count too much on a rapid rise to the top, but who cannot be but disappointed in that respect because of lack of room. On the other hand one would, particularly in The Netherlands, prefer an attitude of wait-and-see, being convinced that only many years of experience with those concerned, in their actual work situation, can bring to light the individual qualities and shortcomings that are relevant to a possible rise to a managerial position.

The 'Dutch' view might draw support from that excellently designed, longitudinal validation study at AT & T,[4] the 'Bell System's Management Progress

---

[4]The first 'assessment centers' in industry were founded by the American companies AT & T and Standard Oil.

Study' (Bray *et al.*, 1974). When later on some of the assessments were repeated, certain capacities of some (adult!) persons turned out to have improved considerably over the years. At the time of the original assessments, such a development was by no means foreseen. It had been assumed that, in young adults, the development of capacities would be more or less rounded off.

Returning to MD as such, we note that, at its beginning, W & O psychology addressed itself to supplying a scientific justification (validation) of the procedures involved, usually oriented towards non-recurring choices and decisions made within the framework of the career plans designed for those concerned. Examples of such validations may be found in Glickman *et al.*, 1969 and Miner, 1977.

In the second half of the sixties, the personnel policy for middle and higher management began to widen its scope. Instead of confining itself to the proportionally small élite of chosen 'growers towards top-level positions', it extended its attention to management as a whole. It was necessary to do so in order to keep this by then very sizable group from getting completely immobile. The fact that their knowledge and skills threatened to become outdated had to be countered and therefore MD programs were made to meet this need (Dubin, 1971; Hinrichs, 1973; Kaufman, 1974, 1975).

In The Netherlands, management itself was among the first to stimulate this extension of policy. The wave of democratization in Western Europe at the end of the sixties did not pass this category of personnel unnoticed. Those years of economic prosperity were bursting with fusions, enlargement of scale, the introduction of information- and other automated systems, reorganizations and so on, which at the same time also caused psychological unrest. Many members of management saw their traditionally safe positions and status in the organization diminishing or even in jeopardy. They felt neglected by top management, which seemed to be interested only in its possible successors. And when decision-making touched on their own existence or took place in areas where they considered themselves more expert, they even felt to be at the mercy of top management. Being thus cut off from the top was experienced as so threatening, that they began looking for formal means of contact, with the purpose to increase their influence on the policy relative to their own group. As a collective they closed ranks and joined the—mostly already existing but till then rather inactive—'unions for middle and higher personnel'. Since then, these unions have been more like labor unions and been taking a more programmatic and more radical stand than they used to (cf. the detailed study on the subject by Smal, 1975).

The managements of various organizations did not remain insensitive to these reactions. Here and there it was attempted to regain the managers' trust. Personnel managements began looking for a compromise—meaningful to both viewpoints—between the protection of organizational interests and the individual interests of members of management. Initiatives were taken to grant the employees concerned their own say in decisions on matters touching on their careers. Furthermore, procedures were designed to provide these employees with the necessary, relevant information and support.

In most organizations this so-called 'career guidance' includes a range of activities, such as supplying information about (expected) vacancies and the capacities, interests etc. required for them, as well as procedures to enable employees to gain experience elsewhere (through job rotation or temporary assignments elsewhere); counseling and advising about the continuation of careers; the exchange between employees and (personnel) management of opinions, needs, and judgements regarding individual career perspectives (via so-called 'performance- or appraisal-interviews'); providing education or training with an eye to career-oriented growth.

In some organizations these activities are not geared to the managerial category only, but to their personnel as a whole and thus to executive employees also.[5] The latter category, however, is sometimes believed to benefit more from collective or structural measures to raise the 'quality of working life', in the sphere of so-called 'organization development' (OD). Meantime, organizations have come to realize that the effect of OD will remain sterile as long as career- and individual development on the 'shop-floor' are neglected (cf. Hoekstra, 1973; Crites, 1976).

A2. Career development and career policy

The term 'career development' plays a major role in the professional literature, but its meaning is sometimes ambiguous. It can refer to both a career as a process of development and to a career that is being developed. The meaning of 'career development' in the second sense can be narrowed down to 'all interventions on the part of personnel management and possibly of the employee himself, that are intended to purposively influence or steer the latter's career'. Viewed thus, 'career development' includes 'career guidance' as mentioned above.

The first step in 'career development' as a system of interventions is to formulate a 'career policy'. Ideally, a career policy is explicitly formulated, representing a synthesis—satisfactory to both parties—of what may be called the 'individual' career policy (from the viewpoint of the person concerned) and the 'institutional' career policy (from the viewpoint of personnel management).

An 'individual' career policy is oriented towards the realization of individual goals. It includes choosing what activities and means are to be used within the limits of the conditions to be created or available in the near future. In devising such a policy, an individual will generally navigate on his self-knowledge, as

---

[5] In many organizations, 'career guidance' is still called by its old name 'management development'; this may cause confusion if other personnel categories are guided as well.

acquired by experience, regarding his capacities, abilities, strong and weak spots, motives, interests, needs, and expectations. He may also take into account the opinions of others, who do not necessarily belong to the context of his work or organization, but are, for example, his family, friends, or influential people. Some aspects of 'career guidance' as described in the previous section allow management to give vent to its views on the person concerned, enabling the latter to incorporate such views into his or her 'individual career policy'.

To individual employees, an 'individual career policy' is the normative basis of their own share in their career development, directing their interventions. Analogously, an 'institutional' career policy serves as a normative touchstone of career developments initiated by (personnel) management.

In an organization, usually two levels of 'institutional' career policy may be distinguished: a *supra-individual level* and an *individual level*. A 'supra-individual' policy applies to a class of employees who share one denominator (e.g. the same level of education, or being of the same generation or in the same job sector). Such a policy will generally ensue from views that are characteristic of the organization's social and personnel managements, such as their views on creating opportunities for development, promoting welfare or well-being, stimulating work motivation, advancing mobility, strengthening the ties with the organization, and the like. This policy takes into account the specific interests of the group concerned as well as the group's significance within the framework of the organization's developments and plans. Ideally, an 'institutional' career policy should coincide with the planning of the human abilities necessary to the organization.[6] *Mutatis mutandis* this also holds for the 'individual', or rather 'individualized' institutional career policy, which is a specialization of 'supra-individual policy'. An 'individualized' career policy takes into account the specific characteristics and the possibilities of growth and performance ascribed to the employee concerned by (personnel) management, on grounds either of its own observations or of information supplied by the person himself in career- or performance interviews. Such a policy may also take account of the needs, expectations, and interests of (or concerning) the employee.[7]

[6]Such 'human resources planning' is directed towards the timely future or present availability of people, human capacities, abilities, and interests, which are considered necessary in connection with the anticipated developments of or in the organization, and with the organizational planning made to fit those developments. Human resources planning should take place in terms of both numbers and qualities of people. For each distinct planning phase, it reflects the expected proportions of supply and demand, i.e. of the sort of employees needed and the potential available, respectively. 'Human resources planning' is an aspect of an organization's so-called 'strategic management' (see e.g. Ansoff, *et al.*, 1976).

[7]The relation between social policy and career development is treated by Bakker and Mulder (1980), who give many concrete examples of policy and research results.

A3. W & O psychology and career development

In its theory formation and research on careers and their determinants, W & O psychology has, over the years, partly been following the developments personnel work has gone through in that respect; for the remaining part it followed its own course. Before the sixties, the emphasis was not on the career-in-its-totality, but rather on the choice of the career to be followed and more in particular on the choice of some specific profession or professional career (cf. Wiegersma, this Handbook, ch. 2.8; also Osipow, 1968). Attention subsequently shifted to various aspects of careers as developmental processes in adults (Miller, 1974).

It is usually assumed that an individual's choice depends on the perceived or suspected matching of his own relevant attitudes or characteristics and aspects which to him are connected with various professions or professional careers. Among the relevant attitudes or characteristics are, *inter alia*: individual interests (Strong, 1955; Campbell, 1971); (development of an) individual identity, the 'self-concept' (Super, 1957; Super *et al.*, 1963); individual needs (Roe and Siegelman, 1964); individual orientations towards, or style of, dealing with the environment (Holland, 1966); attitudes resulting from interactions between the person and the influences of his environment, such as his family, socioeconomic background, job, etc. (Blau *et al.*, 1956).

One of the first process theories on how professional preferences come about is Ginzberg's (1951). The theory assumes that an adolescent's preference for a professional career 'matures' in successive stages. (Incidentally, to have a definite preference does not mean that the preferred profession is actually chosen. Tiedeman and O'Hara (1963) made a study of what happens between the moment of pronounced preference and actual choice and what could be the reasons for a deviating actual choice.)

The range or area of generalization of the early hypotheses and theories was mostly confined to the world of adolescents, or at best to that of young adults. The influence of organizational variables was as yet scarcely recognized (an exception is Holland (1966), who presents a typology of environmental climates with a matching typology of personalities who will feel at home in the different environments).

Moreover, the theoretical statements are formulated so vaguely, that they cannot or only with difficulty be falsified. Yet, we should not underrate the importance of this theory formation. It has yielded a rich harvest of still useful career-theoretical concepts. One example is Ginzberg's (1951) 'maturity concept', mentioned above, which we find in most modern process theories about careers. This concept was further elaborated by Super *et al.* (1957) to include the assumption that a developing person has to pass through various successive maturation processes so as to be up to the problems or tasks he is confronted with at successive stages in his life or career. Such stages, which occur in the life of the average individual from any population, are characterized by mean-ingful events, each of which requires its own specific adjustments. Examples are: accepting one's first job, entering the professional world, raising a family, reaching the 'climacteric age' ('mid-life crisis'), and so on. Each stage presents the individual with its own particular problems. These may be so divergent, that a person's 'maturity' at one stage does not ensure his adequate functioning at another, subsequent stage.

Considering also the development of (measuring) instruments in behalf of career research and career-guidance, the years before the sixties have not been without importance either. Here, the old SVIB (Strong's 'Vocational Interest Blank') (Campbell, 1971) may be mentioned. Next come, for example, the 'Vocational Preference Inventory' and the 'Self Directed Search', resulting from Holland's (1973) theory, which enable a person to determine which occupational environments will more or less match his individual orientation towards the environment.

The above-mentioned 'maturity concept' of Super et al., worked out further in his theory of vocational development, has been instrumentalized also. The 'Career Maturity Inventory' (Crites, 1973) and the 'Career Development Inventory' (Forrest, 1971) measure an adolescent's degree of maturity, i.e. the ability to cope with the problems and tasks that characterize the next stage of his life or career. From the latter inventory a form was derived, suited for use in research on adults (Super and Zelkowitz, 1973; Super et al., 1974).

From the early sixties to the present, W & O psychology's contribution to research and theory formation in aid of MD and career development procedures has been steadily increasing.

Erickson (1959) considered a career as an individual's course of development through chronologically successive life stages. This interpretation was later worked out in more detail by various researchers (e.g. Tiedeman and O'Hara, 1963; Havighurst, 1964). A life or career stage is characterized by its limits or transitions ('career transitions') from, respectively, the preceding stage to the present one and from the present stage to the next. Such a transition takes place when a person is rather abruptly confronted with new circumstances, unfamiliar problems or tasks, for which the ways of behavior and adjustment of the stage at which he finds or found himself, do not suffice. In general, a process of reorientation, re-adaptation or re-adjustment will then be necessary to enable him to stand up to or to feel at home in the new phase.

Every person spends his life in various contexts, each of which makes its particular demands, requires another role behavior, and so on. Relatives, family, school, work, profession, and work organization all confront the individual with their own kinds of problems and tasks, which may also change drastically in the course of time. Thus we can say that, apart from possibly following an occupational career, each person follows a series of other careers as well. Many of these careers are of a predictable nature, i.e. they are characterized by a stage-wise course that is more or less normative for all individuals finding themselves in the career context concerned. An example is the 'school career', which, for most students, has a programmed character with clearly structured 'transitions' and stages, each with its own requirements (cf. Dronkers, 1978).[8] In the 'occupational career' Schein (1978, p. 40 ff.) distinguishes nine successive stages, each of which is characterized by (rough) age limits, certain roles in the work situation, and certain specific problems and tasks for those who happen to have arrived at that stage of their occupational career. Schein defines these successive stages as *1*. a period of growth, exploration, and unfolding fantasies; *2*. the entrance into the world of work; *3*. a period of basic training on the job; *4*. full employment in the first part of the career; *5*; full and permanent employment in the middle part of the career; *6*. a period of crisis in the middle part of the career ('mid-career crisis'); *7*. the late stage of the career, spent either in a managerial or in a non-managerial position;[9] *8*. a period of demotion, detachment, decline; *9*. the pension stage. To illustrate we will now give a few examples of the role- and task specifications mentioned by Schein for each of these stages. At stage *1*, the person, in the role of pupil, student, apprentice, or job-finder, must develop a basis for a realistic choice of profession or career. He must translate his youthful fantasies about professional practice into viable realities. He must also discover the preconditions accompanying his social circumstances. He has to lay the foundations of the knowledge and skills necessary in the world of work. At stage *2*, this person, in the role of applicant or future employee, should try to find a job that can from the basis of a further career. He should try to conclude a formal and 'psychological' contract that meets both his own needs and those of his employer. He must pursue membership of some professional group or work organization. So much for examples. Schein notes, that not everybody passes through all the stages. The order of the stages too may vary in some cases. The age limits he assigns to each stage are at best indications only.

Empirical research among managers (Hall and Nougaim, 1968) supports Schein's stage-model, including its hypothesis about individual problems of re-orientation or adjustment at each new stage. According to Van Maanen and Schein (1977) stage-wise occupational careers are to be found at the level of the 'shop-floor' also.

For a survey of the stages and stage-transitions in contexts other than the work or the organization we refer to Schein (1978) and Hall (1976). Schein, moreover, draws attention to the possibility that the role behaviors of the same

---

[8]The life cycle, the development of the human organism, can also be considered a career. It has stage transitions in the sense described here. The most outstanding example is what is usually called the 'climacteric' or 'climacteric age'. This is accompanied by manifestations of certain hormonal and mental changes, which may greatly shock or disturb some people's lives and which in most cases require adjustments and re-orientations of behavior and attitudes.

[9]Schein makes this distinction because the roles and problems of managers and non-managers are very different at this stage.

person in different environments may interfere with one another. Thus, adaptive behavior resulting from a stage transition in the person's occupational career — e.g. promotion to a managerial position — may, for example, influence his behavior among friends. His usual role behavior there may be seriously disturbed without a change of stage having occurred in that context. A well-known interference phenomenon affecting almost all of a person's careers is the 'climacteric' at middle age. In Schein's scheme, its effect is even recognized as a separate stage: the 'mid-career' or 'mid-life' crisis (Sofer, 1970; Stoner *et al.*, 1974).

When, in whatever career, a transition occurs, there is always the danger that the individual is incompetent or incapable to deal with the newly posed problems. We must all learn how to arm ourselves as well as possible against this danger. One of the means is to gain 'insight-into-oneself', self-confidence, self-esteem, composure, in short a self-assured 'identity'. Schein (1968, 1975) assumes that, at least in principle, everyone is capable of developing such an awareness of his or her own capacities, abilities, motives, attitudes, needs, values, and the like. This awareness will be derived from or based on how a person has experienced himself in the practice of his actual career. This experience-based syndrome of insights-into-and-about-oneself Schein calls a person's 'career anchor'. He notes that it

> 'functions as a way of organizing experience, identifying one's area of contribution in the long run, generating criteria for kinds of work settings in which one wants to function, and identifying patterns of ambition and criteria for success by which one will measure oneself' (Schein, 1978, p. 127).

A career anchor helps a person in the storms of stage transitions to stick to a course that, as experience has taught him, could lead to the personal experience of a 'successful' career. A career anchor is formed by his systematically gaining experience with himself in his interaction with a specific work environment, such as an organization, the occupational sphere to which he actually belongs, and his actual job. Would he have chosen another occupation or another career, he might have gained other experiences with himself and thus have developed another career anchor. That is why Schein believes that individual career anchors cannot be predicted by means of tests at an early stage. According to him, the anchors acquire stability only in the middle phase of the career. Using a 'Career Anchor Self-Analysis Form' Schein identified the career anchors of managers with at least five years of industrial experience and classed them in a typology. To become aware of one's career anchor can be an important aspect of career development, because it may form the basis of career decisions and choices. In the framework of career guidance, Schein's concept deserves more attention than it is presently receiving from personnel managements. The same holds, incidentally, for other (theoretical) insights about career development achieved by W & O psychology. There are quite a few reasons for this phenomenon:

a. Organizational-psychological theories *pur sang*, which—with the aid of system models—describe interactions between persons and organizations, are relatively recent (cf. Porter *et al.*, 1975; see also this Handbook, ch. 4.2, 4.3, and 4.5). This is especially true of the combination of views derived from both work- *and* developmental psychology into one theory (cf. the surveys by Hall, 1976; Super and Hall, 1978). The literature on management mostly disregards these theories.

b. The career-theoretical concepts used by W & O psychologists (but also by personnel management!) are confusingly numerous and frequently poly-interpretable. In addition, their meanings overlap to a considerable extent. Thus Schein's career anchor has its counterpart in a combination of concepts that Hall and Schneider (1973) designate as 'career self-image', 'career sub-identity' and 'career satisfaction'. These are all concepts of 'self defense' referring to the possibilities an individual has, in the course of his career, to arm himself against crises, threatening incompetence, and the like.

c. In most theories and models generated by W & O psychology with regard to career development, the aspect of individual experience prevails (cf. Kroll *et al.*, 1970; Hall and Schneider, 1973). It is recognized, however, that careers may also be defined and perceived from an external viewpoint, e.g. that of the organization's management—whose viewpoint may be totally different and may have a different outcome. However, the psychological theory and the related research do not usually take such an external view as their point of departure. Therefore, most of this theory is not very relevant to the approach of organizational problems relative to careers. There are exceptions: Schein's work is one of them. In *Career dynamics* (1978) Schein discusses his theory about the barriers and *'rites of passage'* employees encounter when they move on to other jobs or positions in the organization that require different role behaviors. This theory corresponds to his three-dimensional model for mobility in the organization (Schein, 1971).[10] Together, the theory and the model provide career guidance with points of reference for 'job rotation', 'horizontal mobility' (changing jobs at the same hierarchical level), MD activities, and so on.

d. Career development concerns the interactions between at least two extremely complex systems: man and organization. This complexity is reflected in nearly all models and theories which, apart from career variables, include organizational and individual variables as well.[11] To people who actually do personnel work such a type of theory is not easily accessible. It is, therefore, not surprising that they feel these erudite, scientific contributions to be insufficiently pragmatic, too difficult to translate into simple techniques and procedures (Walker, 1976).

---

[10]See section B4 below, where the three dimensions are discussed.
[11]Hall and Schneider (1973), testing their model for the determination of 'subjective experiences of success or failure in a career', use dozens of variables.

e. Nearly all presently available theories and models are confined to partial aspects of career development. This may not only be ascribed to the researchers' interests and 'school formation', but no doubt also rests on the need to keep the supportive empirical research under control. In the absence of a common framework of conceptual meanings (see *b*) and of a common paradigm for research and theory formation, our knowledge about the subject matter is disconnected—which does not improve its accessibility either.

Obviously, W & O psychology would do well to reconstruct its theoretical contributions to form a coherent whole and to be more accessible to those who are in the practice of personnel work.

A4. Careers in the framework of developmental psychology

A number of handicaps have long obstructed theory formation pertaining to adult careers in their entirety. One of these was the absence of a developmental-psychological framework for such theory formation and research.

A psychological view of individual careers will emphasize phenomena of growth, development, and change in the personality and behavior of adult individuals as they occur in interaction with or under the influence of the environment, the progress of time, and 'growing older'. With respect to the last point, developmental psychology may reasonably be expected to have given theory formation on career development a major impetus. But what is the real state of affairs? Until about 1960, the world of adults was practically *terra incognita*: developmental psychologists confined themselves to studying non-adults. They probably assumed that, after adolescence, individuals for the most part stopped growing or developing. Considerations of a more practical and methodical nature may also have played a role. Cognitive and behavioral developments can more easily be studied in children and adolescents than in adults. The first two categories are not too mobile and more easily accessible—e.g. through the school—to prolonged, longitudinal research. W & O psychologists may be blamed for having made little effort to introduce developmental-psychological research into organizations. This is regrettable, as it has now been determined that adults go on developing in their work in a rather interesting way with respect to both personal and behavioral aspects (cf. Bray *et al.*, 1974). Developmental psychology has by now discovered this fact, be it in a roundabout way.

In countries with a high or rising affluence and excellent medical provisions there has been a growing social and governmental concern about the consequences of the rapid 'growing grey' of the population. This gave a powerful impulse to the development of 'psycho-gerontological' research, carried out by developmental psychologists like Munnichs (1972) in The Netherlands. This research revealed that as yet unexpected and quite considerable developments and changes take place in the behavior and personality of elderly people, which do not come under the heading of 'mental decline' but, on the contrary, might indicate growth. Many behavioral and personality developments in the last phase of life turn out to be comprehensible or predictable only from the individual's development in earlier life phases (Birren, 1964a, 1964b; Botwinick, 1967; Britton and Britton, 1972).

By studying people who are growing older and quit working, developmental psychologists learnt to appreciate the significance of a view that would encompass the growth and development of a whole life. Around 1970, the publication of reports on the subject really got under way. General developmental-psychological views may be found in Elias *et al.* (1977), Levinson *et al.* (1974), and especially Troll (1975), who not only amply discusses the existing literature up to 1975, but also pays attention to the influence of work and family on the development of adults. LeShan (1973), Rogers (1974), and Sheehy (1976) deal with aspects concerning crisis phenomena in the lives of adults. Next, Chew (1976), who chose the 'inner life' of adults as his subject, and Vaillant (1977), who discusses adjustment phenomena in adulthood. The phasic development of adults is described by, among others, Gould (1972), Sze (1975), and Fiske Lowenthal *et al.* (1975). Noteworthy are the volumes of papers from a series of conferences on 'Life-time Developmental Psychology' (organized by the University of West Virginia), each on a different theme. Two of these volumes are of particular importance, as they deal with fundamental meta-theoretical and methodological aspects of developmental research (Datan and Reese, 1977 and Nesselroade and Reese, 1973, respectively). Two other volumes contain theories on personality development and socialization (Baltes and Schaie, 1973) and on normative life-crises (Datan and Ginsberg, 1975). And, finally, there is a volume on interventions in the development of life, that could be important to 'career guidance' both theoretically and practically (Turner and Reese, 1980).

'Life-span developmental psychologists' have, since 1970, not been idling. The numerous publications they produced in the next ten years are systematically reviewed by Baltes *et al.* (1980). In 1978, Baltes began publishing a yearbook which was to serve as a multi-disciplinary platform for all who are scientifically concerned with man's life-span.[12] W & O psychology, too, makes itself heard in this yearbook. The third volume includes a paper by Abeles (1980) about the career development of 400,000 men and women over a period of fifteen years (the so-called 'Project TALENT').

A5. Researching career development

Riegel, one of the godfathers of 'life-span developmental psychology', takes note of the 'dialectics' of, on the one hand, an individual's developments and

---

[12]'Life-span development and behavior' (Baltes, 1978; Baltes and Brim, 1979, 1980).

changes in the course of time and, on the other, cultural-historical changes in his environment. This 'dialectics' (cf. Datan and Reese, 1977) is essential to the development of individual careers. It requires a multivariate approach to research, which should do justice to the dynamics of time-dependent interactions of both individual and situational variables. The paradigms constructed for that purpose are all of a longitudinal nature (Peeters, 1978). The problems of design, dimension, and measurement associated with such paradigms are more complicated than those associated with the rather more common 'cross-sectional' paradigm.

Wohlwill (1973) and Baltes et al., (1980) are good introductions to longitudinal designs. In all such paradigms, time plays the key role. The concept 'time'— also when used in the framework of careers—has more than one meaning (Wohlwill, 1973). Apart from 'clock time' and 'calendar time', 'psychological time' (i.e. experiencing phases in time), 'biological or fysiological rhythm', and 'social time' are important (Roth, 1963; Gurvitch, 1964; Doob, 1971; Yaker et al., 1971; Fraser et al., 1975; Lauer, 1981).

Baltes and Nesselroade (1979) conclude that the most detailed methodology of longitudinal research is that for 'identifying' changes. Models for the analysis of 'interactions' and 'interrelations' between behavioral changes and their 'causes' or 'determinants' are still in statu nascendi (cf. also Nesselroade and Baltes, 1979). Baltes et al. (1980, p. 74 ff.) describe a model postulating three kinds of influence on the life-span: 1. normative, age-bound ('ontogenetic') influences; 2. normative influences, bound to historical development ('evolutionary' influences); and 3. non-normative influences ('significant life events'). Ontogenetic influences (1) are defined as: biological and environmental determinants which bear a rather firm relation to chronological age and show up in approximately the same way in individuals from the same (sub)culture.[13] Evolutionary influences (2) are biological and environmental determinants related to the historical time or context in which a generation or 'cohort' of peers lives and develops.[14] Significant life events (3) are the biological and environmental determinants occurring in most people individually as to their onset, duration, and/or structure, and implying some major change in an individual's life situation.[15] Baltes et al. suggest that the relative forces of these three sources of influence change proportionally in the course of a life. The category 'significant events', at first of minor importance, will eventually be the prevailing influence on behavioral and personality development.

The pragmatic preference of W & O psychologists for 'cross-sectional re-

[13]Examples (from Baltes et al.): biological maturing processes, age-bound socialization processes, e.g. in the family, at school, or in the occupation.
[14]Examples: economic depressions, wars, epidemics, emancipatory movements.
[15]Examples: change of career, moving house, medical surgery, joblessness, divorce, birth of a descendant, meeting certain persons who are important to the individual.

search' impedes the formation of a theory on career development based on the above model. For, using such an approach, it cannot be determined whether behavioral changes should be ascribed to ontogenetic or to evolutionary influences. When introducing 'quasi-longitudinality' into the research by calling upon the memory of those concerned, there is no way to ascertain to what extent their memories are distorted or colored by intermediate events. Another drawback of the time-bound character of 'cross-sectional research' is, moreover, that the generalizations based upon its results may be valid only for a very limited period (Cronbach, 1975; Elms, 1975; Boerlijst, 1977). Research on career development will profit from a 'mixed' research strategy, retaining the advantages of the 'cross-sectional approach', but simultaneously doing justice to the 'dialectics' of time- and culture-bound factors of influence and the longitudinality of a person's behavioral or personality development. Such research requires a multidisciplinary approach: the science of psychology alone does not suffice to delineate such a 'dialectic design' (cf. Back, 1980).

A6. A look at the future: the development of career development

In numerous organizations, career development has come to be part and parcel of personnel management. The circumstances under which it was possible for these activities to develop (economic boom etc.) have changed radically in the past ten years. The present economic climate is one of stagnation and decline and it looks like the days of old will never come back. Nevertheless, W & O psychology has and will have numerous opportunities to contribute to the 'development of career development', maybe particularly so in these probably structurally changing times. We will very briefly discuss a few of them.

It is a fact of experience that personnel policies in industries and organizations whose survival is no longer self-evident, have come under great pressure. Managements attempt to (sub)optimalize certain chances of survival and more often than not the importance of the employees' 'individual development and growth' will be affected or made subject to objectives of economy and efficiency. We are convinced that, certainly in the long run, W & O psychology will be capable of providing scientifically and ethically justifiable support for the organizations' strategies for survival and innovation. We are thinking of, among other things, the construction of relevant instruments to be used by personnel managements to prevent or check the wasting or, worse still, destruction of the available human potential of ingenuity and interests. W & O psychology could, in principle, supply information about the surplus of human capacities, which, although present in every organization, generally goes unused or even unnoticed, W & O psychology could make a meaningful contribution to organization theory by investigating whether and, if so, to what extent such dormant 'human resources capital' is a factor in organizational development. More generally, W & O psychology could look into the matter of how to integrate 'human resources planning'[16] into the various other planning circuits of organizations.

The basis of these supportive activities will have to be a career-development theory, in which views on the development of organizations and those on the development of their individual employees meet. Currently existing ideas about careers and career development are as yet too disparate to be amalgamated in one whole. A basic framework is needed for such a co-ordinating theory. In section B10 of this chapter we will discuss an attempt of ours at a suitable model for such a framework.

B. DESCRIPTIONS AND DEFINITIONS OF THE CONCEPT 'CAREER'

Although we are by now familiar with terms like 'career planning', 'career guidance', and 'career development', there is little agreement among (and sometimes also in) organizations about the meaning of these concepts or how they should be given substance. In common usage as well as in professional jargon we find a host of descriptions. Now that more and more organizations favor a systematic approach to the problems of careers and scientific interest in the subject is increasing, it is very important that the definitions be agreed upon. Such agreement will make it possible to compare, exchange, connect, and generalize research and theory from different sources.

In the following sections we shall discuss some current interpretations of the concept. Thus, the concept 'career' has been connected with: adjustment to an occupation (section B1); hierarchical careers (section B2); an organization's policy (section B3); individual mobility (section B4); the development of a person's roles in the organization (section B5); the time dimension, i.e. the historical context, in which a person is placed (section B6); 'external' and 'internal' reflections on a person and his development (section B7); the interaction (or transaction) between person and context (section B8); and a person's identity or self-awareness (section B9).

In the last paragraph of section A6 above, we made mention of a model that should serve as a framework for the construction of a career theory. In section B10 we will briefly summarize such a model, as developed by us (Boerlijst, 1982). It is based on a conceptual analysis of the descriptions discussed in sections B1–9. It co-ordinates the conceptual domain of career development. The model's structure not only offers the possibility to accommodate and compare existing theories, but also presents suggestions for new hypotheses and a research design.

B1. Career and the adjustment to an occupation

The classical but still widely held view on careers implies that somehow an individual adjusts in or to a (chosen) occupation or, rather, his image of it.

---

[16]See footnote 6.

This view was expressed at an early date by, among others, the sociologist Hall (1948). Thus, Hall says that a medical career 'may be conceived as a set of more or less successful adjustments to the institutions and to the formal and informal organization (of the medical profession)'.

Those who consider this aspect of adjustment the primary characteristic of an occupational career usually proceed from the following three assumptions: a. time-wise, the social and functional structures, together forming the professional image, are of a stable character; b. when an individual adequately adjusts to the structure-bound professional norms, his career will run a modal and thus predictable course; c. when his adjustment is inadequate, retirement or expulsion from that profession will follow. These assumptions lead to the normative view, that adjustment to an occupation should preferably take place as early as possible, in the first years of adulthood or possibly before that, at the school stage. 'Career' is associated with '(early) adjustment to an occupation', especially so among educational and occupational consultants and in vocational guidance and employment agencies. The assumed relation is also the basic assumption of the approach of 'fitting the man to the job', so familiar in personnel work. This approach was first widely propagated by the University of Minnesota during the depression of the thirties (Paterson and Darley, 1936). Thirty years later, staff-members of this very same institution discovered a theoretical justification of these activities, the so-called 'Work Adjustment Theory' (Lofquist and Dawis, 1969). The theory specifies a number of prerequisites for a person and his social or work environment to agree. The principle described above led to the construction of many instruments to aid occupational consultants and employment agencies as well as occupational research. Surveys may be found in Shartle (1959), Crites (1969), and Holland (1976) (see also this Handbook, ch. 2.8). The 'Vocational Interest Blank' of Strong and his executor Campbell (1971) explicitly takes 'adjustment to an occupation' as its criterion for composing groups of professionals by which the occupational scales of that test are standardized and validated.

Super and Hall (1978) note that the identification of 'career' with 'adjustment to an occupation' has led to conceptual confusion and even conceptual impoverishment:

> 'popular and even professional (as contrasted with scientific) usage have typically used the words 'career' and 'occupation' interchangeably. This has been the great loss of what has since 1971 been known as the "career education" movement, but what is meant (if one studies typical treatises and syllabi) is actually an "occupational education" movement.'

A number of earlier 'career theoretical' contributions, such as e.g. those mentioned in Osipow's volume (1968), would more appropriately be called 'occupational adjustment theories'. The classical ideas about (bureaucratic) organizations find their counterpart in the above view. There, the concept of 'occupational adjustment' is replaced or extended by 'adjustment to an occupation', 'adjustment to the occupational image' or 'adjustment to the occupation-bound position in the organization'. The fact that, until recently, numerous organizations hardly paid any special attention to policy aspects pertaining to the careers of employees could perhaps be ascribed to their opinion that an early and preferably also quick adjustment to a position or job 'secures', so to speak, someone's career (i.e. it will from then on take a steady, predictable course).

B2. Hierarchical vs. non-hierarchical careers

Anyone preaching the principle that a career reflects adjustment to an occupation, is obliged to find a norm for such adjustment. The rise or pace of rising on the 'hierarchical ladder' is a normative principle that is still applied by our society, although it is now subject to serve criticism. This principle usually concerns the increase of responsibilities implied by such a rise. A well-known, normative definition of 'career' that is in keeping with this, is that of the sociologist Slocum (1974):

> 'An "occupational career" may be defined ... as an orderly sequence of development extending over a period of years and involving progressively more responsible roles within an occupation. ... the theoretical model involves entry into a position that requires the performance of occupational duties at the lowest rung of the occupational ladder. This is followed by a sequence of promotions into higher-level positions within an organization, leading eventually to the pinnacle, and finally to retirement.'

This definition retains the old, normative connotation of the concept of career. The original meaning of the word 'career' is 'race-course'. Thus the definition associates 'career' with 'rivalry', 'relative positional progress', 'attaining an (un)favorable position', 'acquiring the highest fame, esteem, or reward', 'crossing the finish'. However, even if a career is not (any longer) a matter of promotion or 'vertical mobility', we can still speak of a 'career' in Slocum's sense. Although Slocum recognizes this difference, he does not feel it is a drawback to his definition: 'Although this generalized model calls for upward progression from the bottom to the top, we know that not every entrant moves through all these steps. Thus there are various degrees of conformity to the model'. According to him, anyone who does not follow a 'career according to the book' is apparently insufficiently adjusted.

B3. Career and career policy

If we wish to use the concept of career with a view to the policy to be applied in organizations or, in a broader sense, society, we should obviously opt for a normative definition whose effect is to confirm the policy involved. Telling examples of such definitions which include the objectives of a policy are given by Schein and Kanawaty in an ILO ('International Labor Office') publication:

'The idea of stages or steps in a progression toward culturally defined higher rewards is the essence of the definition of "career"' (Schein, 1976).
'One is inclined ... to give the word (career) a wider meaning that that of mere promotion in a limited work context. A more useful notion would be to look at this concept as encompassing the events either happening to or initiated by the individual which affect his progression or promotion, his widening and/or changing employment possibilities, and his acquiring a different and usually higher status, better conditions and increased satisfaction with the job' (Kanawaty, 1976).

B4. Career and mobility

The normative definitions discussed above are not very suitable to scientific purposes, because they reflect culture- and time-bound views and interests which are not universally applicable and which, moreover, may easily lose their validity. It is our opinion that descriptive definitions of an open, neutral character are to be preferred. In their study on 'occupational mobility', the sociologists Davidson and Anderson (1937) gave one of the first non-normative descriptions, speaking, however, not of a 'career' but of a 'career pattern' defined as: 'the number of occupations followed and the duration of each'. The same concept turns up again in the first psychological career theory that was to become widely known, that of Super (1957). He describes a 'career pattern' as: 'a sequence of occupations in the life of an individual or of a group of individuals' and specifies this as follows: 'this sequence may be analysed in order to ascertain the major work periods which constitute a career'. Shartle (1959) gave Super's definition a wider scope: 'A career covers a sequence of positions, jobs, or occupations that one person engages in during his working life'.

The application of the above definitions does not necessarily lead to a (work) content analysis of successive positions, jobs, or occupations, but rather to research and the analysis of modal and deviant sequences of positions, etc. Nor does such application lead to the analysis of cognitive, behavioral, and experiential aspects inherent in the performance in (successive) positions. This aspect is crucial in many career definitions. It refers to a person's (capacity for) mobility within the framework of a work organization or some other social context.

Mobility on a (status) hierarchical ladder is called 'vertical' mobility. If someone 'moves' to another position in the organization without thereby acquiring a higher or lower status, we speak of 'horizontal' (or 'functional' or 'lateral') mobility. When someone is moving from or towards the center of power, knowledge, and influence (the 'inner circles'), which exist at all hierarchical levels and in all occupational areas of organizations, we speak of 'centrality' or 'inclusion' mobility (Schein, 1971).

B5. Careers and the development of roles

Van Maanen (1977) considers the concept 'career' as 'a shorthand notation for a particular set of activities with a natural, unfolding history—involvement over time in a given role or across a series of roles.' He points out that most people often play more than one role within one and the same context (e.g. the work organization) and certainly in different contexts (work, school, family, friends, society, and the like). Each person follows 'multiple careers'; obviously, they will influence one another considerably (Tyler, 1978).

B6. Careers and historical context

Crites (1976) emphasizes the importance of time and especially historical context to a person's present position:

> 'What the notion of career introduces to the analysis of work behavior which less dynamic conceptualizations do not is the dimension of "time", and the interrelationship of events along it. More specifically, career refers to the sequence of variables which have preceded a worker's current position'.

Blau and Duncan (1967) and Sewell *et al.* (1969, 1970) developed models for such sequences of position-relevant historical variables. Such a sequence they call a 'career path'. According to them, each type of career has its own characteristic career path. Thus it may be that for a certain type of career the following variables are relevant to the present position in the work career: 1. the socio-economic family background of the career occupants concerned; 2. their parents' occupations; 3. their school results; 4. their (degree of) success in previous jobs. Such sequences of variables are established by means of a statistical 'path analysis' (Land, 1969).

B7. External and internal careers

When a career is described from the viewpoint of an external institution or person (usually belonging to the context in which the career definition is meaningful), we speak of an 'external' career. Generally, the terms in which these 'external' career definitions are couched are important or significant to the context concerned. It is, by the way, very well possible for a person to describe his own career 'externally', concentrating on those aspects that are important from an external point of view. An example of such an 'external'

334 HANDBOOK OF WORK AND ORGANIZATIONAL PSYCHOLOGY, VOLUME 1

career description is the *curriculum vitae* that is customarily required from job applicants.

An individual may of course also develop his own, personal view on his career, which does not necessarily coincide with the external view. Schein (1977) puts it as follows: 'work careers reflect both individual and societal definitions of what is a worthwhile set of activities to pursue throughout a lifetime.' We speak of an 'internal' career when it is described or defined in terms or categories that a person subjectively feels to be meaningful to his own identity or existence. Van Maanen (1977) explains that

'What is most significant about a person's career is . . . the degree to which it serves as the principle around which the person organizes his or her life. And this depends not only upon the status, direction, tempo and length of the career, but upon the meaning the individual ascribes to the career as well.'

Schein (1977) puts it a bit more pointedly:

'The career can be thought of as a set of stages or a path through time which reflects two things: (a) the individual's needs, motives, and aspirations in relation to work, and (b) society's expectations of what kinds of activities will result in monetary and status rewards for the career occupant.'

B8. Career as an interaction between person and context

The relation between the views of an 'external' institution (e.g. a work organization) on a person's career and the 'internal' views of the person himself can sometimes be a rather strained one. To find mutually acceptable 'external' and 'internal' careers that are worth pursuing and can be combined, the parties will have to play a game of give and take. This holds for all types of career, both at work and in an occupation as well as in the family and at school, and so on. Kolb and Plovnick (1977) describe a career as 'the self-mediated progress through time of transactions between person and environment', that is, so to speak, as a synthesis of the 'internal' and 'external' careers.

Transactions in this sense require continuous reconsideration and renewal, because of the developments and changes occurring both in the person and in the relevant context. The above description suggests that the person concerned can take the initiative in determining or arranging his own career. This view— also found in Kanawaty (who speaks of 'events initiated by the individual')— does not necessarily conflict with the 'adjustment principle' mentioned in section B1. According to that principle, the prevailing norms of an (in)formal social system such as an organization do indeed generate stable and consistent, modal careers, but within the limits of the given norms there is in some cases more, in other cases less room available (or prescribed!) for mobility or individual initiatives. Incidentally, concepts like 'individual initiative', 'flexibility', etc., being connected with a person's autonomous actions, should not be lumped together with 'mobility'. Mobility may be a precept or normative principle in organizations that otherwise do not tolerate individual initiatives.

B9. Careers and identity

One of the means by which an individual may protect himself against confrontations with drastic changes in his life, e.g. transition to a new life stage or an unknown, completely different environment, is to form his own 'identity', a self-awareness, from which he can derive self-confidence. By maintaining and guarding his identity a person can, so to speak, stay on his feet in the stormy periods of his life: he knows what he is about, he knows his capacities for adjustment, and so on.

The concept 'identity' plays an important part in many descriptions of the concept 'career' and of the concepts derived from it. As Van Maanen (1977) concisely put it: 'Time and identity are what the notion of a career so nicely conveys'.

With this we may conclude our survey of meaning-variants.

B10. A facet-analytical definition of the concept 'career'

For the unification of theory and research on careers it is important to connect the different meaning-variants of the concept 'career'. On the basis of Guttman's and others' 'facet-analytical model' for structuring definitions (cf. Guttman, 1957, 1965; Foa, 1965; Laumann and Guttman, 1966; Aranya et al., 1976) we construed a co-ordinating definition for the concept 'career', from which all possible definition-variants can, in principle, be derived. We have described this co-ordinating definition in detail in another publication (Boerlijst, 1982); considering the framework of the present Handbook, we can here discuss it only summarily, omitting many important details.

To construe such a definition, appropriate abstractions must be found for all explicit and implicit characteristics that, in the various definition-variants known to us, are thought to be relevant to the meaning of the concept 'career'. All these abstractions or 'facets' should, in principle, be included in the formulation of the definition inasfar as they are logically distinguishable from each other. We arrived at the following list of facets of the concept 'career':

a. the 'career occupant', i.e. the subject or subjects of a career;

b. the 'context' of a career;

c. the 'aspects', or rather 'aspect-variables', in terms of which the career is described or characterized;

d. the 'sequence of successive positions' the career occupant holds or obtains on the aspect variables;

e. the 'period of time', within which the successive positions were or are ascertained or perceived;

f. the 'observing agency' that ascertains or perceives the successive positions of the career occupant;

g. the 'relevant relation' between the aspect-variables and the context of the career.

Some of these facets will not be found in some of the definition-variants, but generally they can be added without any problems. In its most abstract formulation, our 'co-ordinating' definition is as follows:

> 'A career is a representation of the sequence of successive positions as ascertained or perceived by an observing agency, which a career occupant has held or acquired within a certain period of time on aspect-variables that have a relevant relation to a certain context'.

We can develop this co-ordinating definition further by giving as many logically distinct specifications as possible of each facet of the definition. We shall give a few examples.

In facet a, a specifying distinction can be made between, for example, a_1: an individual career occupant, and a_2: a group or category of career occupants. Substituting the facet 'career occupant' of the co-ordinating definition by either of the two specifications or 'elements' of this facet, we obtain a certain type of definition variants or career images. Definitions or images of 'individual' careers are generated by filling in element a_1 and definitions or images of 'modal' careers by filling in element a_2. Element a_2 can be further specified, since persons can be categorized in various ways. We can, for example, distinguish different occupational groups. In principle, each occupation has its own 'modal' career.

In facet b we could, for example, distinguish the following elements: b_1: family or home community; b_2: school; b_3: occupation; b_4: work or work environment; b_5: organization or organizational community; b_6: societal context. Substituting these elements for the facet 'context' in the co-ordinating definition generates as many types of definition-variants or career images, i.e. family careers; school careers; occupational careers; work careers, etc., respectively.

Thus it is possible to dissect each facet into elements (and possibly some elements into sub-elements). The above examples make clear that each combination of elements from each facet will lead to another kind of definition-variant. The combination of, for example, $a_1 \times b_2$ generates definitions of individual school careers; $a_2 \times b_5$ will generate definitions of categorial or modal careers in organizations.

Were we to specify all facets exhaustively, we would, in principle, be able to derive *all* conceivable definition-variants of the concept 'career' from the co-ordinating definition.

However, our facet-analytical, co-ordinating definition has yet another, more important function, if, that is, Foa's (1958) 'contiguity principle' is applied in the specification of the facets by their elements. It implies that, in ordering the elements of each facet, we take into account our hypothetical expectations regarding the empirical structure of the similarities or proximities of these elements. Let us take facet b ('context') as an example. In the sequence b_1, b_2, etc. is embedded our expectation that, for example, the work career of a person or group will, on certain aspect-variables, display more similarities to the occupational career of the person(s) involved than to his (their) school career(s).[17] This implies, among other things, that we are assuming that certain results or conclusions of empirical career research, carried out in work contexts, can be generalized to the occupational context rather (or more so) than to that of the school. In principle, such hypotheses and expectations, formulated on the basis of the 'contiguity principle', can be tested. For this purpose, special non-metrical methods have been developed (Lingoes, 1973); Lingoes and Roskam, 1973; Lingoes *et al.*, 1976). Research designs relevant to such tests may be derived also from the specified co-ordinating definition (cf. Runkel and McGrath, 1972).

We may conclude, that a carefully structured and specified co-ordinating definition of the concept 'career' can have more than just descriptive value and, in particular, is capable of generating fruitful hypotheses about the empirical structure of the affinities between the different manifestations of careers. To find theoretically fruitful specifications is no easy task; and to distinguish the relevant aspect-variables (facet c) and their relative order or contiguity is a particularly complex matter.

Once we dispose of an adequate co-ordinating definition of the career concept, other career concepts, such as 'career development' and 'career guidance', may be derived by simple means, i.e. by adding or omitting facets. Together with the concept 'career', they are then put into one all-embracing framework of facets. Such a framework offers the possibility to analyze and reconstruct existing theories, hypotheses, and models of career development, to compare one with the other or possibly to connect them (cf. the interesting attempt of Van Maanen (1977, p. 169 ff.) to connect the various theoretical contributions to his volume on *Organizational careers: Some new perspectives* and to order them along different dimensions, e.g. along the time axis of 'career stages').

REFERENCES

Abeles, R. P. (1980), Patterns and implications of life-course organization: Studies from Project TALENT. In: Baltes, P. B., Brim Jr., O. G. (Eds.), *Life-span development and behavior. Vol. 3.* New York: Academic Press, 308–337.
Ansoff, H. I., Declerck, R. P., Hayes, R. L. (Eds.) (1976), *From strategic planning to strategic management.* New York: Wiley.

[17] We assume b_1, b_2, etc. to be linearly ordered, so b_4 will be closer to b_3 than to b_2.

Aranya, N., Jacobson, D., Shye, S. (1976), Organizational and occupational commitment: A facet-theoretical analysis of empirical data. *Nederlands Tÿdschrift voor de Psychologie*, 31, 13–22.

Back, K. W. (Ed.) (1980), *Life course: Integrative theories and exemplary populations.* Boulder (Colorado): Westview Press.

Bakker, G. M., Mulder, G. A. (1980), *Projekt Levensloop en Sociaal Beleid. Literatuurstudie en afbakening van het onderzoeksveld, eerste voortgangsverslag* [Project Life-span and Social Policy. Review of the literature and delineation of the research area, first progress report]. University of Utrecht: Dept. of Psychology.

Baltes, P. (Ed.) (1978), *Life-span development and behavior. Vol. 1.* New York: Academic Press.

Baltes, P. B., Brim, Jr., O. G. (Eds.) (1979, 1980), *Life-span development and behavior* (*Vol. 2 en 3*). New York: Academic Press.

Baltes, P. B., Nesselroade, J. R. (1979), History and rationale of longitudinal research. In: Nesselroade, J. R., Baltes, P. B. (Eds.), *Longitudinal research in the study of behavior and development.* New York: Academic Press.

Baltes, P. B., Schaie, K. W. (Eds.) (1973), *Life-span developmental psychology: Personality and socialization.* New York: Academic Press.

Baltes, P. B., Reese, H. W., Lipsitt, L. P. (1980), Life-span developmental psychology. In: Rosenzweig, M. R., Porter, L. W. (Eds.), *Annual Review of Psychology*, 31, 65–110. Palo Alto (Cal.): Annual Reviews Inc.

Baltes, P. B., Reese, H. W., Nesselroade, J. R. (1977), *Life-span developmental psychology: Introduction to research methods.* Monterey (Cal.): Brooks/Cole.

Beach, D. S. (1980), *Personnel: The management of people at work*, p. 381–402. New York: Macmillan (4th ed.).

Birren, J. E. (1964a), *The psychology of aging.* Englewood Cliffs, N. J.: Prentice-Hall.

Birren, J. E. (1964b), *Relations of development and aging.* Springfield, Ill.: Thomas.

Blau, P. M., Duncan, O. D. (1967), *The American occupational structure.* New York: Wiley.

Blau, P. M., Gustad, J. W., Jessor, R., Parnes, H. S., Wilcox, R. S. (1956). Occupational choice: a conceptual framework. *Industr. Labor Rel. Rev.*, 9, 531–543.

Boerlijst, J. G. (1974), *Werk met perspectief: Instrumentontwikkeling ten behoeve van functie- en loopbaanonderzoek* [Work with a perspective: Development of instruments in aid of job position- and career research]. Amsterdam: Academische Pers.

Boerlijst, J. G. (1977), *Op de lange baan: Een verandering van koers in het organisatiepsychologisch onderzoek* [On the long track: A re-orientation in organizational-psychological research]. Assen/Amsterdam: Van Gorcum.

Boerlijst, J. G. (1982), *Facet definitions of career-related concepts.* Enschede: Twente University of Technology.

Botwinick, J. (1967), *Cognitive processes in maturity and old age*, New York: Springer.

Bray, D. W., Campbell, R. J., Grant, D. (1974), *Formative years in business: A long-term AT & T study of managerial lives.* New York: Wiley.

Britton, J. H., Britton, J. O. (1972), *Personality changes in aging: A longitudinal study of community residents.* New York: Springer.

Campbell, D. P. (1971), *Handbook for the Strong Vocational Interest Blank.* Stanford, (Cal.): Stanford University Press.

Chew, P. (1976), *The inner world of the middle-aged man.* New York: Macmillan.

Crites, J. O. (1969), *Vocational psychology: The study of vocational behavior and development.* New York: McGraw-Hill.

Crites, J. O. (1973), *Career Maturity Inventory.* Monterey (Cal.): CTB/McGraw-Hill.

Crites, J. O. (1976), Work and careers. In: Dubin, R. (Ed.), *Handbook of work, organization and society.* Chicago: Rand McNally, 131–165.

Cronbach, L. J. (1975), Beyond the two disciplines of scientific psychology. *American Psychologist*, **30**, 116–127.

Datan, N., Ginsberg, L. H. (Eds.) (1975), *Life-span developmental psychology: Normative life-crises.* New York: Academic Press.

Datan, N., Reese, H. W. (Eds.) (1977), *Life-span developmental psychology: Dialectic perspectives on experimental research.* New York: Academic Press.

Davidson, P. E., Anderson, H. D. (1937), *Occupational mobility in an American community.* Palo Alto: Stanford Univ. Press.

Dawes, R. M. (1972), *Fundamentals of attitude measurement.* New York: Wiley.

Doob, L. W. (1971), *Patterning of time.* New Haven, Conn.: Yale Univ. Press.

Drenth, P. J. D., Willems, P. J., Wolff, Ch. J. de (Eds.) (1973), *Arbeids- en organisatiepsychologie* [Work- and organizational psychology]. Deventer: Kluwer.

Dronkers, J. (1978), Manipuleerbare variabelen in de schoolloopbaan [Manipulable variables in school careers]. In: Peschar, J. L., Ultee, W. C. (Eds.), *Sociale stratificatie* [Social stratification]. Mens en Maatschappij [Man and Society], special issue. Deventer: Van Loghum Slaterus.

Dubin, S. S. (1971), *Professional obsolescence.* Lexington, Mass.: Heath.

Dunnette, M. D. (Ed.) (1976), *Handbook of industrial and organizational psychology.* Chicago: Rand-McNally.

Elias, M. F., Elias, P., Elias, J. W. (1977), *Basic processes in adult developmental psychology.* St. Louis (Mo.): Mosby.

Elms, A. C. (1975), The crisis of confidence in social psychology. *American Psychologist*, **30**, 967–973.

Erickson, E. H. (1959), Identity and the life cycle. *Psychological Issues*, **1**, 1–171.

Finkle, R. B. (1976), Managerial assessment centres. In: Dunnette, M. D. (Ed.), *Handbook of industrial and organizational psychology.* Chicago: Rand-McNally.

Fiske Lowenthal, M., Thurnher, M., Chiriboga, D., *et al.* (1975), *Four stages of life: A comparative study of women and men facing transitions.* London: Jossey-Bass.

Foa, U. G. (1958), The contiguity principle in the structure of interpersonal relations. *Human Relations*, **11**, 229–238.

Foa, U. G. (1965), New developments in facet design and analysis. *Psychological Review*, **72**, 262–274.

Forrest, D. (1971), *The construction and validation of an objective measure of vocational maturity.* London: University Microfilms International (1978).

Fraser, J. T., Lawrence, N., Park, D. (1975), 1978), *The study of time. 3 Vols.* New York: Springer.

Geffen, L. van (1977), *De keuze van werk: Ontwikkeling van een model, een meet-instrument en een begeleidingsmethodiek* [Occupational choice: Development of a model, a measuring instrument, and a method of guidance]. Culemborg: School-pers.

Giesen, R. W. van der (1970), Management development. In: Drenth, P. J. D., *et al.* (Eds.), Bedrijfspsychologie: Onderzoek en evaluatie [Industrial psychology: Research and evaluation]. Deventer: Kluwer, 252–266.

Ginzberg, E., Ginsburg, S. W., Axelrad, S., Herma, J. L. (1951), *Occupational choice: An approach to a general theory.* New York: Columbia Univ. Press.

Glickman, A. S., Hahn, C. P., Fleishman, E., Baxter, A. (1969), *Top management development and succession: An exploratory study.* New York: Macmillan.

Gould, R. L. (1972), The phases of adult life: A study in developmental psychology. *Am. J. of Psychiatry*, **129**, 521–531.

Goulet, L. R., Baltes, P. B. (Eds.) (1970), *Life-span developmental psychology: Research and theory.* New York: Academic Press.

Gurvitch, G. (1964), *The spectrum of social time.* Dordrecht: Reidel.

Guttman, L. (1957), Introduction to facet design and analysis. In: *Proceedings of the*

XVth Intern. Congress of Psychology, Brussels. Amsterdam: North-Holland Publ. Co.

Guttman, L. (1965), A faceted definition of intelligence. *Scripta Hierosolymitana,* **14,** 166–181.

Hall, D. T. (1976), *Careers in organizations.* Pacific Palisades (Cal.): Goodyear.

Hall, D. T., Nougaim, K. (1968), An examination of Maslow's Need Hierarchy in an organizational setting. *Organizational Behavior and Human Performance,* **3,** 12–35.

Hall, D. T., Schneider, B. (1973), *Organizational climates and careers: The work lives of priests.* New York: Seminar Press.

Hall, O. (1948), The stages of a medical career. *Amer. J. Sociol.,* **53,** 327–336.

Havighurst, R. J. (1964), Youth in exploration and man emergent. In: Borow, H. (Ed.), *Man in a world at work.* Boston: Houghton Mifflin.

Heller, F. A., Clark, A. W. (1976), Personnel and human resources development. In: Rosenzweig, M. R., Porter, L. W. (Eds.), *Annual Review of Psychology,* **27,** 405–435. Palo Alto (Cal.): Annual Reviews Inc.

Hinrichs, J. R. (1973), Professional updating [in Dutch]. In: Drenth *et al.* (1973).

Hoekstra, M. H. R. (1973), Manager ontwikkeling en organisatieontwikkeling [Management development and organization development]. In: Drenth *et al.* (1973), 81–90.

Hoesel, A. F. G. van (1969), *Het labyrinth van management development* [The labyrinth of management development]. Enschede: Twente University of Technology.

Hoesel, A. F. G. van (n.d.), Personal communication, Incorporated in: Boerlijst, J. G. (1978), *Assessment of management potential: Experiences and opinions in Holland.* Paper, XIXth ICAP, Munich. Enschede: Twente University of Technology.

Hof, M. A. van't (1977), *Some statistical and methodological aspects in the study of growth and development, with a special emphasis on mixed longitudinal designs.* Nijmegen: Catholic university (doctoral thesis).

Holland, J. L. (1966), *The psychology of vocational choice.* Waltham (Mass.): Blaisdell.

Holland, J. L. (1973), *Making vocational choices: A theory of careers.* Englewood Cliffs (N.J.): Prentice-Hall.

Holland, J. L. (1976), Vocational preferences. In: Dunnette, M. D. (Ed.), *Handbook of industrial and organizational psychology.* Chicago: Rand-MacNally, 521–570.

Holland, J. L., Magoon, T. M., Spokane, A. R. (1981), Counseling psychology: Career interventions, research and theory. In: Rosenzweig, M. R., Porter, L. W. (Eds.), *Annual Review of Psychology,* **32,** 279–305. Palo Alto (Cal.): Annual Reviews Inc.

Kanawaty, J. (1976), In: *Career planning and development.* Geneva: International Labor Office, Management Development Series No. 12.

Kaufman, H. G. (1974), *Obsolescence and professional career development.* New York: AMACOM.

Kaufman, H. G. (1975), *Career development: A guide to combating obsolescence.* New York: IEEE Press.

Kimberley, J. R., Miles, R. H., and associates (1980), *The organizational life cycle: Issues in the creation, transformation and decline of organizations.* London: Jossey-Bass.

Kolb, D. A., Plovnick, M. S. (1977), The experiental learning theory of career development. In: Van Maanen, J. (Ed.), *Organizational careers: Some new perspectives.* New York: Wiley.

Kraut, A. I. (1976), New frontiers for assessment centers. *Personnel,* **53,** 30–38.

Kroll, A. M., Dinklage, L. B., Lee, J., Morley, E. D., Wilson, E. H. (1970), *Career development: Growth and crisis.* New York: Wiley.

Krumboltz, J. D., Becker-Haven, J. F., Burbett, K. F. (1979), Counseling psychology: Developing skill for career transitions. In: Rosenzweig, M. R., Porter, L. W. (Eds.), *Annual Review of Psychology,* **30,** 577–588. Palo Alto (Cal.): Annual Reviews Inc.

Kuip, R. (1979), Van carrièreplanning naar loopbaanbegeleiding: De loopbaan van een specialisme [From career planning to career guidance: The career of a specialism].

PW, Maandblad voor Personeelswerk en Arbeidsverhoudingen [Monthly Journal for Personnel Work and Industrial Relations], **3**, 4–19.

Land, K. C. (1969), Principles of path analysis. In: Borgatta, E. F. (Ed.), *Sociological methodology*. San Francisco: Jossey-Bass.

Lauer, R. H. (1981), *Temporal man: The meaning and uses of social time*. New York: Praeger.

Laumann, E. O., Guttman, L. (1966), The relative associational contiguity of occupations in an urban setting. *Ann. Sociol. Review*, **31**, 169–178.

LeShan, E. (1973), *The wonderful crisis of middle age*. New York: McKay.

Levinson, D. J., Darrow, C. M., Klein, E. B., Levinson, M. H., McKee, B. (1974), The psycho-social development in men in early adulthood and the mid-life transition. In: Ricks, D. F., *et al.* (Eds.), *Life history research, Vol. 3*. Minneapolis: University of Minnesota Press.

Lievegoed, B. C. J. (1972), *Organisaties in ontwikkeling: Zicht op de toekomst* [Developing organizations: A look at the future]. Rotterdam: Lemniscaat.

Lingoes, J. C. (1973), *The Guttman-Lingoes nonmetric program series*. Ann Arbor, Mich.: Mathesis Press.

Lingoes, J. C., Roskam, E. E. (1973), *A mathematical and empirical analysis of two multidimensional scaling algorithms*. Richmond (Virg.): The William Bird Press.

Lingoes, J. C., Guttman, L., Roskam, E.E. (Eds.) (1976), *Geometric representations of relational data structures*. Ann Arbor (Mich.): Mathesis Press.

Lofquist, L. H., Dawis, R. V. (1969), *Adjustment to work*. New York: Appleton-Century-Crofts.

Miller, C. H. (1974), Career development theory in perspective. In: Herr, E. L. (Ed.), *Vocational guidance and human development*. Boston: Houghton Mifflin.

Miner, J. B. (1977), *Motivation to manage: A ten year update on the 'Studies in management education' research*. Atlanta (Ga.): Organizational Measurement Systems Press.

Moses, J. L., Byham, W. C. (1977), *Applying the assessment center method*. Elmsford (N.Y.): Pergamon Press.

Mulder, H. (1970), *The search for the qualities essential to advancement in a large industrial group: An exploratory study*. The Hague: Author.

Munnichs, J. M. A. (1972), *Bouwstenen voor een sociale gerontologie* [Building stones for a social gerontology]. Nijmegen: Dekker & van de Vegt.

Nederlands Tijdschrift voor de Psychologie [Dutch Journal of Psychology]. Deventer: Van Loghum Slaterus.

Nesselroade, J. R., Baltes, P. B. (Eds.) (1979), *Longitudinal research in the study of behavior and development*. New York: Academic Press.

Nesselroade, J. R., Reese, H. W. (Eds.) (1973), *Life-span developmental psychology: Methodological issues*. New York: Academic Press.

Osipow, S. H. (1968), *Theories of career development*. New York: Appleton-Century-Crofts.

Owens, W. A. (1976), Background data. In: Dunnette, M. D. (Ed.), *Handbook of industrial and organizational psychology*. Chicago: Rand-McNally, 609–644.

Paterson, D. G., Darley, J. G. (1936), *Men, women and jobs*. Minneapolis: Univ. of Minnesota Press.

Peeters, H. F. M. (1978), Historiciteit, gedrag en gedragswetenschap: Een pleidooi voor onderzoek van gedrag op de lange termijn [Historicity, behavior, and behavioral science: A plea for long-term research on behavior]. *Nederlands Tijdschrift voor de Psychologie* **33**, 191–218.

Porter, L. W., Lawler, E. E., Hackman, J. R. (Eds.) (1975), *Behavior in organizations*. New York: McGraw-Hill.

Quay, C. L. M. de (1973), Management development en beoordelingen [Management development and appraisals]. In: Drenth *et al.* (1973), 91–107.

Riegel, K. F. (1976), *Psychology of development and history.* New York: Plenum Press.

Roe, A., Siegelman, M. (1964), *The origin of interests.* APGA Inquiry Studies No. 1. Washington, D. C.: American Personnel & Guidance Association.

Rogers, K. (1974), Crisis at the mid-point of life. *New Society,* (1974), 413–415.

Roth, J. A. (1963), *Timetables: Structuring the patterns of time in hospital treatment and other careers.* New York: Bobbs-Merrill.

Runkel, P. J., McGrath, J. E. (1972), *Research on human behavior: A systematic guide to method.* New York: Holt, Rinehart and Winston.

Schein, E. H. (1968), Organizational socialization and the profession of management. *Industrial Management Review (MIT),* **9**, 1–15.

Schein, E. H. (1971), The individual, the organization, and the career: A conceptual scheme. *J. Appl. Behav. Science,* **7**, 401–426.

Schein, E. H. (1972), *Professional education: Some new directions.* New York: McGraw-Hill.

Schein, E. H. (1975), How 'career anchors' hold executives to their career paths. *Personnel,* **52**, 11–24.

Schein, E. H. (1976), In: *Career planning and development.* Geneva: International Labor Office, Management Development Series no. 12.

Schein, E. H. (1977), Career anchors and career paths: A panel study of Management School graduates. In: Van Maanen, J. (Ed.), *Organizational careers: Some new perspectives.* New York: Wiley.

Schein, E. H. (1978), *Career dynamics: Matching individual and organizational needs.* Reading (Mass.): Addison-Wesley.

Sewell, W. H., Haller, A. O., Ohlendorf, G. W. (1970), The educational and early occupational status attainment process. *Am. Sociol. Rev.,* **35**, 1014–1027.

Sewell, W. H., Haller, A. O., Porters, A. (1969), The educational and early occupational/attainment process. *Am. Sociol. Rev.,* **34**, 82–92.

Shartle, C. I. (1959), *Occupational information.* 3rd ed. Englewood Cliffs (N.J.): Prentice-Hall.

Sheehy, G. (1976), *Passages: Predictable crises of adult life.* New York: Dutton.

Slocum, W. L. (1974), *Occupational careers,* 2nd ed. Chicago: Aldine.

Smal, C. A. (1975), *Organisatie van hoger personeel: Een structuurschets* [The organization of higher personnel: An outline of its structure]. Deventer: Kluwer.

Sofer, C. (1970), *Men in mid-career.* Cambridge: Cambridge University Press.

Stoner, J. A. F., Ference, T. P., Warren, E. K., Christensen, H. K. (1974), *Patterns and plateaus in managerial careers—An exploratory study.* Research paper no. 66. Graduate School of Business, Columbia University, August 1974.

Strong, Jr. E. K. (1955), *Vocational Interests. 18 years after college.* Minneapolis (Minn.): University of Minnesota Press.

Strong, Jr., E. K. (1960). An eighteen-year longitudinal report on interests. In: Layton, W. L. (Ed.), The Strong Vocational Interest Blank: Research and uses. Minneapolis: Univ. of Minnesota Press.

Super, D. E. (1957), *The psychology of careers.* New York: Harper & Row.

Super, D. E., Hall, D. T. (1978). Career development: Exploration and planning In: Rosenzweig, M. R., Porter, L. W. (Eds.), *Annual Review of Psychology,* **29**, 333–372. Palo Alto (Cal.): Annual Reviews Inc.

Super, D. E., Zelkowitz, R. (1973), *Vocational maturity in the Thirties: The definition and measurement of coping with career development tasks in mid-career.* Paper presented at the Annual Convention of the APA, August, 1973.

Super, D. E., Crites, J. O., Hummel, R. C., Moser, H. P., Overstreet, P. L., Warnath, C. F. (1957), *Vocational development: A framework for research.* New York: Teachers College Press.

Super, D. E., Starishevsky, R., Matiln, N., Jordaan, J. P. (1963), *Career development: self-concept theory.* New York: College Entrance Examination Board.

Super, D. E., *et al.* (1974), *Measuring vocational maturity for counseling and evaluation.* Washington, D. C.: American Personnel and Guidance Association.

Sze, W. C. (1975), *Human life-cycle.* New York: Aronson.

Taylor, B., Lippitt, G. L. (Eds.) (1975), *Management development and training handbook.* New York: McGraw-Hill.

Tiedeman, D. V., O'Hara, R. P. (1963), *Career development: Choice and adjustment.* New York: College Entrance Examination Board.

Tigchelaar, L. S. (1974), *Potentieel beoordeling en loopbaansucces* [Potential assessment and career success]. University of Amsterdam (dissertation; unpubl.).

Troll, L. E. (1975), *Early and middle adulthood: The best is yet to be—maybe.* Monterey (Cal.): Brooks/Cole.

Turner, R. R., Reese, H. W. (Eds.) (1980), *Life-span developmental psychology: Intervention.* New York: Academic Press.

Tyler, L. E. (1978), *Individuality: Human possibilities and personal choice in the psychological development of men and women.* London: Jossey-Bass.

Vaillant, G. E. (1977), *Adaption to life.* Boston: Little, Brown.

Van Maanen, J. (Ed.) (1977), *Organizational careers: Some new perspectives.* New York: Wiley.

Van Maanen, J. (1977), Introduction: The promise of career studies. In: J. Van Maanen (Ed.), *Organizational careers: Some new perspectives.* New York: Wiley, 1–12.

Van Maanen, J., Schein, E. H. (1977), Improving the quality of work life: Career development. In: Hackman, J. R., Suttle, J. L. (Eds.), *Improving life at work.* Los Angeles: Goodyear.

Walker, J. W. (1976), Human-resource planning: Managerial concerns and practices. *Business Horizons,* **19**, 55–59.

Wohlwill, J. F. (1973), *The study of behavioral development.* London: Academic Press.

Wolk, E. van der (Ed.) (1971), *Loopbaanplanning* [Career planning]. Amsterdam: Intermediair.

Yaker, H., Osmond, H., Cheek, F. (1971), *The future of time: Man's temporal environment.* Garden City (New York): Doubleday.

Yuill, B., Steinhoff, D. (1975), *Developing managers in organizations.* New York: Wiley.

Handbook of Work and Organizational Psychology
Edited by P. J. D. Drenth, H. Thierry, P. J. Willems and C. J. de Wolff
© 1984, John Wiley & Sons, Ltd.

2.9. Interview skills training

Arie Vrolijk

1. INTRODUCTION

Interview skills training implies that there are interview skills which are worth
passing on to others. The question is, what is the best way to do it? Before
any technique is applied generally it should be demonstrated that it works.
Furthermore, the method must be ethically acceptable and the trainees should
agree with the ideas inherent in the method. Having discovered such interview
methods, the question arises as to how they can best be taught to others.
When looking for theories which could support a training program, one soon
encounters Skinner's three-component theory (1953). Bandura (1969) later
expanded Skinner's model to what is now known as the 'Social Learning
Theory'. It is not the purpose of this paper to expound upon the history of the
Social Learning Theory, also called 'observation learning' (Berger, 1961),
or modeling (Goldstein, 1973), which began with McDougall's instinct theory
(1908) and continued via Miller and Dollard's reinforcement theory and Skinner
(1953) to lead up to Bandura. Readers who wish to learn more of this background should refer to Bandura (1969) and Kanfer and Philips (1970). In this
chapter we will consider Skinner's and Bandura's teaching theories, a review
of research on the application of the Social Learning Theory in work- and
organizational psychology and a summary of some modules which are used for
interview tranining.

Dr. Arie Vrolijk, Vrije Universiteit Amsterdam, Subfaculteit der Psychologie, De Boelelaan 1115,
Postbus 7161, 1007 ML AMSTERDAM.

2. SKINNER'S THEORY

The theory can be expressed in the formula: $Sd \rightarrow R \rightarrow Sr$. It says that a student is first shown an example (discriminative stimulus); he is then asked to imitate the example (response) and a reward (reinforcing stimulus) follows if the imitation is successful.

How does this simple expression of Skinner's theory help us to make a training program for an interview technique? The first point is that learning is facilitated by observation of exemplary behavior. This means that we show a student an example and thus prescribe his behavior. In many social-skills training programs, participants are invited to take part in role playing without a previous example. It is questionable whether this method is acceptable. The group members are invited to display a certain behavior, but, because there was no example, the behavior will mostly not be that which is wanted by the trainer; there is a discrepancy between 'actual' and 'should'. The participant cannot do it right because he has no idea what is wanted of him. Thus the volunteer in role playing fails and receives 'punishment' instead of 'reinforcement'. The punishment is often meted out in the guise of 'constructive criticism'. We call this learning without examples, 'trial and error' learning, or 'learning by mistakes'; it is left to chance whether the participant chooses the right approach. In a technical learning situation one would never just put a trainee in front of a machine and tell him: 'Try and get it to work'. On the contrary, one would explain its function step by step and practise its use thoroughly. If the trainer knows a 'should' it is important not to hide it. It is a good idea to show the method on video; then 'learning by imitation' can start. The role player is not vaguely told to 'hold an appraisal interview' but he is explicitly told to 'try to do it using the method we have just seen on video'. This is much less vague and will cause less tension: the trainee knows more precisely what is expected of him. The example contains objective criteria by which one can afterwards judge the participant's performance; if it did not go well we can show another example and try again. The absence of an example has another disadvantage and that is that the (wrong) behavior of the first role player becomes the example for the others. Because they have no concept or idea of the structure of the interview technique, the participants will tend to embrace the first method they encounter, even if it is wrong. If will then cost the trainer a lot of trouble to neutralize the effect of the wrong example. Thus the first rule we derive from Skinner is the need for clear behavior prescriptions.

There are a great many films and video tapes on the market which do not answer to Skinner's rule. Hiring a tape on conflict management, for example, one has a good chance of getting a tape which shows some sort of conflict, but what is missing is a description of how to tackle the conflict situation. In other words, the tape is descriptive and not prescriptive. Descriptive tapes have only a limited value. We already know that conflicts are destructive and are apt to raise the blood pressure. The interesting question is that of how to tackle the conflict. How do you achieve an optimal appraisal interview, for example? That is the point at which most of the films end. If you enquire into the reason for this descriptive approach you will usually hear that the film was not meant to be prescriptive, but meant to generate discussion and to set people thinking. Another excuse that is often heard is that they were not really interested in tranining behavior but were concentrating on more important things, such as a change of attitude or personal growth. Nijkerk (1975) is an important protagonist of this idea.

The second rule we can derive from Skinner is that the example must be followed by imitation by the trainee. The participant must know that when he sees the example he will be obliged to try and follow it. This is another rule that is often broken. If one wants to learn how to run an appraisal interview it is not enough to watch an example and then discuss it: you must do it yourself.

The third rule we get from Skinner is that doing must be followed by feedback. The trainer must comment on the performance of the trainee or ensure that it is commented upon.

We have shown above that Skinner's simple formula has far-reaching consequences for the construction of a social skills training. We must confront the class with an ideal example; we must invite them to follow the example and we must evaluate their performance.

We shall now show how Bandura extends Skinner's ideas in his 'Social Learning Theory'.

3. BANDURA'S THEORY

Bandura's ultimate target is 'matching behavior', that is that the student produces an exact duplicate of the behavior demonstrated. In order to achieve this one must pay attention to factors such as attention, cognition, memory and motivation, as well as imitation and feedback.

Attention can be attracted by presenting attractive material. The construction of the course must be such that the trainees achieve a cognitive appreciation of the method. The handbooks, films, and video tapes must be so constructed that the essential ingredients of the method are easily recognizable. The ingredients must be named so that they can easily be remembered. The characteristics should be so coded that the code can be used in the reproduction of the example.

Bandura's theory gives rise to many useful aids to the construction of training programs.

3.1. Attention

—In order to hold the participants' attention, a video tape should not last longer than 35 minutes.

—The interview method which is presented must answer a specific need. The problem which can be solved by the method must occur fairly frequently. It must have a reasonably wide application and the method must be applicable to the present or future situation in which the class member finds himself.

—The tapes must be as realistic as possible. It is best to design the tapes with people who are conversant with both the situation and the subject matter. The viewer must not be able to dismiss the situation as unreal or irrelevant. If a tape about power in a workers' committee is shown and the situation is atypical for the viewers, then, however right the method is, if the context is irrelevant, the tape will be rejected. Situational factors must be accurately reproduced. A tape about conflict management that shows a row in a workshop should, if possible, be acted by people from a workshop. This guarantees the best face-validity of the tape.

—Attention must be focussed on the main points; it is a great art to be able to leave out irrelevant information. There are always differences of opinion between teacher and producer. The producer wants a good picture while the teacher wants to get the message across. In a tape about interview techniques with Telly Savallas as the interviewee, everybody focusses on his big shoulders instead of on the interview technique. Such things remove attention from the technique to irrelevant factors in the context. The task of the viewer is to sift characteristic elements of the method from the flood of auditory and visual stimuli which confront him. He can be helped by being shown different tapes of the same method. This increases recognition and conservation of the pattern. Conservation is the ability of the viewer to recognize the structure in spite of disturbing or irrelevant factors in the context.

3.2. Cognitive and memory aspects

The student is expected to reproduce the model behavior. After seeing the tape he will be left with vague impressions. These pictorial impressions are not easy to remember. If in a film a chauffeur is shown driving through a town, it is difficult to remember the route if the viewer only uses the visual images he remembers. It becomes easier if he translates the pictorial images into: turn right twice, left twice and right again. If the visual material is coded it is even easier to retain and recall. If the teaching material on the tape is sorted and ordered, the patterns and characteristics of the method become easy to recognize. The introduction to the tape should serve to supply the viewer with cues and labels; the viewer is then relieved of the task of himself discovering the system in the chaos of impressions. A tape about management of an inter-group conflict can be announced as the 'five step method'. The name already tells him that the method consists of five parts. A long film on the management of inter-person conflicts can be coded with the words: complaint-importance-demand. During role playing the code serves as a guide and a memory aid. It is possible to furnish the different parts of an interview with their own code using a commentator's voice, subtitles, drawings, or diagrams. Describing the method beforehand helps the viewer to recognize the patterns. A handout of just a few pages is enough to explain the main concepts and the codes.

You can get the students to repeat the codes by letting them discuss the method in small groups before they see the tape. This sort of discussion of the method, the concepts, and the terms used greatly helps memory retention.

3.3. Motivation

What can we do to increase the participant's motivation?

The trainee must first be convinced of the effectiveness of the method. It helps if the method is 'sold' by the right person ('high credibility'). The viewer will tend to believe someone who has a certain prestige in the field in question.

A second important person is the one who demonstrates the method: the model. Learning by imitation is increased by building in 'modeling-enhancers'. Goldstein *et al.* (1976) state a number of conditions which enhance the effectiveness of the model. Learning is facilitated if the trainee can identify with the model. The model should therefore bear some resemblance to the trainee. The model should have approximately the same age, sex, vocabulary, clothes, and class as the group for whom the tape is intended. Beekers (1980) recounts the tale of a house painter who received a listening training. The wife in the example talked about the children and the model, the husband, listened carefully, asked the right questions and summarized perfectly. After watching the tape the painter shook his head and said: 'That's no good to me; we haven't got any children'.

If you make a tape for heads of social services you need a male model between 30 and 40. It's a mistake to choose a 25-year old woman.

Sometimes it is a good idea to choose a model who is known to have been successful in the past. Pele is a good model for a football instruction tape for young football players.

Another method of increasing the motivation of the viewers is by vicarious reinforcement. This principle is extensively used in advertising. The wife makes good hamburgers and is praised by her husband. The reward has two functions. First, the reward gives information; the viewer sees which behavior is rewarded. It also has a motivational aspect; if the viewer puts himself in the place of the model and behaves like the model, he or she can expect to be rewarded. In this way you can show the man who has just been for an appraisal interview with his boss saying: 'We had a good talk'.

Yet another way to increase motivation is the discussion in groups that we mentioned earlier. The discussions are best done, for example in threes, before showing the tape. It is important that the material in the handout is related to the participants' own experience. If it is about an appraisal interview, a participant will often have his own associations about the subject matter due to his experience as appraiser or appraised. This association with their own past experiences ensures that the discussion is not merely academic. The discussions should serve to break the ice and to motivate.

Finally, one can increase motivation by placing the role playing in the participants' own sphere of reference. In dilemma counseling, for example, it is not necessary to supply role playing instructions. The trainees are told to choose a dilemma of their own to practise with. It is then intrinsically relevant to their own situation.

3.4. Reproduction or imitation

The imitation of a positive example is central to Bandura's theory. Watching the model must be followed by practice; a number of repetitions is necessary before an exact replication of the model behavior is achieved. The trainee must be made to repeat the verbal code at each repetition: 'What did I have to say to the opponents? Oh yes, first the problem, then its importance and then the specific demand.' Silent (covert) repetition of the code means that the participant is going over the strategy in his mind. An overt repetition of the coding takes place if the participants hold a council of war together before starting role playing. Both covert and overt repetitions make the trainee familiar with the method. Sometimes the method is too complex to be repeated as a whole; the components can then be split up. The method for appraisal interviews, for example, is one which can be practised in part. When the parts have been grasped, the whole method can be attempted.

3.5. Feedback

Feedback is an essential part of the Social Learning Theory. All practice attempts must be followed by feedback. The feedback should be concentrated on the discrepancies between the model behavior and its imitation; between 'should' and 'actual'. Feedback can be provided by the trainee himself, by the other participants, or by the trainer.

Lists of questions and category lists (more about these below) can be used as feedback instruments. Obviously 'self-feedback' is the least threatening. We can stipulate that feedback must be precise, must not be attacking, and must not be personal. The feedback: that was a sloppy presentation' could be: 'you muddled up three models, the chronological model, the goal-means model and the question mark method; that made if difficult for your listeners to grasp the gist of what you were trying to say; try to stick to one model next time.' The first form of feedback leads to self-defense, the second could be the start of a learning process.

In concluding this part about Bandura we can say that following the Social Learning Theory leads to a didactic approach that can best be characterized as multimodal. Attention, cognition, memory, and motivation are activated to obtain optimal results.

The general set-up of the training consists of the following elements:
1. reading the handout;
2. discussing the handout;
3. watching an example (video);
4. imitation (role playing);
5. feedback.

4. RESEARCH ON MODELING IN WORK PSYCHOLOGY

In 1970 Sorcher developed a training program for supervisers at General Electric. He concentrated on frequently occuring interaction problems such as giving and taking criticism, asking for and giving help, and creating trust. Research had shown that turnover of trained employees was lower than in a control group. The program was later extended with modules on expressing appreciation, questions of discipline, career counseling, etc. The effect of the course was measured four months later. Using questionnaires the subordinates of the participants were asked whether they had noticed any changes in their bosses' behavior (Burnaska, 1976). No clear differences could be shown between those who had taken part in the training and a control group.

Burnaska explained this by the fact that the subordinates' perception only changed slowly and the boss needed time to display his new behavior pattern. They also tried to measure the effect using a role playing set-up. Behavior during the role playing was scored on a Likert scale. The behaviors scored were: 'leaving the self-confidence of the client intact', 'building up an open communication', 'control of the situation' and 'achieving the goal of the inter-action'. The scores of the role plays were done twice, one month after the course and four months after the course. The trained bosses had better scores than the untrained ones. Moreover, the results after four months were better than after only one month. Burnaska assumed that the managers needed time to absorb their new proficiency.

At AT & T Moses and Ritchie (1976) measured the effect of modeling in the handling of questions of discipline. The measurements were done two months after the course. They also used a role playing situation. There were three themes: 'absenteeism', 'discrimination', and 'theft'. Trained volunteers got higher scores than untrained volunteers.

Byham (1976) trained six chefs in nine modules. Subjects were 'introducing a new colleague', 'resistance to change', 'increasing achievement levels', etc. His method was original: he questioned the subordinates of the trained chefs about specific incidents. The superior's behavior during the incidents was scored as correct if he had followed the steps stipulated in the training program. The interviews were held just before the training and seven months afterwards. This pre-post experiment showed significant improvements.

Smith (1976) did some research at IBM. He trained managers to cope with complaining clients. Measurements were performed just before and just after the training, using written answers to a number of clients' statements, the satisfaction of the clients and the sales statistics. Noticeable improvements were made on all three scores.

5. THE DEPENDENT VARIABLES

It is pertinent to draw attention to the dependent variables. Methodologically speaking there are a number of pitfalls lurking in this area.

Judgement of role playing behavior with a five point scale gives rise to inter-observer problems with reliability, the more so as terms like 'understanding' and 'respect' are poly-interpretable. In practice it appears that the scores 1 (very bad) and 5 (very good) are hardly ever used so that it is in fact a three-point scale. Interviewing employees and asking for specific incidents probably gives rise to a 'peaks and valleys' effect; only the extreme behaviors are remembered so that it is not certain that the incidents are representative.

The method of requesting written reactions to statements by clients is not free of validity problems either. Written reactions probably activate a behavior different from verbal reactions. Written reactions allow more time for thought and will probably show more answers 'according to the book'.

Sales statistics (Smith, 1976) are of course more trustworthy, as are turnover and production statistics (Goldstein and Sorcher, 1974). The problem there is, however, that other factors can also influence these parameters. Vrolijk (1978) developed a category system to tabulate the reactions of participants. He distinguishes:

Ein: Questions seeking further explanation (intrinsic exploration).
Eex: Questions about new aspects or subjects (extrinsic exploration).
S: Summarizing or sorting.
O: Giving an opinion or evaluation.
Inf: Giving information.
As: Expressing an assumption.
I: Interjections such as mm-mm, yes, etc.
By scoring these categories it is possible to construct a so-called interview profile. The categories can be listed horizontally and the scores placed vertically. An ideal interview profile can be developed for different interview techniques.

Let us take the appraisal interview as an example, based on Maier's (1963) problem-solving method. Maier developed this method and described it precisely, using an interview protocol. If we score this protocol using the above-mentioned categories, then it appears to consist of a combintion of equal number of Ein-, Eex-, S- and Inf-reactions.

An exit interview on Schoenfeld's (1957) model mainly consists of S- and Ein-reactions.

Once a method is chosen, it is possible to determine the 'ideal' profile. By comparing the 'own' profile with the 'ideal' profile it is possible to measure the learning effect. The categories are formal and need little or no interpretation, which leads to a high inter-observer reliability (Neuteboom, 1966).

Using the categories as criteria does mean that the goal of the training is limited. The goal is not producing better managers or getting higher production or sales results, but is learning an interview method.

6. SOME INTERVIEW TECHNIQUES

After these rather theoretical considerations we will describe some training modules: much of what follows is the result of experience combined with theory. Results of systematic experimental work in this field are, alas, not widely available.

6.1. Appraisal interviews

The most important model for managers is Maier's problem-solving interview (1963). It is the successor to the old-fashioned 'tell and sell' interview with a form. The interview begins with an open question: 'How's the work going?'. In 90% of the cases the interviewee first mentions some good points and then goes on to some more difficult ones. He then tries to think up some solutions to the tricky points. When he has finished it is his superior's turn to bring up points about his subordinate's work. Here, too, both of them can think up solutions to difficult matters. At the end the boss summarizes the points and the solutions that have been suggested. The points may concern personal functioning or the work itself. Sometimes the interviewee will not behave according to the general model: for example, in answer to the question, 'how's the work getting on' he just replies 'O.K.'.

Vrolijk (1982) wrote down an emergency procedure for these situations.

6.2. Two-column interviews

This method originates from Maier and Lansky (1957). The two-column interview is suitable for use when there is resistance to change. The method homes in on the things that most preoccupy the client, viz. his objections to the change. The client is invited to voice his objections to the new idea until he can't think of any more.

After that the client is invited to see if there might be some advantages to the idea. Grateful for the opportunity he has had to air all his objections, he will be glad to think up a few advantages. When the list of pros and cons is complete, he is asked to think over a revision of the suggestion so that the objections can be met and the advantages retained. For example, if the suggestion of a consultant is to set up the new office on an open plan, an objection might well be that some of the people who will work there produce a lot of noise.

Via the two-column method a compromise can be reached by deciding on an open plan office with noise baffles. The consultant gets most of what he was aiming for and the client sees that his objections are taken seriously. In the two-column approach the opponent is invited to bring forward his objections. The idea is that the interview gathers enough momentum downhill to get up the other side, to the advantages.

6.3. Dilemma counseling

Janis (Janis and Mann, 1977) has developed a method for resolving dilemmas. Suppose that someone cannot decide whether to stay in his old job or to take a new one. He is asked to list the pros and cons of both alternatives in brief headings; the headings are listed in four columns, the first with the advantages of alternative A, the second with the disadvantages, the third with the advantages of alternative B and the fourth with the disadvantages. If the client says that his present work is varied, then 'varied' is listed in the first column. It is important to ask for an explanation of the headings because in a later stage the client is asked to assign a particular value to each heading.

The next step is that the client is asked to project his thoughts into the future. He must shut his eyes, imagine that he has chosen alternative A, and then tell the counselor how he feels in a year's time. He must imagine that he has stayed in the same job, a commerical position and that he now telephones the dilemma counselor to tell him how things have gone in the past year. The idea behind this future-projection-technique is that the client really feels and appreciates the implications of choosing alternative A, i.e. staying in the same job. With this technique it is also possible to discover new aspects to both alternatives and add them to the existing columns. After making the 'telephone call' for alternative A, he does the same for alternative B.

After this the 'accounting' stage follows. If he has to make a choice between two alternatives, some aspects will weigh more heavily than others. In order to make the client realize the difference in importance between the various aspects he is asked to score each of the headings on a 1 to 10 scale. The score is 1 if the item is of low importance to him and 10 if it is very important. Finally the numbers are summed. If there are four columns a, b, c, and d, then if a + d is greater than b + c, the client attributes more importance to alternative A.

In this way it is possible to include all the different elements of the choice in the decision. The dilemma counselor should only concern himself with the procedure. The method also protects the client from disappointment. He knows that the choice he has made has a number of potential disadvantages. When they appear they are not unexpected but have been reckoned with. This minimizes disappointment over the decision that has been made. It has been shown that people have a higher stress tolerance regarding unwanted consequences if they have considered beforehand what they can expect (Gomersall and Meyers, 1966; Macedonia, 1969; Wanous, 1973).

6.4. Exit interviews

The exit interview is an enquiry into the reasons for departure of a member of the organization (Schoenfeld, 1957).

The purpose of the interview is to track down possible shortcomings in the organization. One must of course realize that the departing employee will not tell you everything and that he will not be objective but will relate his experiences from his own, individual point of view. An exit interview provides 'feelings', not 'facts'. However, the exit interviewer should take note of the slogan: 'Feelings are facts'. These feelings have led to the departure of this member of the organization. So it is important to take them seriously.

Schoenfeld advised a non-directive method for the exit interview. The interview begins with an open question: 'What has made you decide to leave the organization?' or 'I heard that you are leaving us; can you tell me something of your reasons for this decision?'.

Often the first sentence will tell you in a nutshell what the reasons are: 'Several factors were involved: the fact that it's a family business was part of it; there was no real place for me and the atmosphere was often a bit heavy'. It is a good idea to note down key words such as 'family business', 'place' and 'atomosphere' and to explore these themes more deeply. Asking for examples is very important in this probing. If the man tells you that the boss's family always gets the good promotions and that when important decisions have to be made the family vote decides the outcome, then you know what he means by a family business.

By asking for examples the employee is compelled to be precise about the statements he made. In the summing up it is important to check whether all the themes have been worked through. The interviewer should confine himself to exploratory questions about unclear points and to summarizing. The commonest mistake is that the interviewer is satisfied with vague answers like:
'I don't agree with the personnel department's ideas.'
'I was really working under my potential.'
'I got no chance to use my own ideas.'
Another mistake is that the interviewer runs through a list of points that he thinks are important; such as 'work satisfaction', 'relationship with colleagues' and 'relationship with superiors', etc. This sort of questions does not stimulate the client to give his own reasons for departure, or to place them in his own order of importance.

The interviewer should watch out for making evaluative comments, such as:

'Did you try to change things in the department?', 'What do you expect as a change for the better with the new firm?'. In a useful and productive exit interview the interviewer should accept the client's own version of the facts without comment, defense, or argument.

6.5. Discipline interviews

Maier (1956) noted that bureaucracies have a marked tendency to handle the breaking of the rules of the organization judicially. The book is opened, the broken rule looked up, and a disciplinary measure is taken accordingly. A judicial approach such as this will usually lead to deterioration of the relationship between superior and inferior, to a diminished motivation and achievement, and possibly to psychosomatic disorders (Maier and Danielson 1956). Maier advises the 'human relations' approach in such cases.

In this approach the superior first tries to find out what the motive was for breaking the rule and this is then followed by problem solving with 'How can we set about this better in the future?' as the most important question.

Maier and Danielson (1956) did some research into the effectiveness of this method. The judicial method was compared to the human relations approach. The latter was the more successful, as appeared from the better relationship between superior and inferior and a higher expected production. The interview contained more problem solving elements and fewer arguments.

6.6. Interpersonal conflict management

Conflicts within organizations are often expensive and are a great waste of time and energy.

Bach (1971) developed a method for the management of interpersonal conflicts. There is a referee or arbitrator who starts off the negotiations between the two parties. The arbitrator first makes a list of the main problems in separate interviews. These are put down on paper and listed in order of difficulty. Then the two parties meet. The problems are dealt with one at a time.

The 'easiest' problems are dealt with first. Chance—the toss of a coin—decides who is going to start. Party A begins with least important problem; he must explain the importance of the problem or complaint and lead up to a specific demand. Party B must first give a summary of what he has heard and party A must approve it. When this approval has been given then it is B's turn to react to the problem and this must again result in a specific demand. This is in turn paraphrased by A, who can then answer. This goes on until a compromise is reached. When A's easiest point has been concluded it is B's turn to bring up his first point. The negotiations continue until all the problems have been dealt with.

The model guarantees equal chances for A and B, for example an equal chance to voice their opionions. By obliging the two parties to formulate specific demands their covert strategies are brought into the open.

Research parameters on the effect of this method are scarce. Vansteenwegen (1976) measured the changes in the perception of the relationship with 36 couples. His hypothesis was that empathy (understanding of the partner's feelings) and transparency (willingness to show oneself to the partner as one really is) would increase after a three weeks' training and would remain constant for six months. The results indeed showed that the participants found their partners more empathic and more transparent after the training. The participants thought themselves more empathic but not more transparent. After six months the results were the same.

6.7. Management of intergroup conflicts

When two groups are highly dependent on each other a conflict quickly leads to malfunctioning through polarisation of points of view and the negative stereotyping of the other group. Both the quality and the quantity of communication decline rapidly. This in turn leads to drastically diminished chances of solving the problem.

The method described here for management of intergroup conflicts is largely derived from Blake et al. (1964). It consists of five stages:

1. The first stage is 'raking up the past'. The members of the two groups take it in turns to rake up past insults and injuries. A member of group A starts with the first incident and then it is group B's turn.

2. The second phase is the exchange of 'images'; each group makes a list of negative characteristiscs of the other. In this way they each construct an image of each other. Descriptions such as lazy, bureaucratic, unimaginative, and antisocial are to be expected.

3. The third step is the exchange of problems. Both groups make a list of the worst bottlenecks. This is by far the most difficult phase, as it is not easy to find formulations for the problems that are neither insulting, nor vague, or personal. You cannot do much with 'You lot are antisocial' as a problem. You can with: 'The vacations of the two departments aren't at the same time'.

4. In the fourth stage the arbitrator makes an agenda from the two lists of bottlenecks and assigns priorities. The problems that occur most frequently, affect most people or form the greatest threat to the organization have the highest priority.

5. In the fifth phase sub-groups, put together from both opposing groups, consider the agenda points. They make propositions which are put before both groups. If the propositions concern matters of policy, they are reported to the management. A bilateral working group makes sure the points are followed up.

Evidence for the effectiveness of this method can be found in Fordyce and Weil (1971) and Truskie (1974).

6.8. Haves and have-nots

This method was developed at the 'Institut für Psychologie' at the Freie Universität of Berlin (*Psychologie Heute*, 1977). The unions developed the method. The 'Haves' are the people with power, status, money, information, and social graces and the 'Have-nots' are those who have fewer of these attributes or none at all. When power differences are manifest, the have-nots will endeavor to reduce the power distance. The haves, however, will try to maintain this power distance or to increase it (Mulder, 1979).

Techniques that the haves employ to maintain the status quo are distracting attention, flattery, putting off decisions, making vague promises, manipulating the agenda, withholding information, holding monologues, making concessions on unimportant points, making light of problems, etc.

What do the have-nots do? The two most important things are: 1. translate emotional frustrations into specific goals; and 2. solidarity; never allow colleagues to be interrupted or attacked from 'behind the lines'.

Then there are other tactics, such as: increasing the amount of speaking time, demanding a point of view, making clear agreements, doing your 'homework' properly, showing understanding for the problems facing the haves, expanding on the advantages to agreeing to your demands and the disadvantages of not doing so, acquiring militant colleagues, exerting pressure by threatening to leave the bargaining table, demonstration meetings, publicity, etc. Most of these tactics come from Deutsch (1973).

6.9. The bad-news interview

The purpose of the bad-news interview is to bring the bad news, to help absorb it and to try to solve the problems that have arisen, together with the client.

Bad news usually means loss of something: a relationship, a job, a part of the body, an object, or the expectation of a future reward. Loss leads to mourning (Bowlby, 1969). Emotions are mobilized: grief, anger, and feelings of guilt are usually uppermost. Most people tend to show evasive behavior when they have to bring bad news (Rosen and Tesser, 1970). This is displayed in the following ways:

—Putting off the interview. Faber (1982) observed this with policemen; they drove more slowly, hung around before leaving the station, went and did other things first, looked for someone else who could do it for them, etc.

—Sugaring the pill: a fatal accident becomes: 'He is badly injured'.

—Worse things could have happened: 'He was killed immediately, so at least he wasn't burnt alive'.

—Justification: the bad-news messenger looks for explanations: 'Your husband was at the end of his tether; it would have happened some time or other anyway'.
—Activism: the messenger tries prematurely to turn attention to the things that have to be done.
—Avoiding personal contact with the recipient of the bad news by sending a letter or telegram, or telephoning.
—The anamnestic method: 'Are you Ms. Peterson? Does your husband drive a blue Cadillac with such and such a number? What time did your husband leave the house this morning?' This method has two advantages for the bringer of the bad news. He can put off the news for a bit and chances are that the recipient discovers the bad news for himself ('Hang yourself' method): 'Has my husband had an accident?', 'Yes, Ma'am'.

A good bad-news interview consists of three parts, telling the bad news, then a phase which concentrates on the client's emotions and giving more information, and a third phase in which the consequences of the bad news are talked through. Vrolijk (1978) advises telling the news as soon as possible, preceded by a sentence such as: 'I'm afraid I have bad news for you'. It should be clear from the tone in which the bad news is brought that the messenger understands the difficulty of the recipient's situation. Start with the worst. If the recipient wants to know 'how' or 'why', the news can be followed by brief information.

When the bad news has been given, the phase of helping the client follows. The client is given the opportunity to vent his feelings of grief, anger, surprise, etc. and the messenger should confine himself to giving information if the client wants it and to making reflections. The following mistakes are often made in this second stage:
—Counter aggression ('You must be really crazy to swim that river, you know');
—sympathetic aggression ('You're absolutely right, Ma'am, they should hang those drunken drivers');
—moralizing ('You really shouldn't let yourself go like that and you mustn't try to play the judge yourself, you know').

The third phase in the bad news interview is the problem solving stage. It is best left to the client to time the start of this phase. A sentence such as: 'The children will be home from school soon, what do I do?' can herald the third stage. It is important that the client himself or herself is active in the problem solving and that the interviewer stimulates him or her to take part actively.

REFERENCES

Bach, G. R., Bernard, Y. (1971), *Aggression lab. The fair fight training manual*. Dubuque: Kendall-Hunt.
Bandura, A. (1969), *Principles of behavior modification*, New York: Holt, Rinehart and Winston.

Beekers, M. (1980a), Videomodellen in vaardigheidstherapieën [Video-models in skill therapies]. *De Psycholoog* [The Psychologist], **15**, 629–636.

Beekers, M. (1980b), *Vaardigheidstherapieën op maat, een regional project* [Taylored skill therapies, a regional project]. Brochure Goldstein-project, Maastricht.

Beekers, M., Gooijen, J. (1980), Spel met grenzen: Een Goldsteintherapie [A game within limits: A Goldstein therapy]. *Tijdschrift voor Psychotherapie* [Journal of Psychotherapy], **6**, 326–337.

Berger, S. M. (1961), Incidental learning through vicarious reinforcement. *Psychological Review*, **9**, 477–491.

Blake, R. R., Shephard, H. A., Mouton, J. S. (1964), *Managing intergroup conflict in industry*. Houston: Gulf.

Bowlby, J. (1969), *Attachment and loss. Vol. 1: Attachment*. London: Hogarth/New York:

Burnaska, R. F. (1976), The effects of behavioral modeling training upon managers' behaviors and employees' perceptions. *Personnel Psychology*, **29**, 329–335.

Byham, W. C. (1976), Transfer of modeling training to the job. *Personnel Psychology*, **29**, 345–349.

Deutsch, M. (1973), *The resolution of conflict*. London: Yale University Press.

Faber, W. (1982), *De politieman als brenger van onheilsboodschappen* [The policeman as bearer of bad news]. Apeldoorn: Police Academy (paper).

Fordyce, J. K., Weil, R. (1971), *Managing with people*. Reading (Mass.): Addison-Wesley.

Goldstein, A. P. (1973), *Structured learning therapy. Towards a psychotherapy for the poor*. New York: Academic Press.

Goldstein, A. P., Sorcher, M. (1974), *Changing supervisor behavior*. New York: Pergamon.

Goldstein, A. P., Sprafkin, R., Gershaw, W. (1976), *Skill training for community living: Applying structured learning therapy*. New York: Pergamon.

Gomersall, E. R., Meyers, M. S. (1966), Breakthrough in on-the-job training. *Harvard Business Review*, **44**, 62–72.

Janis, I. L., Mann, L. (1977), *Decision making. A psychological analysis of conflict, choice and commitment*. London/New York: The Free Press.

Kanfer, F., Philips, J. S. (1970), *Learning foundations of behavior therapy*. New York: Wiley.

McDougall, W. (1908), *An introduction to social psychology*. London: Methuen.

Macedonia, R. M. (1969), *Expectations-press and survival*. New York University (unpublished doctoral dissertation).

Maier, N. R. F. (1963), *Het gesprek als stimulans* [The appraisal interview]. Utrecht: Het Spectrum.

Maier, N. R. F., Danielson, L. E. (1956), An evaluation of two approaches to discipline in industry. *Journal of Applied Psychology*, **40**, 319–323.

Maier, N. R. F., Lansky, L. M. (1957), Effect of attitude on selection of facts. *Personnel Psychology*, **10**, 293–304.

Moses, J. L., Ritchie, R. J. (1976), Supervisory relationships training: A behavioral evaluation of a behavior modeling program. *Personnel Psychology*, **29**, 337–344.

Mulder, M. (1979), *Het spel om macht* [The power game]. 5th ed. Meppel: Boom.

Neuteboom, P. M. C. (1966), *Opleiding in gespreksvoering* [Training in conducting interviews]. Delft: Meinema (dissertation).

Nijkerk, K. J. (1975), *Training in tussenmenselijke verhoudingen* [Training in inter-human relations]. Alphen a/d Rijn: Samsom.

Psychologie Heute (1977), Verhaltenstraining für Betriebsräte. January.

Rosen, S., Tesser, A. (1970), On reluctance to communicate undesirable information: The MUM effect. *Sociometry*, **33**, 253–263.

Schoenfeld, E. (1957), The non-directive exit interview. *Personnel*, **34**, 46–50.

Skinner, B. F. (1953), *Science and human behavior*. New York: MacMillan.

Smith, P. E. (1976), Management modeling training to improve morale and customer satisfaction. *Personnel Psychology*, **29**, 351–359.

Sorcher, M. (1971), A behavior modification approach to supervisory training. *Professional Psychology*, **2**, 401–402.

Tesses, A., Rosen, S., Batchelor, T. R. (1972), On the reluctance to communicate bad news. *Journal of Personality*, **40**, 88–103.

Teulings, A. (1981), *Ondernemingsraadpolitiek in Nederland* [Works council policies in The Netherlands]. Amsterdam: Van Gennep.

Truskie, S. D. (1974), A case study of a union-management: learning encounter in industry. *Personnel Journal*, **53**, no. 4, 277–279.

Vansteenwegen, A. (1976), Gevechtstraining in echtpaartherapie [Fair fighting in marital therapy]. *Tijdschrift voor Psychotherapie* [Journal of Psychotherapy], **2**, 30–39.

Vrolijk, A. (1982), *Communicatiemodellen* [Communication models]. Alphen a/d Rijn: Samsom.

Vrolijk, A., Höweler, M. (1968), De twee-kolommen methode van Maier. Toetsing van een hypothese [Maier's two-column method. Testing a hypothesis]. *Nederlands Tijdschrift voor de Psychologie* [Dutch Journal of Psychology], **23**, 165–178.

Vrolijk, A., Dijkema, M. F., Timmerman, G. (1978), *Gespreksmodellen: Een geprogrammeerde instructie* [Interview models: A programmed instruction]. 4th ed. Alphen a/d Rijn: Samsom.

Wanous, J. P. (1973), Effects of a realistic job preview on job acceptance, job attitudes, and job survival. *Journal of Applied Psychology*, **58**, 327–332.

Handbook of Work and Organizational Psychology
Edited by P. J. D. Drenth, Hk. Thierry, P. J. Willems and C. J. de Wolff
© 1984, John Wiley & Sons, Ltd.

2.10. Job evaluation

John R. de Jong and Henk Thierry

1. INTRODUCTION

When asked what the term 'job evaluation' means, employees of any firm will, in all probability, answer that it refers to a method of establishing the rates of pay. If—in a firm applying job evaluation—one persists, it will probably be added that job evaluation consists of examining what kind of activities are carried out by an individual and what his working conditions are, on which basis it will then be established to which salary grade his work (or job) is related.

The word 'job' has a specific meaning in this context. A concise definition in this sense would be: 'the sum total of an employee's tasks to be carried out, his responsibilities and the appropriate working conditions' (de Jong *et al.*, 1977). The definition excludes the manner in which a job is carried out. The application of job evaluation usually does not involve establishing the worker's wage or salary, but does lead to its penultimate stage: the indication of the wage or salary *grade* relating to that particular job. Therefore, ascertaining the height of the individual income (whether fixed or variable) is the next step: relevant factors may be seniority, performance (assessment), special conditions (as e.g. irregular working hours), etc. (see this Handbook, ch. 4.11).

The need for systematic job evaluation was first felt in large, unclearly structured organizations, in which it was impossible to decide whether the rates of pay

Dr. Ir. John R. de Jong, De Genestetlaan 25, DE BILT.
Prof. dr. Hk. Thierry, Universiteit van Amsterdam, Vakgroep Arbeidspsychologie. Weesperplein 8, 1018 XA AMSTERDAM.

were properly related to each other. It called for an instrument for a systematic (sometimes called 'objective') evaluation of jobs, in order to ascertain wages and salaries.

As early as 1871 the U.S. Civil Service Commission applied a form of job evaluation; another early example is the city of Chicago, in 1909. Through the years, a variety of methods have been developed for job evaluation. In the long run the so-called point-rating method appeared to be favourite. Dating from 1925, it has a well-known example in the system applied by the American National Electrical Manufacturers Association, which led to application in 1200–1500 companies in the U.S., by the year 1945 (Smith and Murphy, 1946). Table 1 shows what job factors were used in this method, and what numbers of 'points' could be awarded to each factor. Also, it was defined what job requirements corresponded to the points recorded. Thus, five points on the factor mental and/or visual demand refers to: 'Little mental and only intermittent visual attention, since either the operation is practically automatic, or the duties require attention only at long intervals'. The maximum of 25 points was described as: 'Concentrated and exacting mental and visual attention, usually visualizing, planning, and laying out very involved and complex jobs'.

Evidently these are rather global descriptions. Therefore, a detailed description was made for each factor of several dozens of 'key jobs': these are various sorts of jobs, whose activities are quite common in the organizations concerned. Also, the number of awarded points was specified. These data

Table 1. Factors and point allocations—The National Electrical Manufacturers Association Plan for hourly rated jobs.

Factors	1st degree	2nd degree	3rd degree	4th degree	5th degree
Skill					
Education	14	28	42	56	70
Experience	22	44	66	88	110
Initiative and ingenuity	14	28	42	56	70
Effort					
Physical demand	10	20	30	40	50
Mental/Visual demand	5	10	15	20	25
Responsibility					
For equipment or process	5	10	15	20	25
For material or product	5	10	15	20	25
For safety of others	5	10	15	20	25
For work of others	5	10	15	20	25
Job conditions					
Working conditions	10	20	30	40	50
Hazards	5	10	15	20	25

served as a standard for analyzing other jobs, by means of making comparisons (we shall briefly return to the use of key jobs in section 3.1). Finally, a table was used which indicated the wage or salary grade, corresponding to the resulting amount of points.

The next section will first deal briefly with the objectives of job evaluation (hence: JE). After that we shall go more deeply into the point rating method (an example of which was mentioned above), as well as other possible methods. We shall then examine to what extent JE systems are applied in Dutch work organizations. Section 3 treats of the current procedures applied in job description and analysis, which occur in many systems. In section 4 we shall discuss the possibilities of applying JE in areas other than the setting of relative pay rates among jobs. Section 5 will pay attention to the question of how much work has been done on JE in the social sciences, particularly in psychology, by way of research and theorizing. Finally, in section 6, we shall take a look at developments in the near future, and briefly comment on the potential contributions of work and organizational psychology.

2. THE APPLICATION OF JOB EVALUATION

2.1. Objectives

It was explained in the introduction that especially unclearly structured organizations felt the need for an instrument to establish a proper relation among the pay rates of jobs. The theme of proper relations is found, whether briefly or elaborately, in many of the generally used definitions of JE. De Jong *et al.* (1977) regard JE as a tool for ascertaining the *relative value* of existing jobs, for the sake of determining the height of incomes. McCormick (1976) distinguishes between an internal and an external objective: JE should be a general basis for, on the one hand, setting salary scales for the jobs *within* an organization, which are felt to be acceptable, relative to each other, by the employees. On the other hand, the resulting salary structure ought to be properly related to the going rates in the *labour market* in general. The Dutch Commission of Experts on Job Classification (1952) does not only refer to the rates of pay, but also to the application of JE for the sake of decisions concerning *organization* and *personnel policy*. This may imply selection, training, career planning, and (re)structuring the content of the job.

But the question is whether these themes—organization and personnel policy—can be qualified as objectives at all, particularly in the light of the development of JE in practice. Perhaps we had better speak of potential applications; we shall elaborate on this in section 4. For the present we consider the setting of relative pay rates to be the essential characteristic of the definition of the objectives of JE, as it appears in the preceding descriptions and in various others too (see e.g. ILO, 1977; Sayles and Strauss, 1977).

But along with a shift of the level of analysis, the objectives change. Thus Scholten (1979, 1981) views JE in the context of labour relations, both nationally, per branch of industry, and in each work organization. He believes that the point is to make the problems of society *controllable*, particularly as regards status and remuneration. JE is an example of bureaucratization by means of which management can control its employees, and the trade union its members. In a more general treatise of JE, the Wage Administration Control Department (WACD) of the Ministry of Social Affairs and Employment takes a similar viewpoint (LTD, 1982). Besides a development from disorder to order in job and wage relations, there is the *purpose of pacification*. JE implies a series of rules which make for legal security and clarity. It meets the employees' need for increased participation—the WACD at this point refers to procedures; see section 3—and the need to legitimatize relative pay rates. JE provides management with a wages structure, a wages policy and control of the total wage amount.

2.2. The first years after the Second World War

The two themes of control and pacification, allegedly, have been detectable in this country's development since 1945. Scholten (1979) remarks that, surprisingly, the government, the employers' associations and the trade unions at that time had reached consensus about JE, although the interests were widely different. The government, for instance, desired to have an instrument for increasing wage differentiation: greater differentiation was expected to incite higher productivity. Moreover, such an instrument fitted quite well into the centralized wages policy of the time. The employers were in favour of greater wage differentiation, partly because it was supposed to create better opportunities for promotion. The trade unions, Scholten says, expected that owing to JE, the content of the job was to be decisive for the height of income rather than the market elements of demand and supply. In addition, greater wage differentiation would relate better to the strongly increased job differentiation. Besides, it could be made more acceptable that certain groups of workers (e.g. in agriculture) had dropped behind in the wages development (for more on post-war wages policy, see Fase, 1980; Koopman-Iwema and Thierry, 1981a).

Whichever way we interpret the developments since 1945, it is a fact that, in The Netherlands as well as elsewhere in Europe, before 1945 JE was applied merely on a small scale. During the war it gained more interest, our country becoming really interested from 1945 onwards. A series of systems was developed: some were intended for a single firm, others for an entire branch of industry. Most of these systems did not survive long. About 1950, they were replaced by two systems, which were applied on a large scale: the 'Normalized Method of Job Classification' (NM), and the 'Metal Industry Method' (MI). Both will be discussed in this section.

They share the characteristics of being point rating systems, of being largely concerned with key jobs in their application, and of being almost exclusively used with respect to manual jobs (therefore, they are of little use for clerical, managerial or other jobs).

The Normalized Method (NM) was designed by the Dutch Commission of Experts on Job Classification that cooperated closely with the Commission on Job Classification for Civil Servants, both founded in 1947. The NM was published in 1952 as a provisional standard (V3000 and 3001), together with over 100 examples (key jobs) of the description and grading of jobs in various branches of industry. In 1959 the definitive standard (NEN 3.000 and 3.001) was published.

The NM lists ten characteristics (called 'viewpoints') and the appropriate tables for finding the number of points to be assigned to a particular job. Each characteristic (and each sub-characteristic, respectively) is first graded, on the basis of a job description, usually on an eight-point-scale. It represents to what degree that (sub)characteristic applies to a job. The result is then multiplied by a weighing factor (or: weighing coefficient) which reflects the relative importance of that characteristic in general. Consequently, weighing factors do not vary according to the job to be evaluated, but they represent the value which

Table 2. Example of how a job is graded by means of NM, in the case of a chauffeur.

Characteristic ('viewpoint')	Grade	Weighing factor	Points
1. Knowledge (type and degree)	3	5	15
2. Independence	3	6	18
3. Contact (type and intensity)	2	2	4
4. Authority (demands and conditions)	1	2	2
5. Skill in communication	0	2	0
6. Motor skill	3	2	6
7. Dexterity with material and machinery	3	1	3
8. Drawbacks inherent to work			
8a. Strenuousness of work	1	1	1
8b. Strenuous posture and one-sided movement	2	1	2
8c. Strenuous attentiveness	4	1	4
8d. Working atmosphere	1	3	3
8e. Personal hazard	2	1	2
9. Special requirements	0	1	0
10. Risk of damage	4	4	16
Total score			76

society puts on each characteristic. Finally, it is determined what salary grade corresponds to the total number of points for the job as a whole.

Table 2 reveals the viewpoints and the weighing factors of the NM; in addition, it contains an example of application to the post of chauffeur.

The Metal Industry Method, officially called 'Method of work classification for manual workers in the metal industry', was designed by Berenschot Consul-

Table 3. The Metal Industry Method.

Main characteristic	Characteristic	Subcharacteristic	Weighing factor
A. DIFFICULTY	1. MANY-SIDEDNESS	1. Nature of work	3
		2. Cycle time	4
		3. Variety and complication in pieces of work	6
		4. Number of machines to be operated	
	2. KNOWLEDGE; ATTENTION; CONSULTATION	1. Setting and operating (machinery or installations)	4
		2. Working with drawings and diagrams	4
		3. Working with measuring tools	2
		4. Working with instruments and dials	2
		5. Judging and selecting materials, tools, etc.	4
		6. Copying, beating out, aligning	8
	3. PRECISION; DEXTERITY	1. Precision in working	7
		2. Small pieces of work	2
		3. Dexterity	4
B. IMPORTANCE	4. RISK OF DAMAGE; RESPONSIBILITY	1. Machinery, installations, tools	4
		2. Pieces of work	4
		3. Responsibility for safety of others	4
		4. Responsibility (working in a group)	5
C. DRAW BACKS	5. EFFORT AND WORKING CONDITIONS	1. Posture	3
		2. Exercising force	4
		3. Atmosphere	3
		4. Health risk	4

tants Bureau by order of the (then) Association of Employers in Metal Industry, in cooperation with the trade unions, and tested in practice by way of numerous committees. It lists five characteristics and 21 sub-characteristics. The tables for each sub-characteristic are clearly keyed to the kind of work done in metal industry. The characteristics and weighing factors are shown in table 3.

By means of an additional Collective Labour Agreement, it became possible, in 1954, to establish classes of work (six in all) for all jobs with the aid of the Metal Industry Method. In principle, the approach of the MI method is the same as that of the NM. The practical differences are that, to make grading easier, the Metal Industry Method had a job list containing 900 key jobs, while the weighing factors vary from 2 to 8 (see table 3).

Considering the developments of the post-war 20–25 years, we can state that the 'controlled wages policy' has promoted the use of JE. Owing to the lack of available employees, most firms aimed at paying the highest possible wages within the limits set by the government; this required the use of JE. But also after the years of controlled wages policy its use kept growing steadily, chiefly because it was applied to non-manual jobs, that is to say, to clerical and managerial posts. With a view to those, separate systems were developed at first, to be followed more and more by systems with which *all* jobs existing in a particular firm could be graded and classed. If required, this bore only upon the area covered by the collective labour agreement, although this restriction was gradually removed. It was, among other factors, the purpose of the 'harmonization' of working conditions of 'blue collar' and 'white collar' workers which contributed to this (de Jong *et al.*, 1977; Colenbrander and Buningh, 1982). This harmonization caused a single set of salary classes to be used for all employees of a firm.

2.3. The extent of application around 1980

The above-mentioned Wage Administration Control Department (LTD) has, in the course of many years, collected data on the application of JE in Dutch work organizations. Initially these data referred to the so-called 'industrial reference group'. As from 1977, however, the investigations have involved firms employing 20 or more people, including the service sector; they did not include the civil service, public utilities, state-subsidized education, and agriculture. The data to be reported by us mainly concern the year 1980; inasfar as we are to make comparisons with other years, we shall go back no further than 1977.

The 1980 sample includes 3,4% of the total number of eligible firms (which is 4% of the total number of employees). In 23% of the organizations, some system of JE is applied, which concerns 33% of the workers. If we look at the develop-

Table 4. Percentage of employees for whom JE is applied, in firms/institutions having at least 20 employees: 1977–1980 (source: LTD).

Year	Employees under JE in %
1977	28
1978	33
1979	36
1980	33

Table 5. Percentage of firms/institutions using JE, according to size: 1979 and 1980 (source: LTD).

Number of employees in each organization	Number of organizations using JE (in %)	
	1979	*1980*
20–49	11	10
50–99	15	20
100–199	31	38
200–499	38	46
⩾ 500	66	52

ments in the immediately preceding years, we find the following data (see table 4).

There is no obvious explanation for the higher percentage in 1979, even less so when we realize that the 1979 figures concern a slightly lower percentage (21%) of work organizations than those of 1980. Possibly, this is a case of sample fluctuation.

Clearly, JE is applied more frequently in larger firms, relatively speaking. Table 5 contains the data on 1979 and 1980.

There are, however, remarkable differences between the branches of industry, both in 1979 and in 1980. In the service sector, JE is applied in 19% of the organizations, in construction in 2% of the firms, and in industry in 33%. Exceptions within the latter category are paint, chemicals, paper, rubber and thermoplastic industry (64% of the firms); another exception is distributive trade (14%).

If we split these data into categories of personnel, we see that in 25% of the organizations JE is used for all the employees, in 54% for the lower and middle categories, in 18% for the lower categories only, and in 3% of the organizations for higher managerial and staff personnel only. Here, too, there are a number of differences between the various branches.

It is an intriguing question, whether the application of JE causes a change in the level of payment, compared with employees whose jobs were not evaluated in this fashion. On this subject, data are available for 1980 with respect to six out of eight job levels distinguished by the LTD: there are hardly any differences

Table 6. Application of various JE systems in the years 1978–1980 (source: LTD).

System	Number of organizations using JE (in %)		
	1978	1979	1980
—Job classification system (FC) or Metal Industry method	31	25	36
—Normalized Method or Extended Normalized Method (UGM; ORBA)	35	35	27
—Bakkenist's system	6	10	8
—Ranking method	1	7	6
—Universal system of job evaluation (USF + USF '78)	6	7	5
—Hay's method	4	3	4
—Zuidema's system	0	3	2
—Other systems	8	3	7
—Individual plant systems	9	7	5
	100	100	100

at the lowest two levels, i.e. very simple, and rather simple work, respectively. At the next four levels (including managing or assistant-managing), the level of payment is always a little lower for employees working under JE. The 1979 figures show a similar picture for five job levels. The LTD fails to mention possible reasons for this.

The nature of the JE-systems applied is represented in table 6. It may be concluded from this table that point rating systems are used in more than 90% of the cases. Naturally, there are immense differences among branches: e.g. the FC system is applied almost exclusively in metal industry. However, this system will be replaced by the Integral System of Job Evaluation (ISF)—an example of a system applicable to all possible jobs in firms—combined with the Standard Method for Working Conditions (SAO) for the evaluation of inconveniences. For banks, moreover, the so-called Basys-system was developed (not represented in the table). Each system is applied in various ways. If we look at the more typical differences between the systems only, we can say that, compared with some ten years ago, the number of different JE systems is now on the decline.

2.4. Types of JE-systems

So far, this chapter has dealt mainly with JE-systems based on a point rating method. Table 6 showed that ranking, for instance, is another possibility. This section begins with a classification, to be followed by a discussion of several types of systems (for more details, see de Jong et al., 1977; Colenbrander and Buningh, 1982).

The first criterion for classification concerns *the number of job characteristics to be evaluated*. There is a distinction between:

1a. Various characteristics (see e.g. the NM);

1b. one characteristic (e.g. Jaques's time span);

1c. the job as a whole.

The second criterion concerns the *method of evaluation*:

2a. the definition of ranks;

2b. grouping in classes (the one-time current term 'work classification' was derived from this);

2c. point rating by means of one- or more-dimensional scales.

Each JE-system can be 'coded' in this way. Thus, the point rating method is denoted as 1a/2c. Figure 1 represents the various current methods.

More detailed information on the structure and nature of a great many JE-systems may be found in De Jong *et al.* (1977) and in Colenbrander and Buningh (1982). ILO (1977) provides a concise survey, as do Wing Easton (1980) and Scholten (1981). We shall here discuss, in brief, three somewhat 'exceptional' methods: Job Classification (as applied by the Dutch government), Time Span (Jaques) and Decision Band (Paterson).

Figure 1 makes clear that *Job Classification* means: grouping jobs into a number of pre-defined classes, on the basis of an evaluation of the jobs as a whole. In the civil service this method is applied up to and including the rank of director-general (Under-Secretary of State). This so-called 'comparative reasoned estimation' has six main groups, each containing three to seven levels. For example, the characteristic of main group III contains the following: 'Those

		2. Evaluation method		
		2a. Ranking	2b. Grouping in classes	2c. Scale or table
1. Evaluated characteristics or entire job	1a. Several characteristics	1a/2a. ranking as to various characteristics		point rating method
	1b. One characteristic		1b/2b. decision band technique (Paterson)	1b/2c. time span method (Jaques)
	1c. Job as a whole	1c/2a. job ranking	1c/2b. job classification	

Figure 1. Various methods of job evaluation.

activities for which capability can, as a rule, be achieved only on the basis of completed secondary occupational training or general education...'. Unlike the growing trend in most other JE-systems, the level of preliminary training is of great importance in this method. The jobs are classed by means of a definition of types of job for each section of a department, and of key or reference jobs. In the end, 18 salary scales are available.

Jaques developed his *Time Span* method during the many years of his association with the London 'Glacier Metal Company' (see e.g. Jaques, 1956, 1961, 1964). According to Jaques, it is nothing but seemingly objective and seemingly logical arguments which are used in negotiations about settling wages, whereas, in his opinion, it is really a matter of emotional considerations. The disadvantage of the usual job evaluation methods is that non-comparable and non-quantifiable criteria are applied to different jobs. Jaques observed that the factor of time plays an essential part in someone's level of job and income. Some examples: the higher his job level, the longer the period over which he receives payment (hourly, weekly, or monthly payment), the longer the breaking-in time, the longer the term of notice in case of discharge, etc. This factor is the core of Jaques' yardstick for defining the level of a job: *responsibility*.

His distinction of two sorts of task is important in this context. Each task has:
1. A 'discretionary content'. That part of the task which the job holder has to carry out at his own discretion.
2. 'Prescribed limits'. The explicit and implicit rules, signs, customs, etc. which the job holder is expected to observe. They establish the limits within which he can use his own discretion.

The higher the job level, the larger will be the discretionary content. Typical of such responsibility that the job incumbent has, is the maximum time span to act at his own discretion, before his superior can assess the quality of his actions. For lower level manual and clerical jobs, for example, the maximum time span—resulting from job analysis—appears to be between one hour and one month, whereas it can be as much as two years or more at top levels. In this connection, Jaques also designed methods for analysing relative salary rates within a firm and the development of an employee's income in the course of several years.

The instruments constructed by Jaques are apt examples of a multi-purpose system, as they can be applied, e.g., in the field of career planning and staffing policy (see section 4). In The Netherlands, the time span method is applied in work organizations on a limited scale only; comparative studies have been done in particular by Wijnberg (1965) and Hazekamp (1966, 1970). The latter pointed out the strong correlations between UGM (see table 6) and time span results. In other countries, research was done by e.g. Atchison and French (1967), Goodman (1967), Richardson (1971) and Kvålseth and Crossman (1974).

Several of Jaques's remarkable theoretical premises have not been discussed in the preceding paragraphs. He believes, for instance, that every human being *unconsciously* knows what level of work he is capable of, what level of work he actually has, what level of payment is equitable, etc. These ideas can be made *conscious* under specific conditions. At present we shall have to confine ourselves to a reference to the available literature; critical comment can be found in, e.g. Thierry (1969).

Paterson shares Jaques's opinion that a single characteristic can be regarded as the basis of the evaluation of all kinds, and all levels, of jobs: *decision making*. He distinguishes six *decision bands* which are essentially different as regards type and level of the decision. Thus, the highest band (E) is characterized by policy-making decisions made by top management; band C is concerned with interpretive decisions at an intermediate level of management within the limits set by the higher band (D); band A, the lowest level but one, concerns operation decisions about when, how and where a process is to be made operational. With the exception of the lowest band (O), each band has two levels, the higher one coordinating the lower. This creates a hierarchical structure of authority on 11 levels. Besides, there are a number of sublevels (see further: Paterson, 1972, 1981). In The Netherlands, this method is used only in a small number of organizations; Great Britain, Canada and South Africa have more examples of it. Research has taken place on a limited scale only.

2.5. Several trends

To conclude this section, we wish to discuss several developments of the present day in the application of JE. As a rule, they are of a very gradual nature: this caused the LTD (1982) to stop publishing annual reports on the use of JE, and to issue reports covering more than one year instead. Still, it is possible to spot certain trends.

Firstly, the number of job characteristics in use is on the decline, partly as a result of the introduction of altered JE-systems (de Jong *et al.*, 1977; Colenbrander and Buningh, 1982). Apart from that, various systems combine the factors into 3–7 main characteristics (Hazekamp, 1982). Generally they are concerned with:
—knowledge and experience;
—responsibility;
—coping with problems;
—supervision;
—social skills;
—working conditions.

It is also apparent that there has been a shift from a work-analytic approach, which distinguishes the concrete, quantifiable characteristics of a job (such as cycle time, precision in working, etc.), to an approach which is often of a more technical-organizational nature: this provides general definitions which the job *incumbent* is expected to meet. It is also remarkable that the feature of education is gradually losing significance—with the exception of the civil service's system, as mentioned earlier—whereas the complexity of the work is emphasized more (see e.g. Kordaszewski, 1969; Malotaux and Dammers, 1978).

A second trend is concerned with the evaluation of the inconveniences related to the work. These were part of the systems of the NM and the Metal Industry Method. A development started around 1964, by which the evaluation of inconveniences was separated from the system, and separate allowances were introduced (as the separate code in the Metal Industry Method). This practice is more common at present: the ISF/SAO in metal industry, and the Basys-system in banking business are examples of it.

It is apparent that the appreciation of inconvenient working conditions has become a highly delicate matter, and that, partly due to that, it changes more easily than the evaluation of other factors. It may be related to the extent to which inconveniences occur, but also—and often much more so—to society's acceptance of inconvenient conditions which in themselves have not or hardly changed at all.

As Hazekamp (1982) says, JE has come to be a matter of millions of guilders. We need only think of the enormous investment of time, which is required of a great many people and groups of people, for the sake of preparing, introducing, applying and maintaining JE (see also section 3.1). Besides, in most cases the cost of (individual) transitional arrangements are considerable. Transitional measures are taken, for example, when the effects of JE cause certain jobs to be rated lower than before, or when certain jobs become redundant in case of a merger or reorganization, etc. As a rule the employees concerned will receive their 'original' income for a couple of years. This leads us to the third trend: the revival of the 'grid approach', which is more time-saving. It implies that a considerable number of jobs, scattered all over the organization, are analysed and evaluated, after which all the remaining jobs can be ordered by means of this grid. If a particular case gives rise to disagreement, that job will be analysed and evaluated in the usual, more elaborate fashion.

The fourth and last trend is concerned with the expansion of the range of application. In section 2.3 we hinted at the developments in some branches of industry. Here we are concerned mainly with the 'vertical' expansion: more and more middle and higher level managers undergo JE, owing to the application of either an 'integral' system or a 'specific' system. Apart from that, JE is increasingly becoming part of the income policy for professional people (like physicians, accountants, etc.) and for the self-employed; section 4 will deal with this further.

The trends illustrated above are directly connected, on the whole, to the nature of JE-systems; the fourth item was concerned with the range of application. However, some other trends can be traced, e.g. as to the procedures applied, the employees' reactions to JE, etc. These will be dealt with in the following sections.

3. JE PROCEDURES

3.1. From description to evaluation

In connection with the NM, section 2.2 provided a concise description of a rather common procedure. We shall now go into that in more detail (but see also Livy, 1975; de Jong *et al.*, 1977; Wing Easton, 1980; Scholten, 1981; Colenbrander and Buningh, 1982). It should be remembered, though, that deviations may occur in practice, depending on the JE-system in question (e.g. job classification), on conceptions of those who provide the system (often an organization consultancy bureau), on the branch (the question whether a single system is applied to the entire branch, as in the printing trade), on local traditions, etc.

It has been observed before that key jobs are frequently used. If not yet available for the branch concerned, they must be selected in each organization, in such a way as to make possible a suitable comparison with the jobs in all other organizations, which are to be described and evaluated.

In the first stage the job is *described*, in which the following distinctions are generally made:

—Recording the name of the job, the relevant department, the job's purpose, and its place in the organization (in relation to higher, lower and same level posts to which it is linked).

—Defining the relevant tasks of the job, contacts, responsibilities, etc.

—Describing it in greater detail, mostly for each 'characteristic' of the system applied.

For this purpose questionnaires, interviews and such are used. All kinds of difficulties may arise when actually implementing the description, which may turn this stage into one of the weakest of the entire cycle from description to evaluation. Apart from the literature already mentioned, we recommend the U.S. Employment Service's handbook (U.S. Dept. of Labor, 1972), which is also useful to various other countries.

The second stage, in the point rating systems, is that of the *analysis* and *grading* of each characteristic in that particular system. The extent to which a particular characteristic applies to a job is established and translated into a number. In the older systems, these scores were multiplied by the relevant *weighing factor*; in the majority of present-day systems the weighing factors are already included in the grading schemes. The total score of the job can now be computed, usually by means of simply adding up.

After that, the ranks are established for a number of 'evaluated' jobs, often by impartial judges, which results are then compared to those of the sum total of points. If there are no discrepancies, the job category or class is established. The decision as to the appropriate salary class is reserved to the negotiations between the employer and the trade unions on the wages policy.

There are many parties who have interests in the preparation and introduction of JE, or in making drastic changes in the way it is applied. Apart from the employees concerned, there is the Works Council. Article 27, paragraph 1 of the Works Councils Act says: 'The employer needs to have the Works Council's consent to any proposed decision to establish, alter or to annul... a system of remuneration or job evaluation ...' (for further detail, see Schoute, 1982). Other interested parties are management, the department of Personnel or Social Affairs, trade unions, employers' association, and often also an organization consultancy bureau (see also Scholten, 1979).

Because there are so many different interests and interested parties involved in the preparation, introduction and application of JE, the practice of it frequently gives rise to all kinds of objections and aversion. Generally, committees are installed to deal with, or if possible prevent, these problems, but not in the least also with a view to enhancing the participation of all those concerned (see section 3.2). Here, too, all kinds of differences occur in practice, e.g. in the composition and the authority of committees (see e.g. Brons, 1982). It is essential that a steering committee be installed and that members of the works council take part in it. Some of this committee's tasks would be the coordination of various activities (each of which may or may not be covered by a separate committee), and control of the progress in general. This (or any other) committee can first make a selection from alternative systems, unless there exists an overall system in the entire branch or a specific tradition, or unless preliminary agreements were made with the trade union, etc. The next important matter is to supply information to the employees on the nature of the system to be applied. Committees can play equally important roles in the ensuing stages and in cases of employees appealing against certain job descriptions, against the ultimately proposed evaluations of jobs, against their classification, etc.

3.2. Participation

It appeared from research done during the second half of the sixties in the metal industry, that employees, as they said, were seldom involved in the evaluation of their jobs (Thierry, 1968). It is a striking fact that, during the last five to ten years, consultants and other agencies that supply JE systems have strongly emphasized the employees' participation during each of the stages distinguished in the previous section (see also Scholten, 1979). The committees mentioned in that section exemplify this phenomenon. It is often said that the suppliers and users of a system attach greater importance to its *acceptability*—and hence to the procedures concerning the design and introduction of JE—than to its measuring properties (see e.g. de Jong *et al.*, 1977; Hazekamp, 1982; Colenbrander and Buningh, 1982). Section 6 will deal further with the possible range and significance of the participation at stake here. For the present we confine ourselves to some comments on its possible form; we shall do so, on the basis of Hazekamp's distinction (1982) between the independence model and the expert model in applying JE.

The first model implies that each employee, whether or not under supervision, describes and evaluates his job himself. No doubt this improves personal involvement and the probability that the results will be accepted, but Hazekamp points out that the authority both of the parties engaged in the negotiation rounds and of the works council have to be taken into account. The JE system must not be too complicated either; still, it makes high demands upon the employee's stylistic and other skills. Considerable differences in e.g. the construction of sentences and the choice of words are quite problematic for those in charge of coordination and internal adjustment. Similar problems may occur as regards the evaluation. Besides, employees lodging an appeal may become problematic, in the sense that sometimes the internally acceptable rates turn out to be not quite in harmony with the going rates on the labour market (the so-called external criterion). The same holds for 'panels' of employees, although this may have the added setback of higher level employees' dominating influence (see also Livy, 1975). On the grounds of these considerations, Hazekamp opts for the expert model: in this model, it is ultimately the experts who decide about the description and the evaluation of jobs, provided that the results are open to discussion and answered to the employees.

In practice, the procedures are widely different in this respect. An important question, in our eyes, is what objectives are chosen in the preparation and introduction of JE. Is it, as was suggested in section 2.1, first and foremost a matter of ordering the jobs for the sake of setting relative pay rates, using an internal as well as an external criterion? Or is the acceptability of the results of primary importance, in which case the internal relations of the organization, and hence the extent of participation, have higher priority? The answer to this question is decisive for the mutual adjustment of social and system-technical requirements (for further detail, see this handbook, ch. 4.5) as well as for the role the consultant is going to play, between the extremes of an expert and a facilitator (see also this handbook, ch. 4.9).

The question as to the objectives of JE is important from another perspective, too; this matter will be dealt with in the next section.

4. MULTI-PURPOSE APPLICATION

In this section we shall deal with the concept of multi-purpose application in a wide sense. First we shall discuss the use of JE in an area other than that of setting relative pay rates among jobs, namely personnel and organization policy. The second sub-section will treat of the proposed role of JE in the context of a national income policy. In the third sub-section we shall pay attention to the significance of JE for equal payment for female employees in relation to their male colleagues.

4.1. Personnel and organization policy

The application of JE in these areas is also denoted by such terms as 'job profiling' (Commission of Experts, 1959; Buningh and Colenbrander, 1982) and 'tool of management' (LTD, 1982). As Kleinendorst (1982) puts it, this is a matter of a systematic and planned use of job-data, assembled by means of JE, for other purposes than wages policy. These may be recruitment, selection, personal appraisal, career planning, education policy, communication, restructuring of jobs, and organizational design (see also Hazekamp, 1982).

According to the LTD's information on 1980, approx. 6% of the work organizations concerned—which is over 25% of the number of organizations applying JE—reported that JE was used, not only for the sake of payment, but also with a view to one or more of the above-mentioned themes. In general they appear to be the larger firms, especially in the chemical branch, in the service sector, and in the transport industry and metal industry. The figures on 1979 are not much different. It is a remarkable fact that, relatively speaking, in 1980 multi-purpose application is more frequent with the use of such JE-systems as Hay, USF, and Zuidema (cf. table 6, section 2.3). In this connection, Hazekamp points out that if one system is used for an entire industrial branch, without specific adaptations for each individual enterprise, the range of possible multi-purpose applications is very limited. In that case the job-data are bound to be too global and insufficiently geared to the specific nature and composition of the tasks and jobs existing in a particular firm.

There is a striking lack of literature reporting of experiences with such applications or of results of research studies (exceptions are e.g. Kleinendorst, 1982; Bindels, 1982; Zwarts, 1982). Kleinendorst supposes that the revival of interest—indeed, it is not new (see also Lawshe and Satter, 1944; Lijftogt, 1966)—may partly be related to the tendency towards decentralization of the negotiations on working conditions, to the high cost of developing and introducing a JE-system (see also Hazekamp, 1982), and possibly to rivalry among consultancy agencies supplying JE-systems. In his own research, Kleinendorst found that a great many firms, which were supposed to practice multi-purpose application of JE according to the LTD-data on 1979, did not in fact do so, although they intended to, in future.

Those four cases which could be detected, reveal first of all that the most detailed applications refer to structuring tasks. Thus, job descriptions were 'cut up' into tiny particles of tasks, so that new (enriched) jobs could be created by means of certain rules of combination. This was felt to be necessary because of previous mergers or reorganizations, because of the need for greater employability of specialists, or for better career opportunities. Other examples are concerned with developing staffing policy.

Kleinendorst's results also make clear that there has not been much development in the applications with respect to personnel administration and personnel policy (selection, appraisal, etc.). He reaches an important conclusion when he says that the multi-purpose character of JE in those four organizations is to be considered as gratuitous, as a side-effect: JE would never have been introduced if not for the purpose of setting relative pay rates. This explains his scepticism as to the future of JE as far as multi-purpose application is concerned. In his opinion, one of the essential conditions is the quality of personnel and organization policy: is there a formulation of concrete objectives, are there means available for policy making, and to what extent are independent initiatives to be realized, etc.

With Kleinendorst, we point out, in this context, that the data collected for the purpose of setting pay rates are not automatically suitable for any other application. For instance, the degree of detail can vary widely in job descriptions: on the one hand they can be extremely detailed—which carries the risk of soon becoming obsolete as a result of alterations—on the other hand the indications may be (too) global, e.g. the level qualifications. They may also vary in consistency (as in the independence model). In addition, it is a question of type of application: data for the purpose of selection are not necessarily identical to the data required for structuring tasks.

4.2. JE and income policy

In the middle of the seventies the Dutch government published the Interim Note on Income Policy. One of the things discussed in it, is the government's responsibility concerning decisions about the rates of pay for all groups of society. On a basis of fundamental equality for all, it states that differences in income may be caused by factors which can be compensated for. Such factors refer to the efforts and sacrifices required for getting an income, such as, in particular: the duration of work, inconvenient conditions, strenuousness and responsibility (see also Pen and Tinbergen, 1977). It also should be accepted, for all practical purposes, that certain factors which cannot be compensated for, in particular talent and education, affect the rates of pay.

The Interim Note assigns a significant role to JE (see also e.g. de Galan, 1973; Roscam Abbing, 1974) in making these viewpoints operational, especially in order to make particular sets of occupations and jobs mutually comparable. On working out these ideas in detail and giving advice on them, several members of the (Wages Commission of the) Labour Foundation—composed of representatives of the employers' federations and the trade unions—initially had in mind a single national JE-system. In time it was felt, rather, that the objectives mentioned might also be achieved by means of a small set of JE-systems existing side by side. Table 6 (section 2.3) makes clear that about 1980 already a very limited number of dominant JE-systems was in fact used (naturally with variations among them).

In section 2 we observed the JE is increasingly applied, though gradually, to middle and higher managerial levels, and that several business branches (e.g. the banks) are in the process of its introduction or expansion. Therefore, the views expressed in the Interim Note have, in the last few years, been particularly relevant to the 'independent' professions—medical doctors, medical specialists, accountants, lawyers, real estate agents—and, possibly, will be for the self-employed. In this context, the Provisional Act on standardization of professional and occupational incomes (1981) is highly significant. The report of the study group installed for that purpose (WUN, 1982) gives a broad sketch of how JE can be applied for that purpose. What it comes down to, briefly, is that for a particular set of occupations a comparison-job in the Civil Service is selected, and that the income related to it is defined as the so-called standard income for those occupations. Those salaries can be adjusted, e.g. due to pension and other social duties, special hazards, exceptional conditions, etc.

It is not surprising that for a great many years this has led to (labour) political arguments. Broadly speaking, the trade unions are in favour of the advocated income policy, whereas the employers' federations state that, in principle, JE is always geared to the relations within a specific firm, and consequently does not lend itself to nationwide application. Various associations of professionals appear to support this last idea. It is contrary to e.g. Van Wijngaarden's (1982) opinion who, partly on the basis of a study on the criteria for justification of income differences carried out among a sample of the Dutch population, advocates a national JE-system.

We shall briefly return to this subject when dealing with the results of empirical research on JE, in section 5.

4.3. JE and equal pay for female employees

A separate chapter of this handbook (4.12) is devoted to the issue of 'women and work', examining in how far the treatment of women on the labour market, on the job and as regards career opportunities is unequal to that of men. In this sub-section we restrict ourselves to the possible role of JE in aiming at equal pay in return for (virtually) equivalent work, regardless of sex.

The equal payment Act (1975) annuls any individual labour contract in which the agreed payment is lower than 'equal' payment. In case of assumed inequality the law requires that the advice of the 'Commission for equal treatment of men and women at work' be asked. Such recommendation is not

Table 7. Discriminative viewpoints in JE (source: Equal Opportunities Commission, England).

Viewpoints (score 1–10)	Maintenance fitter	Nurse
Skills		
Experience in job	10	1
Training	5	7
Responsibility		
For money	0	0
For equipment and machinery	8	3
For safety	3	6
For work done by others	3	0
Effort		
Lifting requirement	4	2
Strength required	7	2
Sustained physical effort	5	1
Conditions		
Physical environment	6	0
Working position	6	0
Hazards	7	0
Total	64	22

absolute, however. If the employer does not act upon the recommendation, a legal claim can be filed, for payment, with the cantonal court or with a committee of settlement provided by a Collective Labour Agreement (see Schoute, 1982). The Commission for equal treatment makes extensive use of JE. If, for example, a female employee thinks she gets paid less than a male colleague in a similar position, her view can be 'tested' by means of a JE-system.

This does not mean that all problems are thus solved. De Bruyn and Kannegieter (1981) point out that the law allows only comparisons within a branch of industry. They wonder what happens to women in the so-called unmixed jobs, i.e. jobs usually held by the members of one sex only (as e.g. in canteens). The British Equal Opportunities Commission (1981) mentions other barriers. To begin with, it refers to the tradition of giving different titles to jobs done by men and women, even though the work content is the same. Examples: shop assistant (women) vs. salesmen (men); operator vs. technician; secretary vs. administrator. Secondly, a JE-system can reveal a male bias in the nature of the chosen viewpoints. Table 7 gives an example of it.

This table does not contain the weighing factors; these, too, can be biased, according to the commission. Comparable difficulties have been spotted in various other countries, such as Ireland, Sweden, Finland and West Germany.

Schippers (1982) has worked out the observations of the LTD in 1975, concerning the wages of men and women. There is little significance in absolute differences between either, since women hold fewer high jobs. As regards direct wage differences—different wages for the same job—he observes that from 1976 to 1979 women earned approx. 25% less then men. There was great variance, though: men earned less in over 25% of the cases. However, the indirect differences turn out to be considerably greater: men and women have equal jobs and equal pay, in this aspect, but the utilization of their qualifications—their 'productivity'—varies. Schippers found that women 'need' more training and/or experience to earn the same wages as men. In other words: women having more experiences and education (compared with male colleagues in the same jobs) do not always earn more, but often the same amount, or even less.

We conclude this review by remarking that the application of JE may certainly contribute to the purpose of equal payment for male and female employees, but that great obstacles exist nevertheless. They are partly beyond the reach of JE; but they can partly influence the JE-system in question, especially in case of a male bias forming part of viewpoints and/or weighing factors.

5. THEORY AND RESEARCH

5.1. Introduction

The reader will have noticed that the preceding sections only briefly mentioned the results of scientific research, and that virtually no theories about (aspects of) JE have been presented. It was rather the various aspects of 'the vicissitudes of JE in practice', as well as aspects of system-technique and procedure, which were discussed.

These features are typical of the developments connected with JE; all the same, this section will deal with the major lines of research. As will become clear, several Dutch psychologists, particularly in the fifties, occupied themselves with important aspects of various problems; after that the interest rapidly faded away, until quite recently. Nor is there appreciable enthusiasm in other countries, for that matter, among psychologists, sociologists and those in business administration. However, there has been more attention in various East and West European countries than in The Netherlands for system-technical changes and innovations. Apparently, this course of affairs has had little or no influence, at least in this country, on the everyday practice, which simply went its own way. Evidently, JE 'works'. Nevertheless, it appeared from the preceding sections that JE is not only applied on an increasing scale, but also that its consequences—if only as regards payment—can be severe for employees, and will therefore be considered of great importance by them. Moreover, apparently a great many people, psychologists among them, are involved with the introduction and application of JE in all sorts of organizations.

It is our opinion, therefore, that more systematic attention for JE by W&O psychologists is essential. In the next sub-section we shall discuss several perspectives which have in fact been taken. Finally, in section 6 we shall suggest what other contributions might be expected of W&O psychology.

5.2. Various perspectives

JE has often been labelled as 'objective' and 'scientific'. We have some objections against this qualification. For, surveying the entire 'course' of events—that is, from the description up to and including the evaluation of the job, eventually— we observe that frequently, depending on the type of system and the chosen procedure, parts of the system do certainly not meet this qualification. In most of the perspectives touched on below some of those parts are referred to.

At the time when experience was gained with the provisional version of the NM and with the Metal Industry Method—the fifties; see section 2.2—various Dutch psychologists had critical questions to ask as regards the premises and characteristics of JE (see e.g. Lijftogt, 1966, app. I and VI). De Groot (1953) found, to his approval, that in the NM, the aim was to avoid psychological traits forming the starting point for the selection of job characteristics, but he also made clear that this never completely succeeded. The question of what an individual is capable of achieving, is after all a psychological one, he says. Thus, a point rating system is bound to impress the psychologist as '... measuring and adding up traits, be it in a veiled way...'. Besides, there is a certain would-be rationality: the differentiation of pay which is partly determined by irrational factors, will hardly change as a result of the application of a sort of system such as NM, but it will be justified by it. With various other psychologists of those days De Groot regrets that the point rating method is used almost exclusively, at the expense of, for instance, ranking. Especially he calls attention to a method of paired comparisons, either of jobs as a whole, or of a particular part, or per viewpoint (see also figure 1, section 2.4). More research will have to inform us as to the reliability and validity of the various methods. Both De Groot and Da Silva (1951) stress the fact that JE can be regarded as a *theory* which is to account for the practice. This leads to the hypothesis that the values of jobs which result from grading and weighing correspond with a sense of justice, or with the existing relative pay rates insofar as they are felt to be fair. To what extent this hypothesis is supported will have to be tested in research. This is also true for the question whether JE will be able to account for the relative pay rates in the course of a number of years.

Furthermore, many authors have referred to the *lack of precision in measuring techniques* in the NM. The grading scores for each viewpoint had been intended, by the Experts Commission (1952), as ranking data (between jobs).

However, the actual use—multiplication by a weighing factor (also a rank number)—led to the assumption that the measuring was done at least on a level of intervals. Then again, the resulting total scores were regarded by the commission as rank indications, etc. The Experts Commission has never given a satisfactory answer to these inconsistencies (for further detail, see Lijftogt, 1966), nor has it ever replied to the questions put by De Groot or to the suggestions he put forward for testing hypotheses.

Wiegersma (1958) called attention to another difficulty. On the grounds of a factor analysis of job-data obtained by means of the NM, he demonstrated that the characteristics of knowledge and independence did not only have a high degree of correlation, but that they, jointly with risk of damage and dexterity with material and machinery, were much more decisive for the differences in scores between the various jobs than all other factors taken together. The factor constituted by these four characteristics was interpreted as *schooling*. Apparently the significance of several characteristics just looks a bit different. Comparable conclusions had previously been reported by Lawshe (1945; Lawshe and Satter, 1944; Lawshe and Maleski, 1946; Lawshe and Alessi, 1946), and are later heard of from Burckhardt and Kallina (1967) and Hazewinkel (1967).

The latter author has demonstrated, in an ingenious experiment, that experienced job-analysts can be misled in the evaluation by *global indications* on a particular job (as e.g. its place in the organization, its status, its present rate of pay) which in themselves may have little or nothing to do with its content. Thus it appeared, that analysts who, in addition, received fictional (though not unrealistic) information on the jobs which had to be graded, generally were systematic in producing results different from those obtained without the additional information.

It is a remarkable fact that these and other critical comments have not really affected the everyday practice. In Varkevisser's (1967) opinion, the effect of the additional information given to the job-analysts in Hazewinkel's experiment, had remained within reasonable limits. The Experts Commission of those days, says Lijftogt, did not only avoid the psychological approach, it also avoided psychologists taking a seat on the commission. From the angle of wages policy, JE was a success: it was often heard, at that time, that the system 'worked'. This general climate, in all probability, has contributed to the considerable decline in the scientists' interest in JE.

Roughly along the same line as the authors mentioned above, Livy (1975) regards JE as primarily a *system of assessment*. This exposes its reliability and validity to highly comparable 'threats' (for further detail, see this Handbook, ch. 2.4). He poses the important question as regards which criterion JE is to be (predictively) valid. A possible criterion could be the relative value of jobs (however much defined), but equally possible would be an income distribution which is socially fair (see also de Groot, 1953). Another possible criterion is equitable payment in return for work performed. Livy points out that in connection with the question as to the validity of JE, it has hardly ever occurred to anyone to take as a criterion the degree of job satisfaction among employees, or their level of performance.

In The Netherlands, virtually no connection has been made between JE and what can, to a certain extent, be considered as a classical field of W&O psychology: *the analysis of tasks and jobs*. The instruments mentioned here— and which are to be distinguished along general lines, henceforth—have not been designed for the purpose of setting relative pay rates among (groups of) jobs. But this does not mean that the results of the analysis of tasks and jobs cannot be used for that purpose. And, indeed, there are many examples of it, some of them in the USA. It is true that it takes a long time to develop such an instrument, or to adapt an existing method for another linguistic or cultural area, or for other jobs, etc. But its use may provide for a likely solution for a number of problems concerning JE which have been referred to here.

Job-analysis can distinguish, for example, between job-oriented activities (such as drilling, weaving, cleaning) and worker-oriented activities (observation, decision-making, action, etc.). An apt example of this approach is the 'Position Analysis Questionnaire' (PAQ) developed by McCormick *et al.* (1969). It has frequently been used for research. A German version of it has been developed (the FAA) by Frieling *et al.* (1973; see also Hoyos and Frieling, 1977). Rohmert and Rutenfranz (1975) added to the PAQ some ergonomic aspects. In The Netherlands, research studies as to the PAQ are only occasionally carried out.

Hemphill (1960) was one of those to follow the job-oriented approach in the development of his 'Executive Position Description Questionnaire' (EPDQ). The same is true of the 'Management Position Description Questionnaire' designed by Tornow and Pinto (1976) and the 'Supervisor Task Description Questionnaire' (Dowell and Wexley, 1978). EPDQ research is rare in our country.

We finally mention in this context some instruments for measuring task and organizational characteristics, such as the 'Requisite Task Attributes Index' (Turner and Lawrence, 1965) and the 'Job Diagnostic Survey' (Hackman and Oldham, 1975; for The Netherlands, see also Algera, 1981; this Handbook, ch. 2.3).

One of the few Dutch sociologists to have been systematically engaged in JE is Scholten (1979, 1981; see also Drukker and Liefferink, 1981). He qualifies some of the topics discussed in this section as criticism concerning 'technical aspects of measuring' (1979, p. 32 ff.). This is an unfortunate phrase, for two reasons: firstly because, in addition to some 'technical' points, admittedly, rather essential arguments were put forth concerning both content and methodology of JE. Secondly, since, as it is, the users of JE tend to look upon matters concerning the 'measuring technique' as less important.

In addition to what was said in section 2.1, Scholten regards JE in the first place as an instrument to make *controllable* certain social questions regarding status and remuneration: JE is an example of 'regulation', i.e. of bureaucratization. It enables the trade unions to control their members, the employers their employees. This control is only partially effective: according to Scholten, important topics—such as workers having more say in matters of payment— are often discarded by the labour-political partners. All sorts of informal ways of escape are created, negotiations need to be continued every time again (e.g. about deviations). Moreover, such control frequently makes for rigidity.

In our opinion Scholten's attempt to integrate the significance of JE into a more comprehensive theory—viz. concerning processes of bureaucratization in organizations—deserves to be followed by others. But it must be understood, on the one hand, that only part of the problems mentioned in this chapter can be viewed from the angle of regulation, and, on the other hand, that this is not a highly specific angle. In other words, there are very few phenomena conceivable in organizations which cannot be viewed (partially) from a bureaucratic angle.

Although there is a great deal of experience with JE in The Netherlands, accounts of them have been published only very rarely. We do not only refer to comparative research studies—e.g. into the consequences of JE for career patterns, staffing policy, performance, motivation, attitudes to payment, etc.— but also to e.g. case-studies rendering the process of introducing JE, or of shifting to a different JE-system. However, the situation seems to be changing somewhat (apart from the information in section 4.1, see Koopman-Iwema and Thierry, 1981b; Wiersum, 1982; Buningh and Colenbrander, 1982). We shall briefly consider five themes:

—Many complaints have been heard about the lack of perspicuity in the structure of JE, partly due to a host of deviations geared to individual (or groups of) workers, as a result of mergers, technological changes, alterations in the labour market, etc.

—Among employees there is an appreciable need for more information on, more control of the various stages in JE.

—JE causes rigidity: individual wage development is fixed, and changes in the content of the job are much too slow in leading to adjustment of the description, analysis and evaluation.

—The problems related to JE closely resemble those formerly resulting from the application of payment by result systems (for further detail, see this Handbook, ch. 4.11).

—The importance of differentiation, e.g. of payment, increases.

The latter theme has received more attention elsewhere (Thierry, 1982). The issue is whether those phenomena, which in themselves are a reason for making more distinctions than usual, can be incorporated into the 'regular' application of a JE-system, or whether these phenomena make us question the *applicability* of JE in principle. These phenomena relate to, among other things, technological developments (both in production processes and in providing services): since most organizations supply more than one product and/or service, these developments may be dissimilar in nature and may consequently cause unequal kinds of effects on JE (e.g. decline and enrichment of the task, simultaneously). Other phenomena are concerned with the perspectives on the organization of work (e.g. redesigning tasks, semi-autonomous groups), with the way in which a 'special' JE-system may emphasize an organization's singular place and position (e.g. with respect to the larger concern, or the industrial branch as a whole), with the desire, among employees, for increased difference in payment (e.g., according to performance; see also Metsch, 1980; Buningh and Colenbrander, 1982; Wijn, 1982; Vinke, 1982), etc. Another example is the multi-purpose applications mentioned in section 4. We believe that these phenomena do not receive sufficient attention, that is to say, as far as consequences for the application of JE are concerned.

The answer to the principal question as to the applicability of JE is, naturally, not only essential for the way in which these phenomena of differentiation are going to be dealt with, but also for the function of JE in setting relative pay rates, in each individual organization as well as in the framework of national income relations.

In the last section we shall go into more detail as to the possible contributions to be made by W&O psychology.

6. JE IN THE FUTURE

6.1. The use of JE

Looking at the future, we expect that, in The Netherlands, the application of JE will grow, be it gradually. On the one hand, this will imply an increased number of organizations (and branches of industry) using JE, as well as more management levels concerned with JE. On the other hand, more and more groups of professional people will become involved with JE. Particularly with a view to the cost, it seems likely that global methods (as the grid approach, general level indications, etc.) will gain favour. If this were to be the case, we shall probably have little to expect in the nature of growth in the multi-purpose application of JE in the area of organization and personnel policy.

A second aspect is concerned with the significance of JE for (national) income policy: we expect that it will be especially (labour) political consider-ations which will affect the developments in this respect, much less so the practical experience of JE. Nevertheless, there are two aspects to this matter which deserve our attention. One is the question in how far the customary evaluation of viewpoints (and weighing factors) would have to be altered, particularly from the idea of a 'modally humane task' (WRR, 1977). The essential theme of this is that jobs lacking certain qualifications—as e.g. any degree of autonomy; the opportunity to use important skills—or having certain negative characteristics (e.g. monotonous work), must be paid higher. Buningh and Colenbrander report that over 40% of their respondents are in favour of a separate award for monotonous work. If the notion of the modally humane task is ever accepted, an important role will undoubtedly be assigned to JE.

The other aspect is concerned with the phenomena of differentiation, discussed in the previous section. It has appeared from recent studies (see e.g. Koopman-Iwema and Thierry, 1981b; Kleinendorst, 1982) that all kinds of informal, and partly illegal, escapes are made in the application of JE. Some examples: lengthening the salary scale for a particular category of employees; inserting preliminary and intermediate scales; creating an 'individual' position; blowing up job descriptions. It is to be expected that, as JE becomes increasingly important as a basis for determining income and income distribution, the urge to find such ways of escape will grow. It is therefore necessary to focus on the opportunity for a more decentralized application of JE, organization-wise or per facility.

6.2. Contributions from W&O psychology

The first, and rather obvious, contribution is concerned with designing strategies and tactics for the preparation and introduction of JE, while making use of what has been learned in other fields of organizational change and development (see also this Handbook, ch. 4.4 and 4.9). A second contribution is performing research studies on attitudes, wants, expectations and motives among employees, previous to, as well as during the application of a JE-system. This, too, might be called a 'classical' contribution, yet it appeared in the foregoing text that this course has seldom been taken. In that context special attention might be paid to the meanings of payment to each worker, to the changes they may undergo (e.g. by comparing the attitudes, after due experience with JE, to the expectations and views held at the start of the preparations), and to the aspects which affect these. The model, presented in chapter 4.11 (present Handbook) on determinants of the meanings of payment may prove to be of use in this respect.

In the third place, such a study might deal with the question to what extent the actual functioning of JE corresponds to the objectives of the groups and individuals concerned (see section 3). In this connection the theme of participation might be concentrated on. We suspect that participation, despite the pains many have taken, can generally play but a modest role, as regards content, because 'only' the procedures (and sometimes the method) are suitable for it. If employees were to ask for drastic changes, e.g. in the mutual weighing of characteristics which would cause the jobs to be ranked other than 'usual', and which would therefore entail different wage relations, then the so-called 'external' criterion would prevent it: the wage and salary structure is supposed to correspond to what is current on the labour market.

A fourth contribution is the further development of instruments for measuring the characteristics of jobs and tasks. Apart from what was said in section 5.2 on this matter, we wish to point out that although the decisions about wage grades and salary classes are reserved to the partners in labour politics, this 'coupling' usually is so evident to the employees, that the quality of both the job description and the job analysis can be negatively affected by it. The use of the previously mentioned instruments will reduce the likelihood of such negative effects (for further detail, see Thierry, 1983).

A fifth possibility: we are in favour of the sort of research which is done from a (rarely followed) organization-theoretical perspective. For this purpose we momentarily disregard the labour-political considerations for applying JE. Thus the following propositions may arise, for example: the application of JE pre-supposes that during a number of years the conditions under which work is done, as well as the content of the work, will remain unchanged, or that the changes, if any, can be controlled. Does this mean that JE is applicable preeminently in bureaucratic organizations, which have a relatively stable and predictable environment? Are the new organizations, which are going through the 'pioneering stage' of the development, suitable for the application of JE? Can the different forms (whether temporary or not) of project and matrix organizations be matched to the use of JE? Will the organization's adaptability be affected by the use of JE, with respect to internal adjustments as well as alterations directly outside?

This is related to a sixth perspective: what processes are followed in making internal decisions concerning (the adaptation of) JE as a result of technological and organizational changes as well as those as regards the job content, whether or not in combination with alterations in the relative power positions among groups of employees?

It is along the same line that we finally underline the importance of doing research on the influence, on the application of JE, of external power relations (both between the government, the federations of employers and the trade unions mutually, and in relation to the individual organizations), and hence on individual working behaviour. A central question is, here, in how far the application of JE can be adjusted to the 'specific' tasks and jobs existing in almost any work organization, to leadership climate, group relations, desires, expectations, attitudes and performance of employees, etc.

Perhaps these contributions will render the following observation made by Wootton (1955) less forceful: 'JE respects in practice the boundaries set by convention to which in theory it might offer serious challenge'.

REFERENCES

Algera, J. A. (1981), *Kenmerken van werk* [Job characteristics]. Lisse: Swets & Zeitlinger.

Atchison, T., French, W. (1967), Pay systems for scientists and engineers. *Industrial Relations*, **20**, 1, 44–56.

Bindels, M. A. F. W. (1982), Multi-purpose gebruik van functieclassificatie [Multipurpose use of job classification]. In: Thierry, Hk. (Ed.), *Differentiatie in beloning?* [Differentiation in remuneration?]. Deventer: Kluwer.

Brons, Th. H. (1982), *Het invoeren en werkbaar houden van functiewaardering* [Introducing and maintaining job evaluation]. Eindhoven: Euroforum (conference paper).

Bruyn, J. de, Kannegieter, G. (1981), Functiewaardering mannelijk of vrouwelijk? [Job evaluation male or female?]. *Zeggenschap* [Co-determination], **8**, 74, 2–4.

Buningh, C. A., Colenbrander, H. B. (1982), *Functie en beloningsverhoudingen. De beloningsproblematiek bij industrie, dienstverlening en overheid* [Job and relative remuneration rates. Problems of remuneration in industry, services and civil service]. Rotterdam: Erasmus University, Dept. of Law, School of Business Administration.

Burckhardt, F., Kallina, H. (1967), Eine Faktorenanalyse der analytischen Arbeitsbewertung. *Arbeitswissenschaft*, **6**, 124–126.

Colenbrander, H. B., Buningh, C. A. (1982), *Functieclassificatiemethoden. Een onderzoek naar toegankelijkheid, aanvaardbaarheid en openheid van methodieken* [Methods of job classification. A study of their accessibility, acceptability and openness]. Alphen a/d Rijn: Samsom.

Commission of Experts on Job Classification = Deskundigencommissie voor Werkclassificatie.

Deskundigencommissie voor Werkclassificatie (1952), *Ontwerp genormaliseerde methode van werkclassificatie* [Draft of a normalized method of job classification]. 2 vols. V3000, part I: Viewpoints; part II: Rating tables. V3001, part III: Examples of descriptions and evaluation. The Hague: Central Bureau of Normalization.

Deskundigencommissie voor Werkclassificatie (1959), *Genormaliseerde methode van beschrijving en gradering van werkzaamheden* [Normalized method of describing and grading tasks]. 2 vols. NEN 3000; part I: Viewpoints; part II: Rating tables. NEN 3001, part III: Examples of grading. Rijswijk: Central Bureau of Normalization.

Dowell, B. E., Wexley, K. N. (1978), Development of a work behavior taxonomy for first-line supervisors. *Journal of Applied Psychology*, **63**, 563–572.

Drukker, E., Liefferink, E. (1981), Functiewaardering als beheersinstrument [Job evaluation as a controlling instrument]. *Mens en Onderneming* **35**, 511–527.

Equal Opportunities Commission (1981), *Job evaluation schemes free of sex bias*. Manchester.

Fase, W. J. P. M. (1980), *Vijfendertig jaar loonbeleid in Nederland: Terugblik en perspectief* [35 years of wages policy in The Netherlands: Retrospective and perspective]. Alphen a/d Rijn: Samsom.

Frieling, E., Kannheiser, W., Hoyos, C. Graf (1973), *Untersuchungen zur Position Analysis Questionnaire PAQ*. Regensburg: Lehrstelle für Angewandte Psychologie, Universität Regensburg.

Galan, C. de (1973), Veranderen van de inkomensverdeling [Changing income distribution]. In: *Inkomensnivellering* [Equalization of incomes]. The Hague: Vereniging voor Staathuishoudkunde.

Goodman, P. S. (1967), An empirical examination of Elliott Jaques' concept of time span. *Human Relations*, **20**, 2, 155–167.

Groot, A. D. de (1953), Genormaliseerde werkclassificatie [Normalized job classification]. *Mens en Onderneming*, **7**, 401–415.

Hackman, J. R., Oldham, G. R. (1975), Development of the Job Diagnostic Survey. *Journal of Applied Psychology*, **60**, 159–170.

Hazekamp, F. C. (1966), Werk, capaciteit en beloning in het Glacier project [Work, capacity and payment in the Glacier project]. *Polytechnisch Tijdschrift* [Polytechnical Journal], **21**, 11 (447–455), 13 (534–538), 14 (578–582).

Hazekamp, F. C. (1970), Enige ervaringen met de timespan-methode van dr. Elliott Jaques [Some experiences with the timespan-method of dr. Elliot Jaques]. In: Drenth, P. J. D., Willems, P. J., Wolff, Ch. J. de (Eds.), *Bedrijfspsychologie: Onderzoek en evaluatie* [Industrial psychology: Research and evaluation]. Deventer: Kluwer.

Hazekamp, F. C. (1982), *De ontwikkeling in techniek en procedures van functiewaardering* [Developments in techniques and procedures of job evaluation]. Eindhoven: Euroforum (conference paper).

Hazewinkel, A. (1967), *Werkclassificatie Een wetenschappelijk instrument?* [Job classification: A scientific instrument?]. Groningen: Wolters.

Hemphill, J. K. (1960), *Dimensions of executive positions*. Ohio State University: Research monograph.

Hoyos, C. Graf, Frieling, E. (1977), Methodik des Arbeits- und Berufsanalyse. In: Seifert, K. H. (Ed.), *Berufspsychologie*. Göttingen: Hogrefe.

ILO (International Labour Office) (1977), Job evaluation. 9th ed. Geneva.

Jaques, E. (1956), *Measurement of responsibility. A study of work, payment and individual capacity*. London: Tavistock.

Jaques, E. (1961), *Equitable payment. A general theory of work, differential payment and individual progress*. London: Heinemann.

Jaques, E. (1964), *Time-span handbook*. London: Heinemann.

Jong, J. R. de, Gaillard, A. W. K., Kamp, B. D. (1977), *Hernieuwde studie functiewaardering in Nederland* [Renewed study of job evaluation in The Netherlands]. The Hague: NIVE.

Kleinendorst, B. F. M. (1982), *De waarde van functiewaardering* [The value of job evaluation]. The Hague: Ministry of Social Affairs and Employment.

Koopman-Iwema, A. M., Thierry, Hk. (1981a), *Prestatiebeloning in Nederland: Een analyse* [Incentive payment in The Netherlands: An analysis]. Dublin: European Foundation for the Improvement of Living and Working Conditions. Amsterdam: University of Amsterdam, Dept. of Work- and Organizational Psychology (rev. ed. to appear 1984, Deventer: Kluwer).

Koopman-Iwema, A. M., Thierry, Hk. (1981b), *Prestatiebeloning: Een vergeten toekomst?* [Incentive payment: A forgotten future?]. Dublin: European Foundation for the Improvement of Living and Working Conditions. Amsterdam: University of Amsterdam, Dept. of Work- and Organizational Psychology (rev. ed. to appear 1984, Deventer: Kluwer).

Kordaszewski, J. (1969), A Polish contribution to job evaluation for non-manual workers. *International Labour Review*, **100**, 2, 140–157.

Kvålseth, T. O., Crosmann, E. R. F. W. (1974), The Jaquesian level-of-work estimators: A systematic formulation. *Organizational Behavior and Human Performance*, **11**, 303–315.

Lawshe, C. H. (1945), Studies in job evaluation. II. The adequacy of abbreviated point ratings for hourly-paid jobs in three industrial plants. *Journal of Applied Psychology*, **29**, 177–184.

Lawshe, C. H., Alessi, S. L. (1946), Studies in job evaluation. IV. Analysis of another point rating scale for hourly-paid jobs and the adequacy of an abbreviated scale. *Journal of Applied Psychology*, **30**, 310–319.

Lawshe, C. H., Maleski, A. A. (1946), Studies in job evaluation. III. An analysis of point ratings for salary paid jobs in an industrial plant. *Journal of Applied Psychology*, **30**, 117–128.

Lawshe, C. H., Satter, G. A. (1944), Studies in job evaluation. I. Factor analysis of point ratings for hourly-paid jobs in three industrial plants. *Journal of Applied Psychology*, **28**, 189–198.

Lijftogt, S. G. (1966), *Werkclassificatie: Waardering en kritiek* [Job classification: Appreciation and criticism]. The Hague: COP/SER.

Livy, B., *Job evaluation: a critical review*. London: Allen & Unwin, 1975.

LTD (Loontechnische Dienst) (1981), *Toepassing van functiewaardering in Nederland* [Application of job evaluation in The Netherlands] **1978**. The Hague: Ministry of Social Affairs and Employment.

LTD (Loontechnische Dienst) (1982), *Functiewaardering in Nederland: Gebruik en toepassing* [Job evaluation in The Netherlands: Use and application] **1980**. The Hague: Ministry of Social Affairs and Employment.

McCormick, E. J. (1976), Job and task analysis. In: Dunnette, M. D. (Ed.), *Handbook of industrial and organizational psychology*. Chicago: Rand McNally.

McCormick, E. J., Jeanneret, P. R., Mecham, R. C. (1969), *A study of job characteristics and job dimensions as based on the Position Analysis Questionnaire*. Lafayette: Occupational Research Center, Purdue University.

Malotaux, P. Ch. A., Dammers, H. F. (1978), Complexiteit: Dominerende factor bij functieclassificatie en-beloning? [Complexity: A dominant factor in job classification and payment?] *Doelmatig Bedrijfsbeheer* [Effective Administration], **12**, 23–29.

Mens en Onderneming [Man and Enterprise].

Metsch, J. C. (1980), *Loonsatisfactie en variable beloning* [Pay satisfaction and variable payment]. University of Amsterdam, Dept. of Work- and Organizational Psychology (research paper).

Paterson, T. T. (1972), *Job evaluation*. Vol. I en II. London: Business Books.

Paterson, T. T. (1981), *Pay for making decisions*. Vancouver: Tantalus.

Pen, J., Tinbergen, J. (1977), *Naar een rechtvaardiger inkomensverdeling* [Towards a fairer income distribution]. Amsterdam: Elsevier.

Richardson, R. (1971), *Fair pay and work*. London: Heinemann.

Rohmert, W., Landau, K. (1979), *Das Arbeitswissenschaftliche Erhebungsverfahren zur Tätigkeitsanalyse(AET)*. Bern: Huber.

Rohmert, W., Rutenfranz, J. (1975), *Arbeitswissenschaftliche Beurteilung der Belastung und Beanspruchung an unterschiedlichen industriellen Arbeitsplätzen (AEG)*. Bonn: Der Bundesminister für Arbeit und Sozialordnung.

Roscam Abbing, P. J. (1974), *Ethiek van de inkomensverdeling* [The ethics of income distribution]. Deventer: Kluwer.

Sayles, L. R., Strauss, G. (1977), *Managing human resources*. Englewood Cliffs: Prentice-Hall.

Schippers, J. J. (1982), Beloningsdiscriminatie van de vrouw in Nederland [Discrimination as to payment of women in The Netherlands]. *Economisch-Statistische Berichten* [Economic-Statistical Reports], **67**, 452–458.

Scholten, G. (1979). Functiewaardering met mate [Analysing job evaluation]. Alphen a/d Rijn: Samsom.

Scholten, G. (1981), *Passen en meten met functiewaardering* [Job evaluation: Cutting and contriving]. Alphen a/d Rijn: Samsom.

Schoute, F. J. (1982), *Juridische implicaties van de invoering van functiewaardering* [Legal implications of the introduction of job evaluation]. Eindhoven: Euroforum (conference paper).

Silva, D. J. da (1951), Werkclassificatie [Job classification]. *Tijdschrift voor Efficiency en Documentatie* [Journal for Efficiency and Documentation], **21**, 186.

Smith, R. C., Murphy, M. J. (1946), *Job evaluation and employee rating*. New York: McGraw-Hill.

Thierry, Hk. (1968), *Loont de prestatiebeloning?* [Does incentive payment pay off?]. Assen: Van Gorcum.

Thierry, Hk. (1969), *Arbeidsinstelling en prestatiebeloning* [Job attitude and incentive payment]. Utrecht: Het Spectrum (rev. ed. to appear 1984, Alphen a/d Rijn: Samsom).

Thierry, Hk. (1982), *Heeft functiewaardering, maatschappelijk en inkomenspolitiek gezien, wel toekomst?* [Does job evaluation, viewed from society and income policy, have a future?]. Eindhoven: Euroforum (conference paper).

Thierry, Hk. (1983²), *Humanisering van arbeid en beloning* [Humanizing work and remuneration]. In: Galan, C. de, Gils, M. J. van, Strien, P. J. van (Eds.), *Humanisering van de arbeid* [Humanizing work]. Assen: Van Gorcum.

Tornow, W. W., Pinto, P. R. (1976), The development of a managerial job taxonomy: A system for describing, classifying, and evaluating executive positions. *Journal of Applied Psychology,* **61,** 410–418.

Turner, A. N., Lawrence, P. R. (1965), *Industrial jobs and the worker. An investigation of response to task attributes.* Boston: Harvard University.

U.S. Department of Labour, Manpower Administration (1972), *Handbook for analyzing jobs.* U.S. Government Printing Office, Superintendent of Documents.

Varkevisser, J. (1967), Werkclassificatie en externe invloedsfactoren [Job classification and factors of external influence]. *Mens en Onderneming,* **21,** 324–326.

Vinke, R. H. W. (1982), *Naar een persoonlijk inkomenspakket* [Towards a personal income package]. University of Amsterdam, Dept. of Work- and Organizational Psychology (research paper).

Wiegersma, S. (1958), Gezichtspunten en factoren in de genormaliseerde werkclassificatie [Viewpoints and factors in the normalized job classification]. *Mens en Onderneming,* **12,** 200–208.

Wiersum, J. (1982), Functiewaardering bij een overheid; Een mono-purpose voorbeeld [Job evaluation in a civil service; A mono-purpose example]. In: Thierry, Hk. (Ed.), *Differentiatie in beloning?* [Differentiation in remuneration?]. Deventer: Kluwer.

Wing Easton, N. J. (1980), *Functiewaardering: Kies zelf uw systeem* [Job evaluation: Choose your own system]. Deventer: Kluwer.

Wootton, B. (1955). *The social foundations of wage policy.* London: Allen and Unwin.

WRR (Wetenschappelijke Raad voor het Regeringsbeleid) (1977), *Over sociale ongelijkheid* [On social inequality]. The Hague: Staatsuitgeverij.

W.U.N. (1982), *Uitgangspunten norminkomen vrije-beroepsbeoefenaren* [Basic principles of norm incomes in the independent professions]. The Hague: Ministry of Social Affairs and Employment.

Wijn, M. M. (1982), *Vrooms valentiemodel en variabele beloning* [Vroom's valency model and variable payment]. Amsterdam: University of Amsterdam, Dept. of Work- and Organizational Psychology (research paper).

Wijnberg, W. J. (1965), *Capaciteit en inkomen* [Capacity and income]. Haarlem: Algemene Werkgeversvereniging.

Wijngaarden, P. J. van (1982), *Inkomensverdelingsbeleid in de verzorgingsstaat* [The income-distribution policy in a welfare-state]. University of Utrecht (dissertation).

Zwarts, H. (1982), Loon naar werken en werk naar loon [Payment according to work and work according to payment]. In: Thierry, Hk. (Ed.), *Differentiatie in beloning?* [Differentiation in remuneration?] Deventer: Kluwer.

Handbook of Work and Organizational Psychology
Edited by P. J. D. Drenth, H. Thierry, P. J. Willems and C. J. de Wolff
© 1984, John Wiley & Sons, Ltd.

2.11. Training

Marc Buelens and Pol Coetsier

1. INTRODUCTION

There are different terms used to indicate an influencing process, which aims at a systematical and purposeful modification of individuals: education, instruction, training, schooling, etc.

The predicate 'systematical' refers to a learning process and distinguishes training from accidental changes, maturation, unconscious influence, etc. The term 'purposeful' shows that the learning process is intentional, planned, set up (usually by others) in view of reaching a previously fixed final situation, e.g. an increase of knowledge or behaviour change. Finally, as appears from the definition, we will confine ourselves to changes in individual behavior. These changes can be focused on the person as well as on the role that the individual performs in the organization. Organizational changes as such are outside the scope of this chapter. This theme is treated at length in this Handbook, chapters 4.4 and 4.9. The restriction to individual change, however, does not mean that the interaction between training processes and the organization are unimportant. In the following pages we will actually put special emphasis on this interaction. The restriction only implies that in this chapter no attention will be paid to direct interventions in organizational variables.

For the sake of completeness it should be added that Glaser (1962) made a distinction between 'training' and 'education': training, then, is aimed at

Dr. Marc Buelens
Prof. Dr. Pol L. Coetsier (R. U. Gent—Lab. v. Toegep. Psychol.), Meersstraat 3, (Pasteurlaan 2), 9830 Sint-Martens-Latem, (9000 Gent—België), België, Tel.: 091/825114—091/240224.

clearly formulated, uniform behavior (e.g. being able to operate a telex-machine), where transfer-possibilities are limited (a new machine requires a new training). Education, on the other hand, would be aimed at complex behavior, impossible to formulate in a precise way (e.g. linguistic feeling), where individual differences increase (everyone develops an individual style) and where the amount of transfer possibilities is important.

This chapter aims at giving a survey of scientific thinking about training. Therefore, we will first (section 2) deal with the question whether there is a training theory or not. Then, two views on training will be discussed (section 3). The rational training model (section 4) is aimed at shedding light upon the most important elements of the training process in their relation to one another. Finally (section 5) a conclusion is formulated.

2. IS THERE A TRAINING THEORY?

Especially striking in the literature on training is *the scanty attention paid to theory formation*. Concepts are borrowed from learning process theories and prescriptions are formulated on the ground of more general theories (e.g. systems theory). Although theory formation related to educational learning processes has made considerable progress (de Klerk, 1979), the same is not true for theory formation related to training in general. The confrontation of theories, of schools of thought, of ways of thinking, which the organizational psychologist may find in the areas of leadership, motivation, and organization theory, is for the most part lacking in the field of training. (For an exception, see Argyris, 1976.) Some trainers 'believe' in sensitivity training: others 'swear by' lecturing; still others 'have good experience' with 'training-on-the-job'. But all this is the (often very firm) belief of a practitioner, and not the—in principle at least—falsifiable belief of a scholar. Besides, training is in the first place *a practice*, which often frustrates the various authors who, in their reviews, try to give a general view on the training process (Campbell *et al.*, 1970; Campbell, 1971; Drenth *et al.*, 1973; Ivancevich and McMahon, 1976; Hinrichs, 1976; Goldstein, 1980). The limited interest in theory formation is also expressed in a striking *lack of conceptual agreement*. Training includes very diverse processes: attitude modification by participating in group discussions; teaching new welding techniques; learning to understand a new method of time series analysis. Can one, in all these cases, speak of a common denominator?

These observations show why theory-oriented research is so scarce. This is a direct result of the preceding point. It is striking how little research is being done in the field of training: most publications are concerned with descriptive research, in which at best a detailed report is given on the circumstances of a (by the way, mainly successful) training program.

3. TWO BASIC APPROACHES TO TRAINING

Roughly speaking, studies on training can be classified into two groups. The first group covers all the studies in which a number of principles and prescriptions for *good* training are being compiled. This 'normative' approach is discussed in section 3.1. The second group includes all the studies which start from the practice of training; these studies, most of which are descriptive in nature, situate training usually in an organization context. This 'organizational practice' approach is explained in section 3.2.

3.1. A normative approach to training

Most publications on training deal with prescriptions for good training. They offer practitioners an ideal to compare with his own efforts in preparing, setting up, and evaluating concrete training activities. This approach is mainly related to systems thinking applied to organizations (see this Handbook, ch. 4.2 and 4.5).

The main recommendations of this approach can be summarized as follows:
—give as much attention as possible to the formulation of precise, and preferably measurable goals;
—take care that every single training activity contributes to these goals;
—give as much attention as possible to the interplay between training and other processes;
—evaluate the training results as a function of the goals.

ASSUMPTIONS OF THE NORMATIVE APPROACH

The normative view on training is based on a number of (mainly implicit) assumptions concerning organizations and views on mankind. The underlying organization-picture considers an organization as a system of interdependent parts, in which each part has a specific function which is conducted in an autonomous—to be sure, interactive—way, and is focused on a common goal which is pursued in an effective way.

An important characteristic of the underlying organization-picture is, in other words, (instrumental) rationality. In this view, training will be rational if it contributes to the realization of the organization's goals. In that way training prescriptions become possible: by way of a specialization process one can rationally deduce concrete goals from the general goals of the organization.

In this way of thinking the idea of harmony is central. Conflicts are regarded as exceptions due to temporary misunderstandings. An organization is a co-operative system in which everyone contributes to the common goals.

Another characteristic assumption of the normative approach is the idea that the quality of an organization is primarily determined by the quality of its individual members (Salaman, 1978). An organization is chiefly considered as a set of individuals where structure, technology, and environmental influence have only minor importance. When an individual learns, an organization will learn as well. In this context it is an axiom that organizational improvement develops via improvement of individuals.

To the extent that training is concerned with socio-psychological domains, it can be said that a human resource model is the basis of the normative approach: the main problem in any organization is the integration of person and organization. For this purpose, it is sufficient for the individuals to be motivated to contribute. Under the influence of humanistic psychology certain needs, such as development, realization of potentialities, growth, etc., are heavily stressed.

THE ROLE OF TRAINING IN THE NORMATIVE APPROACH

In the normative approach, training is an obvious means whenever an individual lacks the knowledge, the attitude, the motivation, or the skill needed for the successful execution of a task or for adequate collaboration with others. Training should contribute to better harmony between the individual and the organization: the individual learning process and the organizational task processes (Simmons, 1978) must be tuned to each other. When a disturbance of the harmony threatens, training in interpersonal relations is indicated. Technical training aims at homogeneity and will consequently be needed whenever two individuals react differently in the same situation: the least effective individual has to be replaced by the more effective one. Non-technical training is focused on insight in and acceptance of common aims, on stimulating the need for growth, and on smooth collaboration. In this sense, training will always have to contribute to an improved general effectiveness of the organization.

3.2. Training as organizational practice

Training hardly even takes place in an organizational vacuum; it is, just like decision-making on communication, an organizational process. A number of studies is clearly less focused on the didactic aspects of training, but rather on training in an organizational context. Goldstein (1980) correctly points out that one can learn a lot about organizations when starting from a study of training processes. But the reverse is also true: one can learn interesting things about training, starting from a number of insights into organizations.

It is of course possible to draw a number of practical lessons from this approach as well; it is, in fact, difficult to maintain that this approach is purely descriptive and therefore the total opposite of the normative approach. There is, however, an important difference between these assumptions.

The underlying organization-picture is related to tendencies in organization theory (cf. this Handbook, ch. 4.1. and 4.2) in which the goal-paradigm is abandoned and in which organizations are conceived as political systems, where different parties, through temporary coalitions, try to realize more of their ultimate aims. This approach is, in other words, much more related to a coalition-model than to a harmony-model. Man is viewed as an actor who tries to realize his aims in a satisfactory way (Crozier and Friedberg, 1977). In this approach, the motivation for training is mainly instrumental: an actor will participate in training as far as training is a help, a path along which he may reach a number of more or less concrete objectives; these objectives are in many cases *not* related to growth or self-realization.

THE ROLE OF TRAINING IN THE ORGANIZATIONAL PRACTICE-APPROACH.

In this approach, training is used by the dominant coalition in order to acquire control of behavior: training is focused on increasing the predictability of behavior and, in this way, on removing an important source of uncertainty. Priority is given to forms of training which can strengthen the dominant coalition's ideology (March and Simon, 1958). Ganzevoort (1981) is right in pointing out that, in this context, training, as a means for controlling organizational culture, shifts from purely instrumental training towards training at an ideological level (attitudes, norms, and values).

What an engineer learns in his specialized engineering course is, in the first place, the affirmation of the priority of technical factors; and a civil servant will only be permitted to attend a training which is sufficiently related to the administrative culture. Sometimes, the ideological component of training is so obvious, that some coalitions stand up against is. We have, for example, witnessed a trade-union protest against social-skills training for first-line supervisors.

4. A RATIONAL TRAINING MODEL

As was pointed out in the introduction, the interest in training is primarily practice-oriented. The practitioner expects theory to provide him with a rational model, preferably a 'one best way', and with unambiguous recommendations. In the following we will supply the material for a rational model, based mainly upon the normative approach. From this model, practical recommendations can be easily derived. We will, however, point to some obviously weak parts in the construction from the organizational practice point of view.

Figure 1. A rational training model.

4.1. Base-structure of a rational training model

In figure 1 a schematic outline of a rational model is given. The starting-point of this model is a consciously formulated training policy, on the basis of which decisions can be made as to what deficiencies should be met. These deficiencies (training needs) must subsequently be translated into training objectives, to be realized by a training program. This process is concluded with an evaluation. In the next sections we will discuss each of these basic components.

4.2 Training policy

A consciously formulated training policy should guarantee that the training efforts are attuned to each other. This policy should be the result of strategic choice. Or, in other words, when looking at the whole of the decisions made in connection with training, a conscious decision strategy should become clear. Strategy can here be defined as a pattern in a stream of decisions (Mintzberg, 1979). In a consciously formulated training policy a coherent answer should be given to questions such as:
—What is the role of training in the complete set of efforts related to the integration of individual and organization?
—Which target groups are aimed at? Training for everyone? For management only? Only for those who fail?
—How much may training cost?
—To what extent should training contribute to modification?

The first question deals with the problem of the relation between training and other integration processes such as leadership or socialization, with special attention to other elements of the staffing policy, such as recruiting, task assignment and promotion (House, 1967; Schafrat, 1978). Some organizations will recruit mainly specialists (trained outside the organization) through an attractive remuneration system (high salary, much autonomy). Other organizations recruit generalists and invest a lot of resources in training.

Training which is not integrated in a broader structure might be beneficial to the individual, but is probably marginal for the organization. It is even possible that a boomerang effect develops. The best-known example in this connection is Fleishman's (1953) study, in which he showed that leadership behavior was negatively influenced by a 'human relations' course: the course aimed at increasing 'consideration' and lowering 'structuring', but the reverse effect was reported in his study.

In order to ensure integration the entire staff is sometimes trained on a certain 'theme'. It is believed that such a procedure intensifies the training's integrational value in two ways: on the one hand, the training effect is increased by the motivating effect that originates from such a theme; on the other hand, the training of everyone, preferably simultaneously, has a smoothing effect on the introduction of modifications.

In the last question the relation between training and other modification processes should be considered. Indeed, it can be desirable to act mainly by means of technological modifications or with structural interventions (e.g. decentralization), or by way of a modification in the stream of information (e.g. transition to computerized systems). According to Leavitt (1978) a 'people' approach is desirable when the problems are unstructured. This remark, however, leaves many questions unanswered.

In practice, a training policy is hardly ever explicitly formulated. In and around the organization different parties think about training, act, and insist on decisions. All these reflections, actions, influences get in some way connected with each other and a kind of decision is taken which can best be described as 'garbage can' decision making. An example: a manager meets a friend who has attended an anti-stress seminar. The manager is interested because in his view such a seminar is a means to improve his physical condition (headache) and because he wants to use the training as a means of communicating to his superiors how busy he is. The training manager has received instructions to economize on external formation. The organizers of the anti-stress seminar have commercial aims. The manager's superior is indifferent to training, as long as the manager is not absent on Mondays, etc. In this way, values, decision makers, and information converge more or less by accident into one external training program, and the decision mirrors a kind of rambling influencing process, rather than a coherent training policy.

This does not, of course, rule out that organizations may follow decision patterns they are not conscious of, or that the decision patterns are hidden from the majority of the observers. In this way the well-known training fashions develop, where solutions (e.g. sensitivity training) are easily connected to problems (of whatever kind), and where many organizations seem to use a 'keeping up with the Joneses' strategy.

4.3. Training needs

Training needs usually develop from a tension-relation, namely the (anticipated) gap between organizational goals and organizational practice, or, in other words, from the evaluation of organizational practice. When this gap can be reduced by systematic modifications of the individuals, one can talk of training needs. In figure 1 this is indicated by the arrow from 'evaluation of organizational practice' to 'training needs'. Laird (1978) distinguishes no less than 23 possible sources of deficiency (such as promotion, complaints, new technology) that can be relieved by training.

The question whether it is worthwhile to cope with deficiencies by means of training should be answered in the training policy. Therefore, in figure 1 there is an arrow between 'policy' and 'needs'. This arrow has a second meaning: training needs may be the direct result of a training policy. In some organizations, for example, all newcomers have to go through an introduction program, or all staff members from a certain level up have to take part in a communication training, a management course, etc.

The interaction between organizational practice ('deficiencies') and training policy determines the training needs. An objective answer to the question 'when is a need a training need?' is consequently hard to find. Training needs as such are defined by a number of bodies. We can therefore agree with Moore and Dutton's (1978) thesis that in deciding on training needs, too little allowance is made for political aspects of what happens in the organization and of the coalition formation. Consequently, the main question is not *how* training needs are determined, but *who* determines them. The relative power position of the different coalitions is more important than an objective analysis of possible deficiencies. One rarely hears of motivation training for the highest management. Apparently only lower management has motivational problems...

Some training needs are objective because the definition is easily accepted. Lack of technical knowledge in newcomers, for example, will be experienced as a clear need by all parties involved, but definitions of reality will conflict with each other when the staff department of a prestigious bank thinks that the higher executives are in need of more creativity. On such occasions the play for the definition power to define dominates.

Newstrom and Lilyquist (1979) developed a contingency model for decision making related to the determination of needs, based on an extensive literature survey. Twelve different methods are discussed: advisory committees, assessment centers, attitude surveys, group discussions, interviews with trainees, exit-interviews, demands from the management, observations by the trainers, evaluation systems, documents, questionnaires, and skill tests. For each of these methods it is checked if they are low, intermediate, or high on five criteria: employee's involvement, management's involvement, requisite time, cost, quantifiability. According to these criteria it is possible to decide which method one wants to apply in order to identify the training needs.

4.4. Training objectives

In the rational training model, training needs must be formulated in terms of training objectives i.e. concrete goals which must be realized, or, as De Block (1975, p. 13) puts it, 'intentionally and systematically pursued, desirable and realizable behavior modifications in the broadest sense'. The methodology of formulating learning goals, especially at the level of transmittal of knowledge, is explained in detail in didactic studies. A more general scheme is offered by Hamblin (1974) and Kirkpatrick (1976). These authors distinguish objectives at five hierarchically ordered levels: a higher level objective can be realized only when all the lower ones have been realized. (The hierarchical arrangement of objectives is not universal; in behavior-modeling (Bandura, 1977) or learning by observation it will be accepted that behavior can take place in a concrete situation without having been trained before.)

Level 1: reactions; i.e. the desired reactions on the training (e.g. interest, satisfaction, active participation).

Level 2: learning, i.e. the desired behavior acquired as a result of the training (e.g. new skills, insights).

Level 3: work behavior; i.e. the desired modification of behavior during working hours, in other words, a successful transfer from the learning situation to the work situation (e.g. better manipulation of a machine, friendlier contact with patients).

Level 4: organization; i.e. desired modifications of organizational variables and processes such as decision making, morale, absenteeism.

Level 5: ultimate values; i.e. desired modifications of the ultimate success indicators which the organization considers relevant (profit, independence, welfare, ...).

Let us take a training in 'rational decision making' as an example.

A level 1 objective could be: the participants prepare the case-study; at the second level: the participants are able to correctly solve a standardized problem situation at the end of the course; at the third level: the trainees also apply the acquired techniques efficiently in real decision situations; on the fourth level: the quality of the decisions in the organization increases; at the fifth level: the organization makes more profit.

The objectives at levels 4 and 5 (results) are in many cases quite remote from the actual training activity, but they remined us of the fact that training for training's sake is an exception. The scheme also shows that the well-known literature on learning objectives (Bloom *et al.*, 1971; De Block, 1975) is almost exclusively limited to level 2. A taxonomy for the other levels would certainly be welcome.

It is clear that training can serve totally different objectives in organizations than to relieve training needs. Training may be used, for example, in order to gain prestige or as an image-builder ('we train all our people in ... '). For many executives it is a status symbol *not* to attend any training. Moreover, training is too often used as a substitute for the correction of organizational errors, which results in a lot of frustration. In an organization with a too bureaucratic structure, for example, an isolated training program on democratic leadership will only create false expectations.

While fixing the training objectives, one should always take competing objectives into account. More particularly, socialization by reference-groups or 'counter training' (Bahn, 1973) can well be stronger than any official training. If the training aims at a conflict with the dominant coalition, acute problems could arise during the training. The realization of objectives of the third level becomes very problematic in such a case: There is no time, there are no means ... It is, consequently, no wonder that one of the 'classical' factors of training success, just as is the case in organization development, is the support of (top) management (House, 1967).

4.5. The training program

In the rational training model, the training program should meet the training objectives: its relation with the learning objectives is the central issue in the different elements of the program. The literature on training has laid an unbalanced and heavy stress on training programs (Hinrichs, 1976). All attention is given to the activities during the training days. Or, as Leach (1979) puts it: 'too much "doing" (classroom teaching) ... too little time conceptualizing'.

In an organization the rewards for action are generally more important than those for conceptualizing. This fact manifests itself even in the attention field of training programs: Burgoyne and Stuart (1978) rightly observe that much attention is paid to manifest characteristics such as duration, residential or non-residential character, method, and only little to the kernel of training activities, namely the transformation process and the underlying learning principles. Therefore, these issues will be dealt with in the next section.

LEARNING PRINCIPLES AND METHODS

The different principles developed in learning psychology can be classified with the help of two questions: 'Is great importance attached to cognitive aspects (information processing)? and 'Is great importance attached to reinforcers (the positive and negative consequences of behavior, reward or punishment)?'.

There are learning principles which are not based on cognitive or reinforcing processes. Learning takes place by experience, by doing. In such an approach a non-systematic feedback effect is central, and in this sense it is not a theoretical,

IMPORTANCE OF CONDITION	IMPORTANCE OF REINFORCERS: LITTLE	IMPORTANCE OF REINFORCERS: GREAT
LITTLE	Principle: experimental learning Methods: simulation, projects, case studies, action learning, training on the job	Principle: conditioning Methods: programmed instruction, behavior modification
GREAT	Principle: information processing system Methods: lectures, syllabi, audiovisual methods	Principle: modeling Methods: role playing, structured social-skill exercises

since feedback is an essential characteristic of training (Komaki *et al.*, 1980). It is, however, not clear how in this approach feedback takes place and there is little guarantee against the incidental learning of the wrong behavior. Methods connected with this approach are mainly simulation and projects, action learning (Revans, 1971) and training on the job.

In conditioning methods the main stress is on manifest behavior which is modified under the influence of reward and punishment. A very well-known application of this principle is programmed instruction. In some industries one has utilized direct behavior modification through manipulation of behavioral consequences (referred to as behavior modification in table 1). The evaluation of this approach is mixed (see survey articles by McGhee and Tullar, 1978; Bobb and Kopp, 1978), although successes are regularly reported (Latham and Saari, 1979; Luthans *et al.*, 1981). Sometimes a spectacular rise in productivity or a clear drop in absenteeism are mentioned—e.g. by rewarding sufficient presence with participation in a lottery—but, on the other hand, this behavior seems to disappear when it is no longer rewarded. The strongest opposition against behavior modification is, however, of a moral nature: conditioning approaches are contrary to all emancipatory movements (Katz and Kahn, 1978)! Circumstances as the picture of the employee in the skinner-box or the 'delusion of brave new world' turn the brakes on all developments in this field.

A number of learning methods start from an image of man as an information processing system, in which each individual possesses a 'cognitive map' by which he classifies information and relations between bits of information. Learning takes place by absorbing new information (emphasis on separate information units) or by changing the cognitive map (emphasis on the whole; gestalt approaches). When the information received by the individual differs highly from previous information, a radical change in the cognitive map may occur, which could be called an attitude change: the fundamentally changed knowledge of the object leads to radically different expectations.

The methods connected with this learning principle are the most classic ones: lectures, syllabi. In a more recent form audiovisual devices are also frequently used.

Modeling combines the cognitive and the reinforcement approach (see Bandura, 1977). There is a cognitive component: the information the individual recieves from others, the way in which others define reality, the observation of behavioral consequences by others; there is also a conditioning effect by way of social reinforcers such as yes-nodding or praise. Methods connected with this learning principle consequently combine information and cognitive aspects with reinforcement: structured social-skill exercises, role playing.

ACCEPTANCE OF THE TRAINING PROGRAM BY THE ORGANIZATION

As pointed out before, acceptance of the entire training cycle by an organization is a prerequisite for success. In this connection, one should bear in mind that training in formal organizations is an important responsibility of the immediate superior. He should be involved in the training of his associates as much as possible. Bare (1978), for example, was able to show a significant correlation between the effectiveness of a work group and the extent to which the participants consider their superior as committed to his subordinates' training. This correlation was even higher than the correlation between effectiveness and the extent to which that superior gives feedback or co-ordinates.

In practice, however, there is, in most cases, total alienation between the actual organization, e.g. management, and the training: the training is happening somewhere 'outside' the organization (not so much physically as psychologically), and in the meantime the 'real' work goes on. The training is encapsulated in a class situation (Haire, 1970); in the work situation other norms are valid, and rewards are given for different kinds of behavior. Afterwards, responsibility for the training is all too easily thrown upon, for example, personnel management or the trainer.

Acceptance by the organization may be increased by involving the hierarchy in the conception and execution. For example, a superior acts as the trainee's tutor and the trainee has to report on his training to his tutor. The mere reporting to the tutor may have important training effects. The immediate superior could help to draft case-studies, formulate training objectives, etc.

4.6. Evaluation

Evaluation is the final stage of the rational training cycle. Two aims may be pursued here: the improvement of the training process (indicated in figure 1 by the arrow from 'evaluation' to 'training program') or the examination of the training's effectiveness (indicated in figure 1 by the arrow from 'evaluation' 'training objectives').

In connection with the first objective (evaluation aimed at improving training practice) it is important to collect as much data as possible *during* the training sessions. Light (1979) has argued in favor of evaluating the underlying structure and training processes on the basis of observations, rather than working with surface structure data obtained by, for example, questionnaires. The questionnaires used after training too often regard training as a 'black box'. Therefore, data should be obtained systematically during the training process.

A complete survey of evaluation methods aimed at training improvement is found in Hamblin (1974). In this study, no less than 38 different methods are discussed, classified according to the five levels (discussed in section 4.4). Some of his examples are the following: diaries, study of the relations between trainees (level 1); tests, group feedback analysis (level 2); critical incident method, questionnaires (level 3); climate studies (level 4); social balance (level 5).

In pursuing the second objective (evaluation aimed at showing effectiveness) experimental and quasi-experimental designs, preferably with control groups, are necessary. In practice, these designs are not easy to realize (the exception that proves the rule is van der Vegt, 1974), not in the least because in most cases it is far from easy to find equivalent control groups.

The evaluation should take place as much as possible at each levels for which training objectives are formulated (ch. section 4.4). This is rather easy at the first level, where observation during the training or satisfaction measurements after the training are sufficient. It is still rather simple at the second level, where progress can be measured (Meuwese, 1970), but at the other levels it is more complex because various variables cannot be sufficiently controlled, and because it is difficult to separate training effects from the effects of social, structural, and even economic changes.

Better preparations for a meeting by means of a plan is an example situated on level 3, and shorter, more efficient meetings may be regarded as a positive outcome at level 4, but how can a better organizational climate or an increase of profits ever be attributed to training? This complexity is caused by the fact that at the highest levels both evaluation objectives as mentioned above, are closely connected with each other, or, in other words, at these levels, 'experimental design' methods should provide information on the training process. This feat of strength is perhaps too much for the present state of science, and, at any rate. requires a lot of resources, time, and organization.

It is also necessary to ask for *whom* the training must be evaluated. For the trainee, the trainer, management, or science (Hesseling, 1966)? The evaluation may offer trainees a better understanding of previous or future learning processes; the trainer might adjust the training process; the management might correct the training strategy; the scientific forum could acquire new insights in the training process. As far as the use of evaluation for trainer and trainee is concerned, it appears that intermediate evaluation is very important so as to allow for corrections on the right moment.

A general remark is, furthermore, that the evaluation of trainees' behavior during the formation process on the basis of criteria not related to the formation itself, is taboo. Data originating from training evaluation must not be used in decisions on selection and promotion. The situation is, however, different in a (leadership) assessment center, where management potential is assessed by different expert judges during simulations, exercises, and individual interviews. In these cases the end report consists of recommendations with regard to promotion as well as to training.

In most organizations training evaluation clearly is a political process, where the following questions are at issue: what data will be used to carry out the evaluation? How will they be used? And by whom? When a training specialist is recommended to 'sell' 'his' training program by means of an influencing program within the organization (Brett, 1979), this will have a distinct effect on the evaluation procedure. As a matter of fact, it is remarkable that so much training evaluation is carried out by the trainers themselves. This is certainly not a guarantee for objectivity.

5. CONCLUSION

5.1. When can the rational model be realized?

Generally speaking, the rational approach to training can be better realized when the underlying assumptions of the normative model are satisfied, i.e. when training can take place according to unambiguous systems. An unambiguous system is characterized by the following features: (a) a clear goal has been formulated and there is consensus about the goal; (b) the learning technology is clear; (c) cause-effect relations are well known.

As far as technical knowledge and skills are concerned these requirements are usually met (e.g. reading a financial balance-sheet, manipulation of apparatus), but the rational model is very problematic when the objectives are related to changes in attitude or interpersonal relations. In these domains there is hardly ever consensus about the behavior to be pursued (e.g. whether the chairman of a meeting should lead discussions in a directive or non-directive way). The learning technology is often unclear (what is the best method to change an attitude?) and cause-effect relations are far from unambiguous (e.g. the relation between attitude and behavior). Does this mean that in this field—which certainly arouses the special interest of organizational psychologists—one is condemned to a political model?

This question partially answered by the pioneering work of Rackham and his colleagues in the United Kingdom (Rackham and Morgan, 1977). They were able to formulate concrete behavioral objectives for a number of social skills. These objectives are collected on the basis of detailed observations of successful and less successful negotiators, chairmen, etc. Comparing this study with most of the other publications on training, one is struck by the amount of systematical preparatory research work done by the authors before the start of the actual training program.

5.2. Some priorities in research on training

Further to the problem formulated in the introduction, we can say that there is a strong need for theory-oriented empirical research in which training is viewed as an organization process.

More in particular, 'decision making' angle would be especially informative. How are decisions made in the field of training problems? By whom? Is it possible to distinguish contingency variables? Are there certain patterns in the decison making, or, in other words, which training strategies can be identified?

In studying training as an organization process, two roads are open to us: a structural approach and an approach connected with symbolic interactionism.

In the first case, questions such as the following may be put: what is the relation between the nature and intensity of training and characteristics such as size of the organization, technology, pressure from the environment . . . ? In the second case, other questions are dealt with: what is the symbolic meaning of training? How do the different groups define the training situation? What are the values or ideologies that play a part?

Finally, a number of 'classical' questions can be dealt with again, such as, for example, when can we speak of a training need? What kind of learning principles are connected with what kind of needs? Is it possible to devise a taxonomy of learning goals at different levels?

REFERENCES

Argyris, C. (1976), Theories of action that inhibit individual learning. *American Psychologist*, **31**, 638–654.

Bahn, C. (1973), The counter training problem. *Personnel Journal*, **26**, 1068–1072.

Bandura, A. (1977), *Social learning theory*. Englewood Cliffs: Prentice-Hall.

Bare, A. C. (1978), Staffing and training: Neglected supervisory functions related to group performance. *Personnel Psychology*, **31**, 107–117.

Block, A. de (1975), *Taxonomie van leerdoelstellingen* [Taxonomy of learning goals]. Antwerp: Standaard Wetenschappelijke Uitgeverij.

Bobb, H. W., Kopp, D. G. (1978), Application of behavior modification in organizations: A review and critique. *Academy of Management Review*, **3**, 281–292.

Brett, R. (1979), You have to sell it to do it. *Training and Development Journal*, **33**, 64–65.

Burgoyne, J., Stuart, R. (1978), Management development programmes: Underlying assumptions about learning. In: Burgoyne, J., Stuart, R., *Management development: Context and strategies*. Westmead: Gower Press, 93–114.

Campbell, J. P. (1971), Personnel training and development. *Annual Review of Psychology*, **22**, 565–602.

Campbell, J. P., Dunnette, M. D., Lawler, E. E., Weick, K. E. (1970), *Managerial behavior performance and effectiveness.* New York: McGraw-Hill.

Crozier, M., Friedberg, E. (1977), *L'Acteuretle système.* Paris: Editions du Seuil.

Drenth, P. J. D., Willems, P. J., Wolff, Ch. J. de (1973), Opleiding en ontwikkeling: Inleiding [Education and development: Introduction]. In: Drenth, P. J. D., Willems, P. J. Wolff, Ch. J. de (Eds.), *Arbeids- en organisatiepsychologie* [Work- and organizational psychology]. Deventer: Kluwer, 77–80.

Fleishman, E. A. (1953), Leadership climate, human relations training and supervisory behavior. *Personnel Psychology,* 6, 205–222.

Ganzevoort, W. (1981), Organisatie-ideologieën [Organization ideologies]. *Intermediair,* 17, 13–21.

Glaser, R. (Ed.) (1962), *Training research and education.* University of Pittsburgh Press.

Golstein, I. L. (1980), Training in work organizations. *Annual Review of Psychology,* 31, 229–272.

Haire, M. (1970), *Psychology in management.* London: McGraw-Hill.

Hamblin, A. C. (1974), *Evaluation and control of training.* London: McGraw-Hill.

Hesseling, P. (1966), *Strategy of evaluation research.* Assen: Van Gorcum.

Hinrichs, J. R. (1976), Personnel training. In: Dunnette, M. D. (Ed.), *Handbook of industrial and organizational psychology.* Chicago: Rand McNally, 823–860.

House, R. J. (1967), *Management Development: Design, evaluation and implementation.* University of Michigan, Ann Arbor.

Ivancevich, J. M., McMahon, J. T. (1976), Group development, trainer style and carry-over job satisfaction and performance. *Academy of Management Journal,* 395–413.

Katz, D., Kahn, R. L. (1978), *The social psychology of organizations.* 2nd ed. New York: Wiley.

Kirkpatrick, D. L. (1976), Evaluation of training. In: Craig, R. L. (Ed.), *Training and development handbook.* 2nd ed. New York: McGraw-Hill, 18–1/18–27.

Klerk, L. F. W. de (1979), *Inleiding in de onderwijspsychologie* [Introduction to educational psychology]. Deventer: Van Loghum Slaterus.

Komaki, J., Heinzmann, A. T., Lawson, L. (1980), Effects of training and feedback: Commponent analysis of a behavioral safety program. *Journal of Applied Psychology,* 65, 261–270.

Laird, D. (1978). *Approaches to training and development.* Reading (Mass.): Addison Wesley.

Latham, G. P., Saari, L. M. (1979), The application of social learning theory to training supervisors through behavioral modeling. *Journal of Applied Psychology,* 64, 239–246.

Leach, J. (1979), Organization needs analysis: A new methodology. *Training and Development Journal,* 33, 66–69.

Leavitt, H. J. (1978), *Managerial Psychology.* 4th ed. Chicago: University of Chicago Press.

Light, D. (1979), Surface data and deep structure: Observing the organization of professional training. *Administrative Science Quarterly,* 24, 551–559.

Luthans, F., Paul, R., Baker, D. (1981), An experimental analysis of the impact of contingent reinforcement on salespersons' performance behavior. *Journal of Applied Psychology,* 66, 314–323.

McGhee, W., Tullar, W. L. (1978), A note on evaluating behavior modification and behavior modeling as industrial training techniques. *Personnel Psychology,* 31, 477–484.

March, J. G., Simon, H. A. (1958), *Organizations.* New York: Wiley.

Neuwese, W. (1970), *Onderwijsresearch* [Educational research]. Utrecht: Het Spectrum.

Minitzberg, H. (1979), *The structuring of organizations.* Englewood Cliffs: Prentice-Hall.

Moore, M. L., Dutton, P. (1978), Training needs analysis review and critique. *Academy of Management Review,* 532–545.

Newstrom, J. W., Lilyquist, J. M. (1979), Selecting needs analysis methods. *Training and Development Journal*, **33**, 52–56.
Rackham, N., Morgan, T. (1977), *Behavior analysis in training*. London: McGraw-Hill.
Revans, R. W. (1971), *Developing effective managers: A new approach to business education*. London: Longman.
Salaman, G. (1978), Management development and organization theory. *Journal of European Industrial Training*, **2**, 711.
Schafrat, W. H. A. (1978), *Mens en werk* [Man and work]. 2nd rev. ed. Deventer: Van Loghum Slaterus.
Simmons, R. E. (1978). *Managing behavioral processes: Applications of theory and research*. Arlington Heights: AHM Publishing Corporation.
Vegt, R. van der (1974), *Opleiden en evalueren. Een veldexperimentele studie naar uitkomsten van een bedrijfsopleiding* [Training and evaluation. A field-experimental study of the outcomes of training on the job]. Meppel: Boom.

Handbook of Work and Organizational Psychology
Edited by P. J. D. Drenth, H. Thierry, P. J. Willems and C. J. de Wolff
© 1984, John Wiley & Sons, Ltd.

2.12. Work and unemployment

Peter Warr

The recent increase in unemployment levels in western countries has been quite dramatic. Rates of unemployment in the early 1970s were typically around three or four per cent of the labour force. At present however most western countries have between 10% and 15% unemployed, a three-fold increase. Tens of millions of people are now out of work. Within each country, there are wide variations around the overall rate, so that for some groups 20% to 30% unemployment is not uncommon. Teenage workers, those approaching retirement, and members of ethnic minorities are particularly likely to suffer in this way. A disproportionate number of unemployed people come from older manufacturing industries which are in decline and are often grouped together in particular regions of a country; rates approaching 30% may be found in those regions (e.g. Wilcock and Franke, 1963; Hill *et al.*, 1973; Sinfield, 1981).

Furthermore, unemployment occurs disproportionately in certain families (with both older and younger adults out of work), and it may occur particularly frequently for certain individuals, interspersed with short spells in work. This recurrence of unemployment is encouraged by the 'last in first out' convention, whereby a company lays off first those employees who have joined most recently. In many cases, especially for older workers, jobs obtained after unemployment are at a lower level of pay then previously (e.g. Parnes and King, 1977). Unemployment may thus have a double cost within the labour market: further unemployment and a movement down the occupational ladder.

There is no doubt that most adults in western countries want to work in the sense of having paid employment (e.g. Kaplan and Tausky, 1974; Cherrington,

Prof. Dr. P. B. Warr, MRC/ESRC Social and Applied Psychology Unit, Department of Psychology, The University, Sheffield S10 2TN, Great Britain.

413

1980; Warr, 1982). The principal material and psychological benefits derived from a job may be summarized as follows:

1. *Money*. Having a paid job is essential for most people as their principal source of income and as a means to individual and interpersonal gains of many kinds.
2. *Raised activity levels*. Employment provides outlets for physical and mental energy, and may permit the exercise and development of personal skills. One basis of mental health is the establishment and attainment of realistic goals, and it is partly through a job that goals may be defined and achieved.
3. *Variety*. Without paid employment a person's behaviours and environments are likely to be relatively restricted. A job takes one out of unchanging domestic surroundings, and permits access to facilities, equipment and behaviours which are not otherwise available. Money received in payment for work allows activities, visits and holidays which otherwise may not be possible.
4. *Temporal structure*. Occupational tasks and routines divide time into segments each with its own built-in structure and goals. Other roles do of course also have this outcome, and as with all potential benefits one can 'have too much of a good thing'. However, for most people the introduction of greater temporal structure into their lives is likely to be a benefit of paid work, albeit one which is not recognized unless it is lost.
5. *Social contacts*. Paid employment gives access through encounters with other people to a range of new ideas and shared experiences, not necessarily related to work tasks. Social support from colleagues may be available to help with current problems in everyday living. Work activities can contribute to group goal achievement and a sense of being valued by co-workers.
6. *Personal identity*. The employed person's social position is in general valued within society, paid work often being seen as a morally correct activity. At a more specific level, particular occupational roles can contribute in important ways to personal identity and self perceptions.

These six principal benefits of paid employment do of course overlap both conceptually and in practice. Jahoda (1981) has drawn upon Freud's (1930) notion that work is a person's strongest tie to reality, suggesting that features of the kind described here provide links to reality which prevent people becoming overwhelmed by fantasy and emotion. Other roles may also provide such ties, but they come together in the employed role in a particularly powerful combination. Note that in this formulation work need not be pleasurable to be beneficial; it is the links with the environment which are important because they sustain and strengthen the self. Indeed, it is clear that having a job may yield certain costs which should be balanced against the benefits. The potential costs of paid employment include boredom, fatigue, reduced freedom, interpersonal conflict, psychological or physical strain, and even impaired health (e.g. Cooper and Payne, 1980; Levi, 1981).

This chapter will review research into unemployment to assess its psychological effects and its impact upon physical health. Particular emphasis is laid on the fact that 'the unemployed' are not a homogeneous group; it is essential to identify features which mediate the impact of being without paid work. Research conducted in the 1930s will first be examined, then more recent investigations into principal indices of psychological well-being will be described. Fourteen mediating variables will be introduced, leading to the notion that unemployment can be psychologically 'good' as well as 'bad', although the latter is more common at present. Finally, research into health effects will be summarized.

EARLY RESEARCH INTO UNEMPLOYMENT

A large number of studies of the impact of unemployment were carried out in the 1930s, when conditions were quite different from today. Major changes since then are the greater availability of guaranteed financial welfare benefits, more widespread free medical care, and marked improvements in nutrition. Role expectations within marriage have also changed. For example, higher rates of employment among married women in the 1980s increase the potential for financial input to the family, but may also increase an unemployed husband's feelings of guilt. Family size is also in general lower nowadays; and divorces and single-parent families are more common, yielding the possibility of additional life-event strain and reduced social support from family members. Differences should also be noted in available research techniques. Most studies in the 1930s were qualitative accounts of particular small groups of unemployed people, and tests of statistical significance and standardized measures of psychological functioning were largely absent.

We must therefore be cautious in generalizing from 1930s research to the present. However, some illustrative themes from that earlier period should be cited. Komarovsky (1940) was concerned to discover the extent to which unemployed men lost their authority within the family. Such 'breakdowns of the husband's status' attributable to unemployment were recorded in 13 out of 58 families in an industrial city outside New York. The husband's role was further examined in New York city by Ginzberg (1943), who also described how status within the family sometimes deteriorated, especially in households with adolescent children where discipline problems were more acute. Ginzberg reports a general increase in family tension, although this was usually kept within bounds.

Ginzberg (1943) and Ginsburg (1942) describe how unemployed men in New York went to considerable lengths to avoid the stigma of accepting relief payments, often waiting for more than a year before drawing them. Bakke (1940) reports that 40% of unemployed men in New Haven waited for more than two years after job loss before applying for relief. Bakke (1940) also studied 24 families in depth over a period of eight years. The general pattern was one of increasing difficulty with continuing unemployment, but in all cases the family was deemed to have made a permanent readjustment to its poorer status. A balance was struck between available income and an accepted standard of living, and stability in family relations and cooperative problem-solving returned. Bakke (1933) had previously studied unemployed men in the Greenwich area of London, concluding that the British system of unemployment insurance had made it possible to keep the diet 'not far below that to which the family is accustomed during normal times' (p. 53), thus alleviating the worst physical effects of unemployment. Unemployment insurance had 'removed the cutting edge of the desperation' which otherwise accompanied the search for work (p. 143).

The Pilgrim Trust (1938) conducted interviews in six British towns with 938 men who had been unemployed for more than a year (54% of the sample had been out of work for more than four years). The families of 30% of these men were considered to be living in 'deep' or 'moderate' poverty, with poverty most common in the families of those men (usually with dependent children) who were aged 25 to 34 (42% in poverty) and 35 to 44 (50% in poverty). However, the authors point out that poverty was also common among working-class *employed* men, so that unemployment did not necessarily yield the financial strains which they observed.

The Pilgrim Trust study paid special attention to the problems of wives of long-term unemployed men, especially those with dependent children. The authors point out that unemployed men in their sample were likely to suffer from nervousness and listlessness. However, 'many of the men concerned do effect a sort of adjustment to unemployment and lead lives that are not unhappy. Their wives only very rarely are able to make such an adjustment' (p. 139). Wives were reported to make substantial personal sacrifices for the benefit of their children and husband. 'In the majority of cases this does not result in specific forms of illness, but in a lowering of vitality, a diminished capacity for full living, and increased proneness to minor ailments. On the other hand there are many cases where serious ill-health and major illnesses have arisen directly as a consequence of undernourishment and wrestling with the domestic problems of long unemployment' (p. 139).

Research in an Austrian village experiencing sudden and widespread unemployment (with 367 out of 478 families having no employed wage-earner) revealed a disintegration of some people's sense of time, a progressive abandonment of financial budgeting, and a reduction in attendance at political clubs or use of the free library (Lazarsfeld, 1932; Jahoda *et al.*, 1933). In Minneapolis, USA, Rundquist and Sletto (1936) developed questionnaire measures of morale, inferiority and economic conservatism, and scales of attitudes to the family, education and the law. Comparisons between employed and unemployed people (almost all aged below 30) revealed differences mainly in respect of morale and economic conservatism. Unemployed people reported more worries, nervousness, disappointments and depression; and also greater agreement that the government ought to take over industry and guarantee jobs for all. No differences were recorded on inferiority and the other measures.

Israeli (1935) examined psychological distress in English and Scottish unemployed men, finding depression and anxiety at a high level which approached that of patients diagnosed as mentally ill. Raised distress levels of this kind were reported in several other studies in the period (Eisenberg and Lazarsfeld, 1938).

Before turning to contemporary research in this field, a later set of studies should be described. These approached psychological aspects of unemployment from a different direction, in response to employers' and governments' need for additional labour during the late 1960s. The aim was to identify people who were reluctant or unable to find and retain work. For example, Tiffany, Cowan and Tiffany (1970) set out to gather information in the United States which would 'foster better work stability and adjustment in the unemployed population' (p. 1). They identified groups of unemployed people described as 'work-inhibited', those who are 'physically capable of work but are prevented from working because of psychological difficulties' (p. 15), and advocated a social psychological approach 'designed to help the individual learn how to work and get along with his cohorts' (p. 3). The general emphasis was upon the development of personal autonomy, self-determination and interpersonal competence.

Related research examined attitudes of the 'hard-core unemployed', seeking through training to encourage their permanent re-entry into the labour force (e.g. Friedlander and Greenberg, 1971; Goodale, 1973). Measures of orientations to employment were devised by Alfano (1973), Goodwin (1972) and others, seeking to characterize important differences between stable employees and those seemingly alienated from the world of work. Unemployment was thus to be explained partly in psychological terms, over and above economic causal factors.

UNEMPLOYMENT AND PSYCHOLOGICAL WELL-BEING

Let us now turn to examine more recent studies of the psychological effects of unemployment. This can helpfully be undertaken through an examination of 'psychological well-being', a term which covers a range of interrelated affective, cognitive and behavioural processes. Low psychological well-being is illustrated in anxiety, depression, low morale, lack of self-confidence, low sense of personal autonomy, inability to cope with the problems of living, and dissatisfaction with oneself and the social and physical environment. Low psychological well-being is not identical with ill-health, since its features may occur in people who are not ill. However, when the features are relatively extreme, generalized and

Table 1. A classification of measures of psychological well-being.

	Positive well-being	Negative well-being	Global well-being
	Type 1	*Type 2*	*Type 3*
	1a. Positive affect	2a. Negative affect	3a. Present life
	1b. Experience of	2b. Experience of strain	satisfaction
	pleasure	2c. Anxiety	3b. Happiness
		2d. Depressed mood	
Less		2e. Psychological distress	
constant		2f. Potential psychiatric	
features		illness	
		2g. Diagnosed psychiatric	
		illness	
	Type 4	*Type 5*	*Type 6*
More	4a. Positive self-esteem	5a. Negative self-esteem	6a. Global self-esteem
constant		5b. Anxious personality	
features			

extended in time, then low psychological well-being may be reflected in psychological ill-health. High psychological well-being is a partly a matter of the absence of symptoms of low well-being, just as health in general is in a limited sense the absence of illness. However, it extends beyond that into more proactive forms, through successful striving for growth and self-actualization (Jahoda, 1958; Maslow, 1970).

It is helpful to view the features of psychological well-being in six groups, as set out in Table 1. That classification distinguishes between positive and negative aspects of well-being, and also includes (in the right-hand column) global aspects of life satisfaction and happiness. A distinction is drawn between the more constant and less constant features of each aspect, although this should be viewed as a continuum rather than a dichotomy. The six sets of features are of course overlapping, and significant intercorrelations are found between some of them.

Several investigators have compared groups of unemployed and employed people in terms of the aspects of psychological well-being listed in Table 1. Results from that research will be summarized next, recognizing at this stage that a cross-sectional difference between groups is not sufficient evidence for a causal interpretation. The issue of causality in unemployment research will be taken up later.

1a POSITIVE AFFECT

Bradburn (1969) has emphasized the need to examine feelings of accomplishment, interest in the environment, and positive happiness over and above the absence of unhappiness. His five-item measure of positive affect is typically found to be uncorrelated with his index of negative affect (2a, below) (cf. Warr *et al.*, 1983).

In two community surveys Bradburn (1969) recorded significantly lower positive affect among unemployed American men (N = 83 and 27) in comparison with those in jobs (N = 1091 and 838). Warr (1978) described interviews with British steel workers six months after closure of their works; at that point 764 were still unemployed and 891 had found jobs. The unemployed workers exhibited very significantly lower positive affect.

1b. EXPERIENCE OF PLEASURE

Warr and Payne (1982) obtained from respondents in a British community survey reports of pleasure experienced on the preceding day. Unemployed men who were looking for work (N = 183) reported significantly less pleasure than those in full-time jobs (N = 1162), but the difference was not significant for women (N = 71 unemployed and looking for work, and 181 full-time employed).

2a NEGATIVE AFFECT

Among indices of well-being identified as Type 2 in Table 1 is Bradburn's (1969) measure of negative affect, containing items about boredom, depression, loneliness and feeling upset. His initial research (described under 1a) failed to yield consistent findings with respect to negative affect and employment status. However, Warr (1978) recorded significantly more negative affect among unemployed members of his sample (see 1a, above).

2b EXPERIENCE OF STRAIN

In the study described under 1b. Warr and Payne (1982) also obtained reports of unpleasant emotional strain experienced on the preceding day. In the case of both men and women, unemployed people reported very significantly more strain than those in jobs.

2c ANXIETY

Three investigations have revealed significantly more anxiety among unemployed people. Cobb and Kasl (1977) and Kasl (1979a) used a seven-item scale in a follow-up study of two plant closures in the United States. Comparisons between responses from the same 46 people in periods of employment and unemployment indicated significantly higher anxiety during the latter times. Warr (1978), in the study of steel workers already described, and Donovan and Oddy (1982), in an investigation of 48 British teenagers, also reported significant associations between unemployment and raised anxiety.

2d DEPRESSED MOOD

Feelings of depression also fall within Type 2 as set out in Table 1. Using an eleven-item self-report measure, comparisons between employed and unemployed married members of an American community sample revealed significantly more depression associated with unemployment in the case of men (N = 24 unemployed, 644 employed) but not for women (N = 77 and 381 respectively) (Radloff, 1975). In a study of male German blue-collar workers (N = 26 unemployed, 15 employed), Frese (1979) reported a significant association between unemployment and high scores on Zung's (1965) self-rating depression scale. Donovan and Oddy (1982) obtained a similar result (see the study described under 2c), but Tiggemann and Winefield (1980) found that the difference in depression scores between 54 employed and 26 unemployed Australian 16-year-olds was not quite significant. Cobb and Kasl (1977) and Kasl (1979a), in comparisons between the same people when in jobs and out of work, recorded no significant difference in feelings of depression.

2e PSYCHOLOGICAL DISTRESS

Several investigators have examined negative psychological well-being through inventories of general psychological distress, covering a range of features associated with both anxiety and depression. For example, Pearlin and Lieberman (1979) in an American study of 92 recently unemployed and 542 continuously employed males and females used a 23-item distress scale. This covered reports in the past week of headaches, stomach upsets, nervousness, tension, fear, boredom, loneliness, hopelessness, sleep problems, lack of energy, etc. Recently unemployed respondents were found to score significantly more highly than those continuously in work. In a British investigation Cochrane and Stopes-Roe (1980) used the Langner (1962) measure of 22 psychophysiological symptoms, similar to those above, and reported significantly higher distress among unemployed men (N = 16) than those in work (N = 107). The difference was not quite significant for women (N = 52 and 57 respectively).

Estes and Wilensky (1978) compared 157 unemployed American professional workers (of both sexes) against 73 employed professionals in terms of a 37-item Index of Emotional Stress, based upon the Langner and other scales. Unemployed members of the sample exhibited significantly more distress. However, comparisons between 46 people when employed and unemployed in the Cobb and Kasl (1977) study revealed no differences in respect of insomnia, anger, resentment or suspicion; a significant difference on a six-item measure of psychophysiological symptoms was found, but in that case respondents reported *fewer* symptoms when unemployed.

2f POTENTIAL PSYCHIATRIC ILLNESS

A small number of measures have been devised as self-report screening instruments to identify people who are likely to be found on more detailed examination to be suffering from psychiatric illness. These are similar in content to the inventories of psychological distress referred to above, but differ in that a cut-off point has been established during standardization, above which a person is more likely to be a psychiatric case. The screening instrument most often used in recent research into unemployment is the General Health Questionnaire (Goldberg, 1972, 1978). This has been shown to be significantly predictive of diagnostic decisions reached in comprehensive psychiatric interviews (e.g. Henderson *et al.*, 1979; Goldberg, 1981; Banks, 1982). It does not directly identify people as ill, but is so constructed that high scores are likely to be associated with illness. Items cover feelings of worry, strain and depression, sleeplessness, loss of concentration, etc.

The General Health Questionnaire (GHQ) has been used in several comparisons of unemployed and employed samples in the United Kingdom. Hepworth (1980) observed significantly higher scores among 78 unemployed men than in a sample of 570 employees. Banks and Jackson (1982) present GHQ data from 2767 interviews with recent school-leavers, reporting a very strong association between unemployment and high scores. This association remained after controlling statistically for differences in sex, ethnic group and educational qualifications. (See also Stafford *et al.*, 1980.) The study by Donovan and Oddy (1982) also revealed a significant difference in GHQ scores between employed and unemployed teenagers. Warr (1983) has summarized a number of investigations using the GHQ: in each case proportionately more unemployed respondents than those in jobs score above the 'potential case' threshold.

2g DIAGNOSED PSYCHIATRIC ILLNESS

Another approach has been in terms of diagnosed illness. In a Canadian study Roy (1981) compared 71 depressed male patients with 71 control patients from an orthopaedic clinic. Fifteen of the former and only four of the latter were unemployed ($P < .01$). Bebbington *et al.* (1981) carried out psychiatric interviews as part of a community survey in London. They identified 6% of employed males as psychiatric cases, compared to 14% of unemployed males ($P < .025$). Causal interpretation is of course particularly difficult in this type of comparison.

3a PRESENT LIFE SATISFACTION

The third type of psychological well-being suggested in the classification of Table 1 is global well-being. Six studies have reported significantly lower life satisfaction among unemployed people in comparison with those who are employed. In an American study which controlled for income levels, Campbell *et al.* (1976) found a difference in life satisfaction for men but not for women. Warr (1978), Hepworth (1980) and Donovan and Oddy (1982), in the British research described earlier, found significant differences between employed and unemployed respondents on bipolar scales describing present life, such as empty-full, frustrating-fulfilling, and discouraging-hopeful. Cohn (1978) studied 537 unemployed and 543 employed American men, using the single question 'Are you more often satisfied or dissatisfied with yourself ?' Unemployed people were very much more likely to be dissatisfied with themselves. Gaskell and Smith (1981) obtained responses from 155 British males aged between 16 and 25, of whom 83 were unemployed. The unemployed group yielded significantly lower scores on satisfaction with attainment of general life goals.

3b HAPPINESS

Community surveys including self-reports of happiness (very happy; pretty happy; not too happy) have been described by Bradburn and Caplovitz (1965) and Bradburn (1969). Men who were unemployed reported significantly less happiness than those in work, but this was not generally found for women. In a combined sample of male and female teenagers, Tiggemann and Winefield (1980) observed significantly lower happiness scores among the unemployed.

4a and 5a POSITIVE AND NEGATIVE SELF-ESTEEM

Self-esteem has often been measured in terms of reported feelings about one's personal worth, and items have been worded either positively or negatively. Examples of items from favourable and unfavourable perspectives respectively are 'I feel I am as good a person as anyone else' and 'I feel I can't do anything right'. Warr and Jackson (1983) have measured separately positive and negative self-esteem of these kinds in five sets of interviews with recent school-leavers in Britain. Despite a correlation between positive and negative scores around 0.25, in each case there was a significant difference between unemployed and employed respondents in respect of negative self-esteem but not in respect of positive self-esteem.

One possible explanation of this differential finding is that unemployed people 'uncouple' their positive and negative self-conceptions in a way which is unnecessary for those in employment. Positive self-conceptions may be psychologically fundamental in the sense that they are retained in the face of moderate adversity, whereas negative self-esteem may in general be more responsive to environmental stress.

One other comparison of negative self-esteem scores of unemployed and employed people has been located. Lawlis (1971) studied 75 employed American men and 75 who had been unemployed for at least six months. The latter group yielded significantly higher scores on the self-depreciation scale of the 16PF personality measure (Cattell, 1962).

5b Anxious personality

In the same study Lawlis (1971) recorded significantly greater emotionality and less placidity on the 16PF among the unemployed members of his sample.

6a Global self-esteem

The final type of well-being measure shown in Table 1 covers global evaluations of oneself, in terms of both positive and negative features. Several unemployment researchers have used Rosenberg's (1965) scale, which contains both positive and negative items. This scale formed the basis of the two separate measured used by Warr and Jackson (1983) (4a and 5a, above). Gaskell and Smith (1981) report no differences between employed and unemployed groups' scores on the overall scale, but Donovan and Oddy (1982) found that employed young people scored significantly more highly than those out of work. Gurney (1980) used a variant of the same scale with 273 Australian 16-year-olds. No differences were observed between employed and unemployed males, but employed females yielded significantly higher scores than those who were unemployed. Hartley (1980) obtained discrepancy scores between actual self and ideal self, using 50 adjectives most of which referred to desirable characteristics (adaptable, cooperative, intelligent etc.). A comparison between 87 unemployed and 64 employed British managers revealed no difference in global self-esteem. Using a six-item measure of self-esteem (four negative, two positive items), Cobb and Kasl (1977) and Kasl (1979a) reported no differences associated with employment status. Results for global self-esteem are thus variable, with the majority of studies finding no association with employment status.

CAUSALITY AND CAUSAL PROCESSES

The literature reviewed here indicates that, in respect of the classification in Table 1, unemployed people are likely to exhibit more negative well-being of Types 2 and 5. They also have lower positive well-being of Type 1 and lower global well-being of Type 3. There appears to be no difference between employed and unemployed people in respect of positive self-esteem (Type 4) and usually no difference in global self-esteem (Type 6). However, this general pattern is mainly restricted to research with men and is less often revealed for women; sex differences in this area will be discussed later.

The results described above were almost all from cross-sectional comparisons of people who were employed or unemployed at the time of an investigation. This leaves open the question whether job loss and unemployment *cause* low psychological well-being or whether people who are chronically more distressed tend to become unemployed while the less distressed stay in work. The latter interpretation has become increasingly unlikely as unemployment levels continue to rise and whole departments or factories are shut down. However, longitudinal studies are clearly desirable, following people as they move from one employment status to another.

Six longitudinal investigations have been located. Cohn (1978) followed up married men who were either employed or unemployed a year after the first interview, at which time they all had paid work. Those unemployed at the second interview were found to express significantly lower satisfaction with self (see 3a, above, for the question wording). Banks and Jackson (1982) examined changes in General Health Questionnaire scores as young people moved from employment to unemployment, or in the reverse direction, observing significant changes across time in two different cohorts. Unemployment was associated with sharply reduced well-being, and employment with a substantial increase. Warr and Jackson (1983) recorded similar transitional changes for negative self-esteem, but not for positive self-esteem. Tiggemann and Winefield (1980) found that Australian school-leavers moving into unemployment became significantly less satisfied with themselves, less happy and more depressed, changes not observed among their employed counterparts. However, Gurney's (1980) similar study of Australian school-leavers revealed no decline in global self-esteem (6a above) on transition into unemployment.

Cobb and Kasl (1977) and Kasl (1979a) examined psychological well-being just before plant closure and six weeks later, by which time 46 men had found jobs and 53 remained unemployed. At the follow-up interviews the unemployed group reported significantly more depression, anxiety and suspicion about other people (but not more psychophysiological symptoms) than those in work. However, this difference did not arise primarily from a significant drop in well-being from pre-closure to post-closure in the unemployed group (although the changes were in that direction), but derived mainly from significant improvements among those workers who obtained jobs after plant closure. Both groups had very low well-being scores at the initial interviews, when they were anticipating with some concern the impending loss of jobs.

It seems clear from these varied data that becoming unemployed does indeed cause the observed decrements in psychological well-being. However, problems at work and anticipation of lay-off can also yield strain for those in employment (see also Wall and Clegg, 1981). It is also likely that in a minority of cases psychological problems may themselves have a causal impact upon job loss.

This is most apparent in the extreme case of problems leading to suicide. Although suicide is more likely to occur among people without a job, their prior personal characteristics are likely to affect both job loss and suicide (e.g. Shepherd and Barraclough, 1980).

In those cases where psychological well-being is negatively affected by unemployment, what causal processes may be expected to yield the decrement? In part, of course, loss of the psychological and material benefits of paid employment is important; these benefits have been illustrated earlier. However, three other features of the transition must also be considered (Warr, 1983).

First, the characteristics of the new role. In comparison with the employed role, unemployed people have few prescribed tasks or routines. Furthermore, those that they have are often unpleasant or threatening. Seeking financial allowances, 'signing on' as unemployed, and applying for jobs where rejection and consequent damage to self-esteem are likely: these are potentially distressing features of unemployment. In terms of social position the unemployed person may have fewer social contacts, and has certainly moved into a position of lower prestige within society. The unemployed role is one from which most incumbents are trying to escape, but the harder they try the more they feel the pain of failure.

Second, we should also examine as causal influences the changes which take place in other non-occupational, roles. For example, the unemployed husband may undertake more domestic chores, and teenagers may spend more time in groups looking for something to do, increasing their chances of getting into trouble with the police (e.g. Murray, 1978). Financial constraints on the unemployed father may lead to fewer outings with the children or fewer visits to the social club. In general, it is to be expected that changes in these non-occupational roles following job loss will be personally disadvantageous, acting to the detriment of psychological well-being.

Finally, role changes of all kinds are in themselves liable to cause personal strain, requiring adaptation, reorientation and learning. In the case of unemployment, the future becomes less predictable, and one is suddenly faced with questions which may not arise in continuing regular employment. What sort of a job do I want? Should I/we move to another part of the country? Why do I fail to get a job when others succeed? What am I good at? For how long will I be out of work? What does the future hold? For many people, the transition into unemployment is thus accompanied by a sense of instability and markedly reduced personal control. The need to cope with experiences of these kinds, perhaps over a period of months, is itself a stressor beyond those associated with changes in roles and role requirements.

In summary, the transition from employment to unemployment is more than the removal of features of the employed role, such as a reduction in money or in required tasks. It also involves introduction of features of a new role as unemployed person, many of which are unpleasant, and it brings with it changes in the number and content of other roles which are not themselves directly linked to occupational issues. Finally, these three types of change generate instability and unpredictability, experienced loss of personal control, a need to cope through the acquisition of new perspectives and skills, and a requirement to resolve questions about oneself which may otherwise never be raised. These four processes in interaction are likely to underlie the causal impact of unemployment upon psychological well-being.

VARIABLES WHICH MEDIATE THE EFFECTS OF UNEMPLOYMENT

Let us now turn to variables which might mediate these effects of unemployment. Knowledge of mediating variables would permit greater precision in statements about the impact of unemployment, and would also enhance understanding of causal processes through an appreciation of features associated with greater or lesser impact. Fourteen different variables will be considered here; they are of course in practice often interrelated.

1. Employment commitment

As was indicated at the beginning of the chapter, most people are personally strongly committed to being in paid employment, for non-financial as well as financial reasons. However, there are variations between people in the strength of this commitment, and these are likely to mediate the psychological effects of unemployment.

Measuring employment commitment through multi-item scales, several studies have found that the personal salience of having a paid job is significantly associated with a number of psychological outcome variables: positive and negative affect, scores on the General Health Questionnaire, and negative self-esteem (Warr, 1978; Stafford et al., 1980; Warr and Jackson, 1983; Jackson et al., 1983; Payne et al., 1983). Feather and Davenport (1981) used single-item measures of need to find a job and of depressed mood in a study of 212 unemployed Australians (mean age 19.76 years); the intercorrelation between need and mood was 0.50. In short, lower psychological well-being is observed in those unemployed people who are more committed to the employed role.

Logically this fact is not very surprising. However, as an instance of the general importance of ego-involvement in all areas of life it has interesting theoretical and practical implications. For example, what factors are likely to give rise to high or low levels of employment commitment? Can, and should, high levels be reduced through counselling, teaching, or social pressures, in periods where unemployment is so high that the probability of finding a job is negligible?

2. Age

It is clear that, at least among men, age is curvilinearly associated with the negative effects of unemployment. Middle-aged men suffer more than those who are both younger and older (e.g. Eisenberg and Lazarsfeld, 1938, p. 375; Daniel, 1974; Hepworth, 1980). In a study of 954 unemployed male manual workers the mean GHQ item scores for age groups 16–19, 20–29, 30–49, 50–59 and 60–64 were 1.02, 1.22, 1.28, 1.20 and 0.87 respectively (P < .001) (Warr and Jackson, unpublished). Employment commitment was also curvilinearly related to age: middle-aged men exhibited both greater distress and greater employment commitment in comparison with those who are younger and older. In this respect, it should be noted that financial problems are likely to be greatest among middle-aged unemployed people (e.g. Wilcock and Franke, 1963; Daniel, 1974; Estes and Wilensky, 1978).

3. Sex

Sex differences in the impact of unemployment are affected by variations in non-occupational roles. For example, a women's marital and parental status can markedly affect her employment commitment and the psychological value to her of paid work. Finlay-Jones and Burvill (1979) used the General Health Questionnaire in a community survey of Australian women. They found markedly higher proportions of unemployed women defined as probable psychiatric cases, but only among those who were unmarried. No differences associated with employment status were found for married women. In respect of satisfaction with self, Cohn (1978) found that unemployment had a negative impact on childless women but not on those with children. Comparisons between employed and unemployed teenagers, typically unmarried and without children, have shown that, although in general the females exhibit lower well-being, there is a large difference in GHQ scores and negative self-esteem between the employed and the unemployed for both sexes (Banks and Jackson, 1982; Warr and Jackson, 1983). Such a similarity between men and women seems likely to be found in all cases where people, male or female, are in effect principal wage-earners.

In other cases, for example among mothers of young children, the value of paid employment may be less. Warr and Parry (1982a) have reviewed the literature on this topic within a conceptual framework whose main elements include employment commitment and quality of non-occupational environment. The latter refers to the extent to which a women's psychological, social and financial needs are already met in the absence of paid employment. When published findings are examined within that framework, a relationship between paid employment and high psychological well-being is observed only among single women and among married women whose non-occupational environment is relatively deprived. For other groups of women there appears to be no association between having a job and experiencing higher psychological well-being.

4. Length of unemployment

It seems reasonable to assume that the increase in distress associated with unemployment is not a single step-function at the point of transition, and that continuing unemployment will be accompanied by further decreases in well-being. Such a relationship is most appropriately studied through longitudinal examination of a cohort of unemployed people, although almost all research has in practice correlated well-being scores at one point in time with each person's current length of unemployment. A moderate negative association is even more to be expected in such cross-sectional data. In addition to expected decreases in well-being with the passage of time, a self-selection process might be assumed: those with higher levels of well-being may be more likely to regain jobs, for example exhibiting greater self-confidence at a selection interview.

It is all the more surprising, then, that those few investigators reporting cross-sectional corrleations of this kind have typically observed no significant associations between duration of unemployment and affective reactions (Goodchilds and Smith, 1963; Little, 1976; Feather and Davenport, 1981; Warr *et al.*, 1982). In a longitudinal investigation, Cobb and Kasl (1977) studied 15 workers continuously unemployed for between six weeks and six months, finding that they improved on most measures and remained stable on others; in no measure was there a significant deterioration with continuing unemployment. (See also Kasl, 1979a, 1982.) However, most participants in these studies had been unemployed for only a few weeks, and longer durations may be required before an association becomes apparent. In Hepworth's (1980) study of 78 unemployed men, approximately half had been out of work for more than six months, and correlations of 0.22 and -0.24 were observed between duration of unemployment and GHQ and life satisfaction respectively ($P < .05$ in each case).

An unpublished investigation by Warr and Jackson examined unemployment lengths up to and beyond 52 weeks, with equal numbers of (male, blue-collar) respondents in each of ten age bands. A very significant association between General Health Questionnaire scores and duration of unemployment was found. For those unemployed less than a month, 42% of respondents scored above the screening threshold. (This compares with around 20% above the cut-off in studies of people in work.) For those unemployed for six months and longer the proportion above the cut-off was consistently around 65%. It thus seems likely that in general well-being drops at the point of transition and continues to decline through the early weeks of unemployment; however, many people adapt to their new role at a stable but significantly lower level of functioning.

The same study obtained measures of employment commitment at each duration of unemployment. There was no evidence of a negative association between expressed commitment and longer duration, although it is well established that continuing failure to find work is associated with fewer job-seeking attempts (e.g. Moylan *et al.*, 1982).

Mention should be made at this point of phase models of unemployment. Several writers have described the movement into and through unemployment in terms of separate phases, suggesting or implying that these are observable and identifiably different from each other. There is some variability between accounts, yet the parallels are marked and the sequence of phases is often said to be similar to that within any major transition. Drawing upon Eisenberg and Lazarsfeld (1938), Harrison (1976), Hill (1978), and Powell and Driscoll (1973), four principal phases may be described:

Shock The announcement that one is to lose a job is said to lead first to surprise, shock, indignation, anger or fury. 'Why me?' is a common response when only certain individuals are selected to lose their job.

Optimism. That initial reaction is said to be followed by a more cheerful phase. This may include a brief holiday, either at home or elsewhere, and domestic jobs may be finished, books read, and hobbies pursued. The feeling is that nothing has greatly changed, money may still be quite plentiful, and the person views him or herself as 'between jobs' rather than 'unemployed'. Active job hunting is said to be frequent, often carried out in a systematic and persistent way, with support from family and friends. The person is reported to be seeking a job similar to or better than the previous one.

Pessimism. However, as job-seeking failures build up a stage of pessimism, anxiety, self-doubt, vacillation, depression, frustration and moodiness is described. One may now increasingly perceive oneself as 'unemployed', and be unsure whether to seek less skilled jobs, accept a markedly reduced wage, or move to another area in search of work. Fears for the future, about money, skill loss, growing unemployability, and about relations within the family, are all said to increase.

Fatalism. A fourth phase is usually described in terms of a sense of hopelessness and apathy. The person is said to adjust to unemployment but with a narrower perspective, lowered aspirations and a continuing depressed outlook. Some writers emphasize swings in mood, between hope and hopelessness, and others stress a reduced sense of personal control, lack of commitment to job seeking, and a general passivity.

Such a sequence of phases certainly seems plausible, yet it should be noted that there is so far almost no direct evidence for a phase model. Support is usually restricted to ad hoc quotations, and contrary instances are never cited. Non-occupational roles are inadequately examined, with attention directed almost entirely to job-related behaviour and experiences. Time bands and criteria for indicating that a person has moved from one phase to the next are not provided. There is a clear need for additional conceptual as well as empirical work in this area.

5. Social class

Job loss and unemployment have traditionally been most common among manual workers, those who might be referred to as of lower social class or lower occupational level. However, middle-class unemployment is becoming more frequent, and social class should be examined as a fifth possible mediating variable.

There have been several suggestions that unemployment is not stressful for some middle-class workers (e.g. Little, 1976; Estes and Wilensky, 1978; Fineman, 1979). Cohn (1978) reported separate analyses for blue-collar and white-collar ex-employees in respect of satisfaction with self. He found that unemployment led to reduced satisfaction only for the blue-collar workers. In a study of unemployed men, Hepworth (1980) recorded significant negative correlations between well-being (in terms of General Health Questionnaire and present life satisfaction scores) and occupational status of last job: lower-status unemployed men exhibited lower well-being. Payne *et al.* (1983) examined 399 unemployed white-collar and blue-collar men; the two groups were matched one age and marital status, each person being between 25 and 39 years and living with his wife. Substantial differences were found in respect of financial problems and difficulties in filling the time, with these being significantly more common among blue-collar respondents. However, in this study there were no differences in psychological well-being measured by the GHQ or in terms of reported strain and pleasure; well-being was low for both groups.

Social class differences appear to be important in the influence of paid employment upon *women's* psychological well-being. A review of the literature and additional analyses of previously published data have indicated that among women in general (where there is overall no correlation with employment status) having a job is likely to benefit working-class women but not significantly those in middle-class samples (Warr and Parry, 1982a, b).

6. Financial strain

Unemployed people in most countries are entitled to two types of financial benefit from the state. Unemployment insurance payments are based upon prior contributions made when employed by the individual, his or her employer and the government. Unemployment insurance was not designed as a protection against long-term unemployment, and in most countries benefits are paid for only a limited period, usually six months or a year. Young people who have never worked and self-employed people are usually excluded, as are those who have made too few contributions, for example through recent periods out of work.

Such people must apply for unemployment or general social assistance payments. These are usually means-tested, dependent upon family commitments and necessary expenditures, and are lower than unemployment insurance payments. Because of their variability it is difficult to make a general assessment of degree of financial deprivation as a result of becoming unemployed. However, it appears that in the United Kingdom approximately two thirds of families with an unemployed man receive in benefits 50% or more of their income in work; a quarter receive more than 80% of their previous income (Davies *et al.*, 1982; Piachaud, 1981). Nevertheless, the absolute level of these benefits is often low: unskilled workers with a low wage when employed receive an even lower sum when unemployed.

Several studies have shown that degree of financial strain strongly affects the psychological impact of unemployment. Estes and Wilensky (1978) examined emotional distress in employed and unemployed professionals, separating the latter group into those reporting heavy financial strain (42% of them) and those not reporting heavy strain. The unemployed people without financial strain yielded emotional distress scores as low as those of employed people, but the scores of the financially strained respondents were very much higher. A five-item measure of economic deprivation yielded similar findings. Estes and Wilensky note that those unemployed people with greatest financial strain were likely to be parents of dependent children. Wilcock and Franke (1963) observed a similar pattern, also recording that financial difficulties were positively correlated with length of unemployment.

A significant association between financial strain and a single-item measure of unfavourable attitude to one's current unemployment was reported by Little (1976) in a study of 100 unemployed American professional men. Klandermans' (1980) study of 41 unemployed Dutch building trade workers revealed a similar finding: greater financial difficulties were associated with greater family strain and lower scores on four well-being items. Eisenberg and Lazarsfeld (1938) have described how this type of relationship was found in several investigations in the 1930s.

Financial strain in unemployment is itself alleviated by payments from a previous employer, occupational pensions, or income from other members of the family. In this last respect it should be noted that a husband's unemployment may sometimes lead to wives taking up jobs. In one sample studied by Wilcock and Franke (1963) the proportions of wives working before and one year after their husbands' plant was closed were 26 and 46 respectively; most of those taking jobs after their husband's lay-off did so primarily for financial reasons. Little (1976) noted that the probability of unemployed professionals having a working wife increased with length of the husband's unemployment.

It is likely that there are social class differences in the availability of finance over and above that received in state benefits. Swinburne (1980) noted that several managers and professional men in her sample had no immediate financial difficulty; and Payne *et al.* (1983) observed that middle-class unemployed men were significantly more likely to have wives with full-time jobs than were men in a comparable working-class sample.

7. Level of personal activity

Level of personal activity is another variable which is associated with the magnitude of the psychological impact of unemployment. Swinburne (1980) describes how her sample viewed activity as maintaining mental alertness, warding off fears and doubts, and providing goals and achievements. Financial constraints are of course influential here, since some activities require money, but variations between people in characteristic activity levels are also to be expected.

Hepworth's (1980) study of 78 unemployed men yielded a correlation of 0.45 between GHQ score and 'whether or not your time is fully occupied'. A sample of 399 unemployed men yielded correlations between GHQ score and a measure of problems in filling the time of around 0.55 (Payne et al., unpublished). The same study included examination of the associations between reported behaviour changes since job loss and several measures of current well-being. It was found that General Health Questionnaire scores were significantly positively associated with extent of reported increase in relatively passive behaviours such as sitting around at home, watching TV, and listening to the radio: the more these forms of inactivity were reported to have increased since job loss, the lower was psychological well-being (Warr and Payne, 1983).

Fryer and Payne (1982) conducted detailed interviews with a sample of people selected because of their positive acceptance of the unemployed role. Despite considerable differences among them in their objectives, each had seen unemployment as an opportunity to work for political, developmental or caring goals, which they could not attain during paid employment. Their main common characteristic was a very high level of personal activity: they were working towards those objectives with a degree of personal investment which exceeded most people's commitment to paid employment, and they exhibited high levels of affective well-being.

8. Attendance on schemes to assist the unemployed

Governments and other institutions in many countries now provide training and advisory schemes which aim to help unemployed people. These often have the primary goal of increasing a person's employment prospects, and should of course largely be evaluated in those terms (Warr and Lovatt, 1977; Schlossberg and Leibowitz, 1980). however, it is also of interest to examine their psychological benefits while the person is attending the scheme.

Stafford (1982) studied the psychological well-being of unemployed recent school-leavers as a function of their attendance on the British government's Youth Opportunities Programme, and Kemp and Mercer (1983) investigated unemployed disabled people attending an Employment Rehabilitation Centre.

In both cases attendance on the scheme clearly provided short-term benefit as evidenced by lower General Health Questionnaire scores.

9. Personal counselling

Personal counselling for unemployed people may also mediate the impact of unemployment. Such counselling is becoming increasingly common, although there appear to be few published evaluations of its effectiveness.

10. Previous experience of unemployment

It is sometimes suggested that previous experience of job loss and unemployment makes the transition less disturbing. Contrary to this expectation, Hepworth (1980) recorded significant negative correlations between number of times previously unemployed and psychological well-being. However, these probably reflect social class differences, in that middle-class men yielded both higher well-being scores and fewer previous episodes of unemployment than working-class men. It is important to control for social class differences in future investigations.

11. Attributed cause of unemployment

A person who loses his or her job while colleagues remain in work may attribute the loss to personal characteristics, whereas in cases of complete plant shut-down causal attributions are more likely to be made in terms of economic conditions, inadequate management, etc. The experience of unemployment might thus be expected to differ between situations of internal and external causal attribution. Feather and Davenport (1981) provided some evidence for this, finding that single-item depressed mood scores among unemployed young people were significantly higher for those who reported that unemployment was their own fault. In a study of 1479 unemployed British workers, Daniel (1974) observed that those who had been dismissed from their last job were more likely to report being 'very concerned' about job loss than those who left of their own accord (65% and 41% respectively).

12. Local unemployment levels

External causal attributions about one's own unemployment are more likely to be made when local unemployment levels are high. In addition, high local unemployment may reduce the sense of personal deviance from normative expectations, and provide more companionship through contact with other unemployed people during the working day. Cohn (1978) found that satisfaction with self is significantly higher for those unemployed men who live in areas where the local unemployment rate is high. However, this may be because unemployed people in areas of high unemployment are more likely to define themselves as out of the labour market; in those cases reduced employment commitment leads to reduced distress. Daniel (1974) has analyzed separately reports that unemployment is 'very bad' from those members of his sample who were still seeking jobs. In areas of high unemployment 55% of job seekers saw their situation as 'very bad', compared to 45% in areas of low unemployment.

13. Social support

It seems plausible that social support available from family and friends should in general mediate the impact of life stress, and this has been demonstrated in several studies in other fields (e.g. Cobb, 1976; La Rocco et al., 1980). Gore (1978) has presented data about the possible mediating role of social support after job loss. Her analyses and tests of statistical significance appear not to permit a definite conclusion, although they are sometimes cited as doing so. Kasl (1982) has discussed the same empirical material, suggesting that 'social support as a buffering influence did not come into play until later, i.e. when it appeared that stable re-employment was not easily attained' (p. 642). This topic clearly deserves further investigation.

14. Personal vulnerability to stress

A final factor which may mediate the impact of unemployment is personal vulnerability. Some people are characteristically more vulnerable than others to depression or anxiety in the face of substantial problems in living. One might expect that those people would suffer more from the difficulties posed by unemployment, but this possibility has not yet been systematically investigated. One promising approach is through the concept of personal 'hardiness', measured through commitment to activity, control over one's environment, and acceptance of challenge (Kobasa et al., 1982). Such a concept does of course embrace several of the preceding variables (perhaps also differing between social classes), and it would be valuable to examine its components separately as well as its overall impact upon the experience of unemployment.

GOOD AND BAD JOBS AND GOOD AND BAD UNEMPLOYMENT

The existence of these 14 mediating variables draws attention to the fact that for some people unemployment may not be particularly troublesome. A 55-year-old middle-class man with a regular income (from an occupational pension or elsewhere) who is active in clubs and societies (perhaps in quasi-managerial or professional roles) may have a level of psychological well-being comparable to that when he was employed, especially after any initial period of adjustment which may have been required.

Furthermore, paid employment may sometimes be seen as undesirable. There are many jobs which are stressful or psychologically demeaning, from which a person may be pleased to escape. It is helpful to consider both individual jobs and individual unemployment in terms of the ratio of costs and benefits of each. In those terms not only unemployment but also employment may be placed upon a dimension ranging from 'good' (yielding high psychological well-being) to 'bad' (low well-being). The main possible costs of paid employment were identified earlier as reduced autonomy, boredom, fatigue, interpersonal conflict, psychological or physical strain, and impaired health. The principal possible benefits were described in terms of money, raised activity levels, variety, temporal structure, social contacts, and personal identity.

Many of these same costs and benefits are also present during unemployment, arising partly from roles which are entirely non-occupational. In assessing the impact of unemployment, we need to examine the ratio of costs and benefits not only of employment and unemployment themselves, but also incorporating other family and social roles (Warr, 1983). In general, unemployment is likely to yield a reduction in benefits and an increase in costs. Such a situation, the usual one, may be classed as 'bad' unemployment, in the sense that it causes low psychological well-being. Relatively 'good' unemployment is however possible, where the cost-benefit ratio has remained the same or shifted favourably after job loss. There are of course many points on the continuum from bad to good unemployment depending upon the cost-benefit ratios.

This brief description is important in placing emphasis on the fact that paid employment is not necessarily desirable, and that unemployment is not inevitably undesirable. We need to find ways to shift both employment and unemployment from the 'bad' pole towards the 'good' pole of this general dimension of contribution to psychological well-being. Technological and economic factors are combining to ensure that unemployment levels will remain high in the foreseeable future. It is important to seek a new societal role and enhanced personal well-being for the millions of people who will inevitably be unemployed. The 14 mediating factors introduced above provide a basis for this search.

UNEMPLOYMENT AND HEALTH

Finally, let us extend this review to ask whether unemployment impairs physical and psychological health. Some studies of this question have been conducted at an aggregate level, investigating overall levels of unemployment and illness within a community as a whole; others (including the investigations described above) have taken the individual as their unit of analysis, studying the health of specific individuals in relation to their own employment status.

Among the aggregate studies are some which have focused upon mortality rates in different groups or geographical regions at one point in time. For example, it is well established that lower socio-economic status is associated with higher mortality rates in cross-sectional comparisons (e.g. Kitiwaga and Hauser, 1973; Spruit, 1982). Community socio-economic status levels can be measured in several ways, one of which is through the proxy variable of local unemployment; unemployment rate and mortality rate are thus sometimes found to be positively correlated in aggregate research at the community level (e.g. Brennan, 1978; Brennan and Lancashire, 1978).

This cross-sectional relationship has been extended into longitudinal inquiries by Brenner (e.g. 1980a, b), who has examined the relationship between several economic variables, including unemployment rates, and mortality rates for the United States between 1909 and 1976. He has reported that mortality rates are significantly related to *earlier* unemployment levels; unemployment is said to have a lagged effect (greatest at two years) upon United States death rate.

Brenner's concern is with rapid economic change of two kinds, growth as well as recession, both of which are said to increase stress and to inhibit the long-term decline in mortality. In respect of increases in unemployment, all members of society (not merely those who lose their jobs) are thought to be at risk. Indeed, his analyses of U.S. data reveal the strongest relationship between aggregate unemployment and mortality for those who are aged below 10 and above 75. The methods and results of this longitudinal aggregate research have been questioned by several writers (e.g. Eyer, 1977; Kasl, 1979b; Spruit, 1982).

Brenner (1979) has repeated his earlier analysis in respect of mortality data from England and Wales between 1936 and 1976, recording a significant relationship with unemployment levels for the period as a whole. However, Gravelle *et al.* (1981) have shown that this relationship is almost entirely due to a substantial decrease in unemployment between 1940 and 1942, at the same time as major improvements occurred in diet, medical treatment and availability of health service facilities. Separate analyses of mortality data for shorter periods within the original range of years (and for a longer period, 1922–1976) failed to reveal any significant relationship with unemployment. Similar differences between the 1930s and 1940s may account for the pattern previously observed in the American data.

Mortality rates are of course rather extreme indices of illness, and other measures should be considered. Brenner (1973) has investigated first admissions to New York state public mental hospitals between 1914 and 1967. He reported a significant lagged relationship with changes in the manufacturing employment index. However, the finding has been questioned on a number of grounds: omission of data from private mental hospitals and state general hospitals, variations between years and sub-samples, and possible failure in matching community areas for economic and psychiatric variables (e.g. Marshall and Funch, 1979, 1980; Ratcliff, 1980). Nevertheless, longitudinal research by

Catalano *et al.* (1981) within a single U.S. county revealed a significant relationship between male admissions to mental health service facilities and local unemployment levels two months earlier. Ahr, Gorodezky and Cho (1981) report a similar finding, but for readmissions rather than for admissions as a whole. Both these research teams tentatively opt for an 'uncovering' rather than a 'provoking' explanation. Mental health service facilities may become more accessible or attractive to people when they are unemployed, so that observed increases in hospital admissions may uncover previous illness more than they reveal new illness caused by unemployment.

Catalano and Dooley (1977) attempted to link local unemployment levels to self-reports of depressed mood within an American city, finding strongest associations after a two-month lag. Such a relationship could provide a possible mechanism for the impact of economic conditions upon mental health facility admissions. However, a second investigation failed to replicate the result (Dooley *et al.*, 1981).

Another approach is to examine specific problems and health-related behaviours at the level of the individual. For example, Smart (1979) and Warr and Payne (1983) studied reported alcohol consumption, finding reports of reduced consumption after job loss. However, Smart also identified a sub-sample of respondents who had personal drinking problems, finding that these people tended to report increasing their consumption when unemployed: alcoholism after unemployment may be more likely among those who are already prone to heavy drinking but not among the population as a whole. Warr and Payne (1983) also obtained reports about changes in smoking since job loss, finding a significant reported increase for working-class but not for middle-class respondents.

What of the individual-level studies summarized earlier in the chapter? In respect of diagnosed psychiatric illness (measure 2g in Table 1), unemployed people have higher prevalence rates in cross-sectional comparisons, but the issues of causality and date of onset remain unresolved. Research with the General Health Questionnaire, a screening measure of potential psychiatric illness (2f in Table 1), showed unemployed people to be substantially more at risk than those in jobs, and longitudinal changes indicate that scores are causally affected by unemployment to a significant degree (Banks and Jackson, 1982). It seems certain from validity studies of the GHQ that some of the high-scoring unemployed people would on full examination be diagnosed as psychiatrically ill, but at present the size of this group is uncertain.

A direct approach to self-reported general health has been taken by Warr and Jackson (unpublished), asking 954 unemployed working-class men whether their health had changed since they became unemployed, and if so whether this was for the better or for the worse. Such an approach reduces the causality problem, although the index of health is rather crude. Sixty-two percent reported no change, 11% an improvement and 27% a deterioration. Improvements were said to come about through less work strain and more relaxation and exercise. Changes for the worse included increased anxiety and depression, as well as an increased frequency of some physical symptoms. Payne *et al.* (1983) found that 26% of a separate sample of men reported a deterioration in health since job loss between six and 12 months previously.

In their follow-up study of plant closures Kasl *et al.* (1975) examined how frequently men recorded in health diaries that they 'did not feel as well as usual'. No differences were observed between days in employment and in unemployment. The same study revealed increases in serum cholesterol levels on transition into unemployment, but continuing unemployment in a sub-sample of 15 people was accompanied by a decline in this measure. No differences associated with employment status were found in respect of blood pressure or body weight (Kasl and Cobb, 1980). However, this investigation covered only relatively brief periods of unemployment (an average of 15 weeks in the subsequent two years), and longer durations may yield different findings.

There remains a need for more studies of physical symptoms and physical ill-health during unemployment. Research to date has not demonstrated unequivocally that unemployment impairs physical health, although it is widely believed that this may be so. However, the results are clear in respect of psychological symptoms: unemployment does reduce psychological health. Experiences of strain, anxiety, depression and hopelessness are likely to increase because of unemployment, and level of aspiration, sense of autonomy and positive involvement in the world are all likely to be negatively affected.

Such consequences are not universal, being mediated by variables discussed in this chapter. From knowledge of mediating variables, we can identify specially vulnerable groups of unemployed people (middle-aged men with high employment commitment and high financial strain, for example), to whom research and ameliorative attention should particularly be directed. This is of major importance as unemployment becomes of much longer duration than in recent decades. A period of 18 months without paid work is qualitatively different from a few weeks between jobs, and the effects of current widespread long-term unemployment on psychological and physical health are likely to be more extensive and severe than have been observed in the past.

REFERENCES

Ahr, P. R., Gorodezky, M. J., Cho, D. W. (1981), Measuring the relationship of public psychiatric admissions to rising unemployment. *Hospital and Community Psychiatry*, **32**, 398–401.

Alfano, A. M. (1973), A scale to measure attitudes toward working. *Journal of Vocational Behavior*, **3**, 329–333.

Bakke, E. W. (1933), *The unemployed man: A social study*. London: Nisbet.

Bakke, E. W. (1940), *Citizens without work: A study of the effects of unemployment upon the workers' social relations and practices.* New Haven: Yale University Press. (Reprinted by Archon Books, 1969.)

Banks, M. H. (1982), Validation of the General Health Questionnaire in a young community sample. *Psychological Medicine*, **13**, 349–353.

Banks, M. H., Jackson, P. R. (1982), Unemployment and risk of minor psychiatric disorder in young people: Cross-sectional and longitudinal evidence. *Psychological Medicine*, **12**, 789–798.

Bebbington, P., Hurry, J., Tennant, C., Sturt, E., Wing, J. K. (1981), Epidemiology of mental disorders in Camberwell. *Psychological Medicine*, **11**, 561–580.

Bradburn, N. M. (1969), *The structure of psychological well-being.* Chicago: Aldine.

Bradburn, N. M., Caplovitz, D. (1965), *Reports on happiness.* Chicago: Aldine.

Brennan, M. E. (1978), Patterns of mortality and the alienation of life: A study using census indicators. In: Armytage, W. H. G., Peel, J. (Eds.), *Perimeters of social repair.* London: Academic Press.

Brennan, M. E., Lancashire, R. (1978), Association of childhood mortality with housing status and unemployment. *Journal of Epidemiology and Community Health*, **32**, 28–33.

Brenner, M. H. (1973), *Mental illness and the economy.* Cambridge: Harvard University Press.

Brenner, M. H. (1979), Mortality and the national economy: A review, and the experience of England and Wales. *The Lancet*, **2**, 568–573.

Brenner, M. H. (1980a), Industrialization and economic growth: Estimates of their effects on the health of populations. In: Brenner, M. H., Mooney, A., Nagy, T. J. (Eds.), *Assessing the contributions of the social sciences to health.* Washington: American Academy for the Advancement of Science.

Brenner, M. H. (1980b), Importance of the economy to the nation's health. In: Eisenberg, L., Kleinman, A. (Eds.), *The relevance of social science for medicine.* New York: Reidel.

Campbell, A., Converse, P. E., Rodgers, W. L. (1976), *The quality of American life.* New York: Russell Sage Foundation.

Catalano, R., Dooley, C. D. (1977), Economic predictors of depressed mood and stressful life events in a metropolitan community. *Journal of Health and Social Behavior*, **18**, 292–307.

Catalano, R., Dooley, C. D., Jackson, R. (1981), Economic predictors of admissions to mental health facilities in a nonmetropolitan community. *Journal of Health and Social Behavior*, **22**, 284–297.

Cattell, R. B. (1962), *The Sixteen Personality Factor Questionnaire.* Champaign (Illinois): Institute for Personality and Ability Testing.

Cherrington, D. J. (1980), *The work ethic.* New York: Amacom.

Cobb, S. (1976), Social support as a moderator of life stress. *Psychosomatic Medicine*, **38**, 300–314.

Cobb, S., Kasl, S. V. (1977), *Termination: The consequences of job loss.* Cinicinatti: US Department of Health, Education and Welfare.

Cochrane, R., Stopes-Roe, M. (1980), Factors affecting the distribution of psychological symptoms in urban areas of England. *Acta Psychiatrica Scandinavica*, **61**, 445–460.

Cohn, R. M. (1978), The effect of employment status change on self-attitudes. *Social Psychology*, **41**, 81–93.

Cooper, C. L., Payne, R. L. (Eds.) (1980), *Current concerns in occupational stress.* London: Wiley.

Daniel, W. W. (1974), *A national survey of the unemployed.* London: Political and Economic Planning Institute.

Davies, R., Hamill, L., Moylan, S., Mee, C. H. (1982), Incomes in and out of work. *Department of Employment Gazette*, **90**, 237–243.

Donovan, A., Oddy, M. (1982), Psychological aspects of unemployment: An investigation into the emotional and social adjustment of school leavers. *Journal of Adolescence*, **5**, 15–30.

Dooley, C. D., Catalano, R., Jackson, R., Brownell, A. (1981), Economic, life, and symptom changes in a non-metropolitan community. *Journal of Health and Social Behavior*, **22**, 144–154.

Eisenberg, P., Lazarsfeld, P. F. (1938), The psychological effects of unemployment. *Psychological Bulletin*, **35**, 358–390.

Estes, R. J., Wilensky, H. L. (1978), Life cycle squeeze and the morale curve. *Social Problems*, **25**, 277–292.

Eyer, J. (1977), Does unemployment cause the death rate peak in each business cycle? *International Journal of Health Services*, **7**, 625–662.

Feather, N. T., Davenport, P. R. (1981), Unemployment and depressive affect: A motivational analysis. *Journal of Personality and Social Psychology*, **41**, 422–436.

Fineman, S. (1979), A psychosocial model of stress and its application to managerial unemployment. *Human Relations*, **32**, 323–345.

Finlay-Jones, R. A., Burvill, P. W. (1979), Women, work and minor psychiatric morbidity. *Social Psychiatry*, **14**, 53–57.

Frese, M. (1979), Arbeitslosigkeit, Depressivität und Kontrolle: eine Studie mit Wiederholungsmessung. In: Kieselbach, T., Offe, H. (Eds.), *Arbeitslosigkeit*. Darmstadt: Steinkopff Verlag.

Freud, S. (1930), *Civilization and its discontents*. London: Hogarth Press.

Friedlander, F., Greenberg, S. (1971), Effect of job attitudes, training, and organization climate on performance of the hard-core unemployed. *Journal of Applied Psychology*, **55**, 287–295.

Fryer, D., Payne, R. L. (1982), Towards understanding proactivity in unemployment. MRC/ESRC SAPU Memo 540.

Gaskell, G., Smith, P. (1981), 'Alienated' black youth: An investigation of 'conventional wisdom' explanations. *New Community*, **9**, 182–193.

Ginsburg, S. W. (1942), What unemployment does to people. *American Journal of Psychiatry*, **99**, 439–446.

Ginzberg, E. (1943), *The unemployed*. (In conjunction with E. L. Ginsburg, S. W. Ginsburg, D. L. Lynn, and L. M. Vickers.) New York: Harper and Brothers.

Goldberg, D. (1972), *The detection of psychiatric illness by questionnaire*. London: Oxford University Press.

Goldberg, D. (1978), *Manual for the General Health Questionnaire*. Windsor: NFER.

Goldberg, D. (1981), Estimating the prevalence of psychiatric disorder from the results of a screening test. In: Wing, J. K., Bebbington, P., Robins, L. N. (Eds.), *What is a case?* London: Grant McIntyre.

Goodale, J. G. (1973), Effects of personal background and training on work values of the hard-core unemployed. *Journal of Applied Psychology*, **57**, 1–9.

Goodchilds, J. D., Smith, E. E. (1963), The effects of unemployment as mediated by social status. *Sociometry*, **26**, 287–293.

Goodwin, L. (1972), *Do the poor want to work?* Washington: The Brookings Institution.

Gore, S. (1978), The effect of social support in moderating the health consequences of unemployment. *Journal of Health and Social Behavior*, **19**, 157–165.

Gravelle, H. S. E., Hutchinson, G., Stern, J. (1981), Mortality and unemployment: A critique of Brenner's time-series analysis. *The Lancet*, **2**, 675–679.

Gurney, R. M. (1980), Does unemployment affect the self-esteem of school-leavers? *Australian Journal of Psychology*, **32**, 175–182.

Harrison, R. (1976), The demoralising experience of prolonged unemployment. *Department of Employment Gazette*, **84**, 339–348.

Hartley, J. F. (1980), The impact of unemployment upon the self-esteem of managers. *Journal of Occupational Psychology*, **53**, 147–155.

Henderson, S., Duncan-Jones, P., Byrne, D. G., Scott, R., Adcock, S. (1979), Psychiatric disorder in Canberra: A standardised study of prevalence. *Acta Psychiatrica Scandinavica*, **60**, 335–374.

Hepworth, S. J. (1980), Moderating factors of the psychological impact of unemployment. *Journal of Occupational Psychology*, **53**, 139–145.

Hill, J. M. M. (1978), The psychological impact of unemployment. *New Society*, **43**, no. 798, 118–120.

Hill, M. J., Harrison, R. M., Sargent, A. V., Talbot, V. (1973), *Men out of work: A study of unemployment in three English towns*. Cambridge: Cambridge University Press.

Israeli, N. (1935), Distress in the outlook of Lancashire and Scottish umemployed. *Journal of Applied Psychology*, **19**, 67–69.

Jackson, P. R., Stafford, E. M., Banks, M. H., Warr, P. B. (1983), Unemployment and psychological distress in young people: The moderating role of employment commitment. *Journal of Applied Psychology*, **68**, 525–535.

Jahoda, M. (1958), *Current concepts of mental health*. New York: Basic Books.

Jahoda, M. (1981), Work, employment and unemployment. *American Psychologist*. **36**, 184–191.

Jahoda, M., Lazarsfeld, P. F., Zeisel, H. (1933), *Marienthal: The sociography of an unemployed community*. English translation. 1972. London: Tavistock Publications.

Kaplan, H. R., Tausky, C. (1974), The meaning of work among the hard-core unemployed. *Pacific Sociological Review*, **17**, 185–198.

Kasl, S. V. (1979a), Changes in mental health status associated with job loss and retirement. In: Rose, R. M., Klerman G. L. (Eds.), *Stress and mental disorder*. New York: Raven Press.

Kasl, S. V. (1979b), Mortality and the business cycle: Some questions about research strategies when utilizing macro-social and ecological data. *American Journal of Public Health*, **69**, 784–788.

Kasl, S. V. (1982), Strategies of research on economic instability and health. *Psychological Medicine*, **12**, 637–649.

Kasl, S. V., Cobb, S. (1980), The experience of losing a job: Some effects on cardiovascular functioning. *Psychotherapy and Psychosomatics*, **34**, 88–109.

Kasl, S. V., Gore, S., Cobb, S. (1975), The experience of losing a job: Reported changes in health, symptoms and illness behavior. *Psychosomatic Medicine*, **37**, 106–122.

Kemp, N. J., Mercer, R. A. (1983), Unemployment, disability and rehabilitation centres and their effects on mental health. *Journal of Occupational Psychology*, **56**, 37–48.

Kitiwaga, E. M., Hauser, P. M. (1973), *Differential mortality in the United States: A study in socio-economic epidemiology*. Cambridge: Harvard University Press.

Klandermans, P. G., Werklozen en de Werklozenbeweging. Mens en Maatschappij, **54**, 1979, 5–53 (unemployed people and the unemployed people's movement).

Kobasa, S. C., Maddi, S. R., Kahn, S. (1982), Hardiness and health: A prospective study. *Journal of Personality and Social Psychology*, **42**, 168–177.

Komarovsky, M. (1940), *The unemployed man and his family: The effect of unemployment on the status of the man in 59 families*. New York: Dryden Press.

Langner, T. S. (1962), A 22-item screening score of psychiatric symptoms indicating impairment. *Journal of Health and Social Behavior*, **1**, 269–276.

La Rocco, J. M., House, J. S., French, J. R. P. (1980), Social support, occupational stress, and health. *Journal of Health and Social Behavior*, **21**, 202–218.

Lawlis, G. F. (1971), Motivational factors reflecting employment instability. *Journal of Social Psychology*, **84**, 215–223.

Lazarsfeld, P. F. (1932), An unemployed village. *Character and Personality*, **1**, 147–151.
Levi, L. (1981), *Society, stress and disease: Working life*. London: Oxford University Press.
Little, C. B. (1976), Technical-professional unemployment: Middle-class adaptability to personal crisis. *Sociological Quarterly*, **17**, 262–274.
Marshall, J. R., Funch, D. P. (1979), 'Mental Illness and the Economy': A critique and partial replication. *Journal of Health and Social Behavior*, **20**, 282–289.
Marshall, J. R., Funch, D. P. (1980), Reply to Ratcliff. *Journal of Health and Social Behavior*, **21**, 391–393.
Maslow, A. H. (1970), *Motivation and personality*. New York: Harper and Row.
Moylan, S., Millar, J., Davies, B. (1982), Unemployment—the year after. *Department of Employment Gazette*, **90**, 334–340.
Murray, C. (1978), *Youth unemployment: A socio-psychological study of 16–19 year-olds*. Windsor: NFER.
Parnes, H. S., King, R. (1977), Middle-aged job losers. *Industrial Gerontology*, **4**, 77–95.
Payne, R. L., Warr, P. B., Hartley, J. (1983), Social class and the experience of unemployment. MRC/ESRC SAPU Memo 549.
Pearlin, L. I., Lieberman, M. A. (1979), Social sources of emotional distress. *Research in Community and Mental Health*, **1**, 217–248.
Piachaud, D. (1981), *The dole*. London School of Economics, Centre for Labour Economics, Discussion Paper 89.
Pilgrim Trust (1938), *Men without work*. Cambridge: Cambridge University Press.
Powell, D. H., Driscoll, P. F. (1973), Middle-class professionals face unemployment. *Society*, **10**, 2, 18–26.
Radloff, L. (1975), Sex differences in depression: The effects of occupation and marital status. *Sex Roles*, **1**, 249–265.
Ratcliff, K. S. (1980), On Marshall and Funch's critique of 'Mental Illness and the Economy'. *Journal of Health and Social Behavior*, **21**, 389–391.
Rosenberg, M. (1965), *Society and the adolescent self-image*. Princeton: Princeton University Press.
Roy, A. (1981), Vulnerability factors and depression in men. *British Journal of Psychiatry*, **138**, 75–77.
Rundquist, E. A., Sletto, R. F. (1936), *Personality in the depression*. Minneapolis: University of Minnesota Press.
Schlossberg, N. K., Leibowitz, Z. (1980), Organizational support systems as buffers to job loss. *Journal of Vocational Behavior*, **17**, 204–217.
Shepherd, D. M., Barraclough, B. M. (1980), Work and suicide: An empirical investigation. *British Journal of Psychiatry*, **136**, 469–478.
Sinfield, A. (1981), *What unemployment means*. Oxford: Martin Robertson.
Smart, R. G. (1979), Drinking problems among employed, unemployed and shift workers. *Journal of Occupational Medicine*, **11**, 731–736.
Spruit, I. P. (1982), Unemployment and health in macro-social analysis. *Social Science and Medicine*, **16**, 1903–1917.
Stafford, E. M. (1982), The impact of the Youth Opportunities Programme on young people's employment prospects and psychological well-being. *British Journal of Guidance and Counselling*, **10**, 12–21.
Stafford, E. M., Jackson, P. R., Banks, M. H. (1980), Employment, work involvement and mental health in less qualified young people. *Journal of Occupational Psychology*, **53**, 291–304.
Swinburne, P. (1980), The psychological impact of unemployment on managers and professional staff. *Journal of Occupational Psychology*, **54**, 47–64.
Tiffany, D. W., Cowan, J. R., Tiffany, P. M. (1970), *The unemployed: A social-psychological portrait*. Englewood Cliffs (N.J.): Prentice-Hall.

Tiggemann, M., Winefield, A. H. (1980), Some psychological effects of unemployment in school-leavers. *Australian Journal of Social Issues*, **15**, 269–276.

Wall, T. D., Clegg, C. W. (1981), Individual strain and organizational functioning. *British Journal of Clinical Psychology*, **20**, 135–136.

Warr, P. B. (1978), A study of psychological well-being. *British Journal of Psychology*, **69**, 111–121.

Warr, P. B. (1982), A national study of non-financial employment commitment. *Journal of Occupational Psychology*, **55**, 297–312.

Warr, P. B. (1983), Job loss, unemployment and psychological well-being. In: Allen, V. Vliert, E. van de (Eds.), *Role transitions*. New York: Plenum Press.

Warr, P. B., Jackson, P. R. (1983), Self-esteem and unemployment among young workers. *Le Travail Humain*, **46**, 355–366.

Warr, P. B., Lovatt, D. J. (1977), Retraining and other factors associated with job finding after redundancy. *Journal of Occupational Psychology*, **50**, 67–84.

Warr, P. B., Parry, G. (1982a), Paid employment and women's psychological well-being. *Psychological Bulletin*, **91**, 498–516.

Warr, P. B., Parry, G. (1982b), Depressed mood in working-class mothers with and without paid employment. *Social Psychiatry*, **17**, 161–165.

Warr, P. B., Payne, R. L. (1982), Experiences of strain and pleasure among British adults. *Social Science and Medicine*, **16**, 1691–1697.

Warr, P. B., Payne, R. L. (1983), Social class and reported changes in behavior after job loss. *Journal of Applied Social Psychology*, **13**, 206–222.

Warr, P. B., Barter, J., Brownbridge, G. (1983), On the independence of positive and negative affect. *Journal of Personality and Social Psychology*, **44**, 644–651.

Warr, P. B., Jackson, P. R., Banks, M. H. (1982), Duration of unemployment and psychological well-being in young men and women. *Current Psychological Research*, **2**, 207–214.

Wilcock, R. C., Franke, W. H. (1963), *Unwanted workers: Permanent layoffs and long-term unemployment*. Glencoe: The Free Press.

Zung, W. W. K. (1965), A self-rating depression scale. *Archives of General Psychiatry*, **12**, 63–70.

Part 3

The interaction between person and group

Introduction

Pieter J. D. Drenth

Part 3 treats of an area that has many connections with classical social psychology in that this branch of psychology is primarily concerned with the relationship between an individual and his immediate, non-physical environment, meaning, in many cases, the concrete group with which that individual interacts: family, friends, fellow students, colleagues, etc. A great deal of research in this field is available to provide insight into the interaction processes between individual and group, paying attention to the development of the behavioral norms shared by the group's members as well as the structure of the group, including role differentiation.

Part of the domain of what is generally described as a psychological group is undoubtedly the work group. Despite the fact that usually the members of a work group do not choose each other, they will in most cases certainly come to share a motivational basis and a number of rules and norms for their behaviour within, or even away from, the group. Work groups are also characterized by their forming some sort of structure that often involves a clear-cut division of tasks and roles. This is not without significance, because it implies that the knowledge and insights of social psychology, directed at the interaction between individual and group, can to a large extent be transferred to the interaction between individual employees and the work groups of which they are part. This involves both the question of what influence the employee feels the work group exercises on him and the question as to the effects of the behaviour, attitudes, and values of an individual employee on the group.

Another topic to be dealt with in the theoretical section concerns one specific role within the work group, i.e. that of the leader, supervisor, coach, boss, or however one might wish to indicate the role of leader. There is much more to this subject than just its application in the field of work organizations. The phenomenon of 'leadership' presents itself in all kinds of social contexts and particularly the changes that occurred in the opinions and expectations concerning this role have in recent days been the subject of much debate and research. Leadership in family life, school, church, or political parties seems to move away from the classical hierarchical role perception to one that would fit in better with the modern sense of life, which—slightly exaggerately—may be called participative rather than hierarchical, serving rather than controlling, and consulting rather than decisive. This gives rise to an interesting question: is leadership in a work organization subject to the same changes as it is in other social systems or do the specific requirements of an organization, whose objective is the efficient production of goods or rendering of services, put distinct limits to such a development or at least require a specific 'colouring'? Of course, much of the research done on this originates from W/O psychology itself. Personality traits, behaviour characteristics, and style differences have very often been analysed with a view to their effects regarding efficiency and acceptance criteria. Obviously, W/O psychologists cannot do without a sound understanding of these research results, while they should also be able to pinpoint the lacunae and shortcomings.

A third fundamental process in W/O psychology is that of the origin and course of conflicts. Once it is recognized that a work organization consists of individuals and groups whose objectives will not always be in line or run parallel, it is also recognized that the occurrence of conflicts—not only about resources (these could still be solved by means of technical approaches), but also about goals—is one of the elementary processes in work organizations. A conflict is then no longer something scary. It is part of the game, so to speak. This does not mean, of course, that the conflict processes in organizations are all desirable or even acceptable, and certainly not that organizations should be indifferent to the course of these processes. Therefore, an analysis of the way in which conflicts take their course, of how certain conditions may have a stimulating or frustrating effect, and of how interventions may promote a favourable settlement definitely has a rightful place in a handbook of W/O psychology. In many cases it is the psychologist who can, as a third party, influence a conflict by choosing an intervention strategy that may have either a preventive, or a curative or an escalating effect.

Another topic drawing increasing attention not only from those outside the work organization but also from within the work organization is what may be called 'stress'. It cannot be denied that modern man has to live and work under ever higher pressure. The number of people suffering from the consequences of stress is growing rapidly and it is apparent that by no means work organizations can be exonerated from actually having created threatening situations. Once one acknowledges that a stress response in not an objective matter of course but depends on what a person feels to be frustrating or threatening or on what he can cope with, psychology enters into the study of this phenomenon.

In the 60s and especially the 70s, interest in the development of organizational stress steadily increased in W/O psychology. Stress research, traditionally and primarily being the province of experimental psychology with a biological orientation and at most clinical application, acquired a social-psychological component. That the objective environment is subjectively perceived in terms of certainty-uncertainty, of clarity-obscurity of roles, of whether or not it meets expectations, etc. is an insight that is gradually gaining ground. Such perceptions may lead to tensions that have a physiological as well as a psychological component, which in turn can influence an individual's health. There are, moreover, individual differences in the extent to which these processes may have undesirable consequences. For W/O psychology, the elaboration of such a social-psychological stress model could be a major contribution towards understanding and improving an employee's physical and psychological well-being.

The topics mentioned above are all discussed in the part on 'Elements and processes'. In the section 'Applications' attention is paid to how a number of these principles are translated into practical measures and applied systems.

The first question put here is how leaders, and especially managers, in a work organization should be prepared and trained for their leadership role. This involves a combination of applications that emanate from two psychological theories: firstly, leadership theory as discussed in the theoretical section and, secondly, learning and educational psychology which is an important subject in the field of experimental psychology. The combination of these two areas provides the building stones for answers to the question of what, when and how in management development.

The next two chapters are concerned with shaping and guiding the work at the work group level. The first one addresses the formal systems according to which the work and work groups are organized and systems such as shorter working weeks, sliding working hours, part-time jobs and shift work may be viewed from a technical/organizational standpoint, but they just as much deserve the attention of W/O psychologists inasfar as their psychological effects on the behaviour and attitudes of a group's individual members are involved.

A discussion of the phenomenon of 'work consultation' makes clear in what way the changing insights into leadership and the stronger emphasis (coming also from society) on more participation and consultation are expressed in concrete procedures within organizations and work groups. It also becomes evident that to devise a work consultation system is one thing, but to introduce and effectively implement this idea quite another. Many preconditions regarding both the organizational context and the nature of the work group's task as well as the orientation and preparation of the members of the work group will have to be met before work consultation will be really effective.

Handbook of Work and Organizational Psychology
Edited by P. J. D. Drenth, H. Thierry, P. J. Willems and C. J. de Wolff

3.1. Group characteristics and individual behavior

John B. Rijsman

1. INTRODUCTION

In the current literature about groups, the connection between group characteristics and individual behavior is often dealt with by, first, seperately defining
the groups' characteristics and regarding them as independent variables which,
then, are assumed to have a certain influence on the individual's behavior.
This is, however, clearly a one-sided approach to the problem. If we start from
the idea that groups are the result of social interaction between individuals,
it is clear that we can just as well (perhaps even better) formulate the problem
the other way round. This means that we first look for the fundamental characteristics of social behavior in general and, from there, reason out the
characteristics of groups. In this chapter, we will cover both approaches.
First, we will discuss the classical approach, i.e. that individual behavior is a
result of group characteristics. We will then reverse our train of thought by
attempting to formulate first the essential characteristics of the social behavior
of human individuals and then to deduce a number of group phenomena.

2. FROM GROUP CHARACTERISTICS TO INDIVIDUAL BEHAVIOR

The term 'group characteristics' can be conceived in two different ways. In
the first place, we can look at the term as a reference to a subdivision of the
psychological definition of a 'real' group. For example, 'mutual dependence'
is a group characteristic in the definitional sense of the word. A set of people

Dr. John B. Rijsman, Katholieke Hogeschool, Hogeschoollaan 225, 5037 GC TILBURG.

whose the members are not mutually dependent can be considered as a social class, but not as a 'real group'. In the second place, however, we can also take the term to refer to the variation within a certain type of group. Of the groups that can fully satisfy the definable 'characteristics' of a 'real group', we can say that one is large and the other small, that one is homogeneously composed and the other heterogeneously, etc. In as much as these characteristics are no longer meant to determine to what extent the group satisfies the definition of a group, but rather to refer to the variation within a certain kind of groups, we call these characteristics 'variation characteristics'.

In the following survey of the influence of group characteristics on individual behavior (this overview is not complete, but serves only as an example), we treat both sorts of characteristics individually. We cover first the definitional characteristics of a group and next the variation characteristics.

2.1. From definitional group characteristics to individual behavior

What are the definitional characteristics of a 'real group'? We will first attempt to answer this question before treating the question of their influence. If we take the definition of the term 'group' as defined by Cartwright and Zander (1968, ch. 3), we find that it is difficult to name a fixed set of characteristics that will always be present in the 'real group'. Cartwright and Zander (1968) believe that it is better to speak of gradations in 'groupness'. They state, literally (p. 48):

'When a collection of people form a group, it is very probable that one or more of the following statements will apply:
a. these people engage in frequent interaction
b. they define themselves as members
c. they are defined by others as belonging to the group
d. they share norms concerning issues of common interest
e. they participate in a system of interlocking roles
f. they identify with one another as a result of the fact that they have set up the same model-object or ideals in their super-ego
g. they find the group rewarding
h. they pursue promotively interdependent goals
i. they have a collective perception of their unity
j. they tend to act in a unitary manner towards the environment
The greater the number of these attributes possessed by a set of people, and the greater their strength, the closer that the collection would seem to come to being the "real group".'

Most of the other authors in the field of group dynamics (for an overview, see, for example, Shaw, 1976, pp. 6–12) provide definitions of the 'real group'

which contain these same characteristics, either a bit more elaborated or a bit more condensed, but essentially the same. Nevertheless, we will present one more, that of Sherif and Sherif (1969), because their definition makes it clearly possible to distinguish between the definitional and variation characteristics of groups. Sherif and Sherif propose (1969, p. 135) that the following four characteristics are essential for the formation and functioning of the real group:
1. A motivational base shared by individuals and conducive to recurrent interaction among them over time.
2. Formation of an organization (group structure) consisting of differentiated roles and statuses and delineated in some degree from that of non-members.
3. Formation of a set of norms (i.e., values, rules, and standards for behavior)
4. More-or-less consistent differential effects on the attitude and behavior of individual members produced by the group properties.

The last point is especially important in this context, becuase it is considered an essential (definitional) characteristic of the 'real group'; i.e., that certain differences between groups (and this, then, must naturally be seen in terms of variation determining characteristics) effectively influence the behavior and attitudes of the group members.

Following this short overview of the most current opinions about the definitional characteristics of the real group, we will now turn our attention to the study of a number of differences in individual behavior that result from the degree to which contact with others does or does not satisfy these definitional group characteristics. We begin with the study of individual behavior in a situation of minimal group level, i.e., the so-called 'minimal social situation', as that described by Sidowski et al. (1956) and by Kelley et al. (1962). The minimal social situation is a situation in which people are definitely dependent upon each other, materially speaking, without realizing it themselves. In other words, as an outsider we can speak of a group, but looking at it from the members' point of view, there is not one form of conscious group membership present.

The proto-typical experimental version of such a situation is as follows: two persons, A and B, are placed in separate rooms, without knowing of each other's presence. In each room there are two push-buttons one on the left (L), and one on the right (R). In each trial, the individuals are given the task of making their own choice as to which of the two buttons they want to press. It is organized such that (without A's and B's knowledge) the pressing of button L has a positive consequence for the person in the other room, and the pressing of button R a negative consequence. In other words, each person receives in the course of the research a number of positive and negative stimuli, but he does not know that these are the result of the choice behavior of the person in the other room. Both subjects consider the situation to be completely individual. The actual interaction structure of the minimal social situation can be expressed in the following matrix form:

$$
A \quad
\begin{array}{c|c}
 & \begin{array}{cc} \text{L} & \text{R} \end{array} \\
\begin{array}{c} \text{L} \\ \text{R} \end{array} &
\begin{array}{c|c}
+/+ & -/+ \\ \hline
+/- & -/-
\end{array}
\end{array}
\qquad (1)
$$

The four cells of this matrix contain the four possible contingencies of the choice of A and B (LL, LR, RL, and RR), and the symbols in each cell show which result (positive or negative) A and B receive as a result of each choice-contingency (the results of A are always indicated to the left of the slash, and that of B always stand right of the slash). A look at the matrix shows that the resulting distribution agrees exactly with the description of the experimental situation described above: a L choice always results in a + for the other person, and a R choice always results in a − for the other person.

The crucial question that we are now concerned with is this: what will people do in such a situation? Will their behavior demonstrate a random pattern? In other words, will they choose L just as often as R, or will they develop a particular systematic preference for one button over the other?

However, before we look at the empirical answer to this question, we will try to determine what would theoretically happen if the behavior of the subject is exclusively determined by the law of effect. By this (in accordance with Kelley et al., 1962) we mean that a subject, after receipt of a positive stimulus, will repeat his choice of the preceding turn, while after receiving a negative stimulus he will change his choice. An application of this law to the four possible starting situations (LL, LR, RL, and RR) results in the four choice sequences represented in table 1 (where the arrow points to the result, + or −, the choice of the one person had for the other).

Table 1 shows that in a complete application of the law of effect, A and B, irrespective of the starting situation, very quickly (i.e., after at most three trials) will systematically push the left button. The results of the empirical research agreed fairly well with these theoretical expectations. Kelley et al. (1962) established that at the beginning of the experiment the subject did not have a clear preference for L or R, and chose, on the average, approximately 50% L. This percentage kept increasing in the course of the experiment. Following 100 trials, the subject chose approximately 75% of the time for L and only 25% for R. In other words, the subjects developed a clear preference for the button which had, in fact, a rewarding effect for the other subject. It would, however, be a mistake to interpret this preference as a symptom of pro-social behavior, i.e., behavior meant to help another. We know that, given the nature of the minimal social situation, this cannot be true, due to the fact that both subjects are subjectively alone. What actually happened was that an unconscious (social) coordination between two persons developed as a function of the posi-

Table 1. The theoretical sequence of choices in the minimal social situation, for simultaneous choices of A and B.

A:	L +	L +	L +	L +	L +	...	L +
B:	L +	L +	L +	L +	L +	...	L +
A:	L −	R −	L +	L +	L +	...	L +
B:	R +	R −	L +	L +	L +	...	L +
A:	R +	R −	L +	L +	L +	...	L +
B:	L −	R −	L +	L +	L +	...	L +
A:	R −	L +	L +	L +	L +	...	L +
B:	R −	L +	L +	L +	L +	...	L +

tive rewards such coordination had for each individual person.

After this analysis of the behavior of people in a minimal social situation, we will now discuss a situation that comes much closer to the definition of a 'real group', i.e. a situation of mutual dependence between people, in which the persons involved are fully informed of the structure and progress of the social interaction. Let us call this a *social situation*. Research on individual behavior in a social situation, which allows for a good comparison with the minimal social situation, is that of Rijsman and Poppe (1977). In this research, the following matrix was used:

$$
\begin{array}{c}
\quad\quad\quad\quad B \\
\begin{array}{c|c|c}
 & L & R \\
\hline
L & +5/+5 & -1/+4 \\
\hline
R & +4/-1 & -1/-1 \\
\end{array}
\end{array}
\quad\quad (2)
$$

with A on the left of the rows.

In the current experiment, this matrix, which structurally resembles matrix 1 (i.e., a L choice always results in a positive consequence for the other and a R choice always results in a negative consequence), was explained to both subjects (who were seated at the same table in full view of one another). They knew, therefore, that with a joint L choice they would both be awarded five points and that with a joint R choice, they would both lose one point, while a dissimilar choice meant that one (the person choosing R) would win four points and the other (the person choosing L) lose one point. They had to make each choice independently of one another and following each choice they received feedback concerning the choice contingency which had developed, the accessory scores, and the cumulative scores of A and B at that moment. In other words, both persons had complete insight in the structure as well as in the progress of the social interaction.

Again, we ask ourselves: what do subjects do in a similar social situation? Do they develop a preference for L or for R, or do they randomly choose from both alternatives? If we take into account that the subjects in the minimal social situation already evolved from 50% to 75% L choices without even the slightest understanding of the matrix, we might, on a naive reasoning expect that in this experiment the subjects, with their full insight in the matrix and the progress of the interaction, would work much faster and for a higher percentage of L. The facts, however, run radically counter to this expectation. The subjects began with approximately 50% of their choices for L, just as in the minimal social situation, but during the interaction the percentage continuously decreased rather than increased. After nearly 100 trials, the subjects chose, on the average, approximately 30% L and 70% R. In other words, almost the opposite was found of what was found in the minimal social situation (75% L versus 25% R). This result is, indeed, not at all unique; in many similar 'social situation' experiments (for an overview, see, for example, Wrightsman et al., 1972) the same high degree of 'unreasonableness' was found between the interacting subjects. Where does this fundamental behavior change come from? The answer is that, by providing insight in the structure and the profits of the social interaction, we simultaneously laid the foundation for a primary *social* motive, that is, the competition motive or, in general, the motive to prove oneself as an individual in front of the other through the relevant comparison channels (in this case, reciprocal profits).

Later on in this chapter, in the discussion of the basic characteristics of human social behavior, we will deal with this motive in detail. This motive is the reason why matrix 2 appears subjectively different for the people involved, A and B. Looking at this from the 'competition' point of view, the scores in matrix 2 are subjectively given the following meaning:

$$
\begin{array}{c}
B \\
\begin{array}{c|c|c}
 & L & R \\
\hline
A \quad L & 0/0 & -5/+5 \\
\hline
R & +5/-5 & 0/0 \\
\end{array}
\end{array}
\tag{3}
$$

Matrix 3, which serves as a shadow matrix of matrix 2, expresses the idea that making the same choice (LL or RR) in matrix 2 produces the same result for both persons (each + 5 or each − 1), while making a dissimilar choice (LR or RL) results in 5-point gain for the R-chooser and a loss of 5 points for the L-chooser. It is obvious that this 'shadow matrix', which is based on competition, is more inviting for a R-choice than for a L-choice.

The research with matrix 2 described above is, undoubtedly, closer to the 'real group' than the minimal social situation, but still does not describe it perfectly. The members, A and B, certainly stand in a conscious social relation to one another, but for the rest they find themselves in a social vacuum. They do not have, for example, the possibility to compare themselves as a group with other groups. This element, the 'intergroup' element, can, however, be easily introduced into the research without foregoing the paradigm used so far. This was done, for example, in the following experiment by Rijsman *et al.* (1979) in which matrix 4 was used.

$$
\begin{array}{c}
& \hspace{2.2em} \text{B} \\
& \hspace{1em} \text{L} \hspace{2.5em} \text{R} \\
\text{A} \quad
\begin{array}{c} \text{L} \\ \text{R} \end{array}
&
\begin{array}{c|c}
+9/+9 & +3/+8 \\ \hline
+8/+3 & +3/+3
\end{array}
\end{array}
\qquad (4)
$$

In one condition of this experiment, which we will call the 'group' condition, persons A and B interact just as in the previous experiment, individually with one another, without having any information about the other groups. In the second condition of this experiment, the 'intergroup' condition, two groups simultaneously performed a task, while the members of each group received not only the customary information about the course of things in their own group, but also the information about the total scores of the two members of the other group. In the group condition, it was again found that A and B chose approximately 50% L at the start of the experiment, but as the experiment progressed the L choice became less and less, with approximately 20% L versus 80% R after 70 trials. In the intergroup condition, on the contrary, the subjects began with approximately 50% L at the start of the experiment, and this percentage remained approximately constant throughout the whole experiment. In other words, we see that the possibility to compare with another group somewhat diminishes the competition within one's own group, but still not to such an extent that L prevails over R; there remains a strong tendency to prove oneself.

We should be able to systematically introduce still other definitional group characteristics (norms and roles, for example), within the framework of this experimental paradigm, and to examine the effects these have upon subjects' the behavior. That, however, is beyond the scope of this chapter and we refer the reader who wishes to study such variables to the excellent works of Thibaut and Kelley (1959) and Kelley and Thibaut (1978).

We shall confine ourselves here to establishing the fact that the transition from an unconscious (minimal) to a conscious social interaction produces a particular dynamics in the behavior of people, i.e., the tendency for an individual or group to distinguish themselves from others. This finding is, naturally, of great importance for anyone who wishes to better understand and control the nature of the daily interactions between people.

The applications of these tendencies are, further examination, so extensive that it is practically impossible to name a sitation in which these tendencies do not occur. Even in the event that people attach importance to self-mortification or humility, we get the paradoxal situation where people, either individually or as a group with which one can identify, want to positively distinguish themselves from others who achieve less or score lower in that area. Just what the origin of these tendencies is and how they function will be discussed in section 3 below.

2.2. From variation characteristics of the group to individual behavior

We will now proceed to an illustrative survey of the influence of variation characteristics of the group on individual behavior. Within the category of variation characteristics, we can, albeit with something of an overlap, distinguish between pre-interaction characteristics and interaction characteristics. By the former we mean those characteristics that can be distinguished ahead of the latter, which ensue from the interaction itself.

A. PRE-INTERACTION CHARACTERISTICS

An excellent example of a pre-interaction characteristic having strong influence on individual behavior is the externally determined timing of A's and B's answering possibilities in the minimal social situation. Throughout our example, we proceeded from the idea that A and B choose simultaneously. Thus, table 1 is based explicitly on the concurrent choice behavior of A and B.

We can, however, also visualize a situation in which the choice behavior of A and B does *not* run simultaneously but alternately (i.e., first A, then B, then A again, etc.). This can easily be accomplished experimentally by making A and B choose at a particular moment by means of signals, administering the signals at alternate times. What is fascinating about such a change is that a pure application of the law of effect now presupposes a completely different choice pattern than when choices are made simultaneously. This is illustrated in table 2.

As we can see in table 2, a stable choice of reciprocally rewarding behavior occurs only when A and B begin with L. In the three other starting combinations, LR, RL, and RR, we get an unstable sequence with 2/3 R and 1/3 L every time. Integrating the four possible starting combinations, we have to conclude that, in theory, the average alternating choice situation should produce only 50% L (in the simultaneous choice situation, this was approximately 100% L).

Kelley *et al.* (1962) have empirically investigated whether it is true that the alternating choice situation produces a lot less L-choices than the simultaneous choice situation, and this indeed clearly turned out to be the case. In the alternating choice situation, approximately 50% L was chosen throughout the experiment, as compared to an increase from 50% to 75% in the simultaneous choice situation.

Table 2. The theoretical sequence of choices in the minimal social situation, for alternating choices of A and B.

```
A:  L           +   L           +   L           +  ...
       \       /       \       /       \       /
        \     /         \     /         \     /
B:       +   L           +   L           +   L

A:  L           -   R           +   R           -  ...
       \       /       \       /       \       /
        \     /         \     /         \     /
B:       +   R           -   L           -   R

A:  R           +   R           -   L           -  ...
       \       /       \       /       \       /
        \     /         \     /         \     /
B:       -   L           -   R           +   R

A:  R           -   L           -   R           +
       \       /       \       /       \       /
        \     /         \     /         \     /
B:       -   R           +   R           -   L
```

After this illustration of behavior changes influenced by a pre-interaction characteristic in the minimal social situation, we will now continue with examples of behavior changes in the more social or 'real group' situation.

In fact, we have already given examples of variation characteristics of the pre-interaction kind in the previous section on definitional group characteristics, where it appeared that they have a certain influence on individual behavior in social situations. Such an example is the difference in absolute level between matrix 2 and matrix 4. As one can see, matrix 4 is nothing more than an upward linear transformation from matrix 2 (matrix 4 is the same as matrix 2, but increased by 4 units). We could say that, by doing this, we have executed a manipulation of the pre-interaction characteristic 'size of the profits in mutual dependence'. As can be seen from the results, this variable has a systematic effect on the behavior of A and B, but differently than one would expect from a naive viewpoint.

In the lower matrix 2, the combined L-choices drop to about 30% in the course of the experiment, but in the high matrix 4, this drop is even more evident, reaching 20%. This too is not just a 'once only' phenomenon. In various other studies, in which this variable was manipulated, every time the same result emerged: the higher the absolute value of the mutual dependence, the less (instead of the more) cooperation or, in other words, the more rivalry or competition (see, for example, Rijsman and Poppe, 1977).

The two matrixes, 2 and 4, can be considered in yet another manner, as an illustration of a pre-interaction variable. That is, they both belong to the family of the so-called 'Maximizing Difference' matrixes. These are matrixes where the private and collective interests of A and B are unequivocally linked to a

L-choice in such a way that a R-choice is functional only in terms of competition. There are still more matrixes, such as the 'Prisoner's Dilemma, matrix, where competition and private interest are not so rigidly divided. We know from research (for a review, see Wrightsman et al., 1972) that these structural variables have certain effects on individual behavior.

In an altogether different context than that of group analysis by means of matrixes, Insko and Schopler (1972) give three examples of pre-interaction variables of which it is known that they clearly influence the behavior of group members, i.e. spatial organization of the members, group size, and group composition. By the first characteristic, spatial organization, one looks for the influence of the physical distance between members, the spatial position of each member, etc. on the behavior of each member individually and on the group as a whole. It has, for example, repeatedly been established that at meetings the people who *are placed* at the end of the table (i.e., not taking their place, because that could be the result of self-selection on the basis of dominance) frequently get their ideas accepted. A classical study in the field of spatial relationships within groups was done by Sommer (1969), *Personal Space*. However, most studies that deal with the influence of spatial factors on individual behavior, are currently found under the heading 'environmental psychology', which field is reviewed by Stokols (1978).

With reference to the variable 'group size' we can encounter variation that ranges from *dyads* to groups the size of a city or country.

Zimbardo (1969), for example, has clearly shown that people in a big city generally behave in a less personal (more de-individualized) way than people in a small town. For a review of the influence of masses on individual behavior, we refer the reader to Freedman (1975). Finally, the variable 'group composition' can, of course, consist of a great many things. For instance, we can refer to groups that are composed only of men, or only of women, or of a combination of both, or to groups that are composed of people of various religions, various nationalities, etc. The trick is to determine what does or does not have an influence on the behavior of group members within a particular context. It is, for example, assumed (Byrne, 1969) that equality in important aspects, such as attitudes, increases the attraction between people, but it has also been shown that this relationship is not as simple as was assumed. For a good survey of such similarities among people and the resulting influence on behavior, we refer the reader to Berscheid and Walster (1978, ch. 5) and to Shaw (1976, ch. 7). We shall give just one example.

Meeuwese and Oonk (1960) wished to investigate the degree to which social stress in a group influenced the behavior of the group leader and, through the behavior of the leader, also the efficiency of the group as a whole. The research was conducted in Amsterdam, and they manipulated social stress by forming, first, small groups whose members were either all catholics or all protestants (homogeneous condition) and, second, groups that were half catholic and half protestant (heterogeneous condition). Depending on the positional power and the personality of the leader (measured by the so-called LPC-scale of Fiedler, 1967) this group composition was indeed shown to influence the extent to which the leader took either a task-directed or social-emotional position, which in turn had a specific influence on the efficiency of the group as a whole.

Apart from the above-mentioned spatial organization, group size and group composition, there are, of course, still other pre-interaction characteristics one can take into consideration; for example, the communication structure and the formally induced hierarchy. The works of Bavelas (1950) and Leavitt (1951), which deal with the difference in efficiency between centralized and de-centralized groups and the differences in satisfaction between central and peripheral group members, have become classics. But the relationship is also less straightforward than was intially assumed in this matter. Shaws' (1964) reanalysis of the problem showed that de-centralized groups can work at least as efficiently as centralized groups, if the task is sufficiently complex or if the de-centralized groups have learned to solve their communication problems (Guetzkow and Simon, 1955). In addition, in the work of Mulder (1972) it has been shown very clearly that the hierarchical structure of a group influences the behavior of its individual members. As a result, people who find themselves in the middle of an inverted Y-structure, exhibit clear signs of being power hungry. To what extent the power-directed behavior of people is influenced by structural variables, was convincingly shown by Sik-Hung NG (1977).

B. THE INTERACTION CHARACTERISTICS

By interaction characteristics we mean those characteristics that are explicitly the product of social interaction between people. The differences between interaction characteristics and pre-interaction characteristics (i.e., the amount of reward, size of the group, etc.) appear to be simple, but we soon realize that the distinction is fairly arbitrary and sometimes difficult to maintain. One could, for instance, rightly suggest that the size of a group is the product of social interaction. But, obviously, the concept 'size' can just as well be applied to a group of trees, while characterization in terms of, for example, norms and roles is applicable only to a 'real' group. Norms and roles are real products of social interaction.

The fact that norms and roles, in essence, result from social interaction does not mean that they cannot be *imposed* on people. This last point, then, gives the impression that norms and roles can exist by themselves, detached from any type of social interaction. This, however, is only seemingly so. First, these imposed norms and roles do actually refer to social interaction, but only in the imagination. Second, and much more important, the acceptance or rejection of certain imposed norms and roles is in itself a phenomenon of social interaction. If I accept what a teacher tells me to do with respect to my behavior with fellow students, then I not only construct an imaginary relationship with my fellow students, but I also derive this construction from my role in relation to the teacher.

There exist not only differences between groups with respect to the content of norms and roles, but—and it is this point we are now especially interested in—there also exist differences in the extent to which norms and roles are formalized. With this, we come to the well-known differences between the so-called formal and informal groups.

It has been repeatedly shown (the clearest illustration are Milgram's (1974) studies of obedience), that formal groups, once contractually accepted by the individual, can have an unbelievably strong influence upon the public behavior of that individual. There are, naturally, also limits to that influence. One of these limits is the so-called 'reactance' process, as described by Brehm (1966). This means that someone will radically oppose what is asked of him and even will do just the opposite, because he feels that whoever asked something of him exceeded the limits of his formal or legitimate rights. We shall discuss this in section 3.

Informal groups can also have a major influence on the public behavior of their members, but it is generally accepted that the strength of informal groups can be found in the inner convictions of the group members. It is usually the case, as a matter of fact, that informal groups are formed on the basis of the human need to give one's opinions a so-called objective character through consensus (Festinger, 1950).

Because the dynamics which lead to the formation of informal groups often differ from the dynamics which lead to the formation of formal groups, it stands to reason that both sorts of groups often differ with respect to the type of task that they want to, or can, perform. The task of the informal group is usually 'social-emotional' in character, i.e., the group serves to support and give value to its individual members. The task of the formal group, on the other hand, is usually material in character. It aims at realizing a particular product and the interaction between certain people is the means to do so. The extent to which the task can be divided among the various members of the group and the manner in which this affects the productivity of each individual member and of the group as a whole are discussed in detail by Steiner (1972) and Taillieu (1975).

In addition to the interaction characteristics, which are formulated in terms of interaction processes 'within' the group, there are also a number of interaction characteristics that can be formulated in terms of the interaction processes 'between' groups.

Such an important group characteristic is the so-called minority or majority of the group. In contrast to what is often thought, it is not true that the group that quantitatively forms a minority is, because of that, deprived of the possibility to influence the majority. Moscovici (1977) has theoretically and empirically shown that an active minority with a consistent behavior style is in a good position to influence a majority group. In connection with this, Moscovici also differentiates between 'nomic' and 'anomic' groups.

Together with Paicheler, Moscovici (1978, ch. 11) attempted to further analyze the effect of both sorts of group on the personal identity of the members, and, therefrom, to make a connection between the general problems of inter-group differentiation and social identity (Doise, 1976; Tajfel, 1978).

We will now end our summary and exemplifying review of what we call the classical approaches, i.e., reasoning from group characteristics to individual behavior. In the following section, we turn the matter around. We will first consider the characteristics of the social behavior of human individuals and attempt to deduce certain group differences from them.

3. FROM THE SOCIAL BEHAVIOR OF AN INDIVIDUAL TO GROUP CHARACTERISTICS

In this section, we first consider the fundamental characteristics of the social behavior of human individuals and, thereafter, determine these characteristics with a view to the characteristics of the 'real' group.

3.1 Fundamental characteristics of the social behavior of an individual

We consider the social behavior of an individual to be a meaningful response of that individual to a reality which, in the eyes of the individual himself, has a social meaning. Reality takes on social meaning as soon as it consists, in the eyes of the observer, of the elements 'self' and 'others like oneself' or, in short, 'congeners'.

On the basis of the two above-mentioned premises, we can conclude that the study of the characteristics of an individual's social behavior really comes down to the study of the characteristics of the psychological process by which the individual translates reality into the elements 'oneself' and 'others' (congeners).

The construction of a meaningful reality existing of the elements 'self' and 'others' can, in our opinion, be described in terms of three processes. The nature of and the relationship between these processes are schematically described as follows:

$$(5)$$

The first process in the whole of 'self-others' perception (represented by the transition of the symbols Gi and Ga to Pi and Pa in the upper half of the diagram) is called *social attribution*. By this, we mean that the individual observer, 'I', perceives a number of behavior signs in himself (Gi) and in others (Ga), which he goes on to attribute to his own personal qualities (Pi) and to the personal qualities of others (Pa).

The term 'behavior sign' must be broadly interpreted here. It involves not only someone's actions (words and deeds, i.e., behavior in the narrow sense of the word) here, but also what someone possesses and his physical features.

It goes without saying, that 'I' perceives his own behavior signs (Gi) from another perspective than that from which he perceives the behavior signs of others (Ga), This difference is most obvious in the case of physical behavior signs: 'I' perceives someone else's physical characteristics from an external viewpoint, whereas he perceives his own physical characteristics from a proprioceptive viewpoint. The fact that one perceives one's own behavior from a different point of view than the behavior of others has certain consequences for the process of social attribution. For example, Jones and Nisbett (1971) have shown that in dealing with their own behavior people generally attach more value to the influence of the situation than in dealing with the behavior of others. One can, however, by means of technical aids such as mirrors, video tapes, film, etc., transform one's own behavior into an imitated version of someone else's behavior. The result of such manipulations is that observers tend less to attribute their own behavior to the situation and hold themselves more responsible for what they do (see, for example, Duval and Wicklund, 1972). It does not seem impossible (but we know of no clear research on this) that objectifying one's own behavior through 'social mirroring' (e.g. external assessment) may likewise lead to a higher degree of subjective responsibility for one's own behavior. In modern psychology, more and more attention is paid to the principles of social attribution, which is increasingly better understood. For a good survey of the current status of this subject matter, we refer the reader to Shaver (1975) and Harvey *et al.* (1976 and 1978).

The second process in the perception of 'self' and 'others' (represented in the upper half of the diagram and indicated by the circles around Pi and Pa with dx and ' + ' next to it) is what is called *social comparison*. This term refers to the fact that, on the one hand, there is a clear separation between self and others (between Pi and Pa, because this is necessary in order to identify the two separately), but, on the other hand, there is also a clear similarity (this similarity is necessary in order to place the two, Pi and Pa, in the same category, i.e. people). This dualism in the 'self-others' perception is symbolized in diagram 5 by the separate circles around Pi and Pa (discrimination) and the one circle around Pi and Pa together (similarity).

It is important for the reader to realize that this dualism in the perception does not only hold for the social objects 'self' and 'others'. The identification of an object, whether a chair, a star, or a human being, will always involve the identification of that object as an element of a group. This means that the identified object is distinguished from similar objects, and at the same time classed as a similar object. This dualism thus is a universal characteristic of the human thinking process.

There is, nonetheless, an important difference between a separation process in which the element 'self' is involved and a seperation process in which this is not the case. The difference lies in the valuation of the involved elements. Valuation occurs when a 'self-involving' distinction is made. The reverse is also true (i.e., a 'self-involving' distinction by definition amounts to a valuation), meaning that one wants to place the element 'self' higher in the area concerned (dx—short for 'dimension x'—in the diagram than the others with whom the comparison is made. (This striving for 'higher' than the other in a similar area, dx, is symbolized by a '+' after Pi and Pa in the diagram.) The striving for higher, however, is limited in the sense that Pi cannot rise too far above Pa because otherwise they can never have the same denominator again. This, then, makes a comparison impossible. It will, after our discussion of social attributes, be clear that not all distinctions between behavior signs are of a 'self-involved' nature. It is, for example, possible to speak of differences in length, weight, assets, certain actions, etc., without assigning a value-aspect to them. This, then, means that, strictly speaking, one does not consider the behavior signs concerned as real 'signs of the person'. Therefore, one does not project them onto some 'personality dimension' or other, but simply regards them as object conditions, rather like one would speak of the weight of a chair. In such a case, the direction of the difference leaves the observer indifferent. However, as soon as one, regards the differences in behavior signs as referring to differences in the person, the Pi position attributed to Pi takes on the meaning of 'superiority'. Subjectively, this superiority can take on different forms. It is, for example, also possible to derive a feeling of superiority from the idea that one attaches less importance to things or to oneself than others do.

From this analysis of the social comparison, we must, therefore, conclude that every experience of social reality elicits primary competitive tendencies or aspirations to positively distinguish oneself from another in one area or another. If this were not so, it would mean that the individual does not identify himself as a 'person' or as a 'social object', which, pursuing this line of reasoning, would mean that he does not experience reality in a social sense. Naturally, this does happen to people; for example, to very young children, whose thinking capacity has not yet so fully developed to enable them to translate behavior signs into a 'person concept' or, in general, to categorize objects conceptually.

In order to succesfully make social comparisons, an individual can take different psychological routes. We will list them here briefly, but they will be further discussed below, when we will go into the characteristics of 'self-others' experiences in terms of group characteristics.

1. An individual may create the necessary behavior signs himself and influence the behavior signs of others in such a way that he comes out better when compared with other individuals in the areas considered important. People can try to improve their physical characteristics, to add to their wealth, to raise their accomplishments, to use words that are closer to the desirability norm, etc. In other words, people can try to positively distinguish themselves from others at a visible and demonstrable level. To give examples is not necessary, because reality constitutes one great example of such behavior.

2. An individual may, without making changes in the external behavior signs, attempt to reinterpret the existing behavior signs in such a way that he likes himself better than the others with whom he is comparing himself. An example of this is to attribute the success of others to luck or external help (and, thus, not to the person himself) and one's own success to knowledge and effort.

3. An individual may also exchange the comparison person for another one. When he finds that he does not compare favorably with someone, he may try to find another person with whom he does compare favorably.

4. An individual may change the comparison environment. If, in a particular environment, one can not distinguish oneself from others, one can subjectively consider this environment as unimportant and subjectively attribute greater importance to another environment where one sees the opportunity to distinguish oneself. In practice, one can go to such extremes as taking another job or even associating with a completely different ideology. The age of the person also plays an important role here. When, for example, he is no longer physically fit, he will no longer choose athletic situations as an important comparison environment.

Before we go on to discuss the third process in the 'self-others' perception (i.e., social validation), we wish to point out that the process of social comparison is just as applicable to groups as to individual persons. The identification of a group, as an element of perception, is only possible by equalizing and distinguishing this group relative to other, comparable groups. When one is subjectively part of the group concerned, then, automatically, one will also want to distinguish it in a favorable sense from other groups.

The 'self-involved' social comparison of groups may be represented as in diagram 6 (in which the elements Pi and Pa are replaced by the elements Pi-group and Pa-group, respectively).

(6)

Finally, the third process in the perception of 'self' and 'others' (represented in the lower half of the figure) is what we call social validation. This term alludes to the fact that observer 'I' tries to have his self-perception confirmed by others. 'I' needs this confirmation to make sure that his own view is 'correct' or 'valid'. It is, of course, impossible for 'I' to immediately determine what other judges think of him. 'I' must deduce this from particular behavior signs. The behavior signs from which 'I' derives the opinion of others, we call Gb (see diagram 5) and the social attributes and social comparison placed after Gb refer not to what the judges really think, but to what 'I' believes they think. In the diagram, the opinion ascribed to the judge agrees with what 'I' thinks of himself. In other words, 'I' gets the feeling that he is socially validated. Consequently, a '+' symbol connects I and Gb. This means that 'I' prefers these judges over other judges, as a reciprocal reaction to the feeling that he is judged positively by these judges. Should 'I', on the other hand, have the feeling that he is judged negatively (which would imply a '−' sign following Pi and Pa in the lower part of the diagram), then 'I' would in turn reject the judges (which would imply a '−' sign between I and Gb).

Of course, rejection of negative judges does not necessarily happen immediately. 'I' may first try to modify their judgment, or he can stimulate the judges to use the same correction mechanisms as those he himself used in constructing a successful social comparison. In other words, 'I' could show them different behavior signs, or he could argue that they should reinterpret the behavior signs, or he could argue that they should make a comparison with other comparison others, or he could argue that they should look at different comparison environments. When this, however, does not help, then 'I' can still save the situation by qualifying the judges as 'unjust', rejecting them and *directing* himself towards other, subjectively just opinions of 'fair' judges (meaning judges who *do* confirm 'I''s own positive self-esteem).

For a more detailed discussion of the processes of social attribution comparison, and validation as described here, we refer the reader to Rijsman (1981). We now turn our attention to the implications of these social behavior characteristics for group phenomena.

3.2. Social behavior characteristics and groups

The following is not a complete, but rather an exemplifying treatment of the subject, in which we will, step by step, take a number of familiar themes from the literature on groups and connect them with the characteristics of the social behavior of individuals discussed above.

A. INGROUP-OUTGROUP AND STATUS DISTINCTION

The comparative classification of social objects is, as we have seen in our

discussion of social comparisons, an unmistakable and fundamental characteristic of human social behavior. In other words, the well-known 'ingroup-
outgroup' phenomenon, which says that an individual judges his own group
(ingroup) to be more important than the comparison group (outgroup) in
certain respects (see Rabbie and Horwitz, 1969; Rabbie and Wilkens, 1971;
Taijfel et al., 1971), must not be regarded as a sign of human maladjustment,
but as an expresion of a fundamental characteristic of human social behavior.
The basis of this distinction is shown in diagram 6 above.

When we proceed from the ingroup (Pi-group) and assume that the individual
'I', at a certain point in time, turns his attention to the members of this group
(instead of to those of the outgroup, as earlier), then these members, in their
turn, become the comparison object and, therefore, the outgroup. This process
of shifts in attention, through which the number of members of the ingroup
becomes steadily smaller, may continue, but it goes without saying that the
limits on this 'social cell division' are set by the individual person I, in other
words, by Pi. The social comparison process, in which 'I' wants to favorably
distinguish himself from others, is, in a sense, the minimal form or nucleus of
the ingroup-outgroup discrimination process.

We can also reverse this reasoning and constract ever larger groups, starting
from Pi. The rivalry between two persons, Pi and Pa, can be eliminated through
the presence of a third comparison person or group, from which Pi and Pa
(who then jointly form one Pi-group) can both successfully distinguish themselves. It is this process in particular, which often forms the basis of what we
call the formation of a coalition: the combination of two parties in order to
successfully make a distinction from a third party on a subjectively important
comparison dimension, for example, the amount of power (see for example,
Wilke, 1968).

In addition to the definition of ingroup-outgroup in terms of social comparison, we can also present definition of ingroup-outgroup in terms of social
validation. The principle of social validation says that the individual 'I' is
attracted to judges who endorse the value of Pi and opposes those who disdain
Pi. This first group of judges is said to form an ingroup for 'I' and the second
group to form an outgroup for I. The two different definitions of ingroup-
outgroup, the one in terms of social comparison and the other in terms of social
validation, may perhaps be more familiar to the reader if we substitute the term
'ingroup-outgroup' by 'reference group'. Reference groups are often divided
into positive and negative reference groups. A positive reference group implies
that an individual identifies himself with a group either to positively distinguish
himself from others or because he feels attracted to that group due to the praise
and appreciation he receives within that group. Negative reference groups can
also be understood in these terms; the individual does not want to become like
some other people because of their negative characteristics, or avoids certain
people because of their disrespect and criticism for the individual. It is possible

in theory and regularly observed in reality, that a group which, according to the social comparison definition, forms an ingroup is considered an outgroup according to the social validation definition, or vice versa. It is, for example, possible that 'I' subjectively considers himself equal to a group of people with a high status (this group then forming a positive reference group or ingroup in the social comparison sense of the word), while specifically this group feels that this is not true and that 'I' represents a lower status than their own (therefore, this group is a negative reference group or outgroup in the social validation sense of the word). Alternatively, 'I' can feel positively distinguished from some people (who then form a negative reference group or outgroup in the social comparison sense of the word), while 'I''s view is confirmed by these people in particular (who are, therefore, a positive reference group or ingroup in the social validation sense of the word). However, this is possible only under very well determined conditions, i.e., those of role differentiation, as we shall see in the next section.

B. Role differentiation in groups

The fact that an individual not only wishes to positively distinguish himself from others, but, in addition, wants the correctness or validity of this positive distinction to be confirmed by others, implies that groups can only be formed or maintained if there are, in this group, various areas in which one can prove oneself, or, in other words, if there exists role differentiation in the group.

To demonstrate this, we will first look at what happens if two individuals, I_1 and I_2, interact without role distinction, i.e. both are interested in precisely the same comparison dimensions. According to the theory, each individual considers himself to be superior to the other (which in itself does not need to present any problem), but, in addition, each individual will want the other individual to confirm the validity of his own opinion. Naturally, this is where the problem starts. When I_1 expresses his desire to have his superiority to I_2 confirmed, then it goes without saying that this is, at the same time, a message about I_2's inferiority. In other words, I_2 feels that he is devalidated (disrespect) instead of validated by I_1. The opposite is also true: as a result of the validation wishes of I_2, I_1 feels devalidated by I_2. The result is that both individuals, each striving for the other's validation, continue to devalidate each other, which, by sheer necessity, leads to mutual hostility and (possibly) the destruction of the group.

The solution to this problem, as already explained in the beginning of this section, is found in creating separate comparison dimensions for both individuals, say dx_1 for I_1, and dx_2 for I_2. In order for this distribution to be psychologically satisfactory, however, a number of conditions must be met. To begin with, it is necessary that both I_1 and I_2 agree to it. They must both be convinced that dx_1 is indeed only of interest to I_1 (and therefore not to I_2), and

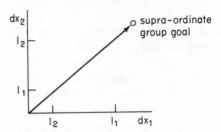

Figure 1. Presentation of a successful role division between two individuals (I_1 and I_2) in view of a supraordinate group goal.

dx_2 is only of interest to I_2 (and therefore not to I_1). We can consider this mutual agreement as the principle of social validation, which means that a subjective view of reality is considered true or valid only if the other subscribes to it. It will further be necessary that dx_1 and dx_2 complementarily contribute to a task which is equally important for I_1 and I_2, but which they will only be able to perform in a combined effort (we call this a 'supra-ordinate goal', which is not the same as an 'equal' goal). The existence of this complementary relationship will, in our opinion, be the only condition in which I_1 and I_2 mutually and spontaneously will accept the division of the dimension. The principle of this division (or role distribution) can, in view of a supra-ordinate goal, be represented as in figure 1.

Looking at figure 1, we see that I_1 and I_2 have absolutely no problem to admit that the other is better in his particular role. I_1 can recognize, without problems, that I_2 is superior in dx_2 because dx_2 is important to I_2 (this is mutually accepted), but not to I_1. Upon closer examination, it is, as a matter of fact, important to both individuals that the other excels in his area, because this ensures a better approach to the supraordinate group goal.

A problem that often occurs in reality is that certain stable complementary relationships are destroyed by technological progress. When, for instance, in a particular company people with unique abilities are replaced by some sort of apparatus, these people, of course, lose the opportunity to invest their personal value in that area. They can then try to establish themselves in areas in which others are also interested. The result, of course, is hostility.

C. CLIQUES AND (AB)NORMAL BEHAVIOR

The principle of role division in the group, can, of course also be applied to the relationships between groups. Groups will also have to specialize in complementary areas within the context of a general organizational purpose, if they want to avoid permanent hostility in their mutual interactions. If a group does not succeed in achieving this, if groups are always compared on identical values, this will (as with individuals) result in mutual demands on each other's appreciation in such a way that mutual devalidation will result. In the latter case, however, the possibility exists that one of the groups involved will chose a value dimension which is not complementary to the original dimension and will then try to recruit the support necessary for the validation of that choice from within its own group. In that case, we speak of a *clique*. Thus, a clique is defined as a group having own values, which differ from those of the society or organizations and which seeks to validate that value within its own group instead of by the consensus of other parties. However, the fact that all members of a clique consider the same things to be important does not mean that they may not become rivals. On the contrary, it will induce rivalry among them; everybody wants to positively set himself apart from the others in the groups in that specific field.

Therefore, a clique is curiously two faced. On the one hand, the members of a clique want to hide themselves from the surrounding society or organizations (their value dimension cannot be coordinated with the value dimension of the environment), but, on the other hand, they try to be as clearly 'visible' as possible within their own clique in order to set themselves apart from the other individuals and in such a way as to gain acknowledgement for doing so. That two-sidedness is well illustrated by so-called vandal cliques. Every vandal tries to remain anonymous to the outside world, but within the group, he wants to set himself apart as conspicuously as possible in order to personally reap the rewards of his vandalism. It is our opinion that this mutual pursuit of recognition within the own group is precisely the basis of the sometimes incomprehensible acts of vandal cliques.

Zimbardo (1969) has tried to explain vandalism in terms of de-individualization (removal of individual identity), but we feel that such a lack of identity can only explain why an individual does not comply with the existing norms. It does not explain why an individual would suddenly engage in extreme behavior in the other direction. To explain this, new dynamics, such as the self-fulfillment tendency (but based then on new norms), are necessary. The tendency towards self-fulfillment with regard to norms which are valid within the group is certainly not limited to the area of violence, but occurs elsewhere too. It appears, for instance, that people (at least in our culture) think it important to make decisions involving a lot of risk and because of that, groups will generally take more risks than individuals. This phenomenon is known in the literature as 'risky-shift'. This phenomenon has been long viewed as a peculiarity on its own, but is presently taken to be a so-called 'extremization' phenomenon (this is a technical term indicating a group moving in one direction; it is the opposite of 'polarization' which means that a group splits up in two parts that move away from each other). This extremization phenomenon may occur with respect to different values (Meertens, 1976).

We assume that every reader, some time or other, has experienced the above described phenomenon himself. When in a meeting or informal discussion with colleages or neighbors, the participants unite behind a certain norm or value, a tendency to exaggerate the norm develops, which usually makes the resulting viewpoint of the group more extreme than that of individual member would have been. To induce such a phenomenon, however, there have to be enough self-involvement and opportunities for discussion (see Moscovici and Doise, 1974).

D. The group as a source of psychological (in)justice

People are inclined to evaluate their own profits and those of others with whom they interact in terms of social justice. According to Adams (1965), people pursue a fair distribution of profits, which means that it is necessary for the distribution of profits to be equal to the input distribution. Adams expressed this attempt towards fairness using the following equation:

$$\frac{\text{Input}_{\text{self}}}{\text{Outcome}_{\text{self}}} = \frac{\text{Input}_{\text{other}}}{\text{Outcome}_{\text{other}}} \tag{7}$$

Adams' formula may, however, be transformed into the following formula:

$$\frac{\text{Input}_{\text{self}}}{\text{Input}_{\text{other}}} = \frac{\text{Outcome}_{\text{self}}}{\text{Outcome}_{\text{other}}} \tag{8}$$

The advantage of the latter equation is that it immediately shows the connection between the pursuit of fairness and the pursuit of social validation as previously described. The left part of equation (8) can be considered the equivalent of social comparison, i.e. the value an individual ascribes to himself in comparison with others. The right part of equation (8) is the equivalent of social validation, i.e. the social comparison value an individual ascribes to himself through external judgement/assessment symbols. Such an analysis of fairness allows us to state that the dynamics of fairness not only exists in pursuing an equalization of both sides of the equation, but also in pursuing an arrangement of both sides of the equation such that the individual himself turns out to be more valuable than the other. Our analysis of social comparison and social validation has shown that the an individual will strive to have his relative 'added value' in the relevant area of comparison confirmed. This upward tendency in the fairness motif was already indicated in Adam's thesis that people react faster to being underpaid than to being overpaid (1965).

When the pursuit of fairness boils down to the pursuit of confirmation of one's own (subjective) added value, then, clearly, fairness for the one will result in unfairness for the other (i.e., for that person who functions as the denominator in the equation). Therefore, it is not surprising that a system in which wages are paid according to the amount of work done is especially attractive for those who are evaluated in a positive way, but not so for those who are evaluated in a more negative way. However, systems in which one receives wages according to work or applications of the fairness rule are not the only ways in which people express their pursuit of justice. For instance, the pursuit of equality and even taking special care of the weak are considered expressions of the pursuit of social justice. We can now ask ourselves to what extent these latter dynamics (the pursuit of equality and care for the weak) are compatible with our idea that, fundamentally, people pursue confirmation of their relative added value, and consider only such a confirmation to be 'correct' or 'just'.

The pursuit of equality as a form of justice can easily be integrated into the social validation model of justice, if we replace the individual social comparison between Pi and Pa (see diagram 5) by the group social comparison as shown in diagram 6, and which was discussed in section 3.2.1 on ingroup-outgroup.

In the pursuit of equality, identification with a certain group (called the Pi group above) will always occur, but this group is meaningful only inasfar as it allows for a comparison to be made with another group (called the Pa group above) in a relevant area. Justice then consists of this Pi group as a whole being positively distinguished from the alternative comparison group. The validity of this statement can be illustrated by a simple fictitious experiment. Let us assume that we succeed in paying all Dutch laborers the same wages. The question then immediately arises: who are the Dutch laborers? Are they the laborers who are actually employed, or are those persons seeking employment included also? Are both women and men included, are only the persons over 18 years of age included, or are those over 17 also included?

It may be noticed immediately that each definition of a group of equals means the exclusion of a group of other people who are not admitted to the privilege of equality and to whom the application of the equality system will mean subjective injustice. For instance, it is certain that the 17-year olds will consider themselves discriminated if they are not included in this group, but as soon as they are included, the 16-year olds will consider themselves discriminated, etc. This fictitious experiment could be extended in such a way that finally all the Dutch, children and adults, are included in the group of people with equal wages, but even then, we would need an alternative group in order to meaningfully define the group of all Dutch. Obviously, we would have to cross the border in order to establish the Dutch group as a positively distinguished group (of course, this is already often happenings; consider, for instance, the comparison of average wages per country, the competitive position of industry, the comparison of morality per country, etc.).

The pursuit of justice in terms of equality boils down to a collective pursuit of fairness. Taking special care of the weak as a goal of justice can also be explained within the social validation model of justice. It is only necessary for us to realize what exactly we mean by 'a weak person who needs help'. A weak person who needs help is, by definition, someone whom we subjectively consider ourselves equal to, with whom we identify ourselves in such a way that we feel his needs to be our needs. When we direct our efforts towards alleviating the needs of these people whom we subjectively feel equal to, then psychologically it seems as if we are taking care of ourselves. The question is, however, who do we chose to be equal to ourselves to such an extent that transferring our energy to them is psychologically experienced as helping ourselves. If we were to confine ourselves to biological criteria, the answer would be simple. It is those who are a duplicate of our genetical code, i.e. our children (or, in a broader sense, nestlings). In this sense, one's loss of fitness in favor of one's nestlings is a means to maintain the species (loss of one's fitness in favor of nonduplicates of one's own code would lead to elimination of the species).

Psychologically, the rule is true also; we may offer our services to those in whom we see a future continuation of ourselves. In that way the loss of one's energy constitutes a reinvestment of that energy in others who will maintain one's self-concept. It is clear, however, that a discrimination process is at work here also: care for nestlings or members of the ingroup whom I consider to be a reincarnation of myself means that I consider the problems of the others or outgroup members to be less important. In other words, when I want extra care to be given to certain needy people, then I am asking, in fact, for extra appreciation of those whom I consider to be a reincarnation of myself. In other words, I am asking for social validation. We refer the reader to Deutsch (1975) for a more thorough discussion of these three forms of the pursuit of justice (fairness, equality, and special care for the needy, all of which, on closer examination, represent a form of pursuing social validation).

E. THE GROUP AS LOCUS OF SOCIAL EXCHANGE AND SOURCE OF LEGITIMATE POWER.

People are dependent upon other people for the fulfilment of many of their needs. Some fellow human beings, however, are better able to fulfil the needs of others than other human beings. Those who are in the immediate environment of an individual, and who are best able to fulfil the needs of that individual, acquire 'potential' power over this person. In other words, they are potentially able to steer the behavior of that individual in any way they want. However, in order to reach that point, it is necessary for the potential authority to have needs of his own which the first individual can satisfy better than others, else there would be no advantage for the potential authority in steering the behavior of the individual in a certain direction. In other words, for two individuals to interact with one another, and thus to have real power over one another, it is necessary that each has potential power over the other, which means that each should consider the other as someone who can fulfil his needs better than someone else. In this sense, the exercise of power is always a two-sided process;

a process of exchange between two parties, each of which considers the other party to be the best source of need fulfilment. A taxonomy (such as, for instance, that of French and Raven, 1959) amounts to a taxonomy of needs which can be used in an exchange process.

For example, when an individual offers his time, expertise and effort (or, in other words, his work) to a group (organization), which in turn offers safety and financial means as well as recognition, etc., then there is a mutually rewarding power: both parties, the individual as well as the organization, can truly influence the behavior of the other party as a function of the exchange that takes place.

Of course, there are goods or services other than rewards which can play a role in social exchange. Examples of this are 'not being punished' (gives force-power to the person who does not punish), 'information' (gives expertise-power to the informant), 'social modelling' (gives reference- or identification-power to the model), and 'the possibility to reincarnate oneself in others' (gives dependence power to those who are to serve as reincarnations). All these and possibly other goods are part of an exchange process wherein (see, for example, Foa, 1979) people will prefer to exchange within a certain area (for example, material goods in exchange for material goods, affection in exchange for affection, etc.). When such an exchange situation develops between people, then a new, typically cognitive and, therefore, typically human form of power will develop within the exchange situation, i.e. that of legitimate power. We should realize that people do not exchange things like marbles do, but as thinking beings. When people exchange, they do that within the framework of the social definition of the reality in which they experience themselves as a 'self' and the exchange partner as an 'other', and in which they are also aware of the fact that an exchange is taking place between the 'self' and the 'other'. Now, this awareness of the exchange between oneself and the other implies that one also knows what exactly is being exchanged and when, what kind of behavior is associated with it, and who does what and where. In short, one is aware of what role both parties play in the exchange. This mutual awareness of the role relationships involved in the exchange constitutes a contract, so to speak. This contract is often implicit, but sometimes explicit; it may even be written down and signed by both parties. Legitimate power is the power that is connected with the perceived roles of both parties within an accepted exchange situation.

Legitimate power is fundamentally two-sided because it originates from an accepted exchange situation, which means that both parties have some need or other and expect the other party to satisfy this need. To illustrate this, we return to our earlier example of the reward exchange between laborer and organization. To accept that an exchange takes place between two parties implies that the one party (for instance, the organization) can require the other to accomplish certain tasks (the work) in a certain time (for example, between 9:00 a.m. and

5:00 p.m.) at a certain location (the factory). But alternatively, the other party (for instance, the laborer) can require the first party to formulate the assignment in a certain way, to provide working clothes, or to pay wages at a certain time and at a fixed amount. In other words, the legitimate role of the one party constitutes at the same time the legitimate role of the other party.

We already referred to the obedience experiments of Milgram (1974) to show how forceful the power can be which results from the acceptance of roles within a social interaction. However, we also (see section 2.2.b) immediately pointed out the limitations of that power. Such a limitation can be found in the fact that no demands can be made which are outside the area covered by the contract between the interacting parties. To do that is to make illegitimate demands, and instead of obedience, an opposite reaction will occur. The opposite of what was asked is done. Brehm (1966) called this reaction 'reactance' (sometimes also called the boomerang effect) and considered it as an attempt by the individual to regain his threatend freedom. We could also call it an individual's attempt to indicate that the request does not form part of the freely accepted exchange system.

This last remark, however, takes us to a new issue, i.e. the issue of changing or expanding an already existing exchange situation. When, for instance, a supervisor wants his employee to perform a certain task under his supervision for half an hour after working hours, the contractual exchange will have to be expanded first; an overtime arrangement will have to be made. In such an extension, the original roles remain unchanged. However, it is also possible that an almost completely new exchange situation is designed. This is, for example, the case when the supervisor asks the employee to voluntarily do something for him which is of great importance and which he will otherwise not get done. When the employee is willing to 'help out' at that time, even for free, then a truely changed exchange situation is said to exist. It is obvious that new goods are exchanged then, i.e., the feeling of recognition, the feeling of having been selected, the feeling of being a part of someone else's goals in life. This new exchange situation requires new roles. It is possible, for instance, that the original employee takes on the role of supervisor or feels he is a supervisor-with-the-supervisor in the eyes of others. New ideas about the job may develop from this shift of roles. It is, for instance, possible, that a task which the employee used to consider boring and useless, will be regarded as much more important by him if he voluntarily participates in solving the problem of the supervisor. It is, however, also possible that, during such a personal service, a supervisor will try to behave in such a way that the original roles are maintained, for instance, by talking about overtime and material rewards. As a consequence, while doing something he considers a personal service the employee may feel to be even more confined, in his original role than he did before. He might show this by aggravating the difficulty, uselessness, etc. of the task to be accomplished.

The way in which extending or changing exchange situations or the accompanying changes in subjective role positions influence the evaluation of the job has not been explicitly studied. In our opinion, however, the so-called 'forced-compliance' experiments (see Elms, 1969) unwittingly are a rich source of information, which can be useful to the study of this problem. What is typical of these experiments, is that a subject is invited by the experimenter to do something which implies an extension or change of the obligations of the experiment originally agreed upon. For instance, in the classic experiment of Festinger and Carlsmith (1959), the subject was suddenly asked to replace the experimenter's sick assistant after he had finished his experimental task. The new task of the original subject was to tell the next subject that the task that he had just completed had been a pleasant one; the original subject was paid either one or 20 dollars for doing this (depending on the experimental condition in which the subject participated). The result was that those who did the work for one dollar judged their original task more positively than those who did the work for 20 dollars. Festinger and Carlsmith explained this result by referring to the theory of dissonance, but one might also say that the poorly paid job gave the original subject the impression that he had rendered the assistant a personal service (thereby siding with the experimenter), while the well paid job created an impression of being paid for overtime and thus indicated a sharp emphasis on the original role. To determine this, one would have to know how exactly the subject experienced the reward, and this depends on the way in which the experimenter offered the reward (small details in the amount can have maximal effects) and on what the subject is used to in terms of rewards. It is not surprising, then, that many attempts to replicate the 'forced-compliance' experiments in different cultures with different subjects, or in different institutions with different habits, show different effects. Therefore, it seems useful to us to critically reanalyze the 'forced-compliance' literature in order to determine for each experiment in what role position the subject ended up relative to the experimenter when the cooperation was induced. Does the original subject take on the position of the experimenter or does the experimenter take on the position of the subject, does the initial distinction become more pronounced or has something completely new developed? It is not unreasonable to assume that the subject's attitudes to his original work can be systematically influenced by these factors.

We have come now to the end of our survey of group characteristics that result from individual characteristics of social behavior. It has not been our intention to be complete, but rather to show by means of examples that the problem can be meaningfully discussed in this manner too and not only, as the classical approach has it, by proceeding from group characteristics to individual behavior.

REFERENCES

Adams, J. (1965), Inequity in social exchange. In: Berkowitz, L. (Ed.), *Advances in experimental social psychology. Vol. II.* New York: Academic Press.

Bavelas, A. (1950), Communication patterns in task-oriented groups. *J. Acoustical Society of America*, **22**, 725–730.

Berscheid, E., Walster, E. (1978), *Interpersonal attraction*. London: Addison-Wesley.

Brehm, J. (1966), *A theory of psychological reactance*. New York: Academic Press.

Byrne, D. (1969), Attitudes and attraction. In: Berkowitz, L. (Ed.), *Advances in experimental social psychology. Vol. IV.* New York: Academic Press.

Cartwright, D., Zander, A. (1968), *Group dynamics*. New York: Harper and Row.

Deutsch, M. (1975), Equity, equality and need: What determines which value will be used as the basis of distributive justice? *Journal of Social Issues*, **31**, 137–150.

Doise, W. (1976), *L'articulation psychosociologique et les relations entre groupes*. Brussels: Editions A. de Boeck.

Doise, W. (1979), Interaction sociale et développement cognitif. In: *Die Psychologie des 20. Jahrhunderts*. Zurich: Kindler Verlag.

Duval, S., Wicklund, R. (1972), *A theory of objective self-awareness*. New York: Academic Press.

Elms, A. (1969), *Role playing, reward and attitude change*. New York: Van Nostrand.

Festinger, L. (1950), Informal social communication. *Psychological Review*, **57**, 271–282.

Festinger, L. (1957), *A theory of cognitive dissonance*. Stanford: Stanford University Press.

Festinger, L., Carlsmith, J. M. (1959), Cognitive consequences of forced compliance. *Journal of Abnormal and Social Psychology*, **58**, 203–210.

Fielder, F. E. (1967), *A theory of leadership effectiveness*. New York: McGraw-Hill.

Foa, U. G. (1971), Interpersonal and economic resources. *Science*, **171**, 345–351.

Freedman, J. L. (1975), *Crowding and behavior*. New York: Viking Press.

French, Jr., R., Raven, B. (1959), The basis of social power. In: Cartwright, D. (Ed.), *Studies in social power*. Ann Arbor: Michigan Institute for Social Research.

Guetzkow, H., Simon, H. (1955), The impact of certain communication nets upon organization and performance in task-oriented groups. *Management Science*, **1**, 233–250.

Harvey, J., Ickes, J., Kidd, R. (Eds.) (1976/1978), *New directions in attribution research. Vol. I* (1976), *Vol. II* (1978). New York: Wiley.

Insko, C., Schopler, J. (1972), *Experimental social psychology*. New York: Academic Press.

Jones, E., Nisbett, R. (1971), *The actor and the observer: Divergent perceptions of the causes of behavior*. General Learning Press.

Kelley, H. H., Thibaut, J. W. (1978), *Interpersonal relations*. New York: Wiley.

Kelley, H. H., Thibaut, J. W., Radloff, R., Mundy, D. (1962), The development of cooperation in the 'minimal social situation'. *Psychol. Mon.*, **76** (12, whole no. 538).

Leavitt, H. J. (1951), Some effects of certain communication patterns on group performance. *Journal of Abnormal and Social Psychology*, **46**, 38–50.

Meertens, R. (1976), *Aspecten van groepspolarisatie* [Aspects of group polarization]. Nijmegen: Stichting Studentenpers (dissertation).

Meeuwese, W., Oonk, S. (1960), *Enkele determinanten van creativiteit: Structuur en proces in kleine experimentele groepen* [Some determinants of creativity: Structure and process in small experimental groups]. Amsterdam: University of Amsterdam (unpublished paper). Quoted in: Fiedler, F. (1967), *A theory of leadership effectiveness*. New York: McGraw-Hill.

Milgram, S. (1974), *Obedience to authority*. London: Tavistock.

Moscovice, S. (1977), *Social influence and change*. European Monographs in Social Psychology. New York: Academic Press.

Moscovici, S., Doise, W. (1974), Decision making in groups. In: Nemeth, C. (Ed.), *Social psychology. Classic and contemporary integrations*. Chicago: Rand McNally.

Moscovici, S., Paicheler, G. (1978), Social comparison and social recognition: Two complementary processes of identification. In: Tajfel, H. (Ed.), *Differentiation between social groups*. European Monographs in Social Psychology. London: Academic Press.

Mulder, M. (1972), *Het speal om macht* [The power game]. Meppel: Boom.

Rabbie, J., Horwitz, M. (1969), The arousal of intergroup bias by chance win or loss. *J. Pers. Soc. Psychol.*, **13**, 296–297.

Rabbie, J., Wilkens, G. (1971), Intergroup competition and its effect on intra- and inter-group relations. *European Journal of Social Psychology*, **1**, 215–234.

Rijsman, J. (1981), Sociale motivatie [Social motivation]. In: Vlist, R. van der, Jaspars, J. (Eds.), *Sociale psychologie in Nederland, Dl. I: Het individu* [Social psychology in The Netherlands, Vol. I: The individual]. Deventer: Van Loghum Slaterus, ch. 2.

Rijsman, J., Poppe, M. (1977), Power difference between players and level of matrix as determinants of competition in a MDG. *European Journal of Social Psychology*, **3**, 347–367.

Rijsman, J., Karel, M., Groenland, E. (1979), *Het effect van intra- en intergroepsvergelijking op het competitieniveau in een spelsituatie* [The effect of intra- and inter-group comparison on the level of competition in a game situation]. Tilburg (dissertation).

Shaver, K. (1975), An introduction to attribution processes. Cambridge (Mass.): Winthrop.

Shaw, M. (1964), Communication networks. In: Berkowitz, L. (Ed.), *Advances in experimental social psychology. Vol. I*. New York: Academic Press.

Shaw, M. (1976), *Group dynamics*. New York: McGraw-Hill.

Sherif, M., Sherif, C. (1969), *Social psychology*. New York: Harper and Row.

Sidowski, J., Wyckoff, L., Tabory, L. (1956), The influence of reinforcement and punishment in a minimal social situation. *Journal of Abnormal and Social Psychology*, **52**, 115–119.

Sik Hung NG (1977), Structural and non-structural aspects of power distance reduction. *European Journal of Social Psychology*, **7**, 317–345.

Sommer, R. (1969), *Personal space: The behavioral basis of design*. Englewood Cliffs (N.J.): Prentice Hall.

Steiner, I. (1972), *Group process and productivity*. New York: Academic Press.

Stokols, D. (1978), Environmental psychology. *Annual Review of Psychology*, **29**, 253–295.

Taillieu, T. (1975), Reward systems, individual and group performance. *Gedrag* [Behaviour], **3**, no. 4/5.

Tajfel, H. (Ed.), *Differentiation between social groups*. European Monographs in Social Psychology. London: Academic Press.

Tajfel, H., Billig, M., Bundy, R., Flament, C. (1971), Social categorisation and inter-group behavior. *European Journal of Social Psychology*, **1**, 149–178.

Thibaut, J. W., Kelley, H. H. (1959), *The social psychology of groups*. New York: Wiley.

Wilke, H. (1968), *Coalitievorming in triades* [Coalition formation in triads]. Rotterdam: Bronder Offset (dissertation).

Wrightsman, L., O'Connor, J., Baker, N. (1972), *Cooperation and competition: Readings on mixed-motive games*. Belmont: Wadsworth.

Zimbardo, P. (1969), *The human choice: Individuation, reason and order versus deindividuation, impulse and chaos*. Nebraska Symposium on Motivation.

Handbook of Work and Organizational Psychology
Edited by P. J. D. Drenth, H. Thierry, P. J. Willems and C. J. de Wolff
© 1984, John Wiley & Sons, Ltd.

3.2. Leadership: theories and models

Erik J. H. Andriessen and Pieter J. D. Drenth

1. INTRODUCTION

The following dictum is from the Chinese book of wisdom Tao Te King (600 B.C.): most leaders are despised, some leaders are feared, few leaders are praised, and the rare good leader is never noticed.

This tells us that even in the very distant past leadership was controversial, but in recent times the position of leaders has become especially complicated. Leadership has come under pressure in politics, in social institutions of all kinds (church, school, family, clubs), and in labour organizations. Matters like authority, responsibility, centralized decision-making power etc., which in the past were never questioned, have now been replaced by new ideas like the primacy of the group, the deposability of the leader, one man one vote, and a dutiful role for the leader. Even where such far-reaching ideas have not been adopted there are, nevertheless, changes. For instance, with respect to the bases of power distinguished by French and Raven (1959) it is clear that in many institutions the rewards and punishments controlled by the leader have, by 1980, been replaced by power based on expertise and at best reference power. Not everyone is finding it easy to adapt to the new expectations—this is especially true of those in business; not infrequently this is a source of serious conflicts.

To a large extent research and development of theories about leadership seem to reflect the confusion already manifest in reality. The theory that the leader has charismatic authority over his followers through his personal qualities

Dr. Erik J. H. T. H. Andriessen, IVA-Instituut voor Sociaal Wetenschappelyk Onderzoek, Tilburg University, Tilburg.
Prof. dr. P. J. D. Drenth, Subfaculteit Psychologie der Vrije Universiteit, De Boelelaan 1081, 1081 HV Amsterdam.

has been abandoned. The scientific approach which attempts to identify specific leadership properties that could, once they had been made measurable, serve as a basis for selection is no longer en vogue. The search for the 'one best way' of management, which could be taught in training courses, has ended. However, this confusion is partly due to the research methodology which has been applied. We will list a number of possible objections to classical leadership research.

This research is conducted almost exclusively through questionnaires. In many cases the psychometrical properties of these questionnaires are, to say the least, dubious. Furthermore, it is well known that many irrelevant factors can influence the answers on questionnaires. This problem is compounded when the aspects of leadership thus measured are compared with dependent variables like satisfaction, attitude towards leadership, or estimated performance, which have also been measured on the basis of questionnaires. It may well be that the common variance that is due to the methods used explains the relations found. It is furthermore not unlikely that the frequent application of 'self-description' aggravates rather than diminishes the problems.

A leader's style or manner of working is often estimated through the computation of an average based on the various judgements of subordinates or superiors. The idea is that differences between group members are due to chance fluctuations which are neutralized by this averaging. But different judgements can actually represent 'true variance', since the leader's behaviour (particularly towards his subordinates) is not as unchangeable as is assumed, and this is all too easily overlooked.

The bulk of leadership research is still correlational. This means that it is often impossible to get at what is really interesting: causal relations. Even if leadership style and satisfaction were measured by different instruments it still remains to be seen whether it is permissible to deduce from the correlation that the style was the cause of the satisfaction. Various other explanations offer themselves, such as:

a. Satisfaction is the cause of the style of management.
b. Satisfied group members attribute certain behaviour to the leader.
c. Style and satisfaction reinforce each other.
d. There is a third variable that influences both (performance, reward).

It is anything but clear what the relevant 'dependent' variables are in leadership research. Campbell (1977) emphatically argues that the following factors—though frequently used—should be avoided: overall judgements of performance, general labour satisfaction indices, objective production measures, and group measures for absenteeism or turnover. The logical distance between these variables and leader behaviour is too great. Besides, they are to a large extent determined by various other technological and/or economic factors.

On the other hand, this confusion is partly due to the use of simplistic theoretical models. Those involved in this research do not sufficiently realize that the interaction between leader and group (members) is a complex socio-psychological phenomenon that in turn forms part of an even more complex organizational system.

In this chapter we hope to bring to light how some of the various approaches indeed suffer from such simplistic assumptions. Moreover, we hope to present a model that takes into account the complexity of the interaction process itself, as well as the complex way in which this is embedded in micro- and macro-organizational sub-systems. Finally we want to show that a number of theories seem to be moving in the right direction.

2. PREMISES

In this chapter we shall focus on the behaviour of leaders in large organizations. That is, we shall mainly focus on the leadership of officially appointed authorities in organizations characterized by hierarchical relations, complex structures and a highly differentiated technology. We shall largely ignore phenomena like the emergence and function of leaders in small informal groups. However, the one cannot always be clearly separated from the other. Even in formal organizations informal groups with informal leaders are formed.

In his *Handbook of Leadership* Stogdill (1974) gives various descriptions of the concept 'leadership'. For instance, it can be seen as a personal property, as the art of inducing obedience, as a way of convincing people or of exercising influence, as an instrument for reaching goals, as the result of interaction, as a role differentiated in group processes, or as a form of structuring. We feel that the last five elements in particular are most important, among other things because they occupy a central place in modern leadership theories. Therefore, we will use the following definition of the concept leadership: *Leadership is that part of the role of a (appointed or elected) leader that in interaction with the group is directly linked to influencing the behaviour of the group, or the behaviour of one or more members of the group and is expressed through directing and coordinating activities that are important in connection with the tasks of the group (in the organization).*

Leadership behaviour, then, is only part of the activity of a leader. It is particularly true of managers in large organizations above the direct supervisoral level that they usually spend their time dealing with affairs that are only indirectly related to supervising group members. Writing reports, administration, calling, maintaining relations with suppliers or customers, and meetings with colleagues all appear to take up much of the manager's time (Campbell *et al.*, 1970; Mintzberg, 1973).

Hemphill (1960) and Stewart (1970) analysed the activities and time allocation of a large number of managers. Stewart identified five groups of functions:
Group 1 (for example sales manager, general director) was characterized by much travel, attending conferences, negotiating, and contacts outside the organization.

Group 2 (for example acting manager, head of accountancy) was characterized by much reading, writing and making reports, and analysis and interpretation of technical affairs.

Group 3 comprised a heterogeneous group of functions that involved divergent managerial activities (simulation, directing, decision-making) carried out in cooperation with colleagues.

Group 4 (for example chief of maintenance) was characterized by short, quick contacts, inspection of the production processes, and solving crises.

Group 5 (for example director of planning, head of training) spent much time in committees, and was mainly preoccupied with coordinating different aspects of personnel management.

This analysis shows that various managerial functions require divergent forms of knowledge and skills, as well as divergent forms of behaviour. Directing subordinates is one aspect of their function; sometimes it is of minor importance.

The fact that we focus on leadership behavior as it takes shape in large complex organization has a few other implications. Direct personal management is an element of the complex of processes taking place in such an organization. The leader's behaviour is not something abstract but is often largely determined by properties of the organization, such as the production process or current ideas about management. Moreover, the behaviour and performance of group members are—quite apart from what their boss says—also directed and limited by all sorts of rules and formal procedures, or by the nature of the production process. This means that in certain cases leadership may well be rather less important than is often assumed. At least it implies that the study of leadership behaviour cannot be separated from the characteristics of the organization as a whole.

3. PERSPECTIVE ON ORGANIZATIONS

Organizations and processes in organizations are complex. One can study them through different approaches and these different approaches produce divergent analyses. Moreover, they can lead to very different recommendations as to what are the most desirable or most effective forms of organization and management. In the course of time a number of such approaches have crystallized; in the following paragraphs we shall briefly describe each of them. For a more detailed discussion the reader is referred to chapter 4.2 of this Handbook.

Taylorism. The rapid industrialization that took place in the previous century and the increasing size and complexity of organizations and production processes gave rise to attempts to find more and more refined methods of controlling the behaviour of large numbers of workers, in order to achieve high productivity and an efficiently conducted business. This development was closely intertwined with the ideal of management characterized by McGregor (1960) as 'Theory X': most workers want to earn as much as possible, and want to work as little as possible; they are unwilling and unable to carry responsibility and must be kept in line by 'stick and carrot' methods, i.e. enticement and coercion. Therefore tasks were carefully analysed and split up so that workers only had to perform a limited number of simple activities. It was 'scientifically' established (hence scientific management) how these activities (e.g. hand-and-arm movements) could be carried out as fast and efficiently as possible. In this context, supervision meant: keeping a strict watch and using the available means of reward and punishment to induce individuals to reach a high level of production.

Human Relations. The first to cast doubt on the idea that the individual pursuit of gain was the primary motive of workers in organizations were social scientists who analysed the actual processes taking place within groups of workers. The well-known Hawthorne studies and investigations on cohesive working groups who limited their own production caused attention to shift to social relations, groups norms and cooperation as important motives of human behaviour (Homans, 1950). At the same time they felt they had traced important determinants of (job) satisfaction.

Leadership was thought to be effective if it satisfied the need for social contacts. A leader had to be sensitive to the feelings and problems of his subordinates, and mutual trust was to be the basis of group relations. It was assumed that this form of supervision would enhance the satisfaction of group members and would in turn result in stronger work motivation. It soon became clear that this model was simplistic. A large number of empirical studies (summarized by Brayfield and Crockett, 1955, and Vroom, 1964 among others) showed that in many cases there was a very weak link between worker satisfaction and motivation.

Later versions of this model (the neo-human relations school) stated that in order to promote both satisfaction and motivation, the leader should not only focus on people but also be task-oriented (Fleishman and Harris, 1962; Blake and Mouton, 1964). Likert (1967) propagated this approach—still more or less exclusively focused on the single group—and turned it into an organization network; as a 'linking pin' the group leader was himself a member of another group on a higher level of the organization. Organizations should consist of a pyramid of such groups, supplemented by work groups particularly created for specific tasks, to be made up of members from various levels and departments. If all these groups had supporting leaders and if high performance was aimed for, the organization would be maximally effective.

Human Resources and Participation. One of the results of post-World War II changes in technology and market relationships, and the quick ageing of products, was that organizations had to adapt more and more rapidly to new circumstances. This required increasing flexibility on the part of the organizations themselves, and increasing creativity and adaptability on the part of the members of these organizations. People became aware of the fact that hitherto too little use had been made of the talents of members of the organization (Miles, 1974). For this reason it was argued that decisions should be made at those levels of the organization where the required knowledge was available (Likert, 1961), that consultation should involve both leader and group members, and that leadership should be participatory. Moreover, it was assumed that participation would not only lead to better decision-making, but would also lead to a lessening in the resistance to change and would motivate people to a higher level of performance. The assumption was that every human being wants to have a say and a certain amount of responsibility; under a participative leader people would be prepared to realize this need. Lammers (1975) calls this approach to participation one of the forms of functional democracy. The assumption is that a certain degree of participation is functional to the aims of the organization, because it makes more effective use of the available information capacities and expertise and because it motivates people.[1]

Systems model. Starting point of many approaches is a perspective—often never made explicit—on organizations referred to by terms such as (structural) functionalism or the Systems model. Organizations are viewed in the light of their goals and their function in society. One talks about the goals of the organization as if one could take for granted that all members of the organization equally work to attain those goals. Organizations are made up of sub-systems whose function can be explained in the light of the goals of the organization as a whole. Conflicts arise when the sub-systems are not well adjusted to each other; alongside other mechanisms, leadership will see both to the attuning of sub-systems to one another and to the attuning of the goals and activities of group members to those of the organization (Katz and Kahn, 1978). This attuning process can be enhanced by appealing to the fact that the formally appointed leader is after all the boss, or by appealing to the members' social obligations to one another, their responsibility with regard to the organization's goal, or to the efficiency and productivity principle.

Multiple Parties model. The multiple parties model of organizations is based on the idea that social systems are the outcome of the process of interaction between various groups or 'parties'. This view implies that organization structures and coordination mechanisms are not so much functional requirements for achieving the organization's goals, which everybody subscribes to, as control mechanisms of the dominant group, or at best as compromises resulting from

---

[1]This functional democracy is to be distinguished from structural democracy in which participation in decision-making is a purpose in itself (see also this Handbook, ch. 4.10).

'negotiations' or exchange relations between various parties. The original Marxist approach only recognizes two parties or classes, i.e. the workers and the representatives of capital. Modern theories acknowledge the existence of more groups which have their own values, goals and interests, their own definition of the situation, and their own strategies for reaching these goals. Two examples of an analysis based on this perspective are Beynon's (1973) study of relations in the British Ford Motor Company, and Baldridge's (1971) study of he organizational structure of New York State University.

This perspective particularly centres on the notion of power. People may derive power from various sources, for instance from their official position, from the fact that they control rewards and punishments, from expertise or personal charm. One reason for the attractiveness of power is that it gives access to privileges. Through various strategies, which are not always consciously pursued, powerholders (particularly managers) try to maintain or increase their power (see for example, Mulder, 1977). According to this perspective, people engage in many, sometimes temporary, coalitions in this power game in order to reinforce their own position.

Conclusion. As is often the case with conflicting approaches, each of the perspectives discussed here contains elements that are valuable. This is especially true of the latter two approaches, the systems model and the multiple parties model: it is impossible to say that the one is more correct or more adequate than the other. The value of either way of thinking depends on its usefulness for specific scientific or social goals. Very often an integration or combination of aspects of the theories will yield useful insights (Lammers, 1980).

4. LEADERSHIP TRAITS AND LEADERSHIP STYLES

The following section discusses leadership perspectives dealing with the personality of the leader. Both the 'trait' and the 'style' approach belong to this category.

4.1 Leadership traits

Since the 1950s, interest in the personality traits or other personal characteristics of leaders has clearly waned, notably because few of such traits or characteristics could be found on the basis of which a distinction could be made between good and bad leaders, or between leaders and followers. Nevertheless, time and again this type of research has been given a new lease of life. Stogdill (1974) discusses hundreds of studies dealing with leadership traits. He too concludes that leadership as such *is not* a personal property, but that there are nonetheless certain fixed personal characteristics that seem to play a part in the role of the leader. House, who developed the path-goal theory which particularly deals with situational and behavioural variables (see section 6), also calls for renewed attention to leadership traits. House and Baetz (1979, p. 352) argue for a more differentiated approach than the traditional one, aimed at finding universal relations, i.e. traits that are important in all situations. They argue that certain characteristics are only important in certain circumstances. This can be demonstrated with the help of Stogdill's correlations of .38, .40, and .60 between athletic capacities and leadership in youth groups, while in other situations the same capacity hardly plays a role at all. House and Baetz offer the following recommendations:

a. Trace the conditions for the relevance of traits by classifying the numerous studies—e.g. those compiled by Stogdill (1948, 1974)—according to population, task, measuring instruments and criteria.

b. Construct specific measuring instruments for measuring leadership.

c. Devote more attention to the interaction of certain traits, for example, competence and dominance.

d. Study the relationship between properties of leaders and leadership behaviour, instead of the relationship between properties of leaders and group performance.

This less universal, strongly differentiated approach may help to dispel the bad reputation that the study of leadership traits has acquired, and thus confirm the common-sense view that some 'have a natural aptitude' for leadership and others do not.

4.2. Leadership styles

Although insight into the personal characteristics of leaders may be useful for selecting leaders, in everyday life it is far more important to know how certain kinds of behaviour affect attitudes and behaviour of the group. It is usually not so very important to know which properties cause a leader to behave as he does. Moreover, the causes for a given behaviour may differ considerably.

'For instance regulating behaviour may be due to a variety of reasons or motives. A person may like to put things in order because he fears unforeseen events, but he may also do it for esthetic reasons. Leaders may want to share power because they are afraid of burning their fingers, or because they adhere to theory Y, or because they appreciate their colleagues, or because they feel that by letting them share they can improve the relationship' (Vollebergh, 1973, p. 235).

Empirical research on leadership as it takes shape both in small informal groups and in formal organizations resulted in the identification of a limited number of dimensions or so-called leadership styles. In the following section, special attention will be devoted to *Consideration, Initiating Structure*, and *Participa-*

tion, the three basic dimensions according to—among others—Campbell *et al.* (1970). The first two have primarily been measured by means of the 'Ohio State Leadership Scales' (see Fleishman *et al.*, 1955). In addition, a few other classifications will be briefly discussed.

Consideration and Initiating Structure. Research on small groups has repeatedly demonstrated the existence of two central functions, viz. fulfilment of the group task and stimulating and taking care of good mutual relations. On the basis of factor analyses of behaviour descriptions of numerous formal organizations, researchers from Ohio State University came to similar conclusions. They named the two dimensions 'initiating structure' and 'consideration'. In the Dutch literature these are usually described as instrumental and social leadership (Philipsen, 1965) or task-oriented and socio-emotional leadership (Mulder *et al.*, 1967).

Consideration reflects the degree to which the leader's behaviour towards the group members is characterized by mutual trust, development of good relations, sensitivity to the feelings of group members, and openness to their suggestions.

Initiating structure reflects the degree to which a leader is bent on defining and structuring the various tasks and roles of group members in order to attain group results.

At first, scholars primarily thought in terms of polar concepts. Later (see for example Blake and Mouton, 1964; Reddin, 1970) it was emphasized that both dimensions were mutually independent. Leaders can focus on socio-emotional matters and be task-oriented at the same time. Various scales were devised with which these dimensions could be measured: the Leadership Opinion Questionnaire—a Likert-type scale which measures how the *leader* thinks he *should* behave—and three versions of the Leader Behavior Description Questionnaire (the 1957 SBDQ, the 1957 LBDQ, and the revised version of the latter, the 1963 LBDQ-XII). The latter three measure how group members perceive the actual behaviour of their leader. With the help of these scales numerous studies have been carried out. Surveys of these studies can be found in Korman (1966), Kerr and Schriesheim (1974) and elsewhere. Stogdill's handbook (1974) also supplies much information on this subject.

Summarizing the results of the many studies we can conclude that socio-emotional leadership is positively related to satisfaction of the group members while task-oriented leadership is positively related to group performance. It should be noted that Fleishman and Harris (1962) concluded that task-oriented leadership without personal attention to group members may have negative effects on satisfaction and even on performance. This conclusion is, however, not confirmed by research carried out by House *et al.* (1971), although it was confirmed by Schriesheim and Murphy (1976). This could imply that socio-emotional leadership has a moderating effect on the relation between task-oriented leadership and performance. If socio-emotional leadership scores high

there is a positive relationship between task-oriented leadership and performance; if socio-emotional leadership scores low the relationship is low or negative.
These and similar results lead to the conclusion that the ideal leader should
combine both aspects of leadership. Consequently, training courses like those
of Blake and Mouton (1964) take this 'one best way' as the gospel truth. Kerr
et al. (1974) expressed some doubts about this approach. It became clear that
there were also negative consequences, partly because preference for an evaluation of a leader's behaviour can vary considerably, depending on the individual
and the situation. These results have induced some to abandon the universal
theories concerning the best combination of leadership styles (see the following
section).

Although the scales mentioned above were carefully constructed, and much
energy was spent in validating and improving them, they have met with rather
severe criticism. Schriesheim and Stogdill (1975) and Schriesheim *et al.* (1976)
in particular studied the comparability of the various scales. They discovered
that the scales only partly measure the same thing, and on the basis of this
discovery they were able to explain the divergent results of various studies.
Notably the early versions of the initiating structure scales appeared to measure
two dimensions. On the one hand, high production is highlighted with items
like: 'he emphasizes the meeting of deadlines', and 'he encourages overtime
work'. On the other hand, there are items that deal with the structuring, i.e.
clarifying, of situations; for example: 'he lets group members know what is
expected of them', and 'he schedules the work to be done'. The original SBDQ
scale contained both kinds of items and therefore produced ambiguous results.
Thus, giving greater weight to performance may have a negatve effect on
 professional workers while structuring the problem may have a postive effect.
The subsequent versions of this scale were clearly oriented towards the structuring of activities.

Moreover, the 'Consideration' scale too does not contain a completely
homogeneous set of items. A distinction can be made between warmth and
trust on the one hand, 'he is friendly and approachable' and participation and
decision-making on the other, 'he acts without consulting the group'. Unfortunately, in the last version of the consideration scale (LBDQ-XIII) the second
dimension is over-represented. Participative leadership will be discussed in
greater detail below. In their analysis of the Ohio State Leadership Scales,
Schriesheim and Kerr (1974, 1977) conclude that the psychometric properties
leave much to be desired. But this does not alter the fact that this type of
research, carried out with the help of the existing versions of the scales, has
yielded valuable results.

Participative leadership. We can be rather brief about this leadership style.
First, this subject is discussed in various other chapters of this Handbook (see
chapters 3.7 and 4.9). Second, an extensive survey of the numerous studies in

this field has recently been published (Locke and Schweiger, 1979). Third, the conclusions drawn in this overview hardly differ from conclusions made by others long ago (see for instance, Drenth and Thierry, 1970). A number of these conclusions can be summarized as follows:

a. Participative decision-making usually leads to satisfaction with this decision-making. According to Locke's survey, this obtains for both laboratory studies and for correlational and longitudinal field studies: in 60% of the studies there was a positive correlation, in 30% no correlation, and in 10% a negative correlation. Similar figures can be deduced from Stogdill's (1974) data (67%, 20%, and 8%). It is not always clear which processes are responsible for this relation. A plausible explanation would be that on the one hand participation meets the need for participation as such, while on the other hand it offers the possibility of attaining other important goals (better decision-making, better relations, more information).

b. Participative decision-making rarely leads to increased motivation, performance, or productivity. According to Locke, in 22% of the cases there was a positive relationship, in 56% there was no relationship, and in 22% there was a negative relationship. Stogdill's results are 30%, 57%, and 13%. Presumably the reason for this is that the relation between the participation concept, which varies considerably according to the situation, and the performance concept, which is determined by numerous factors, are very complex and largely depend on situational variables (see section 5).

c. Many factors have been tested for their moderating effect on the relationship participation/performance. Knowledge and intelligence of the group leaders appear to play a vital part. House and Baetz (1979) add that the nature of the task (routine or complex, structured or unstructured) is also important. Simple routine tasks require little participation and it follows that in connection with these tasks there is no relation between participation and performance; the opposite holds for complex tasks, particularly those requiring the cooperation of group members. This implies that participation is only successful when it is absolutely vital for the task. These tasks often require personnel who have had a reasonable amount of schooling, and who have a reasonable level of knowledge. The moderating effect of task complexity probably runs parallel to the knowledge and experience factor. Finally, House and Baetz mention the need for participation as a moderator variable. They assume, however, that this variable is only important for relatively uninteresting tasks, since everyone will be interested in participation when it comes to interesting tasks.

A completely different research tradition (Mulder, 1977) demonstrates that participation, in the sense of being involved in decision-making, does not always entail an increase in influence. Mulder's participation paradox implies that increased participation can lead to increased power of the leader, as it is ultimately his expertise that determines the outcome of the decision-making procedure, albeit through a strategy that makes the group members more tractable and motivated.

It is indeed remarkable that surveys like Locke and Schweiger's (1979) or those of other authors pay practically no attention to instruments for measuring the degree of participative leadership. From the short descriptions of the various studies we gather that researchers often use their own instruments. Contradictory or at least obscure results are probably partly due to the use of non-comparable or psychometrically weak instruments. The scale of Koopman and Werkman (1973), developed in The Netherlands, has been used often in a shortened version in a variety of studies (Zanders *et al.*, 1978; Andriessen *et al.*, 1983). The psychometric properties of this scale are satisfactory. The scale contains a series of Likert-type items that inquire into the degree to which the leader usually informs or consults group members. Yet, at the same time the nature of this scale is evaluative. A completely different instrument investigates the degree to which group members are involved in decision-making on specific issues. The positions on the response scale usually include the following range: not involved; being consulted; joint decision-making; and the possibility of taking decisions independently (Vroom and Yetton, 1973; Heller, 1971; DIO, 1983; IDE, 1981). This scale also has reasonably good psychometric properties.

Other leadership styles. The 'Survey of Organizations' (Taylor and Bowers, 1972), an extensive questionnaire for organizational diagnostic research, contains four sub-scales for measuring leadership dimensions. The four scales are made up of four to five Likert-type items that are supposed to measure the following dimensions:
— *Support*: letting group members know that they are valuable and important.
— *Goal emphasis*: stimulating enthusiasm for work.
— *Work facilitation*: removing barriers that hamper work.
— *Interaction facilitation*: turning the group into a solid team.

There are two different types of these scales: one describes the behaviour of the leader, the other the behaviour of the group members. Both the meaning of these four dimensions and the value of the instruments involved is still unclear. Schriesheim and Kerr's (1977) evaluation of the psychometric properties is rather negative. A vital problem in the evaluation is that hitherto only scholars from the Institute of Social Research, the place where the instrument was devised, have published results. In most of these publications the four scales are either added into one total score, which is subsequently correlated to other variables, or correlations of the four scales are averaged. It remains to be seen how far these scales are independent of the Ohio State Leadership Scales.

Numerous other leadership dimensions have been distinguished and operationalized. As a result of the small amount of research done up to now, it is generally impossible to establish the value of the distinctions and the instruments. Thus Bass *et al.*, (1975) devised—on the basis of a social system model—an instrument that was to measure five dimensions, viz. *direction, negotiation, consultation, participation,* and *delegation.* The last three dimensions show a relatively high intercorrelation and can therefore be considered aspects of participative leadership. The other two dimensions are more or less independent of each other and of the three participation dimensions. Stogdill (1974) describes the development of twelve sub-scales of the LBDQ-XIII (two of them are Initiating Structure and Consideration). Examples of other scale are: tolerance of uncertainty, tolerance of follower freedom of action, representation, and production emphasis. The various studies have not yet made clear which—if any—new dimensions have thus been identified.

4.3. Summary

The theories and empirical inquiries discussed so far all belong to a rather simplistic tradition, which could be called the trait or style approach. 'Trait' is an underlying individual property. 'Style' refers to the leader's more or less stable way of behaviour. Characteristics of the style approach are: universalism (the one best way' of leadership), defining leadership in terms of a number of broad dimensions, a simple casual model (leadership causes satisfaction and improves performance), and correlational questionnaire research in which perceptions are treated as descriptions and individual variation as error. Campbell (1977, p. 228) sums up the following points of criticism:

'. . . Consideration and initiating structure have been recognized as both too simple and too complex. They are too simple in that two factors simply cannot reflect the complexity of what leaders do . . . They are too complex in that scores on these two variables are several steps removed from behavioral bedrock and represent a considerable amount of inference on the part of the respondent'

To a greater or lesser degree these points of criticism apply to all leadership style dimensions. The dimensions can be seen as factors of a higher order. However, both for research and for leadership practice it is necessary to focus on more specific forms of behaviour. The notion 'leadership style' suggests that leaders always behave in the same way towards all group members. So long as leaders are described in terms of only a few dimensions, we will not gain a deeper insight into the complexity of the behaviour of divergent types of leaders. Besides, in practice and particularly in connection with the training of leaders a much more specific approach of leadership behaviour is called for. It is hardly useful to tell a boss that he should give more support or be more sensitive to certain needs if he is not told how he should react to the behaviour of group members. Theories and approaches that to some degree remedy these problems will be discussed below.

5. CHARACTERISTICS OF MODERN LEADERSHIP APPROACHES

Typical of the traditional leadership approaches was the simplicity of their conceptual schema as illustrated in figure 1.

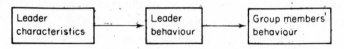

Figure 1. Traditional leadership model.

Behaviour (and attitudes) of group members were believed to be wholly or largely determined by the behaviour of the leader, which in turn was largely determined by his (personal) characteristics. Moreover, leadership behaviour could be described in terms of a permanent 'style' of management. This style of management was to be adjusted to the motives of group members. True, there were different opinions as to the most effective style: directive, open and supporting, or democratic, depending on which human motives one saw as most important, i.e. the need for guidance and stimulation, sociability or participation.

Nevertheless, it was generally accepted that in everyday practice leaders could be characterized by a particular style, and the gospel of a particular leadership style (for instance, Likert's supportive leadership, Blake and Mouton's 9.9. style) was spread with missionary zeal. That this zeal brought grist to the missionaries' mill (witness book sales and the popularity of this kind of leadership training) might well have something to do with the simplicity of these approaches. However, reality appeared to be more complicated than these approaches and theories assumed. Modern insights led to new theories about leadership, which are based on the following psychological and organizational assumptions:

1. Human behaviour is determined by many factors. The traditional motives —money, sociability, participation—are motivating factors only under certain conditions. Moreover, there are other needs that also determine motivation, and other factors besides motivation that determine behaviour.

2. Leadership is one aspect of the total set of activities that take place in an organization. Interaction between leader and group members takes place within the context of various situational factors. Therefore, contextual (e.g. technology, power relations, general climate) and situational factors (e.g. nature of the decision, personality of subordinates) also determine leader behaviour and type of management.

3. Leader and group members influence each other continually, i.e. leadership behaviour is liable to change, partly due to the way a leader reacts to the behaviour of group members.

In the following sections these characteristics of modern leadership theories will be developed and combined into a new leadership model.

5.1. A differentiated model of man

At the start of this chapter various views on people and organizations were discussed. It appeared that most of these views were based on rather one-sided ideas about human motivation. The workers were either motivated only by money, or only by social needs, or only by the need for autonomy. Meanwhile it has become rather clear that people have many needs, and that a number of these needs can be realized in work situations.

The literature provides various classification schemes of human needs. Maslow's (1954) division, despite the criticism on his theory, offers a good starting-point: human needs can be classed into physiological needs, the safety need, belongingness or social needs, extreme needs, and the need for self-actualization. Alderfer (1972) simplified this classification and refers to three types of needs: existence needs, relatedness needs and growth needs. Central to modern leadership theories is the idea that if a leader wants to influence the behaviour of his group members he must adapt to their needs by making rewards (incentives) available that meet these needs. A good leader is sensitive to what group members need in given situations. People's motivation is determined not only by the availability of certain rewards, but also by whether or not they expect to attain these rewards through their efforts. If good relations with colleagues exist independently of whether or not one works hard, this 'incentive' will not motivate people to higher performance.

There are also other factors that determine the behaviour of group members, and if leaders want to direct this behaviour they must take them into account. Campbell and Pritchard (1976) summarized these factors in a model.[2]

In principle the boxed elements in figure 2 can be influenced (at least partly) by a leader. People take their capacities with them to work but the boss can help to develop experience and skills. A boss can also play in important role in

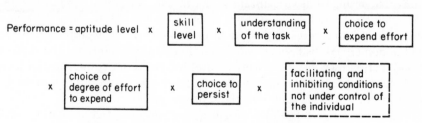

Figure 2. Determinants of human performance.

[2]The sequence of the boxes does not imply that we are dealing with a causal chain.

making clear what is expected of group members. In modern leadership theories, like that elaborated in 'Management by objectives' which focuses on management through formulating joint goals (Drucker, 1954), this is seen as one of leadership's most important functions. Obviously, there are not only official goals (= expectations of the management), but also sorts of more or less explicit expectations of others (colleagues, higher personnel, subordinates, trade unions, family members etc.), which also partly determine behaviour. The following three elements of this model are concerned with motivation, which was discussed in an earlier section. Strictly speaking the last element (enclosed by a dotted line) does not reflect leadership behaviour in the limited sense of exercising influence on the behaviour of group members through direct interaction. But it is part of the supervisor's job to ensure that work conditions for group members are optimal. Modern views about leadership also emphasize this point. Leadership is a 'boundary function' (Katz and Kahn, 1978, p. 532). It is the leader's task to regulate the relations with other sub-systems of the organization (obtaining materials, transport of products, etc.) in such a way that group members can do their work well.

5.2. Leadership as part of organizational processes

Hitherto, the new theories of leadership have hardly taken into account that interaction between leader and group members is embedded in an organization with a formal structure, a given technology, processes of control and an external environment. The contingency theories that were developed during the 1960s (Fiedler, 1967; Heller, 1976) primarily acknowledge the importance of certain micro-situational variables, i.e. characteristics of the work group itself, such as task structure and group relations.

In many organization theories leadership is looked upon as one of the coordinating mechanisms that are used to adjust the behaviour of various individuals and groups to the (top management's) goal of the organization. Both those who think in terms of a systems model and those who think in terms of a multiple parties model postulate that differentiation in the activities of organizational units that result from specialization and division of labour creates the need for integrating mechanisms (Lawrence and Lorsch, 1967). This need stems from the wish to control the behaviour of members of the organization. March and Simon (1958) distinguish two types of control mechanisms. They refer to 'coordination by plan', i.e. a fixed control by means of organization structure and technology, and to 'coordination by feedback', i.e. coordination of activities in situations that cannot easily be pre-programmed.

Van der Ven et al. (1976) distinguish three groups of coordinating mechanisms, namely impersonal mechanisms (rules, plans, systems, procedures), individual mechanisms (leaders, coordinators), and group mechanisms (committees, meetings). Research carried out in 197 departments of large government organizations showed that the impersonal mechanisms were much in evidence, the individual mechanisms less so, and the group mechanisms least frequent. However, as tasks became more unsafe and dangerous, the impersonal mechanism was replaced by group mechanisms of coordination. As mutual dependence of group members increased, so more and more coordination mechanisms were added to the existing mechanisms—notably individual and group mechanisms. Furthermore, in large departments the number of impersonal mechanisms was larger than in small departments (with a comparable degree of consultation).

In addition, Miner (1975) mentions the professional form of control over behaviour, i.e. the behavioural code that many professionals (e.g. physicians, accountants, psychologists) are taught during their training.

It has become clear that management is only one of many coordination mechanisms, and is itself determined by other mechanisms. There are three ways in which external variables and aspects of the situation, like organization structure, technology or group relations, can play a part; these are indicated by arrows a, b, and c, in figure 3. We will devote some attention to these three ways of exercising influence.

a. *Influence of situational characteristics on leader behaviour*

Although traditionally leadership was taken to be an independent variable, many studies have shown that the behaviour of the leader is also dependent on situational factors. The degree to which the leader is forced to behave in a certain way is highly variable. In bureaucratic organizations, first-level supervisors usually have little freedom of movement. On the other hand, the manager and owner of a small enterprise can largely determine his own policy and leadership style (although it should be borne in mind that this type of leader is also constrained by government regulations, collective labour agreements, type of personnel, etc.). This phenomenon is confirmed by various empirical studies. Thus an elected (as opposed to an assigned or appointed) leader appears to take more initiative (Carter *et al.*, 1951), and to have more power and influence (Raven and French, 1958).

Furthermore, many studies have demonstrated the importance of manage-

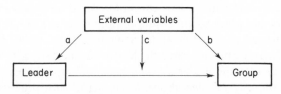

Figure 3. The impact of aspects of the situation on
leader-group relations.

ment expectations and of management philosophy on the one hand, and the nature of decisions on the other (Heller, 1976; Wilpert, 1977). The level of the organization itself is an important differentiating factor with regard to leadership. Katz and Kahn (1978, p. 536) distinguish three basic types of leadership behaviour.

—'*Origination*', i.e. policy making, creating and changing structures (particularly at top level). In order to be able to do this one needs complete insight into both the system as a whole, including its sub-systems, and the demands, developments and possibilities of the environment. According to Katz and Kahn, this 'systemic perspective' is more important to top managers than are interpersonal skills.

—'*Interpolation*', development of ways of effecting policies (particularly at the middle level). This presupposes a two-way orientation whereby ideas can be handed from the top to the bottom, and vice versa. This requires interpersonal skills and a keen insight into organization processes.

—'*Administration*', i.e. making use of the existing structure and effectuating procedures and regulations (particularly at the lower level). This mainly requires technical and procedural knowledge.

Although every level requires its particular dominant type of leadership, a sufficient degree of each of the three types of leadership will have to be represented at each level. Insufficient attention at top level to policy, change, and adjustment can result in a rigid, bureaucratic organization. Insufficient attention at top level to routine control functions can lead to inefficiency and irritations, and to rivalry or lack of integration at lower levels (Katz and Kahn, 1978, p. 570).

b. *Aspects of the situation and the behaviour of group members*

As mentioned above, the behaviour of individuals depends on more factors than leadership behaviour alone. Naturally this also holds for group attitudes and behaviour: these depend partly on all sorts of factors outside the leader's sphere of influence. In the first place we are alluding to task characteristics and group processes. Yet, organizational characteristics also appear—usually in a very complex way—to have considerable impact on the behaviour and attitudes of group members (Hall, 1972; James and Jones, 1976). Kerr and his colleagues go even further (Kerr, 1974; Kerr and Jermier, 1978): they developed the concept of 'leadership substitutes'. This concept is based on the idea that there are situation factors that grant so much support and structure that group members can derive sufficient motivation and satisfaction from them, and as far as support and structure are concerned the leader becomes superfluous. This does not mean to say that the leader as such becomes superfluous. He has more functions than those mentioned above. Examples of substitutes for supportive leadership are: intrinsically satisfying tasks, a professional orientation, and a cohesive work group. Possible substitutes for structuring leadership are: routine tasks, formalized plans, and rules and procedures.

Kerr and Jermier (1978) distinguish between 'substitutes' and 'neutralizers'. 'Substitutes' are factors that replace leadership or a certain type of leadership, 'neutralizers' are factors that simply make leadership impossible, and in so doing create a power vacuum that can lead to all kinds of dysfunctions. Spatial distance is an obvious example, but lack of communication with the top level can also have a neutralizing effect (Pelz, 1951, 1952). Kerr and Jermier's (1978) approach is intriguing and promising, and it may well succeed in establishing a link between organizational-theoretical notions about coordination mechanisms, and theories of leadership. However, at this stage conceptualization, operationalization and testing are still in their infancy (see for instance Jermier and Berkes, 1979). It is therefore too early to consider it as an elaborate theory. All this means that it is doubtful whether a leader is always equally important to group behaviour. Hall (1972) therefore wonders whether there is convincing evidence that leadership has significant effects. Practical experience and common sense suggest that it does; but Pfeffer (1978) warns against such reasoning. Human beings constantly search for the causes of what happens to them, partly because that enables them to effectively control events. They particularly look for factors that are controllable, and dislike attributing causality to an obscure complex of human interaction, rules, structures, and objects. Where there is success there must be a hero; where there is a failure there must be a scapegoat.

We would like to argue that the need for leadership is in evidence not only in practice but also in theory and empirical research. Katz and Kahn (1978, p. 530) mention a number of reasons:

—No organization scheme or scenario can be so exhaustive as to cover all activities.

—Organizations are open systems and are embedded in a constantly changing environment. Every change in the environment brings on changes in the organization.

—An organization consists of sub-systems that are often not completely adjusted to each other, as they have different goals. The leader typically has a boundary function; that is to say, it is his task to regulate relations with other groups so as to create optimal working conditions for his own group.

—Members of an organization are at the same time members of other systems (family, trade union, club). These systems may also cause changes in the leader's behaviour. It is the leader's task to react to these changes in order to keep the organization running.

c. *Situational aspects and the part they play in the relationship between leadership (behaviour), group attitudes and group behaviour*

Theories that contend that the effect of a certain type of leadership on the performance and satisfaction of group members is partly determined by aspects of the situation, are called contingency theories. A well-known (if strongly criticized) example is Fiedler's theory (1967), which states that the success of task-oriented or relation-oriented leadership is dependent on the leader's formal power, task structure and group relations (see the following section).

Drenth and Thierry (1970) discuss a number of studies that demonstrate the importance of characteristics of *group members* (capacities, needs personality), of the *group* at large (size, degree of interaction and interdependencies of tasks, homogeneity, the system of norms and values), of the *leader* (capacities, influence at the top), the *task* (the degree to which it is routinized) and the *organization* (nature, size, and structure).

Kerr *et al.*, (1974) present at a long list of moderator variables, based on an elaborate analysis of studies carried out with the help of the Ohio State Leadership Scales, 'consideration' and 'initiating structure'. Their most important findings are:

—Structuring leadership will be most desired and appreciated in crisis or at least stress situations, e.g. as a result of pressure of time, conflicts, physical danger or other factors (see also Mulder *et al.*, 1967). Recently this was confirmed by Katz (1977) with respect to group conflicts.

—If tasks are very routine or if the person in question is very experienced or competent there is no insecurity and therefore little need for structuring leadership. In such cases, satisfaction of group members is primarily linked to 'considerate' leadership.

—Contrary to expectation the effects of hierarchical position, expectations of group members with respect to the most adequate leadership style, concurrence between leadership style of the direct supervisors and the manager on the next rung of the ladder, communication with the top level, appear to be rather unclear. In some studies they had positive moderating effect; in others effect was negatively moderating, or completely absent.

These conclusions confirm House's Path–Goals theory (House 1971; House and Dessler, 1974), in which many of the variables mentioned above are integrated into a consistent model (see the following section). However, these studies pay little attention to the moderating effect of the characteristics of the organization structure, technology, and other 'macro' variables. Vollebergh (1973) deals with the subject in a rather impressionistic way; he defines certain types of leadership with the help of two dimensions, viz. the degree of planning (improvisation vs. bureaucracy) and the degree of participation (hierarchical vs. participative). The four types that can be defined on the basis of these dimensions are each taken to be effective in certain organizations. Classical entrepreneurship (hierarchical but not very bureaucratic) is suitable for small organizations that require quick decisions. The inspiring leader (non-bureaucratic, oriented towards participation) suits the smaller organizations or departments in which various types of competent people should form a solid team, e.g. a project organization. The controller (hierarchical as well as bureaucratic) suits those organizations that need to be rigidly structured in order to avoid mistakes (for instance, administrative organizations). Finally, the role of manager (both structuring and oriented towards participation) is primarily effective in large organizations with complex links between divergent departments.

Interesting but as yet unverified is Melcher's (1977) attempt to develop a model in which eight structural variables (for example, size, departmentalization, task complexity, and spatial barriers), five leadership dimensions ('representation', 'rule organizations', 'participation', 'direction', and 'inducement'), and a personality trait (dogmatism) are all included. According to Melcher the impact of all these variables as such is not so extensive, but the interaction of the three types of variables is particularly important for group performance and satisfaction.

Finally, in this context it is worth noting the 'multiple influence model of leadership' (Hunt and Osborn, 1980), which includes macro-organization moderators like complexity of environment, contextual complexity (size, technology) and structural complexity (specialization and diversity). The moderator variables discussed so far are all more or less permanent aspects of the situation. Moreover, leadership behaviour is always described in terms of certain stable leadership styles.

The approach of Shull et al. (1970), Duncan (1973), DIO (1983), and Vroom and Yetton (1973) differs from the preceding studies in that they assume that moderating factors are to be sought in characteristics of specific decision-making processes. The latter developed a theory that postulates that the effect of participative or autocratic ways of decision-making depends, among other things, on the urgency of the decisions, the amount of information the boss has, and whether the acceptance of the decision is vital for its implementation (see the following section). The DIO International Research Team (Heller, Drenth, Koopman and Rus) emphasizes a.o. the importance of conflictuousness, amount of trust and clarity of goal in this respect (DIO, 1983; Koopman and Drenth, 1980). They further show that this differentiation can also be linked to the *phase* of the decision-making process.

Graen and his assistants (Graen and Cashman, 1975; Dansereau and Dumas, 1977) go one step further. They reject the traditional approach, which links the general leadership style of a leader to the 'average' reaction of a group. In many such studies it is assumed that the differences in the group members' descriptions of the leader are the result of accidental fluctuations, and that in fact leader and group member behaviour is 'homogeneous'. In other words, it is postulated that the interaction between leader and all group members is more or less alike. However, the authors mentioned above focus on the analysis of 'vertical dyadic linkages', i.e. interaction between a leader and a specific group member. In analysing a series of groups in a large organization, they concluded that the nature of dyadic interaction varies in many groups. To be sure, in his reaction to this article Cummings (1975) states that to presuppose heterogeneity of behaviour is as generalizing as to presuppose homogeneity.

Dansereau and Dumas (1977) present a method by which one can decide in a concrete research situation which of the two suppositions corresponds to reality. It can safely be assumed that in some situations—for instance where group members work close to each other and on the same tasks—the leader shows rather consistent behaviour, if only because unequal treatment is likely to be seen as unfair. Besides, in very cohesive groups it is probably more effective if the leader approaches the group as a whole instead of approaching each member individually (Schriesheim and Kerr, 1977, p. 38). Nevertheless, the authors' call for a more differentiated approach is very important, as it appears to take account of the notion that leader behaviour is not always as consistent and unchangeable as traditional theories suppose.

5.3. Mutual influence of leader and group members

Most studies dealing with the relation between leadership and group satisfaction, group performance or other criteria are correlational. Positive correlations often lead to the conclusion that the behaviour of the leader is the reason behind, and a determining factor in the attitudes and performance of the group. Of course there are many situations in everyday life in which a new leader 'sets a new course', and is consequently the reason for changes in the attitudes and behaviour of the group. Systematic studies (laboratory experiments or longitudinal field studies) have demonstrated that a change of leader can cause a change of group behaviour. House and Baetz (1979, p. 347) give a survey of studies that show that leadership has influenced the dedication and motivation of group members, their adjustment to change, their turnover and absenteeism, the quality of their decisions, their acceptance of decisions taken, their group productivity, and the profits of the enterprise. It seems appropriate in this context to note the importance of the time factor. Leadership behaviour comes into being and grows in permanent interplay with the group and the environment. However, other studies have shown that there is often no relationship between the leader and group performance (Stogdill, 1974; Locke and Schweiger, 1979), or that the cause-effect relation can be the other way around (Lowin and Craig, 1968; Farris and Lim, 1969). For example, higher performance by the group can lead to less close supervision by the leader.

Studies by Graen and Cashman (1975) show that the process of interaction can be even more complex. When new members join the group, a long process may follow whereby leader and group members (and group members among themselves) will feel each other out as it were, and test each others' reactions. During this process an exchange relation develops which determines whether or not the leader will assign a group member certain tasks, give information, or support the group member in his relations with other members of the organization. The group member in turn shows a degree of dedication, conformity, cooperation etcetera (Jacobs, 1970).

As a rule, in such an interaction process the attitude of one person is a reaction not so much to the observable behaviour of the other as to what he assumes to be the causes of that behaviour. When a worker comes in late his boss' reaction will differ depending on whether he attributes his being late to indifference or laziness, or to external factors (circumstances beyond his control). The same holds for the worker himself—he too attributes his own performance to certain causes. If boss and workers have different explanations for the same behaviour the chance of conflict increases. In order to further analyse such interaction processes between leader and group members Green and Mitchell (1979) use insights from attribution theory (see the following section).

5.4. Conclusions

At the end of this section we can conclude that theories concerning leadership should be complex, that is they should take into account many variables and the way these variables interact. But this does not mean that one should aim at drawing up long lists of factors that are all relevant in one way or another. The effects of the various kinds of variables should be further specified. Thus Osborn and Hunt (1975) have argued that micro-situational variables (characteristics of group members and tasks) have a *moderating* effect on the relationship between leadership and group behaviour, while macro-situational variables (the characteristics of the environment, e.g. organization structure and complexity of the organization environment) have a directing and/or limiting effect on leadership behaviour as such. Although their own study of environmental complexity seems to lend some support to this theory, there are sufficient indications that the organization characteristics have a moderating effect, and that group characteristics can have a direct effect.

The assumption that a stable, firm leader always reacts in the same imperturbable (autocratic) way towards his group members was perhaps adequate at times when and under circumstance in which the leader's power was strong and unchallengeable. In many modern and complex work situations the relative power positions of the various participants are less divergent and the leader will have to adjust his behaviour to those participants and to the situation.

6. A model and a number of theories

Based on the considerations discussed above we constructed a model (see figure 4) that attempts to integrate the relevant variables and relations discussed above. The interaction processes (within leader and group members) that have a direct determining or moderating effect on the central process are placed at

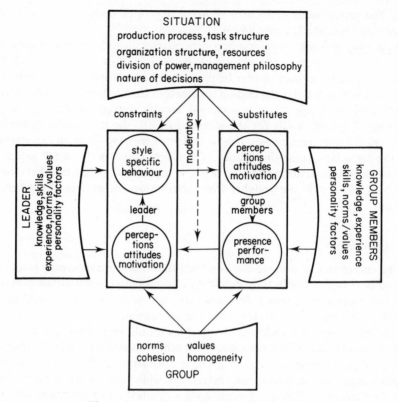

Figure 4. An integrated model of leadership.

the centre of the model. Naturally this is not an empirically tested, ontological, but rather a heuristic model.

The model clearly shows that, in our opinion, leadership can hardly be isolated from the whole complex of dynamic processes. It can be assumed, however, that the determining effect of leadership on the attitudes and behaviour of group members will be stronger when aspects of the situation are less clearly structured and less pressing.

With the help of this model we will now discuss a number of the better known and more recent theories in the field of leadership.

1. Fiedler's contingency theory. Fiedler's theory (1967) is certainly worth mentioning since it is one of the first of the contingency models. The central idea is that the effect of a certain type of leader behaviour on group performance depends on the situation (see figure 5). Rather than measure leadership behaviour, Fiedler measures (with the help of a semantic differential questionnaire)

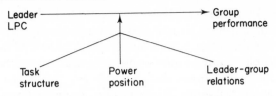

Figure 5. Fiedler's contingency theory.

a personal property, *an attitude* of the leader, i.e. his attitude towards the 'least preferred coworker' (LPC). A high LPC score is interpreted as strongly relation-oriented, a low LPC score as strongly task-oriented.

At the same time three aspects of the situation are measured with the help of questionnaires, i.e. the degree to which the task is routine and/or clearly structured, the degree to which the power position of the leader is guaranteed by the organization and the degree to which the group climate is favourable.

On the basis of numerous empirical studies, Fiedler concludes the following:
—Highly task-oriented leadership is most effective in groups in which conditions are relatively favourable (i.e. good relations and the presence of one or both of the other factors), or in those cases where all these factors are unfavourable.
—Highly relation-oriented leadership is most effective when the other condi-
1tions prevail, i.e. when the task is sufficiently structured yet the leader-group relations and/or the leader's formal power position are rather poor.
—The leader's attitude (as represented in the LPC score) is hard to change. Consequently it is suggested that the selection and appointment of the leader should happen in such a way that he ends up in the right groups, or that the leader's attitudes are being diagnosed, whereupon the aspects of the situation might be changed so as to create the most favourable combination of leader and situation (Fiedler *et al.*, 1976).

Fiedler's theory has met with severe criticism (for example Graen *et al.*, 1970; Schriesheim and Kerr, 1977). The most important critical observations are:
—The LPC scale shows insufficient conceptual, substantial, and predictive validity. One important issue is the fact that the LPC variable is unidimensional, while the Ohio State Studies have demonstrated that task and relation-oriented behaviour can occur simultaneously. 'Thus we must conclude that after twenty-five years the LPC remains a measure in search of a meaning' (Stinson, 1977). Furthermore, homogeneity often scores high, but it appears that in many studies stability (test-retest) is very low. The latter is important since the LPC variable is supposed to measure a stable personality trait.
—The selection, measuring and differential weighting of the three aspects of the situation are conceptually obscure, and in various studies they have been

changed in an *ad hoc* manner. Moreover, the model in figure 4 shows that the choice of these three aspects is rather arbitrary and incomplete.

—The theory is static. There is no room for change; the LPC variable is taken to be unchangeable, and if a leader wants to be effective he must see to it that the situation does not change either. According to the theory, the leader can afford to be strongly task-oriented when leader-group relations are favourable. It remains to be seen whether these relations continue to be favourable if the leader is exclusively task-oriented.

These and other criticisms show that the theory is rather vulnerable. Nevertheless, during the 1960s and the early 1970s this model has stimulated much theorizing and research; in this respect it certainly has exerted important influence.

2. *The Path–Goal theory*. Following Evans (1970), House based his theory about leadership behaviour on the expectation theory of work motivation. According to this theory, people's motivation to work depends both on the importance (the valence) they attach to certain results that are to be attained (the outcomes) and on the expectation that their behaviour will actually cause them to obtain those results (see also Vroom, 1964). The behaviour of the leader should supply rewards (valent outcomes), e.g. by reacting with open and social leadership to desired behaviour (= consideration). Besides, the leader's instructions and structuring (= initiating structure) should be such that they help the group members to attain their goal. The latter, also called role clarification, means that the group members' expectations about their chances of attaining their goals (path-goal relation) are reinforced. This leads to two conclusions: (1) The leader is effective (i.e. he motivates his people) if he makes satisfaction of group member needs (i.e. receiving valent outcomes) dependent on their behaviour (2) The leader is effective insofar as his behaviour (rewarding or structuring) is complementary to what the situation is already producing.

House (1979) distinguishes two groups of situational factors, viz. characteristics of group members (notably perception of their own skills, 'locus of control' orientation and authoritarianism), and characteristics of the environment (notably task structuring and structuring of the organization). In discussions and empirical studies the degree of task structuring received most attention. The second proposition implies that if the task itself is very structured, i.e. routine, the leader should not give instructions or do much supervising, since this is superfluous and causes frustration. He should instead adopt a considerate and supportive form of leadership, i.e. he should be friendly, open, and helpful, in order to compensate for the monotonous task or the formalistic organization. Tests of the Path–Goal theory have been limited to an analysis of the moderating effect of task structure on the relationship between leadership behaviour and performance, satisfaction, or expectations of group members. In their survey article Schriesheim and Kerr (1977) conclude that hitherto the empirical support for the theory, notably the above-mentioned effect on task structure, is rather weak. Possible explanations are: first, the rather unfortunate operationalization of leadership behaviour (for lack of any better, the Ohio State Leadership Scales for 'consideration' and 'initiating structure' were used in many cases[3]); and second, the fact that all kind of other factors that could influence relations were not taken into account. The study by Downey *et al.* (1976) demonstrates that hierarchical differences (with the attending differences in task preferences) interact with task structure. Managers appear to prefer a great deal of independence. As a result, structuring leadership did enhance their performance but it also caused dissatisfaction. In the long run this could lead to lower performance. Hammer and Dachler (1975) argue for a more explicit use of the expectation theory, which they believe will improve the conceptualization of notions like 'path' and 'goals'.

Partly on the basis of our model (figure 4) we can make the following criticisms of the Path–Goal theory:
a. House and Dessler's (1974) formulation in particular pays little attention to the actual behaviour of the members, to group performance as a whole, and to the feedback effect on the perception and behavior of the leader. The longitudinal research carried out by Downey *et al.* (1976) illustrates the importance of these factors.
b. Apart from task structure there are various other aspects of the environment that, either by themselves or in a process of interaction, might influence the relationship between leader behaviour and the group.
c. Although the theory explicitly postulates that leadership behaviour should be adjusted i.a. to the performance of group members, most empirical studies only use operationalizations of general leadership styles.
　　Despite these criticisms the Path–Goal theory offers a model that in principle can encompass many variables and phenomena relevant to the effects and determinants of leadership behaviour. For further verification of the theory many of these variables and their effects should be defined and operationalized more explicitly (Schriesheim and Kerr, 1977).

3. *Leadership as decision-making.* Vroom and Yetton (1973) have developed a detailed theory about the conditions under which different ways of decision-making are most effective. The five ways of decision-making[4] vary with respect to the degree to which group members are involved in the decision-making of the leader:

---

[3] Recently Schriesheim developed specific Path–Goal scales for measuring Consideration and Initiating structure (Kerr and Jermier, 1978, p. 392).
[4] The various decision-making strategies can be compared with the levels in the Influence-Power Continuum (IPC), mentioned by Heller (1971), and the participation levels used in recent research on industrial democracy in Europe (IDE, 1981), and complex decision-making (DIO, 1983).

—*autocratic–1* (AI): the leader makes the decision without making enquires in the group;
—*autocratic–2* (AII): the leader makes the decision after selective enquiries;
—*consultative–1* (CI): the leader makes the decision after he has asked individual group members for solutions;
—*consultative–2* (CII): the leader makes the decision after consulting and discussing with the whole group;
—*group method* (GII): the group (which includes the leader) makes the decision.

Certain aspects of the situation are important in determining what strategy is chosen. Unlike other contingency theories Vroom and Yetton's model focuses not so much on general organization, group, or task characteristics as on the characteristics of specific decisions. According to the theory, seven characteristics are important (see the questions in figure 6). The effectiveness of decisions is defined in terms of the quality of the solution and the motivation of group members to cooperate in its implementation. In fact the model consists of a number of rules for decsion-making that determine which methods of decision-making are more and which less effective, given a certain combination of decision-making characteristics.

The 'acceptance-rule' can serve as an example: if effective implementation of a decision requires that group members accept it, and if it is not certain that an autocratic decision will be accepted, then strategies AI and AII (autocratic decision-making) are unsuitable.

The theory is in the first place meant to be normative. That is to say, on the basis of an extensive study of the literature Vroom and Yetton have drawn up rules that specify how a leader should behave in order to reach a given goal. This normative model is represented in figure 6.

Definition of decision characteristics

A. Is there a quality requirement such that one solution is likely to be more rational than another?
B. Do I have sufficient information to make high quality decisions?
C. Is the problem structured?
D. Is acceptance of decision by subordinates critical to effective implementation?
E. If I were to make the decision myself, is it reasonably certain that I would be accepted by my subordinates?
F. Do subordinates share the organizational goals to be attained in solving this problem?
G. Is conflict among subordinates likely in preferred solution?

Vroom and Yetton (1973) and Jago and Vroom (1975) have investigated whether the normative model has also an empirical character, i.e. to what degree leaders actually behave according to this model. They conclude that leaders do indeed adjust their behaviour to the situation, i.e. the nature of the problems confronting them. However, they only do this within limits. Apparently, many leaders showed less variation in their behaviour than the model postulates.

Characteristics of decisions

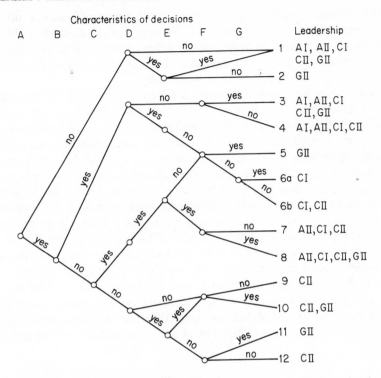

Figure 6. Contingency model of decision-making by Vroom and Yetton (1973).

Some are less, others more participative than the model prescribes. From this the authors deduce that to some extent leaders adopt a certain personal style, which manifests itself in various situations. Nevertheless, the theory needs further testing. Vroom and Yetton have actually used two research strategies, both of which are reputational in character. First, managers were asked to mention decisions they had had to make in the past and to describe the decision-making process followed. Second, managers were confronted with a series of standardized problems and subsequently asked how they would go about making a decision.

Jago and Vroom's (1975) research seems a step in the right direction. They asked group members to describe (predict) how their leader would make certain decisions. This study also led to the conclusion that the leader adjusts his decision-making style to the problem. However, there was practically no agreement in the descriptions that the group members and the leaders themselves gave of the latter's strategy.

The model is therefore not yet empirically tested, and it remains uncertain whether managers who do make decisions in the 'prescribed' manner are really more effective than those who do not. No matter how self-evident the links, empirical research can lead to completely different results. Thus Koopman and Drenth (1980) found that in a situation of conflict rather than of consensus, decision-making is indeed linked to effectiveness.

Finally, when we compare Vroom and Yetton's theory with the model in figure 4 it becomes clear that the theory's scope is limited. First, it is only concerned with a specific part of leadership, namely ways of decision-making. Other forms of interaction between leader and group members, such as daily contact, supervision of work, or discussion of a group member's personal problems, are not taken into account. Furthermore, no attention is devoted to conditioning characteristics of the organization or the group. However, it is likely that the same decision-making style applied to the same problems in (departments of) organizations with varying power relations or managerial climate would yield wholly different results. This may explain the limited variance of the decision-making style of Vroom and Yetton's managers. It is possible that some of them behaved more autocratically or participatively than prescribed by the model, since they bore in mind the general climate of the organization, and their own bosses' wishes. Nevertheles, this theory is clearly an improvement on the traditional universal theories. One does not often come across such an accurate specification of leader behaviour and aspects of the situation.

4. *Attribution theory.* Green and Mitchell (1979) have used notions from the attribution theory to understand an aspect of leadership that is often neglected, namely the impact of behaviour of group members on leader behaviour. According to this theory, the reactions of a leader to the behaviour of his group members is dependent on how he interprets and explains this behaviour. The leader will attribute that which a group member does to his specific characteristics and/or the nature of the task and/or the nature of the context within which the group member performs his task (group and organization characteristics). For instance, he will compare the behaviour of one group member with that of another, or performance on one task with performance on another, or behaviour at one moment with behaviour at another. The more complex the situation (for instance, as a result of the size of the workgroup, heterogeneous tasks, geographical space, etcetera), the less the leader will be inclined to seek or use all available information; instead, he will confine himself to very simple causal interpretation schemes in order to 'explain' a given level of performance of a group member (see, for instance, figure 7). The leader's reactions (e.g. rewards, punishments, nature of supervision, expectations of the group members) will depend on what he considers to be the cause of that behaviour. If he thinks that a group member's failure is due to external factors, he will give support and consideration; if he feels that it is due to group member's remiss-

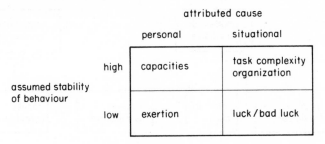

Figure 7. Causal interpretation schema.

ness, he will be inclined to motivate him through either negative or positive sanctions. If he feels that high performance of group members is a result of his close supervision, he will be inclined to continue this type of leadership. And if he attributes a group member's behaviour to lack of understanding of the task, he will probably react with structuring behaviour.

The central idea behind the attribution theory is that the leader's reaction is not directly linked to the observable behaviour of a group member, but to causes that determine that behaviour *according to the leader*. The group member himself goes through a similar process of attributing causes to his *own* behaviour. In cases where these two attribution processes lead to different conclusions, the odds are that conflicts will arise. In fact this is extremely likely, according to Green and Mitchell. A variety of socio-psychological processes lie at the root of this:

—Observers are rather inclined to attribute an actor's behaviour to *internal* factors, while the actors themselves are strongly inclined to emphasize the importance of *external* causes.

—People are inclined to attribute success to their *own* capacities or devotion, and to attribute failure to external factors.

Apart from these general processes there are also variables that influence the leader's interpretation of the behaviour of his people. Characteristics of group members and leader (sex, race, etcetera), the degree to which they match, the psychological distance between group and leader, the complexity of the situation, and the effect of behaviour can influence the leader's explanation of group members' behaviour. This process is represented in figure 8.

However, leaders in formal organizations cannot determine their behaviour and reactions solely on the basis of their own causal explanations. They are tied to rules and procedures and to the conduct of higher managers. Thus a boss may attribute the tardiness of a group member to external factors (his car tyres were slashed), but the rules of the organization prescribe that the missed hours shall not be paid. In such cases it is important to know what leaders do when their own attributions are in conflict with the policy of the organization. One can

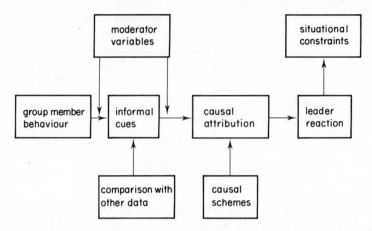

Figure 8. Attribution theoretical model of leadership reactions.

assume that factors such as the leader's power position (partly) determine the extent to which either his own attributions or those or organizational policy will prevail.

5. *The operant-conditioning theory.* Another theory that explicitly focuses on interaction of leader and group members is the operant-conditioning theory (Scott, 1977; Sims, 1977). With the help of notions developed by this theory, attempts have been made to explain the behaviour of both the leader and group members. Scott (1977) does the former and defines leadership as 'human operant behaviour reinforced by its effects on the behaviour of others'. Sims (1977) studies in particular the stimuli and reinforcements leaders supply to group members. He defines leadership as 'a process of supervisory structuring of reinforcement contingencies in the environment'. Sims' operant-conditioning theory is based on the idea that group member behaviour is particularly determined by stimulus-response-reward chains in the work environment.

In an organization there are various sources of reward: colleagues supply friendship; the organization supplies wages, promotion, secondary labour conditions; the task supplies intrinsic satisfaction and the leader gives compliments, acknowledgement, and pleasant tasks. The leader therefore plays an often crucial role in devising 'contingencies of reinforcements'. He does this in two ways. If tasks are not completely routine he is the one who determines the 'discriminative stimuli' (i.e. he indicates how group members should act), among other things by assigning tasks. Sims (1977, p. 134) believes that what is called 'initiating structure' or 'goal specification' in leadership style traditions in fact comes down to defining the stimuli and indicating the correct response.

Besides indicating the correct stimulus and response, the leader's task consists in giving a reward for the correct response.

It is well known that the conditioning theory states that giving rewards should be directly dependent on the nature of the response and should follow closely on the response. Furthermore, conditioning experiments have yielded all sorts of reward schemes. According to Sims, some of them can be used in a work situation. He devised a questionnaire—the Leader Reward Behaviour Questionnaire—with which this reward behaviour of the leader can be evaluated by group members. With the help of factor analysis three dimensions could be identified:

—*Positive Reward Behaviour* (example: Your boss would be very interested if you would suggest new and better ways of working);
—*Advancement Reward Behaviour* (example: If you asked him for transfer your boss would help you get it);
—*Punitive Reward Behaviour* (example: Your boss would be angry with you if your work wasn't as good as that of the others in your department).

Whereas 'Initiating Structure' and 'Goal Specification' specify that which precedes group member behaviour, 'Leader Reward Behaviour' specifies what comes after it. The theory was tested in a study of 61 workers at various levels in different types of organization. Positive Reward Behaviour and to a lesser degree Advancement Reward Behaviour appear to be positively correlated with performance. Punitive Reward Behaviour was not related to performance level.

Leadership research within this conceptual framework has only recently begun, and its usefulness remains to be proved. Besides, there is a real danger that this approach to leadership is mechanistic or even manipulative. Nevertheless, some ideas have already proven to be valuable. Among them is the distinction between response-specifying (initiating structure) and reward-assigning behaviour (reward behaviour), and the attention to the fact—also illustrated in figure 4—that a leader's effectiveness depends on the way in which he reacts directly to the behaviour of group members.

7. CONCLUSIONS

Recent surveys about leadership (for example Hunt and Larson, 1977; McCall and Lombardo, 1978) present a rather pessimistic picture of the field. There is certainly little optimism in the discussion of research results and theories. This negative assessment primarily concerns research and theories within the realm of what we called the 'style' paradigm. This approach is characterized by:
—exclusive attention to a number of general leadership styles;
—the assumption that leadership and group behaviour are homogeneous;
—confinement to shopfloor level work groups in large organizations;

—confinement to only a few dependent variables (satisfaction, motivation, and performance);
—scant attention to aspects of the situation other than qualities of the leader and the group;
—a simplistic cause-and-effect model (leadership → result);
—an exclusive reliance on correlational questionnaires in gathering data.

Moreover, as a consequence of this approach, training courses focused on teaching leaders 'the one best way': i.e. a leadership that was both task-oriented and, human-oriented, and—more recently—preferably also participative.

During the 1960s in particular, the contingency approach led to more attention to the environment in which leaders and group members function. In leadership training courses leaders were now taught that there were environments in which other combinations of the two leadership styles could be effective (Reddin, 1970, 1971). In the 1970s, however, the 'style' paradigm came under more vigorous attack. This is not to say that then the route to new approaches, theories and research became clearly mapped. In his concluding remarks at the third Southern Illinois University Leadership Symposium, Miner (1975) described the situation as follows:

'This state of high uncertainty and its concordant frustrated desire for real understanding presently characterizes the leadership field more than any other single thing; we simply do not know what we want to know.'

The only point of agreement is that existing approaches have largely lost their usefulness for the further development of the field. It is therefore striking that one of the most ambitious projects in the field of leadership research, Stogdill's *Handbook of Leadership* (1974)[5] which includes literally thousands of studies, is hardly referred to at all.

Nonetheless, some new and promising developments have emerged, although so far they have been little tested; some of them have been discussed in this chapter. Future approaches to the problem of leadership should focus on a number of elements brought to light in this review. We will finish by enumerating those elements, and thus—in a sense—summarize and present our conclusions on the arguments we have developed in this chapter:
—Leadership is part of an organization process. Leader behaviour, like the behaviour of group members, is strongly determined and restricted by structure, technology, role expectations, control mechanism, and other characteristics of the environment.
—Leaders at various levels of the organization have widely differing functions and tasks that appeal to divergent capacities, cognitive processes and social skills.

---

[5] A revised edition of this handbook has been published by Bass (1981).

—The effect of leader behaviour is dependent on the expectations and goals of the group members and on the conditions in the environment.

—Leader and group members constantly interact. In the course of this interaction they create complex exchange relations which, through changes in the composition of the group or in the environment, are themselves constantly subject to change.

—Developing one specific style and sticking to it may be dysfunctional. It is more important that a leader understands the expectations and goals of group members, the complexity and dynamics of the situation, and the possible changes that may occur.

—Leadership research will have to make use of other techniques besides questionnaires. Longitudinal research will be needed to discover the dynamics of certain processes. One should also focus on those independent variables that are directly related to leadership, i.e. perceptions and expectations of individual group members and their direct reactions to the leader.

—Leaders only devote a limited amount of their time to direct supervision. Often their work is extremely fragmentary and their function is largely a boundary one, i.e. they maintain contacts with colleagues, superiors, suppliers, clients, trade unions, etcetera. In these contacts they serve their own interests and the interests of the group, in order that it may function optimally. They enter into coalitions or into conflicts. In short, they play their role in the organization's power game.

REFERENCES

Alderfer, C. P. (1972), *Existence, relatedness and growth: human needs in organizational settings*. New York: Free Press.

Andriessen, J. H. T. H., Drenth, P. J. D., Lammers, C. J. (1983), *Medezeggenschap in Nederlandse bedryven* [Participation in Dutch enterprises]. Amsterdam: North-Holland Publ. Co.

Baldridge, J. V. (1971), *Power and conflict in the university*. New York: Wiley.

Bass, B. M. (1981), *Stogdill's handbook of leadership*. Rev. ed. New York: Free Press.

Bass, B. M., Farrow, D. L., Valenzie, E. R., Solomon, R. J. (1975), Management styles associated with organizational task, personal and interpersonal contingencies. *Journal of Applied Psychology*, **60**, 720–729.

Beynon, H. (1973), *Working for Ford*. London: Penguin.

Blake, R. R., Mouton, J. S. (1964), *The managerial grid*. Houston: Gulf Publishing.

Brayfield, Crockett (1955), Employee attitudes and employee performance. *Psychological Bulletin*, **52**, 396–424.

Campbell, J. P. (1977), The cutting edge of leadership: An overview. In: Hunt, J. G., Larson, L. L. (Eds.), *Leadership, the cutting edge*. Carbondale: Southern Illinois University Press.

Campbell, J. P. Pritchard, R. D. (1976), Motivation in industrial and organizational psychology. In: Dunnette, M. D. (Ed.), *Handbook of industrial and organizational psychology*, Chicago: Rand McNally.

Campbell, J. P., Dunnette, M. D., Lawler, E. E., Weick, K. E. (1970), *Managerial behavior, performance and effectiveness*. New York: McGraw-Hill.

Carter, L. F., Kaythorn, W., Schriver, E., Lanzetta, J. (1951), The behavior of leaders and other group members. *Journal of Abnormal and Social Psychology*, 22, 396–424.

Cummings, L. L. (1975), Assessing the Graen/Cashman model and comparing it with other approaches. In: Hunt, J. G., Larson, L. L. (Eds.), *Leadership frontiers*. Kent: Kent State University.

Dansereau, F., Dumas, M. (1977), Pratfalls and pitfalls in drawing inferences about leader behavior in organizations. In: Hunt, J. G., Larson, L. L. (Eds.), *Leadership, the cutting edge*. Carbondale: Southern Illinois University Press.

Dawson, J. A., Messe, L. A., Philips, J. L. (1972), Effects of instructor-leader behavior on student performance. *Journal of Applied Psychology*, 56, 369–379.

DIO International Research Team (1983), A contingency model of participative decision making: An analysis of 56 decisions in three Dutch organisations. *Journal of Occupational Psychology*, 56.

Downey, H. K., Sheridan, J. E., Slocum, J. W. (1976), The path-goal theory of leadership: A longitudinal analysis. *Organizational Behavior and Human Performance*, 16, 156–176.

Drenth, P. J. D., Thierry, Hk. (1970), Onderzoek naar effectief leiderschap [Studies on effective leadership]. In: Drenth, P. J. D., Willems, P. J., Wolff, Ch. J. de (Eds.), *Bedrijfspsychologie. Onderzoek en evaluatie* [Industrial psychology: Research and evaluation]. Deventer: Kluwer.

Drucker, P. (1954), *The practice of management*. New York: Harper.

Duncan, R. B. (1973), *Modifications in decision making structures in adapting to the environment*. Evanston: Northwestern University.

Evans, M. G. (1970), The effects of supervisory behavior on the path-goal relationship. *Organizational Behavior and Human Performance*, 5, 277–298.

Farris, F., Lim, F. (1969), Effect of performance on leadership cohesiveness, influence, satisfaction and subsequent performance. *Journal of Applied Psychology*, 53, 490–497.

Fiedler, F. E. (1967), *A theory of leadership effectiveness*. New York: McGraw-Hill.

Fiedler, F. E., Chemers, M. M., Maker, L. (1976), *Improving leadership effectiveness; The leader match concept*. New York: Wiley.

Fleishman, E. A., Harris, E. F. (1962), Patterns of leadership behavior related to employee grievances and turnover. *Personnel Psychology*, 15, 43–56.

Fleishman, E. A., Harris, E. F., Burt, H. E. (1955), *Leadership and supervision in industry*. Columbus: Ohio State University.

Graen, G., Cashman, J. F. (1975), A role making model of leadership in formal organizations: A developmental approach. In: Hunt, J. G., Larson, L. L. (Eds.), *Leadership frontiers*. Kent: Kent State University Press.

Graen, G., Alvares, K., Orris, J. B., Martella, J. A. (1970), Contingency model of leadership effectiveness: Antecedent and evidential results. *Psychological Bulletin*, 74, 286–296.

Graen, G., Dansereau, F., Minami, T. (1972), Dysfunctional leadership styles. *Organizational Behavior and Human Performance*, 7, 216–236.

Green, S. G., Mitchell, T. R. (1979), Attributional processes of leaders in leadermember interactions. *Organizational Behavior and Human Performance*, 23, 429–458.

Hall, R. M. (1972), *Organizations: Structure and process*. Englewood Cliffs: Prentice-Hall.

Hammer, T. H., Dachler, H. P. (1975), A test of some assumptions underlying the path goal model of supervision: Some suggested conceptual modifications. *Organizational Behavior and Human Performance*, 14, 69–75.

Heller, F. A. (1971), *Managerial decision making: A study of leadership styles and power sharing among senior managers*, London: Tavistock.

Heller, F. A. (1976), Decision processes: An analysis of power sharing at senior organizational levels. In: Dubin, R. (Ed.), *Handbook of work, organization and society*. Chicago: Rand McNally.

Hemphill, J. K. (1960), *Dimensions of executive positions*. Ohio State University: Bureau of Business Research, no. 98.

Herold, D. M. (1971), Two way influence processes in leader follower dyads. *Academy of Management Journal*, **20**, 224–237.

Homans, G. C. (1950), *The human group*. New York: Harcourt.

House, R. J. (1971), A path goal theory of leader effectiveness. *Administrative Science Quarterly*, **16**, 321–328.

House, R. J. (1977), A 1976 theory of charismatic leadership. In: Hunt, J. G., Larson, L. L. (Eds.), *Leadership, the cutting edge*. Carbondale: Southern Illinois University Press.

House, R. J., Baetz, M. L. (1979), Leadership: Some empirical generalizations and new research direction. In: Staw, B. (Ed.), *Research in organizational behavior I*. Greenwich: JAI Press.

House, R. J., Dessler, G. (1974), The path-goal theory of leadership: Some post hoc and a priori tests. In: Hunt, J. G., Larson, L. L. (Eds.), *Contingency approaches to leadership*. Carbondale: Southern Illinois University Press.

House, R. L., Filey, A. C., Kerr, S. (1971), Relation of leader consideration and Initiation of structure to R & D subordinates' satisfaction. *Administrative Science Quarterly*, **16**, 19–30.

Hunt, J. G., Larson, L. L. (Eds.), *Leadership, the cutting edge*. Carbondale: Southern Illinois University Press.

Hunt, J. G., Osborn, R. N. (1980), *Beyond contingency approach to leadership*. Birmingham: Management Center, University of Aston.

IDE, International Research Group (1981), *Industrial democracy in Europe*. Oxford: Oxford University Press.

Jacobs (1970), *Leadership and exchange in formal organizations*. Alexandria: Human Resources Research Organization.

Jago, A. G., Vroom, V. H. (1975), Perceptions of leadership style: Superior and subordinate descriptions of decision-making behavior. In: Hunt, J. G., Larson, L. L. (Eds.), *Leadership frontiers*. Kent: Kent State University Press.

James, L. R., Jones, A. P. (1976), Organizational structure: A review of structural dimensions and their relationships with individual attitudes and behavior. *Organizational Behavior and Human Performance*, **16**, 74–113.

Jermier, J. M., Berkes, L. J. (1979). Leader behavior in a police command bureaucracy: A closer look at the quasi military model. *Administration Science Quarterly*, **24**, 1–23.

Katz, D., Kahn, R. L. (1978), *The social psychology of organizations*. 2nd ed. New York: Wiley.

Katz, R. (1977), The influence of group conflict on leadership effectiveness. *Organizational Behavior and Human Performance*, **20**, 265–286.

Kerr, S. (1974), Substitutes for leadership. In: Hunt, J. G., Larson, L. L. (Eds.), *Contingency approaches to leadership*. Carbondale: Southern Illinois University Press.

Kerr, S., Jermier, J. M. (1978), Substitutes for leadership: Their meaning and measurement. *Organizational Behavior and Human Performance*, **22**.

Kerr, S., Schriesheim, C. A. (1974), Consideration, initiating structure and organizational criteria: An update of Korman's 1966 review. *Personnel Psychology*, **27**, 555–568.

Kerr, S., Schriesheim, C. A. Murphy, C. J., Stogdill, R. M. (1974), Toward a contingency theory of leadership based upon the consideration and initiating structure literature. *Organizational Behavior and Human Performance*, **12**, 62–82.

Koopman, P. L. (1979), *Besluitvorming in organisaties* [Decision-making in organizations]. Assen: Van Gorcum.

Koopman, P. L., Drenth, P. J. D. (1980a), Komplexe besluitvorming in organisaties [Complex decision-making in organizations]. *Gedrag* [Behavior], **8**, 361–379.

Koopman, P. L., Drenth, P. J. D. (1980b), Een contingentie-model voor participatie in complexe besluitvorming [A contingency model for participation in complex decision-making]. *Mens en Onderneming*, **6**, 464–478.

Koopman, P. L., Werkman, B. (1973), Het verhoudingsmodel bij de meting van satisfactie [The ratio model in the measurement of satisfaction]. In: Drenth, P. J. D., Willems, P. J., Wolff, Ch. J. de (Eds.), *Arbeids- en organisatiepsychologie* [Work- and organizational psychology]. Deventer: Kluwer.

Korman, A. K. (1972), 'Consideration', 'initiating structure' and organizational criteria: A review. *Personnel Psychology*, **19**, 349–362.

Kuhn, T. (1962), *The structure of scientific revolutions*. Chicago: University of Chicago Press.

Lammers, C. J. (1975), Self-management and participation: Two concepts of democratization in organizations. *Organization and Administrative Sciences*, **5**, 17–33.

Lammers, C. J. (1980), *Ontwikkeling en relevantie van de organisatiesociologie* [Development and relevance of organizational sociology]. Leiden: University of Leiden.

Lawrence, P. R., Lorsch, J. W. (1967), Differentiation and integration in complex organizations. *Administrative Science Quarterly*, **12**, 1–47.

Likert, R. (1961), *New patterns of management*. New York: McGraw-Hill.

Likert, R. (1967), *The human organization*. New York: McGraw-Hill.

Locke, E. A., Schweiger, D. M. (1979), Participation in decision making: One more look. In: Staw, B. (Ed.), *Research in organizational behavior I*. Greenwich: JAI Press.

Lowin, A., Craig, J. (1968), The influence of level of performance on managerial style. *Organizational Behavior and Human Performance*, **3**, 440–458.

Lowin, A., Hrapchak, W. J., Kavanagh, M. J. (1969), Consideration and initiating structure: An experimental investigation of leadership traits. *Administrative Science Quarterly*, **14**, 238–253.

McCall, Jr., M. W., Lombardo, M. M. (Eds.) (1978), *Leadership: Where else can we go?* Durham (NC): Duke University Press.

McGregor, D. (1960), *The human side of enterprise*. New York: McGraw-Hill.

Mahoney, T. A., Frost, P., Crandall, N. F., Weitzel, W. (1972), The conditioning influence of organization size upon managerial practice. *Organizational Behavior and Human Performance*.

March, J. G., Simon, H. A. (1958), *Organizations*. New York: Wiley.

Maslow, A. (1954), *Motivation and personality*. New York: Harper and Row.

Melcher, A. J. (1977), Leadership models and research approaches. In: Hunt, J. G., Larson, L.L. (Eds.), *Leadership, the cutting edge*. Carbondale: Southern Illinois University Press.

Miles, R. E. (1974), Leadership: Human relations or human resources. In: Kolb, D. A., Rubin, I. M., McIntyre, J. M. (Eds.), *Organizational psychology*. Englewood Cliffs: Prentice-Hall.

Miner, J. B. (1975), The uncertain future of the leadership concept: An overview. In: Hunt, J. G., Larson, L. L. (Eds.), *Leadership frontiers*. Kent: Kent State University Press.

Mintzberg, H. (1973), *The nature of managerial work*. New York: Harper and Row.

Mulder, M. (1977), *Omgaan met macht* [Managing power]. Amsterdam: Elsevier.

Mulder, M., Ritsema van Eck, J. R., Van Gils, M. R. (1967), *Structure en dynamiek van een grote organisatie: Een veldstudie op zee* [Structure and dynamics of a large organization: A field study at sea]. Leiden: NIPG.

Osborn, R. N., Hunt, J. G. (1975), An adaptive-reactive theory of leadership: The role of macro-variables in leadership research. In: Hunt, J. G., Larson, L. L. (Eds.), *Leadership frontiers*. Kent: Kent State University Press.

Pelz, D. (1951), Leadership within a hierarchical organization. *Journal of Social Issues*, **7**, 49–55.

Pelz, D. (1952), Influence: A key to effective leadership in the first-line superior. *Personnel*, **29**, 209–217.

Pfeffer, J. (1978), The ambiguity of leadership. In: McCall, M. W., Lombardo, M. M. (Eds.), *Leadership: Where else can we go?* Durham: Duke University Press.

Philipsen, H. (1965), Het meten van leiderschap [The measurement of leadership]. *Mens en Onderneming*, **3**, 153–171.

Raven, B. H., French, J. R. P. (1958), Group support, legitimate power and social influence. *Journal of Personality*, **26**, 400–409.

Reddin, W. J. (1970), *Managerial effectiveness*. New York: McGraw-Hill.

Reddin, W. M. (1971), *Effective management by objectives: The 3-D method of MBO*. New York: McGraw-Hill.

Schriesheim, C. A., Kerr, S. (1974), Psychometric properties of the Ohio State Leadership scales, *Psychological Bulletin*, **81**, 756–765.

Schriesheim, C. A., Kerr, S. (1977), Theories and measures of leadership: A critical appraisal of current and future directions. In: Hunt, J. G., Larson, L. L. (Eds.), *Leadership, the cutting edge*. Carbondale: Southern Illinois University Press.

Schriesheim, C. A., Kinicki, A. J., Schriesheim, J. F. (1979), The effect of leniency on leader behavior descriptions. *Organizational Behavior and Human Performance*, **23**, 1–29.

Schriesheim, C. A., Murphy, C. J. (1976), Relationships between leader behavior and subordinate satisfaction and performance: A test of some situational moderators. *Journal of Applied Psychology*, **61**, 634–641.

Schriesheim, C. A., Stogdill, R. M. (1975), Differences in factor structure across three versions of the Ohio State Leadership scales. *Personnel Psychology*, **28**, 189–206.

Schriesheim, C. A., House, R. J., Kerr, S. (1976), Leader initiating structure: A reconciliation of discrepant research results and some empirical tests. *Organizational Behavior and Human Performance*, **15**, 297–321.

Scott, W. E. (1977), Leadership: A functional analysis. In: Hunt, J. G., Larson, L. L. (Eds.), *Leadership, the cutting edge*. Carbondale: Southern Illinois University Press.

Shull, F. A., Delbecq, A. L., Cummings, L. L. (1970), *Organizational decision making*. New York: McGraw-Hill.

Sims, H. P. (1977), The leader is manager of reinforcement contingencies: An empirical example and a model. In: Hunt, J. G., Larson, L. L. (Eds.), *Leadership, the cutting edge*. Carbondale: Southern Illinois University Press.

Stewart, R. (1970), *Managers and their jobs*. London: Pan.

Stinson, J. E. (1977), The measurement of leadership. In: Hunt, J. G., Larson, L. L. (Eds.), *Leadership, the cutting edge*. Carbondale: Southern Illinois University Press.

Stogdill, R. M. (1948), Personal factors associated with leadership: A survey of the literature. *Journal of Psychology*, **25**, 35–71.

Stogdill, R. M. (1974), *Handbook of leadership: A survey of theory and research*. New York: Free Press.

Taylor, J. C., Bowers, D. G. (1972), *Survey of organizations: Toward a machine scored standardized questionnaire instrument*. Ann Arbor: Institute for Social Research.

Thierry, Hk., Jong, J. de (1979), *Naar participatie en toerekening* [Towards participation and imputation]. Assen: Van Gorcum.

Ven, A. H. van de, Delbecq, A. L., Koenig, R. (1976), Determinants of coordination within organizations. *American Sociological Review*, **41**, 322–338.

Vollebergh, J. J. A. (1973), Leiderscap en organisatie [Leadership and organization]. In: Drenth, P. J. D., Willems, P. J., Wolff, Ch. J. de (Eds.), *Arbeids- en organisatiepsychologie* [Work- and organizational psychology]. Deventer: Kluwer.

Vroom, V. H. (1964), *Work and motivation*. New York: Wiley.

Vroom, V. H. (1967), Leadership. In: Dunnette, M. D. (Ed.), *Handbook of industrial and organizational psychology*. Chicago: Rand McNally.

Vroom, V. H., Yetton, E. W. (1973), *Leadership and decision making*. Pittsburgh: University of Pittsburgh Press.
Wilpert, B. (1977), *Führung in deutschen Unternehmen*. Berlin: De Gruyter.
Zanders, H. J. G., Büchem, A. L. J. van, Berkel, J. J. C. van (1978), *Kwaliteit van arbied 1977* [The quality of work]. The Hague: Ministry of Social Affairs.

Handbook of Work and Organizational Psychology
Edited by P. J. D. Drenth, Hk. Thierry, P. J. Willems and C. J. de Wolff
© 1984, John Wiley & Sons, Ltd.

3.3.   Conflict—prevention and escalation

Evert van de Vliert[1]

In the last decades, conflict, especially the parties' behavior in a conflict, has been attracting increasing academic attention. The results of this effort are considered here in the light of the so-called *prevention-escalation model*. First, some restrictions on this survey will be discussed as well as definitions of conflict and conflict management and my own view of the customary approaches of conflict.

1. POINTS OF DEPARTURE

In constructing their theories, organizational psychologists usually restrict themselves to conflicts between two individuals or groups. Following in their footsteps, we will not consider purely intrapersonal conflicts or conflicts between three or more parties. And, except for a typology of intervention strategies in the last section, conflict management by an intervening third party will not be discussed either.

Two individuals, an individual and a group, or two groups are said to be in conflict when at least one of the parties feels it is being obstructed or irritated by the other (for other definitions see Fink, 1968; Mack and Snyder, 1957; Pondy, 1967; Schmidt and Kochan, 1972). Important elements of this definition are: (a) the nature of the frustration may be both cognitive and affective (blocked goals and/or feelings of repulsion, hostility, fear, and the like); (b) the frustration is a subjective experience and does not necessarily have an

Dr. E. van de Vliert, Vrije Universiteit, Vakgroep Sociale Psychologie, De Boelelaan 1081, 1081 HV Amsterdam.
[1]I wish to thank Willem F. G. Mastenbroek for various discussions and suggestions.

objective basis; (c) the conflict arises as soon as one party feels frustrated (cf. Murray, 1975; Thomas, 1976); (d) the conflict exists independently of the reaction to the frustration experienced (but not in e.g. Mulder, 1978). The reaction to the frustration experienced as well as all reactions to that reaction come under the heading of conflict management, irrespective of whether the reactions are those of the frustrated party or of the opposite party.

In the study and management of conflicts two kinds of model have been used: process models and structural models. Process models are oriented primarily towards the cyclic and dynamic courses of conflicts where one event follows another, such as frustration, conceptualization of the conflict, behavior, reaction, consequence, renewed frustration, etc. (Filley, 1975; Pondy, 1967; Thomas, 1976; Walton, 1969). Structural models, on the other hand, are oriented primarily towards factors influencing the conflict and the behavior of the parties: the parties' predispositions, the degree of mutual dependence and incompatibility of interests, pressure from others, rules and procedures, and the like (Katz and Kahn, 1978; Prein, 1978; Thomas, 1976; Walton and Dutton, 1969). Whereas process models hardly pay any attention to the causes of conflicts, structural models neglect the dynamics and consequences of conflicts. In this chapter we shall therefore attempt to integrate the two models instead of differentiating them any further.

A disadvantage of both the process approach and the structural approach is their lack of systematic concern for the central mechanisms of prevention and escalation (but see Robbins, 1974) and for the extent to which conflict management constitutes a strategic choice. Therefore, the intention is to blend both models into what is called the *prevention-escalation model*. This compound model not only puts the conflict parties both in a sequence of events (process model) and in a constellation of forces (structural model), but also emphasizes, respectively, the preventive or escalating nature of all kinds of spontaneous and strategic conflict management. From the models it integrates, it adopts the assumption that the causes, characteristics, and consequences of conflicts between individuals do not differ essentially from the causes, characteristics, and consequences of conflicts between groups.

2. THE PREVENTION-ESCALATION MODEL

As schematized in figure 1, there are characteristic phenomena underlying a conflict: the *antecedent conditions*. There are some who call these potential determinants of conflict 'latent conflicts'—a misleading and unfruitful term, according to Glasl (1980). For at least one of the parties involved they may cause a certain cognitive and/or affective frustration: the perceived *issue of the conflict*. Because what one author calls 'antecedent conditions' is called 'conflict issues' by another, the explicit criterion chosen here is that of feeling obstructed or irritated. The conflict management subsequent to this experience represents the model's essence. The central issue here is, to be sure, to distinguish between

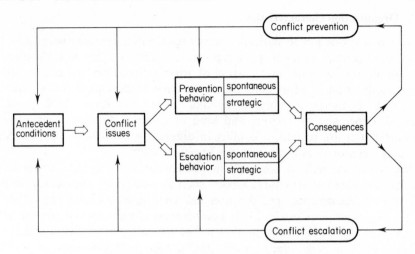

Figure 1. The prevention-escalation model.

mainly spontaneous or strategic preventive behavior on the one hand, and mainly spontaneous or strategic escalation behavior on the other.

Prevention behavior involves a range of behaviors, including (a) reducing the chances of the other party also getting frustrated; (b) reducing the chances of a related conflict in the future; (c) resolution of the current conflict; (d) reducing or preventing the intensification of the conflict. Obviously, the opposite is *escalation behavior*. All such behavior is *spontaneous* inasmuch as it is not intentional. It is *strategic*, however, inasmuch as it forms part of a conscious plan either to prevent or to stimulate conflict or intensification of conflict. Spontaneous or strategic conflict management has preventive or escalating *consequences* for the antecedent conditions, the conflict issues, or the parties' subsequent behavior, as well as for the accompanying opinions, feelings and behavioral tendencies. With direct consequences this feedback is direct (e.g. conflict resolution or vengeful behavior). With indirect consequences conflict management first influences other variables, such as positive or negative feelings, which in their turn influence the antecedent conditions, conflict issues, or subsequent prevention- or escalation behaviors.

Having presented the prevention-escalation model, we shall now discuss the constituent parts of the model in more detail, while also taking account of the relevant literature.

3. ANTECEDENT CONDITIONS

A natural classification of the potential causes of conflict would be: organization characteristics, group characteristics, individual characteristics, and relationship characteristics.

3.1. Organization characteristics

It is a precarious job to indicate which organization characteristics may be a source of conflict. In the first place, potential conflict is inherent in the phenomenon of organization: "every aspect of organizational life that creates order and coordination of effort must overcome other tendencies to action, and in that fact lies the potentiality for conflict" (Katz and Kahn, 1978, p. 617). Second, depending on context and kind of conflict, the same organization characteristics are related to conflict in different ways (Corwin, 1969). And third, correlation does not necessarily imply causality.

We would do well to keep this in mind when learning that, apparently, conflict is related to structural aspects such as number of hierarchical levels, number of departments, specialization and heterogeneity among the members of the organization (Corwin, 1969), combination of uniform and non-uniform tasks (Litwak, 1961), differentiation in the formality of structure and time-orientation (Lawrence and Lorsch, 1967), and joint resources or means. Ambiguity of tasks, input, or criteria of evaluation, which is often caused by physical and spatial communication barriers, also goes hand in hand with conflict (Walton and Dutton, 1969; Walton et al., 1969; Zald, 1962). Role conflicts are found especially with incumbents of managing, controlling, and innovative positions (Kahn et al., 1964; Miles and Perreault, 1976) and with those in representative or other boundary roles (Frey and Adams, 1972; Rozema et al., 1980; Walton and McKersie, 1965).

At the same time, conflict appears to be associated with cultural organization characteristics, such as goals, values, and norms. On the one hand, conflicts prosper by differences in e.g. goals, reciprocal openness, or tolerance (Aubert, 1963; Lawrence and Lorsch, 1967). On the other hand, conflicts may arise from the norm that competition is to the benefit of the organization or from the absence of the norm that quarreling is 'not done' (Blake et al., 1964; Boulding, 1964).

The organizational regulation mechanisms constitute a case in its own right. These formal and informal rules influence not the rise of the conflict as such, but rather the form it takes on and the subsequent preventive course of the conflict process: rights and duties, weapons allowed, procedures in cases of disagreements and complaints, the administration of justice, possibilities for appeal, and so on (Dubin, 1957; Evan, 1965; Scott, 1965). Thomas (1976) distinguishes and discusses decision rules, negotiation procedures, and mediation and arbitration mechanisms, each of which imposes its restrictions upon conflict management. Unfortunately, no-one explicitly distinguishes between the rules regulating the management of existing conflicts and the rules stimulating or preventing conflicts. This is confusing and has undoubtedly slowed down developments in this field.

3.2. Group characteristics

Of course, many conflict determining organization characteristics operate via groups. But there are also group characteristics which, in themselves, may be considered independent antecedent conditons of conflict. Among them are group polarization, construction of a constituency, and ingroup-outgroup differentiation. The first phenomenon entails that groups, more so than individuals, tend to take up extreme positions (Meertens, 1976; Lamm and Myers, 1978), which increases the chance of conflict. Thus, after internal deliberations about the delivery date desired by the sales department, the production department may take up a more radical position than originally favored by its individual employees.

Furthermore, dividing a group into representatives and constituency is just begging for problems between the representatives and either their constituency or the outsiders involved. Walton and McKersie (1965) describe why and how trade union negotiators usually negotiate both with their constituency and with the official opposite party. If the latter also consists of a group, group polarization on both sides may reinforce the role conflict of the representatives, who must choose between a conflict with their constituency, or with the other group, or with both. On the basis of his experience, Glasl (1980) distinguishes three types of representative: those who are strongly dependent on their constituency ('Volkstribunen'), those who take up an independent position ('Senatoren'), and quasi-representatives ('Könige im Exil').

Ingroup-outgroup differentiation is the phenomenon whereby the members of a group judge their own group and their fellow members more favorably and give it/them more preference than they would another group and its members, which stimulates intergroup conflicts (Rabbie and Wilkens, 1971; Tajfel et al., 1971; see also Rijsman, this Handbook, ch. 3.1). The fact that such discrimination also occurs when the members of the group have never met one another nor the members of the other group, indicates that what is involved here is not exclusively a consequence but also a cause of intergroup conflict (Doise and Sinclair, 1973; Rabbie, 1979; Tajfel and Billig, 1974). Such initial ingroup-outgroup differentiation gains force when interaction with one's own group occurs, provided interaction with the other group is not still more frequent.

Discord within the group and endangered leadership are two other, probably mutually related sources of intergroup conflicts (Deutsch, 1973; Rabbie and Bekkers, 1976; Rabbie and Visser, 1976).

3.3. Individual characteristics

As indicated by a survey of Boekestijn (1979), various explanations of conflict behavior can be traced to individuals. It is assumed that relationships exist

Antecedent conditions
Organizational characteristics
Group characteristics
Individual characteristics
Relational characteristics

between education and aggression, personal frustration and aggression, categorization and conflict, mistaken perceptions and conflict, and so on. In view of such explanations, Blake and Mouton (1962) warn against the 'psychodynamic fallacy' of unjustifiably ascribing conflicts to individuals. Like Sherif (1966), they believe the extra- and supra-individual determinants of conflict to be much more important than the individual ones. The question is, however, whether the latter is true, since even stimulation of certain parts of the brain may elicit hostile behavior (Mark and Ervin, 1970; Moyer, 1968). Also, there is increasing evidence that aggressive behavior is related to hormonal unbalances and to the configuration of chromosomes (Weitz, 1977).

Researchers have been concerned more with the influence of personality traits and attitudes than with the biological basis of conflicts. Using experimental games, they find a more combative attitude with increase of, among other things, the need of power, dogmatism, machiavellism, suspiciousness, and a sense of inferiority (Deutsch, 1971; Křivohlavý, 1974; Terhune, 1970). In actual organizational situations, conflicts seem to occur more often and to be more serious when the people involved are more neurotic or introvert or when people have a high degree of internal control and are readier to take risks (Cummings *et al.*, 1972; Kahn *et al.*, 1964).

One of the most important causes of conflicts between individuals or groups is the intrapersonal conflict (Sanford, 1964). Examples may be found elsewhere in this volume, in the chapter on stress. Role ambiguity and various kinds of role conflict are especially well known (Kahn and Quinn, 1970; only when one holds others responsible for these frustrations, a two-party conflict arises!). One could think of the role ambiguity experienced by members of an organization following unexpected disappointment or events they were not told about, or of a department manager who got stuck between the conflicting desires of his superiors and his subordinates, or of the above-mentioned role conflict of a representative having a constituency. Apparently, there are three ways for such internal tension to become manifest and, thus, to result in external conflicts. Firstly, as a discharging, aggressive explosion (Coser, 1956; Wardwell, 1955). Next, as a deliberate attempt at changing role expectations or at foisting the conflict upon others (Goode, 1960; van de Vliert, 1979). And finally, as some form of non-conforming behavior, such as innovation, withdrawal, and rebellion (Merton, 1957).

Individual characteristics influencing the course but not the rise of the conflict represent styles of conflict management. Common practice, following Blake and Mouton (1964, 1970), distinguishes five styles: (1) *avoiding*, or withdrawing from, discord and confrontation, because of indifference regarding the relationship with the opposite party; (2) *smoothing*, or accommodating, in order to retain a good relationship; (3) *compromising*, in which case each party is partly satisfied; (4) *forcing* in order to win and beat the opponent; (5) *problem solving*, so that both parties get rid of their frustrations completely (cf. Prein, 1976). If the manner of conflict management favored most turns out to be unsuitable or ineffective, one might fall back upon another style, the 'back-up' style.

3.4. Relationship characteristics

Obviously, the characteristics of each party will increase the chance of conflict only when they stand in some relation to one another (Apfelbaum, 1974; Deutsch, 1973). Thus, in many of the antecedent conditons discussed, aspects of the relationship between the parties are implicitly present. It is, therefore, all the more remarkable that the research tradition of experimental conflict games usually ignores relationship characteristics.

The most general formulation of the influence of relationship characteristics is that perceived inequality stimulates conflict (Apfelbaum, 1974). This proposition, however, is rather unsophisticated, as it does not take account of the extent to which perceived differences may be acceptable. Thus, organizations exist by favor of some form of accepted inequality that could be associated with harmonious cooperation rather than with conflict: the complementary fulfilment of functions. This acceptance seems to be important also for Mulder's viewpoint, based on research, that relatively small and extremely big differences in power constitute conditions for conflicts (Mulder, 1978). An additional condition, not mentioned by Mulder, seems to be that the parties reject the imbalance of powers, otherwise there would be no basis for conflicts. Horwitz's (1964) results and view are more sophisticated: hostility does not result from differences in influence as such, but rather from an influence ratio turning out more unfavorably than expected. Raven and Kruglanski (1970) represent a completely different point of view. According to them, conflicts are tempered by possibilities of positive sanctioning, whereas they are intensified by possibilities of negative sanctioning.

A point often mentioned is the extent of mutual dependence among the parties. The opinions are contradictory, however. On the one hand, there are many who confirm that mutual dependence is a source of conflict (see e.g. Molnar and Rogers, 1979; Mulder, 1978; Prein, 1979; Walton and Dutton, 1969); on the other hand, there is some consensus, based partly on Sherif's field experiments (1966), that mutual dependence in the form of shared interests prevents or reduces conflict. According to Coser (1956), closer relations may intensify both the existing harmony and the existing conflict. In short: we do not know. We would need exact definitions of dependence and conflict as well as a more precise specification of the conditions under which a relationship obtains between them. The distinction of Deutsch (1973) between 'promotive interdependence', with the parties needing one another to attain their goals, and 'contrient interdependence', with the goals being irreconcilable, appears to be a step in the right direction.

Finally, other determinants of conflict, such as communication failures among the parties (Burton, 1969; March and Simon, 1958), mutual prejudices (Harding *et al.*, 1968), and mutual suspiciousness (Lindskold, 1978), though obvious, are not less important.

In my opinion, the relationship characteristics could well turn out to be more important than the other antecedent conditions, since they are not restricted (a) to one of the conflict parties, as are individual characteristics; (b) or to a characteristic both parties have in common, as is the case with most organization characteristics; (c) or to groups, as are group characteristics.

4. ISSUES OF CONFLICT

A slight change in the classifications of Walton (1969, p. 73) and Mastenbroek (1979) will produce four kinds of frustration resulting from the antecedent conditions: conflicts of interest over scarce resources, disagreements about collective policies or procedures, role conflicts over individual behaviors, and social-emotional conflicts whereby identity comes into play (dozens of other typologies may be found in Deutsch, 1973; Fink, 1968; Glasl, 1980).

The *scarce resources* one tries to secure in a conflict of interests may be both material and social. They concern money, materials, space, and manpower, but also information, attention, prestige, authority, and power. As long as the two parties share the same interests and their conflict is embedded in accepted rules of play, we usually speak of competition (e.g. Filley, 1975).

In case of disagreements about *collective policies or procedures*, it is not the available resources but a group's activities, intended or accomplished, that constitute the stumbling block (Schmidt and Kochan, 1972). The conflict is about the intention, planning, execution, coordination, results, or control of group activities (Blake *et al.*, 1964; Pondy, 1967; Walton *et al.*, 1969). Thomas (1976) calls these common problems. According to Brickman (1974), diverging goals or procedures that concern the rules regulating the management of conflict, as

Conflict issues
Scarce resources
Collective goals or procedures
Individual role behaviors
Identity

discussed in section 3.1, represent revolutionary conflicts; haggling about democratization is a good example.

Conflicts about *individual role behaviors* are concerned with what a member of an organization should or should not do under certain circumstances. They are subdivided by some according to the social position(s) a member of an organization holds (Biddle, 1979). On the basis of a survey by Van de Vliert (1974, p. 146), four kinds of role conflict between two parties may be distinguished. That is, the role expectation of a group or individual A concerning the role behavior of an individual member B of the organization may come into conflict with (1) the role expectation of a group or individual C concerning B's role behavior; (2) B's own role perception (Dunkin, 1972; van de Vliert, 1976); (3) a personality trait of B's (Getzels *et al.*, 1968); (4) B's actual role behavior (van de Vliert and Boekestijn,1978). Strangely enough, it is not among the adherents of role theory in the first place where we must look for studies of role conflicts between two parties, since they generally concern themselves with such intrapersonal role conflicts as discussed in section 3.3.

Frustration of an individual's or group's *identity* occurs when others affect or deny their self-image or their characteristic identifications, including their values and sensibilities (Mastenbroek, 1979; Walton, 1972). This often occurs in mergers (Zwart, 1977). It comprises Turner's (1975) forms of social competition, where one compares oneself or one's own party to another, intending nothing but to come out of it well, to win. Identity conflicts may be recognized by their intense emotional involvement: feelings of being insulted, of fear, suspicion, resentment, contempt, anger, hate, etc. When accumulated tension explodes suddenly in the face of just anyone, we speak of an unrealistic conflict (Coser, 1956).

It appears that, with escalation, cognitive conflicts of interest and disagreements easily turn into affective conflicts of identity (Walton, 1969). This process is sometimes also called the personalizing of conflicts (Filley, 1975; Pondy, 1967) and greatly resembles that of ideological polarization as studied by Druckman and Zechmeister (1973). Conversely, rationalization may turn deeply rooted affective frustrations partly into manifest surface problems (Deutsch, 1969, 1973; Walton, 1969). Colleagues aspiring to the same management function can get so personally involved in that conflict, that they will begin to obstruct one another in other respects too. As the social-emotional issues may result both from and in other conflict issues, they have a central function that, to date, has been insufficiently recognized, let alone researched.

5. PREVENTIVE CONFLICT MANAGEMENT

Each direct or indirect reaction of the parties to a conflict issue constitutes conflict management. It is preventive if it does not increase, or decreases or reduces to zero the joint frustration. On paper, such a description causes no problems, but in practice it does. Because the amount of frustration perceived is a personal matter, it is not always easy to establish whether a behavior has a preventive effect. Nor is it always easy to establish whether a party's attempt at preventing further frustration is a conscious one (strategic prevention) or not (spontaneous prevention). But these problems in characterizing certain behaviors would be overrated if, merely because of them, we would ignore such important distinctions as those between prevention- and escalation behavior and between spontaneous and strategic behavior.

5.1. Spontaneous prevention behavior

Spontaneous conflict management of a mainly preventive nature is encountered in the form of the rejection or talking down of frustration, of typically individual styles of behavior, and other automatic reactions to a frustrating situation, such as blindly conforming to organizational regulation mechanisms.

Repression of a minor conflict occurs if one suppresses awareness of it or does not pay any attention to it (Pondy, 1967). Another way of rejecting an experience of conflict is to revise immediately one's own perception or opinion which evokes the conflict (Hall, 1972; Kahn and Quinn, 1970; Sarbin and Allen, 1968). It appears that a person, unable to avoid a conflict, will often unconsciously attenuate his frustration by, for example, considering it of minor importance, reformulating the issue in such a way as to take the sting out of it, by viewing it less egocentrically, or by not attributing any design to the other party (Deutsch, 1973; Thomas, 1976; Thomas and Pondy, 1977).

Of the personal styles of conflict management mentioned in section 3.3, withdrawing, smoothing, compromising and problem solving usually have at least a short-term preventive effect. For example, at a meeting the closing down of part of a plant is to be discussed. A member of the works council, being against the management doing so, may unintentionally be absent from that meeting (withdraw), be silent (smooth), propose to carry out the plan only partly or not yet (compromise), or try to find out what the management actually wants to attain and how that can be done without closing down that part of the plant (problem solving). Each of these spontaneous reactions will decrease rather than increase the council member's frustration, while frustration of the management does not occur or is kept within bounds. Those scoring low on traits like internal control and risk taking will most probably tend to withdraw and to smooth (Cummings et al., 1972). People predisposed to react in a confronting and problem solving manner are both more assertive and more cooperative (Prein, 1976) and score higher on internal control and risk taking.

While some view the above-mentioned ways of preventive conflict management primarily as personality traits (following Blake and Mouton, 1964, 1970), others view them rather as organization characteristics (following Lawrence and Lorsch, 1967) or as reactions to conflict, strongly influenced by the type of situation (following Thomas and Kilmann, 1974). No doubt each view contains some grain of truth.

Examples mentioned in the literature make clear that, indeed, spontaneous prevention behavior is sometimes more determined by the situation. Thus, in certain situations, confrontation is automatically avoided because there is no time for it, or the issue is considered trivial, or one does not particularly need the other party, or one is too much in favor of, too involved with, or has too much in common with the other(s), and so on. But there are also situations in which negotiating about a compromise is just a foregone conclusion, as in the case of a mild conflict of interest about scarce material resources or in conflict situations urgently requiring a mutually satisfactory settlement (Blake *et al.*, 1964; Thomas, 1976).

Spontaneous problem solving behavior may be expected to occur when the attitude towards the phenomenon of conflict is a positive one, when one does not feel threatened, believes that everyone else is of equal value, appreciates the other party's contribution, or when one trusts the other party because one considers it trustworthy, willing, cooperative, non-manipulative, and so on (Deutsch, 1969, 1973; Filley, 1975). Because of these prerequisites, it is unlikely that problem solving behavior will occur in social-emotional conflicts, where one's own identity is at stake.

The last determinant of spontaneous prevention behavior consists of conflict inhibiting regulation mechanisms (see section 3.1)—e.g., task assignments, delivery dates, backroom consultations, voting in writing, and loyal cooperation—which one obeys without really thinking about it. Murray (1975) notes with amazement that although such customs, rules, and procedures are applied most in organizations, they nevertheless have been studied least. A favorable exception is the study of La Tour *et al.* (1976), showing that conflict parties are more in favor of involving a third party in the conflict when one party's winning means loss for the other, when some criterion for resolving the issue is available, or when under pressure of time. But in all their experimental conditions an objective, arbitrating third party is preferred over a mediator without real power.

In a hierarchical organization, the most appropriate third party is someone higher up (Scott, 1965), certainly in civil service organizations (Evan, 1965). In conflicts between superiors and subordinates, the latter will usually unquestioningly comply to the decisions, wishes, or irritating behavior of their superiors, as these happen to be in power legitimately (Raven and Kruglanski, 1970). If they do not, the boss or department manager will usually suppress the conflict promptly and successfully by insisting on his rights (Shepard, 1964). In a very different way, the hierarchical principle automatically has a preventive effect also when one reverts to established priorities, such as are often laid down in a hierarchy of role obligations (Merton, 1957; Toby, 1952).

5.2. Strategic prevention behavior

As soon as a party consciously pursues prevention, its behavior changes from spontaneous to strategic. With figure 1 as our guide, we can differentiate between strategic conflict management directed mainly towards more preventive antecedent conditions, towards eliminating the frustrating issue itself, or towards promoting further prevention behavior.

The first category of strategic prevention behavior includes, in particular, changing the organization or relationship characteristics, which usually goes beyond an incidental conflict. Structural operations often propagated are: diminishing power differences by institutionalizing joint consultations, explicating the decision-making and executive responsibilities or dividing them up more appropriately, establishing an expert and impartial point of coordination, or establishing or clearing communication channels. A decrease rather than increase of mutual dependence occurs with decentralization, job enlargement or job enrichment, creation of a buffer, or even total separation of roles. When personnel or financial means are involved, further frustration can be prevented by adding personnel, through early retirement, transfers, different working hours, reconsideration of remuneration rules, changing allocated budgets, and the like. Leeds (1964) makes a plea for the absorption of protest, legalizing a group's non-conforming behavior which cannot be changed anyway (see also Gamson, 1968). Finally, a well-known procedure is to look for a superordinate goal to be reached only through the efforts of both parties (Sherif, 1966). However, it has been demonstrated that this may have an escalating rather than preventive effect when not a third party, but one of the conflict parties takes such an initiative (Johnson and Lewicki, 1969).

Basically, the above means that arrangements are made that should completely or partly eliminate a current conflict and, at the same time, prevent similar conflicts from occurring in the future. They represent deliberate changes in the antecedent conditions in order to remove the conflict. Furthermore, it turns out that, sometimes, those directly involved introduce formal or informal regulation mechanisms that should ensure more preventive conflict management without preventing further conflicts (Walton, 1969). This mostly involves rules concerning the manner in which the parties should deal with one another or the steps they must or are allowed to take externally (cf. section 3.1). For example, 'management by exception' contains such a rule, i.e. when the members of an organization are in conflict, they should first try everything in their

PREVENTIVE CONFLICT MANAGEMENT
Spontaneous prevention behavior
Denying the conflict
De-escalating styles of behavior
Situational determination
Automatic regulation mechanisms
Strategic prevention behavior
Changing the antecedent conditions
Problem solving
Re-conceptualization of the conflict
De-escalating reaction models
Negotiation

power to find a solution, before calling in the management (Lievegoed, 1969).

Both the agreements intended to end a conflict and the regulation mechanisms will only have an appeal if they are known, clear, and unprejudiced, if they are supported and adhered to by others and promise to bring about improvement, while deviations will soon come to light (Deutsch, 1973). In this case, rules have the advantage of being impersonal and legitimate, which in itself will have a more preventive effect than taking a personal stand will or, for example, applying negative sanctions (Raven and Kruglanski, 1970). Moreover, as elucidated in section 5.1, eventually they often elicit spontaneous prevention behavior. In individual cases, however, rules may discourage problem solving, promote black-white thinking encouraging win-lose competition, and tend to lead to new rules (Thomas, 1976) as well as ignore attitudes, views, and feelings (Glasl, 1980, pp. 154, 368).

The most advocated preventive strategy, problem solving behavior, is oriented towards the incidental conflict issues themselves instead of towards the antecedent conditions. Filley (1975), who speaks of the win-win method of integrative problem solving, worked out this strategy in detail (see also Egan, 1976; Levi and Benjamin, 1977; Walton and McKersie, 1965). That this is, as a rule, the most effective way of managing a conflict is supported by persuasive arguments (Blake and Mouton, 1970; Schmidt and Tannenbaum, 1960), anecdotal evidence (Blake *et al.*, 1964; Filley, 1975), and systematic empirical research (Burke, 1970; Lawrence and Lorsch, 1967; Lewis and Pruitt, 1971), although the latter has been criticized (Prein, 1976). Yet, resolution of an existing problem is to be advised only when the issue is worthwhile and is possible only when agreement is not out of the question (Blake *et al.*, 1964; Mastenbroek, 1976). Moreover, it is difficult to apply if negotiations are also required or if the issue is sensitive because identity is involved (Walton, 1972; Walton and McKersie, 1965, 1966). As for social-emotional conflicts, Walton stated that any satisfactory resolution will always contain elements of conciliation.

A kind of alternative to conflict resolution is the conscious reconceptualization of the conflict issue in such a way that frustration decreases or even disappears (Thierry, 1977; Thomas and Pondy, 1977). Reconceptualization causes one to view a conflict as less abstract and therefore easier to solve, as redeemable, as less threatening to one's identity, less a matter of all or nothing or of 'it's me or him', 'us or them'. Much attention has been paid to the approach of Fisher (1964), who divides big conflicts into a number of small ones, each of which involves fewer people, topics, principles, or related issues. Another kind of reconceptualization is to remind oneself that, in spite of the conflict, the relationship with the opposite party is essentially one of cooperation (Deutsch, 1969; Druckman and Zechmeister, 1973). The attractive thing about these strategies is that they can often dispense with the opposite party. But there is the risk of getting stuck with a shifted conceptualization of the problem, thus obscuring the real conflict (Thierry, 1977). Walton (1969) and Deutsch (1973) do not consider this a very serious drawback, because working on some less threatening manifest problem may often clear the way for and encourage resolution of the more fundamental frustrations.

It often happens that both the realization of more preventive conditions and the elimination of the conflict issue itself are undesirable or impossible. Strategic prevention must then be directed towards stimulating de-escalating behavior. There are two reasonably verified strategies for changing from hostile behavior to less frustrating behavior: Deutsch's realization of cooperation (Deutsch, 1973; Deutsch et al., 1967) and Osgood's graduated and reciprocated initiatives in tension reduction (GRIT).

Through laboratory experiments, Deutsch and his colleagues, carrying on from Solomon (1960), did research on the usefulness of various strategies in their ability to induce the opponent to more cooperation. The most effective one is to react defensively, always reciprocating an attack with self-defense and never with a counterattack. Least effective is a strategy of deterrence, in which one does counterattack. The strategy of consistently turning the other cheek apparently stimulates exploitation rather than cooperation. The most preventive strategy is the one where one does not react in a hostile fashion, but does not allow intimidation either. This is in accord with the experimental result that threats—however preventively intended—intensify rather than attenuate the conflict, especially when the opposite party deems the threat illegitimate. (Deutsch and Krauss, 1962; Kelley, 1965). Making promises is, on the other hand, a good preventive tactic (Deutsch, 1961, 1973; Cheney et al., 1971).

Osgood's GRIT-strategy (1959, 1966), developed in order to realize a step-by-step way to relieve international tension, entails that one expounds one's strategy, then publicly makes some unequivocal conciliatory gesture and subsequently invites the opposite party to reciprocate. If the opposite party does not reciprocate, these de-escalating initiatives are continued anyhow. Attacks are countered by measured retaliation, after which a relieving measure is announced again, etc. Gaining trust and credibility is crucial. This according to experimental data successful strategy can also be applied by groups or individuals in conflict (Lindskold, 1978).

Negotiating is an approach that consciously walks the middle road or fluctuates between cooperation and arguing. It usually emphasizes distribution and compromise rather than integration and resolution (Mastenbroek, 1980; Thomas, 1976). Although negotiating is especially appropriate for managing conflicts of interest over scarce resources, it is also applied to, e.g., role conflicts (Adams, 1976; Goode, 1960). Here, one should think not only of market situations, rate fixing, and the granting of licences, or of the allocation of personnel, material means, or time, but also of discussions about goals, priorities procedures, powers, and duties. In the course of time, attention has been paid to types of negotiation (Walton and McKersie, 1965), the phasing of the process (Himmelmann, 1971; Karrass, 1970), inherent dilemmas (Mastenbroek, 1980; Morley and Stephenson, 1977), tactical tricks (Karrass, 1974), the relationship between a negotiator and his constituency (Megginson and Gullett, 1970; Rabbie et al., 1976; Walton and McKersie, 1965), and the like. Rubin and Brown (1975) and Druckman (1977) also present good surveys of the research. But all this divided effort has not yet resulted in an overall theory about negotiating.

Among the other activities on behalf of short-term stimulation of prevention behavior are: agreeing on a cooling off period, deliberately avoiding the opposite party or the issue, throwing dice, voting, or giving in after mature consideration. If one goes to talk with the opposite party, one may safeguard the reliability of the communication (Burton, 1969; Walton, 1969), replace subjective judgements by objective descriptions (Filley, 1975), and exchange views on and feelings about one's own and the other party (Blake et al., 1964; Goodstein and Boyer, 1972; Walton, 1969). The latter three tactics have proved useful, particularly in de-escalating social-emotional conflicts. It is remarkable and disappointing that, for the so important affective conflicts of identity, relatively few preventive strategies have been developed.

5.3. Consequences of prevention behavior

Consequences may be of longer or shorter duration. Thus, feedback to antecedent conditions is more lasting than feedback to conflict issues or to behavior. Consequences may also be direct or indirect: preventive conflict management, for example, may result in conflict resolution both directly and through joint goals, or through more reciprocal empathy. However, the two distinctions have much in common. That is to say, direct consequences involve a shorter term than do indirect consequences.

A direct consequence of changing the antecedent organizational or relational characteristics is the partial or complete removal of the conflict. But there exist, too, various indirect consequences, such as destroying healthy competition and elasticity (Prein, 1978), about which hardly anything is known. We do not know exactly how the parties experience the various structural operations and cope with them individually and socially. Nor is it clear whether the party taking the initiative for some operation experiences consequences different from those for the opposite party. This lacuna is partly due to the separation, criticized above, of the structural and the process approach.

Successful conflict resolution not only removes, according to plan, frustration, but leads, moreover, to higher effectiveness (Blake et al., 1964; Lawrence and Lorsch, 1967), trust and openness (Deutsch, 1969, 1973; Zand, 1972), attraction (Thomas, 1976), and de-personalization of future conflicts (Filley, 1975). A negotiator striving for compromise is considered to be just as willing and attractive (Ruble and Thomas, 1976), although the compromise may leave both negotiators with some residue of frustration. And since an opposite party that gives in or that covers up an issue also makes a constructive impression (Burke, 1970; Thomas, 1976), it may very well be that the same holds for an opposite party that eliminates a conflict issue by reconceptualizing it.

A much-favored proposition is that prevention behavior in one party will elicit prevention behavior in the other party. Above it was made sufficiently likely that this view is generally correct. Here, it is more interesting to note that spontaneous or strategic prevention behavior quite often has indirect consequences entailing or realizing escalation of conflict. In hierarchical organizations, preventive rules sometimes appear to result in more rather than less frustration (Pondy, 1967). Unilateral openness intended as a preventive tactic (Walton, 1969), drawing attention to overall interests (Johnson and Lewicki, 1969), tough negotiating (Filley, 1975; Thomas, 1976), and arbitration (Blake et al., 1964) can all have a boomerang effect. Often, it turns out after a while that management functionaries who want to prevent further conflict by suppressing the current disagreement, in fact attain the opposite (Deutsch, 1973). It has been mentioned already that threats have an intensifying rather than attenuating effect. Avoidance of any confrontation is experienced negatively too (Ruble and Thomas, 1976), which often has the consequence that, in the end, a destructive, so-called underground or cold conflict arises (Glasl, 1980; Walton, 1969). Thus, like the hierarchical suppression of conflict, avoidance may for a while have a direct, preventive effect, but in the long run it will have an indirect, escalating effect.

It may be concluded that the indirect consequences of prevention behavior can be of a preventive as well as of an escalating nature, depending on the kind of behavior and how it is experienced by the opposite party.

6. ESCALATING CONFLICT MANAGEMENT

Any reaction of either party to the conflict issue or to the other's behavior by which the total amount of cognitive and affective frustration increases, constitutes an escalating reaction. Therefore, anyone familiar with conflict management will recognize as such certain behaviors that are intended to be preventive, for instance threats and suppression. A reaction escalates a conflict if it brings about, directly or indirectly, an expansion of, *inter alia* "the size and number of the immediate issues involved; the number of motives and participants implicated on each side of the issue; the size and number of the principles and precedents that are perceived to be at stake" (Deutsch, 1973, p. 351). The increased frustration in its turn again elicits fresh reactions from the parties. Since, apparently, expanding conflicts tend to become more complex, it is no great step from this line of thinking to the assumption that with continuing escalation the strategic aspects of behavior will eventually supersede the spontaneous ones.

6.1. Spontaneous escalation behavior

Ways to escalate conflict management, in which spontaneity usually predominates, are: magnifying the issue, attacking the opposite party, and restricting the amount of interaction. These are characteristic of conflicts with strongly emotional aspects.

In the literature, it is agreed that parties tend to connect a conflict about facts with their own identities and emotions. This may be observed to occur in any strike. According to Walton (1969, p. 87), there are two mechanisms that largely explain this escalation: 'One is the need for consistency. If one dislikes the position another takes, or if he is in competition with him, there is a psychological tendency to develop similar attitudes toward the person. The second mechanism involves the tactics of competition, debate and bargaining over substantive differences; such tactics contain many points of friction and are likely to result in feelings of being attacked, in perceptions that the other is unfair, etc.'.

Not only may cognitive conflicts lead to affective identity conflicts. As some issue comes to affect identity more and more, there will, conversely, be a growing tendency to exaggerate the issue (Walton, 1972; see also above, section 4). This occurs often by unconsciously shifting the problem from, for example, an 'and-and' issue to one of 'either-or', or from a secondary or isolated position to a central one (Louis, 1977; Thierry, 1977; Thomas, 1976). Because the rules imposing restraints on conflict management constitute an additional frustration, the regulation mechanisms themselves will sometimes be challenged (Brickman, 1974). As a consequence of the reduction of their cognitive dissonance (Deutsch, 1973; Festinger, 1964), simplification of their line of thinking under stress (Walton, 1969), and attributions of cause and intention (Louis, 1977), the parties come to consider themselves as being good, reasonable, cooperative, and victim, and the opposite party as bad, unreasonable, hostile, and instigator. Such black-and-white mirror images constitute an excellent stimulus for escalation behavior.

The impulsive attack on the opponent(s), the attitude of win or perish, is represented by terms such as win-lose fight, dominance, forcing, and competition. It is a power context, in which all the available means of power are brought into play: convincing information, attraction as a relation, legitimate claims, expertise, positive and negative sanctions (Raven and Kruglanski, 1970). The main determinant of this type of spontaneous conflict management is, according to some, personality (Blake and Mouton, 1970; Filley, 1975) and according to others the organizational situation (Lawrence and Lorsch, 1967; Thomas and Kilmann, 1974). Terhune (1970) concludes that both factors are important, but that certain situations minimize the influence of certain personality traits on conflict management. Going by the results of experimental games, like Terhune did, Kelley and Stahelsky (1970) argue that the influence of the perceived social situation can ultimately be traced to personality. This view contains the danger that, despite the warning given in section 3.3, one may unjustifiably tend to hold individuals too much responsible for the escalation of conflicts.

Anyone knows from experience that a deeply rooted conflict may go hand in hand with a decline in contact between the parties (sometimes starting with avoidance behavior intended as prevention). Groups or individuals at war prefer to deal with one another as little as possible (Deutsch and Krauss, 1962; Katz and Kahn, 1978; Sherif, 1966). Sometimes, new issues may even arise from the subconscious of an emotional party, ensuring the isolation of the opponent (Walton, 1969). The less contact, however, the less chance of prevention behavior (Burton, 1969; Rapoport, 1960) and the more so of escalating misinterpretations, stereotypes, and distrust (Deutsch, 1973; Newcomb, 1947).

According to Glasl (1980), a conflict increasing in force passes through nine stages of escalation. The first is characterized by incidental frustration which puts a strain on cooperation and mutual understanding. The second stage of escalation entails that the parties have come to think in a polarized way and that their disputes are irrational and unfair. At the third stage, readiness to fight, lack of understanding, and nonverbal communication are predominant in both parties: deeds, not words! Escalation stage four involves stereotyped image building, win-lose behavior, and asking others for support. With the fifth stage, the opponent's immoral character comes to the fore and one tries to expose him and make him lose face. Escalation stage six is that of all-pervasive and determined threatening. The seventh stage is reached when each party tries to destroy the other's weapons and to inflict more harm than one has suffered oneself. Finally, escalation stages eight and nine represent the splitting up and total destruction of the enemy, respectively; both parties lose or even go to ruin.

Glasl combines the first three stages of escalation into a main phase I, where both parties still consider the substantial aspects of their conflict to be central and cooperate to search for a resolution. In main phase II, containing escalation stages four through six, the opponents' reciprocal image building and interaction become more of a problem and cooperation turns into obstruction. The last three stages of escalation, constituting main phase III, have in common that the opponents deny the other's human value, thus clearing the way for manipulation, retaliation, elimination, and destruction. In the first main phase, spontaneous escalation behavior is predominant, in the second main phase it is strategic escalation behavior, while in the third main phase the spontaneous and strategic elements and strongly interconnected.

6.2. Strategic escalation behavior

The goal one may have in mind when applying conscious escalation of conflict varies from conquering or adversely affecting the opposite party to creating a more effective level of tension so as to bring the conflict to an end that is satisfactory to both parties. The first extreme occurs, for example, when an important conflict is considered inevitable and insoluble, because it ran aground on bad people, ideological differences, or scarce resources (Blake et al., 1964). At the other extreme, we have to do with a constructive escalation to some desired point of greater intensity (Robbins, 1974), through which the ability of the parties to produce, process, and utilize information increases (Walton, 1969). Although this may sound fine, compared to the preventive strategies discussed, the goals nor the means of escalation have been studied satisfactorily. Our framework suggests that escalating conflict management may be directed towards changing the antecedent conditions or towards extending the issues or promoting further escalation behavior.

Continuous escalation is a powerful weapon in the hands of those wishing to bring about fundamental changes in existing organizational and relational characteristics. As in such a case a conflict functions as a lever for changes, it is sometimes called a strategic conflict (Glasl, 1980; Pondy, 1969; it comprises the revolutionary conflict of section 4). The ever more forcible ways by which certain action groups bring far-reaching demands to the attention of directors and politicians, such as obstruction and even occupation of buildings or terrains, may serve as an example. By making use of every conceivable escalation behavior, they try to realize other structures and opinions, which, of course, in their turn will serve as antecedent conditions of conflict. This radical strategy differs from operations that are intended to render the existing antecedent conditions more conflict stimulating. In this case, structural or cultural barriers to escalation will be lowered or potential triggers reinforced (Walton, 1969). Alternatively, the chance of frustration is enhanced through such reorganizations as recommended by Robbins (1974): a more complex structure, irreconcilable collective goals, a changeable style of leadership, carefully contrived transfers, unacceptable role prescriptions, and so on.

An extension of issues that is not directed towards fundamental changes often serves some hidden goal. Mulder (1978) mentions the raising of prestige, diverting attention, and removing internal discord. Here, it does not seem to matter very much which frustrations are increased or introduced. The original conflict may be reconceptualized in a direction opposite to that set out in section 5.2 and thus be concerned with various other things, become more threatening to identity, or grow into a matter of life and death. But one may also seize upon other fairly arbitrary items, keep back information, or supply threatening intelligence (Robbins, 1974). Creating new issues in order to gain a tactical advantage over the opposite party, however, constitutes a different case (Glasl, 1980; Walton, 1969). Then, it appears to be important to choose one's main goals carefully.

Finally, deliberate escalation is also possible through influencing further behavior, that is, without first changing the antecedent conditions or conflict issues. If a party decides on such a course, that decision will most likely be based on one or more of the following factors: (a) old wounds that were a consequence of earlier conflict; (b) current frustration; (c) norms existing as antecedent conditions: one should not be soft-hearted, should fight injustice, etc.; (d) the role expectations of a constituency or some other encouraging audience; (e) one's own role conceptions: 'Being a manager I cannot afford to lose face', 'It is my task to interfere now', etc.; (f) the imagined hostile intentions of the opponent; (g) the expected benefits after deduction of the expected costs, or: the balance of the positive and negative consequences of escalation behavior, including external and inner sanctions.

The behaviors that characteristically effect further escalation behavior are

---

ESCALATING CONFLICT MANAGEMENT
Spontaneous escalation behavior
Exaggerating the conflict
Attacking the opponent(s)
Restricting contact
Strategic escalation behavior
Changing the antecedent conditions
Extension of conflict issues
Re-conceptualization of the conflict
Escalating reaction models
Looking for allies

familiar to us: twisting information, lying, not listening, ignoring, laughing at someone, interrupting, belittling, accusing, using abusive language, etc. Not any less well-known but certainly less studied is the tactic of looking for allies. This means trying to improve one's own position and impairing that of the opposite party by obtaining the moral and active support of outsiders (Dalton, 1959; Kopytoff, 1961; Schattschneider, 1974). In an industrial conflict, for example, an employee will turn to his trade union or the local employment bureau or he may try to get the support of his colleagues. Whether such activities will result in victory depends not only on the opposite party's conflict management, but also and especially on the kind and amount of power the opponents and their possible allies can and will exert over the others (van de Vliert, 1981). A relatively powerless party, by the way, will prefer a more acceptable escalation behavior, such as arguing and protesting, thus making it all less grim (unless tension has mounted too high: Mulder, 1978).

A party wanting to create unilaterally a more effective tension level so as ultimately to bring the conflict to an end satisfactory to both parties, will prefer controlled escalation. It will state conditions, emphasize differences, defend its own interests or its being right, undermine the views of the opposite party, outline its own identity, vent and clarify feelings, and so on. Such an approach will benefit the quality of decision making (Cosier and Rose, 1977; Mason, 1969). Therefore, it is sensible to have each preventive phase of integration preceded by a controlled phase of escalation or differentiation (Walton, 1969; see also: Guetzkow and Gyr, 1954; Schmidt and Tannenbaum, 1960). Bach and Wyden (1969) even go so far as to teach married couples to cope more constructively with their problems and with each other by fighting fairly.

In retrospect, permanent stimulation of frustration through the antecedent conditions seems a very unsophisticated instrument. Extension of issues emerges as a pivotal subject, because stimulation of escalation behavior will fairly quickly change into just that. Here the need of research is greatest, especially concerning those points at which conflicts of interest and disagreements come to touch upon the identity of an individual or group.

6.3. Consequences of escalation behavior

Whereas prevention behavior quite often leads indirectly to escalation, escalation behavior does not lead so easily to prevention by means of other variables. From section 6.2 it is apparent that, in the end, moderate escalation is conducive to problem solving behavior. Exceptional is Coser's proposition (1956) that conflict brings the parties closer together and that it restores the unity and stability among them, unless the relationship is affected too badly. He finds support in Bach and Wyden's (1969) practical experience and Corwin's (1969) interesting research results, that if the number of minor disagreements increases, the number of major clashes decreases.

Thanks to the experiments of Sherif (1966) and Blake and Mouton (1962) we know, furthermore, that escalation of a conflict between groups is accompanied by prevention of conflict within those groups. Identification with one's own group, feelings of solidarity, and tractability increase, while internal differences and irritations dissolve. Negotiators with a constituency know this mechanism from experience and will, for that reason, take a more rigorous stand externally (Walton and McKersie, 1965). Rabbie (1979), however, has shown that the mechanism works only if a group expects to win; if it expects to lose, cohesion will rather diminish. Indeed, not only the group's expectation of losing may undermine the relation between external escalation and internal prevention. An attacked group will, at the same time, develop a more centralized and task-oriented leadership (Mulder and Stemerding, 1963; Rabbie et al., 1974; Rabbie and Wilkens, 1971) and become less tolerant internally—qualities which increase rather than decrease the chances of internal conflict.

The relationship between the groups will come to be marked more and more by communication distortions, ingroup-outgroup differentiation, exaggerated mutual prejudices and mutual distrust (Deutsch, 1973; Rabbie, 1974, 1979). The defeated group grows divided internally and starts looking for a scapegoat (Blake and Mouton, 1962; Shepard, 1964). These are all direct or indirect consequences functioning also as antecedent conditions, so that a vicious spiral of feedbacks and further frustration may easily arise. Escalating personal conflicts take the same course. Moreover, they draw attention to the intrapersonal conflicts that result from conflicts between individuals or groups (Krauss, 1966; Sanford, 1964) and that also constitute antecedent conditions for further conflicts (see section 3.3). In this interaction between a two-party conflict and an intrapersonal conflict we again come upon an important area yet unattended to by organizational psychologists.

Deliberately creating and spontaneously magnifying conflict issues are among the escalation behaviors discussed, which lead to further frustration without mediation of antecedent conditions. Furthermore, extension of conflict issues occurs through the disapproval and disgust evoked in the opponent by escalating conflict management as such (Ruble and Thomas, 1976). In particular, exertion of force and taking illegitimate steps have such an effect (Deutsch, 1973; Raven and Kruglanski, 1970), albeit probably less so on people who enjoy conflicts (Berkowitz, 1962; Pondy, 1967). Similar to these consequences is the fact that escalation behavior directly instigates the opposite party to defensive and other escalation behavior. Renwick (1975) found that members of an organization will behave hostilely if they think the opposite party is doing the same. Thus, this readiness to fight which is ascribed to the other party, works as a self-fulfilling prophecy, without this being noticed (Kelley and Stahelski, 1970; Thomas and Pondy, 1977).

Another strongly escalating tactic is looking for allies. According to Van de Vliert (1981b) its direct consequences are that, by informing a third party, the conflict issue becomes more defined and that, moreover, the relationship itself between the parties in conflict and the outsider will become a stake in the conflict as well. If an original outsider does take sides, various indirect consequences are added: (a) siding implies that the outsider adopts the win-lose conceptualization and thus reinforces it; (b) it creates a winner (the party chosen) and a loser (the party rejected), which also precipitates escalation; (c) it increases the number of those actively involved in the conflict; (d) it complicates the conflict issue and the conflict management by adding other views; (e) the energy the siding outsider invests in the conflict raises the total stake of the conflict; (f) siding encourages the outsider to show behavior supporting the correctness of his choice.

As is generally known, the escalation process, if not checked, will result in delays, impasses, disintegration of subdivisions, personnel turnover, absenteeism, and other inefficiencies in the organization (Burke, 1970; Lawrence and Lorsch, 1967; Thomas, 1976). At the same time, the psychological and physical condition of the organization members deteriorates, which will not fail to have its effect either. They become, for example, inwardly frayed, dependent, indifferent, cynical, oversensitive, restless, or ill (Kahn *et al.*, 1964). Against the background of the above this means, basically, that as a rule escalation is a self-reinforcing, destructive process, unless the whole system of antecedent conditions, spontaneous prevention behavior, or strategic conflict management curbs excess escalation.

7. USE OF THE MODEL

In my opinion, the model developed here has the following advantages: (a) it integrates the customary process and structural approaches; (b) its focus really consists of the central mechanisms of prevention and escalation; (c) it may inspire new research on conflict and conflict management; (d) it provides the practising organizational psychologist with a typology of strategies of conflict management.

Of these points, c and d have not yet been discussed. As for c, the present survey already presented some important research questions and assumptions. First, there is the question of the relative influence of the various antecedent conditions on the rise of the four kinds of conflict issues and on the preventive or escalating course of conflict processes. This problem thus meets the need of Thomas (1976) for more complex research, simultaneously taking into account more independent, intervening, and dependent variables. Next, there are questions regarding the pivotal function of social-emotional conflicts: when and how does a conflict of interest or a disagreement begin to affect the identity of an individual or group? Conversely, when and how does an affective identity conflict become a source of cognitive problems? What strategic behavior can control escalation brought about by social-emotional issues?

Furthermore, future research might throw more light on the differences as to the causes and effects between the three feedbacks on the antecedent conditions, conflict issues, and behavior, respectively. The indirect escalating consequences of prevention behavior and the indirect, preventive consequences of escalation behavior in particular still are a challenging void. Also, very little is known about the interaction between two-party conflicts and intrapersonal conflicts. If we really want to do something about that, longitudinal studies of conflict processes are urgently necessary (cf. Murray, 1975). Longitudinal studies may, moreover, improve our insight into the phases of escalating conflicts.

The practising organizational psychologist training clients in constructive conflict management or intervening in conflicts—as a third party—will certainly benefit from the results of such research (point d). Both the conflict parties and any third party may use the prevention-escalation model first as a diagnostic instrument providing questions about causes, issues, reactions, and consequences, and subsequently as a means for selecting certain prevention or escalation behaviors.

On the basis of the diagnosis, the third party may single out the antecedent conditions, the conflict issue of the parties, their conflict behavior, or the consequences as its point of action for intervention. Regardless of the point of action, the intervention strategy may then be directed towards either prevention or escalation. Combination of both choices results in a typology of eight strategies of conflict management, as represented in figure 2 and worked out in more detail elsewhere (van de Vliert, 1981a).

Each of the four prevention and four escalation strategies corresponds to

Conflict management by a third party		Point of action for intervention			
		Antecedent conditions	Conflict issues	Conflict behavior	Consequences
Intervention strategy	Prevention	I	II	III	IV
	Escalation	V	VI	VII	VIII

Figure 2. Typology of eight strategies of conflict management by a third party.

the changing of certain aspects of the relationship between the two conflict parties on the one hand, and to certain roles of the intervening party on the other. The former was discussed in the above sections on conflict management, the latter—the roles of the third party—would really require a separate chapter (see Blake et al., 1964; Fisher, 1972; Glasl, 1980; Kohn, 1972; Mastenbroek, 1979; Prein, 1978, 1979; Walton, 1969).

REFERENCES

Adams, J. S. (1976), The structure and dynamics of behavior in organizational boundary roles. In: Dunnette, M. D. (Ed.), *Handbook of industrial and organizational psychology.* Chicago: Rand McNally.

Apfelbaum, E. (1974), On conflicts and bargaining. *Advances in Experimental Social Psychology*, 7, 103–156.

Aubert, V. (1963), Competition and dissensus: Two types of conflict and of conflict resolution. *Journal of Conflict Resolution*, 7, 26–42.

Bach, G. R., Wyden, P. (1969), *The intimate enemy.* New York: Morrow.

Berkowitz, L. (1962), *Aggression: A social psychological analysis.* New York: McGraw-Hill.

Biddle, B. J. (1979), *Role theory: Expectations, identities and behaviors.* New York: Academic Press.

Blake, R. R., Mouton, J. S. (1962), The intergroup dynamics of win-lose conflict and problem-solving collaboration in union-management relations. In: Sherif, M. (Ed.), *Intergroup relations and leadership.* New York: Wiley.

Blake, R. R., Mouton, J. S. (1964), *The managerial grid.* Houston: Gulf.

Blake, R. R., Mouton, J. S. (1970), The fifth achievement. *Journal of Applied Behavioral Science*, 6, 413–426.

Blake, R. R., Shephard, H. A., Mouton, J. S. (1964), *Managing intergroup conflict in industry.* Houston: Gulf.

Boekestijn, C. (1979), De psychologie van relaties tussen groepen [The psychology of intergroup relations]. In: Jaspars and van der Vlist (1979).

Boulding, E. (1964), Further reflections on conflict management. In: Kahn, R. L., Boulding, E. (Eds.), *Power and conflict in organizations.* London: Tavistock.

Brickman, Ph. (1974), *Social conflict: Readings in rule structure and conflict relationships.* Lexington (Mass.): D.C. Heath.

Burke, R. J. (1970), Methods of resolving superior-subordinate conflict: The constructive use of subordinate differences and disagreements. *Organizational Behavior and Human Performance*, 5, 393–411.

Burton, J. W. (1969), *Conflict and communication.* London: McMillan.

Cheney, J., Harford, T., Solomon, L. (1971), Effects of communicating threats and promises upon the bargaining process. *Journal of Conflict Resolution*, 16, 99–107.

Corwin, R. G. (1969), Patterns of organizational conflict. *Administrative Science Quarterly*, 14, 507–520.

Coser, L. (1956), *The functions of social conflict.* Glencoe (Ill.): Free Press.

Cosier, R. A., Rose, G. L. (1977), Cognitive conflict and goal conflict effects on task performance. *Organizational Behavior and Human Performance*, 19, 378–391.

Cummings, L. L., Harnett, D. L. Schmidt, S. M. (1972), International cross-language factor stability of personality: An analysis of the Shure-Meeker personality/attitude schedule. *Journal of Psychology*, 82, 67–84.

Dalton, M. (1959), *Men who manage.* New York: Wiley.

Deutsch, M. (1961), The interpretation of praise and criticism as a function of their social context. *Journal of Abnormal and Social Psychology*, **62**, 391–400.

Deutsch, M. (1969), Conflicts: Productive and destructive. *Journal of Social Issues*, **25**, 7–42.

Deutsch, M. (1971), Toward an understanding of conflict. *International Journal of Group Tensions*, **1**, 42–54.

Deutsch, M. (1973), *The resolution of conflict: Constructive and destructive processes.* New Haven: Yale University Press.

Deutsch, M., Krauss, R. M. (1962), Studies of interpersonal bargaining. *Journal of Conflict Resolution*, **6**, 52–76.

Deutsch, M., Epstein, Y., Canavan, D., Gumpert, P. (1967), Strategies of inducing co-operation: An experimental study. *Journal of Conflict Resolution*, **11**, 345–360.

Doise, W., Sinclair, A. (1973), The categorization process in intergroup relations. *European Journal of Social Psychology*, **3**, 145–153.

Druckman, D. (Ed.) (1977), *Negotiations: Social-psychological perspectives.* Beverly Hills (Calif.): Sage.

Druckman, D., Zechmeister, K. (1973), Conflict of interest and value dissensus; Propositions in the sociology of conflict. *Human Relations*, **26**, 449–466.

Dubin, R. (1957), Industrial conflict and social welfare. *Journal of Conflict Resolution*, **1**, 179–199.

Dunkin, M. J. (1972), The nature and resolution of role conflicts among male primary school teachers. *Sociology of Education*, **45**, 167–185.

Egan, G. (1976), Confrontation. *Group and Organization Studies*, **1**, 223–243.

Evan, M. (1965), Superior-subordinate conflict in research organizations. *Administrative Science Quarterly*, **10**, 52–64.

Festinger, L. (1964), *Conflict, decision, and dissonance.* Stanford: Stanford University Press.

Filley, A. C. (1975), *Interpersonal conflict resolution.* Glenview (Ill.): Scott, Foresman.

Fink, C. F. (1968), Some conceptual difficulties in the theory of social conflict. *Journal of Conflict Resolution*, **12**, 412–460.

Fisher, R. (1964), Fractionating conflict. In: Fisher, R. (Ed.), *International conflict and behavioral science: The Craigville papers.* New York: Basic Books.

Fisher, R. J. (1972), Third party consultation: A method for the study and resolution of conflict. *Journal of Conflict Resolution*, **16**, 67–94.

Frey, R. L., Adams, J. S. (1972), The negotiator's dilemma: Simultaneous in-group and out-group conflict. *Journal of Experimental Social Psychology*, **4**, 331–346.

Gamson, W. A. (1968), *Power and discontent.* Homewood (Ill.): Dorsey.

Getzels, J. W., Lipham, J. M., Campbell, R. F. (1968), *Educational administration as a social process.* New York: Harper & Row.

Glasl, F. (1980), *Konfliktmanagement: Diagnose und Behandlung von Konflikten in Organisationen.* Bern: Haupt.

Goode, W. J. (1960), A theory of role strain. *American Sociological Review*, **25**, 482–496.

Goodstein, L. D., Boyer, R. K. (1972), Crisis intervention in a municipal agency: A conceptual case history. *Journal of Applied Behavioral Science*, **8**, 318–340.

Guetzkow, H., Gyr, J. (1954), An analysis of conflict in decision-making groups. *Human Relations*, **7**, 367–381.

Hall, D. T. (1972), A model of coping with role conflict: The role behavior of college educated women. *Administrative Science Quarterly*, **17**, 471–486.

Harding, J., Proshansky, H., Kutner, B., Chein, I. (1968), Prejudice and ethnic relations. In: Lindzey, G., Aronson, E. (Eds.), *Handbook of social psychology Vol. V.* 2nd ed. Reading (Mass.): Addison-Wesley.

Himmelmann, G. (1971), *Lohnbildung durch Kollektivverhandlungen*. Berlin: Duncker & Humblot.

Horwitz, M. (1964), Managing hostility in the laboratory and the refinery. In: Kahn, R. L., Boulding, E. (Eds.), *Power and conflict in organizations*. London: Tavistock.

Jaspars, J. M. F., Vlist, R. van der (Eds.) (1979), *Sociale psychologie in Nederland: II. De kleine groep* [Social psychology in The Netherlands: II. Small groups]. Deventer: Van Loghum Slaterus.

Johnson, D. W., Lewicki, R. J. (1969), The initiation of superordinate goals. *Journal of Applied Behavioral Science*, **5**, 9–24.

Kahn, R. L., Quinn, R. P. (1970), Role stress: A framework for analysis. In: McLean, A. (Ed.), *Mental health and work organizations*. Chicago: Rand McNally.

Kahn, R. L., Wolfe, D. M., Quinn, R. P., Snoek, J. D., Rosenthal, R. A. (1964), *Organizational stress: Studies in role conflict and ambiguity*. New York: Wiley.

Karrass, C. L. (1970), *The negotiating game*. New York: Crowell.

Karrass, C. L. (1974), *Give and take: The complete guide to negotiating strategies and tactics*. New York: Crowell.

Katz, D., Kahn, R. L. (1978), *The social psychology of organizations*. 2nd ed. New York: Wiley.

Kelley, H. H. (1965), Experimental studies of threats in interpersonal negotiations. *Journal of Conflict Resolution*, **9**, 79–105.

Kelley, H. H., Stahelski, A. J. (1970), Social interaction basis of cooperators' and competitors' beliefs about others. *Journal of Personality and Social Psychology*, **16**, 66–91.

Kohn, M. (1972), Intervenor roles II: The community advocates. *Crisis and Change*, **2**, 1–6.

Kopytoff, I. (1961), Extension of conflict as a method of conflict resolution among the Suku of the Congo. *Journal of Conflict Resolution*, **5**, 61–69.

Krauss, R. M. (1966), Structural and attitudinal factors in interpersonal bargaining. *Journal of Experimental Social Psychology*, **2**, 42–55.

Křivohlavý, J. (1974), *Zwischenmenschliche Konflikte und experimentelle Spiele*. Bern: Hans Huber.

Lamm, H., Myers, D. G. (1978), Group-induced polarization of attitudes and behavior. *Advances in Experimental Social Psychology*, **11**, 145–195.

La Tour, S., Houlden, P., Walker, L., Thibaut, J. (1976), Some determinants of preference for modes of conflict resolution. *Journal of Conflict Resolution*, **20**, 319–356.

Lawrence, P. R., Lorsch, J. W. (1967), *Organization and environment: Managing differentiation and integration*. Boston: Harvard University.

Leeds, R. (1964), The absorption of protest: A working paper. In: Cooper, W. W., Leavitt, H. J., Shelley, M. W. II (Eds.), *New perspectives in organization research*. New York: Wiley.

Levi, A. M., Benjamin, A. (1977), Focus and flexibility in a model of conflict resolution. *Journal of Conflict Resolution*, **21**, 405–425.

Lewis, S. A., Pruitt, D. G. (1971), Organization, aspiration level, and communication freedom in integrative bargaining. *Proceedings of the American Psychological Association*, **6**, 221–222.

Lievegoed, B. C. J. (1969), *Organisaties in ontwikkeling: Zicht op de toekomst* [Developing organizations: A look at the future]. Rotterdam: Lemniscaat.

Lindskold, S. (1978), Trust development, the GRIT proposal, and the effects of conciliatory acts on conflict and cooperation. *Psychological Bulletin*, **85**, 772–793.

Litwak, E. (1961), Models of bureaucracy which permit conflict. *American Journal of Sociology*, **67**, 177–184.

Louis, M. R. (1977), How individuals conceptualize conflict: Identification of steps in the process and the role of personal/developmental factors. *Human Relations*, 30, 451–467.

Mack, R. W., Snyder, R. C. (1957), The analysis of social conflict: Toward an overview and synthesis. *Journal of Conflict Resolution*, 1, 212–248.

March, J. G., Simon, H. A. (1958), *Organizations*. New York: Wiley.

Mark, V. H., Ervin, F. R. (1970), *Violence and the brain*. New York: Harper & Row.

Mason, R. O. (1969), A dialectical approach of strategic planning. *Management Science*, 15, B403–B414.

Mastenbroek, W. F. G. (1976), Conflicthantering in organisaties [Conflict management in organizations]. *Intermediair*, 12, no. 23.

Mastenbroek, W. F. G. (1979), Conflicthantering: Een procesbenadering [Conflict management: A process approach]. *M & O, Tijdschrift voor Organisatiekunde en Sociaal beleid*, 33, 69–89.

Mastenbroek, W. F. G. (1980), Negotiating: A conceptual model. *Group and Organization Studies*, 5, 324–339.

Meertens, R. W. (1976), *Aspecten van groepspolarisatie* [Aspects of group polarization]. Groningen: University of Groningen (dissertation).

Megginson, L. C., Gullett, C. R. (1970), A predictive model of union-management conflict. *Personnel Journal*, 49, 495–503.

Merton, R. K. (1957), *Social theory and social structure*. New York: Free Press.

Miles, R. H., Perreault, W. D. (1976), Organizational role conflict: Its antecedents and consequences. *Organizational Behavior and Human Performance*, 17, 19–44.

M & O, Tijdschrift voor Organisatiekunde en Sociaal Beleid [Journal of Organization Science and Social Policy].

Molnar, J. J., Rogers, D. L. (1979), A comparative model of interorganizational conflict. *Administrative Science Quarterly*, 24, 405–425.

Morley, J., Stephenson, G. (1977), *The social psychology of bargaining*. London: Allen & Unwin.

Moyer, K. E. (1968), Kinds of aggression and their physiological basis. *Communications in Behavioral Biology*, 2, 65–87.

Mulder, M. (1978), *Conflicthantering: Theorie en praktijk in organisaties* [Conflict management: Theory and practice in organizations]. Leiden: Stenfert Kroese.

Mulder, M., Stemerding, A. (1963), Threat, attraction to group, and need for strong leadership: A laboratory experiment in a natural setting. *Human Relations*, 16, 317–334.

Murray, V. V. (1975), Some unanswered questions on organizational conflict. *Organization and Administrative Science*, 5, 35–53.

Nederlands Tijdschrift voor de Psychologie [Dutch Journal of Psychology].

Newcomb, T. M. (1947) Autistic hostility and social reality. *Human Relations*, 1, 69–86.

Osgood, C. E. (1959), Suggestions for winning the real war with communism. *Journal of Conflict Resolution*, 3, 295–325.

Osgood, C. E. (1966), *Perspective in foreign policy*. Palo Alto (Calif.): Pacific Books.

Pondy, L. R. (1967), Organizational conflict: Concepts and models. *Administrative Science Quarterly*, 12, 296–320.

Pondy, L. R. (1969), Varieties of organizational conflict. *Administrative Science Quarterly*, 14, 499–505.

Prein, H. C. M. (1976), Stijlen van conflicthantering [Styles of conflict management]. *Nederlands Tijdschrift voor de Psychologie*, 31, 321–346.

Prein, H. C. M. (1978), De diagnose en hantering van conflicten [Diagnosing and managing conflicts]. In: Hazewinkel, A., Boekholdt, M. G., Knip, J. L., Prein, H. C. M. (Eds.), *Conflicten tussen groepen in organisaties* [Conflicts between groups in organizations]. Deventer: Kluwer.

Prein, H. C. M. (1979), Rollen van een derde partij bij conflicthantering [The third party's roles in conflict management]. *M & O, Tijdschrift voor Organisatiekunde en Sociaal beleid*, **33**, 100–124.

Rabbie, J. M. (1974), Effecten van een competitieve en coöperatieve intergroepsoriëntatie op verhoudingen binnen en tussen groepen [Effects of competitive and cooperative intergroup orientation on intra- and intergroup relations]. *Nederlands Tijdschrift voor de Psychologie*, **29**, 239–257.

Rabbie, J. M. (1979), Competitie en coöperatie tussen groepen [Intergroup competition and cooperation]. In: Jaspars and van der Vlist (1979).

Rabbie, J. M., Bekkers, F. (1976), Bedreigd leiderschap en intergroepscompetitie [Endangered leadership and intergroup competition]. *Nederlands Tijdschrift voor de Psychologie*, **31**, 269–283.

Rabbie, J. M., Visser, L. (1976), Gevolgen van interne en externe conflicten op verhoudingen tussen groepen [Consequences of internal and external conflicts for intergroup relations]. *Nederlands Tijdschrift voor de Psychologie*, **31**, 233–251.

Rabbie, J. M., Visser, L., Tils, J. (1976), De vertegenwoordiger en zijn achterban: Een exploratieve studie [The representative and his constituency: An exploratory study]. *Nederlands Tijdschrift voor de Psychologie*, **31**, 233–268.

Rabbie, J. M., Wilkens, G. (1971), Intergroup competition and its effect on intra- and intergroup relations. *European Journal of Social Psychology*, **1**, 215–234.

Rabbie, J. M., Benoist, F., Oosterbaan, H., Visser, L. (1974), Differential power and effects of expected competitive and cooperative intergroup interaction upon intra-group and outgroup attitudes. *Journal of Personality and Social Psychology*, **30**, 46–56.

Rapoport, A. (1960), *Fights, games and debates*. Ann Arbor: University of Michigan Press.

Raven, B. H., Kruglanski, A. W. (1970), Conflict and power. In: Swingle, P. G. (Ed.), *The structure of conflict*. New York: Academic Press.

Renwick, P. A. (1975), Perception and management of superior-subordinate conflict. *Organizational Behavior and Human Performance*, **13**, 444–456.

Robbins, S. P. (1974), *Managing organizational conflict: A nontraditional approach*. Englewood Cliffs (N. J.): Prentice-Hall.

Rozema, R., Visser, A.Ph., Boekestijn, C. (1979), Roloriëntatie en rolgedrag in een brugpositie: Een onderzoek onder praktijkbegeleidsters [Role orientation and role behavior in a bridge position]. In: Jaspars and van der Vlist (1979).

Rubin, J. Z., Brown, B. R. (1975), *The social psychology of bargaining and negotiation*. New York: Academic Press.

Ruble, T. L., Thomas, K. W. (1976), Support for a two-dimensional model of conflict behavior. *Organizational Behavior and Human Performance*, **16**, 143–155.

Ryan, S. G., Clemence, J. B. (1973), Conflict resolution behavior, influence and organizational effectiveness: An integrative study. *Proceedings of the 10th annual meeting of the Eastern Academy of Management*, 1973.

Sanford, R. N. (1964), Individual conflict and organizational interaction. In: Kahn, R. L., Boulding, E. (Eds.), *Power and conflict in organizations*. London: Tavistock.

Sarbin, T. R., Allen, V. L. (1968), Role theory. In: Lindzey, G., Aronson, E. (Eds.), *Handbook of social psychology Vol. I*. 2nd ed. Reading (Mass.): Addison-Wesley.

Schattschneider, E. E. (1974), The scope and bias of the pressure system. In: Brickman, Ph. (Ed.), *Social conflict*. Lexington (Mass.): D.C. Heath.

Schmidt, S. M., Kochan, T. A. (1972), Conflict: Toward conceptual clarity. *Administrative Science Quarterly*, **17**, 359–370.

Schmidt, W. H., Tannenbaum, R. (1960), The management of differences. *Harvard Business Review*, **38**, 107–115.

Scott, W. G. (1965), *The management of conflict: Appeal systems in organizations.* Homewood (Ill.): Irwin-Dorsey.

Shepard, H. A. (1964), Responses to situations of competition and conflict. In Kahn, R. L., Boulding, E. (Eds.), *Power and conflict in organizations.* London: Tavistock.

Sherif, M. (1966), *In common predicament.* Boston: Houghton Mifflin.

Solomon, L. (1960), The influence of some types of power relationships and game strategies upon the development of interpersonal trust. *Journal of Abnormal and Social Psychology*, **61**, 223–230.

Tajfel, H., Billig, M. (1974), Familiarity and categorisation in intergroup behavior. *Journal of Experimental Social Psychology*, **10**, 159–170.

Tajfel, H., Billig, M., Bundy, R., Flament, C. (1971), Social categorisation and intergroup behaviour. *European Journal of Social Psychology*, **1**, 149–175.

Terhune, K. W. (1970), The effects of personality in cooperation and conflict. In: Swingle, P. G. (Ed.), *The structure of conflict.* New York: Academic Press.

Thierry, Hk. (1977), *Organisatie van tegenstellingen* [The organization of antitheses]. Assen: Van Gorcum.

Thomas, K. W. (1976), Conflict and conflict management. In: Dunnette, M. D. (Ed.), *Handbook of industrial and organizational psychology.* Chicago: Rand McNally.

Thomas, K. W., Kilmann, R. H. (1974), *Thomas-Kilmann conflict mode intrument.* Tuxedo (N. Y.): Xicom.

Thomas, K. W., Pondy, L. R. (1977), Toward an 'intent' model of conflict management among principal parties. *Human Relations*, **30**, 1089–1102.

Toby, J. (1952), Some variables in role conflict analysis. *Social Forces*, **30**, 323–327.

Turner, J. C. (1975), Social comparison and social identity: Some prospects for intergroup behaviour. *European Journal of Social Psychology*, **5**, 5–34.

Vliert, E. van de (1974), *Rolgedrag in de organisatie* [Role behavior in organizations]. Deventer: Kluwer.

Vliert, E. van de (1976), Role conflict between supervisor and subordinate. *Personnel Review*, **5**, 19–23.

Vliert, E. van de (1979), Gedrag in rolconflictsituaties: 20 jaar onderzoek rond een theorie [Behavior in role conflict situations: 20 years of research on a theory]. *Nederlands Tijdschrift voor de Psychologie*, **34**, 125–146.

Vliert, E. van de (1981a), Het preventie-escalatiemodel van conflictinterventie [The prevention-escalation model of conflict intervention]. *M & O, Tijdschrift voor Organisatiekunde en Sociaal beleid*, **35**, 332–347.

Vliert, E. van de (1981b), Siding and other reactions to a conflict: A theory of escalation toward outsiders. *Journal of Conflict Resolution*, **25**, 495–520.

Vliert, E. van de, Boekestijn, C. (1978), Floyd Allport's J-curve hypothese over conformerend gedrag [Floyd Allport's J-curve hypothesis on conforming behavior]. *Nederlands Tijdschrift voor de Psychologie*, **33**, 15–32.

Walton, R. E. (1969), *Interpersonal peacemaking: Confrontations and third party consultation.* Reading (Mass.): Addison-Wesley.

Walton, R. E. (1972), Interorganizational decision making and identity conflict. In: Tuite, M., Chisholm, R., Radnor, M. (Eds.), *Interorganizational decision making.* Chicago: Aldine.

Walton, R. E., Dutton, J. D. (1969), The management of interdepartmental conflict: A model and review. *Administrative Science Quarterly*, **14**, 73–84.

Walton, R. E., McKersie, R. B. (1965), *A behavioral theory of labor negotiations: An analysis of a social interaction system.* New York: McGraw-Hill.

Walton, R. E., McKersie, R. B. (1966), Behavioral dilemmas in mixed-motive decision making. *Behavioral Science*, **11**, 370–384.

Walton, R. E., Dutton, J. M., Cafferty, T. P. (1969), Organizational context and interdepartmental conflict. *Administrative Science Quarterly*, **14**, 522–542.

Wardwell, W. I. (1955), The reduction of strain in a marginal social role. *American Journal of Sociology*, **61**, 16–25.

Weitz, S. (1977), *Sex roles: Biological, psychological and social foundations*. Oxford: Oxford University Press.

Zald, M. N. (1962), Power balance and staff conflict in correctional institutions. *Administrative Science Quarterly*, **7**, 22–49.

Zand, D. E. (1972), Trust and managerial problem solving. *Administrative Science Quarterly*, **17**, 229–239.

Zwart, C. J. (1977), *Gericht veranderen van organisaties* [Planned change in organizations]. *Vol. I.* Rotterdam: Lemniscaat.

3.4   Stress in organizations

Jacques A. M. Winnubst

1. WORK AND HEALTH: A GROWING PROBLEM

It is an ever striking fact that so little attention is paid to employee health in the industrial world, government agencies, hospitals and other organizations. Always the task, the job to be done, seems to dominate. The job should be done as efficiently as possible—after all, 'time is money'—and stagnation of production or service should be avoided.

An organization selects the most 'appropriate' people for the job to be done, draws up job descriptions and takes care of management. Adequate working conditions are created and precautionary measures are taken. On a short-term basis, many employees can come to terms with such a situation. The situation is precarious however, when seen on a long-term basis. In many organizations, one is not aware of the fact that people have to last a life-time and that tasks can eventually become too arduous. One often does not think in terms of work and health.

In The Netherlands, the number of people on social security has increased dramatically. Between 1967 and 1978 this number increased by 68% (van den Bosch and Petersen, 1980). Additionally, between 1951 and 1976 the number of Dutch people to die of cardio-vascular diseases increased by 59.5% (Grosfeld, 1978). Since 1981, however, the figures have been showing a drop for women and a rise for men. Total mortality is decreasing, although morbidity remains as high as it was.

The following aspects are among those playing a role in the 'stress problem':

Dr. J. A. M. Winnubst, Katholieke Universiteit, Vakgroep A & O psychologie, Montessorilaan 3, 6500 HE NIJMEGEN.

the enormous increase of traffic, the explosion of information, economic instability, the necessity for organizations to keep adjusting to ever-changing conditions. Also, it may well be possible, that modern man is more vulnerable, because the old, familiar stress-regulating mechanisms have disappeared: formerly strong family-ties are breaking down, religious orientations are disappearing, impersonal newly-built apartment buildings form the new scenery of life.

It is not so surprising that interest in 'stress' is rising. Stress is considered a phenomenon to be fought in any case, as something to investigate and to be 'managed'. A surplus of stress is indeed undesirable, but it should nevertheless be remembered that a certain amount of stress is often necessary to achieve something. People actually look for stress, create stress, challenge themselves and thus achieve something.

What exactly should be understood by 'stress' is a continuing source of discussion: some researchers use the word as a general indication for a field of research, others define stress as a physical response (emphasizing the response-aspect) or as an environmental factor (emphasizing the stimulus-aspect). In this chapter we will use the concept of 'stressor' for the stimulus-aspect, while the concept of 'strain' is to be reserved for the response-aspect. The term 'stress' will be used to apply to the entire field of research.

Below, we will present a review of the state of affairs in the field of stress research, in which the emphasis will be on stress as defined by organizational factors. The manner in which personality traits can play a part in the occurrence of stress will also be discussed, and especially how an individual and an organization can be adjusted to each other in order to keep the stress manageable. Finally, an inventory is made of a number of approaches to 'coping', that is: the way in which individuals and organizations cope with stress.

Readers interested in a critical treatment of stress research, are recommended to study McGrath (1976) and Kleber (1982). Such an analysis, however, is not the primary objective of this review. Good review articles about coping and stress are those of Beehr and Newman (1978), and Newman and Beehr (1979).

2. A CHRONOLOGICAL SURVEY OF STRESS-APPROACHES

Stress is a term derived from the technical sciences and indicates an excessive, detrimental overloading of objects. Steel has a certain strain capacity. If certain values are exceeded, a rupture or fracture occurs. The term was used in this sense in the 19th century.

In the beginning of the 20th century, the concept appears in medical jargon and as such indicates the overloading of the human body. The physician Cannon (1935) related the stress concept to equilibrium tendencies in the body.

When the sympathic nervous system and the endocrine system are activated in a certain way, for example by extreme coldness or great excitement, then an individual is said to be under stress. The endocrinologist Selye adopted this theory. This pioneer in the field of stress research has played a key-role in the propagation of the concept. Only after World War II was the stress concept granted a place in psychological jargon. Grinker and Spiegel (1945) wrote *Men under Stress* and Stouffer published a number of studies about battle-fatigue, war-neurosis and demoralization in the army in *The American Soldier* (1950). Within psychology, Lazarus especially paid attention to the stress concept. Around 1950, this researcher started a series of research projects that are of great importance (Lazarus, 1966; Lazarus *et al.*, 1974).

Lazarus broke through the prevailing biased interest for the biological aspects of the stress phenomenon and elaborated a cognitive stress theory: he pointed out that perception and individual colouring play an important, if not essential part in the development of stress. The stress reaction depends on what an individual considers dangerous or threatening. A yound child, walking along a ravine, does not perceive any dangers; an adult, however, will experience fear and, as a consequence, may lose his balance. In this approach cognitive factors are assigned the most important place.

Characteristic for the development of the stress-theme is (1) the fact that more and more different scientists are interested in stress; it is increasingly a matter of an interdisciplinary approach; (2) the fact that there has been a shift from the biologically, more individually oriented approach, towards a more environmentally oriented one.

In the field of work- and organizational psychology too the stress concept obtained its own position under the label 'organizational stress' (Kahn *et al.*, 1964). Characteristic for the 20th century is the growing complexity of organizations: increasing specialization, more mutual interdependence, more complicated tasks. Organizations can make people prosper, but the opposite is also possible: people can be frustrated in their career and fall ill because of bad working conditions.

As early as the 1920s, physicians were interested in the pathological aspects of industrial society. During that period Southard, Jarett and Adler, pioneers in the USA, addressed themselves actively more to a 'mental hygiene of industry'. Thus, the field of 'occupational psychiatry' (McLean, 1974) was developed.

After World War II more socio-psychologically oriented research was conducted on the phenomenon of alienation (estrangement, helplessness) in industry. Blauner (1964) and also Kornhauser (1965) found that alienation from work, together with a number of physical complaints accompanying such an alienation, are found more often in people who perform monotonous, strictly controlled and supervised work at an assembly line. This research was the precursor to other developments.

A number of universities in the USA engaged in 'occupational mental health'. The most important influence emanated from the Institute of Social Research of the University of Michigan in Ann Arbor, where in the early 1960s Kahn, French, Caplan, Cobb and Quinn developed a research programme. These researchers succeeded in finding a number of stress-inducing factors within organizations and in precisely defining these factors and indicating how they are connected with unfavourable mental and physical effects: strains (French and Caplan, 1972).

3. THE STRAINED BODY: STRESS AS A PHYSIOLOGICAL PHENOMENON

The notion that various physical processes can be extremely activated is an old one. It was only in 1956, however, that Selye developed a theory about this phenomenon. He found that extreme stimulations of a divergent nature brings about a certain typical endocrine reaction pattern. He did not connect specific stimulations with specific reactions: stress can be induced by many different means. Actually, he was not particularly interested in those causes (stimuli); more important to him was the universal reaction pattern (General Adaptation Syndrome or GAS) occurring in characteristic phases.

The GAS consists of three phases: an alarm-response accompanied by a shock and a counter-shock reaction, next a resistance phase and finally exhaustion or recovery. Incidentally, Selye believes that some stress is necessary for people to function. He wanted to demonstrate, however, the especially damaging effect of excessive and continuous stress.

Cannon has contributed much to the development of psychosomatic and socio-biological medicine (see Henry and Stephens, 1977). In this branch of medical science a lot of knowledge was accrued about the relation between stress and the development of cardio-vascular diseases, intestinal disorders, etc.

In addition, psychologists also have an eye for the fact that the human body is not equally strained under all circumstances. We find these ideas in the so-called activation theory, in which the concept of 'arousal' is the most important one. Over a period of 24 hours, great changes take place in the physiological activation of individuals; this condition can vary from deep sleep to extreme arousal (as in conflicts).

Hebb (1955) assumed that the organism needs an 'optimal level of arousal'; organisms function most effectively when this level is reached. Behaviour that helps the organism to achieve this optimum will be reinforced. In certain situations the activation of an organism can be too strong or too weak, and in both cases it overshoots its mark and the most probable result is stress.

On the basis of these views, Defares (1976) presents the following descriptions: 'Negative stress can be described as a state of activation that affects the homeostasis, whereby this disturbance performs no function for the individual's chances of survival but, on the contrary, can be seen as harmful. If this happens frequently and over a longer period of time, then permanent tissue damage can be the result'. 'Positive stress can be explained as: an activation that temporarily affects the homeostasis, however, it is *instrumental* for the individual's chances of survival'.

In the following section we shall further explore the conditions that allow the disturbance mentioned in the definition to occur.

4. PROBLEMS IN STRESS RESEARCH: THE SOCIO-PSYCHOLOGICAL APPROACH

In spite of the progress made in the medical field, a number of marginal notes can be made concerning these developments. The first concerns the neglect of the possible causes of stress: stress researchers generally have little insight into the causal connections between stimulus and response.

At the same time, there is a growing confusion in stress terminology. Some researchers define stress as unpleasant physical and mental reactions, others exhaustively search for the causes of stress, defining their stress concept in terms of these causes, others again emphasize the interactional aspects of stress. The complexity of this becomes clear from the description by Lazarus (1978): 'If, as we suggested, the meaning sphere encompassed by the term stress is any event in which environmental or internal demands (or both) tax or exceed the adaptive resources of an individual, social system, or tissue system, this makes stress a very broad concept, encompassing as it does a social system, an individual system (psychological) or a tissue system (physiological)' (p. 16). In the interaction between individual and environment, the individual's adaptive resources are *exceeded*; this is the essence of the modern theories.

When 'individual' and 'environment' are mentioned, other levels than the strict physiological ones emerge. Since Selye, various developments, pointing more towards psychology, have surfaced. Thus, Lazarus and Launier (1978) developed the 'appraisal'-concepts, of which the perception of stress is the most important one. The epidemiologists Holmes and Rahe (1967) developed methods for scoring and processing in a stress-index events that cause a lot of stress in people's lives, an approach in which the environment holds a key-position. The cardiologists Rosenman and Friedman (1974) designed a coronary risk-profile, the A/B typology, outlining a behavioral pattern connected with stress and coronary heart disease. In Michigan, French and Caplan, Kahn, Cobb and many others collaborated on a stress research project and arrived at an integrated research approach. They distinguished a number of stressors (i.e. what individuals experience as stress in the environment) and a number of strains (the consequences for the individual). They also assumed that personality traits exert a mediating influence on the relation between stressors and strains.

The central position of the role concept in the thinking of the Michigan researchers is striking. Particularly Kahn *et al.* (1964) in this respect based themselves on Merton (see his classical article on the 'role-set'; Merton, 1957).

Below, some of the most important aspects of this model are discussed and documented from the literature. We shall proceed from the integration model of De Wolff, Reiche and Van Dijkhuizen; for a detailed description of all elements, we refer to Van Vucht Tijssen *et al.* (1978).

5. STRESS RESEARCH MODELS

The stress literature knows a multitude of complex models. In these models, various variables and levels of variables—sociological, psychological, physiological—and various feedback mechanisms are built in. Unfortunately, it seems that these models only rarely function in the research. A favourable exception are the models of researchers working in the Michigan tradition. One of these models is Kahn's (1970), represented in figure 1, where the main elements of the chain are assumed to be causally connected. The objective environment has a direct causal influence on the perceived environment, which in its turn has a causal influence on the individual's reactions which may lead to sickness. The interpretation of the situation holds a key-position in this model. How an individual will respond to his environment is influenced also by the conditioning variables 'personality traits' and 'interpersonal relations'. Other members of the Michigan group, French and Caplan (1972) among others, constructed different models. Striking differences with Kahn are:
—the objective environment is assigned a less important role: according to

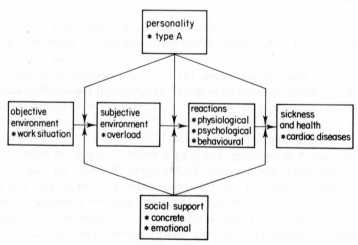

Figure 1. The stress model of Kahn (1970).

these authors, the impact of subjective factors is the main issue in the development of strain;

—all elements in the model are elaborated and precisely specified;

—social support is regarded as a stressor rather than a moderator variable;

—the personality traits are worked out in more detail and have the position of moderator variable.

As Driessen (1979) notes, the members of the Michigan group have generally confined themselves to research on a number of separate relations between the variables, usually from a cross-sectional rather than a longitudinal perspective.

The models of Kahn (1964, 1970) and French and Caplan (1972) were integrated into one new model, represented in figure 2. The Stress Group at Nijmegen University uses this model pursuing the line of research begun at Michigan in a more advanced form. Thus, a longitudinal framework has been realized and documentation is collected for the cross-validation of research results across various professional groups. Additionally, a revised version of

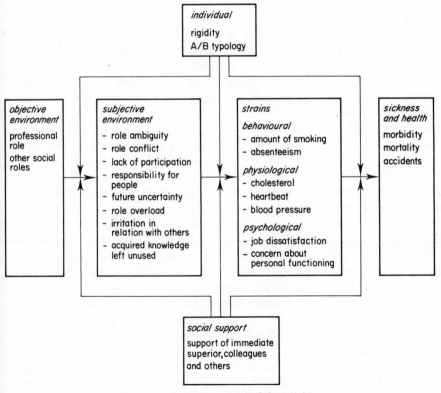

Figure 2. The stress model of the Michigan group.

the Questionnaire on Organizational Stress (VOS) is now available (Winnubst, 1980; van Dijkhuizen, 1980; Reiche, 1981; van Bastelaer and van Beers, 1982).

6. TIME-PRESSURE AND TIME-ANXIETY: STRESS AT THE PERSONALITY LEVEL

Personality is an important factor in the development of stress. Lazarus already indicated that the way in which a person interprets a situation is of great importance for the occurrence or non-occurrence of stress problems.

The interpretation of a situation is related to an individual's personality structure. A very competitive person will regard a situation in which he had the worst of it as more threatening than someone who is not competitive. There are all kinds of personality aspects that correlate with the development of stress: a conformist will feel threatened by situations that require originality, a submissive person will not be able to adjust to a situation that requires initiative, etc.

At present, one personality syndrome in particular plays a major role in stress research: the so-called A/B typology of Rosenman and Friedman (1974). There are many indications that the clock and the watch have become more and more important in industrial society. The measurement of time has become more sophisticated over the past hundred years and the pace of life has increased. Winnubst (1975) called this 'The Western time syndrome'. Modern man sees time as a quantitative, economic property; 'time is money', time can be wasted.

Rosenman and Friedman called this mental and behavioural pattern the type-A behaviour. On the basis of experience and research, they adopted a theory that is unacceptable to many cardiologists: 'In the absence of a type A behaviour pattern, coronary heart disease almost never occurs before seventy years of age, regardless of the fatty foods eaten, the cigarettes smoked or the lack of exercise. But when this behaviour pattern *is* present, coronary heart disease can easily erupt in one's thirties or forties' (Rosenman and Friedman, 1974, p. 9).

Verhagen *et al.* (1982) demonstrated in their research that people who have had a coronary tend to be more depressive than healthy people, show more positive fear of failure and worry more about lack of time (time-anxiety). Jenkins (1971) arrived at a 'coronary prone behavioural syndrome'. Individuals who are subject to this syndrome are characterized by extreme competitiveness, an urge to achieve, aggression, haste, impatience, restlessness, hyper-alertness, tension, and time-pressure.

This competitive person, who continually lives under time-pressure and worries about lack of time, is found in many organizations. To what extent do organizations call for such a behavioural pattern? Are there functions for which an A-type behavioural style is required? Some authors say that this type of behaviour is an extreme variant of what is socially highly recommended and positively rewarded. Others think the A-type behaviour is dysfunctional and that the better jobs are only for the quiet, detached, contemplative B-types (see also Matthews, 1982).

Generally, the personality traits mentioned in stress research have a mediating status (Caplan et al. 1975). From the above-mentioned research on middle managers it appeared 'that for A-type middle managers the dimension "relations to others", for example, shows a strong relation to psychical and psychosomatic complaints and that the dimension "role ambiguity" shows a clear relation to "higher blood pressure"' (van Vucht Tijssen et al., 1978, p. 228).

It is of interest to relate this type-A behaviour to the above-mentioned physiological processes. The theory of the psychologist Glass (1977) is important in this respect. A-types demonstrate hyper-responsiveness with regard to challenging situations, meaning that they always expose themselves to fight-situations. If they fail to succeed, they will, much more so than B-types, start to achieve less and to feel helpless (learned helplessness).

It should also be pointed out that many more personality traits are of importance in stress research than those mentioned here, such as rigidity, conformism, suppression of aggression, dogmatism, authoritarianism, internal versus external control, etc. It is impossible to elaborate all of these factors here. For good overviews see Glass (1977), Dembroski (1978), and Reiche (1981).

Having emphasized the personal style, we can now move on to the contextual factors that affect an individual. What environmental factors will induce A-type behaviour and, frequently, excessive arousal? One influential context factor is the work-atmosphere. This has links with the concept of organizational stress and with role theory. The Michigan group especially (e.g. French and Caplan, 1972); Kahn et al., 1964) made room for concepts such as role conflict, role ambiguity, and role overload. In the following section, the main elements of the Michigan approach are further elaborated.

7. THE OVERLOADED ROLE

Role overload is one of the factors in research on organizational stress. Sales (1969) described this concept as follows: 'role overload means a condition in which the individual is faced with a set of obligations which, *taken as a set*, requires him to do more than he is able to in the time available' (p. 325).

Such a description offers a number of interesting starting points. Role overload obviously has to do with lack of time and too many activities. In the case of too many activities, we speak of quantitative overload; when an individual has to perform tasks that are too difficult for him, we speak of qualitative overload (French and Caplan, 1972). Lack of time is also essential for type-A behaviour: for example, the 'hurry sickness' described by Rosenman and Friedman, 1974 (see section 6). It is important to know the origin of this haste: does an individual seek for role overload within the organization, or does the organization confront the individual with overload up to some breaking-point?

The relation between the role bearer and the other employees is essential in role overload: it is a complex transaction. The role bearer may be bombarded by expectations; a force which he eventually cannot cope with. A sensible tactic then is to organize 'role negotiation' or 'role bargaining' (Harrison, 1973), whereby the threatened individual tries to organize his obligations with or without outside help. Nevertheless, some individuals do not appreciate a simplification of their tasks and continue their 'Sysiphus complex' (Wolf, 1961).

In research on middle management (van Vucht Tijssen et al., 1978), role overload was shown to be related to physical complaints and, even more clearly, to greater obesity, higher blood pressure and more smoking. In Sales' (1969) and House's (1974) review articles the assumed relation between role overload and a higher coronary risk was documented. Many studies emphasize the harmful increase of serum-cholesterol that occurs with stress. Friedman et al. (1958) demonstrated that this is caused by a higher stress level (influenced, for example, by working under a deadline).

It is, thus, no exaggeration to say that role overload is an element to be rejected within organizations, especially because of the, in the long run, higher risk of illness and exhaustion. However, research is still needed on whether self-inflicted overload and overload inflicted by others make a significant difference.

8. CONFLICTING ROLE-ASPECTS

Organizations usually are complex networks; the people who come to work for them have many connections with other social institutions (family, political parties, community life, church, etc.). Working people are on the crossroads of various conflicting expectations. Kahn et al. (1964) described role conflict as 'the simultaneous occurrence of two (or more) sets of pressures, such that compliance with one would make more difficult compliance with the other' (p. 19).

Some professions or jobs are characterized by a higher degree of role conflict than others. People in mediating positions appear to be the most vulnerable: bosses, personnel managers, head-nurses; in general, middle management. These individuals are in the centre of a network of pressures. The personnel manager is in a sandwich position. The organizational staff is often his prime frame of reference and he wants to belong to this group in the first place. However, his subordinates will often expect his solidarity in many different situations. He must dare to stand up for the man at a lower level. This forces him to compromise, which results in both parties mistrusting him (van Beers and Winnubst, 1977).

The above is an example of the so-called 'inter-sender conflict' (two different role senders make contradictory demands) and 'inter-role conflict' (one and the same person holds contradictory positions).

Research by Kahn et al. (1964), Shirom et al. (1973), and Caplan et al. (1975) suggests that being in a role conflict situation is often associated with little job satisfaction, obesity and a higher coronary risk. Moreover, House and Rizzo (1972) found more feelings of anxiety and tension and a higher degree of fatigue in cases of role conflict.

The conclusion is that role conflict is an important stressor, although there are indications that this is more the case for the white collar professions than for blue collar factory workers (Caplan et al., 1975).

9. THE AMBIGUOUS ROLE

The adverse effects of role conflict can be compared to the adverse effects of so-called role ambiguity. People in an organization sometimes do not have sufficient information about what they are expected to do and especially about how they are to perform a task. Lack of structure is characteristic of jobs, expecially of those implying work with a kind of open assignment. This deficiency can be remedied through job evaluation, job descriptions and education.

In the Dutch research on middle management (van Vucht Tijssen et al., 1978), ambiguity emerged as the most powerful stressor. Too much role ambiguity correlated significantly with psychological and psychosomatic complaints, with higher heartbeat frequency, with concern for personal functioning, and with higher absenteeism (see also van der Graaf and Huizinga, 1969).

Obviously, in many cases, there is a need for more structure Nonetheless, fulfillment of these needs imposed from above can overshoot its mark since autonomy is also highly appreciated by many people.

10. THE FIXED ROLE AND THE MALE MENOPAUSE

Many people experience the frightening feeling of being fixed in their role within the organization. Most threatening is monotonous work, or work without challenge, whereby time seems to stand still (Kornhauser, 1965; Shephard, 1971).

Some people develop a strong aversion to their job or their position in the organization. Freedom of movement can be restricted through different circumstances. Secondary working conditions are sometimes so favourable that people often stay on 'unvoluntarily'.

Middle age is an especially problematic period for many employees, particularly for those in middle and higher management. One's career is no longer growing, tension has vanished and there are no further possibilities. Constandse (1972) terms this the 'male menopause'. Kets de Vries (1978) suggests that the midcareer crisis is actually appropriate to our society; a society, based on achievement and spurred on by the dominant work-ethos. This orientation implies that one should rise in one's career and rising means promotion. Room at the top of the pyramid is limited, however. As a result, employees get frustrated exactly during that period of their life when their career opportunities are becoming decisively clear. Because of, among other things, career frustrations, middle age is often accompanied by a series of vague psychoneurotic and psychosomatic complaints, including heart neurosis, headaches, lower back complaints, fatigue, and overweight.

In view of these problems, organizations should spend more time on career supervision. Employees should be made aware of the problems they may expect to occur. Also, by making a psychological cost/benefit analysis, male menopause victims can come to understand that not being promoted within the organization may also have its positive side.

Being promoted too quickly may also lead to psychological and physical problems, especially when the type-A behaviour is extremely activated. However, individuals who rise too fast within an organization do not show more stress than those who do not (Hinkle, 1968). This is attributed to the following mechanism: 'Success in career may be perceived as having control over one's destiny and can serve as a buffer to lessen frustration and combat stress' (Kets de Vries, 1978).

These days, lack of perspective can also be found in terms of industries that threaten to be closed down, early retirement, the increased chance (and possibility) of ending up living on social security, etc. In research on middle management, uncertainty about the future was found to be strongly related to psychological and psychosomatic complaints (van Vucht Tijssen et al., 1978).

On the other hand, too much mobility of individuals within or between organizations can also have detrimental effects. A change of career, such as moving house, settling into a new job, a change of life style, participation in training programmes, can also cause a lot of stress (Kets de Vries et al., 1977).

11. THE IMPORTANCE OF SOCIAL SUPPORT

There are quite a few people who manage to do a lot of work in rather unstructured situations, without this leading to health problems. On closer examination, one finds that their functioning is determined by environmental supports, including a superior who socializes in the right way, colleagues who help out at the right moment, as well as a domestic situation in which it is possible to relax and get the necessary rest.

The relations with others, both at home and at work, are often crucial for an employee's well-being. This makes high demands upon social skills. An employee should build up a good relation of trust with his environment. On the one hand, he should defend his rights and prove himself but, on the other, he should not rely too much on his capacities only.

As mentioned earlier, every member of an organization is exposed to a 'bombardment' of expectations while not all expectations can be met. The question then arises as to how to change or divert these expectations, and as to which expectations can be met. In organizational psychology, too little attention was paid to these subtle exchange processes. The contribution of the social exchange theory has been unjustly ignored here (Chadwick-Jones, 1976). Another important question is whether the individual has access to mechanisms to realize this social exchange in a legitimate and open manner. In other words, are there possibilities for job evaluation, participation, job description, etc.?

In research on middle management it was found that inadequate willingness of others to help at work is related to considerably more smoking as well as to anxiety about one's own functioning, job dissatisfaction and physical complaints (van Vucht Tijssen *et al.*, 1978).

French (1973) emphasized the fact that a good relationship between employer and employee serves as a buffer against the occurrence of stress. He found a significant positive relation between role ambiguity and serum-cortisol level for employees who had a bad relationship with their employer. This pattern disappeared if a good relationship existed between employer and employee. Winnubst *et al.* (1982) showed that social support buffers the impact of work-related stressors on psychological and behavioural strains, but that there is no such buffering effect on health strains.

12. THE MUTUAL ADJUSTMENT OF INDIVIDUAL AND ROLE

The stress-themes dealt with thus far emphasize the role of either the individual or the environment. In this respect, questions arise resembling those concerning type-A behaviour. To what extent does such behaviour cause trouble for an individual within the organization, or does the organization actually reward this life-style? In the past few years, an approach was developed that offers more insight into these problems: the 'person-environment fit' theory of French *et al.* (1974). They distinguish two kinds of agreement between an individual and the job environment. The first 'fit' is between an individual's capabilities and the possibilities presented by the job. If there is no such adequate co-ordination between the individual and the environment, then strains like anxiety, depression and dissatisfaction have an increasing chance of occurrence.

By calculating the discrepancy between questions about actual job strain and desired job strain, quantitative insight into the 'p-e fit' can be gained (French, 1973; French *et al.*, 1974). Van Harrison (1976) points to the significance of this approach for, for example, job design. General improvements in the organization cannot be effectively made if the possibilities and wishes of those involved are not considered. Many job design programmes assume that their proposed changes meet the need for more challenge and participation of those involved. The 'p-e fit' theory differentiates these assumptions by explaining that not every employee is willing to co-operate in this. Van Harrison notes in this respect: 'Those who want more complex and challenging jobs can take advantage of the opportunities opened up to them. Those individuals who prefer simpler jobs can choose to delegate decision making to others who want this job demand' (van Harrison, 1976, p. 31).

Adequate adjustment of the individual to his job environment and vice versa is therefore important. This is often not the case and the individual consequently experiences strain. In such cases, a number of individual tactics are available that can bring temporary relief. The individual can defend himself against strain, even if structural improvement is not immediately possible. In such cases the Anglo-Saxon literature speaks of 'coping techniques'.

13. COPING WITH STRESS

We can state that in modern life stress is inevitable and certainly so in complex organizations. The question of how to cope with stress therefore is almost more important than the question of its origin. Some researchers closely connect 'stress' and 'coping' and point out that the amount of strain depends on the number of coping tactics available to an invidual. Stress arises only when people discover that they cannot cope adequately with a difficult situation (Mechanic, 1974).

In the literature, generally two different styles of coping with stress are distinguished: the 'avoider' as opposed to the 'coper'. The avoider solves his stress problems simply by denying them, while the coper seeks out stress situations in order to learn how to cope with them. The coping issue is extensively dealt with in the classic survey of Lazarus et al. (1974).

Another distinction is that between repression and sensitization, which is closely related to the afore-mentioned division. With repression the emphasis lies on defense mechanisms that keep the individual from adequately facing reality, but at the same time protect him from too much stress. Sensitization means looking for solutions by turning one's attention to the outside world.

Lazarus et al. strongly criticize the literature on coping. Most studies emphasize the psychological aspects of the coping process and neglect the interaction between individual and environment.

Moreover, the above-mentioned division of coping-styles is too narrow. In organizational psychology a much broader coping-literature has developed (Kets de Vries, 1977; Cooper and Marshall, 1978; van Vucht Tijssen et al., 1978; Newman and Beehr, 1979). Kets de Vries distinguishes two trends of coping with stress: the courses an individual can take on the one hand, and the possibilities to arrive at stress-coping within organizations, on the other.

The individual can start off by tackling the so-called risk factors: smoking less, eating less, taking more exercise, more relaxation, using less salt, etc. This will supposedly lead to improvement of his physical condition and, through this, he will experience less strain. Also, techniques promising people more control over various physical processes are being rapidly developed. Benson's research (1974) on the relaxation-response should be mentioned, as well as Transcendental Meditation, Zen, Yoga, Biofeedback, Autogenic Training, Bio-energetics, etc. Unfortunately, there is a lot of chaff among the wheat.

Other courses are those of psychotherapy, by which traumas can be lessened and ways for re-orientation discussed. It is often very difficult for people to find course of another life-style. Rosenman and Friedman (1974) present some suggestions, such as substituting the hectic, competitive A-type life-pattern by a more contemplative and balanced B-type pattern. However, these authors are not so clear about how to bring about such a change. The concern with type-A behaviour has recently led to programmes designed to modify these behaviours. Relaxation, rational emotive therapy, and biofeedback are some of the techniques used (Roskies, 1979).

We are also faced with a number of meta-psychological questions such as the extent to which B-type behaviour is desirable, especially in an economic recession. Ambivalence regarding this issue is also found in research on middle management. On the one hand, for certain categories type-A behaviour plays a mediating role between stressors and strains (stress experienced personally) and, thus, can sometimes contribute to the development of a coronary. It is, on the other hand, doubtful whether it is desirable to exclude, via selection, the A-type from certain functions. It has been noted, for example, that 'Often the A-types are exactly the ones who perform well in an organization. They are the hard workers, who want to make progress, who aspire after a middle management position themselves' (van Vucht Tijssen et al., 1978).

With the possibility to intervene via selection, we arrive at yet another category of intervention possibilities, viz. the measures that can be taken at the organizational level. Kets de Vries mentions measures that have to do with the career of employees, such as careful selection and appointment, good training programmes, adequate supervision of critical moments in the career, such as entrance upon one's duties, promotion and retirement or discharge. '. . . the social contact between individual and organization should be clearly spelled out to limit confusion and prevent the existence of unrealistic expectations, much care should be given to arrive at compatibility between organizational role and individual' (Kets de Vries, 1977, p. 52).

In conclusion, it can be stated that 'coping' at an individual level can possibly bring about some temporary relief. Beech et al. (1982) present a good and recent review of behavioural techniques for managing stress. If the structural causes remain unchanged, however, exhaustion of the individual may be expected. An impending stress problem requires activities at various levels simultaneously. Job overload will have to be reduced to more workable proportions; roles with too many ambiguities should be restructured; the non-supporting role should be revised and be given more support by employer and colleagues.

Such processes require knowledge of the individual's possibilities and wishes, of his 'arousal' and 'stress' levels, and also knowledge of the organizational possibilities. Mutual adjustment of these levels demands a continuous and systematic approach, while no one should think that a realistic optimal adjustment is easily, if ever, attainable.

REFERENCES

Bastelaer, A. van, Beers, W. van (1982), *Organisatiestress en de personeelfunctionaris* [Organizational stress and the personnel manager]. Lisse: Swets & Zeitlinger.

Beech, H. R., Burns, L. E., Sheffield, B. F. (1982), *A behavioural approach to the management of stress. A practical guide to techniques.* New York: Wiley. 1982.

Beehr, T. A., Newman, J. E. (1978), Job stress, employee health, and organizational effectiveness: A facet analysis, model, and literature review. *Personnel Psychology*, **31**, 665–699.

Beers, W. van, Winnubst, J. (1977), *Het rolconflict van de personeelchef; Een literatuurstudie.* [The role conflict of the personnel manager; A study of the literature]. Stressgroep Nijmegen, publication no. 1. University of Nijmegen, Psychological Laboratory.

Benson, M. (1974), Your innate asset for combating stress. *Harvard Business Review*, **52**, 4, 49–60.

Blauner, R. (1964), *Alienation and freedom: The factory worker and his industry.* Chicago: University of Chicago Press.

Bosch, F. A. J. van den, Petersen, C. (1980), *Economisch-Statistische Berichten* [Economic-Statistical Reports], **65**, 3238, 52–58.

Cannon, W. B. (1935), Stresses and strains of homeostasis. *American Journal of Medical Science*, **189**, 1.

Caplan, R. D., Cobb, S., French, J. R. P., Van Harrison, R., Pinneau, S. R. (1975), *Job demands and worker health.* HEW Publication (NIOSH).

Chadwick-Jones, J. K. (1976), *Social exchange theory: Its structure and influence in social psychology.* London: Academic Press.

Constandse, W. J. (1972), Mid-40's man: A neglected personnel problem. *Personnel Journal*, **51**, 2, 129.

Cooper, C. L., Marshall, J. (1978), *Understanding executive stress.* London: MacMillan.

Defares, P. B. (1976), *Socialisatie, adaptatie en stress* [Socialization, adaptation and stress]. Amsterdam: Van Gorcum.

Dembroski, T. M., Weiss, S. M., Shields, J. L., Haynes, S. G., Feinleib, M. (Eds.) (1978), *Coronary-prone behavior.* New York: Springer.

Dijkhuizen, N. van (1980), *From stressors to strains. Research into their interrelationships.* Lisse: Swets & Zeitlinger.

Dirken, J. M. (1967), *Het meten van stress in industriële situaties. Een multidisciplinaire ontwikkeling van een algemeen diagnosticum* [Measuring stress in industrial situations. A multidisciplinary development of a general diagnostics]. Groningen: Wolters.

Driessen, J. G. M. (1979), *Stressoren, sociale steun en strains* [Stressors, social support and strains]. Stressgroep Nijmegen, publication no. 13. University of Nijmegen, Psychological Laboratory.

French, J. R. P. (1973), Person-role fit. *Occupational Mental Health*, **3**, 1.

French, J. R. P., Caplan, R. D. (1972), Organizational stress and individual strain. In: Marrow, A. J. (Ed.), *The failure of success*. New York: Amacom, 30–67.

French, J. R. P., Rodgers, Cobb, S. (1974), Adjustment as person-environment fit. In: Coelho, G., Hamburg, D. A., Adams, J. E. (Eds.), *Coping and adaptation*. New York: Basic Books.

Friedman, M., Rosenman, R. H., Carroll, V. (1958), Changes in serum cholesterol and blood clotting time in men subjected to cyclic variation of occupational stress. *Circulation*, **17**, 852–861.

Glass, D. C. (1977), *Behavior patterns, stress, and coronary disease*. Hillsdale (N. J.): Lawrence Erlbaum.

Graaf, M. H. K. van der, Huizinga, J. (1969), *Bedrijfsenquête staf- en kaderpersoneel* [Industrial questionnaire for staff- and managerial personnel]. The Hague: SER (Commission on Stimulation of Productivity).

Grinker, R. R., Spiegel, J. P. (1945), *Men under stress*. Philadelphia: Blakiston.

Grosfeld, J. A. M. (1978), *Arbeidsongeschiktheid in Nederland: Omvang van het probleem en inventarisatie van onderzoek vanuit de gedragswetenschappen* [Disablement in The Netherlands: Size of the problem and inventory of the research done from the behavioral science perspective]. Stressgroep Nijmegen, publication no. 9. University of Nijmegen, Psychological Laboratory.

Harrison, R. (1973), Role negotiation: A tough-minded approach to team development. In: Bennis, W. S., Berleer, D. E., Schein, E. H., Steek, F. I. (Eds.), *Interpersonal dynamics*. Homewood (Ill.): Dorsey Press, 467–479.

Hebb, D. O. (1955), Drives and C.N.S. *Psychological Review*, **62**.

Henry, J. P., Stephens, P. M. (1977), *Stress, health and the social environment. A sociobiologic approach to medicine*. Berlin: Springer.

Hinkle, J. E. (1968), Occupation, education and coronary heart disease. *Science*, **161**, 230–246.

Holmes, T. H., Rahe, R. H. (1967), The social adjustment rating scale. *Journal of Psychosomatic Research*, **11**, 2, 213–218.

House, J. S. (1974), Occupational stress and coronary heart disease: A review and theoretical integration. *Journal of Health and Social Behavior*, **15**, 12–27.

House, R. J., Rizzo, J. R. (1972), Role conflict and ambiguity as critical variables in a model of organizational behavior. *Organizational Behavior and Human Performance*, **7**, 467–505.

Jenkins, C. D. (1971), Psychologic and social precursors of coronary disease. *New England Journal of Medicine*, **284**, 244–255, 307–317.

Kahn, L. (1970), Some propositions towards a researchable conceptualization of stress. In: McGrath, J. W. (Ed.), *Social and psychological factors of stress*. New York: Holt, Rinehart and Winston, 97–104.

Kahn, R. L., Wolfe, D. M., Quinn, R. P. (1964), *Organizational stress; Studies in role conflict and ambiguity*. New York: Wiley.

Kalsbeek, J. W. H. (1967), *Mentale belasting, theoretische en experimentele exploraties ter ontwikkeling van meetmethoden* [Mental load, theoretical and experimental explorations in behalf of the development of measuring methods]. Amsterdam: Van Gorcum.

Kets de Vries, M. F. R. (1978), The midcareer conundrum. *Organizational Dynamics*, Autumm, 54–62.

Kets de Vries, M. F. R., Zaleznik, A., Howard, J. H. (1977), *Stress reactions and organizations: The minotaur revisited.* Working paper 7530. Montreal: McGill University.

Kleber, R. J. (1982), *Stressbenaderingen in de psychologie* [Stress approaches in psychology]. Deventer: Van Loghum Slaterus.

Kornhauser, A. (1965), *Mental health of the industrial worker.* New York: Wiley.

Lazarus, R. S. (1966), *Psychological stress and the coping process.* New York: McGraw-Hill.

Lazarus, R. S., Averill, R., Opton, Jr., M. (1974), The psychology of coping: Issues of research and assessment. In: Coelho, G., Hamburg, A., Adams, J. E. (Eds.), *Coping and adaptation.* New York: Basic Books, 249–316.

Lazarus, R. S., Launier, R. (1978), Stress-related transactions between person and environment. In: Pervin, L. A., Lewis, M. (Eds.), *Perspectives in interactional psychology.* New York: Plenum.

McGrath, J. E. (1976), Stress and behavior in organization. In: Dunnette, M. D. (Ed.), *Handbook of industrial and organizational psychology.* Chicago: Rand McNally, 1351–1396.

McLean, A. A. (Ed.) (1974), *Occupational stress.* Springfield: Thomas.

Matthews, K. A. (1982), Psychological perspectives on the Type A behavior pattern. *Psychological Bulletin,* **91**, 2, 293–323.

Mechanic, A. (1974), Social structure and personal adaptation: Some neglected dimensions. In: Coelho, G., Hamburg, D., Adams, J. E. (Eds.), *Coping and adaptation.* New York: Basic Books.

Merton, R. (1957), *Social theory and social structure.* Glencoe (Ill.): Free Press.

Newman, J. E., Beehr, T. A. (1979), Personal and organizational strategies for handling job stress: A review of research and opinion. *Personnel Psychology,* **32**, 1–43.

Reiche, H. M. J. K. I. (1981), *Stress aan het werk* [Stress at work]. Lisse: Swets & Zeitlinger.

Rosenman, R. H., Friedman, M. (1974), *Type A behavior and your heart.* Greenwich (Conn.): Fawcett.

Roskies, E. (1979), Considerations in developing a treatment program for the coronary-prone (Type A) behavior pattern. In: Davidson, P. (Ed.), *Behavioral medicine: Changing health life styles.* New York: Bruner/Mazel.

Sales, S. M. (1969), Organizational role as a risk factor in coronary heart disease. *Administrative Science Quarterly,* **14**, 325–336.

Selye, H. (1956), *The stress of life.* New York: McGraw-Hill.

Shepherd, J. M. (1971), *Automation and alienation.* Cambridge (Mass.): MIT Press.

Shirom, A., Eden, D., Silberwasser, S., Kellerman, J. J. (1973), Job stresses and risk factors in coronary heart disease among occupational categories in kibbutzim. *Social Science and Medicine,* **7**, 875–892.

Stouffer, S. A. (1950), *The American soldier.* Princeton: Princeton University Press.

Van Harrison, R. (1976), *Job stress as person environment misfit.* A symposium presented at the 84th Annual Convention of the APA, September 1976.

Van Harrison, R., Person Environment fit and job stress. In: Cooper, C. L., Payne, R. (Eds.), *Stress at work.* New York: Wiley, 175–205.

Verhagen, F. H., Nass, C. H. Th., Winnubst, J. A. M. (1982), *Hart en stress: Een psychosociale benadering* [Stress and the heart: A psychosocial approach]. Deventer: Van Loghum Slaterus.

Vucht Tijssen, J. van, Broecke, A. A. J. van den, Dijkhuizen, N. van, Reiche, H. M. J. K. I., Wolff, Ch. J. de (1978), *Middenkader en stress. Een onderzoek naar de problemen van het middle management* [Middle management and stress. A study of the problems of middle management]. The Hague: COB/SER.

Winnubst, J. A. M. (1975), *Het westerse tijdsyndroom* [The western time syndrome]. Amsterdam: Swets & Zeitlinger.
Winnubst, J. A. M., Marcelissen, F. H. G., Kleber, R. J. (1982), Effects of social support in the stressor-strain relationship: A Dutch sample. *Social Science and Medicine*, **16**, 475–482.
Wolf, S. (1961), Disease as a way of life. *Perspectives on Biological Medicine*, **4**, 288.

Handbook of Work and Organizational Psychology
Edited by P. J. D. Drenth, H. Thierry, P. J. Willems and C. J. de Wolff
© 1984, John Wiley & Sons, Ltd.

3.5.   Management development: A view from psychology

Jaap Huijgen and Roger Williams

1. INTRODUCTION

Management development has had a bad press in the psychological literature. For example, Campbell (1971, p. 565) concluded that although the training and development literature was voluminous, it was also 'non-empirical, non-theoretical, poorly written, dull and faddish to an extreme'. Hinrichs (1976) in his review refers to similar worries. And although another psychologist, Goldstein (1980), does appear to be slightly more positive in general, even he can still find cause enough for some trenchant observations. For example, in relation to the literature on management development, he comments (p. 254), 'much of the material in this area is dominated by low utility anecdotal presentations'.

There are many possible reasons why psychologists have voiced such criticisms of management development. For example, Hinrichs cites management developers lack of interest in theory, in contrast to their deep concern for face validity and attention getting. There is more emphasis on doing something than on analysing what ought to be done. There is a concentration on achieving short-term immediate goals to the exclusion of longer term issues.

The criticisms could also have their base in the difficulty of pinpointing exactly why an organization might undertake to develop its managers. There are a multitude of possible reasons. The most obvious ones are to improve performance in the current job or to equip the individual for some future role. But there may be much more subtle reasons. For example, using a manage-

Drs. J. H. Huijgen Prof. dr. A. R. T. Williams, Erasmus Universiteit, Fac. der Economische Wetenschappen. Burg. Oudlaan 50, 3062 PA ROTTERDAM.

ment development exercise primarily in order to bring individuals from different outlying parts of an organization together, so that they can get to know one another. Or sending a manager to an expensive programme in a foreign country as a mark of status. Or letting him relax for a week in a luxury hotel in the country as a reward for hard work or as a way of moving him quietly right out of the organization. And so on.

And if the possible reasons why organizations indulge in management development are so diverse, it is small wonder that such research as has been carried out has resulted in so few clear guidelines. But above all, perhaps psychologists have not appreciated much of the management development literature because of the vagueness of the term 'management'. Management for example can be (Becker 1968):

an activity of policy making and execution
a team in the organization
a group within a society
a body of knowledge.

If we have such difficulty in defining management, we naturally could face similar problems in discussing its development.

In this chapter we will attempt to side-step potential difficulties firstly by regarding as a manager anyone who has an element of policy making and execution in his job, and secondly by accepting the definition of management development as suggested by Hawrylyshyn (1979). He differentiates management development from, on the one hand, management training and, on the other, organizational development. He suggests we use management training to describe activities aimed at developing in managers highly specific and immediately useful skills. Whereas he sees management development as encompassing the whole complex process by which managers as individuals learn, grow and improve their ability to perform professional management tasks. And finally he suggests that organizational development should be used to describe a somewhat similar complex process but one whose aim is different. It is not only concerned with the manager as an individual, but its goal is much wider; the development of either the whole or at least major parts of an organization.

Given this broad definition of management development, this chapter will attempt to look at the processes involved from a psychological rather than from a practitioner's point of view.

And indeed, it could be said another reason why psychologists have been so dissatisfied with the work of researchers and practitioners in this field of management development may be because they have so often forsaken some psychological inputs that might have directed their efforts into different and perhaps more fruitful paths.

In order to clarify this point of view, in this chapter we will approach management development as a form of instructional plan and will use for our framework

those developed by Bruner (1966) and Glaser (1966). They suggested that an instructional plan comprises the following elements:
formulation of learning objectives
diagnosis of needs
organization of contents of learning experience
evaluation.

In accordance with this scheme our first section will be concerned with what the organization should develop in its managers, our second with the problem of when the organization should develop it, and our third with how the organization should develop it. Finally we will examine an evaluation of how successful our development attempts have been. Thus our emphasis throughout will be on management development from the organization's, as opposed to the individuals', point of view.

2. WHAT TO DEVELOP?

The emphasis in management development as far as the 'what to develop' issue is concerned has tended to be in one of two directions. Either, on a simple single topic approach where particular skills, techniques, attitudes or values are looked at in isolation from the environment in which they are used. Or secondly on a view that emphasizes the limited use, given the pace of modern change, of learning anything specific and the importance therefore of learning instead the general skill of how to learn.

The single topic approach in perhaps the most common form of management development and indeed the myriad of topics involved are truly amazing. Management developers who take this approach have in common a view of the manager as essentially a pro-active rather than a reactive individual. That is, as someone who could make things happen as opposed to someone who is primarily having to react to forces outside his own immediate control. The theory being that if a manager learns X, then he can also put X into operation, whether X be a new costing system, democratic leadership style, or how to be interviewed on television by journalists. Secondly, management developers take for granted that the manager can implement these new ideas or techniques, irrespective of the situation or organizational process in which he may find himself.

A psychologist might, in contrast, have stressed the necessity of examining both the manager's job itself and the organizational environment in which he is called upon to operate, before deciding on the kind of training to which he is to be submitted. Research which has attempted to carry out such examination has yielded some interesting observations (Fores and Sorge, 1981).

For example, it suggests that managers in general tend to be concerned with immediate day-to-day issues and to have very little time for reflection or planning. Stewart (1968) has described the 'grasshopper' nature of the managerial job jumping from one thing to another. Such 'jumps' can be very rapid and studies in activity rates have shown that two hundred separate incidents or episodes occurring during the normal eight hour day are not unusual for a middle manager, and Mintzberg (1973) found that, even for Chief Executives, more than half of their activities lasted less than nine minutes.

Again experience from research suggest that executives handle problems in fire fighting order—interspersing the significant and the trivial with no apparent particular order. They handle issues as they arise. They are thus clearly more reactive rather than pro-active.

We could also conclude that managers are very unlikely to be able to delegate. They spend between twenty-five and fifty per cent of their total time getting and receiving information (compared to spending between five and fifteen per cent of their time taking decisions and giving instructions). And the major way in which they obtain their information is by word of mouth. Thus most of their time is spent talking, normally in face to face situations at formal meetings or during informal contacts, and mostly with peers and colleagues and relatively seldom with superiors or subordinates (McCall, 1978).

Now to the extent that the information managers have is carried in their own heads and gleaned from their own network of contacts, the more difficult it will be to transfer that information to others. And because the job is so fragmented and so often interrupted, delegating to someone else may take more time than handling the issue oneself. Thus probably only straightforward, well defined problems and activities can ever be delegated easily. Not only is delegation likely to be difficult unless managers drastically change their work patterns, but so is any form of participative decision making. Their contacts with subordinates occur often but are very brief. Their work day is full of interruptions. They are used to reacting very fast to new problems based on their own personally gathered information and then taking a series of quick decisions. They have thus neither the time, the means nor the information for participation.

Clearly these are generalizations, and much more research needs to be done but, equally clearly, if there is any truth in the suggestions that the manager's job is as it has been described, then we must call into question some current management development activities. For example, those which advocate rational decision making or stress delegation and participative leadership styles. We can also suggest that there has been undue emphasis in the past on developing a leader's relations with his subordinates instead of developing the more frequent and often more difficult leader/peer group relations (Dubin, 1962).

And perhaps we need to think instead of how to improve our managers' abilities to plan in the midst of chaos' and to help them to become proficient at superficiality (Mintzberg, 1973).

Again we should perhaps spend more time, since our managers' job seems to depend primarily upon the spoken word, in developing their communication skills. The successful manager must have the ability to selectively 'hear', retain and transmit vast quantities of aural information and perhaps, even more difficult, selectively utilize the large amount of written information to which he is exposed, even though he has no more time left at the end of the day for reading (McCall, 1978).

And, finally perhaps we should rethink how we categorize managerial jobs. Grouping them according to level in hierarchy or to functional specialization is the classic approach. But already some (e.g. Stewart, 1976) have suggested other possible ways of grouping—for example according to the nature of the contacts required, or the nature of the work patterns. In terms of managerial development the latter would lead naturally to a suggestion that we should rotate managers through jobs not just according to functional differences, but also according to the work characteristics. Clearly, therefore, more detailed studies of what managers actually do are needed.

But there is also an approach which maintains that, because of the current pace of change in some organizations, it is not sensible to teach managers any specific job-related skills at all. This view stresses that any development must be at the level of learning how to learn rather than that of learning specific skills because the latter may soon become obsolete.

Such an approach is exemplified by the work of Argyris and Schön (1978) who describe their approach as 'deutero-learning' in which persons reflect on and enquire into their own previous learning. They try to discover what they have done in the past that facilitated or inhibited their previous learning and they then try and invent new strategies for learning based on this, the results of which can then become included in their individual images and maps of how the organization operates. It is important, in this view, that individuals should learn to question their own value structures. Such ideas about basic adult learning should be of interest to management developers (Argyris, 1976), but unfortunately as yet little research is available as to their usefulness (Eden et al., 1979).

Approaches which concentrate on what has been learnt in the past and why should also help to highlight another factor which has been conspicuously absent from most management development thinking for some time and yet which would be regarded, certainly by many social psychologists, as being of prime importance. This is the process side of management development (Goldstein, 1980). By this is meant the importance of considering management development as a system within the organization rather than as a separate entity.

There has been perhaps to date too much concern with what has been learnt and too little with why anything has or has not happened (Locke, 1977). Some studies concerning the hard-core unemployed in the United States and others which concentrated on the successful development of second careers (Kaufman, 1978) have both emphasized the important influence that the characteristics of an organization can have on the success of a development programme.

A simple first step towards further examination of this relationship has been suggested by Handy (1976). He has identified four alternative approaches to management development—each approach related to a particular organizational culture. In the 'power' culture key individual managers have great influence on decisions in the organization. The appropriate management development approach aims to help others model themselves on these key figures. In contrast, in the more bureaucratic 'role' culture, the job is more important than its holder. Development should therefore be additive, picking up the knowledge and skills relative to the job. In the 'task' culture the completion of project work provides a priority and the emphasis of development is upon the individual increasing his capacities. Finally, in the 'personal' culture where the organization exists only for the people in it, development cannot be planned at all but will occur through new work experiences.

Handy's ideas are based more on experience than experiment, but would suggest to us that developers need perhaps to spend less time actually running training courses and more in observation in the field, trying to tease out over time the subtle interplay of individual and organization.

So, in conclusion, we would take issue with the two simple models used to date in much of the work related to the 'what' issue in management development. We would prefer instead that more note should be taken of what managers actually do in the course of their jobs, and, since their amount of control over their situations is often so small that more emphasis should also be placed on investigating their relationships with their organizations.

3. WHEN SHOULD WE DEVELOP MANAGERS?

The possibility that the actual timing of the management development input might be of importance as well as its content and environment has not received much notice in the literature. It is as if, in the past, we have concluded that, if the content is interesting and the environment favourable, learning will automatically result. And yet common sense will tell us quite clearly that this is unlikely to be so. For example, training and development, however efficiently organized and presented, demand time and energy on the part of the learner and therefore an individual's willingness to undergo such experience will be dependent, at the very least, on his current work-load.

The problem of when an organization should expose an individual to a development input is thus primarily one of motivation: when is he most likely to be motivated to learn? Unfortunately, our knowledge of the conditions under which adults are motivated to learn leaves a lot to be desired, but we have some rough guidelines (see Knowles, 1973). Adults seem to be primarily motivated to solve what they perceive as important problems needing solutions. Thus they must see any profferred learning experience as being of immediate relevance to current issues. Secondly, they value their own experience highly and will not take kindly to being placed in situations where such experience is regarded as irrelevant or under-valued. Finally, mature adults see themselves as capable independent beings used to being able, to a degree at least, to control their own destinies. Therefore, they can be disturbed by being placed in essentially subordinate positions vis-à-vis others—for example in the classic teacher pupil situation.

Given these simple conclusions we can see that some situations are more likely to motivate learning in adults than others. These will be situations where they are faced with immediate important problems to which they do not have the answers. And such situations are most likely to occur at stages in their careers where the essence of their job, or of their basic life interests, changes.

For example, according to Katz and Kahn (1978), the essence of the job which a manager does will change at certain critical levels in the hierarchy. They have differentiated between three different levels. These are the policy formation or top management level, the policy implementation or middle management level, and finally the operational or junior management level. They maintain that the exercise of these three patterns of management calls for different cognitive styles, different types of managerial knowledge, and different affective characteristics. Hence the managerial skills appropriate to one level of the organization may be irrelevant or even dysfunctional at another level.

For example, they suggest that, at the top level of policy formulation, the cognitive skills required are to be able to conceptualize, appraise, predict and understand the demands and opportunities posed to the organization by its environment. And such top managers do not really need the persuasiveness, warmth and inter-personal skills which the middle management level of policy implementation will find irreplaceable as they endeavour to exercise their responsibility, without the necessary attendant power to control.

Again, the critical affective requirement for a top leader, according to Katz and Kahn, is that he or she be able to generate charisma, that magical aura with which people sometimes endow their leaders. Charisma derives from people's emotional needs and from the dramatic events that can be associated with the exercise of leadership. These can either stem from the fact that the situation itself is dramatic, such as in time of high danger or tension, or, in more normal circumstances, can be produced as a result of bold and imaginative acts of leadership. It is not an objective assessment by followers of a leader's ability to meet their specific needs. It is a matter of trust and requires social distance between leader and follower. It would thus be impossible for a lower level manager, caught up in the day-to-day intimacy of implementing or operating policy, to attempt to manage by charisma.

In contrast, middle management concerned primarily with implementing policy, will need, as far as cognitive skills are concerned, a high degree of knowledge about how the internal company systems work. They must be able to work out how much real freedom of manoeuvre they have. And as far as their affective skills are concerned, their major need is to be able to integrate the needs of their own primary group—their department or constituency or whatever—with the needs of the total organization. They need to be able to use referent power—a kind of power that depends on a bond of personal liking and respect.

Finally, at lower levels, where managers are engaged in operating routine procedures, we find that technical know-how is most often the critical cognitive skill required. They must be able to ensure that their people have an adequate flow of materials, proper tools and appropriate directives. And they must know enough about the tasks involved to be able to help them in cases of need and to be able to evaluate their subordinates' performance. The critical affective skill at this level will be an ability to be fair and equitable in the treatment of their subordinates. The rules themselves do not have to be seen as equitable but the ways in which they are applied, do.

Now clearly, if we follow Katz and Kahn's thinking, at least at the three gross levels of management which they distinguish, then when the individual passes from one to the other he is more likely to be ready for major development and change.

This concept of ripeness or maturity, of readiness to develop, has existed in other areas of psychology for some time. For example in considering the development of the human infant, Jordan (1968) suggests that critical periods can often be distinguished. He cites the example that if a child is kept tied to a crib so that it cannot stand, it will suffer no harm as long as it physically cannot stand. But once it reaches a maturation state wherein it is possible for it to stand, further restraint would definitely be harmful. After a given period of construction its legs will atrophy and it will remain a cripple for life. Seligman and Hager (1972) develop the argument further and conclude that all organisms appear to show a readiness to acquire certain forms of learning at certain times—and a gross unwillingness to acquire any other forms of learning (for a recent view of the critical period concept see Columbo, 1982).

Consideration of such concepts of ripeness and maturity has not yet penetrated deeply into thinking about management development. There are some exceptions. For example Katz (1977) suggests that time in a particular job is crucial in determining an individual's response to job enrichment. The implication is that employees, including managers, may be amenable to job redesign efforts only during particular phases of their careers. And Wanous (1977) has explored the socialization process newcomers face entering organizations as a kind of critical stage in which they are more open than usual to be influenced by others and thus to being developed. And in a somewhat similar vein, Berlew and Hall (1966) have pointed out that the way the initial job is perceived appears to have a relationship to later career success. There is a positive relationship between the amount of challenge in the initial job and later success.

A related concept to ripeness and maturity is that of the importance of the sequencing with which various activities occur. Again, in other areas of psychology this has been widely used. For example by Piaget (1957) in his approach to the development of logical thinking or Kohlberg (1969) in his studies of development of moral reasoning. The clinical literature concerning the various stages of life (see Erikson, 1950; Levinson, 1978) could also be cited in this context. And, of direct relevance to our field, Gagné (1977) sees learning as essentially a sequential process in which complex skills can be built up more efficiently if systematic prior training has first been given on simpler subordinate skills. Simpler subordinate skills should be taught first and then the more complex superordinate skills later.

As far as any possible stages in skill development for managers are concerned, we have too little information to be able to draw conclusions. We need to study managerial jobs in order to be able to identify possible subordinate and superordinate skills. Again, bearing in mind such conceptualizations as the Katz and Kahn hierarchy of managerial positions already referred to, we need to look at possible relationships between successful performance at various levels of management. For example, is it necessary for all top managers first to have been through the lower and middle levels or can some individuals go straight from business school into a policy formulating role without first having had to work their way up through the normal organizational hierarchy?

Thus, these questions of when individual managers might be especially ripe to be exposed to developmental inputs, and of the sequential order in which such inputs might best be given could well repay further study by psychologists involved in the field of management development.

The traditional way to increase ripeness or readiness development in the work context has been the annual assessment procedure. During this an individual's strengths and weaknesses and thus his development needs are often identified and discussed. Now, despite major criticisms of traditional assessment procedures by psychologists (see Sofer, 1974) they are still widely in existence, if not widely respected. However a newer, and for management development at least, potentially more powerful form of assessment appeared during the late 1960s and early '70s in the United States: the assessment centre approach.

A typical programme, as described by Stewart (1973), might consist of two days of assessment, followed by three days of development work based in part on the initial assessment period. There might be around twelve participants who would be observed by four specially trained managers who would preferably be at least two levels senior to the participants.

The assessment phase might consist of leaderless group discussions, individual and team based business games and case studies, in-tray exercises and possibly a variety of psychological tests for mental abilities and personality.

After this assessment phase the four observers would come together and agree on a summary statement about each participant. This would form the basis for the feedback to the individual, which would then be given in a series of interviews aimed at enabling him to explore his own strengths and weaknesses as shown up in his performance during the previous two days of tests and exercises.

Finally, during the third and fourth days a variety of activities which participants may utilize for their own personal development are offered. For example, in Stewarts case, these included training in communication skills, effective group behaviour, in efficient organization of one's own work schedules and self development planning.

The assessment centre approach has not gone without its share of criticism. As Finkle (1976) in a comprehensive review of the development of the technique has pointed out, organizations can use it for many different purposes, primary amongst which has been selection rather than development. For example, programmes have been especially popular in selection situations when there are large numbers of potential candidates and a major difference between what is required for successful performance in their current function and in the function for which they are applying. Typical situations would be selecting foremen from amongst assembly-line employees and sales managers from amongst salesmen (See Stewart and Stewart, 1976).

In this context of selection some important points have been raised. For example, Dunnette and Borman (1979) have warned that the rapid growth of these centres may be accompanied by sloppy or improper application of assessment procedures. Hinrichs and Haanpera (1976) have expressed reservations about the reliabilities of the ratings that are made of the assessees, and Klimoski and Strickland (1977) were equally concerned about their validity. They may be predicting the organization's subsequent promotion decisions accurately, but have little predictive validity as far as future individual behaviour is concerned.

Such legitimate sources of concern about assessment centres may be of somewhat less importance when such techniques are being used primarily for individual developmental purposes rather than for selection, providing of course, those involved are made aware of such possible weaknesses. However, individuals should be able to get the feel, for example, of the different demands the new level of job might make upon them during these two days and be able to test themselves out as to their suitability for such a post in comparison with some of their natural competitors. In other words they should become far 'riper' for development.

And another reason why the assessment centre approach may be useful for management development purposes is that it may mirror some of the characteristics that have been suggested as being typical of managerial work. For example the exercises tend to be short, fragmented and varied. Much of the activity is oral, and time pressure is often perceived as being high. Thus, as we have seen in the previous section, maybe this method can enable individuals to decide for themselves whether they can handle these aspects of the managerial environment or not.

We should conclude this section on the timing of management development activities by remarking that despite some evidence from other areas within psychology concerning the importance of the timing and sequencing of activities, possible related concepts such as those of ripeness and maturity and their relationships to management development have not been adequately explored. And that such areas might well repay further study.

4. HOW SHOULD WE DEVELOP MANAGERS

This third area, which is concerned primarily with the methods and techniques of management development, has seen perhaps the most publications in the whole management development field. And generally speaking we could say that many such writings can be grouped into two categories. One category we could call the instrumental view and the other the existential view.

Those who hold an instrumental view are likely, in management development, to talk of teaching things to people and to evaluate the success of the development in terms of the individual's contributions to effectiveness. For them, education is a shaping process. This view tends to be subject-based and deductive in its assumptions about reasoning and learning. That is, it assumes that practice can be deduced from theory. Learning or development should follow a similar path—theory, practice and then application. Such an instrumental philosophy sees therefore the teacher as a subject expert, permits of large classes with fairly distant learner/trainer relations and formalized learning mechanisms like prescribed problems, programmed learning assignments and timetabling.

In contrast, the existential view concentrates on the individual and sees the trainer essentially as a coach or mentor who helps the learner to formulate his own concepts and to perfect his own skills and talents. The learner does this by induction, by repeated trials, by testing hypotheses until he arrives by himself at his own theories or viewpoints. Inputs by the trainer are regarded as interesting possibilities for future consideration rather than as dictates to be absorbed and adhered to. There will only be a tenuous timetable, small classes, a vague syllabus and development is more by discovery and by experimentation than by absorption (See Handy, 1975).

A major consequence of these contrasting views is the difference in the amount of active involvement in the learning process which the learner is expected to take. The two views could be seen as being the two end points of a continuum, with the instrumental approach at the passive end, expecting very little involvement from the learner in the initiation and subsequent learning process, and with the existential school at the active end of the continuum, requiring a large amount of active involvement. Burgoyne in a discussion paper published in 1975, was able to distinguish, despite some degrees of overlap, six major approaches which could be spread along this continuum from the instrumental to existential:

1. The Conditioning Approach.
2. The Trait Modification Approach.
3. The Information Theory Approach.
4. The Cognitive Approach.
5. The Pragmatic Approach.
6. The Experiential Approach.

Direct application of the Conditioning Approach is perhaps best exemplified by programmed learning which sets out to evoke correct responses for learning and to reward and punish with the news that they are right or wrong. Two other recent applications which could be of especial interest to those working in the management development field are organizational behaviour modification and behaviour modelling.

Although there has been but little direct application of behaviour modification to management development (Andrasik, 1979) to date reported in the literature, interest is growing. This was first stimulated by popular reports of the success of the work done in increasing individual productivity by Feeney at the Emery Air Freight Company in the USA (*Business Week*, Dec. 18, 1971). Although research conducted under more controlled conditions has been limited in scope, results so far do seem as predicted by the theory in that reinforcement increases the required behaviour more than non reinforcement does (Komaki et al., 1977) and that differing schedules of reinforcement can have differing effects on this behaviour (Pritchard et al., 1976). However, criticism has been made of this approach both on ethical grounds and on the basis that the theory plays down the importance of the individual's own internal states (Locke, 1977). Despite such criticisms, the possible relevance of such techniques for developing particular skills in managers must still be great.

In contrast to the classical conditioning model lying behind behavioural modification techniques, advocates of 'modelling' or social learning approaches believe that learning often occurs just from watching others perform and from imitating their performance. They therefore assume that there is something about watching others perform the target behaviour that actually facilitates learning. Behaviour modelling practitioners carefully sequence and control the nature of the observations made by the learner (Goldstein and Sorcher, 1974), and lay especial emphasis on social reinforcement from other learners and from supervisors for appropriate behaviour. Research supporting this approach has been encouraging, in particular where the techniques have been used in training first and second line supervisors in interpersonal skills and in solving subordinate centred problems (Burnaska, 1976; Moses and Ritchie, 1976; Latham and Saari, 1979). There is, however, very little evidence to date that the techniques can be used successfully in the areas of acquisition and development of other types of skill.

Indirectly, the Conditioning Approach has given support to the traditional 'carrot and stick' approach to teaching and learning. And it has shed interesting light on such areas as whether massed or spaced practice (all at once or in short periods) is better for certain learning problems, and on the role that over-learning—that is continuing to practice even though you have reached one hundred per cent learning—plays in delaying the point at which forgetting sets in. The critical aspect about the approach is that the trainer has to know exactly what the learner has to learn in behavioural terms. And therefore it is only suitable for very clearly defined and structured learning tasks.

In contrast, Bourgoyne suggests that the second approach, the Trait Modification Approach, can cope with somewhat less structured tasks. It views a person as having one set of knowledge skills and attitudes but as needing another. The 'have' set is determined by studying the person, preferably by the use of psychometric measures, and the 'need' set is discovered by studying the job he has to perform. The difference between these two forms the learning goals for the individual. Here again the learner is shown primarily as being a passive entity being shaped by the developer.

The third approach, based on Information Theory, conceives that the person is basically a system which takes in, stores, processes and outputs information. This often results in careful emphasis being laid on the actual process of the transfer of knowledge from trainer to learner. For example, what is the right rate at which information should be given, what sequence is the most appropriate for the material, and so on.

Whereas all these approaches, conditioning, trait and information theory start with supposed realities external to the individual, that is with some form of external observable reality in which meaningful patterns exist independent of anyone's knowledge of them, in contrast, cognitive theorists start from the premise that each person, through his own experience, builds up his own 'map' as it were of his world; it is this map, representing his conscious or unconscious knowledge and understanding, that steers his action. Learning is the process by which these cognitive maps change and develop. Such an approach aims to improve managers' practical understanding and skills by starting with those which they already possess, and helping the individuals involved to extend them by further thinking. New ideas are introduced when this is judged likely to help him make sense of his existing experience and extend the existing cognitive map.

This Cognitive Approach is typified by normal subject based teaching methods, about which we, certainly as far as children and schools are concerned, have some information regarding factors leading to effectiveness (Gage, 1978). For example, there is a strong relationship between how much children actually learn and the amount of time they are engaged in activities related to the objectives of the instruction. The actual nature of the activities in which they engage does not seem to matter very much, it is the time spent which is the critical variable. Again, individual independent activity seems to be less productive than teacher initiated activity; that is, the teacher just asking simple questions leads to greater learning gains than does pupil initiated interaction.

Whether such conclusions are equally relevant for managers as opposed to their children has yet to be studied, but surely such a possibility should at least be borne in mind by any management developer using such a teaching based approach.

The Pragmatic Approach is really a further development based on the ideas of the cognitive theorists and it summarizes much thought and practice in current management development. Its rationale is, according to Burgoyne, that we do not really know what it is that managers have to have in order to be effective, or, in detail, precisely by what processes they actually learn. However, we do know, on a common sense basis, that managers achieve a reasonable degree of competence and that they do so over time, through working on managerial problems. They learn thus from experience. Therefore, a good way to help managers learn is to give them as much varied experience as possible, in as short a time as possible. This kind of rationale underlies the much used case study as a management development technique. Here the learner can be confronted with what are felt to be important managerial problems and given the chance to analyse proposed actions and solutions and test them out in some way.

However, the major problem with the case study approach is that the learner may begin to see his world as, rather than through, a series of case studies. He may go on to analyse and deal with the real situations with the same detached rationality and practical efficiency that he has shown in the classroom, relatively unaffected by the personal feelings in himself and those he is dealing with. That is why recent developments in the pragmatic approach to learning are concerned with enabling managers to tackle problems which are real-life issues, normally in organizations other than their own, in order that they should be exposed to their own attitudes and feelings as well as to their competences and weaknesses.

Despite these advances there are still at least two problems with learning through experience. Firstly, unless careful control is exercised, as for example behaviour modelling theorists do, then what is actually learnt from an experience may not be the most effective way of carrying out the particular task or function. It may just be the way the model individual has been doing it for the last few years, rather than the way which will suit the trainee best. And, secondly, learning by experience requires the individual to pay attention to nonoccurrences of the event in question as well as to actual occurrences. And we have some evidence that the tendency to ignore nonoccurrences is initimately related to the lack of search for disconfirmatory evidence (Wason and Johnson Laird, 1972; Mynatt *et al.*, 1978) and that attempts to alter this tendency, even at a simple level, have been generally unsuccessful (Tweney *et al.*, 1980). Individuals just do not seem to seek out disconfirmatory evidence with which they can test out the efficiency of what they have already learnt. Unless the learning by experience theorists can overcome this problem, the power of this approach must remain suspect.

The approaches considered so far have in common the assumption that from a learning point of view the individual is a relatively passive entity whose behaviour is determined by those characteristics which he has and the things that happen to him. The Experiential Approach, in contrast, recognizes that initiatives for new behaviour may also come from 'within' the person. Indeed such an approach considers that the more of this 'agent like' behaviour the individual indulges in, that is the more he takes responsibility for himself and the things that he influences, the less he will be likely in the future to accept his original passive or 'patient' role. Thus, experiential learning is closely linked with the personal growth movement and with humanistic psychology (Rogers, 1969; Maslow, 1970). It is perhaps more of an ideology than a theory.

However, this approach has been influential within management development over the last 20 years or so and has taken many forms ranging from unstructured sensitivity and encounter type groups to team building packages (for a view of the latter see Woodman and Sherwood, 1980). One of the often noted problems with these methods, which tend to stress learning about the self as such rather than learning about how to improve performance, is the conflict which can emerge between these values and those of the organizations in which such individuals have to work (Smith, 1973).

Thus we have seen that the two general views about management development, the instrumental and the existential, can be seen as two extremes of a continuum spreading from active through to passive learner involvement in the learning process. They can also be seen as differing in the degree to which they require structure of the learning concerned. The more instrumental approaches require that the behaviour to be learned can be precisely predicted and structured. In contrast, the more existential techniques are suited to the examination of unstructured problems where there are no clear right or wrong answers.

Since we could argue that most management problems will be composed of some elements which lend themselves to structure and others which will usually be far less well defined, we could conclude that therefore most management development programmes should have elements within them of both instrumental and existential approaches to management learning.

And this is indeed the result that we see, for example, in the programmes of perhaps the best known current proponent of the pragmatic or action learning approach (Revans, 1971). In the initial part of his programme, there is a very strong element of structuring and straight teaching. This is aimed at spreading a common language across all participants so that they can understand one another's concepts during the later parts of the programme. And yet in the course of the participant's field work, where they are involved in tackling real-life problems in organizations other than their own, Revans puts emphasis on their meeting regularly in small groups with a trainer whose role is primarily a counselling one to encourage them to share and learn from their own personal experiences.

Similarly, in one of the best researched programmes which could well serve as a model to any aspiring management developer, that of McClelland (1965) and his need achievement training, we see again in the course of one short but sophisticated course that he uses a variety of approaches ranging from conditioning to experiential learning.

It is possible that what is critical in the design of a management development programme is not which approach, instrumental or existential, the programme developer supports, but rather if he can achieve the right balance in his programme between the various possibilities. And, judging by the two cited above, it is most sensible to begin such programmes along clearly structured instrumental lines and then gradually to develop into more open existential inputs.

However, it is not only in the design of whole training programmes that the amount of active involvement and initiative should vary between trainer and learner. It may also be the case that such variation is needed even within a particular learning session. Snell and Binsted (1981) for example, examined whether trainer or learner took the responsibility for factors such as the truth and relevance of the content and ideas of the training, the process of learning and discussion, or the overall structuring of the session, across a variety of management training activities. They concluded that, within every one of the 15 different sessions studied, the relationship between trainer and learner was dynamic rather than static in that responsibility for these various aspects was constantly shifting, from one to the other and back again.

It is sad that such research, carefully examining by means of videotape actual learning situations together with follow-up over time, is still in its infancy, since more detailed work will be needed before we can reach more definite conclusions on this issue of the sequencing required in both the total development programme and in the individual sessions between trainer structure and learner responsibility for his own learning.

A final point concerning method and techniques of management development to which we should turn is the degree of structure needed on a task in order for it to result in high motivation to learn. Here the relevant psychological work is that of Locke (1968, 1978, 1981) and his colleagues, which would lead us to conclude that the minimum degree of structure needed is the ability to define clear objectives. For Locke, any teaching of specific techniques or ways of how to achieve goals is not so important as the fact that the individual possesses a clear goal. It is as if, given that he knows what he is aiming at and is motivated to achieve it, the mature individual will somehow find a way to get there. And Locke maintains that specific goals are seen as more motivating than general goals like 'do your best', and that difficult goals, if internalized, will lead to greater effort than more easy goals.

The research in this area is refreshingly rigorous (see Mitchell, 1979) and needs careful examination by aspiring management developers who are concerned with the initial motivation of participants on their programmes. One area of importance however on which there is as yet no clear evidence is how to persuade individuals to internalize goals which may have been set by the organization for them. Unless such goals are internalized, individuals will not be so motivated to achieve them. Joint participation in the setting of such goals does not seem to be the answer here, in that, although it seems to lead to higher satisfaction (Arvey *et al.*, 1976), it has no clear relationship with performance, although in some circumstances participation in goal setting has resulted in raising the difficulty of the set goals (Latham *et al.*, 1978).

Although the degree of structure along this dimension from passive through to active learner involvement may well be of importance in the design of management development programmes, another dimension which may equally repay further research is the perceived reality of the learning situation involved in the programme. By reality is meant here how managers can relate their learning experience back to their day-to-day working behaviour within their organizations.

Binsted and Stuart (1979) have recently attempted to summarize much work in this field in their series of articles on 'designing reality into management learning events'. They suggest it is useful to distinguish three separate components or dimensions of reality—those of content, process and environment.

Content reality has to do with how closely the content and activities a manager experiences in a training programme accord with the content and activities that he undertakes in his normal work role. For example, if we use simulation, requiring participants in a programme to build a tower of lego bricks in order to develop understanding of leadership roles in the group, this could well be perceived as having very low content reality since managers seldom spend much time building towers with lego bricks.

On the other hand, such a task could well be perceived as having high process reality since the decision making processes required in order to achieve the (unreal) task, might be very similar to the decision making processes which the manager experiences in the work groups to which he normally belongs. The word 'process' is used here in the behavioural sense and refers to the human interactions involved in achieving this task.

Finally, the third dimension of reality concerns the extent to which the environment of the learning or development event is perceived to accord with the manager's own work environment. For example, an activity where managers are given special assignments or projects within their own organizations is likely to be seen as having high environmental reality. In contrast, where managers are asked to make factory floor type decisions in a learning event held in a luxurious hotel, this might be perceived by many as rating low on environmental reality.

Binsted and Stuart insist that building a high degree of perceived reality into learning situations can often be counter-productive. For example, it can create a situation of potential threat which might inhibit rather than encourage self-questioning. It may be very helpful to step out of the world of real work and to have the opportunity to experiment in a safe, low risk environment such as a hotel in the country or through experience in running some outside work activity. This would rate as low environmental reality but might provide an appropriate context for radical experimentation which could well not be possible on the job itself.

So it is important, in designing any management development exercise, to define carefully what the goals of the programme are and then to look at the degree of perceived reality of content, process and environment which might be most likely to lead to the attainment of that goal. Such an approach may hopefully lead management developers to take note of the possibilities of development off as well as on the job and stimulate them to look also at the structuring of the learning programme both in the sense of the desired goal attainment and also of the amount of active participant involvement in the learning process.

5. HOW GOOD

A few general observations on the question of how good a particular programme may be will conclude this chapter. It is important in any evaluation procedure, not least in one related to management development, to distinguish between the two stages of evaluation. Firstly, has any change occurred? This is a straightforward measurement issue. And secondly, how do we regard this change—positive, negative or neutral? Clearly, there can be as many answers to this second question as there are individuals involved in the issue. For example, participants, their wives, the organizers, those who did not go on the development programme, and so on, can all have very different views. However, the question of defining what changes has actually occurred, lends itself somewhat more easily to objective study and so we will restrict ourselves in this section to this initial phase of evaluation without which the secondary phase cannot occur.

Now, if we are concerned to measure the degree of change that has taken place as a result of the management learning exercise, then we must ask ourselves at what level of learning we are most interested. A useful taxonomy in this context is that of Bloom (1966). He suggested that there are four levels of learning. Firstly the category of simple comprehension and repetition. That is the repetition of what has been learnt by rote, given that the same cues are present as when the original learning took place. The second stage of learning, which Bloom calls analysis, is really a form of insight which occurs when an individual can himself join together a number of simple rote learning facts because he has been able to identify general principles which connect them all together.

And then there are two further stages of learning which Bloom distinguishes which are more concerned with changing behaviour than just with changes in cognitions. The first of these is the direct application of learning. That is being able to apply what has been learnt in a similar situation to the one in which it was originally absorbed. And the second stage of learning concerned with changing behaviour is that of synthesis. This is a deeper level in that it involves learning being applied in new ways, in new situations, automatically.

A major problem with evaluating management development is that, although it is at this final level of synthesis that most of our development programmes are aimed, unless we are constantly monitoring an individual's behaviour, we will seldom be able to make judgements as to any changes which may have occurred at this level. This is because the essence of such changes is that they are unpredictable: they will be only triggered by the relevant external situation.

Nor, for similar reasons, are we easily able to measure change in learning at the level of insight. The occurrence of discovery or insight is similarly unpredictable and thus bears no specific relationship to the length of time passed since the original development activity. Development of insight may again have more to do with the incidence of triggers or stimuli occurring in the normal day-to-day environment—or just with the provision of time available for reflection.

Thus we find that most evaluation of change as a result of management development programmes has taken place at the levels of immediate personal reactions, of initial comprehension or rote learning and at the level of immediate application of knowledge in very similar situations.

Besides defining what level of learning we wish to examine in evaluating management development, we must also define at what stage or time we wish to examine its effects. Hamblin (1974) for example has suggested four possible evaluation stages in any management development programme.

The first and crudest stage would be the immediate reaction to the input. For example, asking participants for their general views about the programme by means of immediate post-course questionnaires and interviews. The second stage is not so interested in immediate emotional reactions, but is rather aimed at measuring any actual learning that has taken place, such as the kinds of problems which executives might be able to answer after the programme which they could not have answered before. Stage three is not so much concerned with learning as with changes in individual work behaviour that may follow from a development effort.

And finally, at a still deeper level, the evaluator may be interested in measuring changes resulting at the organization level. For example any changes in profit and loss figures.

Now clearly, the number of possible contaminating variables influencing why any change may have taken place, increases dramatically as we progress from stage 1 up through to stage 4. Participants' immediate reactions to a particular development activity are, one may reasonably suppose, mainly influenced by their initial expectations of and experiences on the activity itself. As indeed to a degree, may also be the changes in any desired learning which they exhibit. However, any changes in behaviour on the job would clearly be subject to many other influences in addition to the training activity— for example, attitudes of relevant other people, changes in their job environment and so on. And finally, any changes at the fourth level such as those in overall company profitability, are clearly difficult to relate specifically to any particular aspect of management development.

So it is at stages 1 and 2 of Hamblin's typology, which are measurable and predictable that we find most attempts at evaluating management development concentrated.

Thus both in Bloom's typology regarding levels of learning and in Hamblin's regarding timing of evaluation, we find that our attempts at evaluation have been largely restricted to that which is, on the one hand, predictable and, on the other hand, easily measurable. And such evaluation information is of but restricted relevance to those designing management development programmes which are aimed primarily at achieving very different levels of learning.

6. A FINAL WORD

This short review of possible relationships between psychology and management development has concentrated on the four areas of formulation of learning objectives, sequencing of training inputs, organization of input content and evaluation of product.

With regard to the initial formulation of learning objectives, we suggested that a first step towards clarification of the necessary super- and subordinate skills in a managerial job would be to undertake more rigorous study of what managers actually do at work than has heretofore been undertaken.

As far as the sequencing of training inputs is concerned, we put forward the idea that managers might be more motivated to learn at some stages in their careers than at others which might be more administratively convenient, and we hypothesized that the effectiveness of the actual content of such training input could be improved, as we have already implied, by taking into account Gagné's (1977) distinction between super- and subordinate skills.

Methods and techniques of management development are many and diverse. They can be thought of as differing in the degree to which they require active participation and involvement of the learner in the training process, and in the degree to which they demand structured training material—for example with learning objectives able to be formulated in behavioural terms.

This problem of the amount of unstructured learning material lies also at the heart of the difficulties we experience in evaluating much management development. In spite of some promising recent work (Thomas et al., 1979; Lodewijks, 1981), we are still uncertain as to how we can attempt to evaluate learning which has objectives such as improved insight or ability to synthesize new material.

In the light of all these factors—the difficulty of studying managerial behaviour in terms of super- and subordinate skills, the problem that management readiness to learn might not occur at the administratively most convenient times, the need to relate active learner involvement in the training process to the degree of structure of the material under consideration, and finally the complexity of measuring unpredictable events—it is hardly surprising that, as we noted in our introduction, psychologists have been so negative about management development. It is to be hoped that more research in the areas mentioned might cast some much needed light on the matters at issue.

REFERENCES

Andrasik, F. (1979), Organisational behavior modification in business settings; a methodological and content review. *Journal of Organisational Behavior Management*, **2**, 85–102.

Argyris, C. (1976), Leadership, learning and changing the status quo. *Organizational Dynamics*, winter 1976, 29–43.

Argyris, C., Schön, D. (1978), *Organizational learning: A theory of action perspective.* Reading: Addison-Wesley.

Arvey, R. D., *et al.* (1976), Relationships between goal clarity, participation in goal setting and personality characteristics on job satisfaction in a scientific organisation. *Journal of Applied Psychology*, **61**, 103–105.

Becker, H. A. (1968), *Management als beroep* [Management as a profession]. Den Haag: Martinus Nijhoff.

Berlew, D. E., Hall, D. T. (1966), The socialisation of managers: Effect of expectations on performance. *Administrative Science Quarterly*, **11**, 207–223.

Binsted, D., Stuart, R. (1979), Designing 'reality' into management learning events, parts 1, 2 and 3. *Personnel Review*, **8** (3), 12–19, **8** (4), 5–8, **9** (1), 12–18.

Bloom, B. S. (Ed.) (1966), *Taxonomy of educational objectives. Handbook I: Cognitive domain.* New York: McKay.

Bruner, T. (1966), *Toward a theory of instruction.* Boston: Harvard.

Burgoyne, J. (1975), *Learning theories and design assumptions in management development programmes, a note for discussion.* Discussion paper, University of Lancaster.

Burmaska, R. F. (1976), The effects of behavior modelling training upon managers behaviours and employees perceptions. *Personnel Psychology,* **19,** 329–335.

Campbell, J. P. (1971), Personnel training and development. *Annual Review of Psychology,* **22,** 565–602.

Columbo, J. (1982), The critical period concept: Research, methodology and theoretical issues. *Psychological Bulletin,* **91,** 2, 260–275.

Dubin, R. (1962), Business behavior behaviourally viewed. In: Strother, G. (Ed.), *Social science approaches to business behavior.* Homewood: Dorsey.

Dunnette, M., Borman, W. (1979), Personnel selection and classification systems. *Annual Review of Psychology,* **30,** 477–526.

Eden, C., *et al.* (1979), *Thinking in organisations.* London: Macmillan.

Erikson, E. H. (1950), *Childhood and society.* New York: Norton.

Finkle, R. B. (1976), Managerial assesment centres. In: Dunnette, M. D. (Ed.), *Handbook of industrial and organizational psychology.* Chicago: Rand McNally.

Fores, M., Sorge, A. (1981), The decline of the management ethic. *Journal of General Management,* **6** (3), 36–50.

Gage, N. L. (1978), *The scientific basis of the art of teaching.* New York: Teachers College Press.

Gagné, R. H. (1977), *Conditions of learning.* 3rd ed. New York: Holt Rinehart.

Glaser, R. (1966), The design of instruction. In: *Changing American School.* NSSE Yearbook Part II. Chicago: University of Chicago Press.

Goldstein, I., Sorcher, M. (1974), *Changing supervisory behaviour.* New York: Pergamon.

Goldstein, I. (1980), Training in work organisations. *Annual Review of Psychology,* **31,** 229–272.

Hamblin, A. C. (1974), *Evaluation and control of training.* London: McGraw-Hill.

Handy, C. (1975), The contrasting philosophies of management education. *Management Education and Development,* **6** (3), 56–62.

Handy, C. (1976), *Understanding organisations.* London: Penguin.

Hawrylyshyn, B. (1979), Management education: A conceptual framework. In: *Management education in the 80s,* New York: American Management Association, 85–98.

Hinrichs, J. R. (1976), Personnel training. In: Dunnette, M. D. (Ed.), *Handbook of industrial and organizational psychology.* Chicago: Rand McNally, 829–860.

Hinrichs, J. R., Haanpera, S. (1976), Reliability of measurement in situational exercises. *Personnel Psychology,* **29,** 31–40.

Jorden, N. (1968), *Themes in speculative psychology.* London: Tavistock.

Katz, D., Kahn, R. L. (1978), *The social psychology of organisations.* 2nd ed. New York: Wiley.

Katz, R. (1977), Job enrichment: Some career considerations. In: Maanen, J. van (Ed.), *Organisational careers.* New York: Wiley.

Kaufman, H. G. (1978), Continuing education and job performance. *Journal of Applied Psychology,* **63,** 248–251.

Klimoski, R. J., Strickland, W. J. (1977), Assesment centres—valid or merely prescient. *Personnel Psychology,* **28,** 563–575.

Knowles, M. (1973), *The adult learner: A neglected species.* Houston: Gulf.

Kohlberg, L. (1969), The cognitive developmental approach. In: Goslin, D. (Ed.), *Handbook of socialisation theory and research.* Chicago: Rand McNally.

Komaki, J., *et al.* (1977), The applied behavior analysis approach and individual employees: Improving performance in two small businesses. *Organisational Behavior and Human Performance,* **19,** 337–352.

Latham, G. P., Saari, L. M. (1979), The application of social learning theory to training supervisors through behavioural modelling. *Journal of Applied Psychology*, **64**, 239–246.

Latham, G. P., *et al.* (1978), The importance of participative goal setting and anticipated rewards on goal difficulty and job performance. *Journal of Applied Psychology*, **63**, 163–171.

Levinson, D. J., *et al.* (1978), *The seasons of man's life*. New York: Knopf.

Locke, E. A. (1968), Toward a theory of task motivation and incentives. *Organisational Behaviour and Human Performance*, **3**, 157–189.

Locke, E. A. (1977), The myths of behaviour modification in organisations. *Academy of Management Review*, **2**, 543–552.

Locke, E. A. (1978), The ubiquity of the technique of goal setting in theories of and approaches to employee motivation. *Academy of Management Review*, **3**, 594–601.

Locke, E. A., *et al.* (1981), Goal setting and task performance 1969–1980. *Psychological Bulletin*, **90**, 1, 125–152.

Lodewijks, J. G. I. C. (1981), *Leerstofsequentie* [Learning sequencing]. Tilburg, Catholic University (thesis).

McCall, M. W. (1978), *Studies of managerial work: Results and methods*. Technical report no. 9. Greenboro: Centre for Creative Leadership.

McClelland, D. C. (1965), Toward a theory of motive acquisition. *American Psychologist*, **20**, 321–333.

Maslow, A. H. (1970), *Motivation and personality*. 2nd ed. New York: Harper and Row.

Mintzberg, H. (1973), *The nature of managerial work*. New York: Harper and Row.

Mitchell, T. R. (1979), Organisational behaviour. *Annual Review of Psychology*, **30**, 243–282.

Moses, J. C., Ritchie, R. J. (1976), Supervisory relationships training. *Personnel Psychology*, **29**, 337–343.

Mynatt, C. R., *et al.* (1977), Confirmation bias in a simulated research environment. *Quarterly Journal of Experimental Psychology*, **29**, 85–95.

Mynatt, C. R., *et al.* (1978), Consequences of confirmation and disconfirmation in a simulated research environment. *Quarterly Journal of Experimental Psychology*, **30**, 395–406.

Piaget, J. (1957), *Logic and Psychology*. New York: Basic Books.

Pritchard, R. D., *et al.* (1976), The effects of varying schedules of reinforcement on human task performance. *Organisational Behaviour and Human Performance*, **16**, 205–230.

Revans, R. W. (1971), *Developing effective managers*. New York: Praeger.

Rogers, C. (1969), *Freedom to learn*. Ohio: Merrill.

Seligman, M., Hager, J. (1972), *Biological boundaries of learning*. New York: Appleton Century Crofts.

Smith, P. B. (1973), *Groups within organisations*. London: Harper and Row.

Snell, R., Binsted, D. (1981), The tutor learning interaction in management development. *Personnel Review*, **10** (3), 3–13.

Sofer, C. (1974), Management and appraisal. In: Tilley, K. (Ed.), *Leadership and management appraisal*. London: English University Press.

Stewart, A., Stewart, V. (1976), *Tomorrow's man today*. London: Institute of Personnel Management.

Stewart, A. M. (1973), *The identification of management potential*. London: Institute of Manpower Studies.

Stewart, R. (1968), Management education and our knowledge of management jobs. *International Social Science Journal*, **20**, 77–89.

Stewart, R. (1976), *Contrasts in management*. London: McGraw-Hill.

Thomas, L. F., Harri Augstein, E. S. (1977), Learning to learn. In: Howe, M. S. A. (Ed.), *Adult learning*. London: Wiley.

Tweney, R. D., *et al.* (1980), Strategies of rule discovery in an inference task. *Quarterly Journal of Experimental Psychology*, **32**, 109–123.

Wanous, J. P. (1977), Organisational entry: Newcomers moving from outside to inside. *Psychological Bulletin*, **84**, 601–618.

Wason, P. C., Johnson Laird, P. N. (1972), *Psychology of reasoning: Structure and content.* London: Batsford.

Woodman, R. W., Sherwood, J. J. (1980), The role of team development in organisational effectiveness. *Psychological Bulletin*, **88**, 166–186.

Handbook of Work and Organizational Psychology
Edited by P. J. D. Drenth, Hk. Thierry, P. J. Willems and C. J. de Wolff
© 1984, John Wiley & Sons, Ltd.

3.6. Work and working time

Henk Thierry and Ben Jansen

1. INTRODUCTION

1.1. The 'normal' working time?

The words by which we refer to the time in which work is done tend to be normative. Thus, we speak of a 'normal' work-day: in The Netherlands this is understood as a continuous 8-hour working period—be it interrupted by a brief lunch-break—which frequently starts between 7.00 and 9.00 hrs. a.m. and ends between 16.00 and 18.00 hrs. What is called a 'normal' or 'complete' working week of approx. 40 hours as a rule refers to five such work-days outside the weekend. Other familiar examples are: the normal working year, usual or normal working life.

The normative nature of such terms becomes more evident when we pay attention to the terms denoting different—we had almost written: deviating—working time agreements. Someone who works longer than is agreed by contract, works *over*time. Someone who averages less than 40 hours a week, is a *part*-timer, etc. Such use of words is far from innocent. It suggests that what is labelled as 'normal' should be like that, or possibly, has always been like that, as if it were a law of nature (Levitan and Belous, 1979). Moreover, the use of such words reveals a discriminatory disposition, particularly with regard to shift workers, who work at different times of the day or night periodically, and in case of continuous work, frequently in the weekends too. These shift workers

---

Prof. dr. Hk. Thierry, Universiteit van Amsterdam, Vakgroep Arbeids- en Organisatiepsychologie, Weesperplein 8, 1018 XA Amsterdam.
Drs. B. Jansen, Universiteit van Amsterdam, Vakgroep Arbeids- en Organisatiepsychologie. Weesperplein 8, 1018 XA Amsterdam.

are said to work during 'unsocial' hours; further on in this chapter we shall see that shift workers have no access to various *normal* facilities, that is, those in accordance with daytime work. However, is there any reason to assume that the working time agreements which we at present seem to take for granted, also prevailed in the past, and were taken for granted then? This question causes us to cast a brief glance at history.

In Roman times, according to Scherrer (1981), the armed forces were regularly made to move, and even wage battle, at night. The Vestal Virgins guarded the sacred fire in the city of Rome, also by night. The Emperor's mail was transported during the night, whether by land or water. The streets in the towns were often narrow and as a rule crammed with the booths of various streetvendors. This was why Caesar enacted the law forbidding transport by horsed vehicles during the day with only a few exceptions (such as transport for construction). Because of this, supplies were transported at night, which caused the citizens to complain of the noise that kept them from sleeping.

During the Middle Ages—still according to Scherrer—the practice of night-work declined. An important factor was the development of a socio-economic structure (the guilds), according to which the practice of trades was bound to strict rules and was supposed to take place usually during the day. This was not only cheaper (saving the expense of artificial lighting), it also enabled anybody to judge with his own eyes the quality of the product to be made. Depending on the season, a work-day lasted 9–14 hours. Only few categories of people were permitted to do night-work, e.g. taylors, monks in the monasteries, and soldiers.

Between the Renaissance and the Industrial Revolution, night-work increased considerably, particularly in the field of transport (of goods as well as people). More and more, time came to be a precious thing, especially during industrialization. With the use of gaslight, kerosine lamps and, later, electric light continuous labour in factories became possible. By the end of the 18th century a work-day in, for example, France or England, contained 14 hours on the average, although it included a lunch-break of 1–2 hours; those engaged in employment at home made even longer days. In the 19th century various countries put a stop to child labour and enacted laws prescribing a weekly period of rest (e.g. in England 1854, from Saturday 14.00 hrs.) In that era, there occurred, on the one hand, a general increase in functions requiring periodical night-work, whereas, on the other hand, the number of people regularly working at night decreased.

Scherrer points out that the average weekly working time in France was between 60 and 64 hours at the end of the 19th century. This does not deviate very much from the figures mentioned by Levitan and Belous (1979) for the United States: where the average working week amounted to 68 hours in 1860, in 1901 it had been reduced to 58.4 hours. In the second half of the 19th century The Netherlands set a record in the Franeker brickworks (Ruppert, 1953):

the average work-day was 20 hours, including mealtimes. Work-days of 12–18 hours were made elsewhere, with an average of 16 hours. At the beginning of this century, according to Harmsen and Reinalda (1975), the average was still over 11 hours; among the exceptions, also in The Netherlands, were the bakers: they averaged more than 80 hours a week, partly at night. In 1919, the Labour Act was passed which determined the industrial work-day at eight hours, and the working week at 45 hours. If desired, exemption from this rule could be granted. In 1922, the decline of the economic situation caused the work-day to be determined at $8\frac{1}{2}$ hours again, and the working week at 48 hours (Bakels and Opheikens, 1978). In the early sixties the five-day working week was introduced on a large scale. Gradually, the average weekly working time was further reduced.

This brief exposition reveals that the present-day working time agreements to a certain extent are of an arbitrary nature and that there is no reason whatsoever to qualify them as normal—that is, in the normative sense of the word. However, it is evident that there are certain trends in history, be it that in the different countries they have had developments, each of their own kind. Thus, reductions of working time and the restriction of night-work and weekend-work have practically always been accompanied by fierce social struggles, whether or not related to the rise of trade unions for employees. From a macro-economic perspective, this reduction could be accomplished, according to Levitan and Belous (1979), because of the considerable increase in productivity. Various authors point out (e.g. de Koning, 1980) that initially the employee's health was the principal reason for adjusting working time agreements. Later on, the emphasis was on the importance of, and the desire for, more spare time.

1.2. Alternative working time agreements

During the last few years it has repeatedly been pointed out, also in the literature, that, considering what happened in most Western countries during the sixties and seventies, more drastic changes of working time agreements are desirable or even essential. This will be the theme of the present chapter. In some cases, however, the total amount of working time is not at issue. For example, in the case of *flexible working hours*, the point is that personnel can decide for themselves when to begin and when to stop working. The *compressed working day or week* means that the number of work-days is reduced, but the number of working hours per day increased. Those alternatives implying a reduction to less than 40 hours a week on the average, are generally summed up by the term *part-time work*. Incidental or periodical work exceeding the requirements of the contract is called *overtime work*. When there is no permanent employment, but the work is done for short periods and on a voluntary basis, it is called *temporary work*. When work is periodically done at irregular hours—

e.g. during rush hours (in public transport) or in combination with the crossing of one or more time zones (as in airline travel)—we speak of *irregular working hours*. When the work is regularly done in the evening and/or at night, whether or not during the weekends as well, it is named *shift work*. In this type of working time agreements not only the schedule is a vital point of consideration, but the number of working hours increasingly so too.

A curious thing is, that in the pleas made for or against the above-mentioned agreements, widely differing considerations are put forward. The creation of more jobs by means of a redivision of the existing amount of work, often is one of the primary arguments for introducing part-time work, working in five or more shifts, and against permitting overtime, respectively (see e.g. de Koning, 1980). Besides, part-time work is being considered from the angle of the emancipation of women, whether or not related to any views on alternative role divisions between (married) partners (see e.g. Schoemaker *et al.*, 1981). Other viewpoints in connection with part-time work are, e.g., the employment of people partially unfit to work, dividing particularly hard or unattractive work among more people, coping with peak hours at work, the unavailability of qualified personnel for the entire working time, etc.

While the foregoing motives refer to some working time agreements in particular, there are various considerations of a more general nature. Marić (1977) holds that working time in general is and has been viewed far too much from a quantitative angle. He advocates a more *qualitative* approach, which aims at a balance between work, rest, and leisure, according to the needs of the individual and society, but which maintains productivity (see also Rosow, 1979). Another and more general consideration refers to changing *norms and values* concerning work and leisure. Jehoel-Gijsbers and Schepens (1981) in this connection draw our attention to, broadly speaking, two kinds of opinion: in the eyes of those supporting a 'leisure-time cult', work will devaluate, whereas leisure time will take the first place in life. Particularly among young people, work ethics are subject to change, which, for one thing, will lead to a growing preference for temporary instead of permanent work. Work is then a means for realizing objectives outside the scope of the job: if the need and the necessity to work grow smaller, by contrast the need for leisure time will increase. In the second trend—'the defenders of work ethics'—it is emphasized that work in itself may be valuable, providing people with a social and individual identity, for example. Leisure time activities are meaningful only if accompanied by meaningful work.

In the literature dealing with alternative working time agreements, one regularly comes across one consideration in particular: the promotion of *flexibility* (see e.g. Robison, 1976; Marić, 1977; Levitan and Belous, 1979; Thierry, 1980, 1981; van Mill and van Schagen-Gelder, 1980; Ronen, 1981; Thierry and Jansen, 1981). One basic point here is the views of the individual, of (married) partners and groups of employees on such topics as being allowed to decide on the starting and finishing times of one's own daily work, on the number of working hours per day, on the number of working days each week or month, on the duration of holiday periods per year, on the working schedule in shiftwork, etc. Another essential point is the importance of the organization of work: the necessity to react to crises and recession, to cope with booms and slumps in the demand for labour, to be able to retain scanty workers, etc.

1.3. The organization of this chapter

It appears, from what was said above, that a considerable number of different considerations and viewpoints are at issue in the discussion of working time agreements other than the usual ones. In the course of this chapter we shall first deal with the theme of flexible working hours (section 2), followed by the compressed working day and working week (section 3). Section 4 deals with part-time work, section 5 with overtime. After these, a brief exposition on temporary work (section 6), followed by section 8 which concerns irregular work and shift work.

Each of these sections opens with a summary description of the working time agreement in question. Then we proceed with a discussion of the research. Since very little psychological research has been done on the agreements to be discussed in sections 2–6 (with a few exceptions), we offer some psychological viewpoints, in section 7, which may lead to relevant research issues in the future.

2. FLEXIBLE WORKING HOURS.

2.1. The type of agreement

As was briefly pointed out in section 1.2, flexible working hours do not imply a change in the total number of working hours in a particular period. What is concerned are options for all the personnel as to *the time when* they start working, finish working, have a lunch-break etc. The terms 'flexible working hours' or 'flex(i)time', have, at times, appeared to suggest an adaptation of the number of working hours (Ronen, 1981).

Diagram 1 shows two examples of flexible working hours. Both examples are based on an eight-hour working day, with a lunch-break of half an hour at least. In schedule A all personnel are expected to be present between 9.00 and 15.30 hrs.; this period includes the fixed lunch-break too. However, employees may choose at what time between 7.00 and 9.00 hrs. they start work. Schedule B offers, besides, the possibility of lunching between 11.00 and 13.00 hrs., going home, taking a longer lunch-break, etc. Presence is compulsory between 9.00 and 11.00 and between 13.00 and 16.00 hrs. This opportunity to choose, in parts, or in the form of clusters, is absent in the so-called 'staggered hours'. In this case, one group of employees works, lunches, goes home, etc., at

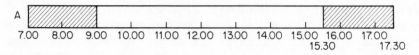

Diagram 1. Two possible schedules with flexible working hours.

earlier times than another group. Such agreements mostly are made to ease traffic, the use of elevators, lunchrooms, etc.

It is obvious that many variations of schedules with flexible working hours are possible. As a rule the choice of one particular variety depends, on the one hand, on the 'needs' of the organization (the supply of work, outside contacts, internal consultation, etc.), and, on the other, upon the preferences of the personnel. Thus, schedule B might appeal to employees living close to their firm or institute, to parents who wish to await their school-going children at home, etc. In all cases, the business hours outnumber the individual working hours. Sometimes employees are not permitted to work longer or shorter per day than was agreed by contract. But it is permitted more often than not: one can then think of various agreements (see e.g. Fleuter, 1975; Robison, 1976; Marić, 1977; Cohen and Gadon, 1978; Ronen, 1981). The 'debit' and 'credit' of working hours—often recorded by means of clocking-in registration—is to be settled, for example, per week. If it happens that too many or too few hours have been made, they will be transferred to the following week; it also occurs that an excess of working hours has to be compensated by e.g. (half) a day off. In other agreements the period of reference is a month, three months or even a calendar year. This, in turn, can be combined with e.g. an agreement that a given minimum and/or maximum number of hours is required per week or month.

There are no statistical data on the extent to which flexible working hours are practised in The Netherlands; one 'senses', however, that it is done on a large scale. In the American literature 'flexitime' is regarded as a typically European invention (see e.g. Fleuter, 1975; Robison, 1976; Cohen and Gadon, 1978; Ronen, 1981). As a rule reference is made to the West-German industry of Messerschmidt-Bölkow-Blohm, which is said to have been the first to introduce this working time agreement in the mid-sixties (the reason being that the personnel had traffic and parking problems) Marić (1977) holds, however, that a

Swiss enterprise was experimenting with it as early as the beginning of the sixties. Of these countries no exact figures are available, either: but various authors contend (see also Keppler, in Robison, 1976) that approx. 40% of the Swiss working population (only 10% of which belong to the labour category) have flexible working hours, the percentage in Germany being 30% (of which 3% labourers). In other European countries, according to these authors, flexible working hours are less common, but the practice is evidently spreading (see also Marić, 1977; Ronen, 1981). As far as the United States are concerned, Cohen and Gadon (1978) estimate that over 400,000 people have flexible working hours: moreover, again, in the civil service and the service sector. Ronen (1981), as well as Fleuter (1975), describes a number of case studies in this field, mentioning in an appendix 250 American work organizations practising flexible working hours.

Some French experiences are particularly remarkable in this connection (Ronen estimates that in that country about 2000 organizations have an 'horaire variable'). Perret (1980), for example, reports of an experiment with cashiers in a very big supermarket in Toulouse (Mammouth). The number of cashiers required varies according to the hour of the day and according to the day of the week. Small groups of cashiers determine their own schedules, the boundary conditions, set by the manager, being only the number of tills that have to be open each hour, and the agreed number of working hours of each individual cashier. For this purpose, each group elects a coordinator once every three months, who draws up a basic plan: each member states her preferences for the next two weeks. One of the effects was that absenteeism was reduced to 50%. Another experiment mentioned by Perret concerns a hospital in Roubaix. Each task of the approx. 50 nurses was checked on the extent to which it was bound to any fixed times (e.g. mealtimes) and the extent to which it could be accomplished at variable times, the object being to relieve the nurses' time-tables and to improve the patients' service. It resulted in obligatory attendance between 8.00 and 14.00 hrs. with flexible starting and finishing times added. Those registering for at least 80 hours over two weeks were allowed to form a credit or debit of eight hours over that period.

2.2. Results

In the literature, the opinions about the objectives of the practice of flexible working hours are not really divided: to provide personnel with options—as managers have them, Marić (1977) adds—, to enhance the quality of working life, to improve motivation etc. Of course the immediate reasons for shifting to flexible working hours may vary. But to what extent are these, or other, objectives achieved in practice?

In The Netherlands, hardly any data are available from systematic research. If we go by 'impressions', the results appear to be modest: it is frequently declared that although, on the introduction of such working hours, each employee does indeed decide on a schedule which suits him,[1] another stabilization ensues with few alterations.

In the literature on experiences in other countries predominantly positive effects are found, although it is remarkable that they are seldom founded on scientific research. Among the favourable effects for the work organization are: less (especially short-term) absenteeism; less turnover; fewer accidents at work and in traffic; fewer late-comers; less overtime; higher morale; easier recruitment of personnel; education and training of deputy foremen and supervisors. Experiences as to the impact on productivity and work motivation are contradictory: in some cases there appears to be no evidence for it, other cases involve a positive or negative impact.

If we consider the individual employee, the positive effects mentioned are: more control of one's time; more undisturbed working time (no telephone calls etc.); better child-minding; better career development for women; fewer traffic and transport problems; more satisfying leisure time activities; learning more skills as a result of periodical substitution for colleagues; more sense of freedom.

In addition, several negative consequences were found too: extra demands are made on the foremen (the so-called first level of management), e.g. on their capacity for coordination. Communication may run less smoothly, the more so as managers are not always in attendance. The way in which work is done and the workflow proceeds, requires accurate analysis (which may be profitable in the long run). Buildings must stay open longer, which involves higher costs of energy. An employee may find it harder to get short-term leave, e.g. for a doctor's consultation (for further reading see Fleuter, 1975; Sloane, 1975; Robison, 1976; Marić, 1977; ILO, 1978; Cohen and Gadon, 1978; Ronen, 1981).

In one of the few more systematic research studies in this field, Schein *et al.* (1977, 1978) report the objections of 63 managers of an insurance company to the possibility of flexible working hours for their personnel. In interviews, they expressed their doubts as to the question whether employees would be able to work with less supervision, whether they could abide by the terms, whether they, the managers themselves, would be able to deal with that changing demand for their time and attention. Then, for four months they experimented with a schedule requiring attendance between 10.00 and 15.15 hrs. (see diagram 1, type A). The results of a questionnaire—administered shortly before the end of the trial period—show, for one thing, that their attitudes had become much more positive, that they assumed the employees stuck to the agreement, and that they felt productivity had risen. However, that last point turned out to be untrue: the researchers had gathered, independently, information regarding

---

[1] Wherever in this chapter we speak of 'he' or 'him', 'she' and 'her' are equally implied.

this point. One must add though that this research has its shortcomings: no control group (or another experimental condition) was used, where in fact no more than one test was done.

These shortcomings are absent in Orpen's (1981) experiment. Both an experimental group and a control group were formed at random, with the consent of his subjects: 64 female clerks at a large governmental office, who had routine clerical jobs. The first group changed to a new schedule for six months: attendance was compulsory between 10.30 and 15.30 hrs., the optional hours being between 7.30 and 10.30, and between 15.30 and 18.30 hrs., respectively. The members of the second group continued working according to the existing 'fixed' schedule: from 9.00 to 17.00 hrs. The results of the tests, administered beforehand as well as afterwards, reveal that those experiencing the new schedule had become significantly more satisfied; the level of achievement had not undergone any change.

Evidently, the topic of flexible working hours still requires a great deal of research. Indeed, Shamir (1980) points out that, in this field, authors usually make 'uniform' statements without allowing for the potential significance of individual differences. He found, in a research study in a bank, that age was not the only vital factor, but also e.g. the importance attached to suitable working hours. We shall return to this theme—perspectives for research—in section 7.

3. THE COMPRESSED WORKING DAY AND WORKING WEEK

3.1. The nature of the agreement

Many people have long been accustomed to one of the forms of a compressed work-day: whereas in the past most working people went home at noon, nowadays this two-part work-day is generally substituted by one interrupted only by a short lunch-break (at work). In schools, this type of arrangement is generally called a tropical or continuous schedule.

As a rule, the number of working hours per day does not alter in this type. This is in contrast to another type, which was mentioned in section 2.1, where we spoke of the opportunity, in connection with flexible working hours, to make more than the usual hours per day. This second type will be dealt with here in relation to the compressed working week.

With Cohen and Gadon (1978) we distinguish two ways of using this type of working week: firstly, in work organizations having semi-continuous or continuous systems, the work continues five or seven days a week, 24 hours a day (see also section 8). Secondly, the compressed working week is applied in organizations operating less than five days a week. In either case, each employee will work $3\frac{1}{2}$ to four days a week on the average: in the first case, the cluster of free days will vary per week as to *when* they are enjoyed; in the second case, this will always be in the (long) weekend.

	Monday	Tuesday	Wednesday	Thursday	Friday	Saturday
Group 1	X	X	X	X		
Group 2			X	X	X	X
Group 3		X	X		X	X

Diagram 2. Example of a compressed working week for three groups of employees having a ten-hour work-day.

Based on a 40-hour-working week, the system of four days of ten working hours each is the most common. Apart from that, there are such things as the $4\frac{1}{2}$-day working week (e.g. four days of nine hours, one day of four hours), the $3\frac{1}{2}$-day and the three-day working week (see e.g. Fleuter, 1975; Marić, 1977). With the last two examples, a work-day may amount to 12 hours or more; in such a case, however, it will usually be a matter of a shorter working week (e.g. 37, 5 or 36 hours).

Let us assume that a work organization, e.g. a department store, must be in business six days a week. On some days there is more work than on others, and a compressed working week for all employees is preferred. Then the following schedule might be designed (see diagram 2). It is based on a ten-hour work-day from 9.00 a.m. to 7.00 p.m.

Diagram 2 reveals that Wednesday is a peak-day, whereas Monday affords work for one group only; on the other four days two groups of employees are available all the time. Groups 1 and 2 have four successive work-days; Group 3 has two sets of two days.

It stands to reason that many variations are possible. Whatever the agreement, the employees' wishes and conditions should be taken into account. From the perspective of the work organization, the following factors are significant too (more details are to be found in Marić, 1977; Cohen and Gadon, 1978):
—The nature of particular activities (such as the delivery of goods, by truck-drivers, to a great many customers, which requires covering great distances).
—The use of capital intensive equipment (e.g. a computing centre operated by two shifts per 24 hours, for six days).

When examining to what extent the compressed working week is applied, one has to take into account the differences, between various countries, in labour legislation and/or in regulations contained in Collective Labour Agreements: such regulations may either prevent its application or regulate it by a system of licences. In The Netherlands, no statistical data are available. In other countries, too, figures are incomplete or non-existent. Marić (1977) points out that the first applications occurred in Great Britain and West-Germany in the sixties. It is usually a question of smaller organizations. According to Sloane (1975) and Walker (1978), in Great Britain, the compressed working week is practised primarily in relation with a two-shift system, which is wide-spread in that country. This so-called alternating day and night shift system involves one watch during daytime and another—but with a break in between—during the night. This night-watch may at times involve four ten-hour shifts. According to Cohen and Gadon (1978) (as well as Marić), this type of working week was introduced on a relatively large scale in the United States at the beginning of the seventies. Estimates concerning the year 1976 vary from 750,000 to 1,000,000 workers; since that time, the number of U.S. organizations introducing this system is said to have been equal to the number of those abolishing it.

3.2. Experiences

There is very little research in this field. Generally speaking, this type of working week was introduced on the one hand to afford employees more days off in succession, and on the other hand with the aim of expanding the organization's service, employing the personnel at times when they are most needed, and making optimal use of costly equipment. What results have been gained?

From the perspective of the work organization we take notice first of the development of productivity: this is either constant or has risen. It saves expenses, particularly when starting the production process is costly, expensive equipment can be used longer, and overtime can be reduced. As regards morale, this has regularly been reported to have improved. Experiences concerning absenteeism, turnover and being late at work were extremely mixed: now they appear to decrease, now they tend to increase, while in some cases there have been no changes in these phenomena at all. Less favourable effects ensue when employees grow too tired, and, consequently, their achievements are of low quality, more errors are made etc. Furthermore, it requires a great deal of attention to compose good schedules: communication problems may arise if foremen and supervisors have no compressed working week. Besides, there may be problems with the receipt of orders, supplying firms, buyers and clients etc., if they use different working weeks.

One of the main advantages for the individual worker, it is found, is the prolonged period of free days, especially if the weekend is included. In this way the control of one's own time is increased. Apart from that, one's travelling time and expenses are reduced: with the four-day working week one has to travel but four days a week, usually before and after rush-hours. This would also reduce the risks of traffic accidents. Another point is that this type of working week is easier to combine with household activities. Moreover, it is stressed that it enables men to do more household work and other jobs which previously were in the hands of their wives. The extra day off also appears to be used for second employment or for overtime. As regards the disadvantages there are, apart from the afore-mentioned factor of fatigue, in the first place, the effects on family life. Particularly in the case of women with a compressed working week, can the long work-day be a considerable burden, with child-minding, cooking meals etc.

Furthermore, the long work-day may prevent participation in social activities during the evening. And often the extra day off is not felt to be 'real' leisure time, expecially when it is needed to take a rest, and or to finish jobs left undone during the working days. Also, quite a few workers have a hard time returning to work after a long weekend; in research done by Sloane (1975) this mainly concerned single men and women (for more details, see Poor, 1972; Fleuter, 1975; Sloane, 1975; Marić, 1977; ILO, 1978; Cohen and Gadon, 1978; Perret, 1980; Kabanoff, 1980). Ivancevich (1974; Ivancevich and Lyon, 1977) points out that, in the short run, the compressed working week offers more advantages than in the long run. For this purpose he compared two groups (of equal size) employed in a food company, the experimental group having a four-day working week of 40 hours, the control group retaining the five-day working week (also 40 hours). Repeated measurements over a period of 13 months showed that the former group had more job satisfaction and yielded better performance. But it appeared, in a follow-up study, that these effects had virtually disappeared after 25 months. Another interesting thing is that a second experimental group, set up during the follow-up study, produced the same short-term effects as the first group.

As to the literature on compressed working days and weeks, involving, broadly speaking, day-time working hours, it is remarkable to find that there is never any reference to data resulting from shift work research, concerning comparable longer day-time shifts. These might prove profitable for future studies on the effects of a compressed working week on working behaviour. What we have in mind is, for example, the degree to which performance, health, job attitudes and leisure time activities are affected by biological functions having an almost 24-hour cycle, by environmental factors such as temperature and noise (see also Willems, 1981, p. 225ff.), by the characteristics of the task, by the required qualifications, by individual differences, by domestic circumstances, etc.

4. PART-TIME WORK

4.1. A matter of definition

Whoever works part-time, by definition averages less than 40 working hours a week. Does this mean that a 39-hour working week should be regarded as part-time work? And what about a seven-hour working week (e.g. two days of $3\frac{1}{2}$ hours)? Unfortunately, there is no such thing as a clear, unambiguous definition of part-time work (indicated hereafter as PTW). Many writers, though, use the definition provided by the International Labour Office: 'work voluntarily accepted and regularly performed in a number of working hours considerably smaller than usual'. But we remain in doubt as to the implications of the words 'considerably smaller' and 'usual'. Driehuis and De Vrije (1981) formulate it as follows: '. . . a period shorter than the customary working time in the branch in question'. Schoemaker et al. (1981) add: '. . . pursuing permanent employment'. It is obvious that we are dealing with paid work and that irregular and temporary work are excluded from PTW, as are agreements concerning shorter working hours on a temporary basis, e.g. due to lack of work.

PTW may occur in various forms. We can first distinguish them on a basis of the unit of time (see e.g. de Koning, 1980):
—Per day: the number of working hours.
—Per week: the number of (half) working days.
—Per year: the number of holidays.
What is attractive about de Koning's definitions is their independence from each other. The terms used in practice are, of course, another matter. Perret (1980) describes a fascinating example of an annual system. A large clothes manufacturing concern ('Albert') is faced with seasonal periods of high and low business activity. At peak-times the maximum number of hours a week can be extended to 45 hours: 25% of the individual employee's credit-hours thus gained are remunerated as overtime, while the remainder is preserved. The remaining credit can be used by that employee at 'low times', e.g. when the firm is closed down for a number of days (such a system, of course, can be applied just as well without PTW).

Various authors make a serious plea for a fourth unit of time: PTW per working life (see e.g. Marić, 1977; Emmerij and Clobus, 1978; de Koning, 1980). The idea would be a flexible system in which every working individual can acquire a sort of 'drawing rights': on this basis he will periodically return to a training centre for an updating course or for retraining, while with advancing age the average working time can be reduced, old-age pension can be granted earlier, etc. Such a system is practised, for example, in France, by Peugeot-Citroën (the so-called 'Plan Individuelle D'Espargne Congés', see Perret, 1980; RCO, 1980). Anyone having been absent from work no more than 15 days a year can amass these so-called 'rights': they amount to 15 minutes ('points') per week for factory workers and nine minutes for clerks. Anyone with a non-attendance record of under five days receives an allowance of 50%, on a yearly basis, while those with a blank non-attendance record receive an extra 100% points. When in a two-shift system (of the day-and-night type), or in permanent night-work, a worker receives an extra six points a week; Sunday work gains 15 points extra, etc. All allowances may be spent immediately. If anyone prefers not to make use of acquired rights within a particular age-period—of which three are distinguished: < 35; 35–50; > 50—his rights are doubled. Then, where the first age-group is concerned, one third of the rights is available immediately, one third when the second age-period is reached, and another third in the last period. For those between 35 and 50 years of age half of their rights are immediately available, the other half after 50. If over 50, employees can make use of their rights immediately. Coetsier (1979) advocates a different approach: if anyone aims at a reduction of his working time and is, besides his actual job, engaged in social or cultural work, he will receive credit-hours, to be remunerated out of different funds.

A second criterion refers to the *organizational form* of PTW (see e.g. de Koning, 1980; Driehuis and de Vrije, 1981; Schoemaker et al., 1981; Hartzuiker, 1981):

—Split jobs: an existing job is divided into two or more new jobs. This may occur e.g. according to phase of production, to specialization, to client etc.
—Twin jobs: two PT workers occupy one job requiring the usual working time; together they are responsible for its fulfilment.
—Joint job: unlike twin jobs, each 'partner' is only responsible for his part of the job.
—Mini-shift: fixed groups of PW workers run shifts according to schedule for a short period of time.
—Min-max-system: based on agreements, a minimum number of hours must be made within a given period of time, excess hours being bound to a maximum (see the above-mentioned annual system).
—Availability at summons: whenever the employer needs it, work is to be done by a given pool of employees on call.

4.2. Part-time work in various countries

PTW is, besides shift work, one of the rare instances of working time agreements 'other than usual' on which statistics are assembled in various countries. The figures to be presented below, however, need to be interpreted with a due measure of caution. One important factor is, as was mentioned in the previous section, the question of how to define PTW. The Dutch 'Central Bureau of Statistics' (CBS) distinguishes the following categories: < 15, 15–25, 25–34, > 34 hours a week. Not all Dutch sources apply this division. The European Community understands PTW as a working week of less than 25 hours. But in the United States the 'Bureau of Labor Statistics', when referring to PTW, speaks of less than 35 hours, etc. Consequently, this means that certain—and, unfortunately, often different—categories of workers without a full-time job are left out of consideration. What appears, too, is that different sources do not always produce the same figures on the subject for the same country, even if the periods of observation as well as the norms applied concerning PTW were identical.

When considering the data in table 1 in relation to each other, the first thing that strikes us is that the percentage of female employees in PTW is, in all countries, considerably higher than that of male ones. Secondly, from 1973 onwards, it is particularly women who have taken more PTW in many countries. It is also apparent that PTW is practised most in the three Scandinavian countries and in the U.K. The Netherlands merely take up a middle position. In absolute figures this country had, in 1977, 426,000 women and 86,000 men in PTW, i.e. less than 25 hours a week (see van der Veen and Roosma, 1981).

In The Netherlands there are, however, considerable differences among the various branches and professions (see tables 2 and 3). Table 2 reveals that in the majority of the branches the percentage of women working less than 25 hours a week has risen in the course of the years. Within each business branch re-

Table 1. PTW done by men and women in percentages of the working populations in various countries.

	DTA	WOMEN				MEN			
		1973[a]	1975[a]	1977[a]	Otherwise	1973[a]	1975[a]	1977[b]	Otherwise
Denmark	< 25	—	40.3	49		—	1.9	3.5	
Norway	< 30	—	—	44		—	—	—	
Sweden	< 34	—	—		42.5 ('78)	—	—	—	5.5 ('78)
United Kingdom	< 25	38.3	40.9	42.5		1.5	2.2	2.5	
Australia	< 35	—	—		35 ('78)	—	—		5.5 ('78)
United States	< 35	—	—	26.5		—	—	9.5	
New Zealand	< 30	—	—		26 ('79)	—	—		5 ('79)
West Germany	< 25	20.0	22.8	25		1.0	1.1	1	
Canada	< 30	—	—		22.5 ('78)	—	—		6 ('78)
The Netherlands	< 25	15.5	18.6	19		1.1	1.5	1.5	
Austria	14–36	—	—		18.5 ('76)	—	—		1.5 ('76)
Japan	< 35	—	—		17.5 ('78)	—	—		—
Portugal	15–34	—	—	16.5		—	—	2.5	
Belgium	< 25	8.2	11.6	14.5		0.4	0.6	1	
France	< 25	11.2	14	13		1.4	2.1	2	
Luxemburg	< 25	13.4	15.4	12.5		0.9	0.9	—	
Finland	< 29	—	—		12 ('78)	—	—		3 ('78)
Ireland	< 25	—	9.9	7.5		—	1.8	1	
Italy	< 25	8.5	9.9	4		2.3	2.7	1	

[a]Data European Community.
[b]Data OCED (derived from de Koning, 1981; Schoemaker et al., 1981; Driehuis and de Vrije 1981).

Table 2. Part-time work done by men and women; its percentage of the total number of employees per branch.

	1971		1975		1977		1978	
	f.	m.	f.	m.	f.	m.	f.	m.
Agriculture and fishery	25.5	—	39.2	2.4	30.0	2.6	39.9	3.2
Mining, industry and public utilities	14.9	—	20.9	1.7	21.4	1.8	21.5	1.0
Construction and installation	19.6	—	28.5	0.6	39.1	1.0	36.5	1.0
Commerce, hotel and catering, repairs	14.2	—	24.6	2.6	27.9	2.8	31.1	3.1
Transport, storage and communication	18.3	—	26.5	1.2	34.3	1.4	37.5	2.1
Banking, insurance and other commercial services	18.1	—	24.5	2.3	24.8	3.5	24.9	3.1
Other public services/ administration, education, health care, etc.	23.1	—	35.1	2.4	38.7	4.6	42.1	5.2

Derived from van der Veen and Roosma, 1981; Sources: General census 1971; Labour census 1975, 1977, Employment Survey, 1978.

Table 3. Part-time work of men and women according to profession (whether mainline of sideline) × 1000.

	1975 f.	1975 m.	1977 f.	1977 m.
Academic, trained specialists, artists	70	19	81	25
Managerial and higher jobs	0	2	0	2
Clerks	75	10	91	12
Commercial jobs	43	9	48	10
Service jobs	127	6	165	6
Agricultural occupations	18	6	18	6
Craftsmanship, industry, transport	23	20	23	21

Derived from van der Veen and Roosma, 1981, and Driehuis and De Vrije, 1981; Sources: Labour censuses, 1975, 1977.

markable differences can be detected between men and women, in the sense of figures on PTW. It holds for both categories that, relatively speaking, PTW is practised most in the branch of other public services, and—especially in the case of women—least in mining, industry and public utilities. If we base ourselves on the absolute figures, not mentioned in table 2, it appears, for example, that in 1977 fewest PT workers were employed in construction (9000 women, 8000 men), while most PT workers were found in other public services: 241,000 women and 30,000 men.

The data contained in table 3 show that the large majority of women employed in PTW are to be found in (lower level) service jobs, closely followed by those employed as clerks. With men, PTW is most common, at least in 1977, among academic workers, other trained specialists and artists. In public service (Schoemaker et al., 1981) a similar division can been found; in various other countries patterns appear to be analogous.

4.3. Experiences

In section 2.1 we mentioned various considerations concerning and objectives of PTW, namely: to create more jobs; the emancipation of women; a suitable answer to peak-time at work; and the employment of people partially fit to work. We may add: more opportunities for employees to choose their working time, e.g. in relation to individual domestic circumstances (as with working mothers).

A relatively large number of publications has appeared on the subject of PTW. This is not surprising, especially when a government—such as the Dutch government—is seriously considering the possibility of using PTW as an important instrument to create more employment, or when it has already done so. Nevertheless, the literature is predominantly contemplative, although gradually more case studies are being reported. Especially from a (macro- and business) economic perspective, several sound analyses have recently been made. But, again, only very little empirical research has been done in the social sciences; one of the reasons for this possibly relates to a problem we mentioned earlier, namely the all-too-comprehensive, ambiguous definition of PTW. In the following, we shall merely touch on several main points (for more details, we refer to the publications mentioned below).

An important question, to be put first, is to what extent PTW affects productivity. Opinions and experiences are divided on this point: the introduction of the five-day working week in The Netherlands, 1961, probably caused a slight rise in productivity (based on estimated figures). More recent experience with PTW presents this confusing picture: no correlation at all; productivity declines (e.g. in tasks requiring a great deal of knowledge and experience); productivity increases (especially in the case of individual tasks and in seasonal work). Various economists have pointed out that, if PTW leads to higher productivity, the number of newly-created job in PTW will be less than proportional (negative effect on employment), assuming that the total amount of work does not alter.

Another important question refers to the developments in costs. A number of economists have stated that a large-scale introduction of PTW is possible only, provided that wages are reduced proportional to the reduction of working time. Driehuis and De Vrije (1981)—summarizing much of the literature— found that the cost of labour might increase, especially due to higher premium duties. There is a maximum income level for levying social premiums: if the original job, in normal working time, was above that maximum, the employer will have to pay more premium duties for two PT jobs. Even if one half of the original salary remains above that level—as in the case of certain members of Dutch County Councils (*NRC*, 1981)—there may be a slight increase in costs: in our example, due to old-age-pension premiums, widow-pension premiums and allowances for the costs of medical care. If the original job was under that level, the exemption from premium duties at the bottom will cause the premium for two PT jobs to be lower. In addition, refunds of travelling expenses and such may increase. But the costs of labour will decrease if productivity increases. The capital costs will decrease if more intensive use is made of the means of production; such costs will increase, however, if capital goods have to be extended as a result of PTW.

PTW may also lead to employees being more attracted to overtime work or taking a second job (which has a negative effect on the availability of work). It was found, on the other hand, that in organizations practising PTW the amount of overtime decreases. Furthermore, PTW may cause mobility in the labour market to decline if both (married) partners are employed part-time. There is a reduction of absenteeism and delay of work; the data on turnover are contradictory.

Supervising becomes more demanding when done part-time, e.g. as regards supplying information, the transfer of work, communication, and composing more elaborate working schedules. This last aspect, though, has its advantages too, since it enhances flexibility. It greatly depends on the form of PTW chosen, to what degree PTW is to promote flexibility (e.g. in coping with peak-times at work).

In the view of the individual employee an essential question is that of the consequences of PTW on his legal status. It is often said that PTW will sooner lead to dismissal. Social security provisions generally are not different for PT workers: partial benefits are granted according to the rate of pay. It is true that, at times, it is hard to become eligible for a benefit. The type of work and the rate of pay are important factors in this connection: complaints are frequently heard of their low levels. It is for this reason, among others, that the objective of emancipation is often questioned: PTW not only is said to be inadequate, it also tends to lay too heavy a burden on those who combine it with household work. This effect will even be heightened if the average work intensity is greater than in the case of normal working days, particularly if resting periods occur partly outside working hours. Another complaint of the same nature is that work cannot be finished within the agreed time and must therefore be taken home.

It may be said, on the positive side of the balance, that people grow less tired, have more options as to working times, find more opportunities for hobbies, study and recreation. However, there are setbacks to PTW which make one wonder whether they are just growing pains or a permanent condition, in that workers often feel to be outside the general run of things, that they tend to be aware of differences in status between themselves and full-time workers, that their career opportunities are more limited, etc.

It is apparent from this account that various experiences concern very specific types of PTW (especially the shorter working day or week), with the result that different effects might ensue if a different sort of PTW were to be applied. That is why various authors are in favour of selecting a type of PTW which is adapted to the actual situation as much as possible. This cannot be achieved without a sound analysis of costs and benefits. In spite of this, there is widespread doubt as to whether PTW can be introduced on a large scale at all, or whether it ought to be restricted to particular business branches and professions. It is possible that biased attitudes towards PTW play a role in this: gaining practical experience apparently makes for a more balanced judgement (see also: de Jong et al., 1974; Nollen, in Robison, 1976; Marić, 1977; Cohen and Gadon, 1978; Levitan and Belous, 1979; Miller and Terborg, 1979; van Mill and van Schagen-Gelder, 1980; RCO, 1980; Driehuis and de Vrije, 1981; de Koning, 1981; Siddré and de Regt, 1981; van der Veen and Roosma, 1981; Cornuit, 1981; WRR, 1981; Bruyn-Hundt, 1982).

This last theme formed the central subject of the research of Schoemaker *et al.* (1981). In five widely different work organizations (a bakery, a publishing firm, etc.), that had been working with PTW for some time, 14 jobs in all were selected of which it was generally assumed that they did not lend themselves to PTW. Ten of these involved leadership activities, such as shift supervisor in continuous shift work, chief reporter of a weekly, etc. Data were assembled with the aid of various methods; for each of the 14 jobs, three informants were interviewed. The researchers came to the remarkable conclusion that, *in principle*, PTW is feasible in any job whatsoever, which does not mean that it is desirable under all circumstances. There is no general recipe: it always depends on local circumstances and on the work in question, what solution is preferable. Thus, in some cases it may be advisable to introduce PTW for a whole group of personnel—e.g. an entire department—and not to any individual employee. Furthermore, the researchers discovered that, at the close of their study, opinions on PTW were more favourable in the organizations concerned. This raised the interesting question as to whether PTW would not be more widely accepted if one were to realize that a 'legitimate, inconspicuous supply of PTW' does indeed exist: i.e. among those who, although having normal working hours, in fact carry out their true job in part-time because they do work in commissions, on Works Councils, on Boards of Directors, because they attend training courses, etc. The same conclusion—that PTW is always feasible—is expressed by van Mill and van Schagen-Gelder (1980) in a study concerning the municipality of Rotterdam.

5. OVERTIME

One speaks of overtime whenever the working time is longer than agreed by contract, whether incidentally or periodically. This description is quite acceptable for those having a regular working week. According to Driehuis and de Vrije (1981), in the case of PTW, problems may arise when the work is done only during certain parts of the day, and the criterion for overtime is 'anything over 8 hours a day'. In The Netherlands, when settling the case of a civil servant a judge will always take the individually agreed working time as the basis, which means that for a large category of workers this type of problem will not occur.

Various countries keep records of data concerning the extent of overtime. In the case of The Netherlands we may refer to the annual reports of the Labour Inspection and to the publications of the Central Bureau of Statistics. It appears from the Statistics Pocket Book (CBS, 1981), for instance, that, in the case of manual workers, there are a great many differences among various business branches as to the average weekly working time (including overtime). Between 1970 and 1978 working time was gradually diminished; between 1978 and 1979, though, there appeared a slight increase in several branches, e.g. in transport, storage and communication companies. For data concerning other EEC-countries we refer to Münstermann and Preiser (1978).

In the field of overtime hardly any (social science) research has been done. As far as The Netherlands are concerned, the only two studies known to us are those carried out by the General Employers Association around 1970 (AWV, 1969, 1972). On the one hand, they contain a survey of those types of company (classed according to size, activity, place of residence) which have employees engaged in production work doing overtime, and of their views on overtime. On the other hand, an inquiry was made among the employees of four companies. It revealed that pay-rise formed an important motive for many employees, but that evidently other motives, too, played a role in working overtime (e.g. as regards the sort of work).

It has been pointed out by Baird and Beccia (1980) that, essentially, there are two causes for the existence of overtime. First, the external demand for goods and services may be greater than the organization's capacity to meet it within the usual working hours. Second, productivity may be low as a result of inadequate coordination, lack of motivation, etc. Therefore, to meet the regular demand, overtime is necessary, another tendency being to employ more personnel. On the grounds of data assembled in 42 offices of a U.S. governmental institution, they discovered first of all a considerable negative correlation between the amount of work done and the average number of overtime hours for each employee. It also turned out that, as more overtime hours were made per office, more employees were recruited. Finally, there was a negative correlation between overtime, job satisfaction and satisfaction with pay.

Although the design of this research does not allow any conclusions as to cause and effect—e.g., there were no repeated tests—we may safely assume that overtime is a far less innocent phenomenon (to the work organization as well as to the individual) than the virtual absence of systematic empirical research would suggest.

6. TEMPORARY WORK

Above, we defined this working time agreement as work done voluntarily, without permanent employment, and for shorter periods. This may or may not involve a regular working day or week. It involves, in fact, a great variety of forms and agreements, whose proportions are hard to estimate. For example, we may think of someone who, for whatever reason, occasionally undertakes to find a job, or of measures, taken by government and industry, to promote employment. This section will be restricted to a brief exposition of two forms: working via employment agencies and working at home.

Working through *employment agencies* is forbidden in The Netherlands, unless the Minister of Social Affairs and Employment has granted a licence for supplying personnel (Bakels and Opheikens, 1978). The Monthly Social Statistics, published by CBS, mention the number of licence-holders as well as the number of temporary employees. The number of the latter category lay between

30,000 and 40,000 in the past years. In this country, opinions on the desirability of 'agency work' vary (for more details, see van Haasteren, 1977). Some say, for example, that at a time when labour is scarce temporary employees are paid too much, which, understandably, is disturbing to those employed permanently. And with an abundance of labour, the use of temporary employees would tend to prevent permanent employment. Others, however, stress that by means of employment agencies more people can find work. In connection with this, the position of the Labour Exchanges in all districts is at issue.

Attention is also called to the greater flexibility arising from agency work, to the benefit of the temporary employee as well as to the work organization. In connection with this point, some exploratory research has been done. In their inquiry, Van Haasteren and Van Overeem (1976) were able to class five types of temporary employees:

—those looking for a permanent job;
—those working part of the year: e.g. married women, students;
—occasional workers;
—the 'professionals': those who find a permanent job unappealing and prefer the 'carefree' existence of working through an agency;
—the 'transitionals': those wishing to avoid inactivity between periods of other employment.

In 1977, research was done among those employing temporary employees (van Haasteren, 1977). One of the things it shows is that the government is the most regular user, while in industry the practice shows seasonal and peak-time influences. It is remarkable that most users are rather pleased with agency work: when asked what problems had arisen, 43% of the informants in industry, 59% in the civil services and 63% in public services answered 'none'. Especially the civil service informants frequently remarked that an entire department may depend on it, that great arrears can be made up. Such underlying motives strongly remind one of the results found by Baird and Beccia (see section 5) in their research on the causes of overtime.

Work-pools can be regarded as a special form of agency work (Leegwater, 1979). Examples are to be found among dockers in Amsterdam and Rotterdam, and among teachers and construction workers in the Rotterdam area (Rijnmond).

Bruijn-Hundt (1981a, 1981b, 1982) finds reason to believe that *paid work at home* may be on the increase, particularly owing to the economic decline. On this point no quantitative data whatsoever exist. Indeed, she mentions two small studies produced by a Dutch women's union (Vrouwenbond, NVV), from which it appears that women working at home are unwilling to cooperate in any research, for fear of losing their jobs. The answers given by those women who where ready to cooperate, yield grim images of working conditions, payment and social security.

7. SOME WORK- AND ORGANIZATIONAL-PSYCHOLOGICAL PERSPECTIVES

7.1. Domain demarcation

One remark repeatedly made in the foregoing sections was that, with the exception of irregular work and shift work, there are virtually no results of empirical psychological research studies in the field of working time agreements. Inasfar as such research was done at all, it was mostly of an exploratory nature. Of course, exploratory research does have its values. It is, for instance, important to know that various groups of the population prefer more spare time to higher incomes (see e.g. Chapman and Otterman, 1975; Best, 1980). Apart from this, there is a need for more research of this kind on the impact of organizational characteristics on the selection and functioning of working time agreements. Nevertheless, such studies are no more than a first step; research of a different nature is required in order to understand, and subsequently predict, certain forms of behaviour. We will now proceed to make some remarks on this subject.

Broadly defined, the object of work- and organizational psychology is *man's behavior at work* (in the context of an organization) as well as *his spare time behaviour*, the latter being relevant, on the one hand, inasfar as spare time has an influence on working behaviour and, on the other, inasfar as spare time behaviour is influenced by work. Relevant psychological perspectives on work and working time may be concerned with:
—Processes of weighing arguments and making choices, e.g. in the wider context of decision-making processes.
—Knowledge, skills, opinions, attitudes, preferences, motives, etc., as determinants of behaviour.
—Actual observable behaviour, such as patterns of recreation, performance behaviour, etc.
—Meanings of (working and spare time) behaviour, e.g. from a perspective of norms and values.
—A policy angle; the design and the evaluation, respectively, of a working time agreement in relation to specific characteristics of the work organization.

Of course, more perspectives are conceivable, but those mentioned here offer sufficient starting-points with regard to the theories below. But first there is one concept which needs to be clarified.

What is typical of *spare time* is the meaning emerging from words such as 'leisure' (French 'loisir'; Latin 'licére'): 'being permitted to . . . ' (*The American Heritage Dictionary of the English Language*). This implies that the emphasis is on having opportunities, being able to choose, etc., not on what one need *not* do (such as; e.g., not working). There are, however, quite a few definitions and views of spare time (for more details, see Burch, 1969; Parker and Smith, 1976; Neulinger, 1978; Kabanoff, 1980). We adopt Parker and Smith's (1976) classification, which distinguishes four broad categories (after having mentioned 'working time' first):

—Work-related time: commuting time, preparation of work, etc.
—Existence time: meals, sleep, etc.
—Semi-leisure: activities of an obligatory nature, such as walking the dog, paying calls, etc.
—Leisure: time to be spent at liberty.

We wish to add that the meaning of (working and spare) time can be affected by the concomitant 'calendar period'. One might think of the hour of the day or night, the day of the week, the week of the month, the season, the year, and the time of one's individual life. Particularly with respect to the first ones, research perspectives taking into account the impact of biological rhythms may be quite relevant.

7.2. Some approaches

In the last few years, the issue of how the worlds of working and non-working are related to one another has been receiving a gradually increasing amount of attention. It is, in particular, a question of whether working behaviour and non-working behaviour influence one another, and, if so, how. Three types of hypothesis have been developed on this issue (the third of which has received relatively little attention):

A. *Compensatory hypothesis* (also denoted by such terms as 'oppositional' or 'contrasting'): it is usually defined in the sense that people 'get rid of the pressure' in their spare time. They do things for which there is no occasion while at work. Of course, the argument can be reversed: men seek or accept such work as will meet with those qualifications which they lack in their spare time. On the basis of research we may indicate two possible patterns:

—supplemental compensation: as the work offers little satisfaction, the spare time prevails as the central life interest;
—reactive compensation: the work is found to be highly satisfying, while the spare time is of little significance.

B. *Spill-over hypothesis* (other terms: extension, generalization, congruence): originally this implied that alienation at work evolves into alienating spare time behaviour. Again, the argument can be reversed, of course, nor does it necessarily concern alienation only. This appears, for instance, from the following two patterns, based on research:

—passive spill-over: both work and spare time receive low scores on attributes generally held important (such as autonomy or the use of skills);
—active spill-over: both work and spare time receive high scores on these attributes.

C. *Segmentation hypothesis*: there is no relation whatsoever between working behaviour and spare time behaviour; they are two separate worlds (in this chapter we cannot go into relevant research or into the alternative theories developed in this context; for further reading see e.g. Wilensky, 1960; Wippler, 1968; Burch, 1969; Parker and Smith, 1976; Rousseau, 1978; Champoux, 1980; Staines, 1980; Kabanoff, 1980; Kabanoff and O'Brien, 1980; O'Brien, 1981).

Nevertheless, on the basis of research (whose amount by now has grown considerably) on the validity of these hypotheses, we can conclude that, among other things, a great many conditioning and intervening variables may affect the results, and that a particular hypothesis may, for one facet (of work and spare time) have an explanatory meaning which need not apply to another facet. It is somewhat surprising, though, that this sort of hypotheses has so far played no role at all in the (W & O psychological) research on working time agreements. And yet, many research questions might be formulated in which they could be profitably used. We shall mention just a couple of examples:

— Let us suppose initial research to shed light on the spare time behaviour of an unemployed person (a category of unemployed people, respectively). Each of the three hypotheses will yield different conclusions when we go into the question of what qualifications an unemployed man will require of any work, or what work will be just acceptable, respectively.

— For full-time workers, acceptance of flexible working hours, a four-day working week of 40 hours, forms of part-time work, etc. may depend on the type of spare time (existence time? leisure?) gained, and on the degree to which working and spare time behaviour are related for these people.

Theoretically speaking, the above-mentioned hypotheses are akin to what Allport (see Katz and Kahn, 1978) understands as '*partial inclusion*'. This concept implies that organizations profit by particular aspects of individual behaviour only. Apart from this, the working behaviour of employees is also influenced by the fact that their participation in the work organization is merely a part of their time and existence. The positions and roles they occupy in other social systems affect their values, attitudes, behaviour, etc. in working. This approach resembles that of *role transitions*: people regularly find themselves in 'boundary positions', and frequently shift from one role set (e.g. their daily work) to another (e.g. a particular recreation activity). In doing so they are confronted with widely different, if not ambiguous or contradictory, role prescriptions and expectations. In our opinion, research in the field of work and working time can gain much by these two approaches; apart from the examples above, we may call attention to, for example, working through employment agencies.

Research in this field may also make use of theories concerning *social comparison processes* (see this Handbook, ch. 2.2, 3.1, and 4.11), for example in the tradition of Homans and Adams. In connection with working time agreements, attention should be paid—according to e.g. Miller and Terborg (1979)—first of all to the frame of reference and the reference groups used by the employees in question. These same authors proceed to pose the interesting question as to what extent the more general concepts of *motivation* are valid for employees dealing with unusual working time agreements (concepts such as expectations concerning means-goal relationships in expectancy-theory; see this Handbook, ch. 2.2).

Finally, we wish to call attention to the potential meaning, for future research, of the theory of *life cycles*: depending on the time in one's life, certain working time agreements may be less suitable than others (see also Cohen and Gadon, 1978).

8. IRREGULAR WORK AND SHIFT WORK

8.1. Introduction

In section 1.1 we ascertained that for centuries there have been working systems far removed from what might be called 'common practice'. An important category, in this connection, is formed by those systems involving irregular work and shift work (henceforth summarized as 'work at unusual hours'). This category is important, on the one hand because a relatively large part (approx. 15–20%) of the Dutch working population is employed in such systems, and on the other, because many of these systems deeply affect the lives of those concerned: one need only remember the current discussions on the necessity to abolish night work and to introduce a five-shift system (which would imply a considerable reduction of working time).

The subject of this section is of a pre-eminently interdisciplinary nature. While rendering the theme all the more fascinating, it also makes greater demands on scientific research. There is hardly any major review on work at unusual hours, which does not include a section on the host of methodological weaknesses of past research studies (see e.g. Münstermann and Preiser, 1978; Haider *et al.*, 1981). Apart from the problems relating to the comparability of research results, there is a remarkable lack of theory formation.

Besides the various perspectives from which work at unusual hours may be viewed, one can distinguish several levels of analysis (individual, family, organization, society). The positive and negative effects of these working systems are rather varied for each level of analysis. Processes of balancing gains and losses may, therefore, lead to different net-results per level. It is generally thought that for large numbers of shift workers the advantages hardly outweigh the disadvantages, while the advantages often prevail for the work organizations. Here we come to the reasons and motives which are at the roots of work at unusual hours.

Economic considerations are one of the major reasons for the existence of shift work, in particular in industry. These concern not only the returns on investments but also employment and the demand for products (de Jong, 1974; de Jong and Ruys, 1979; Bosworth and Dawkins, 1979a, 1979b).

Technology is another causal factor. There are, for example, processes in chemical industry that have a 'reaction-time' far exceeding the eight-hour working day; paper-mills use machinery with very long 'starting times'.

A third factor relates to the nature of the product: the processing of perishable products may require a (temporary) prolongation of business hours. Our society's need for continuous service activities (public utilities, transport, hospitals, police) plus the existence of different time-zones, depending on the degree of latitude (tele-communication, airline traffic), are, finally, the main reasons for the existence of work at unusual hours in the service sector.

8.2. Nature and extent of work at unusual hours

8.2.1. NATURE

As in the preceding sections, by 'usual working hours' we mean the hours between 7.00 and 18.00 hrs., Mondays to Fridays (in conformity with the Dutch Labour Act 1919, section 24). This implies that we understand by *unusual working hours* the hours *between 18.00 and 7.00 hrs.* (i.e. in the evening and at night) and those *during the weekend.* If we confine ourselves to those systems involving working hours which regularly occur at unusual hours, we can distinguish two main categories:
—shift work;
—irregular work.

Shift work refers to working systems involving two or more watches (or duties). During every watch a particular number of workers (the shift) is responsible for the tasks to be carried out. Depending on the number and the specific part of the 24-hour-periods during which work is done each week, one can make roughly the following distinction (cf. Rutenfranz *et al.*, 1976, who offer a more specific classification):
—*Discontinuous systems*, with one interruption of the work every 24 hours (mostly at night).
—*Semi-continuous systems*, in which the work is continued for several periods of 24 hours, and interrupted weekly (mostly during the weekend).
—*Fully continuous systems*, with little or no interruptions in the work.

Those systems which do not involve shift work, but regularly entail working at unusual hours, we call *irregular working systems.* One usually encounters such systems in the service sector, as the need for service often varies in the course of the day or night (Hoek and de Jong, 1979; Rutenfranz *et al.*, 1979). Moreover, storage of 'products' (services) is possible only in a limited measure. In short, there is a varying need of personnel in the course of 24 hours. There would not be any point in working with 'shifts' of equal force which pass the work on to each other at regular shifting times, as is usual with shift work in industry.

It is barely possible to make a broad classification of irregular working systems, because the applied solutions are of a highly individual character.

8.2.2. THE EXTENT

In 1976, at the initiative of the European Community's Bureau of Statistics, a second sample survey of Dutch manpower was made. Some of the data assembled relate to unusual working hours. The sample comprised approx. 130,000 addresses (3%). Some of the outcomes are presented in table 4.

The table shows that there are about 700,000 people regularly working at unusual hours. No data are availabe on the exact classification of this number of people into shift work systems and irregular work systems. What we know is that in 1975 the number of shift workers in industry totalled 126,000 (Directorate-General of Labour, 1975).

Since 1950, the number of shift workers has increased in a great many countries. But it is hard to predict what number of people will have unusual working hours in times to come. It has been said, admittedly, that the number of people working in industry will decrease, and that the service sector will show the reverse tendency. However, extrapolations merely based on figures of the past do not form a valid picture. From data produced by Dutch public utilities it appears, for example, that productivity and production grew considerably between 1960 and 1970, but that the number of shift workers was diminished (Hoek and de Jong, 1979).

Münstermann and Preiser (1978) have established that estimates should allow for, at least, the following factors: reduction of working time, business concentration, technological developments, changes in the societal structure (including economics and the provision of services), the state of trade and legal measures. It has been pointed out (Colquhoun and Rutenfranz, 1980, Reading 1), in this connection, that the most essential factor might very well be the extent to which any individual, and society itself, in time, will opt for the economic advantages of shift work and accept any alterations in the way of life, particularly when it concerns night work.

8.3. Effects of working at unusual hours on the individual worker

In the framework of this chapter there is no place for an elaboration on all effects (at all levels of analysis) of working at unusual hours: we shall deal with the effects on individual workers in particular.

Table 4. Numbers of people regularly on night duty or Sunday-duty in 1975 (according to industrial branch and sex).

Branch of industry	numbers × 1000		% of the number of working people			
	People employed	People on night and/or Sunday duty	People on night and Sunday duty	People on night duty only	People on Sunday duty only	People on night and/or Sunday duty
Agriculture and Fishery	264	123	5	1	41	47
Mining	11	3	15	7	3	24
Industry	1,132	137	5	6	1	12
Public utilities	47	6	10	6	1	13
Construction	475	8	1	0	1	2
Commerce, hotels catering, repairshops	802	77	2	1	7	10
Whole-salers	251	8	1	1	1	3
Agents	12	0	0	0	0	0
Retailers	385	12	1	0	2	3
Hotels, restaurants, public houses	81	53	12	1	53	65
Repair shops (of utensils)	73	3	1	0	3	4
Transport and communication	300	100	16	8	9	33
Railways	28	23	23	5	17	46
Road transport	110	31	11	1	12	28
Navigation	39	21	35	14	6	54
Inland navigation	15	8	34	8	10	51
Airlines	16	8	40	2	9	51
Supply industry	22	3	6	4	5	15
Communication	70	16	6	13	3	22
Banks, Insurance, Business Service	316	12	1	1	2	4

	1,097	209	10	1	8	19
Other services						
Public administration, defence, social insurance	284	45	11	1	4	16
Religious organizations	12	8	3	0	62	64
Education	254	6	1	0	1	2
Health care and veterinary service	217	90	25	1	15	41
Social service	125	30	10	1	13	24
Social-cultural and cultural institutes	11	2	5	1	16	22
Sport and recreation	54	20	7	1	29	37
Employers' organizations, trade unions, research institutes, other social organizations	41	2	3	0	2	5
Other services	77	4	2	0	3	5
Private households	22	3	2	0	11	12
Total	4,444	678	6	2	7	15
men	3,370	543	6	2	7	15
women	1,074	135	5	0	7	12

Source: *Manpower census 1975* (ed. A. Corpeleijn), CBS, 1978.

8.3.1. AETIOLOGY: WORKING AT UNUSUAL HOURS AS A PROBLEM OF RHYTHM

For the individual worker (and often for his family), the consequences of working at unusual hours are closely related to the disturbed rhythms inherent in such working systems. These are twofold:

a. disturbance of biological rhythms;
b. disturbance of social rhythms.

Re a: An appreciable number of bodily functions, varying from cell division to the menstrual cycle, shows periodical fluctuations. It is especially the circadian (= approx. 24 hours) rhythms which are relevant in this context. These rhythms can be found in numerous bodily functions, such as electric brain activity, heartbeat, respiration and body temperature. As a rule these rhythms have peaks during the day, and falls during the night. These states of activation and de-activation run largely parallel to the cycle of sleeping and waking.

Changes in the sleeping/waking cycle, e.g. the shifting of phases as a result of working at unusual hours, will frequently lead to inadequate adaptation of the circadian rhythm (see e.g. van Loon, 1980; Knauth and Rutenfranz, 1980). Changes occur in the amplitudes of periodical functions (flattening) and mutual phase relations between functions are disturbed (desynchronization), mainly because the social 'Zeitgebers'—i.e. stimuli from the social environment— greatly influence, in the case of human beings, the course of biological rhythms (see e.g. Wever, 1979). This indicates both the significance of a phase-shift in itself, and the relevance of social rhythms.

Re b: Section 1.1 explains what is meant by 'normal' working time. The organization of our society is tuned to it: we need only remember the accessibility of all sorts of recreation, educational institutes, public service, etc. This has at least three consequences with regard to working at unusual hours:

1. The need for, e.g., recreation outside 'business hours' *demands* work to be done at unusual hours.
2. Those working at unusual hours have *in fact restricted* opportunities to participate in social recreation activities.
3. Awareness of social rhythms promotes, in the individual working at unusual hours, disturbances of *biological rhythms* (social 'Zeitgebers').

Although, as indicated above, the social 'Zeitgebers' often conflict with the work rhythm of individuals engaged in shift work or a comparable system, there are exceptions. A pilot, for instance, when passing time zones, will experience disturbances of his sleeping/waking rhythms and, hence, of his biological clock, whereas the social rhythm may preserve a measure of harmony with his working rhythm (the social 'Zeitgebers' will shift accordingly). We refer, in this connection, to the relevant time-lag studies (e.g. Aschoff, 1980; Desir *et al.*, 1981; Fuller *et al.*, 1981).

The various disturbances of rhythm described here, often cause appreciable problems for those concerned. It is for this reason that we wish to refer to working at unusual hours as a rhythm problem.

8.3.2. SHIFT WORK SYSTEMS VERSUS IRREGULAR WORK SYSTEMS

Although shift work systems can be distinguished from irregular work systems, e.g. from an organizational angle, the two types greatly overlap as regards the consequences for the individual employees. This is because the disturbances of biological and social rhythms frequently apply to both types of work system. A few additional remarks need to be made here, though.
—After the Second World War a great deal of research was done on shift work in industry. There was far less research on the service sector, where many irregular work systems occur nevertheless. During the past few years the emphasis has shifted a little: e.g. the European Foundation for the Improvement of Living and Working Conditions commisioned a number of studies concerning work at irregular hours in the service sector (Hoek and de Jong, 1979; Rutenfranz et al., 1979). One of the reasons of this difference in attention, Rutenfranz et al. declare, lies in the fact that in the service sector the (legal) working time agreements were more vaguely formulated, which caused a great diversity of systems. Night work, as well as Sunday work, also have always been more readily accepted in the service sector (Hoek and de Jong, 1979).
—It appears from research that in the service sector extremely irregular working times occur. It is true that being able to start working at any time of the day may seem appealing (flexibility), but studies have made abundantly clear that the setbacks increase as a family, particularly one with children, has to deal more and more with the irregularity of those working times.
—It is an advantage of irregular work systems that they lend themselves very well to part-time work (e.g. when coping with peak-times).

8.3.3. DISADVANTAGES FOR THE SHIFT WORKER

The harmful effects of shift work (especially in industry) have been studied and recorded at length during the last decades. This does not mean that no questions remain at present. Within the scope of this chapter we must confine ourselves to a brief sketch of the main points: see table 5, which we shall briefly explain first.

Not every shift work system causes unambiguously harmful effects on those concerned. The effects of this type of work should rather be considered as— sometimes strongly—*promoting risk*. There are many factors acting as conditioning or intervening variables in a network of relationships. The following features are among the important ones:
—the nature of the system (changeover times, speed of rotation, recovery times);
—personal characteristics (age, married state, motivation);
—characteristics of the private environment (family, friends, residence);
—characteristics of the work situation (type of work, special facilities (in)available, multiple load).

Table 5. Potential inconveniences of shift work for the employee.

Main factor	Sub factor	State-of-affairs research			Sources
		1	2	3	
1. Health	*increasing number of subjective complaints*				Aanonson, 1964
	—sleep problems (qualitative, quantitative)	×			Angersbach *et al.*, 1980
	—fatigue	×			Harrington, 1978
	—more feelings of overload	×			Rutenfranz, *et al.*, 1977, 1980, 1981
	—nervous complaints (headache, depression, irritability, trembling hands)	×			Taylor and Pocock, 1980
					Thiis–Evensen, 1958
	—digestive complaints (dyspepsia, gastritis, lack of appetite, nausea, diarrhoea, constipation)	×			Münstermann and Preiser, 1978
					Ulich, *et al.*, 1979
					Walker, 1978
					Rentos and Shepard, 1976
					Meyman, 1981
					Thierry *et al.*, 1979, 1980, 1981
					Carpentier and Cazamian, 1977
	growing number of objective infirmities				Hoolwerf, *et al.*, 1974
	—greater mortality	(×)			Siersema, 1981
	—gastric and intestial ulcers		×		Hoolboom and Van Alphen, 1980
	—coronary diseases			×	TNN, 1979
	—respiratory diseases			×	Agervold, 1976.
	—rheumatoid arthritis			×	
	—neurological diseases			×	

2. Social life			
more domestic problems			Bunnage, 1979
—limited partner role (in company, sexually)		X	Carpentier and Cazamian, 1977
—limited parent role (upbringing of children)		X	Münstermann and Preiser, 1978
—more problems of coordination (planning)		X	Walker, 1978
—household problems (extra meals, silence during the day after night duty)		X	Hoolwerf et al., 1974
—more divorce cases	X		Maasen, 1978
			Rutenfranz et al., 1977, 1979
less opportunities for socially bound spare time activities			Mott et al., 1965
—participation in formally organized activities (societies, clubs, cinema, theatre)		X	Siersema, 1981
—visiting friends and acquaintances		X	Ulich et al., 1979
—visiting relatives		X	Jugel et al., 1978
more restricted to individual-oriented spare time activities		X	Koller, 1980
			Industriebond NVV, 1978

3. Separation			
stronger sense of belonging to a separate, perhaps isolated group			Banning et al., 1961
—with regard to the family (see social life)		X	Thierry et al., 1979, 1980, 1981, 1982
—with regard to the work organization (status, communication)	X		Hoolwerf et al., 1974
—with regard to society (status)	X		Walker, 1978

Main factor	Sub factor	State-of-affairs research			Sources
		1	2	3	
4. Personal development	*less opportunities for training and/or education*		×		Thierry *et al.*, 1979, 1980, 1981, 1982
	dependence on shift allowance, resulting in a restriction of mobility between jobs		×		Bunnage, 1979
5. Outlook	*limited prospects of the future*	×			Thierry *et al.*, 1979, 1980, 1981, 1982
	—as regards health (e.g. sleeping problems)		×		Carpentier and Cazamian, 1977
	—as regards personal development (see 4)		×		Åkerstedt and Torsvall, 1981
	fear of not being able to cope with shift work				
6. Support	*greater dependence on support and aid*				Thierry *et al.*, 1979, 1980, 1982
	—by the supervisor (social-emotional leadership)		×		Hoolboom and Van Alphen, 1980
	—by colleagues (shift climate)		×		Loskant, 1980
	—by medical service	×			Walker, 1978
	—by social workers			×	
7. Facilities	*greater dependence on special facilities*		×		Thierry *et al.*, 1979, 1980, 1981, 1982
	—need for well-equipped canteen		×		Walker, 1978
	—need for good transport arrangements				

*1 = research results converge considerably.
2 = some corroborating results, insufficient grounds for generalization.
3 = few corroborating results.

This implies that the factors mentioned in table 5 are to be considered as potential inconveniences. The extent to which they will become manifest depends on the concrete situation.

We learn from table 5 that the relation between shift work and health is much studied. Åkerstedt (1976) and others say that, in general, the research concerning that relation has been unsatisfactory and has left numerous questions unanswered. A first problem concerns the definition of the term *health*. In everyday language, health usually equals the absence of objective physical malfunctioning. But it is often noted—and justifiably so, as we see it—that this is a very restrictive idea of health (e.g. Åkerstedt, 1976; Webb, 1981). The importance of, for example, the subjective dimension of health might be overlooked in this way. But to decide on a broader definition—in terms of well-being—would inevitably lead to questions as to the possibilities of, and the consensus on, operationalization.

Apart from such problems with regard to the dependent variable(s), the research is incomplete as far as research designs and the choice of subjects are concerned. Let us illustrate this by just two examples. An example of the first topic is *pre-selection*: Thiis-Evensen (1969) estimates, on the basis of official figures of 'drop-outs', that 20% of the shift workers cannot adjust to irregular work at unusual hours. Since this group of ex-shift workers is left out of consideration in many research designs, the research results may well be based on data derived from a select, 'stronger' population (see e.g. Aanonson, 1964).

To illustrate incompleteness as a result of the (limited) selection of subjects, we may mention the knowledge available on the relation between shift work and *the state of health of women* engaged in it. Although, on rational grounds and on the basis of existing studies, it would be unlikely that the potential inconveniences mentioned in table 5 would not apply to women shift workers, yet, little is known about any specific risks to their health (e.g. Carpentier and Cazamian, 1977; Jugel *et al.*, 1978; Ulich *et al.*, 1979; Siersema, 1981). Besides the 'double load' (work in as well as outside the home), the greater instability— compared with men—of their vegetative nervous systems might be an aggravating factor (Siersema, 1981). A closer examination of this subject seems highly relevant, bearing in mind the discussion on the abolition of specific labour protection for women, prompted by, for one thing, the Directive of the Council of European Communities, 9 February 1976, 'concerning the implementation of the principle of equal treatment for men and women regarding access to work...'.

Other questions which have so far remained unanswered concern, for example, the performance of shift workers and their absenteeism caused by illness. A great deal of research reveals that the human level of performance depends on the time of day (or night). Initially it was thought that this level ran roughly parallel to the circadian temperature rhythm. This general finding has proved to be too crude. The parallelism is fairly true for driving tasks and other motor activities, but it is hardly found in, for instance, more cognitive tasks (Folkard, 1981; Willems, 1981). Other factors, too, influence the momentary performance level. Folkard and Monk (1979) mention, for example, the nature of the shift-work system, as well as a number of varying individual factors, such as pace of adjustment in circadian rhythms, motivation, subjective health and the normal performance rhythm. It appears from various studies that factors such as activities outside the job, the length of tasks, characteristics of the (physical) work environment, eating habits and lack of sleep, can certainly carry weight (see e.g. Wilkinson, 1969; Colquhoun, 1971; Wojtczak-Jaroszowa et al., 1978; Spijkers, 1980; Willems, 1981).

From the factors listed it will be evident that, in the case of a number of studies, we will have to reconsider the conclusion that performance (qualitative and/or quantitative) declines with unusual working hours. However, we wish to point out that an equal level of performance need not imply an equal level of effort. To reach the daytime norms during the night might very well mean an extra load for the individual worker, for the very reason that his body is then partly de-activated.

Considering the amount of complaints expressed by shift workers, we may pose the hypothesis that their absenteeism owing to illness is higher than that of daytime workers. Research results based on global indices of absenteeism (e.g. average duration and frequency), seldom support this hypothesis, however (Taylor et al., 1972; Hoolwerf et al., 1974). There is reason to suppose though that there is in fact a relationship, suggested by certain studies relating specific patterns of absenteeism to specific work schedules (Nicholson et al., 1978). But the question arises as to what factor might be of importance. The research literature yields three aspects, viz.:

—Pre-selection: the largest risk group, as far as absenteeism is concerned, has left shift work.

—Social control: absenteeism usually implies that a colleague has to sacrifice part of his spare time.

—Underrating physical dysfunctions: Andersen (1970) found that shift workers, more so than daytime workers, regard their complaints (about sleep, digestion, etc.) as a 'natural' element of their work situation.

8.3.4. ADVANTAGES TO THE SHIFT WORKER

The relatively large proportion of shift work makes one suspect that, apart from the potential disadvantages, there must be advantages to the individual worker. We shall presently point to three of these. What goes for the disadvantages holds good here: it depends on the concrete situation whether a potential advantage is to become manifest.

One advantage concerns the possibility to have *extra income*. Although the amount may vary, working at unusual hours generally involves receiving a financial bonus (shift allowance). This calls for two side-notes, however:

—shift workers often declare they are bound to spend more on account of working at unusual hours;

—the government claims a large part of the extra pay by means of levying taxes (in this context, see Berendrecht *et al.*, 1980).

In addition to the shift allowance (a small?) part of the shift workers earns extra wages in a second job. They are enabled to do this because they have more spare time, compared to daytime workers, during 'office hours' (see e.g. Maurice and Monteil, 1965).

Another advantage of shift work is *more/or a different kind of spare time*. Again, two side-notes:

—a smaller number of working hours than in daytime work does not automatically cause a proportional increase of true leisure time hours (e.g. Meyman, 1981, stresses the greater need for recuperation time);

—it has not been established to what extent the appreciation of 'the different kind of spare time' is affected by adaptation, habituation, etc. (see also section 7).

A third advantage is *the increased responsibility and the greater freedom to plan one's work* at unusual working hours.

There is a fourth 'advantage' which we did not touch upon yet, although it is questionable whether the term 'advantage' applies in this case. We are referring to the fact that, in some cases, the choice between working in shifts or not working in shifts is, in fact, the choice between working or not working at all, owing to the absence of alternative employment. For the individual worker, to decide to work in shifts implies enjoying the advantages of having a job, i.e. social contacts, status, etc.

8.4. Interventions concerning shift work

8.4.1. Interventions: necessity or luxury?

The attitudes of shift workers to their working schedules may be considered an indicator of the necessity to take measures. This attitude is, more often than not, negative in the case of night work (see the review of Bunnage, 1979); yet it would provide for an ambiguous criterion. On the one hand the attitude is based upon a comparison of unequal components (e.g. health compared to pay); on the other it is affected by many factors—such as the availability of alternative employment—that are hardly related to shift work. A relevant distinction is made by Nachreiner (1978): attitudes contain an evaluative element as well as an element bearing upon the decisions to be made. We think it better to justify the necessity of interventions on the basis of the risks shift workers run regarding their well-being. With reference to table 5 our conclusion can be very clear-cut: interventions are not a luxury.

8.4.2. THE NATURE OF THE INTERVENTIONS

The interventions concerning shift work may generally be divided into five categories:
a. restriction of the occurrence of shift work;
b. restriction of the number of years individuals spend in shift work;
c. selection of shift workers;
d. offering counter-value compensations;
e. removing multiple work load.

Re a: Although it is unrealistic to suppose that shift work can be entirely abolished, it certainly appears possible to restrict working at unusual hours. This is made evident by innovatory studies recently carried out in several EE C-countries. Reorganization of activities and/or automation can enable shift workers to be transferred to daytime work. In this connection Pollet (1979) remarks that to abolish night work always seems to require capital investment, but ' . . . the required amount is not, of necessity, unreasonably high'. We add that the existence of shift work is based on choices made by our society. However, the need for 24-hour service, an established standard of life, etc., are not unalterable characteristics.

Re b: The duration effect of this potential stressor can be restricted by turning shift work into a minor part of someòne's professional career. Interventions in this context are, e.g., setting age-limits for shift workers and determining a maximum number of years permitted to work in shifts. These interventions are closely connected with more general measures to promote mobility, such as agreements for the gradual reduction of shift allowance, development of qualifications for the sake of alternative employment, etc. (in connection with the professional careers of shift workers, see Streich and Jansen, 1979).

Re c: Selection of shift workers may stimulate (special) interventions like rejection, extra supervision, etc. for those that run more risks. Some criteria for selection are available, whereas some will need to be developed. From a medical angle, attention is called to the potentially unfavourable effect of shift work on diseases with a decidedly circadian rhythm: e.g. diabetes mellitus, asthma, epilepsy (Winget *et al.*, 1978). According to Rutenfranz *et al.* (1977), people having a background of gastric and intestinal complaints are unfit for shift work.

Although not pretending completeness, we finally wish to point out the—promising—indication supplied by chronobiology: the amplitude of certain biological rhythms (temperature, 17-OHCS) could be considered as a measure for the individual adaptability to shift work (Reinberg *et al.*, 1981).

Re d: In those cases where shift work actually is applied, reduction of risks could be attempted by means of counter-value compensators (Thierry *et al.*, 1979, 1980, 1981, 1982). A compensation model was developed, as a result of earlier industrial-psychological research on shift work (Hoolwerf *et al.*, 1974). In this model, the concept of compensation is based on two of its meanings. First, compensation in terms of *counter-weight*: a disadvantage is balanced by an advantage of a different kind, but, in principle, the disadvantage remains. Recent practice offers many examples of such counter-weight compensation: sleep problems, fatigue, etc. are compensated for by payment (shift allowance).

Second, compensation is conceived in terms of *counter-value*. If such an intervention is to be effective, it must meet two requirements:

1. The intervention is to have positive effects within the same category, or in other words, relating to the *same denominator*, as that of the aspect of shift work which the worker perceives or experiences as harmful.

2. The effects must be rewarding in relation to the *motives* and the situational outcomes which the workers concerned feel to be essential.

This approach distinguishes between three types of counter-value interventions, interrelated by means of hierarchic order. Type I is the reduction or removal of the *causes* of the inconveniences. Such interventions may be aimed at working time: e.g. a reduction may cause less disturbance of biological rhythms, etc. Type II is the reduction or removal of the *effects* of the inconveniences: social isolation, for example, can be (partially) compensated for by organizing social activities that fit in the shift worker's schedule. Type III, finally, is aimed at compensating for the *psychological meanings* of the inconveniences. If shift work is experienced as a decline in status, interventions aimed at a rise in status are qualified as counter-value compensators.

There is no end to the counter-value interventions conceivable. The choice, however, will eventually always depend on the concrete situation (time and place). The counter-value approach, therefore, can be qualified as pluriform and flexible.

Re e: The interventions mentioned in the last category are not immediately related to shift work, but to other aspects of the work situation. The starting-point is, that shift work is a potential stressor, whose effect may be enhanced by other forms of loading. We mention, for example, the potentially harmful effects of particular aspects of the physical work environment, such as noise, heat, toxic substances, etc. (Münstermann and Preiser, 1978; Bergman and Bolm, 1980). The interventions discussed here aim at a reduction of such additional stressors.

We conclude this chapter by a more general remark. Relatively much research (psychological, for one) has been done on shift work, compared to that on other types of working time arrangements; in spite of this, there is a considerable

636   HANDBOOK OF WORK AND ORGANIZATIONAL PSYCHOLOGY, VOLUME 1

number of gaps and as yet unanswered questions. This emphasizes the necessity
of more and better research, but at the same time we think that what research
has yielded so far could be used much more often in the policy-making and the
implementation of shift work than is usually the case.

REFERENCES

Aanonson, A. (1964), *Shift work and health*. Oslo: Universitetsforlaget.
Agervold, M. (1976), Shift work—a critical review. *Scand. J. of Psychology*, **17**, 181–188.
Åkerstedt, T. (1976), Shift work and health: Interdisciplinary aspects. In: Rentos, P. G.,
    et al. (Eds.), *Shift work and health ... a symposium*. Washington D.C.: U.S. Department
    of Health, Education and Welfare.
Åkerstedt, T., Torsvall, L. (1981), Age, sleep and adjustment to shift work. In W. P. Koella
    (Ed.), *Sleep 1980*. Basel: S. Karger.
Andersen, J. E. (1970), *Treskiftsarbejde—a sociomedical study*. Copenhagen: Social-
    forskningsinstituttet.
Angersbach, D., Knauth, P., Loskant, H., Karvonen, M. J., Undeutsch, K., Rutenfranz, J.
    (1980), A retrospective cohort study comparing complaints and diseases in day and
    shift workers. In: Colquhoun, W. P., *et al.* (Eds.), *Studies of shift work*. London: Taylor
    & Francis Ltd.
Aschoff, J. (1980), Features of circadian rhythms relevant for the design of shift schedules.
    In: Colquhoun, W. P., *et al.* (Eds.), *Studies of shift work*. London: Taylor & Francis Ltd.
AWV (1969), *Overwerk: Verslag van een schriftelijke enquête* [Overtime: Report on a
    survey]. Haarlem (The Netherlands).
AWV (1972), *Overwerk: Verslag van een onderzoek in vier bedrijven naar de opvattingen
    rond het overwerken* [Overtime: Report on an investigation of attitudes towards over-
    time, held in four firms]. Haarlem (The Netherlands).
Baird, L. S., Beccia, P. J. (1980), The potential misuse of overtime. *Personnel Psychology*,
    33, 557–565.
Bakels, K. L., Opheikens, L. (1978), *Schets van het Nederlandse arbeidsrecht* [Outline of
    Dutch labour law]. Deventer: Kluwer.
Banning, W., Bonjer, W., Bast, G. H., Jong, J. R. de, Werff, H. M. A. van der (1961),
    Ploegenarbeid medisch, psychologisch, sociologisch, technisch, ekonomisch belicht
    [Shift work considered medically, psychologically, sociologically, technically, and
    economically]. The Hague: COP.
Berendrecht, A. J. *et al.* (1980), *Vijf voor vier*. Eindrapport van de kommissie volkon-
    tinudienst [Five to four. Final report of the commission on continuous-shift work] of
    Shell Nederland Raffinaderij BV and Shell Nederland Chemie BV, Rotterdam/Pernis.
Bergmann, E., Bolm, W. (1980), Beanspruchungen von Schichtarbeitern—eine Folge
    ihrer Mehrfachbelastung? In: Brenner, W., *et al.* (Eds.), *Arbeitsbedingte Gesundheits-
    schäden—Fiktion oder Wirklichkeit*. Stuttgart: Gentner Verlag.
Best, F. (1980), *Exchanging earnings for leisure: Findings of an exploratory national survey
    on work time preferences*. Washington: U.S. Government Printing Office.
Bosworth, D. L., Dawkins, P. J. (1979a), *The spread of shiftwork—United Kingdom*.
    Contract no. EF/SC/78/12/SW, Dublin, European Foundation for the Improvement of
    Living and Working Conditions.
Bosworth, D. L., Dawkins, P. J. (1979b), *Advantages and disadvantages of shiftwork—
    United Kingdom*. Contract no. EF/SC/78/12/SW, Dublin, European Foundation for
    the Improvement of Living and Working Conditions.

Bruyn-Hundt, M. (1981a), Huisindustrie [Home industry]. *Economisch-Statistische Berichten* [Economic-Statistical Reports], **66**, 536–537.

Bruyn-Hundt, M. (1981b), Voor jou tien anderen [Ten others for your job]. *Intermediair*, **17**, no. 38, 47–53.

Bruyn-Hundt, M. (1982), *Deeltijdwerk* [Part-time work]. Deventer: Van Loghum Slaterus.

Bunnage, D. (1979), *The effects of shiftwork on social and family life*. Contract no. EF/SC/78/20/SW, Dublin, European Foundation for the Improvement of Living and Working Conditions.

Burch, W. R. (1969), The social circles of leisure: Competing explanations. *J. of Leisure Research*, **1**, 125–148.

Carpentier, J., Cazamian, P. (1977), *Nightwork*. Geneva: International Labour Organisation.

CBS (Central Bureau of Statistics) (1981), *Statistisch zakboek* [Statistics Pocket Book]. The Hague: Staatsuitgeverij.

Champoux, J. E. (1980), The world of nonwork: Some implications of job re-design efforts. *Personnel Psychology*, **33**, 61–75.

Chapman, J. B., Otterman, R. (1975), Employee preference for various compensation and fringe benefit options. *Personnel Administrator*, November, 30–36.

Coetsier, P. (1979), Arbeidsduurverkorting, maar hoe? [Reduction of working time, but how?] *Economisch en Sociaal Tijdschrift* [Economic and Social Journal], **4**, 405–418.

Cohen, A. R., Gadon, K. (1978), *Alternative work schedules: Integrating individual and organizational needs*. Reading: Addison-Wesley.

Colquhoun, W. P. (Ed.) (1971), *Biological rhythms and human performance*. London: Academic Press.

Colquhoun, W. P., Rutenfranz, J. (Eds.) (1980), *Studies of shift work*. Reading/London: Taylor & Francis Ltd.

Cornuit, J. R. N. A. (1981), De 'glamour' van deeltijdarbeid [The 'glamour' of part-time work]. *Intermediair*, **17**, no. 40, 49–53.

Corpeleyn, A. (1978), *Arbeidskrachtentelling 1975* [Labour force census 1975]. Central Bureau of Statistics. The Hague: Staatsuitgeverij.

Desir, D., Cauter, E. van, Golstein, J., Fevre, M., Jadot, C., Reftoff, S., Copinschi, G. (1981), Adaptation of the nycthemeral variations of pituitary and related hormones after transmeridian transportation in normal man. In: Reinberg, A., *et al.* (Eds.), *Night and shift work, biological and social aspects*. Oxford: Pergamon Press.

Direktoraat-Generaal van de Arbeid [Directorate-General of Labour] (1975), *Ploegenarbeid 1975* [Shiftwork 1975]. Voorburg (The Netherlands).

Driehuis, W., Vrije, P. A. de (1981), *Vooronderzoek experiment bevordering deeltijdarbeid* [Preliminary study to an experiment to stimulate part-time work], part I: Study of the literature. The Hague: Ministry of Social Affairs.

Emmerij, L. J., Clobus, J. A. E. (1978), Volledige werkgelegenheid door creatief verlof [Full employment through creative sabbaticals]. Deventer: Kluwer.

Fleuter, D. L. (1975), *The workweek revolution*. Reading: Addison-Wesley.

Folkard, S. (1981), Shiftwork and performance. In: Johnson, L. C., *et al.* (Eds.), *Biological rhythms, sleep and shift work*. New York: SP Medical & Scientific Books.

Folkard, S., Monk, T. H. (1979), Shift work and performance. *Human Factors*, **21**, 483–492.

Fuller, C., Sulzman, F., Moore-Ede, M. (1981), Shift work and the jet-lag syndrome: Conflicts between environmental and body time. In: Johnson, L. C., *et al.* (Eds.), *Biological rhythms, sleep and shift work*. New York: SP Medical & Scientific Books.

Haasteren, F. C. A. van (Ed.) (1977), *Uitzendureaus ter sprake* [Discussions on temporary employment agencies]. Scheveningen: Stichting Maatschappij en Onderneming.

Haasteren, F. C. A. van, Overeem, M. van (1976), *Arbeid à la carte* [Work à la carte]. Scheveningen: Stichting Maatschappij en Onderneming.

Haider, M., Kundi, M., Koller, M. (1981), Methodological issues and problems in shift work research. In: Johnson, L. C., et al. (Eds.), Biological rhythms, sleep and shift work. New York: SP Medical and Scientific Books.

Harmsen, G., Reinalda, B. (1975), Voor de bevrijding van de arbeid [For the liberation of work]. Nijmegen: Socialistiese Uitgeverij (SUN).

Harrington, J. M. (1978), Shift work and health: A critical review of the literature. London: Her Majesty's Stationery Office.

Hartzuiker, J. G. (1981), De opmars van de deeltijdwerker [The advance of the part-timer]. Gids voor Personeelbeleid, Arbeidsvraagstukken, Sociale Verzekering [Guide to Personnel Policy, Labour Issues, Social Security], 3, no. 2, 14–24.

Hockey, G. R. J., Colquhoun, W. P. (1972), Diurnal variation in human performance: A review. In: Colquhoun, W. P., (Ed.), Aspects of human efficiency—diurnal rhythm and loss of sleep. London: English Universities Press.

Hoek, C. Jong, J. R. de (1979), Shiftwork in the service sector—The Netherlands. Contract no. EF/SC/78/24/SW, Dublin, European Foundation for the Improvement of Living and Working Conditions.

Hoolboom, H., Alphen, M. H. (1980), Ploegendienst en ziekte: Een literatuuroverzicht [Shiftwork and illness: A review of the literature]. Leiden: NIPG.

Hoolwerf, G., Thierry, Hk., Drenth, P. J. D. (1974), Ploegenarbeid: Een bedrijfspsychologisch onderzoek [Shiftwork: An industrial-psychological research study]. Leiden: Stenfert Kroese.

ILO (International Labour Organisation) (1978), Management of working time in industrialised countries. Geneva: ILO.

Industriebond NVV (1978), Leven om te werken om te leven, ervaringen en meningen van volkontinudienstwerkers bij Shell-Pernis en hun partners [Living to work to live, experiences and opinions of continuous-shift workers at Shell-Pernis and their partners]. Amsterdam: NVV.

Ivancevich, J. M. (1974), Effects of the shorter workweek on selected satisfaction and performance measures. J. of Applied Psychology, 59, 717–721.

Ivancevich, J. M., Lyon, H. L. (1977), The shortened workweek: A field experiment. J. of Applied Psychology, 62, 34–37.

Jehoel-Gijsbers, G., Schepens, Th. (1981), Gedeelde arbeid: Gedeelde vreugd [Shared work: Shared joy]. The Hague: Ministry of Social Affairs and Employment.

Jong, J. R. de (1974), Ploegenarbeid: Waarom, wanneer en hoe? [Shift work: why, when and how?]. Leiden: Stenfert Kroese.

Jong, J. R. de, Ruijs, Th. G. P. M. (1979), Economic aspects of shift work. Contract no. EF/SC/78/25/SW, Dublin, European Foundation for the Improvement of Living and Working Conditions.

Jong, J. R. de, Intven, C. H. J., Visser, P. (1974), Beter ten halve gewerkt? [Maybe better work half-time?]. Leiden: Stenfert Kroese.

Jugel, M., Spangenberg, B., Stollberg, R. (1978), Schichtarbeit und Lebensweise. Berlin, Dietz Verlag.

Kabanoff, B. (1980), Work and nonwork: a review of models, methods, and findings. Psychological Bulletin, 88, 60–77.

Kabanoff, B., O'Brien, G. E. (1980), Work and leisure: a task attributes analysis. J. of Applied Psychology, 65, 596–609.

Katz, D., Kahn, R. L. (1978), The social psychology of organizations. New York, Wiley, 2nd ed.

Knauth, P., Rutenfranz, J. (1980), Experimental shift work studies of permanent night, and rapidly rotating, shift systems, In W. P. Colquhoun et al. (Eds.), Studies of shiftwork, London, Taylor & Francis Ltd.

Koller, M. (1980), Psychosoziale Störungen bei Nacht- und Schichtarbeit. In: W. Brenner et al. (Eds.), *Arbeitsbedingte Gesundheitsschäden—Fiktion oder Wirklichkeit*, Stuttgart, Gentner Verlag.

Koning, J. de (1980), *Optimalisering van de verdeling van de werkgelegenheid* [Optimalization of the distribution of employment]. Rotterdam: Netherlands Economic Institute.

Leegwater, D. K. (1979), *Arbeids-'pools'* [Work-pools]. *Intermediair*, **15**, no. 39, 11–19.

Levitan, S. A., Belous, R. S. (1979), *Minder werk, meer werk* [Less work, more work]. Deventer: Kluwer.

Loon, J. H. van (1980), Diurnal temperature curves in shiftworkers. In: Colquhoun, W. P., et al. (Eds.), *Studies of shiftwork*. London: Taylor & Francis Ltd.

Loskant, H. (1980), Arbeitsmedizinische Vorsorgeuntersuchungen bei Nacht- und Schichtarbeit. In: Brenner, W., et al. (Eds.), *Arbeitsbedingte Gesundheits schäden— Fiktion oder Wirklichkeit*. Stuttgart: Gentner Verlag.

Maasen, A. (1978), *The effects of shiftwork on health, social and family life*. Contract no. EF/SC/78/14/DW, Dublin, European Foundation for the Improvement of Living and Working Conditions.

Marić, D. (1977), *Adapting working hours to modern needs*. Geneva: International Labour Organisation.

Maurice, M., Monteil, C. (1965), *Vie quotidienne et horaires de travail: Enquête psychosociologique sur le travail en équipes successive*. Paris: Université de Paris I, Institut des sciences sociales du travail.

Meyman, T. F. (1981), Een onderzoek naar het herstel in een volkontinu schema [A study on recuperation in a continuous-shift schedule]. *Tijdschrift voor Sociale Geneeskunde* [Journal of Social Medicine], **59**, 378–383.

Mill, R. van, Schagen-Gelder, M. van (1980), *Deeltijdarbeid op de proef gesteld* [Part-time work put to the test]. Rotterdam: Municipal Office.

Miller, H. E., Terborg, J. R. (1979), Job attitudes of part-time and full-time employees. *J. of Applied Psychology*, **64**, 380–386.

Mott, P. E., Mann, F. C., McLoughin, Q. (1965), *Shift work: The social, psychological and physical consequences*. Ann Arbor: University of Michigan Press.

Münstermann, J., Preiser, K. (1978), *Schichtarbeit in der Bundesrepublik Deutschland: sozialwissenschaftliche Bilanzierung des Forschungsstandes, statistische Trends und Massnahmeempfehlungen*. Bonn: Der Bundesminister für Arbeit und Sozialordnung.

Nachreiner, F. (1978), Ueber Determinanten der Einstellung zur Schichtarbeit. *Zeitschrift für Arbeitswissenschaft*, **32**, 6–11.

Neulinger, J. (1978), *The psychology of leisure*. 3rd ed. Springfield: Thomas.

Nicholson, N., Jackson, P., Howes, G. (1978), Shift work and absence: An analysis of temporal trends. *J. of Occupational Psychology*, **51**, 127–137.

NRC/Handelsblad (1981), Deeltijd voor gedeputeerden van de provincie Zuid Holland [Part-time work for deputees of the county of Zuid Holland]. Newspaper article.

O'Brien, G. E. (1981), Leisure attributes and retirement satisfaction. *J. of applied psychology*, **66**, 371–384.

Orpen, C. (1981), Effect of flexible working hours on employee satisfaction and performance: A field experiment. *J. of Applied Psychology*, **66**, 113–115.

Parker, S. R., Smith, M. A. (1976), Work and leisure. In: Dubin, R., (Ed.), *Handbook of work, organization and society*. Chicago: Rand McNally.

Perret, D. (1980), Experiments involving productivity and 'work sharing'. Paper 5th EFPS/ EAPM Congress on 'Rewarding Work', Amsterdam.

Poan, R. (Ed.) (1972), *4 days, 40 hours: Reporting a revolution in work and leisure*. London: Pan Books.

Pollet, P. (1979), *An alternative policy for the organization of shift work*. Contract no. EF/SC/78/18/SW, Dublin, European Foundation for the Improvement of Living and Working Conditions.

RCO (Raad van de Centrale Ondernemingsorganisaties [Council of the Central Employers' organizations]) (1980), *De arbeidsduur* [Working time]. The Hague: VNO.

Reinberg, A., Andlauer, P., Vieuw, N. (1981), Circadian temperature rhythm amplitude and long term tolerance of shift working. In: Johnson, L. C., *et al.* (Eds.), *Biological rhythms, sleep and shift work*. New York: SP Medical & Scientific Books.

Rentos, P. G., Shephard, R. D. (Eds.) (1976), *Shift work and health ... a symposium*. Washington D.C.: U.S. Department of Health, Education and Welfare.

Robison, D. (1976), *Alternative work patterns*. Scarsdale: Work in America Institute.

Ronen, S. (1981), *Flexible working hours*. New York: McGraw-Hill.

Rosow, J. M. (1979), Quality-of-Work-Life issues for the 1980s. In: Kerr, C., Rosow, J. M. (Eds.), *Work in America, the decade ahead*. New York: Van Nostrand Reinhold.

Rousseau, D. M. (1978), Relationship of work to nonwork. *J. of Applied Psychology*, **63**, 513–517.

Ruppert, M. (1953), *De Nederlandse vakbeweging* [The Dutch trade unions] I. Haarlem: Bohn.

Rutenfranz, J. (1980), Befindlichkeitsstörungen und Erkrankungen bei Nacht- und Schichtarbeitern. In: Brenner, W., *et al.* (Eds.), *Arbeitsbedingte Gesundheitsschäden — Fiktion oder Wirklichkeit*. Stuttgart: Gentner Verlag.

Rutenfranz, J., Colquhoun, W. P., Knauth, P., Ghata, I. N. (1977), Biomedical and psychosocial aspects of shift work. *Scand. J. of Work and Environmental Health*, **3**, 165–182.

Rutenfranz, J., Knauth, P., Angersbach, D. (1981), Methodological and practical issues related to shift work research. In: Johnson, L. C., *et al.* (Eds.), *Biological rhythms, sleep and shift work*. New York: SP Medical & Scientific Books.

Rutenfranz, J., Knauth, P. Colquhoun, W. P. (1976), Hours of work and shift work. *Ergonomics*, **19**, 331–340.

Rutenfranz, J., Knauth, P., Küpper, R., Romahn, R., Ernst, G. (1979), *Model study on physiological and psychological consequences of shift work in some branches of the service sector*. Contract no. EF/SC/78/20/SW, Dublin, European Foundation for the Improvement of Living and Working Conditions.

Schein, V. E., Maurer, E. H., Novak, J. F. (1977), Impact of flexible working hours on productivity. *J. of Applied Psychology*, **62**, 463–465.

Schein, V. E., Maurer, E. H., Novak, J. F. (1978), Supervisor's reactions to flexible working hours. *J. of Occupational Psychology*, **51**, 333–337.

Scherrer, J. (1981), Man's work and circadian rhythm through the ages. In: Reinberg, A., *et al.* (Eds.), *Advances in the study of night- and shift work*. Oxford: Pergamon Press.

Schoemaker, N., Gageldonk, A. van, Demenint, M., Vianen, A. van (1981), *Deeltijdarbeid in het bedrijf* [Part-time work in the firm]. Alphen a/d Rijn: Samsom.

Shamir, B. (1980), A note on individual differences in the subjective evaluation of flexetime. *J. of Occupational Psychology*, **53**, 215–217.

Siddré, W., Regt, E. de (1981), Macro-economische gevolgen van arbeidstijdverkorting [Macro-economic consequences of a reduction of working time]. *Beleid en Maatschappij* [Policy and Society], **8**, no. 2, 42–52.

Siersema, J. (1981), *Vrouwenarbeid — nachtwerk?* [Women's work — night work?]. Amsterdam: Pegasus.

Sloane, P. J. (1975), *Changing patterns of working hours*. London: Department of Employment Manpower Paper No. 13, HMSO.

Spijkers, W. (1980), Slaapdeprivatie en taakprestatie: Een literatuuroverzicht [Sleep deprivation and task performance: A survey of the literature]. *Nederlands Tijdschrift voor Psychologie* [Dutch Journal of Psychology], **35**, 151–172.

Staines, G. L. (1980), Spillover versus compensation: A review of the literature on the relationship between work and nonwork. *Human Relations*, **33**, 111–129.

Streich, W., Jansen, R. (1979), *Shift work as part of the occupational career: New ways of planning occupational careers of employees working in shifts.* Contract no. EF/SC/78/27/SW, Dublin, European Foundation for the Improvement of Living and Working Conditions.

Taylor, P. J., Pocock, S. J., Sergean, R. (1972), Absenteeism of shift and day workers: A study of six types of shift system in 29 organizations. *Brit. J. of Industrial Medicine,* **29**, 208–213.

Themagroep Noord Nederland (TNN) (1979), Belasting en herstel in de volkontinu [Load and recuperation in continuous shift work]. Groningen: Inst. of Social and Industrial Psychology.

Thierry, Hk. (1980), Compensation for shift work: A model and some results. In: Colquhoun, W. P., Rutenfranz, J. (Eds.), *Studies of shift work.* London: Taylor & Francis.

Thierry, Hk. (1981), Arbeidstijdverkorting: modaal of in modaliteiten? [Shortening the working time: modally or in modalities?]. *Beleid en Maatschappij* [Policy and Society], **8**, no. 2, 76–88.

Thierry, Hk., Jansen, B. (1981), Potential interventions for compensating shift work inconveniences. In: Reinberg, A., *et al.* (Eds.), *Advances in the study of night- and shift work.* Oxford: Pergamon Press.

Thierry, Hk., Jansen, B., Hirtum, A. van (1982), *Ploegenarbeid-in-konveniënten* [Shift work in conveniences] *IV.* Contract no. 81/3030/11/SW/MK, Dublin, European Foundation for the Improvement of Living and Working Conditions.

Thierry, Hk., Jansen, B., Smits, P., Hirtum, A. van (1981), *Shiftwork-in-conveniences III.* Contract no. 80/3030/30/SW/MK, Dublin, European Foundation for the Improvement of Living and Working Conditions.

Thierry, Hk., Jansen, B., Smits, P,, Hoolwerf, G. (1979), *Shiftwork-in-conveniences I.* Contract no. EF/SC/78/27/SW, Dublin, European Foundation for the Improvement of Living and Working Conditions.

Thierry, Hk., Jansen, B., Smits, P., Hoolwerf, G. (1980), *Shiftwork-in-conveniences II.* Contract no. EF/SC/79/29/SW, Dublin, European Foundation for the Improvement of Living and Working Conditions.

Thiis-Evensen, E. (1958), Shift work and health. *Industrial Medicine and Surgery,* **27**, 493–497.

Thiis-Evensen, E. (1969), Shift work and health. *Studia Laboris et Salutis,* **4**, 81–83.

Ulich, E., Baitsch, C., Straumann, M. (1979), *Schicht- und Nachtarbeit im Betrieb: Probleme und Lösungsansätze.* Zürich: GDI-Verlag.

Veen, A. van der, Roosma, S. I. J. (1981), Deeltijdarbeid: Instrument voor herverdeling van arbeid? [Part-time work: An instrument for redistributing work?]. *Economisch-Statistische Berichten* [Economic-Statistical Reports], **66**, 104–108.

Walker, J. (1978), *The human aspects of shift work.* London: Institute of Personnel Management.

Webb, W. B. (1981), Work/rest schedules: Economic, health, and social implications. In: Johnson, L. C. (Ed.), *Biological rhythms, sleep and shift work.* New York: SP Medical & Scientific Books.

Wever, R. A. (1979), *The circadian system of man, results of experiments under temporal isolation.* Berlin: Springer Verlag.

Wilensky, H. L. (1960), Work, careers, and social integration. *International Social Science Journal,* **12**, 543–560.

Wilkinson, R. T. (1969), Some factors influencing the effect of environmental stressors upon performance. *Psychological Bulletin,* **72**, 260–272.

Willems, P. J. (1981), *Inleiding in de psychologie van menselijke verrichtingen* [Introduction to the psychology of human performance]. Deventer: Van Loghum Slaterus.

Winget, C. M., Hughes, L., Ladou, J. (1978), Physiological effects of rotational work shifting: A review. *J. of Occupational Medicine*, **20**, 204–210.

Wippler, R. (1968), *Sociale determinanten van het vrijetijdsgedrag* [Social determinants of leisure-time behavior]. Assen: Van Gorcum.

Wojtczak-Jaroszowa, J., Makowska, Z., Rzepecki, H., Banaszkiewicz, A., Romejko, A. (1978), Changes in psychomotor and mental task performance following physical work in standard conditions, and in a shift working situation. *Ergonomics*, **21**, 801–809.

WRR (Wetenschappelijke Raad voor het Regeringsbeleid) (1981), *Vernieuwingen in het arbeidsbestel* [Innovations in the employment system]. The Hague: Staatsuitgeverij.

Handbook of Work and Organizational Psychology
Edited by P. J. D. Drenth, Hk. Thierry, P. J. Willems and C. J. de Wolff
© 1984, John Wiley & Sons, Ltd.

3.7. Work consultation as a channel of communication and as a consultative framework

Paul L. Koopman and A. F. M. Wierdsma

1. DEFINITIONS OF TERMS

The term work consultation has a wide variety of meanings in the many publications on this subject. Illustrative of this is Van Dongen's (1972) total of no less than 16 definitions, even after he has sifted some out. The diffuse meaning of 'work consultation' stems from a lack of consensus about the form it should take and the goals it should serve. Before going into these aspects, we would like to give several characteristics which, in our definition, differentiate work consultation from ordinary consultation (cf. van Hoof, 1972).

Work consultation is (1) a *regular and organized* form of consultation (2) between a supervisor and his subordinates as a *group* or representatives of the group (3) in which the prime objective is to participate in and exert *influence* on *decision making* (4) with the emphasis on issues concerning the *work* and working conditions (Koopman *et al.*, 1981).

Work consultation is subject to *rules and regulations* which govern certain matters. Some kind of regularity is also a requirement in the above definition. We feel that consultation on work between a supervisor and one of his subordinates cannot be considered work consultation. The oft-heard remark: 'Work consultation? We have been doing that for years' is correct only if we look at the subjects discussed. But the *group nature* of work consultation gives it an entirely different character and opens up new possibilities. The collective element requires a different attitude on the part of both supervisor and group members. We do wish to include in our definition forms of work consultation through

Dr. P. L. Koopman, Vrije Universiteit, Vakgroep Arbeids- en Organisatiepsychologie, De Boelelaan 1081, 1081 HV Amsterdam.
Drs. A. F. M. Wierdsma, Standertmolen 18, 3481 AG Harmelen.

rotation or representation, although we agree with Kuipers (1975) that work consultation through direct participation of the entire work group should be preferred in most situations. The first and foremost consideration must be whether or not the disadvantages of a representative form of work consultation (such as the formation of an élite, or disagreements between the person elected and those who have elected him) outweigh the advantages.

The third element in our definition—*influence* on decision making—implies that the purpose of work consultation is more than just giving instructions, improving the atmosphere, etc. The issue of changing the distribution of influence in an organization definitely comes under the heading of work consultation. So it is not easy to say exactly what forms of consultation can be called work consultation. The extent to which it is integrated in the decision making structure will vary according to the phase of development it is in. The *content* and radius of work consultation may also change with time. The definition focuses on the content aspect of work consultation in the starting-up phase. The extent to which one succeeds, in the long run, to include matters of a broader range in the discussions will, for the greater part, determine the integration of work consultation in the existing information and decision making structure. This is of essential importance for the continuity of work consultation (Ramondt, 1974).

In actual practice, the term 'work consultation' is usually reserved for consultation at the lowest levels in the organization. Without wanting to depart from this usage, we wish to point out that consultation at lower and middle management levels, which is systematically linked to work consultation, seems an essential condition for the success of work consultation.

We would now like to define some terms that will be frequently used in this chapter. For co-determination we adopted Scholten's (1975) definition: 'the extent to which the members of an organization have at their disposal the means to effectuate their definition of the situation'. By 'definition of the situation' we mean the way in which the work and its context are experienced. So, co-determination denotes the means the members of an organization have for putting forward in discussions the subjects they feel are important and for influencing decision making on these subjects. If this is done without representatives, we speak of participation.

In the literature, terms such as co-determination, industrial democracy, and self-management are generally reserved for highly institutionalized forms of consultation having far-reaching jurisdiction. For instance, Walravens (1977, p. 5) applies the term industrial democracy at the organizational level exclusively to situations where the members of an organization have a say in assessing and deciding on the goals for which and the conditions under which they are working.

This chapter is organized as follows. First, three basic orientations from which work consultation is approached in the literature will be distinguished. Some results of evaluative studies will also be discussed. The position of work consultation in society as well as the attitudes towards it of government and employees' and employers' organizations will be briefly considered. Then we will attempt to show, using a socio-psychological model, what factors reinforce the introduction and continuity of work consultation. On the basis of the dimensions 'latitude for work consultation' and 'need for co-determination', two types of work consultation will be distinguished: work consultation as a channel of communication and work consultation as a consultative framework. A discussion on the developmental possibilities of both types of work consultation will close this chapter.

2. THE THEORETICAL BASIS

Using an adapted version of a classification made by Dachler and Wilpert (1978), we distinguish three groups of theories or views from which participation in work situations is approached. The first approach may be labelled 'quality of work'; concepts such as humanizing, alienation, and work motivation and satisfaction belong to this orientation. Although slightly different definitions of these concepts are found in the literature, the primary criterion almost always is the way in which the organization members experience their work. The second approach is 'co-determination'. Concepts such as democratization and power equalization belong to this category. The primary criterion here is the redistribution of power in the organization. The third approach can perhaps best be indicated by the word 'control'; the criterion then is effective management. An important consideration is the coordination and control of the behaviour of the employees to maximize the realization of the organizational goals. Many management and leadership theories have their roots in this orientation. Below, these three categories are used to classify the most relevant literature. It should be kept in mind that some sources make use of aspects from different orientations.

2.1. Quality of work

In the sixties and seventies, the literature in the field of work motivation and satisfaction was largely dominated by the 'growth theories'. Personal development, utilization of human potential, and health of the organization are seen as compatible (Herzberg et al., 1959; McGregor, 1960; Argyris, 1964; Likert, 1967). This emphasis on the realization of one's own potential is also found in literature on psychotherapy, emancipation, etc. (Rogers, 1961; Perls et al., 1973; Negt, 1975).

The origins of this approach can partly be found in the theories of motivation, which assume a hierarchy of needs, emphasizing a need for growth or self-actualization (Maslow, 1954; Alderfer, 1972). Although the theoretical assumptions of these theories have been questioned (Duijker, 1976; Salancik and Pfeffer, 1977) and the research results have varied widely (de Kleer-Wilander, 1973; Thierry and Drenth, 1970), the growth model largely determined thinking on organization in the seventies. In this view, participation in the work situation is one of the ways of countering the frustrating effects of organizations with a traditional structure. Following the ideas of the 'Scientific Management' movement many organizations can be characterized by a high degree of specialization, short-cycle tasks, a strict division into management and workers, and a remunerative system primarily based on extrinsic factors. In these organizations there is little room for the satisfaction of 'higher' needs. In the contemporary literature, there is an increasing tendency to give suggestions for changes in the organization design to meet the demand for greater latitude and variety in tasks (Hackman, 1975; Davis, 1976; Galbraith, 1977; de Sitter, 1978; van Assen, 1980; den Hertog, 1980). Job enrichment and changes in production set-up play an important role here, along with work consultation.

The issue of the quality of the work has often been approached by sociologists from the point of view of *alienation*. The concept of 'alienation', which has its roots in nineteenth-century thought (Marx, Durkheim), received attention after World War II, particularly through the work of Seeman, Fromm, and Blauner (van Strien, 1975). Seeman (1959) distinguishes the following dimensions of alienation: powerlessness, meaninglessness, normlessness, social alienation, and self-estrangement. Blauner (1964) uses the same dimensions, with the exception of normlessness. But the operationalizations of these concepts are very much psychological ones, because of the stress placed on the subjective perception of work situations. Blauner's example is followed by Blumberg (1968), Arzensek (1977), and Allegro (1980), who study the relationship between participation and 'subjective' alienation from work. Van Strien (1975) advocates including both 'subjective' and 'objective' alienation in research.

Essential to Van Strien's view is that, to prevent alienation, changes must be worked out and implemented in collaboration with those involved. The concept of humanizing requires no further explanation, as it can be regarded as the opposite pole of the concept of alienation. To humanize a work situation, alienating elements must be eliminated (Allegro, 1980).

The costs of alienation to the organization have been studied by many, including McGregor (1960), Argyris (1964), and, in The Netherlands, De Sitter (1977) and Van Strien (1978). As the Dutch social insurance system enables firms to shift many of the negative results of stress and illness on the community, the costs to society are also considerable (Lubbers, 1978, 1979; Bomers, 1980).

Research results on the relationship between direct participation and job satisfaction mostly indicate a positive relationship (for survey studies see Lowin, 1968; Blumberg, 1968; Filley et al. 1976; Locke and Schweiger, 1979). Nineteen of the 20 laboratory experiments, correlational studies, and field experiments discussed by Filley et al. showed a positive relationship between participation and satisfaction. Even more extensive is the literature study by Locke and Schweiger. Twenty-six (60%) of the 43 studies they investigated yielded a positive relationship between participation and satisfaction. Thirteen cases showed no clear relationship, and four cases even showed a negative one. To summarize, in about 40% of the research studied, no positive relationship was found between participation and satisfaction. In a very critical analysis of the literature, Wall and Lischeron (1977) reach the conclusion that the above research results can partly be attributed to methodological shortcomings. This primarily concerns the correlational studies. The results based on experiments are, according to these authors, much less consistent. Other recent research seems to indicate that the relationship between participation and satisfaction is also dependent on other circumstances, such as the nature of the task and the complexity of the subjects discussed (House and Baetz, 1979; Koopman, 1980; Koopman et al., 1981). In addition, because of habituation to participation more participation may be necessary to increase satisfaction again; the 'level of aspiration' may rise with experience (Córdova, 1982). This could partly explain the lack of consistence in the research findings.

2.2. Co-determination

Quite different from this view is the orientation we simply call 'co-determination': participation as a value in itself. To have a say in determining the goals and means which concern one's own actions is viewed either as a right (Walravens, 1977) or a duty (van Zuthem, 1978). Participation falls under the heading of democratization of the organization. Power equalization is the central concept here.

Sociologists in particular have supported this view in their publications, from the famous 1911 study of Michels ('iron law of oligarchy') to the more recent work of Bachrach (1967), Naschold (1970), and Pateman (1970). In The Netherlands the evaluative studies of the Institute of Industrial Sociology of the Free University (Amsterdam) have dominated the discussion (van Zuthem, 1973; Ramondt, 1974; Kuipers, 1975). Contributions of psychologists primarily aimed to understand how people function in groups. Mulder (1973, 1977) takes the approach of reducing the power distance between those with more and those with less power. He bases his case on the assumption that, in general, the fact that one possesses power leads to satisfaction. Less powerful people will strive to decrease the power distance between them and the more powerful, as long as the costs of doing so are not too high. Behavioural choices are determined not only by the valency of the outcome, but also by the 'instrumentality' of the behaviour, that is, the chance that it will lead to the result desired (Vroom, 1964; Koopman-Iwema and Thierry, 1977). An important condition for the learning process of the 'power game' to have any chance of success, is that the difference in power among the participants is not too great. From this perspective, work consultation offers better starting conditions than does representative consultation as, for instance, in a works council. If the differences in power are great from the outset, participation may, in certain circumstances, even increase the power distance between the participants (Mulder, 1971, 1973).

The *evaluative studies*, which investigate to what extent consultation contributes to a greater degree of co-determination for employees, lead to quite dismal conclusions. In a report, made for a trade union research foundation, Looise (1976, p. 213) concludes that 'these experiments are generally quite unsuited for bringing about any form of co-determination'. Co-determination here refers to the organizational level. This can only be realized if, with the introduction of work consultation, a number of important changes takes place in the power relationships in an organization. The report is much more positive about the contribution of work consultation towards humanizing work situations. On the basis of the results of a trade union discussion project concerning 'the place of work', Looise reaches the conclusion that the large majority of employees seems to take a positive stand on work consultation: 91% of the approximately 550 participants in this project agreed with the statement: 'Work consultation can be a real step towards the democratization of organizations' (SWOV, 1975, p. 47). Apparently, trade union members are more optimistic on this point than union leaders, and also more optimistic than research results would seem to justify. Kuipers (1972), Ramondt (1974), and Scholten (1975) also feel that work consultation does little in the way of promoting other forms of co-determination.[1] In his thesis, tellingly entitled 'Industrial democratization without workers' Ramondt reaches the following conclusions:

—Work consultation is a one-sided, management-oriented, management-controlled form of consultation. It does little to promote the interests of employees.

—Work consultation does not stimulate the employees to organize themselves independently. It functions isolated from other ways of promoting employees' interests, such as the works council or the union.

—Work consultation generally is barely structured or formalized and its life-span is uncertain (Ramondt, 1974, pp. 185–186).

Kuipers (1975) and Scholten (1975) approach work consultation as a process. They emphasize that its character should be established in consultation with the employees involved and that readjustments should be made in the same manner. Ramondt (1974) expects that a more independent attitude of and

---

[1] The fact that direct participation at the shop-floor has so little influence on an organization's policy is not an exclusively Dutch problem; see Drenth *et al.* (1979) and IDE (1981).

greater solidarity among employees, coupled with influence on the preconditions, will result in a form of work consultation which will increasingly contribute to co-determination. Looise (1976) and Walravens (1977) chiefly emphasize changes in power relationships, because work consultation can facilitate co-determination by employees at the organizational level only under the condition of an altered power structure.

All of these authors mention one dominant condition, i.e. that the power to make decisions about the contents of work consultation (such as the matters to be discussed or the powers of that body) and about the course the development of work consultation should take, cannot exclusively be an affair of the management. Essential to this condition is that the design and readjustments of work consultation be effected in consultation with the people who will be involved, preferably all of them. The employees and the works council must have a real say in formulating the pre conditions under which work consultation is to be developed. Some examples would be budget agreements, the right to information, training, and education, meeting facilities, etc. Although the authors particularize these conditions to varying degrees, they all mention demands for a more structured (institutionalized) form of consultation, agreements on the supply of information and authority, and guarantees that the process of work consultation be open to all.

2.3. Control

Although, considering the studies cited above, the possible contribution of work consultation to co-determination has received a good deal of attention, the reason such projects are started often lies in concrete problems of the work situation (Scholten, 1975) or in the management's need for greater efficiency and control of the behaviour of the organization members (Kuipers, 1972). Scholten concludes that the criterion of co-determination in the work consultation experiments evaluated is 'inappropriate, at any rate external'. In this section we will consider to what extent work consultation can be seen as a tool of management, along with other means to control the behaviour of organization members, such as systems of remuneration and evaluation.

As stated in section 2.1, there are often large discrepancies between the characteristics of a classic organization and the demands of the employees with respect to their work situation. This tension is vented in various reactions, all expressing the tendency to keep mentally aloof from the work situation. Argyris (1964) mentions as examples daydreaming, doodling, making mistakes on purpose, and aggression. Employees can also avoid work situations through absenteeism or frequent changes of job. More subtle forms of sabotage are also used. De Sitter (1977) discusses a number of 'defensive strategies'; for instance, creating extra manoeuvring room beyond that strictly necessary for carrying out the task. He estimates the 'system loss' at assembly lines due to absenteeism, waiting times, unused capacities, and such at 40 to 50%! Considering this, it is hardly surprising that managements show an increasing interest in techniques aimed at increasing the employees' involvement in organizational goals. This interest is further enhanced by the fact that the classic motivation techniques, such as individual merit ratings, have gradually fallen into discredit (see Industriebond NVV, 1977) and are disappearing (Thierry, 1979).

Attempts to increase productivity and efficiency through direct participation are not something new. One need only think of classic studies such as those of Coch and French (1948), or Morse and Reimer (1956). Such experiments fit well in the train of thought of the 'Human Relations' movement, i.e. that participation has a positive effect on morale, and that high morale leads to less resistance and higher productivity. But the introduction of participation also fits in the ideas of the 'Human Resources' movement, its goal being to increase the effectiveness of organizations. This school assumes that participation will lead to greater use of human capacities, which should positively affect the quality of decisions, the control of production processes, and work satisfaction (Miles, 1965). The experiments with the 'Scanlon plan' may also be classed in this tradition (see Thierry and de Jong, 1979; this Handbook, ch. 4.11).

   We return now to the question whether work consultation can be of use in increasing organizational effectiveness. Many studies show participation and decentralization of decision making to be positively related with the effectiveness of organizations (Likert, 1967; Tannenbaum, 1968; Argyris, 1972; Pennings, 1976; Dickson, 1981). All in all, however, research results on the relationship between participation and productivity vary greatly (Filley et al., 1976; Locke and Schweiger, 1979). When work consultation is defined as 'consultation with the emphasis on issues concerning the work and working conditions', obviously, such consultation will become more useful according as the work itself requires more consultation and as the employees, through their taking part in work consultation, increasingly contribute to an optimal functioning of the production process. This is why recent studies on the feasibility of forms of participation in work situations pay much attention to the type of technology and the organization of production processes (Hedberg et al., 1976; Galbraith, 1977; Davis, 1977; den Hertog, 1977; de Sitter, 1977; van Assen, 1980). We will come back to this in section 5.

3. THE POSITION OF WORK CONSULTATION IN SOCIETY

In The Netherlands, the outlook of work consultation is largely determined by the attitudes of the government and of the employers' and employees' organizations. We shall briefly discuss this.

   The *government*, at least until recently, has kept rather aloof from the forms participation may take at the lower levels of organizations, although the Works

Council Act of 1971 did state that it is the task of the works council to encourage the introduction of work consultation.

But for a few years now, the government seems to want to take a more active part. For instance, the Department of Labour of the Ministry of Social Affairs undertook a programme for the improvement of work quality in which work consultation plays a considerable role. Another example of the government's increasing attention to the shop-floor are the special funds: in 1974 some 2.25 million guilders was made available for a number of experiments with co-determination in organizations. After a long drawn-out discussion between employers and employees about how these experiments should be set up, ten projects were started (van der Molen, 1977; COB/SER, 1981). Some of them have since been completed (Allegro and de Vries, 1979; Becker et al., 1981; Bolweg et al., 1982).

Since then, special funds have also been made available for the qualitative improvement of work at the workers' level. Each year, there are millions of guilders involved (in 1977, for example, Dfl. 45 million). The new Works Council Act (1979), confers on works councils more authority as to the organization of work consultation: all regulations must be approved by the works council. Since the introduction of the new Working Conditions Act in 1980, work consultation is more or less compulsory (Koopman, 1981). Article 14 of the bill states that there must be some form of consultation between management and employees in each work unit. However, the government leaves the concrete definitions of work consultation (as to content and design) entirely to the organizations themselves. Thus, work consultation is much less 'thrust upon' an organization from without than is the case with the works council.

In general, *employers' organizations* seem to take a fairly positive stand on work consultation. A report on labour relations policy in organizations by two employers' organizations even calls work consultation indispensable to social management. The employers feel work consultation can contribute to 'a genuine recognition of people with ideas and views in their concrete need for responsibility, opportunities, and appreciation'. They also see work consultation as a means to stimulate efforts on the part of the employees. They speak of 'the redress of dissatisfaction and the decline of performance' (VNO/NCW, 1971).

Another report by one of these organizations (NCW, 1977) says that 'designing effectively proportioned participation and meaningful work is not a matter of courtesy, but a matter of social justice'. Mes (1978), speaking on behalf of the NCW at an open seminar on 'Co-determination in organizations' (Free University, Amsterdam) advocated the extensive restructuring of the entire work organization, which includes work consultation.

A constructive approach to work consultation is found in a report by yet another employers' organization (AWV, 1977). It should be noted, that this study supports the trade unions' criticism of many work consultation experiments—one-sided, management oriented, little employee influence on the preconditions, etc.—and that it partly concurs with the preconditions also formulated by these trade unions. However, in their view, 'those involved' in work consultation should be restricted to management and works council, and they feel it is not desirable to involve the employees in the starting-up phase.

It is difficult to judge to what extent this standpoint reflects the attitude of employers. In his opening speech to the above-mentioned seminar on co-determination, the chairman of the employers' organization VNO took a much less constructive stand on co-determination in organizations. He so unequivocally emphasized the restrictions he felt ought to be placed on co-determination that the audience was almost obliged to conclude that the VNO wants to put the whole thing on ice (van Veen, 1978).

The SWOV report (Looise, 1976, p. 214) asserts a growing industrial interest in forms of work consultation which do not go beyond improving the atmosphere and having a voice in social management. In section 6 we will consider what course of development is open to work consultation if potential changes in the apportionment of participation are precluded.

Until recently, the *trade unions* have shown only a minimum of concern. After World War II, the unions primarily played a role at the national and industry branch levels. In the sixties, however, attention to individual firms and to the workshop became more pronounced (Windmuller and de Galan, 1977; Albeda, 1975). The unions' standpoints on work consultation are divided, due to differences in opinion on the direction in which industrial democracy should be accomplished and on their appraisal of work consultation as a possible step in the desired direction. The trade unions have explicit expectations of the democratizing effects of work consultation: to them, it is part of a pattern of ever increasing means for employees to exert influence on decisions. Their ultimate goal is a 'situation in which all members of an organization discuss and take part in decisions about the goals for which and the conditions under which they want to work' (Looise, 1976). Up to this point, the standpoints of the various federations of trade unions run more or less parallel. But when it comes to the actual form of co-determination, the views begin to diverge considerably (see also Andriessen and Coetsier, this Handbook, ch. 4.10).

The federation of trade unions CNV sees an organization primarily as a joint undertaking in which co-determination should not be a right, but a duty. Proceeding from a view of humanity in which concepts such as equality and responsibility are central, they want to strive for organizations in which each individual can develop himself in an optimal way. The structure of organizations should be such that they provide all employees the opportunity to experience freedom and responsibility (Lanser, 1978). To achieve this ideal, they advocate strengthening employee participation through work consultation, the work council, and the broad of directors. The board should assume the form of joint management where the most important decisions in the organization are made. In the view of the CNV, half of the board members should be elected by the employees. Shared responsibility on the basis of delegation and trust is the CNV's central theme.

The federation of trade unions FNV is much more sceptical of its chance to realize its goals under the existing economic system. Eventually, the FNV has in mind some form of self-management, but it has not yet worked out this idea in detail. It is, at any rate, important that employees do not find responsibility is thrust upon them unless it is offset by genuine power. Until this can be effected, the FNV sees the 'control strategy' as an intermediate stage (Spit, 1978; Industriebond NVV, 1977).

This strategy involves turning the works council into an employee-representative body and stimulating the system of union representatives on the shop floor. Work consultation is primarily seen as a new 'tool of management' which management would want to use to increase contact with the employees at 'the basis', just like the trade unions do with their system of having representatives on the shop floor. They are not very optimistic about the ability of work consultation to change the apportionment of participation: on this point, they have adopted a wait-and-see attitude. However, inasfar as work consultation brings more variety to jobs as well as more responsibility and means for self-development, they view it as compatible with their goals (NKV, 1975; Looise, 1976). But what they do not want is a 'pound of responsibility for an ounce of co-determination'.

In reality, this means that the FNV can hardly be said to play a stimulating role. They limit themselves mainly to formulating preconditions which are aimed at tightening the hold of the works council on work consultation and diminishing the chance of work consultation being manipulated by the top management (Looise, 1976).

To summarize, we can say that the trade unions approach work consultation chiefly from the point of view of co-determination (the CNV also stresses humanizing); the employers see work consultation from the view of coordination and control (Kuipers, 1972); and the government's approach is primarily one of humanizing, aimed at the quality of the work.

4. A SOCIO-PSYCHOLOGICAL MODEL

As we have seen, the government has left the organization of co-determination at the work place to the employers' and employees' organizations, and the trade unions are generally not very positive in their attitude. Thus, the initiation and the continuity of work consultation depends almost exclusively on the members of a particular firm. We have therefore taken this fact into account in our model.

Like Scholten (1975), Kuipers (1975), Allegro (1980), and Revans (1981), we see work consultation primarily as a learning process. This is in contrast to such authors as Ramondt (1974) and Walravens (1977) who put much more stress on the importance of structural conditions. In addition to results from the field of psychology of learning, we will chiefly use elements from socio-psychological theories of motivation, to wit the 'exchange theory' (Shaw and Constanzo, 1970, pp. 69–116; Chadwick-Jones, 1976) and the 'cognitive expectancy theory' (Vroom, 1964; Lawler, 1973). Learning how to work with work consultation is a laborious process. In our view, the introduction of work consultation is impossible without a definite *extra effort* over a longer period of time on the part of top management, lower management (the supervisors who must chair the discussions), and the workers, sometimes with the temporary aid of professional staff groups.

For the top management, this extra effort or investment may mean providing time and facilities for work consultation, and ensuring timely and efficacious feedback on the questions and suggestions arising from it. The lower management will also find themselves faced with extra demands. They will have to consult regularly with the employees as a group and another, more participative, style of leadership will be expected from them. This requires not only a different attitude, but also different skills than those on which supervisors used to be selected and trained in the past. Finally, from the workers, greater involvement in the organization's doings and active contribution of ideas is expected. This is no small offering, if we realize that withdrawal of their 'involvement' is often the only means workers can employ against the much more powerful management.

We assume that these groups will only want to make this extra effort if they are sufficiently confident that it will improve their own position, or—in the terms of the expectancy theory—that it will lead to outcomes with a positive valency (Pollard and Mitchell, 1972; Kipnis, 1976). Each group makes an estimate of these outcomes. The management wonders what the employees' potential contribution, through work consultation, will be to the organizational goals as formulated by the management. The employees will make their further co-operation dependent on the results they anticipate. Figure 1 shows a diagram of our model. To keep its presentation clear, we distinguish only two groups, management and employees.

The following is in explanation of figure 1. We call this a flow model, and by that we mean a learning process in which expectations, moments of choice, behaviour, and reinforcement succeed one another, where tomorrow's choices are influenced by today's experiences. Behaviour often precedes a change in attitude here (Bem, 1970). Continuity in work consultation is determined by the extent to which behaviour is reinforced in the cyclic learning process, by the extent to which *both* groups see their primary goals and interests strengthened as a result of work consultation (Lowin, 1968; Veen, 1973). Putting it like this

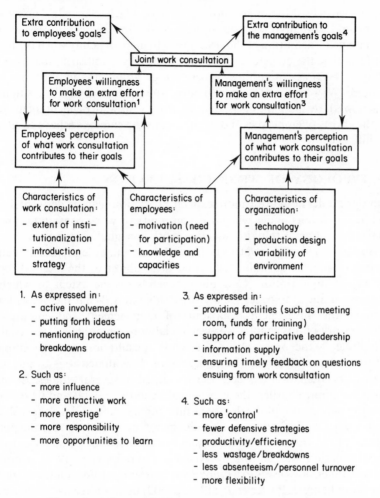

Figure 1. A flow model for success of work consultation.

is an implicit indication that we do not believe in the continuity of work consultation if it is instrumental only to the interests of one of the partners. The oft-encountered discussion in the literature on the 'real' motives of management to introduce work consultation (e.g. Kuipers, 1972) is therefore of limited value. The suggestion arising from this, that work consultation has less chance to increase co-determination if the management sees it primarily as a 'tool of management', is, we feel, only partially true. This idea presumes that only management is capable of determining the content of work consultation. But work consultation that does not obtain the approval of the employees involved has no means of sustaining itself or of developing (den Hertog, 1980).

Below we will attempt to show that particularly when the management feels it could gain anything from work consultation, the employees' chance to effectuate their 'definition of the situation' will increase. Only when the management feels that the contribution of the employees is indispensable does withholding it become interesting, which brings about an 'implicit bargaining situation' (Wierdsma, 1978, p. 80). For, the extent to which a situation is characterized by bargaining is determined by how dependent management is on the efforts of employees and by the means the employees have to effectuate their influence.

5. A TYPOLOGY OF WORK CONSULTATION

From our model in figure 1 more explicit predictions can be derived about the concrete conditions under which the continuity of work consultation may get a chance. Our line of thinking was that work consultation is not 'thrust upon' an organization from without, as is the works council, by legislation or collective bargaining agreements; this means that it is subject to the internal forces at work in the organization. Continuity depends on the extent to which both management and employees see a lasting value in it. What factors will mainly determine the 'investment behaviour' of management and employees? In the framework of this chapter we wish to elaborate on only two factors, namely the latitude in the organization for work consultation and the employees' need for co-determination. The relevance of these dimensions to the successfulness of participation has been demonstrated in several studies. Besides the sources mentioned earlier, the research of Schouten (1974) and Cliteur (1973) shows the importance of the degree of functionalization and task specialization (in other words: the amount of latitude the job design allows) for the potential influence of the workers. The importance of the need for personal growth and co-determination was shown by Hackman and Lawler (1971). Combining these two dimensions leads to a typology with four work consultation situations, as shown in figure 2. Porter et al. (1975, p. 309) use a somewhat more extensive model: besides the need for growth, they distinguish the factors 'organization design' (organic vs. mechanistic) and 'job design' (routine vs. 'enriched').

5.1 Work consultation as a channel of communication

If an organizational structure offers little latitude for work consultation, whereby participation is not very functional in the production process, and employees are only moderately interested in co-determination (situation 1) then work consultation will not contribute to increasing co-determination. After the 'complaint phase' (Kuipers, 1975) there are very few points left in the actual work situation which are suitable for work consultation. Topics for work consultation are the working conditions shared by all participants, and individual jobs.

Work consultation will then be of a restricted nature and the realization of employees' interests will depend strongly on the willingness of the supervisor to make an effort for it. This type of work consultation in situation 1 we will call 'work consultation as a channel of communication'. Forms of type-1 work consultation are chiefly found in organizations with a relatively simple technology and a stable environment, for example in mass or serial production industry (Woodward, 1965). Such organizations often have a very extensive division of labour with established production norms and precisely defined tasks. The behaviour of the workers is allowed little freedom because of its close relation to the production process. In case of production difficulties established procedures must be followed or a higher hierarchical level called in. There is only very little 'voluntary behaviour' and a great deal of 'necessary behaviour' (Lammers, 1965). In this sort of situation one often finds a very utilitarian attitude adapted to the available means. Co-ordination of the production process is not done in the work unit, but at higher levels. The control system has many procedures and rules and its co-ordination runs through higher levels in the hierarchy.

Work consultation will contribute only little to such an organization; the control system is based on non-participation of the workers in the organization's decision making or in control tasks. At best, work consultation can here fulfil a function in improving communication. Matters of a broader scope may be the subject of discussion, but considering the lack of pressure brought to hear by the employees, the chances of this actually occurring are slight. In work consultation, the employees' behaviour is very individualistic and there is nothing even resembling a well-organized presentation of interests and wishes

	Need for co-determination	
	little	much
Latitude in the organization for work consultation	1. Work consultation as a channel of communication	2.
	3.	4. Work consultation as a consultative framework

Figure 2. A typology of work consultation. —Situation 1 is extremely unfavourable, situation 4 extremely favourable to the course of development of work consultation. Situation 2 and 3 are considered mixtures of the 'ideal' situations or intermediate stages.

on the part of the employees as a group. Here, work consultation can have little continuity: not one group can really improve its position through it. The evaluative studies show that, in the absence of short-term results, management will no longer invest much in work consultation. Ramondt (1974) speaks of 'letting work consultation bog down'. Such work consultation has few possibilities of expansion, unless active measures are taken in the organization, so that more latitude is created (van Assen, 1980). The contribution of this type of work consultation to greater co-determination is negligible.

5.2 Work consultation as a consultative framework

The type-4 situation is entirely different. In this situation, there is a great deal of latitude for work consultation, in view of the nature of the tasks and the information and decision making structure geared to this. Consultation becomes part of the control of the production process and makes an unmistakable contribution to it. The more effect participation has (measured by instrumental criteria), the more chance the employees have of effectuating their definition of the situation. In the 'bargaining process', the participants in work consultation have something to say about the concrete form work consultation should take (topics and power). Besides, here the people feel a need for co-determination. Whether the participants are in a position to turn their potential influence on the definition of the situation into real influence depends on many factors, some of which lie outside the issues under discussion. Group formation among the employees and a supportive management policy are, however, essential.

Opportunities to expand such work consultation to more co-determination are no longer exclusively dependent on factors outside the participants themselves. Their involvement in the functioning of the production process gives them the means to exert influence on defining the margins of work consultation. We therefore call this 'work consultation as a consultative framework'. This type of work consultation is possible especially in organizations with a flexible production process, which allows many control tasks to be done in the work units with relatively highly qualified personnel. According to Woodward (1965, p. 64) such flexibility is chiefly found in organizations with unit production and in the processing industry.

Of course, in real situations usually mixtures of the 'ideal' types 1 and 4 will be found. It should also be stressed that, over time, organizations can shift their positions on these dimensions. Particularly the need for co-determination, often latent at first, may manifest itself more and more in the course of time. It is often possible to introduce adaptations in the production set-up and co-ordination in such a way that it creates more room for work consultation (van Assen, 1980; den Hertog, 1977).

6. POSSIBLE COURSES OF DEVELOPMENT

For an accurate evaluation of the contribution of work consultation to the interests of both management and employees, it is important that the goals and design of work consultation not be considered as fixed. In this section we will elaborate on the reasoning underlying our model as to aspects of continuity and courses of development open to both types of work consultation.

As we have seen, to date, experiences with work consultation have been quite disappointing, especially if compared with the expectations in the early sixties (Lammers, 1965). Work consultation often lasts but two or three years. Improving its continuity would thus appear to be a first condition for development.

In section 3 it was stated that the content and design of work consultation are not prescribed by legislation. This is one reason why the management is more or less in a position to put its own stamp on work consultation. And there are no indications that this will change in the near future. It is possible that the government's interest in humanizing work situations will further increase, under the influence of, inter alia, the effects the 'work drain' (van der Graaf, 1975) has for the government. For example, a quite considerable part of the costs of social security results from early exits from the labour market due to stress. It has been pointed out that the new Working Conditions Act provides for compulsory consultation. But even then, the initiative to work consultation as well as its continuity are still largely in the hands of the most powerful group in the organization, top management. This is even true when the recommendations as formulated in the SWOV report (Looise, 1976, pp. 213–214) are met. These are:
—Work consultation should be set up in a systematic way in the entire organization.
—The employees and their representatives must be involved from the outset in the design and implementation of work consultation.
—There must be a body for co-ordination and assistance.
—There should be an affiliation between work consultation and the representative forms of consultation.
—The authority of work consultation must be laid down in rules and regulations.

Such conditions are indeed essential if those involved are to have a better hold on work consultation (see Koopman and Drenth, 1977). But in spite of this, we agree with De Sitter (1977, p. 23) that, in the future, the initiative and control of work consultation will largely remain in the hands of management. For the continuity of work consultation, this means that only if it is functional for the organizational goals as formulated by the management can one count on their lasting support. Employees, on the other hand, will withdraw their necessary contributions if work consultation does not sufficiently meet their interests, which would include a greater degree of co-determination in the work situation. We therefore feel that, in the long run, the outlook for work consultation will be favourable only if, in Lammers' (1975) terms, 'functional' and 'structural' democratization go hand in hand. Before working out in more detail the possible courses of development of both types of work consultation (figure 2) we will first consider to what extent clear *advance agreements* on the design and manner of introduction of work consultation could contribute to its continuity.

6.1 Preconditions

When work consultation is to be set up, the question always is what conditions should be considered minimum preconditions. This discussion, which has quite some influence on the design and scope of work consultation, is more explicitly of a bargaining nature.

Authors who feel the primary goal of work consultation is to facilitate the redistribution of power in the organization, will formulate conditions delineating the structure within which work consultation can further develop. Their object is an institutionalized form of work consultation with clearly defined authority, so that the continuity is not only dependent on its contribution to the production process (Walravens, 1977; Ramondt, 1974; Looise, 1976).

A dilemma confronts us in setting the preconditions: the more conditions involving redistribution of power are put before the management in advance, the smaller the chance that work consultation will be introduced (Kanter, 1982). Walravens (1977) formulates conditions which are nearly identical to the goals!

But not to lay down any preconditions would mean to ignore the results of the evaluative studies on work consultation. They show that work consultation which hinges on the supervisor's willingness, and has no 'backbone' in the form of agreements which the employees can appeal to, has little or no chance of development. In such situations, the course of development will depend on supervisors, who find their tasks growing and their positions weakening through work consultation. Philipsen (1965) speaks of an intensified role conflict at lower and middle management levels, resulting from the introduction of work consultation, if done without sufficient recognition and support from the higher management levels.

Authors puting less emphasis on power dimensions will formulate conditions which, rather than outlining an initial framework, concentrate on ensuring the involvement of the employees in setting up and carrying out work consultation. They often advocate participation in steering committees and emphasize the necessity of taking each step in consultation with all those involved (Kuipers, 1975; Scholten, 1975; Koopman and Drenth, 1977; van Hooft and Koopman-Iwema, 1978; Allegro, 1980). But the realization of these preconditions assumes some kind of structure in the consultations with the employees involved. In our view, work consultation, in its initial phase, can play a useful role here. In this way there can be an interaction between the introduction of a consultative system and consultation on the preconditions and manner of introduction. To put it another way: a participative system should be introduced in a participative way (Thierry and de Jong, 1979). A 'shuttle strategy' (Kuipers, 1975; p. 42), paying attention alternately to the conditions which make possible the process of development and the conditions which serve to stimulate the learning process, appears to be a way to stay on top of the problem of minimum preconditions. But this also means that all those involved must be prepared, in joint consultation, to make interim changes in the conditions.

In the long run, the outlook of work consultation is not only—not even in the first place—determined by the preconditions. The primary requirement is that it 'fits' in the organization, is not an 'ugly duckling'. Work consultation that meets the need for consultation which the work itself requires offers both management and employees results that reinforce their investment behaviour. The greater the contribution of work consultation to the organizational goals, the more serious will be the consequences for the management if the employees withdraw their cooperation. Thus, the more functional work consultation is to the organizational goals, the greater the chance that the employees can put forward their definition of the situation; their position in the 'implicit bargaining process' becomes stronger. Since the latitude for work consultation in organizations is such a determining factor, we will have to differentiate the possible courses of development according to the work consultation forms in situations 1 and 4 in figure 2.

6.2. Work consultation as a channel of communication

In organizations with little latitude for work consultation, because of either the technology used or the production design, work consultation will, as we already suggested, only be able to act as a channel of communication. The importance of this is mainly that it improves communication and possibly has positive effects on work satisfaction (Veen, 1973). Such work consultation has little room for development and only limited continuity.

However, the importance of work consultation as a channel of communication rises if an organization's management decides to make a change in the production process or a change in the organization design, so that the work offers greater challenges and more responsibility. Such changes in organization design may be prompted by several considerations:
—tension between the organization and its members;
—tension between the organization and increasing uncertainty in its environment;

—tension due to the limited means of the bureaucratic processes to reduce internal uncertainty.

In sections 2.1 and 2.3 it was noted that there generally exists a *discrepancy* between the *demands* of employees regarding their job and the *possibilities* the job offers (Maher and Piersol, 1971). This discrepancy leads to high costs, both for the organization and for the community—in the form of illnesses, absenteeism, 'defensive strategies', etc. It is only realistic to expect that this discrepancy will not decrease in the near future, and even may increase. Some recent developments may illustrate this.

In education, for example, big changes have taken place. We see not only a rising level of education, but also a change in the nature of education. More than in the past, there is room for the development of children's individuality and creativity. This may well result in tomorrow's employees being less willing to do uninteresting work exclusively for the money (den Hertog, 1977, pp. 36–44).

Considerations involving the *adaptation of the organisation to its environment* can also be a reason for restructuring an organization. Studies of the development of organizations show that increasing variability in the organization's environment ought to be countered by an organizational structure with more room for manoeuvring and more decision powers at lower levels. Burns and Stalker (1961) point to the shift from a mechanistic to an organic type of structure. Compared to the mechanistic type, the organic type shows more group responsibility and an increasing importance of consultation and 'involvement' of the employees (Argyris, 1970, p. 104). Lawrence and Lorsch (1969) note that a change is taking place from a bureaucratic to a more non-bureaucratic pattern. (See further Hazewinkel, this Handbook, ch. 4.3.)

The *bureaucratic process* has only limited means to reduce internal uncertainty, even in a relatively stable environment. The study by Crozier (1964) suggests a spiral motion. A bureaucratic organization will, by establishing rules and standardizing procedures, attempt to make the behaviour of its employees controllable. To attempts of the employees to obtain more room for manoeuvring it will usually react by increasing the number of rules and procedures; actually a strategy of 'more of the same'. The result often is an even more defensive attitude of and withdrawal of 'involvement' by the employees (van Dijck, 1974, p. 46). Increasing the means of control therefore is, considering its undesirable side effects, possible only to a limited extent.

In short, work consultation as a channel of communication, as far as it concerns a greater contribution to organizational effectiveness and co-determination, chiefly depends on changes in the organization design. But by the same token it is an *indispensable element* of organization design. Alterations in the production design result in an increasing need for consultation, in order to facilitate the coordination of tasks within a group.

Changes in organization design can radically alter the employees' level of aspiration, because the tasks demand more from the employees' capacities and sense of responsibility. This activation brings them closer to the demand for changes in the power distribution, and leads to demands for changing the style of leadership and decision making. Leadership which used to be geared to supervision and control of individual employees must now become geared to coordination of the activities of a working group.

For organizational effectiveness, the contribution of such changes lies in the increasing internal control capacity and the decreasing chance of breakdown, because control and operating tasks are integrated. The change contributes to the means available to the employees to effectuate their definition of the situation mainly in that it has an activating effect. By abolishing the strict division between operating and control tasks, one of the marbles of the organisational game, 'prestige', is also redistributed (Lammers, 1965). But work consultation remains instrumental to the goals of management. The nature of such work consultation may be typified in the terms of Van Dijck (1974) as 'work situational participation'.

6.3. Work consultation as a consultative framework

We will conclude with some remarks on the outlook for work consultation of 'situation type 4', in which there is quite a lot of latitude and also a very evident need on the part of the employees for co-determination.

The course of development of this type of work consultation will mainly depend on the amount of agreement between management and employees on which subjects work consultation pertains to and what means of influence should be linked to them. Considering the often divergent views of management and employees on this point, it would be a misconception to assume that employees will only wish to discuss subjects suggested by management. In work consultation as a consultative framework, the amount of effort employees will make depends on the type of subject receiving genuine attention in work consultation. Work consultation as an organized form of consultation creates a situation by which employees, as a group, can enter into discussions with their supervisor. Because the problems are related to their experience, the means to reduce the power distance are available (Mulder, 1973). The employees can temporarily withdraw their active involvement which is needed for the production process. This means they have potential influence. Whether they will be in a position to effectuate this influence will largely depend on the extent to which they manage to manifest themselves *as a group*. For the employees, the contribution of work consultation as a consultative framework will primarily lie in the opportunities to learn and to participate in decision making; alongside work situational participation 'participation in the control structure' becomes possible (van Dijck, 1974). For the organization, the importance of this type of work consultation must primarily be sought in a systematic structuring of the consultation necessary for the work. Due to the latitude in the task, the regulation and carrying out of production are already integrated to a certain degree. Through consultation, experience with the production process can be directed at anticipatory steering (de Sitter, 1977). It may be expected that the increased latitude will allow fewer defensive strategies to develop.

There is always a chance that work consultation will be used by the management to keep the employees 'in line' (see Teulings, 1974), but under these circumstances (situation type 4) this chance seems smaller. The 'anti-demo-cratization syndrome' (Ramondt, 1974), the 'sounding out' behaviour of employees in the complaint phase, and the active attitude of the employees will not give this type of work consultation much chance to become biased to the interests of only one party. Den Hertog (1980) studied several cases and demonstrates that employees may react in two ways if they are not taken seriously in their contribution to consultation: passively—a wait-and-see, indifferent attitude—and actively, implying that their contribution to the consultation depends on certain demands being met. On the basis of these cases, Den Hertog concludes that the introduction of work consultation and job design as an anaesthetic only, generally produces effects that are undesirable to the management as well.

REFERENCES

Albeda, W. (1975), *Arbeidsverhoudingen in Nederland* [Industrial relations in The Netherlands]. Alphen a/d Rijn: Samsom.

Alderfer, C. P. (1972), *Existence, relatedness, and growth: Human needs in organizational settings*. New York: Free Press.

Allegro, J. T. (1980), Stromingen en achtergronden [Trends and backgrounds]. In: van Assen *et al.* (1980).

Allegro, J. T., Vries, E. de (1979), *Projekt humanisering en medezeggenschap bij Centraal Beheer te Apeldoorn*. The Hague: COB/SER [English transl.: Project: Humanization and participation in Centraal Beheer, in: *Working on the quality of working life: Developments in Europe* (1979). Boston: Nijhoff].

Argyris, C. (1964), *Integrating the individual and the organization*. New York: Wiley.

Argyris, C. (1970), *Intervention theory and method: A behavioral science view*. Reading (Mass.): Addison-Wesley.

Argyris, C. (1972), *The applicability of organizational theory*. Cambridge: Cambridge University Press.

Arzensek, V. (1977), *Alienation and self-management*. 2nd International Congress of Participation, Workers' Control and Self-Management, Paris.

Assen, A. van (1980), Organisatie-ontwerp, een analytisch model voor werkoverleg en werkstructurering [Organization design, an analytical model for work consultation and job design]. In: van Assen *et al.* (1980).

Assen, A. van, Hertog, J. F. den, Koopman, P. L. (Eds.) (1980), *Organiseren met een menselijke maat* [Human organization]. Alphen a/d Rijn: Samsom.

AWV (1977), *Werkoverleg: Inzichten, ervaringen, adviezen* [Work consultation: Experiences and recommendations]. Haarlem: AWV.

Bachrach, P. (1967), *The theory of democratic elitism*. Boston: Little, Brown.

Becker, N. J., Verstegen, R., Pekelharing, B. G. (1982), *Medezeggenschap en coöperatie* [Co-determination and cooperation]. The Hague: COB/SER.

Bem, D. J. (1970), *Beliefs, attitudes, and human affairs*. Belmont: Wadsworth.

Blauner, R. (1964), *Alienation and freedom*. Chicago: University of Chicago press.

Blumberg, P. (1968), *Industrial democracy*. London: Constable.

Bolweg, J. F. Dunnewijk, M., Schafrat, W. H. A. (1982), *Van ondernemingsstatuten naar medezeggenschap?* [From industrial regulations to co-determination?]. The Hague: COB/SER.

Bomers, G. B. J. (1980), *Organisatie en gezondheid: Op steeds meer gespannen voet?* [Organization and health: Increasing tensions?]. Breukelen: Nijenrode, Netherlands School of Business.

Burns, T., Stalker, G. M. (1961), *The management of innovation*. London: Tavistock.

Chadwick-Jones, J. K. (1976), *Social exchange theory: Its structure and influence in social psychology*. London: Academic Press.

Cliteur, H. A. M. (1973), Werkoverleg en organisatie [Work consultation and organiza-tion]. *Gids voor Personeelsbeleid* [Guide to Personnel Policy], **2**, 62–74.

COB/SER (1981), *Voortgang van het programma Experimenten Medezeggenschap* [Progress in the programme Experiments Co-determination]. The Hague: SER.

Coch, L., French, J. P. R. (1948), Overcoming resistance to change. *Human Relations*, **1**, 512–533.

Córdova, E. (1982), Workers' participation in decisions within enterprises: Recent trends and problems. *International Labour Review*, **121**, 125–140.

Crozier, M. (1964), *The bureaucratic phenomenon*. London: Tavistock.

Dachler, H. P., Wilpert, B. (1978), Conceptual dimensions and boundaries of participation in organizations: A critical evaluation. *Administrative Science Quarterly*, **23**, 1–39.

Davis, L. E. (1976), Current developments in job design. In: Warr, P. (Ed.), *Personal goals and work design*. London: Wiley.

Davis, L. E. (1977), Evolving alternative organization designs: Their sociotechnical bases. *Human Relations*, **30**, 261–273.

Dickson, J. (1981), The relation of direct and indirect participation. *Industrial Relations Journal*, July/August, 27–35.

Dijck, J. J. J. van (1974), *Organisatie in verandering* [Organization in transition]. Rotter-dam: Universitaire Pers.

Dongen, H. J. van (1972), Verslag discussies [Report discussions]. In: *Werkoverleg: Rapport van de studiegroup werkoverleg* [Report on work consultation]. The Hague: NIVE.

Drenth, P. J. D., Koopman, P. L., Rus, V., Odar, M., Heller, F. A., Brown, A. (1979), Participative decision making, a comparative study. *Industrial Relations*, **18**, 295–309.

Drenth, P. J. D., Willems, P. J., Wolff, Ch. J. de (Eds.) (1973), *Arbeids- en organisatiepsy-chologie* [Work- and organizational psychology]. Deventer: Kluwer.

Duijker, H. C. J. (1976), De ideologie der zelfontplooiing [The ideology of self-actuali-zation]. *Pedagogische Studiën* [Pedagogical Studies], **53**, 358–373.

Filley, A. C., House, R. J., Kerr, S. (1976), *Managerial process and organizational behavior*. Glenview (Ill.): Scott, Foresman.

Galbraith, J. R. (1977), *Organization design*. Reading (Mass.): Addison-Wesley.

Graaf, M. H. K. van der (1975), *Psychologische aspekten van de organisatie* [Psychological aspects of the organization]. Alphen a/d Rijn: Samsom.

Hackman, J. R. (1975), On the coming demise of job enrichment. In: Cass, E. L., Zimmer, F. G. (Eds.), *Man and work in society*. New York: Van Nostrand.

Hackman, J. R., Lawler, E. E. (1971), Employee reactions to job characteristics. *Journal of Applied Psychology*, **55**, 259–286.

Hedberg, B. L. T., Nystrom, P. C., Starbuck, W. H. (1976), Camping on seesaws: Prescriptions for a self-designing organization. *Administrative Science Quarterly*, **21**, 41–65.

Hertog, J. F. den (1977), *Werkstrukturering* [Job design]. Alphen a/d Rijn: Samsom.

Hertog, J. F. den (1980), Organisatorische vrijheidsgraden voor veranderingen in de direkte werksituatie [Organizational degress of freedom for change in the immediate work situation]. In: van Assen *et al.* (1980).

Herzberg, F., Mausner, B., Snyderman, B. B. (1559), *The motivation to work*. New York: Wiley.

Hoof, J. A. P. van (1972), Staalkaart van vragen [A range of questions]. In: *Werkoverleg: Rapport van de studiegroep werkoverleg* [Report on work consultation]. The Hague: NIVE.

Hooft, P. L. R. M. van, Koopman-Iwema, A. M. (1978), Van werkoverleg nåar overleg [From work consultation to consultation]. *Intermediair*, **14**, no. 14.

House, R. J., Baetz, M. L. (1979), Leadership: Some empirical generalizations and new research directions. *Research in Organizational Behavior*, **1**, 341–423.

IDE—International Research Group (1981), *Industrial democracy in Europe*. London: Oxford University Press.

Industriebond NVV (1977), *Breien met een rooie draad* [Knitting with a read thread]. Brochure Industriebond NVV.

Kanter, R. M. (1982), Dilemmas of managing participation. *Organizational Dynamics*, Summer, 5–27.

Kipnis, D. (1976), *The powerholders*. Chicago: University of Chicago Press.

Kleer-Wilander, B. de (1973), *Maslows behoeftentheorie en het verschilmodel bij het meten van werk satisfactie* [Maslow's need theory and the measuring of job satisfaction]. Amsterdam: Free University.

Koopman, P. L. (1980), *Besluitvorming in organisaties* [Decision making in organizations]. Assen: Van Gorcum.

Koopman, P. L. (1981), De Arbeidsomstandighedenwet: En nieuwe impuls voor werkoverleg? [The Working Conditions Act: A new stimulus for work consultation?]. *Intermediair*, **37**, 51–55.

Koopman, P. L., Drenth, P. J. D. (1977), '*Werkoverleg*' [Work consultation],*Experiments in participative decision making on the shop floor*. 2nd International Conference on Participation, Workers' Control and Self-Management, Paris.

Koopman, P. L., Drenth, P. J. D., Bus, F. B. M., Kruyswijk, A. J., Wierdsma, A. F. M. (1981), Content, process, and effects of participative decision making on the shop floor: Three cases in The Netherlands. *Human Relations*, **34**, 657–676.

Koopman-Iwema, A. M., Thierry, Hk. (1977), Participatie, motivatie en machtsafstand [Participation, motivation and power distance]. *Mens en Onderneming* [Man and Enterprise], **31**, 263–284.

Kuipers, J. H. (1972), *Verantwoordelijkheidsverruiming in de directe werksituatie* [Expanding responsibility on the shop floor]. Amsterdam: Free University/COP.

Kuipers, J. H. (1975), *Beleidsvoering door werkoverleg* [Management by work consultation]. Alphen a/d Rijn: Samsom.

Lammers, C. J. (Ed.) (1965), *Medezeggenschap en overleg in het bedrijf* [Co-determination and consultation in the organization]. Utrecht: Het Spectrum.

Lammers, C. J. (1975), Self-management and participation: Two concepts of democratization in organizations. *Organization and Administrative Sciences*, **5**, 17–33.

Lanser, L. (1978), Samen verantwoordelijk [Jointly responsible]. In: de Sitter *et al.* (1978).

Lawler, III, E. E. (1973), *Motivation in work organizations*. Monterey: Brooks/Cole.

Lawrence, P. R., Lorsch, J. W. (1969), *Developing organizations: Diagnosis and action.* Reading (Mass.): Addison-Wesley.

Likert, R. (1967), *The human organization: Its management and value.* London: McGraw-Hill.

Locke, E. A., Schweiger, D. M. (1979), Participation in decision-making: One more look. *Research in Organizational Behavior,* 1, 265–339.

Looise, J. C. (1976), *De proef op de som* [The proof of the puding]. Utrecht: SWOV.

Lowin, A. (1968), Participatory decision-making: A model, literature critique and prescription for research. *Organizational Behavior and Human Performance,* 3, 68–106.

Lubbers, R. F. M. (1978/79), Interviews in the newspaper *NRC/Handelsblad* of 7 Dec. 1978 and in *ED* of 24 Jan. 1979.

McGregor, D. M. (1960), *The human side of enterprise.* New York: McGraw-Hill.

Maher, J. R., Piersol, D. T. (1971), The motivation to work; Outlook for the future. In: Maher, J. R. (Ed.), *New perspectives in job enrichment.* London: Van Nostrand, Reinhold.

Maslow, A. (1954), *Motivation and personality.* New York: Harper and Row.

Mes, J. B. M. (1978), Verruiming en verdieping van de medezeggenschap [Extending and deepening of co-determination]. In. de Sitter *et al.* (1978).

Michels, R. (1925), *Zur Soziologie des Parteiwesens in der modernen Demokratie,* Stuttgart.

Miles, R. E. (1965), Human relations or human resources. *Harvard Business Review,* 43, 148–163.

Molen, R. A. J. van der (1977), Het COP-programma experimenten medezeggenschap [COP-programme experiments co-determination]. *M & O,* 31, 362–375.

Morse, N C., Reimer, E. (1956), The experimental change of a major organizational variable. *Journal of Abnormal and Social Psychology,* 52, 120–129.

Mulder, M. (1971), Power equalization through participation? *Administrative Science Quarterly,* 16, 31–38.

Mulder, M. (1973), Moeilijkheden van de minder machtigen bij het leren van participatie [Problems of the less powerful in learning to participate]. In: Drenth *et al.* (1973), 280–291.

Mulder, M. (1977), *Omgaan met macht* [Managing power]. Amsterdam: Elsevier.

Naschold, F. (1970), *Organisatie en democratie* [Organization and democracy]. Utrecht: Het Spectrum.

NCW (1977), *Verantwoordelijkheden voor onderneming en ondernemer* [The company's and the employer's responsibilities]. The Hague: NCW.

Negt. O. (1975), *Sociologische verbeeldingskracht en exemplarisch leren* [Sociological imagination and learning by example]. Groningen: Tjeenk Willink.

NKV (1975), *Een visie ter visie* [A view on view]. Utrecht: NKV.

Pateman, C. (1970), *Participation and democratic theory.* London: Cambridge University Press.

Pennings, J. M. (1976), Dimensions of organizational influence and their effectiveness correlates. *Administrative Science Quarterly,* 21, 688–699.

Perls, F. S., Hefferline, R. F., Goodman, P. (1973), *Gestalt therapy: Excitement and growth in the human personality.* London: Penguin.

Pilipsen, H. (1965), Medezeggenschap in de vorm van werkoverleg [Co-determination in the form of work consultation]. In: Lammers, C. J. (Ed.), *Medezeggenschap en overleg in het bedrijf* [Co-determination and consultation in the organization]. Utrecht: Het Spectrum.

Pollard, W. E., Mitchell, T. R. (1972), Decision theory analysis of social power. *Psychological Bulletin,* 78, 433–446.

Porter, L. W., Lawler, III, E. E., Hackman, J. R. (1975), *Behavior in organizations*. New York: McGraw-Hill.

Ramondt, J. J. (1974), *Bedrijfsdemocratisering zonder arbeiders* [Industrial democratization without workers]. Alphen a/d Rijn: Samsom.

Revans, R. W. (1981), Worker participation as action learning. *Economic and Industrial Democracy*, **2**, 521–541.

Rogers, C. (1961), *On becoming a person: A therapist's view of psychotherapy*. London: Constable.

Salancik, G. R., Pfeffer, J. (1977), An examination of need-satisfaction models of job-attitudes. *Administrative Science Quarterly*, **22**, 427–546.

Scholten, G. (1975), *Medezeggenschap en organisatieverandering* [Co-determination and organizational change]. The Hague: COP/SER.

Schouten, J. (1974), Vrijheid in het werk. [Freedom in the work situation]. *Intermediair*, 19 July.

Seeman, M. (1959), On the meaning of alienation. *American Sociological Review*, **24**, 783–791.

Shaw, M. E., Constanzo, P. R. (1970), *Theories of social psychology*. New York: McGraw-Hill.

Sitter, L. U. de (1977), *Produktieorganisatie en arbeidsorganisatie in sociaal-economisch perspectief* [A socio-economic perspective on production organization and work organization]. The Hague: NIVE.

Sitter, L. U. de (1978), Medezeggenschap, arbeid en arbeidsorganisatie [Co-determination, work and work organization]. In: de Sitter *et al.* (1978).

Sitter, L. U. de, *et al.* (1978), *Medezeggenschap in de onderneming* [Co-determination in the organization]. Nijkerk: Callenbach.

Spit, W. J. L. (1978), Medezeggenschap: Een kwestie van democratie en humaniteit in de arbeidsorganisatie [Co-determination: A matter of democracy and humaneness in the work organization]. In: de Sitter *et al.* (1978).

Strien, P. J. van (1975), Vervreemding en emancipatie—theorie en praktijk van vervreemdingsonderzoek [Alienation and emancipation—theory and practice of alienation research]. In: Strien, P. J. van (Ed.), *Vervreemding en emancipatie* [Alienation and emancipation]. Meppel: Boom.

Strien, P. J. van (1978), *Om de kwaliteit van het bestaan* [On the quality of life]. Meppel: Boom.

SWOV (1975), *De plaats van de arbeid* [The place of work]. Part I. Utrecht: SWOV.

Tannenbaum, A. S. (1968), *Control in organizations*. New York: McGraw-Hill.

Teulings, A. (1974), Chef, kunnen we even overleggen ... [Boss, can we talk now]. *De Groene Amsterdammer*, 9 Oct.

Thierry, Hk. (1979), Humanisering van arbeid en beloning [Humanizing work and remuneration]. In: Galan, C. de, Gils, M. van, Strien, P. J. van (Eds.), *Humanisering van de arbeid* [Humanizing work]. Assen: Van Gorcum.

Thierry, Hk., Drenth, P. J. D. (1970), De toetsing van Herzbergs 'two-factor' theorie [Testing Herzberg's 'two-factor' theory]. In: Drenth, P. J. D., Willems, P. J., Wolff, Ch. J. de (Eds.), *Bedrijfspsychologie* [Industrial psychology]. Deventer: Kluwer.

Thierry, Hk., Jong, J. R. de (1979), *Naar participatie en toerekening* [Towards participation and imputation]. Assen: Van Gorcum.

Veen, C. van (1978), Mogelijkheden en grenzen van de medezeggenschap [Possibilities and boundaries of co-determination]. In: de Sitter *et al.* (1978).

Veen, P. (1973), Participatie: Een poging tot synthese [Participation: An attempt at synthesis]. In: Drenth *et al.* (1973), 261–279.

VNO/NCW (1971), *Sociaal beleid in ondernemingen* [Social policy in the firm]. The Hague.

Vroom, V. (1964), *Work and motivation*. New York: Wiley.

Wall, T. D., Lischeron, J. A. (1977), *Worker participation*. London: McGraw-Hill.

Walravens, A. H. C. M. (1977), *Veldexperimenten met industriële demokratie* [Field experiments with industrial democracy]. Assen: Van Gorcum.

Wet op de Ondernemingsraden [Works Council Act] (1979).

Wierdsma, A. F. M. (1978), *Werkoverleg, zowel middle als doel* [Work consultation, a means as well as a goal]. Amsterdam: Free University.

Windmuller, J. P., Galan, C. de (1977), *Arbeidsverhoudingen in Nederland* [Industrial relations in The Netherlands]. Utrecht: Het Spectrum.

Woodward, J. (1965), *Industrial organization: Theory and practice*. Oxford: Oxford University Press.

Zuthem, H. J. van (1973), *Macht en democratie binnen de onderneming* [Power and democracy within the organization]. Amsterdam: De Bussy.

Zuthem, H. J. van (1978), *Spanningsvelden rondom bedrijfsdemocratie* [Tensions concerning industrial democracy]. Baarn: Ten Have.

Author Index

A1

A18

Reid, L. D., 1156, 1172, 1173
Reimann, B. C., 704, 705
Reimer, E., 650, 798
Reinalda, B., 599
Reinberg, A., 635
Reisberg, D. J., 224
Renwick, P. A., 542
Revans, R. W., 405, 588, 654
Revel, J. F., 1148
Rhenman, E., 824
Rhode, J. G., 874, 1055
Rice, A. K., 812, 814, 821, 822, 892, 893, 910, 924
Richards, M. G., 1181, 1182
Richardson, A. J., 1183
Richardson, R., 373
Richardson, S. A., 39
Rieken, J., 1090
Riemersma, J. J., 1172
Rijsman, J., 146, 455, 457, 459, 467
Rijsman, J. B., 146
Rissler, A., 283
Ritchie, R. J., 351, 585
Ritzen, J. M. M., 76
Rizzo, J. R., 563
Robbins, S. P., 522, 539, 540
Roberts, K. H., 189, 1201, 1208
Robison, D., 600, 602, 604
Rodenburg, K. J., 1061
Rodgers, W. L., 1108, 1113
Roe, A., 116, 320
Roe, R. A., 58, 59, 108, 109, 111, 120, 121, 219, 291, 1024, 1025, 1040
Roeleveld, C. L. G., 1047
Roethlisberger, F. J., 5, 717, 756, 795
Rogers, C., 587, 645, 795
Rogers, D. L., 528
Rogers, K., 326
Rohmert, W., 262, 263, 283, 386
Romein, J., 789
Ronan, W. W., 159, 166, 211, 212
Ronen, S., 600, 601, 602, 603, 604, 1208
Roosma, S. Y., 610, 614
Roscam Abbing, P. J., 380
Rose, G. L., 541
Rosen, S., 358
Rosenberg, M., 53, 423, 842
Rosenman, R. H., 557, 560, 561, 567
Rosenzweig, J. E., 861
Roskam, E. E. Ch. I., 27, 337
Roskies, E., 567
Rosow, J. M., 600

Ross, A., 1147
Ross, J., 836
Rossi, R. J., 1108
Roszak, T., 890
Roth, J. A., 327
Rothengatter, J. A., 1175, 1179
Rothman, J., 929
Rotter, J. B., 138
Rounds, J. B., 117
Rousseau, D. M., 191, 192, 620
Rowe, R. H., 199
Roy, A., 421
Royce, J. R., 115
Rozema, R., 524
Rubin, I. M., 927, 929
Rubin, J. Z., 535
Ruble, T. L., 536, 542
Ruigh, A. de, 261
Rundquist, E. A., 293, 416
Runkel, P. J., 13, 18, 26, 31, 337
Ruppert, M., 598
Rus, V., 500, 842, 844, 845, 848, 971
Russell, J. A., 1185, 1189
Rutenfranz, J., 386, 622, 623, 626, 627, 634
Ruter, W. H., 218
Ruijs, Th. G. P. M., 622

Saaksjarvi, M., 1055
Saari, L. M., 405, 585
Saipukas, A., 895
Saito, Y., 270
Salaman, G., 398, 936
Slancik, G. R., 41, 646, 727, 842, 1081, 1087
Sales, S. M., 561, 562
Samuelson, P. A., 983
Sanders, A. F., 262, 266
Sanford, R. N., 526, 542
Sarbin, T. R., 530
Sashkin, M., 798, 936
Satter, G. A., 379, 385
Saunders, D. R., 30
Sayles, L. R., 366
Schachter, S., 143
Schaddelee, C., 1047
Schaff, A., 1039
Schafrat, W. H. A., 400
Schagen-Gelder, M. van, 600, 614
Schaie, K. W., 326
Scharpf, F. W., 1083, 1085
Schattsschneider, E. E., 541

Subject Index

S1